**THE VICTORIA HISTORY
OF THE
COUNTIES OF ENGLAND**

A HISTORY OF
YORKSHIRE EAST RIDING

VOLUME III

THE VICTORIA HISTORY OF THE COUNTIES OF ENGLAND

EDITED BY R. B. PUGH, D.LIT.

THE UNIVERSITY OF LONDON
INSTITUTE OF
HISTORICAL RESEARCH

Oxford University Press

OXFORD LONDON GLASGOW NEW YORK
TORONTO MELBOURNE WELLINGTON CAPE TOWN
IBADAN NAIROBI DAR ES SALAAM LUSAKA ADDIS ABABA
KUALA LUMPUR SINGAPORE JAKARTA HONG KONG TOKYO
DELHI BOMBAY CALCUTTA MADRAS KARACHI

© *University of London 1976*

ISBN 0 19 722744 9

Printed in Great Britain at the Alden Press, Oxford

INSCRIBED TO THE
MEMORY OF HER LATE MAJESTY
QUEEN VICTORIA
WHO GRACIOUSLY GAVE THE TITLE TO
AND ACCEPTED THE DEDICATION
OF THIS HISTORY

HEMINGBROUGH CHURCH FROM THE SOUTH-WEST

A HISTORY OF THE COUNTY OF
YORK
EAST RIDING

EDITED BY K. J. ALLISON

VOLUME III

PUBLISHED FOR
THE INSTITUTE OF HISTORICAL RESEARCH
BY
OXFORD UNIVERSITY PRESS
1976

Distributed by Oxford University Press until 1 January 1979
thereafter by Dawsons of Pall Mall

CONTENTS OF VOLUME THREE

	PAGE
Dedication	v
Contents	ix
List of Illustrations	x
List of Maps and Plans	xii
Editorial Note	xiii
Classes of Documents in the Public Record Office used	xiv
Note on Abbreviations	xv

Topography . . . . . Architectural investigation by A. P. Baggs

Ouse and Derwent Wapentake	By K. J. Allison	1
Dunnington	By J. D. Purdy	5
Elvington	By J. D. Purdy	12
Escrick	By K. J. Allison	17
Fulford	By K. J. Allison	29
Hemingbrough	By K. J. Allison	37
Hemingbrough		37
Barlby		47
Brackenholme with Woodhall		52
Cliffe with Lund		55
South Duffield		60
Menthorpe with Bowthorpe		63
Osgodby		64
Heslington	By K. J. Allison	66
Naburn	By K. J. Allison	74
Riccall	By K. J. Allison	82
Skipwith	By K. J. Allison	89
Stillingfleet	By J. D. Purdy	101
Thorganby	By J. D. Purdy	112
Wheldrake	By K. J. Allison	120
Harthill Wapentake	By K. J. Allison	129
Wilton Beacon division (western part)		
Allerthorpe	By G. H. R. Kent	133
Barmby Moor	By G. H. R. Kent	140
Catton	By K. J. Allison	147
High and Low Catton and Stamford Bridge East		147
Kexby, Scoreby, and Stamford Bridge West		158
Fangfoss	By G. H. R. Kent	164
Full Sutton	By K. J. Allison	170
Sutton upon Derwent	By K. J. Allison	173
Thornton	By G. H. R. Kent	179
Wilberfoss	By K. J. Allison	190
Index	By K. J. Allison and G. H. R. Kent	198

LIST OF ILLUSTRATIONS

Thanks are rendered to Aerofilms Ltd., the British Library, Mr. Keith Gibson, Hull Central Library, the National Monuments Record of the Royal Commission on Historical Monuments (England), the architects of the University of York (Robert Matthew, Johnson-Marshall & Partners), the vicar of Riccall, and the *Yorkshire Post* for permission to use material in their care or to use photographs in their possession as indicated below. Photographs dated 1972, 1973, and 1974 are by A. P. Baggs.

Hemingbrough church. Photograph, 1974	*frontispiece*
Moreby Hall. Photograph by Aerofilms Ltd., 1968	*facing page* 16
Escrick Hall. Photograph by Aerofilms Ltd., 1968	,, ,, 16
Escrick Church. Photograph, 1972	,, ,, 17
Elvington Church. Photograph, 1972	,, ,, 17
Hemingbrough: the remains of Loftsome Bridge. Photograph, 1973	,, ,, 32
Wheldrake: Ings Bridge. Photograph, *Yorkshire Post*, 1963 (Hull Central Library)	,, ,, 32
Stamford Bridge: the railway viaduct. Photograph, 1974	,, ,, 33
Cliffe: the former malting. Photograph, 1973	,, ,, 33
Dunnington: an old chicory kiln. Photograph, 1973	,, ,, 33
Thorganby: the coach-house and stables to the hall. Photograph, 1972	,, ,, 64
Kexby: Manor Farm. Photograph, 1973	,, ,, 64
Lund: Oak Wood Farm. Photograph, 1974	,, ,, 64
Dunnington: the village. Photograph by Aerofilms Ltd., 1972	,, ,, 65
Heslington: the University of York. Photograph by Keith Gibson, *c.* 1970	,, ,, 65
Naburn: Bell Hall. Photograph, 1972	,, ,, 80
Riccall: the old Vicarage. Photograph, 1973	,, ,, 80
Skipwith Church. Photograph, 1973	,, ,, 81
Riccall Church. Drawing of *c.* 1862 in church	,, ,, 81
Stillingfleet: the church, bridge and Town greens. Photograph, 1974	,, ,, 112
Allerthorpe: the village street. Photograph, 1974	,, ,, 112
Thorganby: Thicket Priory. Drawing by the architect, Edward Blore, for the design that was carried out. From B.L. Add. MS. 42028, f. 98	,, ,, 113
Heslington Hall, before restoration. From J. P. Neale, *Mansions of England* (1847), vol. ii	,, ,, 113
Thorganby Church. Photograph, 1972	,, ,, 128
Wheldrake Church. Photograph, 1974	,, ,, 128
Wheldrake: no. 51 Main Street. Photograph, 1973	,, ,, 129
South Duffield: Holmes House. Photograph, 1974	,, ,, 129
Barmby Moor House. Photograph, 1974	,, ,, 129
Barmby Moor: Barmby Manor. Photograph, 1974	,, ,, 129
Elvington Bridge. Photograph, 1972	,, ,, 160
Catton: Kexby Bridge. Photograph, 1973	,, ,, 160

LIST OF ILLUSTRATIONS

Thornton: Walbut Lock. Photograph, 1974 . . . . . . *facing page* 161

Thorganby: the former station. Photograph, 1974 . . . . . ,, ,, 161

Fangfoss: the former station. Photograph, 1974 . . . . . ,, ,, 161

Stamford Bridge: the former water-mill. Photograph, 1974 . . . . ,, ,, 176

Sutton upon Derwent: disused water-mill and Elvington Lock. Photograph by Aerofilms Ltd., 1968 . . . . ,, ,, 176

Stillingfleet Church: the south doorway. Photograph, 1972 . . . . ,, ,, 177

Sutton upon Derwent: fragment of an 11th-century cross-shaft. Photograph, National Monuments Record, 1965 . . . . ,, ,, 177

LIST OF MAPS AND PLANS

The maps were drawn by K. J. Wass, from drafts by K. J. Allison; the plans were compiled and drawn by A. P. Baggs. The maps are based on Ordnance Survey maps with the sanction of the Controller of H.M. Stationery Office, Crown Copyright reserved. The help of the Escrick Park Estate Office, Mr. and Mrs. R. J. Perry, and the late Cmdr. G. B. Palmes in giving access to original material is gratefully acknowledged.

	PAGE
The Wapentake of Ouse and Derwent	2
Escrick, *c.* 1600. From a map in the Escrick Park Estate Office	18
Growth plan of Escrick Hall	21
Deighton, 1619. From a map *penes* Mr. and Mrs. R. J. Perry	24
Hemingbrough Parish, *c.* 1915	38
Hemingbrough Church	44
Heslington, *c.* 1850	68
Naburn, 1739. From a map *penes* the late Cmdr. G. B. Palmes	76
Skipwith, 1769. From a map in the Escrick Park Estate Office	90
North Duffield, 1760. From a map in the Humberside Record Office	92
Harthill Wapentake (Wilton Beacon division)	130, 131
Catton and Stamford Bridge, 1616. From a map at Petworth House, Sussex	148
Thornton, 1616. From a map at Petworth House, Sussex	180
Wilberfoss and Newton upon Derwent, 1755. From a map at Petworth House, Sussex	192

EDITORIAL NOTE

The arrangement of the Victoria History of the County of York in five distinct sets of volumes is described in the Editorial Note to Volume I of the East Riding set. The present volume, the third in that set, relates the history of the parishes in Ouse and Derwent wapentake and of the more westerly parishes in the Wilton Beacon division of Harthill wapentake; the remainder of that division and the other divisions of the wapentake are reserved for treatment in later volumes.

The East Riding County Council, which in 1970 had assumed the responsibility for compiling the remaining East Riding volumes, was dissolved on 31 March 1974 under the Local Government Act, 1972, and the area which it had administered was transferred to the new counties of Humberside and North Yorkshire. Before the end of its existence the Council made a loan, free of interest, to the University of London to enable the University to take over the Council's purpose of completing the history of the East Riding. The staff of the *East Riding History* were accordingly transferred to the University's employment, and have continued their work under the direct supervision of the general Editor of the *History*. The University of London gratefully acknowledges the generosity of the former County Council both for its earlier collaboration and particularly for providing for the continuation of the project. The new arrangement was made possible by the resolute initiative of Lt.-Col. Sir John Dunnington-Jefferson, Bt., D.S.O., D.L., and the former Clerk of the East Riding County Council, the late Mr. R. A. Whitley, D.L.

In September 1972 the Revd. J. D. Purdy, who before taking orders had been assistant editor of the *East Riding History* since 1968, resigned his post. He was succeeded in August 1973 by Mr. (later Dr.) G. H. R. Kent.

Many have helped in preparing this volume. The names of those who assisted with a particular part are indicated in the footnotes or in the preface to the list of illustrations. Among those who made documents available and provided information for several places or passages were the Librarian of York Minster, the Director and acting Director of the Borthwick Institute of Historical Research, University of York, the Diocesan Registrar, the Librarian of the North Yorkshire County Library at York, the Librarian of the Humberside County Library at Beverley, and the City Archivist of Leeds: to them and their colleagues, as also to Mr. N. C. Forbes Adam, and to parochial incumbents collectively, thanks are gratefully offered. In particular, acknowledgement is made of the extensive help given by Mr. N. Higson, formerly East Riding County Archivist and now Archivist to the University of Hull, and by Mr. C. N. Snowden, Acting Registrar of Deeds for the East Riding.

The *General Introduction* to the *History* (1970) outlines the structure and aims of the series as a whole.

LIST OF CLASSES OF DOCUMENTS IN THE PUBLIC RECORD OFFICE
USED IN THIS VOLUME
WITH THEIR CLASS NUMBERS

Chancery
    Proceedings
  C 1   Early
  C 2   Series I
  C 3   Series II
  C 5   Six Clerks Series, Bridges
  C 54   Close Rolls
  C 66   Patent Rolls
  C 94   Survey of Church Livings
    Inquisitions post mortem
  C 132   Series I, Hen. III
  C 133   Edw. I
  C 134   Edw. II
  C 135   Edw. III
  C 136   Ric. II
  C 138   Hen. V
  C 139   Hen. VI
  C 140   Edw. IV and V
  C 142   Series II
  C 145   Miscellaneous Inquisitions

Court of Common Pleas
    Feet of Fines
  C.P. 25(1)   Series I
  C.P. 25(2)   Series II
  C.P. 40   De Banco Rolls
  C.P. 43   Recovery Rolls

Duchy of Lancaster
  D.L. 29   Ministers' Accounts

Exchequer, King's Remembrancer
  E 134   Depositions taken by Commission
  E 142   Ancient Extents
  E 152   Inquisitions, Enrolments
  E 164   Miscellaneous Books, Series I
  E 178   Special Commissions of Inquiry
  E 179   Subsidy Rolls, etc.
  E 199   Sheriffs' Accounts, etc.

Exchequer, Augmentation Office
  E 301   Certificates of Colleges and Chantries
  E 303   Conventual Leases
  E 309   Enrolments of Leases
  E 310   Particulars for Leases
  E 311   Counterparts or Transcripts of Leases
  E 315   Miscellaneous Books
  E 318   Particulars for Grants

Exchequer, Lord Treasurer's Remembrancer's and Pipe Offices
  E 370   Miscellaneous Rolls

Ministry of Education
  Ed. 7   Public Elementary Schools, Preliminary Statements
  Ed. 49   Endowment Files, Elementary Education

Home Office
    Various, Census
  H.O. 107   Population Returns
  H.O. 129   Ecclesiastical Returns

Justices Itinerant, Assize and Gaol Delivery Justices, etc.
  J.I. 1   Assize Rolls, Eyre Rolls, etc.

Court of King's Bench (Crown Side)
  K.B. 27   Coram Rege Rolls

Exchequer, Office of the Auditors of Land Revenue
  L.R. 2   Miscellaneous Books

Map Room
  M.P.E.   Maps and Plans

Court of Requests
  Req. 2   Proceedings

Special Collections
  S.C. 2   Court Rolls
  S.C. 6   Ministers' Accounts

Court of Star Chamber
  Sta. Cha. 2 Proceedings, Hen. VIII

Court of Wards
  Wards 7   Inquisitions post mortem

NOTE ON ABBREVIATIONS

Among the abbreviations and short titles used the following may require elucidation:

Acreage Returns, 1905	Board of Agriculture, Acreage Returns of 1905, from a MS. *penes* the Editor, Victoria History of the East Riding
Aveling, *Post Reformation Catholicism*	H. Aveling, *Post Reformation Catholicism in East Yorkshire 1558–1790* (East Yorkshire Local History Series, xi)
B.I.H.R.	University of York, The Borthwick Institute of Historical Research
B.L.	British Library (used in references to documents transferred from the British Museum)
Baines, *Hist. Yorks.* (1823)	E. Baines, *History, Directory and Gazetteer of the County of York*, vol. ii, East and North Ridings (1823)
Boulter, 'Ch. Bells'	W. C. Boulter, 'Inscriptions on the Church Bells of the East Riding', *Yorkshire Archaeological Journal*, vol. iii (1875)
Bulmer, *Dir. E. Yorks.* (1892)	T. Bulmer & Co. *History, Topography and Directory of East Yorkshire* (1892)
Char. Com. files	Records held by the Charity Commission at its Northern Office, Liverpool
1801 Crop Returns	School of Economic Studies, University of Leeds, typescript based on the original returns in the Public Record Office (H.O. 76/26), being an appendix to P. A. Churley, 'The Yorkshire Crop Returns of 1801', *Yorkshire Bulletin of Economic and Social Research*, vol. v (1953)
D. & C. York	The Dean and Chapter of York
E.R.R.O.	East Riding Record Office, County Hall, Beverley; since 1 April 1974 the Humberside Record Office. After the East Riding County Council was dissolved, and at an advanced stage in the compilation of this volume, many of the private collections deposited at Beverley were removed by their owners to the Brynmor Jones Library, University of Hull, which has retained the old references. A few private collections were transferred elsewhere.
E.Y.C.	*Early Yorkshire Charters*, ed. W. Farrer and Sir Charles Clay (Yorkshire Archaeological Society Publications, Extra Series, 1914–65)
Educ. Enquiry Abstract	*Abstract of Answers and Returns relative to the State of Education in England*, H.C. 62 (1835), xliii
Educ. of Poor Digest	*Digest of Returns to the Select Committee on the Education of the Poor*, H.C. 224 (1819), ix (2)
G.R.O.	General Register Office, St. Catherine's House, 10 Kingsway, London
Herring's Visit. i–v	*Archbishop Herring's Visitation Returns, 1743* (Yorkshire Archaeological Society, Record Series, vols. lxxi, lxxii, lxxv, lxxvii, lxxix)
Hodgson, *Q.A.B.*	C. Hodgson, *Queen Anne's Bounty* (1845)
H.U.L.	Brynmor Jones Library, University of Hull
Inst. Bks.	Institution Books, being Public Record Office MS. indexes to Bishops' Certificates of Institutions to Benefices (E 331)
Inventories of Ch. Goods	*Inventories of Church Goods* (Yorkshire Archaeological Society, Record Series, vol. xcvii)
Lawton, *Rer. Eccl. Dioc. Ebor.*	G. Lawton, *Collectio Rerum Ecclesiasticarum de Diocesi Eboracensi* (1840)
Morris, *E. Yorks.*	J. E. Morris, *The East Riding of Yorkshire* (Little Guides, 3rd edn. 1932)
Pevsner, *Yorks. E.R.*	N. Pevsner, *The Buildings of England: Yorkshire: York and the East Riding* (1972)
R.D.B.	Registry of Deeds, Beverley
Reg. Corbridge, i–ii	*Register of Thomas Corbridge* (Surtees Society, vols. cxxxviii, cxli)

NOTE ON ABBREVIATIONS

Reg. Giffard	*Register of Walter Giffard* (Surtees Society, vol. cix)
Reg. Gray	*Register, or Rolls, of Walter Gray* (Surtees Society, vol. lvi)
Reg. Greenfield, i–v	*Register of William Greenfield* (Surtees Society, vols. cxlv, cxlix, cli, clii, cliii)
Reg. Romeyn, i–ii	*Registers of John le Romeyn and of Henry of Newark* (Surtees Society, vols. cxxiii, cxxviii)
Reg. Wickwane	*Register of William Wickwane* (Surtees Society, vol. cxiv)
10th, 11th, and 12th Rep. Com. Char.	*Reports of the Commissioners for Inquiry concerning certain Charities in England and Wales*, H.C. 103 (1824), xiii; H.C. 433 (1824), xiv; H.C. 348 (1825), x
Rep. Com. Eccl. Revenues	*Report of the Commissioners appointed to Inquire into the Ecclesiastical Revenues of England and Wales* [67], H.C. (1835), xxii
3rd Rep. Poor Law Com.	*3rd Annual Report of the Poor Law Commissioners for England and Wales*, H.C. 546 (1837), xxxi
Returns relating to Elem. Educ.	*Returns relating to Elementary Education*, H.C. 201 (1871), lv
Sheahan and Whellan, *Hist. York & E.R.*	J. J. Sheahan and T. Whellan, *History and Topography of the City of York, the Ainsty Wapentake, and the East Riding of Yorkshire*, vol. ii, East Riding (1856)
T.E.R.A.S.	*Transactions of the East Riding Antiquarian Society*
Test. Ebor. i–vi	*Testamenta Eboracensia* (Yorkshire Archaeological Society, Record Series, vols. iv, xxx, xlv, liii, lxxix, cvi)
White, *Dir. E. & N.R. Yorks.* (1840)	W. White, *History, Gazetteer and Directory of the East and North Ridings of Yorkshire* (1840)
White, *Dir. Hull & York* (1846)	F. White & Co. *General Directory of Kingston-upon-Hull and the City of York* (1846)
White, *Dir. Hull & York* (1858)	F. White & Co. *General Directory and Topography of Kingston-upon-Hull and the City of York* (1858)
Y.A.J.	*Yorkshire Archaeological Journal*
Y.A.S.	Yorkshire Archaeological Society, Leeds
Yorks. Ch. Plate	*Yorkshire Church Plate*, begun by T. M. Fallow, completed and edited by H. B. McCall, Yorkshire Archaeological Society Publications, Extra Series, vol. i (1912)
Yorks. Deeds, i–x	*Yorkshire Deeds* (Yorkshire Archaeological Society, Record Series, vols. xxxix, l, lxiii, lxv, lxix, lxxvi, lxxxiii, cii, cxi, cxx)
Yorks. Fines, i–iv	*Feet of Fines of the Tudor Period* (Yorkshire Archaeological Society, Record Series, vols. ii, v, vii, viii)
Yorks. Fines, 1218–31; 1232–46; 1246–72; 1272–1300; 1300–14	*Feet of Fines* (Yorkshire Archaeological Society, Record Series, vols. lxii, lxvii, lxxxii, cxxi, cxxvii)
Yorks. Fines, 1327–47; 1347–77; 1603–14; 1614–25	*Feet of Fines* (Yorkshire Archaeological Society, Record Series, vols. xlii, lii, liii, lviii)
Yorks. Inq. i–iv; Hen. IV–V	*Yorkshire Inquisitions* (Yorkshire Archaeological Society, Record Series, vols. xii, xxiii, xxxi, xxxvii, lix)

OUSE AND DERWENT WAPENTAKE

THE WAPENTAKE lies in the heart of the Vale of York, at the western extremity of the East Riding; it adjoins both of the other ridings, and the city of York stands at its northern edge. The rivers Ouse and Derwent form the greater part of the boundaries of the wapentake, enclosing a gently undulating countryside relieved by few marked natural features. The area is still largely rural with a mainly agricultural economy.

Much of the land lies at about 25 ft. above sea-level and large tracts are lower still. It consists mostly of drifts of clay, sand, and silt, deposited in the shallow water that occupied the vale during the final stage of glaciation in northern England. Successive limits of the Vale of York glacier during that period are marked by two pronounced terminal moraines of boulder clay and gravel: the Escrick moraine crosses the centre of the wapentake and the York moraine forms its northern boundary. These ridges are the most prominent features of the Ouse and Derwent landscape, the first in places exceeding 50 ft. above sea-level, the second even passing 100 ft. More recent deposits include extensive areas of alluvium occupying the flood plains of the rivers, more especially in the south of the wapentake.[1]

In prehistoric and Roman times the moraines served as routeways across the marshy vale, and Anglian and Scandinavian settlers established several villages upon them, like Escrick, Wheldrake, and Dunnington. Elsewhere subtle variations in relief and drainage determined the settlement pattern, and riverside villages like Naburn and Elvington were planted at points where the meandering Ouse and Derwent swing close to the firm valley sides. The Ouse has in places changed its course in historic times and several small areas thus became detached from their ancient parishes. These anomalies were tidied up by late-19th-century boundary changes, like that which brought Newhay (now in Hemingbrough), a former monastic grange, into the East Riding.

In the early Middle Ages much of the wapentake lay within the royal forest of Ouse and Derwent, disafforested in 1234.[2] Widespread woodland and common wastes long characterized the area, however, and the methods by which they were assarted helped to produce a distinctive agricultural landscape. The small open fields, large commons, and extensive early inclosures contrast strongly with the predominantly open-field economy of the wolds in, for example, Dickering wapentake.[3] Much common land remained in Ouse and Derwent until well into the 19th century, and one waste, the 600-acre Skipwith common, survived in 1973 as a nature reserve.

A few timber-framed buildings still survive in the area, but the villages now consist largely of brick houses of the 17th century and later. Several outstanding mansions in the more northerly parishes reflect the proximity of York and the interest of its citizens in country property. Much of Gate Fulford has become part of the built-up area of the city since the 19th century, and recently several villages have been developed as York dormitories. In addition, the University of York was established at Heslington in 1960.

[1] *The Pennines and Adjacent Areas* (Brit. Regional Geol.) (H.M.S.O.), 72–4; Geol. Surv. Map 1″, solid and drift, sheets 63 (1967 edn.), 71 (1973 edn.); drift, sheet 79 (1973 edn.).
[2] *V.C.H. Yorks.* i. 501.
[3] See especially pp. 123–5; cf. *V.C.H. Yorks. E.R.* ii, *passim*.

A HISTORY OF YORKSHIRE: EAST RIDING

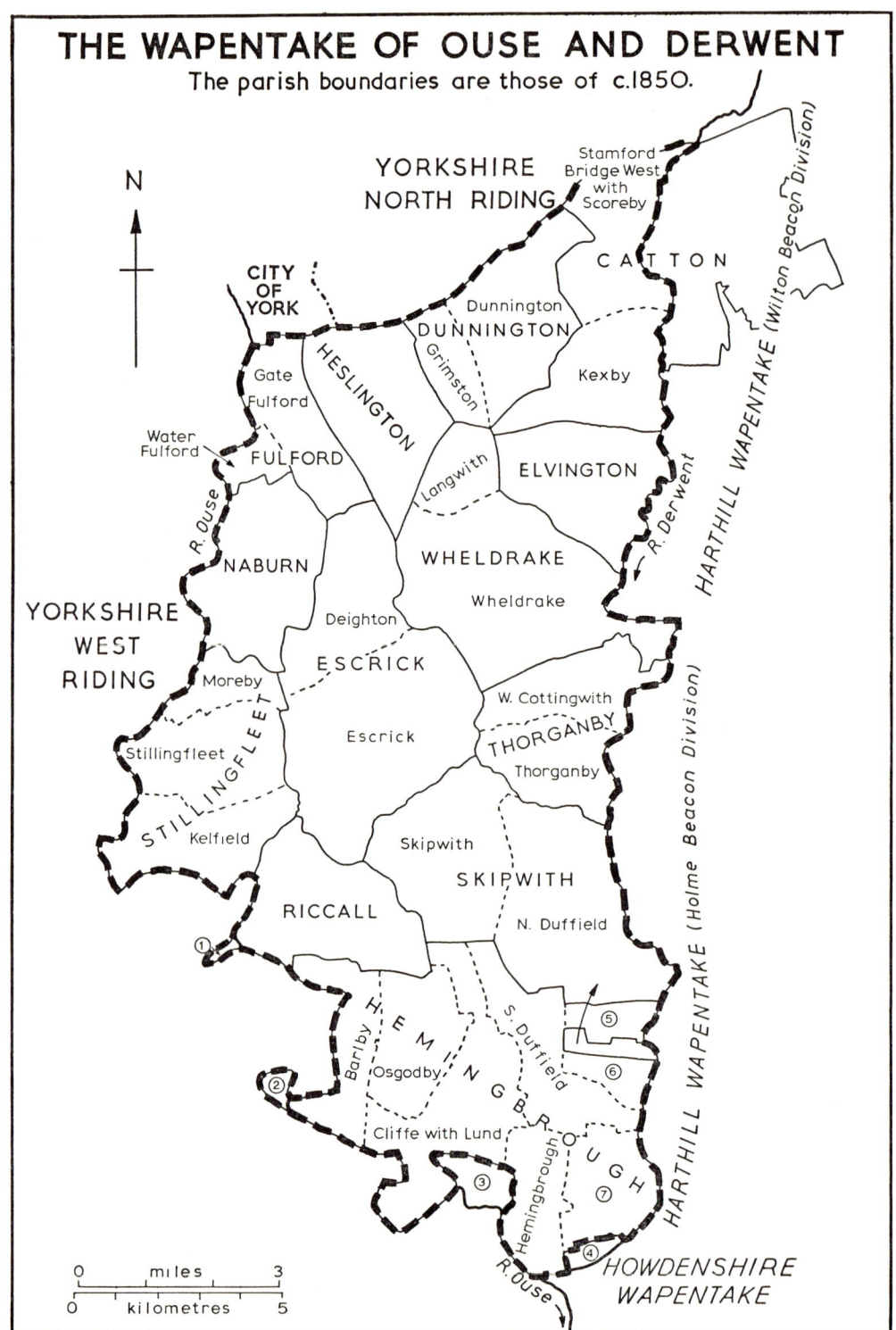

1 The Nesses (later W.R.), 2 The Holmes (later W.R.), 3 Newhay (later in Hemingbrough), 4 part of Barmby on the Marsh (later in Hemingbrough), 5 Menthorpe, 6 Bowthorpe, 7 Brackenholme with Woodhall.

OUSE AND DERWENT WAPENTAKE

Industrial development has largely been confined to Barlby, where riverside mills and housing estates form a suburb of Selby, across the Ouse in the West Riding.

As has been explained elsewhere[4] the Domesday hundreds in the East Riding were during the 12th century transformed into wapentakes. Ouse and Derwent wapentake, first mentioned in 1200,[5] was made up of parts of Cave, Howden, Pocklington, Sneculfcros, and Warter hundreds, though the Howden townships may not have been included until the 14th century.

From Cave hundred the wapentake drew part of the township of West Cottingwith. From Howden it took Babthorpe, Barlby, Bowthorpe, Brackenholme, Cliffe, the rest of West Cottingwith, North Duffield, South Duffield, Hagthorpe, Hemingbrough, Osgodby, Riccall, Skipwith, and Thorganby. Menthorpe and Woodhall, not mentioned in Domesday, were also included in the wapentake. From Pocklington hundred the wapentake drew the townships of 'Chetelstorp' (in Escrick), Elvington, Escrick, Deighton, Kelfield, Moreby, Stillingfleet, and Wheldrake. Kexby, not mentioned separately in 1086, was also included. Sneculfcros hundred contributed the townships of Dunnington, Grimston, 'Janulfestorp', and Scoreby, and Warter hundred those of Water Fulford, Heslington, Langwith, and Naburn.[6] Also included in Ouse and Derwent wapentake was Gate Fulford, which in the Survey had been described, along with other places, 'in the geld of the city' of York.[7]

The early relationship between Howden hundred and the new wapentake is not entirely clear. The hundred comprised the liberty of the bishop of Durham's manor of Howden, and by the later 12th century the liberty was known as Howdenshire. Not until the mid 14th century was Howdenshire regarded as a wapentake, when those townships which became part of Ouse and Derwent wapentake were finally excluded. In the mean time Howdenshire was for certain purposes apparently regarded as lying partly in Harthill and partly in Ouse and Derwent wapentakes. Thus 'the wapentake of Harthill with part of Howdenshire' was mentioned in 1230.[8] The whole of the later Ouse and Derwent wapentake was curiously described in 1284–5 as 'the wapentake in Howdenshire between Ouse and Derwent'.[9] In 1316 only the northern townships were listed under Ouse and Derwent, the rest being included with the liberty of Howden.[10] In 1354, for taxation purposes, the southern parishes were still separated under the liberty of Howden, but by 1446 the distinction was no longer made.[11] The wapentake of Howdenshire had itself been mentioned in 1354[12] and perhaps emerged as a distinct unit in the later 14th century, just as Ouse and Derwent then assumed its modern identity. Various townships and parts of townships in Ouse and Derwent were also taxed separately in 1354 as belonging to the liberties of St. Leonard's hospital and St. Mary's abbey in York and to York minster.[13]

The township of Gate Helmsley was included in Ouse and Derwent wapentake in 1284–5 and still in 1446,[14] but it was subsequently reckoned part of Bulmer wapentake in the North Riding.[15]

The area dealt with here under Ouse and Derwent includes Newhay, gained from the West Riding in 1883, as well as the Nesses and the Holmes, transferred to the West Riding that year. Kexby and Scoreby, which were parts of Catton parish, itself mainly in the Wilton Beacon division of Harthill wapentake, are reserved for treatment later in this volume.

[4] *V.C.H. Yorks. E.R.* ii. 2.
[5] O. S. Anderson, *English Hundred-Names*, 19.
[6] *V.C.H. Yorks.* ii. 318–22.
[7] Ibid. 193; *V.C.H. City of York*, 19.
[8] Anderson, op. cit. 18–19.
[9] *Feud. Aids*, vi. 32.
[10] Ibid. 172–3.
[11] E 179/202/53, 120.
[12] Anderson, op. cit. 18.
[13] E 179/202/53.
[14] E 179/202/120; *Feud. Aids*, vi. 32.
[15] See *V.C.H. Yorks. N.R.* ii. 139.

The wapentake remained with the Crown until at least the 16th century. The office of wapentake bailiff was granted for life to successive holders in 1542, 1552, and 1567.[16]

It is not certainly known where the wapentake met. In 1280, however, it was recorded that the king claimed suit from the prioress of Thicket at the county and wapentake courts at York once a year.[17] They may both have been held at the castle.[18] Many of the townships paid a share of the wapentake fine and owed suit at the court.[19]

The sheriff accounted for 6 marks from the wapentake in 1236–7 and 5 marks in 1399–1400.[20] In the 16th and 17th centuries he received less than £1 in blanch farm from Ouse and Derwent. The bishop of Durham was said in 1542–3 to be quit of suit at the wapentake courts.[21]

[16] *L. & P. Hen. VIII*, xvii, p. 33; *Cal. Pat. 1550–3*, 295; *1566–9*, p. 82.
[17] *Yorks. Fines, 1272–1300*, pp. 45–6.
[18] See *V.C.H. City of York*, 522–3.
[19] *Feud. Aids*, vi. 32–7; *Plac. de Quo Warr.* (Rec. Com.), 191, 201.
[20] E 370/6/18, 27.
[21] E 370/6/28; /13/217; /15/28, 43, 57, 60.

DUNNINGTON

THE VILLAGE of Dunnington, which was an Anglian settlement,[1] lies about 4 miles east of York on the southern flank of the York moraine.[2] The small hamlet of Grimston, also Anglian, occupies a similar situation in the west of the parish, and surviving wells near both settlements suggest that a supply of water was readily available. In 1086 there was another hamlet in the parish, a Scandinavian settlement called 'Janulfestorp',[3] but no later reference to it has been found and its site is not known. The irregularly-shaped parish covers 3,837 a., of which Grimston township accounts for 797 a.[4]

The boulder clay, sand, and gravel of the moraine,[5] along the northern margin of the parish, lie mostly at a height of between 75 ft. and 100 ft. above sea-level, although the area around Mill hill in the north-east is higher. Other sections of the moraine are called Thorn, Thorntree, and Stock hills. The village lies at about 50 ft. to 75 ft. and the rest of the parish to the south occupies the more low-lying outwash sand and clay. The open fields of Dunnington lay for the most part on the moraine and an area of assarts and ings on the adjoining lower ground. The pattern of long narrow fields reflects the inclosure of these grounds by 'flatting' in 1707. Much of the lower ground in the south of the parish was occupied by the common, and there the larger more compact fields are the result of the inclosure of 1772. In Grimston township more irregular fields may reflect its earlier inclosure.

The low grounds are drained by several dikes and streams, some of which form sections of the parish boundary, notably Common drain in the north-east. Common, Ings, and Howden Jury drains unite in Dunnington as Tilmire drain, which flows southwards towards the former Tilmire[6] and becomes Bridge dike in Escrick parish. The name 'Howden Jury', recorded by 1850, suggests that the drain may have been the responsibility of the court of sewers for the west parts of the East Riding.[7]

The former Roman road from Brough to York via Stamford Bridge follows the moraine along the northern edge of Dunnington, where it forms the entire parish boundary. The Dunnington stretch is now part of a main road to the coast. A second Roman road to York, more southerly and more direct, crosses the centre of the parish and meets the first road at Grimston. This later became the main York–Beverley road. Both roads were turnpiked in 1765 and the trust was not discontinued until 1872. A bar was built at the junction and the still-surviving milestones were erected.[8] The roads have been widened and straightened in the 20th century.[9] Dunnington village lies between the main roads and is linked to them by four minor roads. One of the latter, Common Lane, continues southwards beyond the Beverley road at Four Lane Ends. It crosses Common drain by a small 19th-century brick bridge, known in 1709 as Byart bridge,[10] in 1850 as Scauders bridge,[11] and in the 20th century as Hassacarr bridge. From Grimston a road formerly known as Grove Lane[12] leads southwards to Elvington. The Derwent Valley Light Railway, opened in 1912 with a station at Four Lane Ends, crosses the parish west and south of the village. The line was closed for passenger traffic in 1926[13] but in 1974 was still used for goods from York as far as Dunnington station. A York bypass road was being constructed across Grimston township in 1974.

The older houses and cottages of Dunnington village, all of brick and dating from the 18th and early 19th centuries, lie for the most part along the closely built-up York and Church Streets and Common Road. Characteristically they have plat bands, brick cornices, and rising sash windows. Several of those of early date appear to have been of only one storey with attics, but, with the exception of one close to the church, they have been heightened to the full two storeys which are normal until the 19th century. At the road junction in the centre of the village stands a cross, replacing a medieval shaft and socket stone which in 1972 were in the Rectory garden. The present shaft, with ball finial and stepped socket stone, was put up in 1840;[14] it was restored in 1900.[15] Near by stood a lock-up with two cells, built in 1850 and largely demolished by 1908.[16] Other older houses stand along Water Lane, and back lanes around the village include Church, Garden Flat, Pear Tree, and Peter Crofts Lanes.

The most noteworthy dwelling in the village is Dunnington House in Common Road, a later-18th-century house of three bays, with additions of the early 19th century which include the central doorcase and flanking screen walls with round-headed recesses and ball finials. The house was a private lunatic asylum owned by the Hornby family from at least 1817 until the 1880s. In 1826 it was said that only a limited number of patients 'of distinction' were admitted, but in 1838 11 out of 16 were paupers. Later there were usually about 20–40 patients.[17]

A great expansion of Dunnington as a dormitory for York has been in progress since c. 1960 and estates of private houses and bungalows have appeared in all parts of the village.[18] There are also some 30 council houses in Church Lane and York Street and 19 west of the village beyond the railway line.

The Temperance Hall, which in 1903 became a

---

[1] *P.N.E.R. Yorks.* (E.P.N.S.), 273.
[2] This article was written in 1972.
[3] *V.C.H. Yorks.* ii. 293; *P.N.E.R. Yorks.* 317.
[4] O.S. Map 6", Yorks. (1853–4 edn.). Most of the parish is covered by sheet 175, the rest by sheet 174.
[5] Geol. Surv. Map 1", solid and drift, sheets 63 (1967 edn.), 71 (1973 edn.).   [6] See p. 29.
[7] June A. Sheppard, *Draining of the Marshlands of S. Holderness and the Vale of York* (E. Yorks. Loc. Hist. Ser. xx), 17.
[8] K. A. MacMahon, *Roads and Turnpike Trusts in E. Yorks.* (E. Yorks. Loc. Hist. Ser. xviii), 21–3, 70.
[9] E.R.C.C. *Mins.* 1919–20, 173, 270; 1920–1, 317; 1960–1, 345; 1967–8, 28; 1968–9, 19.
[10] E.R.R.O., DDGD/Box 1.
[11] O.S. Map 6" (1853–4 edn.).
[12] Ibid.
[13] *V.C.H. City of York*, 479.
[14] Sheahan and Whellan, *Hist. York & E.R.* ii. 616.
[15] *Kelly's Dir. N. & E.R. Yorks.* (1901), 469.
[16] Sheahan and Whellan, *Hist. York & E.R.* ii. 616; *Yorks. Gaz.* 29 Feb. 1908.
[17] E.R.R.O., QAL/3/21–9, 57.
[18] See plate facing p. 65.

club and reading room, was built in Church Street in 1889.[19] In 1823 there were two inns, the Cross Keys and the Greyhound,[20] and both still existed in 1972. By 1840 the Smith's Arms, later successively known as the Blacksmith's Arms and the Three Horseshoes, had appeared, also in the centre of the village;[21] it closed in the 1930s.[22]

The now much shrunken hamlet of Grimston consisted in 1606 of 10 houses and 8 cottages standing in north, south, and east rows.[23] An undated 18th-century map shows that some houses then lay west of the Elvington road as well as alongside it as at present. By that time there was also a group of houses at the junction of the Beverley and Stamford Bridge roads,[24] and by 1850 they were known as Grimston Smithy,[25] later simply as Grimston. Of the older houses Manor House or Manor House Farm is a mid-18th-century building with a stringcourse, a dentil eaves course, and a doorcase with panelled pilasters surmounted by a cornice. Hill Farm is a similar but plainer 18th-century building. There are earthworks, possibly representing former house-sites, in near-by fields, where there is also a 19th-century brick well-head. Three alehouses were licensed at Grimston in the 1750s and one in the 1760s and later.[26] By 1823 it was known as the Blackwell Ox[27] and by 1840 as the Bingley Arms.[28] It was presumably on the site, at the junction of the Bridlington and Beverley roads, occupied by the New Inn in 1850.[29] It had closed by 1872.[30]

In the 19th and especially the 20th centuries a scattered collection of houses has grown up on the York–Beverley road and on the side roads north and south of Four Lane Ends. They include the Windmill inn, first mentioned in 1872.[31] The isolated farm-houses in Dunnington township apparently all date from after the inclosures of 1707 and 1772. Dunnington Hall, known throughout the 19th century as East Field House,[32] stands in its own grounds in East Field Lane. It is a large early-19th-century three-storeyed building, extended later, and has a coach-house and stable block. The house was owned by a York druggist in 1821[33] and may be an early reflection of the proximity of the city. Clock Farm in Grimston has a large barn surmounted by an ornate brick and stone clock tower with a wooden bellcot.

In 1377 there were 127 poll-tax payers at Dunnington.[34] In 1672 74 households there were included in the hearth-tax return, 19 of them discharged from paying. Of those chargeable 45 had one hearth, 7 had 2, and one each had 3, 4, and 8 hearths.[35] There were about 78 families in the whole parish in 1743[36] and 70 in 1764.[37] The population of Dunnington township was 430 in 1801 and it rose steadily to a peak of 842 in 1861. It then decreased to 741 in 1881 and 654 in 1901[38] before again rising to 738 in 1921 and 818 in 1931. The population of the whole parish was 958 in 1951 and 983 in 1961, but with the subsequent building of housing estates it rose to 2,442 in 1971.[39]

There were 41 poll-tax payers at Grimston in 1377[40] and 14 households were included in the 1672 hearth-tax assessment. Two were discharged from paying, 4 had one hearth, 6 had 2, and one each had 4 and 13 hearths.[41] In 1801 the population of the township was 51 and until 1901 it varied only between 50 and 81.[42] In 1921 there were 77 inhabitants and in 1931 66.[43]

MANORS AND OTHER ESTATES. In 1066 Slettan and Edwin held two manors totalling 4 carucates at Dunnington, which in 1086 were held as one estate by the chapter of York. Before the Conquest two other estates there, totalling $5\frac{3}{4}$ carucates, had been held by Norman and Alden. In 1086, despite a claim that 14 bovates belonged to William Malet, they were held as one estate by Geoffrey of William de Percy.[44] The chapter of York subsequently became the under-tenant of the Percies and the whole of the chapter's Dunnington estate was set aside for the support of two prebendaries.

The land held under the Percys became part of the endowment of Dunnington prebend, which had apparently been formed by 1175 when, on the division of the Percy barony, a York prebend, presumably Dunnington, was assigned the share of Jocelin of Louvain.[45] The Percy interest in the prebend was finally extinguished in 1225, when Richard de Percy quitclaimed all his rights in the prebendal lands in Dunnington, Grimston, and elsewhere to the archbishop of York.[46] The prebend's estate in Dunnington township was later known as the manor of *DUNNINGTON*. It consisted of 18 bovates, 68 a., and some 20 tofts and crofts c. 1295.[47] About 1330 2 bovates were alienated without royal licence,[48] and in 1349 they were ordered to be restored to the prebendary.[49]

The manor was let by the prebendary in 1548 to John Boyce and in 1692 to Thomas Rhodes for short terms,[50] and in 1703 to Tobias Jenkins for lives. At the inclosure of 1707 the last-named received 138 a. for his demesne. About 600 a. were then allotted to copyholders.[51] The manor was let to J. S. Smith in 1767[52] and at the inclosure of 1772 he received 110 a. for his demesne. Copyhold tenants

---

[19] R.D.B., 54/393/374 (1903); Bulmer, *Dir. E. Yorks.* (1892), 593.
[20] Baines, *Hist. Yorks.* (1823), ii. 199.
[21] White, *Dir. E. & N.R. Yorks.* (1840), 325, and later directories.
[22] Local information.
[23] Leeds City Archives, Lane-Fox 83/1.
[24] Ibid. 117/24.
[25] O.S. Map 6" (1853–4 edn.).
[26] E.R.R.O., QDT/2/15.
[27] Baines, *Hist. Yorks.* (1823), ii. 211.
[28] White, *Dir. E. & N.R. Yorks.* (1840), 325.
[29] O.S. Map 6" (1853–4 edn.).
[30] *Kelly's Dir. N. & E.R. Yorks.* (1872), 355–6.
[31] Ibid. 356.
[32] O.S. Map 6" (1853–4 edn.); directories.
[33] E.R.R.O., DDBH/5/2.
[34] E 179/202/58 m. 18.
[35] E 179/205/504.
[36] *Herring's Visit.* i. 171.
[37] B.I.H.R., Bp. V. 1764/Ret. 156.
[38] *V.C.H. Yorks.* iii. 497.
[39] Census.
[40] E 179/202/58 m. 7.
[41] E 179/205/504.
[42] *V.C.H. Yorks.* iii. 497.
[43] Census.
[44] *V.C.H. Yorks.* ii. 211, 262, 293, 320.
[45] *E.Y.C.* xi, p. 66.
[46] *Percy Charty.* (Sur. Soc. cxvii), p. 17.
[47] *Miscellanea*, iv (Y.A.S. Rec. Ser. xciv), 7–8.
[48] *Yorks. Fines, 1327–47*, p. 31.
[49] *Cal. Inq. Misc.* ii, p. 516.
[50] Minster Libr., D. & C. Archives, Wb. f. 47; Wf. ff. 20d.–21d.
[51] E.R.R.O., DDGD/Box 1.
[52] B.I.H.R., CC. Ab. 10.

were awarded about 700 a.[53] The manor was let to the Revd. William Lowth in 1772 and to the Revd. Frederick Dodsworth in 1796. In 1829 the estate was let in three parts, Dodsworth's devisees receiving the manor and 92 a. and two other men a total of 181 a.[54] In 1847 the manor was vested in the Ecclesiastical Commissioners upon a voidance of the prebend.[55] The commissioners sold 156 a. to Thomas Barker in 1853[56] and 77 a. to the Revd. E. Prest in 1855–6.[57] A total of 353 a. of copyhold land was enfranchised between 1898 and 1922,[58] and the remainder under the Law of Property Act of 1922.[59] The commissioners sold a further 38 a. between 1947 and 1964.[60]

In 1672 a house of eight hearths at Dunnington, which may have been the prebendary's manor-house, was occupied by a Mr. Hall.[61] The manor-house was let to Thomas Barker in 1829[62] and sold to him in 1853.[63] It stood west of the church[64] and was described as a 'neat residence' in 1872.[65] The house was demolished c. 1966 and a housing estate built on the site.[66]

The rest of the chapter's estate in the township was assigned to Ampleforth prebend, presumably at its formation before 1219–34.[67] The prebendal estate consisted of 20 bovates, 100 a. of pasture, and 6 tofts and crofts c. 1295.[68] It was let for a short term to William Witham in 1639,[69] and was later attached to the prebendary's manor of Heslington, the lessee of which, Henry Wickham, received 103 a. for his demesne at the inclosure of 1707. Copyholders received about 200 a.[70] Wickham's lease was renewed for lives in 1722[71] and at the inclosure of 1772 the Revd. Henry Wickham received 6 a. as lord of Heslington manor. Copyholders were allotted 133 a.[72] The estate followed the descent of Heslington manor,[73] and in 1853 the Ecclesiastical Commissioners sold 52 a. to Elizabeth Appleby.[74] The rest of the estate was subsequently merged with Dunnington manor.[75]

The prebendary of Ampleforth had a manor-house at Dunnington c. 1295.[76]

In 1066 Sonulf held an estate of 2 carucates at Grimston and in 1086 it was held by Niel of the count of Mortain, despite claims by William de Percy and Ernuin the priest.[77] In 1166 it was apparently held by Matthew de Punchardun of Bertram of Bulmer[78] and in 1284–5 Alan Roald and Hugh of Methley, described as chaplains, held it of 'the heirs of Punchardun', and they of Ralph de Neville.[79] In 1287 Hugh de Punchardun granted the manor of GRIMSTON to York minster to support a chantry he had founded there.[80] In 1346 a carucate was held of Richard de Neville by the heirs of Simon de Hescheheld.[81]

The Punchardun chantry in the minster was dedicated to Saints Agatha, Lucy, and Scholastica.[82] After the suppression its Grimston property was granted by the Crown to William Tanckard in 1599, when it comprised 7 houses and cottages, 4 closes, and 11 bovates. At the same time Tanckard acquired the former lands of St. Nicholas's hospital, York, and in 1606 his estate in Grimston amounted to 268 a. He still had the manor-house in 1630.[83] Tanckard conveyed property in the township to Sir Henry Jenkins in 1622,[84] and by 1697 the manor was held by Tobias Jenkins.[85] Like Scoreby manor Grimston was settled on Tobias's daughter Mary and her husband Sir Henry Goodrick, and it passed in 1715 to Mark Kirkby. Whereas Jenkins surrendered his life interest in Scoreby to Kirkby's sons Mark and Christopher in 1723, he regained Grimston from them that year and promptly sold it to Robert Benson, Lord Bingley.[86]

Lord Bingley's daughter Harriet married in 1731 George Fox, who became Lord Bingley in 1762,[87] and by 1779 it had passed to his nephew James Fox-Lane (or Lane-Fox).[88] It descended in the family until 1856 when George Lane-Fox sold it, comprising 761 a., to T. S. Watkinson.[89] In 1890 Watkinson's devisees sold the manor to William Hotham[90] and his heir Edward Hotham Newton sold it to J. J. Hunt in 1899.[91] In 1954 the executors of Reginald Hunt (d. 1941) sold the estate, then comprising about 1,000 a. in Grimston and Dunnington, in various lots.[92]

In 1672 Tobias Jenkins occupied a house of thirteen hearths at Grimston,[93] presumably that described as Grimston Hall and owned by him or another Tobias Jenkins in 1719.[94] George Fox's lessee did much work on the house in 1750.[95] In 1772 it stood on the west side of the Elvington road.[96] It may have been demolished when Grimston Hill was built in the early 19th century and it had certainly gone by 1839.[97] Grimston Hill, which apparently replaced the hall as the manor-house of the

[53] E.R.R.O., DDGD/Box 1.
[54] B.I.H.R., CC. Ab. 10.
[55] Ibid. Inst. AB. 21, p. 167.
[56] B.I.H.R., PR. DUN. 40/2; R.D.B., HB/187/246.
[57] R.D.B., HK/287/296; HL/382/385.
[58] Ibid. e.g. 5/483/464; 6/140/125 (1898); 72/202/178 (1904).
[59] 12 & 13 Geo. V, c. 16; R.D.B., e.g. 327/38/32.
[60] R.D.B., 752/253/187; 797/517/430; 841/556/476; 1351/439/394.
[61] E 179/205/504.
[62] Minster Libr., D & C. Arch., Wm. f. 534.
[63] B.I.H.R., PR. DUN. 40/2.
[64] O.S. Map 6" (1853–4 edn.).
[65] Kelly's Dir. N. & E.R. Yorks. (1872), 355.
[66] Local information.
[67] York Minster Fasti, i (Y.A.S. Rec. Ser. cxxiii), 60.
[68] Miscellanea, iv. 25.
[69] Lamb. Pal. Libr., COMM./XIIa/18/23.
[70] E.R.R.O., DDGD/Box 1.
[71] H.U.L., DWB/1/10.
[72] E.R.R.O., DDGD/Box 1.
[73] See p. 70.
[74] R.D.B., HB/136/182.
[75] See above.

[76] Miscellanea, iv. 25.
[77] V.C.H. Yorks. ii. 225, 293, 320.
[78] E.Y.C. ii, p. 114.   [79] Feud. Aids, vi. 34.
[80] Minster Libr., Torre MS., 'Peculiars', p. 641.
[81] Feud. Aids, vi. 223.
[82] F. Harrison, York Minster, 184.
[83] Leeds City Arch., Lane-Fox 83/1.
[84] Yorks. Fines, 1614–25, 191.
[85] C.P. 25(2)/895/9 Wm. III Hil. no. 59; R.D.B., A/137/200; /175/241.
[86] R.D.B., H/569/1144; /570/1145; Leeds City Arch., Lane-Fox 70/6, 8.
[87] J. W. Clay, Ext. & Dorm. Peerages of N. Cos. of Eng. 13–14.
[88] R.D.B., BC/135/193; BD/216/339.
[89] Ibid. HK/265/282. See Burke, Land. Gent. (1965), 288.
[90] R.D.B., 41/114/108 (1890).
[91] Ibid. 16/128/121 (1899).
[92] Ibid. 692/15/14; 976/189/166; /331/295; /332/296; 986/151/137; 992/66/60.
[93] E 179/205/504.
[94] R.D.B., G/309/681.
[95] Leeds City Arch., Lane-Fox 83/27; 99/3.
[96] T. Jefferys, Map of Yorks. (1772).
[97] B.I.H.R., TA. 304M.

Lane-Fox family, stands beside the Beverley road. The brick and slate building, painted white, has a canted bay window rising through both storeys and a porch with Ionic columns and an entablature. Grimston Hill was replaced in its turn as the manor-house by Grimston Court, a large Jacobean-style red-brick building standing in its own grounds on the opposite side of the road. It was built in 1903 by J. J. Hunt.[98] It was sold in 1958 by the executors of R. Hunt[99] and in 1972 was an old people's home.

In 1086 an estate of one carucate at Grimston, which Ulchil had held before the Conquest, was in the hands of William de Percy.[1] It had evidently passed to the chapter of York by 1225, when Richard de Percy quitclaimed his rights in the chapter's lands there,[2] and in 1284–5 the chapter held a carucate in the township.[3] In the late 15th century the estate was known as *GRIMSTON* manor and was held by Henry Annas of the chapter. Annas later granted the manor to Thomas Barton, and it was subsequently held by John Barton (d. 1506), John Barton (d. 1553), and Thomas Barton (d. 1565).[4] Thomas's son Edward Barton died in 1610 seised only of common rights in Grimston.[5] In 1606 the estate was represented by 8 bovates of copyhold land, held by several tenants of the manor of Dunnington.[6]

The hospital of St. Nicholas, York, bought 3 bovates at Grimston between 1260 and 1291,[7] and in 1346 it held 2 bovates of the Neville fee.[8] The estate was let by the Crown to Leonard Beckwith in 1553[9] and granted to William Tanckard in 1599, then comprising 2 houses, a close, and 5 bovates.[1] Thereafter it formed part of the manor.[11]

ECONOMIC HISTORY. In 1086 the chapter's estate in Dunnington township had land for two ploughs and, although two villeins had only one plough, the estate had increased in value from 10s. before the Conquest to 15s. The Percy estate had land for three ploughs and Geoffrey had one plough and two villeins half a plough. The estate had fallen in value from £1 4s. in 1066 to 10s.[12]

Though little is known of the process, considerable reclamation was evidently carried on in the Middle Ages. Peter Crofts, adjoining the village on the east,[13] may represent part of the nucleus of land cultivated by the chapter's tenants at the time of Domesday. The Intake, south-east of the village, may have been subsequent reclamation, and other reclaimed land went to form the later open fields.

About 1295 the prebendary of Dunnington held in demesne 8 bovates and 12 a. of arable land, 20 a. of meadow, 30 a. of moor, and 6 a. of wood. There were 38 bond tenants, of whom one held 4 bovates, 2 held 2, and 8 held one bovate, and the remainder held only tofts and crofts. The tenants performed boon-works and rendered money rents, hens, and eggs. The lord enjoyed pannage, merchet, leyrwite, and multure.[14] At the same time the prebendary of Ampleforth's demesne comprised 6 bovates, each consisting of 10 a. of arable and one of meadow. There were also seven bond tenants, each holding 2 bovates for boon-works, money rents, hens, and eggs. Each tenant was to provide a haymaker and five reapers, perform carting services, provide an assistant for the lord's thatcher, and pay small sums known as 'wodepeny' and 'Romepeny'. The lord had merchet and relief. There were also six cottars and grassmen holding tofts and crofts. The tenants all had common rights in about 100 a. of pasture.[15]

Three of the open fields, Undergate, Mill, and East fields, were named in 1628 and the fourth, Thornhill field, in 1631. New field, or Ox close, and the Intake, both of which were evidently divided into strips or subject to common rights, were mentioned in 1621 and 1631 respectively.[16] Together with the ings, all these areas were laid out in flats and inclosed by agreement in 1707,[17] confirmed by a Chancery decree of 1709.[18] In all, 1,049 a. were dealt with. Undergate field, which adjoined the village on the south-west, contained 117 a., Thorntree field, evidently the earlier Thornhill field, to the north, 155 a., Mill field, north-east of the village, 126 a., and East field 295 a. The ings, beyond Undergate field, occupied 118 a., the Intake 75 a., and New field, between the ings and the common, 163 a.[19] Tobias Jenkins, as lessee of Dunnington manor, received 138 a. and Henry Wickham, as lessee of Heslington manor, 342 a. There were also 2 allotments of 50–100 a., 14 of 10–49 a., and 16 of under 10 a.

The extensive common, which was unstinted in 1709, occupied the southern part of the township. The south-east section of it was evidently used at one time as a rabbit warren.[20] The common was inclosed in 1772,[21] under an Act of 1770,[22] and 937 a. were allotted. J. S. Smith, as lord of Dunnington manor, was awarded 110 a., the Revd. Henry Wickham, as lord of Heslington manor, 6 a., and the rector 103 a. There was one allotment of 57 a., 25 of 10–50 a., and 34 of under 10 a.

At Grimston in 1086 the count of Mortain's estate had land for one plough. Niel had a plough there and three villeins half a plough. The estate had decreased in value from £1 in 1066 to 10s. There was also land for a plough on the Percy estate. Before the Conquest it had been worth 10s. but in 1086 it was waste.[23] About 1295 four bond tenants of the prebendary of Dunnington at Grimston held a total of one carucate and two cottars held tofts for money rents, hens, eggs, and boon-works.[24] By 1606 there were 389 a. of open-field land in the township, including 71 a. in New field and 60 a. in Low field. The commons then included the 25-

---

[98] F. Horner, *Dunnington, a Hist. of a Village Community*, 61.
[99] R.D.B., 1117/437/379.
[1] *V.C.H. Yorks.* ii. 262, 320.
[2] *Percy Charty.* p. 17.
[3] *Feud. Aids*, vi. 34.
[4] C 142/23 no. 315; C 142/100 no. 31; C 142/142 no. 119.
[5] C 142/317 no. 92.
[6] Leeds City Arch., Lane-Fox 83/1.
[7] *Yorks. Inq.* ii, pp. 125–6.
[8] *Feud. Aids*, vi. 223.
[9] *Cal. Pat.* 1563–6, p. 12.
[10] Leeds City Arch., Lane-Fox 83/1.
[11] See p. 7.
[12] *V.C.H. Yorks.* ii. 211, 262.
[13] O.S. Map 6" (1853–4 edn.).
[14] Minster Libr., Torre MS., 'York Minster', p. 1047; *Miscellanea*, iv. 7–8.
[15] *Miscellanea*, iv. 25.
[16] Minster Libr., D. & C. Arch., F. 6.
[17] E.R.R.O., DDX/195/9, 11.
[18] Ibid. DDGD/Box 1.
[19] O.S. Map 6" (1853–4 edn.).
[20] Ibid.; E.R.R.O., DDGD/Box 1.
[21] E.R.R.O., DDGD/Box 1.
[22] 10 Geo. III, c. 32 (Priv. Act).
[23] *V.C.H. Yorks.* ii. 225, 262.
[24] *Miscellanea*, iv. 8.

acre Bymoor and the 335-acre Great moor, in the south of Grimston. There was also a stinted cow pasture in which William Tanckard had seven gates in 1630. Several small closes were already mentioned in 1599, and by 1656 a close of 6 a. had been taken out of Bymoor, and the 22-acre Far pasture and the 39-acre 'new intake' called Cony hill out of Great moor. Thirteen acres of Cony hill were ploughed up in 1657.[25] The township was apparently mostly inclosed by 1708 and certainly by 1719. Among the closes mentioned in the former year were Merial ings, West ings, and Summer pasture.[26] An undated 18th-century map shows the whole township inclosed except 89 a. of Great moor, then called Grimston common and reached by an outgang on the line of the later Elvington road. The inclosed parts of Great moor included several called Tilmire which were attached to three of the nine farms in the township.[27]

In 1801 475 a. of the whole parish were under crops, mainly oats (200 a.) and rye or maslin (100 a.).[28] The number of farmers in the parish in the 19th and 20th centuries was usually between 20 and 30.[29] In 1851 7 held 100–200 a. and 20 held smaller amounts,[30] and in 1937 4 farms had an acreage of 150 or more and 13 were smaller.[31] There was a score of marl pits on the former common and New field in the mid 19th century.[32] In 1905 there were 1,224 a. of arable of 535 a. of grassland at Dunnington and 547 a. of arable and 161 a. of grassland at Grimston. There were then only 85 a. of woodland in the parish, mostly in Grimston.[33] Grimston wood has been managed by the Forestry Commission since 1963.[34] In the 1960s the parish was still largely under arable, but there was a substantial amount of grassland in the south; the former rabbit warren, which in the 1930s was heathland, had been planted with trees.[35]

In 1840 it was said that a hiring-fair was held annually in November.[36] By 1872 a pleasure fair was held each July and it continued into the 1930s.[37]

For most of the later 19th century much of the country's home-grown chicory was cultivated in and near Dunnington, which was described as 'the English chicory-growing metropolis'.[38] The crop was probably introduced c. 1840[39] and in 1851 there were three chicory merchants in the parish.[40] In 1856, when it was apparently declining, the industry was said to have formerly employed 400 people for much of the year. There were then nine disused kilns in the parish in which the roots had been dried.[41] The industry evidently revived, and in 1872 'a great quantity' of chicory was said to be grown.[42] By 1902, however, none of the twelve surviving kilns was still in use. It was then reported that 200–300 a. of chicory were formerly grown in the parish and that hundreds of itinerant labourers had been employed during harvest. Only 50 a. of the crop were then grown, mainly in small plots which the farmers kept 'for luck', and for many years the chicory had been taken to York for drying as well as processing.[43] A small amount continued to be grown until the 1930s.[44] Three kilns still stood in 1972, the largest, in Common Lane, a long two-storeyed building with a half-hipped roof and a flight of stone steps leading to the first floor.[45] Another kiln, in York Street, had been converted into a shop.

Dunnington was also well known in the 19th century for the manufacture of agricultural implements, machinery, and carts. In 1851 there were two firms, one employing ten men and the other six.[46] Implement manufacture was described as the main industry of the parish in 1856 and the quality of the products was said to be widely renowned.[47] Fifty workmen were employed by one manufacturer in the later 19th century and several new types of implement originated at Dunnington.[48] By 1908 the numbers employed had greatly decreased,[49] but two firms continued throughout the 1920s and 1930s[50] and one, Hornshaw's, remained in 1972, although implements were then only repaired, their manufacture having ceased c. 1967.[51]

A weaver, a rope-maker, and a tanner were mentioned at Dunnington in 1772,[52] a brewer in 1872, and a maltster in 1879.[53] There were two bicycle manufacturers from at least 1909 until the late 1920s.[54] In 1972 two firms of grain handlers had premises at Four Lane Ends.

The prebendary of Dunnington had a water-mill and a windmill c. 1295,[55] and a windmill in 1723.[56] The windmill may have stood in the area known as Mill hill, on the moraine north-east of the village, where Mill field was mentioned in the earlier 17th century.[57] There was a miller from at least 1823 onwards[58] and in 1850 a windmill stood near Four Lane Ends.[59] It closed down c. 1900[60] and has since been demolished.

LOCAL GOVERNMENT. There are surviving court rolls for the capital manor of Dunnington for the years 1606–40 and 1724–1925. The court was largely concerned with land transfers; officers

[25] Leeds City Arch., Lane-Fox 83/1.
[26] R.D.B., A/137/200; G/309/681.
[27] Leeds City Arch., Lane-Fox 117/24.
[28] 1801 Crop Returns.
[29] Directories.
[30] H.O. 107/2351.
[31] Kelly's Dir. N. & E.R. Yorks. (1937), 451.
[32] O.S. Map 6" (1853–4 edn.).
[33] Acreage Returns, 1905.
[34] Ex inf. Forestry Com., York, 1972.
[35] [1st] Land Util. Surv. Map, sheet 27; 2nd Land Util. Surv. Map, sheets 699 (SE 64–74), 709 (SE 65–75).
[36] White, Dir. E. & N.R. Yorks. (1840), 325.
[37] Kelly's Dir. N. & E.R. Yorks. (1872), 355, and later directories.
[38] Yorks. Gaz. 31 May 1902; 29 Feb. 1908.
[39] Ibid. 14 June 1902.
[40] H.O. 107/2351.
[41] Sheahan and Whellan, Hist. York & E.R. ii. 616.
[42] Kelly's Dir. N. & E.R. Yorks. (1872), 356.
[43] Yorks. Gaz. 14 June 1902.
[44] Directories; local information.
[45] See plate facing p. 33.
[46] H.O. 107/2351.
[47] Sheahan and Whellan, Hist. York & E.R. ii. 616.
[48] Yorks. Gaz. 31 May 1902.
[49] Ibid. 29 Feb. 1908.
[50] Directories.
[51] Local information.
[52] E.R.R.O., DDGD/Box 1.
[53] Kelly's Dir. N. & E.R. Yorks. (1872), 356; (1879), 387.
[54] Directories.
[55] Minster Libr., Torre MS., 'York Minster', p. 633; Miscellanea, iv. 7.
[56] B.I.H.R., Bp. C. & P. XIX.
[57] O.S. Map 6" (1853–4 edn.); see above p. 8.
[58] Baines, Hist. Yorks. (1823), ii. 199.
[59] O.S. Map 6" (1853–4 edn.).
[60] Directories.

were not mentioned until the 1860s, but thereafter two bylawmen, two affeerors, and a bailiff were usually sworn.[61]

Constables' accounts survive for 1765–1844, churchwardens' accounts for 1818–66,[62] overseers' accounts for 1816–31,[63] and surveyors' accounts for 1843–56.[64] Dunnington was a member of the Rillington union and maintained one or two paupers in the workhouse there throughout the period 1816–31. Until 1820 there was one overseer and thereafter two. Two poorhouses were built in 1816 and two more in 1821. Dunnington joined York poor-law union in 1837.[65] In 1850 two rows of poorhouses still stood in the south of Dunnington village and another row on the Elvington road at Grimston;[66] one set survived until 1936.[67] Dunnington was included in Escrick rural district in 1894, Derwent rural district in 1935,[68] and the Selby district of North Yorkshire in 1974.

CHURCH. Although parts of the fabric are earlier, a church at Dunnington was not mentioned until 1220, when Richard de Percy and the archbishop were in dispute over the advowson.[69] The living was described, apparently erroneously, as a vicarage in 1225.[70] In that year the archbishop quitclaimed the advowson to Richard de Percy,[71] in whose family it descended[72] until 1537, when it apparently passed with the rest of their Yorkshire estates to the Crown.[73] Presentations were made by the Crown in 1556 and 1558,[74] Robert Cripling in 1568, John Gibson in 1582, and Ralph Eure, Lord Eure, in 1610.[75] The advowson had passed by 1642 to John Egerton, earl of Bridgwater, and descended in the Egerton family[76] until 1823, when it passed to John Home-Cust, Viscount Alford, the heir of John Egerton, earl of Bridgwater.[77] In 1722 and 1755 the archbishop of York presented,[78] presumably by lapse. In 1950 the patronage was transferred from Peregrine Cust, Baron Brownlow, to the archbishop of York.[79]

The church was valued at £13 6s. 8d. in 1291, reduced to £8 n the new taxation,[80] and still at the lower figure in 1428.[81] It was worth £19 net in 1535.[82] In 1650 the value was £80.[83] In 1829–31 the average net income was £349 a year,[84] in 1884 about £420, and in 1914 £313.[85]

Tithes accounted for most of the income in 1535 and later. In 1546 the tenant of an area in the south of the parish called Grey leys claimed to pay a modus of 3s. 4d. a year for tithes there.[86] The prebendary of Ampleforth owned the tithes arising from his estate at Dunnington and they were let with it in the 17th century and later.[87] In 1685 the rector received tithes from 63 bovates at Dunnington and 7 at Grimston.[88] In 1716 the lord of Grimston manor paid a composition of £6 a year for the remaining Grimston tithes.[89] At the inclosure of 1707 the tithes of the whole of Dunnington township, except for New field and the common, were commuted for 1s. 8d. a year from each acre.[90] In 1225 the archbishop granted two tofts and common rights to the rector[91] and at the inclosure of 1772 the rector was awarded 4 a. for common rights. He also received 98 a. for half his tithes from the common and a rent-charge of about £16 for the rest.[92] In 1838 the remaining tithes and existing moduses were commuted for a rent-charge of £348 a year.[93] The living was endowed with another 2 a. by the Ecclesiastical Commissioners in 1858.[94] In 1925 98 a. of glebe were sold[95] and the remaining 6 a. in 1949.[96]

There was a parsonage house in 1535.[97] About 1610, when it was in disrepair, it was a thatched building containing a hall, parlour, 'great chamber', and study.[98] In 1727 it was said to comprise three bays of building and in 1743 to be of two storeys. In 1764 it was a brick building with a tiled roof, containing four bedrooms.[99] It is said to have been rebuilt in 1777, but a new house was built in 1823–4[1] and it was still the Rectory in 1972.

There is no certain reference to a chapel at Grimston in the Middle Ages, but Chapel garth there was mentioned in 1606.[2]

In the 1440s the rector also held the living of Huggate.[3] It was reported in 1579 that the rector had been non-resident for two years and that the cure had been served by an assistant curate.[4] In 1612 it was claimed that Christopher Lindley, the previous rector, had allowed the church and parsonage house to fall into disrepair.[5] Henry Ayscough, rector 1610–42, who also held the living of Elvington, was a Puritan.[6] In 1628 he was licensed to be absent because of ill-health,[7] and in the 1630s and 1640s he employed an assistant curate.[8] In 1743 the rector resided on his other living at Settrington and employed an assistant curate, who was also vicar of

---

[61] Minster Libr., D. & C. Arch., F. 6; B.I.H.R., CC. P. Dunnington 12/1–3.
[62] B.I.H.R., PR. DUN. 22–4, 41.
[63] York City Archives, Acc. 104 par./1.
[64] E.R.R.O., PR. 1.
[65] 3rd Rep. Poor Law Com. 171.
[66] O.S. Map 6″ (1853–4 edn.).
[67] Horner, Dunnington, 65.
[68] Census.
[69] Cur. Reg. R. viii. 183.
[70] Reg. Gray, p. 2.
[71] Percy Charty. p. 17.
[72] Cal. Inq. p.m. v, p. 323; x, p. 28; xii, p. 227; Y.A.J. xxxvi. 233.
[73] G. Brenan, Hist. of House of Percy, i. 250.
[74] Cal. Pat. 1555–7, 366; 1557–8, 356.
[75] Minster Libr., Torre MS., 'Peculiars', p. 633.
[76] e.g. B.I.H.R., Inst. AB. 6, pp. 331, 409–10; Inst AB. 8, p. 114.
[77] Complete Peerage, s.v. Bridgwater, Brownlow.
[78] Inst. Bks.   [79] B.I.H.R., PR. DUN. 38.
[80] Tax. Eccl. (Rec. Com.), 300, 323.
[81] Feud. Aids, vi. 332.
[82] Valor Eccl. (Rec. Com.), v. 98.
[83] C 94/3 f. 76.
[84] Rep. Com. Eccl. Revenues, 930.
[85] B.I.H.R., Bp. V. 1884/Ret.; Bp. V. 1914/Ret.
[86] Ibid. CP. G. 360.
[87] Lamb. Pal. Libr., COMM./XIIa/18/23; see p. 7.
[88] B.I.H.R., TER. N. Dunnington 1685.
[89] Ibid. 1716.
[90] E.R.R.O., DDX/195/9.
[91] Yorks. Fines, 1218–31, p. 57.
[92] E.R.R.O., DDGD/Box 1.
[93] B.I.H.R., TA. 304M.
[94] Lond. Gaz. 13 Aug. 1858, pp. 3780–1.
[95] R.D.B., 318/144/117.
[96] Ibid. 824/314/273.   [97] Valor Eccl. v. 98.
[98] B.I.H.R., CP. H. 706.
[99] Ibid. TER. N. Dunnington 1727, 1743, 1764.
[1] Horner, Dunnington, 10.
[2] Leeds City Arch., Lane-Fox 83/1.
[3] Y.A.J. xxxvi. 233.
[4] B.I.H.R., CP. G. 914.   [5] Ibid. CP. H. 706.
[6] R. A. Marchant, Puritans and the Ch. Courts in Dioc. York., 1560–1642, 226–7, 320.
[7] Cal. S.P. Dom. 1627–8, 568.
[8] Marchant, op. cit. 224, 272.

Osbaldwick (Yorks. N.R.) and curate of Rufforth (Yorks. W.R.), and who lived at York.[9] An assistant curate was also employed in the 1860s and 1870s.[10]

There were two services each Sunday in 1743 and Holy Communion was celebrated three times a year, with 30–50 communicants.[11] By the 1860s and 1870s there were three services each Sunday and communion was celebrated fortnightly, usually with 14–28 communicants. In 1884 there was a weekly celebration and in 1894 four services were held each Sunday. In 1914 two Sunday services were held[12] and in 1972 three. From 1865 until it was removed in 1911 services were also held in a mission room at Grimston.[13]

The church of ST. NICHOLAS is built of freestone and rubble and has a chancel with north aisle and south vestry and organ chamber, aisled and clerestoried nave with north porch, and west tower with south vestry. The nave is small and perhaps 11th-century in origin. In the 12th century aisles with arcades of two bays were added to north and south, the former slightly the earlier, and the plain west tower is probably of the same date. The east end of the church was completely rebuilt late in the 13th century to provide a new chancel, in which the piscina and sedilia survive, and north aisle with a three-bay arcade. The removal of the chancel arch may date from that time or it may be a more recent alteration. The upper stage of the tower dates from the 15th century.

The tower was repaired in 1717[14] and in 1738–40 the pulpit was rebuilt and the church repewed.[15] All three aisles were rebuilt in 1839–41. The nave aisles have small round-headed Norman-style windows and three-light clerestory windows, and the chancel aisle windows are in the Decorated style. At the same time the main entrance was moved from the south to the north side and the north porch was built. The west gallery was removed and replaced by a smaller one, the chancel and tower were repaired, and the church was repewed.[16] The plain font also probably dates from this restoration. Another restoration, by C. H. Fowler, took place in 1877 and a vestry and organ chamber were added to the east end of the south aisle.[17] In 1930 the north chancel aisle was converted into a side chapel.[18]

The windows are all filled with 19th- and 20th-century stained glass. A grave slab with an incised floriated cross is in the south aisle.

In 1743 it was reported that a house and 23 a. had been left for repairs to the church.[19] In 1824 the church estate, the origin of which was then unknown, consisted of a house, a shop, and 28 a., 5 a. having been awarded for common rights at the inclosure of 1772.[20] The rents, totalling about £62, were used in place of church-rates for repairs to the church.[21] Most of the property was sold in 1921. In 1972 the income was £128 from £2,111 stock.[22]

The tower contained three bells in 1770[23] and there are still three: (i) 1639; (ii) 1700, Samuel Smith of York; (iii) 1727.[24] The plate includes a silver chalice and paten, both made in London by 'I.F.' in 1876, and a silver flagon made in Sheffield in 1828 by 'T.B.' There is also a brass alms-dish dated 1677.[25] The registers begin in 1584 and are complete.[26]

The churchyard was extended in 1866[27] and 1911.[28] It contains the base and part of the shaft of a stone cross, perhaps of the 14th century.

PROTESTANT NONCONFORMITY. There were seven protestant dissenters in the parish in 1676.[29] A Quaker was reported at Dunnington in 1743[30] and a house was registered for Quaker worship in 1748.[31] In 1764 there were said to be 'four or five' Methodists,[32] and houses were registered for dissenting worship in 1765, 1788, 1803, 1807 (two), and 1819.[33] The Wesleyan Methodists built a chapel in 1805 in York Street[34] and this was replaced by a new one in Common Lane in 1868.[35] In the latter year the Wesleyans were said to have a strong hold on the minds of the people[36] and in 1884 they had 38 members.[37] In 1871 the former 'meeting-house', presumably the old chapel, was owned by the rector and occasionally used for Anglican services;[38] it was used as a store-house in 1900[39] but was later demolished. The new chapel was still used for services in 1972.

The Primitive Methodists built a chapel in 1852.[40] In 1908 they had a 'comparatively small' membership.[41] The chapel was used as a store-house in 1972.

EDUCATION. In 1640 the assistant curate was also the schoolmaster,[42] and a schoolmaster was again mentioned in 1725.[43] In 1743 there were three unendowed 'English' schools in the parish.[44]

[9] Herring's Visit. i. 171–2.
[10] B.I.H.R., V. 1865/Ret. 145; V. 1868/Ret. 136; V. 1877/Ret.
[11] Herring's Visit. i. 171.
[12] B.I.H.R., V. 1865/Ret. 145; V. 1868/Ret. 136; V. 1871/Ret. 137; V. 1877/Ret.; Bp. V. 1884/Ret.; Bp. V. 1894/Ret.; Bp. V. 1914/Ret.
[13] Ibid. PR. DUN. 35/1; Kelly's Dir. N. & E.R. Yorks. (1872), 356 and later directories; Horner, Dunnington, 19.
[14] B.I.H.R., Inst. AB. 10A, f. 29. The date appears on the outside of the west wall.
[15] B.I.H.R., Fac. Bk. i, pp. 31–2; Fac. 1740/1.
[16] Ibid. PR. DUN. 25; Sheahan and Whellan, Hist. York & E.R. ii. 616.
[17] E.R.R.O., DDX/234/7.
[18] B.I.H.R., Fac. Bk. xi, p. 30; inscription in church.
[19] Herring's Visit. i. 171.
[20] E.R.R.O., DDGD/Box 1.
[21] 11th Rep. Com. Char. 753.
[22] Char. Com. files.
[23] B.I.H.R., TER. N. Dunnington 1770.
[24] Boulter, 'Ch. Bells', 31. The third bell is said to be by Sam. Smith the younger of York: Horner, Dunnington, 13.
[25] Yorks. Ch. Plate, i. 68.
[26] B.I.H.R.
[27] Ibid. PR. DUN. 32.
[28] York Dioc. Regy., Consecration deeds.
[29] Bodl. MS. Tanner 150, ff. 27 sqq.
[30] Herring's Visit. i. 171.
[31] G.R.O. Worship Returns, Vol. v, no. 38.
[32] B.I.H.R., Bp. V. 1764/Ret. 156.
[33] G.R.O. Worship Returns, Vol. v, nos. 234, 723, 1765, 2101, 2108, 3350.
[34] H.O. 129/23/515.
[35] G.R.O. Worship Reg. no. 18766.
[36] B.I.H.R., V. 1868/Ret. 136.
[37] J. Lyth, Glimpses of Early Methodism in York and Dist. 288.
[38] B.I.H.R., V. 1871/Ret. 137.
[39] R.D.B., 22/224/215 (1900).
[40] Date on building.
[41] Yorks. Gaz. 29 Feb. 1908.
[42] Marchant, Puritans and Ch. Courts in Dioc. York, 272.
[43] B.I.H.R., Schools index.
[44] Herring's Visit. i. 171.

No school was reported in 1764[45] but a master was again mentioned in 1781 and later.[46] In both 1819 and 1835 there were three unendowed schools, containing in the former year 80–90 children and in the latter 109.[47] The churchwardens repaired the school-house several times in the 1820s[48] and they built a new school in the centre of the village in 1836. In 1864, when it was largely supported by school pence, the school contained 65 pupils.[49] It first received an annual government grant in 1864.[50] It was enlarged in 1905–6,[51] and from 1908 to 1936 the attendance varied between 105 and 142. In 1938 attendance was 98.[52] In the 1950s and 1960s the Methodist chapel schoolroom and the village reading room were used as additional classrooms.[53] A new school was built in 1969–70 in Church Lane[54] but in 1972 the former building was still used as well. In April 1972 the number of pupils on the roll was 324.[55]

In the 1860s an unsuccessful evening school was held.[56]

CHARITIES FOR THE POOR. Timothy Overend, by will dated 1728, gave £10, the interest of which was to be distributed annually in bread to the poor of the parish. In 1824 the income was 10s. James Twinam, by will dated 1733, devised a 4-acre close, half the income of which was to be distributed to the poor of Dunnington and half to those of Holtby (Yorks. N.R.); in 1824 £4 8s. was received by Dunnington.[57] Dinah Richardson, by a codicil to her will dated 1787, left £2 10s. a year to be distributed in bread in church every Sunday to the poor who attended service. Her executor Thomas Wilson increased the annual sum in 1816 to £3 15s.[58] These three charities were administered together for much of the 19th century and a joint distribution in bread was made. From 1844 to 1884 a total income of £8–10 was usually received, and from 1885 to 1895 £5–8. In 1896 the administration of the Overend and Twinam charities was transferred to the parish council.[59]

In 1972 Richardon's charity was represented by £79 stock and the income of £2 was kept in an accumulating fund. The income had been distributed to the sick poor in 1967. The land belonging to Twinam's charity was sold in 1967, Dunnington's share of the proceeds being £413.[60] The income was £22 in 1973–4, used to help a club for local pensioners. Income is no longer received from Overend's charity.[61]

John Hodgson, a guardian of the poor, by will proved in 1891, bequeathed £5,000 for the benefit of the sick poor, not in receipt of poor relief, living within the area of York poor-law union or at Sheriff Hutton (Yorks. N.R.). In 1949 £4,643 was added to the endowment under the will of H. A. Phillips (d. 1940). The income in 1972 was £446 from £9,799 stock, and 38 cash grants were made,[62] including one to a resident of Dunnington.[63]

ELVINGTON

THE VILLAGE of Elvington lies about 6 miles south-east of York on the west bank of the river Derwent.[1] It faces Sutton village on the opposite bank and it seems likely that this was a natural crossing-point of the river from early times. Elvington, which was an Anglian settlement,[2] stands alongside a small stream near its confluence with the Derwent, and another stream forms the southern parish boundary. The entire eastern boundary follows the Derwent except where the course of the river has been straightened across a small meander. Near the river the ings occupying the flood-plain lie at less than 25 ft. above sea-level and the rest of Elvington lies at 25 ft. to 50 ft. The area of the parish, which is roughly triangular in shape, is 2,372 a.[3]

A small area of boulder clay and glacial sand and gravel in the south of the parish represents the northern edge of the Escrick moraine. The rest of the parish, including the sites of the former open fields around the village, consists of outwash sand and clay.[4] The common moor lay on the sand in the north-west where much of the parish is now occupied by an airfield.

The road from York, forming the main village street, is carried over the river to Sutton upon Derwent by a stone bridge of two arches. A bridge was mentioned in 1396, when Robert Holme, a York merchant, left money to build a new one.[5] It was of stone by 1535[6] and was constantly repaired by the county in the 18th century.[7] The road was straightened near Elvington Hall in 1937.[8]

From the village Dauby Lane leads northwards to Kexby. Church Lane leads southwards and formerly continued to Wheldrake. About 1767, however, a new road was laid out from the York road 1½ mile west of the village to link up with the old Wheldrake road, and at inclosure two years later part of the old road was evidently blocked up.[9] Stray Lane, men-

[45] B.I.H.R., Bp. V. 1764/Ret. 156.
[46] Ibid. PR. DUN. 41.
[47] *Educ. of Poor Digest*, 1079; *Educ. Enquiry Abstract*, 1083.
[48] B.I.H.R., PR. DUN. 22.
[49] Ibid. PR. DUN. 25; Ed. 7/135 no. 36.
[50] *Rep. of Educ. Cttee. of Council, 1864–5* [C. 3533], p. 530, H.C. (1865), xlii.
[51] E.R. Educ. Cttee. *Mins.* 1905–6, 58–9, 223; Horner, *Dunnington*, 21.
[52] *Bd. of Educ. List 21* (H.M.S.O.).
[53] E.R. Educ. Cttee. *Mins.* 1956–7, 116; 1960–1, 147; 1967–8, 119; 1969–70, 137.
[54] Ibid. 1967–8, 206; 1970–1, 48.
[55] Ex inf. Chief Educ. Officer, County Hall, Beverley, 1972.
[56] B.I.H.R., V. 1865/Ret. 145; V. 1868/Ret. 136.
[57] *11th Rep. Char. Com.* 752.
[58] Ibid.; B.I.H.R., PR. DUN. 29/1.
[59] B.I.H.R., PR. DUN. 28.
[60] Char. Com. files.
[61] Ex inf. clerk to Dunnington Par. Counc. 1975.
[62] Char. Com. files.
[63] Ex inf. Mr. A. R. Tunnah, Haxby, 1974.
[1] This article was written in 1972.
[2] *P.N.E.R. Yorks.* (E.P.N.S.), 272.
[3] O.S. Map 6″, Yorks. (1854 edn.). Most of the parish is covered by sheet 192, the rest by sheet 175.
[4] Geol. Surv. Map 1″, solid and drift, sheet 71 (1973 edn.).
[5] *V.C.H. City of York*, 98.
[6] Y.A.S., MS. 530(d).
[7] E.R.R.O., QAB/1/1–3. See plate facing p. 160.
[8] Ibid. HD/116.
[9] 8 & 9 Geo. III, Sess. 2, c. 21 (Priv. Act); T. Jefferys, *Map of Yorks.* (1772); O.S. Map 6″ (1854 edn.).

tioned in 1774,[10] follows part of the northern parish boundary and gave access to the common. Ings Lane formerly led from Church Lane towards the river.[11]

The river Derwent was improved for navigation in the early 18th century and by 1723 a cut with a lock had been made at Elvington, bypassing a new weir across the river. A lock-keeper's house had been built by 1782 but the present house dates from the 19th century. In 1807 an Elvington trader regularly used the navigation[12] and in the mid 19th century coal yards lay on the river bank near the bridge.[13] The navigation ended c. 1900[14] and the Derwent was closed as a public waterway in 1932.[15] The lock subsequently decayed, but it was restored for pleasure craft in 1972.[16] About a mile upstream of the weir Sheffield corporation built a water intake and treatment plant, completed in 1965.[17]

The Derwent Valley Light Railway, opened in 1912, crossed the parish and the former station adjoins the York road west of the village. The line was closed for passenger traffic in 1926[18] and the sections south and north of the station for goods in 1968 and 1972 respectively.[19] The track has been lifted.

The village houses and cottages, which are all of brick and date from the 18th century and later, stand in the long main street and around its junction with Church Lane. In the village centre a stream runs alongside a small green, and in the mid 19th century Cross bridge carried Church Lane over the stream.[20] The church stands a short distance from the green and Elvington Hall at the east end of the village overlooking the river.[21] Noteworthy buildings include Belvoir House, beside the green, a later-18th-century building, and the early-19th-century Roxby Farm. The Grange, known in the mid 19th century as Annfield Villa,[22] stands in its own grounds to the south of the village. It is an early-19th-century stuccoed house with a cast-iron ground-floor veranda. Later-19th-century buildings include in Church Lane a row of thirteen mottled-brick cottages, dated 1860, with ornamental barge-boards and entrance porches; they were built by A. J. Clarke, rector 1865–85.[23] There are several substantial detached Victorian houses, including the Villa, Bank House, and Derwent House. Much 20th-century development has taken place, reflecting the proximity of York, notably at the west end of the village where three new streets have been laid out and about 50 private houses built. There are also 22 council houses, and seven houses were built c. 1965 for the employees of Sheffield corporation.[24] An alehouse was licensed in the village from 1754 onwards[25] and in 1823 it was called the Bay Horse.[26] Since at least 1840 it has been known as the Grey Horse.[27] From 1916 to 1962 the building which formerly served as a Primitive Methodist chapel and later a school was used as a church hall. In 1972 the school building of 1858 was used as a village hall.[28]

Buildings away from the village include Brinkworth Hall, a large early-19th-century house. It stands in a small park about a mile west of the village and was probably built between 1803 and 1823 for Alexander Mather, who held a small estate at Elvington.[29] The isolated farm-houses all date from after the inclosures of 1743 and 1769. Two had been built on the former common by 1772[30] and Cheesecake House in the south of the parish had also appeared by that date.[31]

A Royal Air Force station has occupied the western part of the parish since 1943[32] and was still in use in 1972. A long new runway extending into Langwith was built in 1956.[33] Beside the York road west of the village is a memorial to a Free French air force squadron which was based at Elvington in 1944–5.

There were 59 poll-tax payers in 1377.[34] In 1672 48 households were recorded in the hearth-tax assessment, of which 14 were discharged from paying. Of the 34 chargeable households 27 had one hearth each, 4 had 2, and the others had 4, 5, and 7 hearths, the last being the manor-house.[35] There were 26 families in the parish in 1743 and 29 in 1764.[36] The population rose from 225 in 1801 to 478 in 1841. It fell to 372 in 1851 but rose again to 472 in 1861, before decreasing steadily to 335 by 1901[37] and 301 by 1911. It rose to 423 in 1951 and was 559 in 1971.[38]

MANORS AND OTHER ESTATES. In 1066 there was one estate of 6 carucates at Elvington held by Ulchil.[39] It passed to William Malet who held it until c. 1070;[40] in 1086, despite a claim that it was the right of William's son Robert, it was held by Alulf of William de Percy.[41] The overlordship descended in the Percy family until at least 1368.[42]

William de Morers was enfeoffed of the estate probably between 1166 and 1175[43] and in 1284–5 Richard de Morers was demesne lord.[44] *ELVINGTON* manor descended in the Morers family[45] until

[10] E.R.R.O., DDFA/4/26.
[11] O.S. Map 6″ (1854 edn.).
[12] B. F. Duckham, 'Fitzwilliams and Navigation of Yorks. Derwent', *Northern Hist.* ii. 48–9, 57.
[13] O.S. Map 6″ (1854 edn.).
[14] *Northern Hist.* ii. 60.
[15] *Wheldrake; Aspects of a Yorks. Village* (Wheldrake Loc. Hist. Soc.), 40.
[16] *Hull Daily Mail*, 28 Aug. 1972. See below plate facing p. 176.
[17] Sheffield corp. *River Derwent Scheme, Progress Reps. 1961–4; Water Supply to Sheffield and Dist.* (1966) (all in York Pub. Libr.).
[18] *V.C.H. City of York*, 479.
[19] *Wheldrake*, op. cit. 41; local information.
[20] O.S. Map 6″ (1854 edn.). [21] See p. 14.
[22] O.S. Map 6″ (1854 edn.). The gatehouse is dated 1857 and the gate-posts bear the initials J.E.C.: they were presumably added by the Revd. J. E. Clarke.
[23] Local information. They bear his initials.
[24] *R. Derwent Scheme, Progress Reps. 1961–4; Water Supply to Sheffield and Dist.*

[25] E.R.R.O., QDT/2/15.
[26] Baines, *Hist. Yorks.* (1823), ii. 202.
[27] Directories.
[28] See p. 17.
[29] R.D.B., CF/294/475; HK/17/20; Baines, *Hist. Yorks.* (1823), ii. 202.
[30] R.D.B., AR/134/264.
[31] Jefferys, *Map Yorks.*
[32] Ex inf. Ministry of Defence, 1972.
[33] *Yorks. Eve. Press*, 4 Oct. 1956.
[34] E 179/202/58 m. 12.
[35] E 179/205/504.
[36] B.I.H.R., Bp. V. 1764/Ret. 170; *Herring's Visit.* i. 181.
[37] *V.C.H. Yorks.* iii. 497.
[38] *Census.*
[39] *V.C.H. Yorks.* ii. 263.
[40] Ibid. 167.
[41] Ibid. 263, 293.
[42] *Feud. Aids*, vi. 33; *Cal. Inq. p.m.* v, p. 319; xii, p. 226.
[43] *E.Y.C.* xi, p. 284.
[44] *Feud. Aids*, vi. 33.
[45] Ibid. 173, 222; *Rot. Litt. Pat.* (Rec. Com.), 164.

1394, when William Morers granted it to three men, apparently trustees of Ralph, Lord Neville,[46] created earl of Westmorland in 1397.[47] The manor, still comprising 6 carucates, was held by Ralph's widow Joan in 1428.[48] It was forfeited by her grandson Richard Neville, earl of Salisbury, on his attainder in 1459 and restored to him the following year when his attainder was reversed.[49] His son Richard Neville (d. 1471), earl of Warwick, 'the kingmaker', succeeded him and held the manor until his death.[50] Upon the forfeiture and partition of his estates by Act of Parliament in 1474 between the dukes of Clarence and Gloucester, Elvington was assigned to the latter and was confirmed to him in 1475.[51] On ascending the throne Richard III kept it in hand and in the 1490s it was accounted for along with Sheriff Hutton (Yorks. N.R.).[52] It was let to members of the Eglesfield family for much of the 16th century.[53] In 1628 it was alienated to the Ditchfield grantees as security for the City of London's loan to the Crown.[54] The grantees sold it to Sir John Gibson and Ralph Radcliffe in 1632,[55] and Radcliffe and Sir Arthur Ingram to Sir Roger Jacques in 1646.[56] The manor passed to the Sterne family on the marriage c. 1700 of Mary, daughter of another Roger Jacques, and Simon Sterne.[57] The writer Laurence Sterne (1713–68) was their grandson.[58]

The manorial estate, comprising about 1,500 a. in 1772,[59] descended in the Sterne family until the later 18th century. In 1774 Richard Sterne sold 837 a. to Ralph and John Dodsworth,[60] 83 a. to Ambrose Etherington, and 172 a. to John Daniel.[61] The following year he sold the manor and 321 a. to John Ramsey.[62] After Ramsey's death in 1801[63] the manor, divided into moieties, passed to his nieces Susannah Spence and Dorothy Garwood[64] and in 1857 the trustees of their six children sold the whole manor with about 200 a. to Smith Wormald.[65] Wormald's devisees sold the 125-acre Manor farm to John Barker in 1871[66] and the manor and about 30 a. to John Dobby in 1876.[67] Thomas Dobby sold the manorial rights to Thomas Masterman in 1891[68] and no more is known of them.

The manor-house occupied by Sir Roger Jacques in 1646 had 7 hearths in 1672.[69] Elvington Hall was apparently built by the Sternes in the later 18th century. It remained the manor-house until 1881, when John Dobby sold it to Harriet Whitaker.[70] On the death of her daughter Harriet Von Beverhoudt in 1934 the hall passed to the latter's cousin Judith Bury-Barry (d. 1947),[71] whose executors sold it to Mr. K. Wadham in 1957.[72] He sold it in 1962 to Mr. R. M. Pontefract,[73] the owner in 1972. The house has been extended and remodelled in the 20th century. The oldest part appears to be the north front, which may be 17th-century in origin. A new drawing room and staircase were added on the south-west in the later 18th century, perhaps from designs by Carr of York, and the south front was made symmetrical by the addition of another room in the earlier 19th century.

Ralph Dodsworth (d. 1794) devized his share of the estate purchased from Richard Sterne to his brother John[74] who, in 1803, sold 416 a. to the Revd. Thomas Preston.[75] In 1837 Dodsworth's trustees sold about 150 a. to P. B. Lawley, later Baron Wenlock, and in 1838 a further 125 a. to Lawley and 195 a. to William Massey.[76] P. B. and B. R. Lawley also increased their Elvington estate by the purchase of 75 a. from Joseph Dresser in 1846 and 168 a. from Henry Preston in 1847.[77] The estate descended like Escrick manor[78] until 1920, when Irene Lawley sold about 400 a. in two farms.[79] She sold the remaining 165 a. in 1927.[80]

ECONOMIC HISTORY. There was land for three ploughs at Elvington in 1086, on which Alulf had one plough and three villeins another, as well as woodland a league long and half a league broad and 10 a. of meadow. The estate had decreased in value from £2 in 1066 to 10s.[81] Between 1182 and 1197 William de Morers granted Meaux abbey a cartload of rods a year from his woodland.[82] In the 13th century Elvington and Wheldrake intercommoned in their fields and woodland. Thus an Elvington holding in 1228 had commonage in Wheldrake[83] and later in the century the lords and inhabitants of the two townships agreed that each should have commonage in the territory of the other. It was further agreed that reclamation of the waste, which had evidently been carried on extensively at Elvington since 1235, should proceed at an equal pace in both townships.[84]

The manor was worth about £50 in 1487[85] and the rents of four freeholders amounted to 13s. in 1510.[86] In 1569 a 64-acre wood called Ragarth and in 1583 waste land called Norwood were let by the Crown.[87]

---

[46] *Cal. Close*, 1392–6, 360, 362.
[47] J. W. Clay, *Ext. & Dorm. Peerages of N. Cos. of Eng.* 146.
[48] Ibid. 147; *Feud. Aids*, vi. 271.
[49] *Cal. Fine R.* 1452–61, 273–4; *Cal. Pat.* 1452–61, 578.
[50] For pedigree of the Nevilles see *Complete Peerage*, s.v. Salisbury, Warwick, Westmorland.
[51] *Cal. Pat.* 1467–77, 483.
[52] D.L. 29/650/10510.
[53] *N. Country Wills*, i (Sur. Soc. cxvi), 281; *Cal. Pat.* 1563–6, p. 513.
[54] C 66/2488 m. 11; Y.A.S., MS. 530(d).
[55] Y.A.S., MS. 530(d).
[56] Ibid.; E.R.R.O., DDFA/4/4.
[57] E.R.R.O., DDFA/4/4.
[58] *D.N.B.*; for pedigree of the Sterne family see *Y.A.J.* xxi. 91.
[59] R.D.B., AR/134/264.
[60] See below.
[61] R.D.B., AU/127/204; /128/205; E.R.R.O., DDFA/4/26.
[62] R.D.B., AU/390/645; /593/982.
[63] Ibid. CD/184/277.
[64] Ibid. CM/299/462.
[65] Ibid. HI/81/104; HQ/80/85.
[66] Ibid. KX/270/352.
[67] Ibid. LU/392/581.
[68] Ibid. 44/435/380 (1891).
[69] E 179/205/504; *Royalist Composition Papers*, i (Y.A.S. Rec. Ser. xv), 196.
[70] R.D.B., NK/210/310.
[71] Ibid. 165/518/437; 507/242/189; 754/297/251.
[72] Ibid. 1086/132/122.
[73] Ibid. 1287/484/430.
[74] E.R.R.O., DDFA/4/5.
[75] R.D.B., CG/540/877.
[76] Ibid. FD/385/421; FF/194/233; /196/234.
[77] Ibid. GL/310/395; E.R.R.O., DDFA/8/110.
[78] See p. 20.
[79] R.D.B., 211/133/115; 216/242/206.
[80] Ibid. 343/435/369.
[81] *V.C.H. Yorks.* ii. 263.
[82] *Chron. de Melsa* (Rolls Ser.), i. 230.
[83] *Cal. Pat.* 1225–32, 208.
[84] *Fountains Charty.* ed. W.T. Lancaster, ii. 834–5.
[85] D.L. 29/650/10510.
[86] B.L. Harl. MS. 6288, ff. 81–7.
[87] E 310/27/162 f. 38; E 310/27/163 f. 39.

Two waste plots were brought into cultivation c. 1600[88] and closes called West intake and Penridding were first mentioned in 1624. The 40-acre Wood close was recorded in 1670.[89] In the 17th century the remaining waste covered much of the north and west of the parish. Turbary rights in it were mentioned in 1620[90] and it was unstinted in 1624. In the latter year the manor contained 34 bovates of openfield land and 224 a. lying in about 30 closes. Nine free tenants held a total of 9½ bovates and 11 a. by suit of court and there were 29 leaseholders, 20 of whom held only cottages and garths. The other nine leaseholders held a total of 20½ bovates and 107 a. The demesne, held by two lessees, contained 4 bovates and 93 a. The manor was then worth about £150 but was let for only about £53.[91]

The open fields were first named in 1663, when they were West or Boondike, North, East, and South or Little fields. East came to be known as Innam field by 1685[92] and as Cocking field by 1769.[93] The main areas of common meadow in 1663 were North ings, Thackmire, West carr, Mask, and Agles, the last-mentioned no doubt the area in the south-east of the parish known as Hagghill Leas ings in the mid 19th century. Hawk ing had been inclosed from Agles by 1663 and Ellerker and Chancellor ings, mentioned in 1685, may also have been inclosed meadow land.[94] In 1763 40 a. of meadow lay in 17 closes.[95]

Much of the remaining common or moor, but not the most northerly part, was inclosed in 1743[96] under an Act of the same year.[97] In all, 576 a. were allotted, Richard Sterne as lord of the manor receiving 469 a. and the rector 91 a. There were three other allotments totalling 16 a. The rest of the common, together with the open fields and ings, was inclosed under an Act of 1769.[98] About 800 a. were involved, of which at least 250 a. were from the common.[99] The rector received 147 a. and two other men a total of 54 a. The rest went to the lord of the manor.

In 1795 the parish contained about 1,000 a. of arable, 800 a. of pasture, 300 a. of waste, and 30 a. of woodland. Oats (375 a.) was the main crop grown.[1] In 1801 697 a. were under crops, mainly oats (268 a.) and wheat (185 a.).[2] There have usually been 12–16 farmers in the 19th and 20th centuries.[3] Of the 13 farms in 1851 7 were of 100–200 a. and 2 of over 200 a.,[4] and of the same number in 1937 3 covered 150 a. or more.[5] In 1905 there were 1,192 a. of arable, 760 a. of grassland, and 58 a. of woodland.[6] The proportion of pasture has increased in more recent years and in 1965 it represented over half the area of the parish not covered by the airfield.[7]

In 1086 there were two fisheries at Elvington rendering 1,000 eels a year.[8] In 1332 Henry of Moreby had a weir, presumably for fishing, which was said to obstruct boats and cause flooding.[9] It was ordered to be diminished in 1337 but this had not been done by 1356, when it was held by William de Morers. Another of William's weirs at Elvington had recently been destroyed by floods.[10] The fishing rights, which have since descended with the manor, were worth £1 in 1510, about 10s. in 1624,[11] and £10–12 a year in 1769.[12] Salmon fishing was carried on in the 19th and early 20th centuries[13] but ceased in the 1940s.[14]

Weavers at Elvington were mentioned in the 1390s.[15] A brick and tile works beside the Wheldrake road existed by 1850[16] and brick-making continued there until the 1930s.[17] In 1972 the site was marked by a 19th-century brick wind-pump and a water-filled pit. There is no evidence of a mill at Elvington and the three corn-millers who lived in the parish in 1851[18] were presumably employed in the large mill at Sutton upon Derwent. In 1892 willows were said to be grown in the parish for basket-making.[19] In 1972 a firm of fertilizer manufacturers provided some employment and huts formerly belonging to the airfield were occupied by several industrial concerns, including a manufacturer of pre-cast concrete and an agricultural engineer.

LOCAL GOVERNMENT. Although the assize of ale was a franchise of the court, matters dealt with and recorded in estreats for manorial courts held by the Crown in 1610, 1621, 1623, and 1624 were mostly agricultural offences and petty misdemeanours.[20]

No parochial records before 1835 are known. In 1743 there were 'three or four' unendowed almshouses[21] and in the mid 19th century a row of poorhouses adjoined the York road west of the village.[22] In 1837 Elvington joined York poor-law union.[23] It became part of Escrick rural district in 1894, Derwent rural district in 1935,[24] and the Selby district of North Yorkshire in 1974.

CHURCH. There was a church at Elvington in 1086.[25] The advowson descended with the manor in the Middle Ages and later[26] but was retained by the Crown in 1628 when the manor was granted away.[27]

[88] B.I.H.R., CP. H. 120.
[89] B.L. Harl. MS. 6288, ff. 81–7; E.R.R.O., DDFA/8/59.
[90] Y.A.S., MS. 530(d).
[91] B.L. Harl. MS. 6288, ff. 81–7.
[92] B.I.H.R., TER. N. Elvington 1663, 1685.
[93] 8 & 9 Geo. III, Sess. 2, c. 21 (Priv. Act).
[94] B.I.H.R., TER. N. Elvington 1663, 1685.
[95] Y.A.S., MS. 530(d).
[96] E.R.R.O., Enrolment Bk. D, p. 37.
[97] 16 Geo. III, c. 18 (Priv. Act).
[98] 8 & 9 Geo. III, Sess. 2, c. 21 (Priv. Act).
[99] B.I.H.R., TER. N. Elvington 1770; R.D.B., AR/134/264.
[1] E.R.R.O., DPX/84.
[2] 1801 Crop Returns.   [3] Directories.
[4] H.O. 107/2356.
[5] Kelly's Dir. N. & E.R. Yorks. (1937), 454.
[6] Acreage Returns, 1905.
[7] 2nd Land Util. Surv. Map, sheet 699 (SE 64–74).
[8] V.C.H. Yorks. ii. 263.
[9] Cal. Inq. Misc. ii, pp. 320–1.
[10] Public Works in Med. Law, ii (Selden Soc. xl), 276–7.
[11] B.L. Harl. MS. 6288, ff. 81–7.
[12] E.R.R.O., DDFA/4/2.   [13] Directories.
[14] Local information.
[15] V.C.H. Yorks. ii. 409.
[16] O.S. Map 6" (1854 edn.).
[17] Local information.   [18] H.O. 107/2356.
[19] Bulmer, Dir. E. Yorks. (1892), 604.
[20] S.C. 2/211/28, 37.
[21] Herring's Visit. i. 181.
[22] O.S. Map 6" (1854 edn.).
[23] 3rd Rep. Poor Law Com. 171.   [24] Census.
[25] V.C.H. Yorks. ii. 263.
[26] Reg. Giffard, i, p. 45; Reg. Corbridge, ii, p. 173; Reg. Greenfield, v, p. 182; Cal. Close, 1392–6, 360; 1422–9, 238; 1476–85, p. 189; Cal. Pat. 1557–8, 448.
[27] Inst. Bks.

Between 1856 and 1866 it passed to the Revd. J. E. Clarke[28] and the Clarkes have since retained it.[29]

The church was valued at £5 6s. 8d. in 1291[30] and about £6 net in 1535.[31] It was worth £50 in 1650[32] and £45 in 1706.[33] The net income in 1829–31 was on average £280,[34] in 1884 it was £290, and in 1914 £249.[35]

Most of the income in 1535 and later was from tithes. Their payment from a plot of newly cultivated waste was disputed in 1603.[36] Only part of the ings was tithable in 1685[37] and by 1698 the lord of the manor paid a composition of £1 a year for the meadow called Mask.[38] In 1535 the glebe comprised 2 bovates of land and 2 a. of meadow[39] and in 1685 it amounted to about 30 a.[40] The rector was awarded 91 a. for tithes and glebe at the inclosure of 1743[41] and 147 a. and a rent-charge of about £23 at that of 1769.[42] Tithes on certain old-inclosed lands were commuted in 1844 for a rent-charge of about £20.[43] The glebe, comprising 208 a., was sold in 1920.[44]

There was a parsonage house in 1535[45] and it was said to be in disrepair in 1582.[46] It had five hearths in 1672,[47] and in 1770 was a thatched brick building with three ground-floor rooms and three bedrooms. It had been rebuilt by 1809, when it contained six rooms on each floor.[48] The house, close to the church, was sold in 1970 and a new Rectory built near by in 1971–2.[49]

Land given to support a light in the church was granted to Francis Barker and Thomas Blackway in 1566.[50]

The rector was licensed to be absent for three years in 1309.[51] In 1743 the incumbent stated that he spent only one night a week at Elvington and the rest at York.[52] The rector resided on his other living at Sutton upon Derwent in 1764[53] and Knaresborough (Yorks. W.R.) in 1835, in the latter year employing an assistant curate at Elvington.[54] In 1972 the rector was also curate-in-charge of Sutton upon Derwent.[55] Henry Ayscough, rector 1618–25, who also held the living of Dunnington, was a Puritan.[56]

There were two services each Sunday in 1743 and Holy Communion was celebrated four times a year, with about 40 communicants.[57] In 1764 services were held fortnightly. By 1865 there were two services each Sunday. In the 1860s and 1870s communion was usually celebrated monthly, with 16–18 people receiving. In the 1880s and 1914 it was celebrated fortnightly and in 1936 weekly.[58] There were still two services each Sunday in 1972.

Little is known of the medieval church of *HOLY TRINITY*. It was out of repair in 1663[59] and 1744[60] and was entirely rebuilt, largely at the rector's expense, in 1803. The new church was of brick with stone dressings and had an embattled west tower and an apse. The windows were in 'semi-gothic' style and there was a west gallery.[61] The church was repaired in 1849[62] and 1868[63] before being rebuilt on a site a little to the south in 1876–7.[64] The new building, of stone, was designed by William White and consists of chancel with polygonal apse, nave with north aisle and vestry, and north-west tower. The belfry stage of the tower is wooden and is capped by a short spire. The aisle arcade has four semicircular red-brick arches on red sandstone columns with leaf capitals. A round Norman font with a scalloped base remains in the church and in the churchyard is a font dated 1685.

There were two bells in 1552 and later,[65] and two still: (i) 14th century, Thomas de Wald; (ii) n.d.[66] The plate consists of a flagon, cup, and paten of silver plate.[67] The registers date from 1600 and are complete, except for gaps for 1643–53 and 1741–4.[68]

The churchyard was extended in 1968.[69] Income for its upkeep derives from Spence's charity.[70]

NONCONFORMITY. There were two recusants at Elvington in 1586 and three were discovered in the 1630s.[71] Houses, barns, and other buildings were licensed for worship in 1785, 1789, 1819, 1821, 1830, and 1833.[72] Between 1790 and 1816 the Wesleyan Methodists usually had 18–29 members at Elvington[73] and they built a chapel in 1810.[74] It was rebuilt or extensively repaired in 1833[75] and restored in 1899.[76] It was said in 1914 to be not well attended.[77] It was still used in 1972.

---

[28] Sheahan and Whellan, *Hist. York & E.R.* ii. 617; *York Dioc. Cal.* (1866).
[29] *York Dioc. Year Bk.*
[30] *Tax. Eccl.* (Rec. Com.), 300.
[31] *Valor Eccl.* (Rec. Com.), v. 97.
[32] C 94/3 f. 76.
[33] B.I.H.R., PR. ELV. 3.
[34] *Rep. Com. Eccl. Revenues*, 932.
[35] B.I.H.R., Bp. V. 1884/Ret.; Bp. V. 1914/Ret.
[36] Ibid. CP. H. 120.
[37] Ibid. TER. N. Elvington 1685.
[38] Ibid. PR. ELV. 3.
[39] *Valor Eccl.* v. 97.
[40] B.I.H.R., TER. N. Elvington 1685.
[41] E.R.R.O., Enrolment Bk. D, p. 37.
[42] B.I.H.R., TER. N. Elvington 1770.
[43] Ibid. TA. 290S.
[44] R.D.B., 211/5/4.
[45] *Valor Eccl.* v. 97.
[46] B.I.H.R., V. 1582/CB.
[47] E 179/205/504.
[48] B.I.H.R., TER. N. Elvington 1770, 1809.
[49] R.D.B., 1658/415/369; 1670/428/383.
[50] *Cal. Pat.* 1563–6, pp. 474–5.
[51] *Reg. Greenfield*, iii, p. 39.
[52] *Herring's Visit.* i. 181.
[53] B.I.H.R., Bp. V. 1764/Ret. 170.
[54] *Rep. Com. Eccl. Revenues*, 932.
[55] *Crockford*.
[56] R. A. Marchant, *Puritans and the Ch. Courts in Dioc. York, 1560–1642*, 226–7, 320.

[57] *Herring's Visit.* i. 181.
[58] B.I.H.R., Bp. V. 1764/Ret. 170; V. 1865/Ret. 166; V. 1868/Ret. 153; V. 1871/Ret. 154; V. 1877/Ret.; Bp. V. 1884/Ret.; Bp. V. 1894/Ret.; Bp. V. 1900/Ret. 114; Bp. V. 1914/Ret.; Bp. V. 1936/Ret. 145.
[59] Ibid. V. 1663/CB. 1.
[60] *Herring's Visit.* i. 181 n.
[61] B.I.H.R., Fac. Bk. iii, p. 332; White, *Dir. E. & N. R. Yorks.* (1840), 326; Sheahan and Whellan, *Hist. York & E.R.* ii. 617.
[62] B.I.H.R., PR. ELV. 9.
[63] Ibid. V. 1868/Ret. 153.
[64] Ibid. Fac. Bk. vi, p. 134; Fac. 1876/4; CD. 437. See plate facing p. 17.
[65] Ibid. TER. N. Elvington 1764; *Inventories of Ch. Goods*, 84.
[66] Boulter, 'Ch. Bells', 31; *V.C.H. Yorks.* ii. 451.
[67] *Yorks. Ch. Plate*, i. 76.
[68] B.I.H.R.
[69] York. Dioc. Regy., Consecration deeds.
[70] See p. 17.
[71] Aveling, *Post Reformation Catholicism*, 64.
[72] G.R.O. Worship Returns, Vol. v, nos. 661, 761, 3307, 3577, 4227, 4293.
[73] E.R.R.O., MRP/1/7.
[74] G.R.O. Worship Returns, Vol. v, no. 2402; H.O. 129/23/515.
[75] E.R.R.O., MRP/1/48.
[76] Ibid. MRP/1/74.
[77] B.I.H.R., Bp. V. 1914/Ret.

Moreby Hall from the south, close to the banks of the Ouse

Escrick Hall from the south, with the village beyond

ESCRICK CHURCH FROM THE SOUTH-EAST
Built in 1857

ELVINGTON CHURCH FROM THE NORTH-EAST
Built in 1876–7

Elvington was the base for the Primitive Methodist mission to York in 1819.[78] A Primitive Methodist 'chapel' mentioned in 1840[79] seems to have been a licensed house or barn. It had ceased to be used by 1856.[80]

EDUCATION. A master, supported by fees, taught at Elvington in 1764.[81] The school was still unendowed in 1819, when it contained about 50 children, 20 of whom were supported by subscriptions.[82] By 1835 there were two schools with a total of 55 pupils[83] but in 1856 there was only one, housed in the former Primitive Methodist 'chapel'.[84] It was rebuilt in 1858 on a new site and in 1864 the average attendance was 56.[85] It first received an annual government grant in 1870.[86] Between 1908 and 1938 the attendance varied between 30 and 50.[87] A new school was built in 1969[88] and in April 1972 there were 78 on the roll.[89] Both the former school buildings were later used as village halls.[90]

The vicar held a night school 'with little success' in the 1860s.[91]

CHARITIES FOR THE POOR. Robert Spence, by will proved in 1906, left £50, part of the interest on which was to be used for the upkeep of family memorials in Elvington and Durleigh (Som.) churches and the residue for the poor of Elvington. In 1972 £50 stock and £21 cash produced an income of £4, all of which was transferred to the churchyard account.[92]

Elvington benefited from the charity of John Hodgson for parishes in York poor-law union.[93]

ESCRICK

THE VILLAGE of Escrick lies 6 miles south of York on the moraine to which it gives its name.[1] The landscape in and about the village was largely created during the half century after 1781 when the church and many of the houses were moved to a new site, when new roads were laid out, and when an extensive park was made around the hall. The old village had been firmly planted astride the moraine, which in places exceeds 50 ft. above sea-level, and the element 'ric' in its name refers either to the ridge itself or to a stream known as Bridge dike which flows along its northern flank.[2] A smaller, almost imperceptible, ridge runs northwards from Escrick; it is followed by the York road and the hamlet of Deighton lies beside it. Both settlements were Anglian. The area of the ancient parish, which is roughly triangular in shape, is 6,348 a., of which Deighton township and civil parish accounts for 2,002 a.[3] The vill of 'Chetelstorp' in Escrick, presumably a Scandinavian settlement, was mentioned in 1086 and during the 12th century[4] but it was not recorded again and its site is unknown.

The boulder clay, sand, and gravel of the higher ground[5] were in part occupied by the relatively small open fields of both Escrick and Deighton. Away from the moraine most of the land lies at between 25 ft. and 50 ft., and a large area in the south of the parish lies lower still. The outwash sand and clay of the low ground were occupied by extensive assarts, as well as carrs and woods. The large common wood of Escrick lay in the extreme south, and Deighton common formed part of the waste land centred on Tilmire which extended into Fulford and Heslington to the north. An area of alluvium alongside Bridge dike was formerly used as carr and meadow land. Several dikes drained the lower ground, including those which formed much of the parish boundary. Flooding was apparently frequent in the Middle Ages, especially from Bridge dike which flowed across the middle of the parish and formed the internal township boundary.[6] To the west of Escrick village, the main channel of Bridge dike was moved to a more southerly course between 1809 and 1847.[7]

The road pattern in Escrick township remained a simple one until the changes of the late 18th and early 19th centuries. The road from York divided at the village, one branch leading south-westwards to Riccall, the other south-eastwards to Skipwith. In 1362 the latter was described as the Howden road and the former as only a trackway.[8] A cross road from Wheldrake to Stillingfleet followed the crest of the moraine. The village was in the form of a reversed L, at the junction of the York and Stillingfleet roads, and it contained 60–80 houses about 1600.[9] Hall, church, and Rectory all stood near its centre. Sir Henry Thompson is said to have made a carriage way from York to Escrick in 1672,[10] presumably an improvement to the existing York road. The bridge by which that road crossed Bridge dike was rebuilt by Beilby Thompson in 1776,[11] and in 1781 he secured an Act of Parliament to facilitate

[78] V.C.H. City of York, 413.
[79] White, Dir. E. & N.R. Yorks. (1840), 326.
[80] Sheahan and Whellan, Hist. York & E.R. ii. 617.
[81] B.I.H.R., Bp. V. 1764/Ret. 170.
[82] Educ. of Poor Digest, 1080.
[83] Educ. Enquiry Abstract, 1084.
[84] Sheahan and Whellan, Hist. York & E.R. ii. 617; see above.
[85] Ed. 7/135 no. 46.
[86] Rep. of Educ. Cttee. of Council, 1870–1 [C. 406], p. 549, H.C. (1871), xxii.
[87] Bd. of Educ. List 21 (H.M.S.O.).
[88] E.R. Educ. Cttee. Mins. 1967–8, 107; local information.
[89] Ex inf. Chief Educ. Officer, County Hall, Beverley, 1972.
[90] See p. 13.
[91] B.I.H.R., V. 1865/Ret. 166; V. 1868/Ret. 153.

[92] Char. Com. files. [93] See p. 12.
[1] This article was written in 1972.
[2] P.N.E.R. Yorks. (E.P.N.S.), 268–9.
[3] O.S. Map 6″, Yorks. (1851 edn.). The whole of Deighton is covered by sheet 191 and most of Escrick by sheets 191 and 206.
[4] See p. 20.
[5] Geol. Surv. Map 1″, solid and drift, sheet 71 (1973 edn.).
[6] Cal. Pat. 1343–5, 593; Cal. Inq. Misc. i, pp. 454–5; Public Works in Med. Law, ii (Selden Soc. xl), 239–41.
[7] Escrick Park Estate Office, 1809 map; O.S. Map 6″ (1851 edn.).
[8] Pub. Works in Med. Law, ii, 240, 247.
[9] E 179/205/504; Escrick Park Estate Office, undated map (internal evidence suggests a date soon after 1600).
[10] W. H. M. Baines, Old Naburn, 57.
[11] Inscription on bridge.

A HISTORY OF YORKSHIRE: EAST RIDING

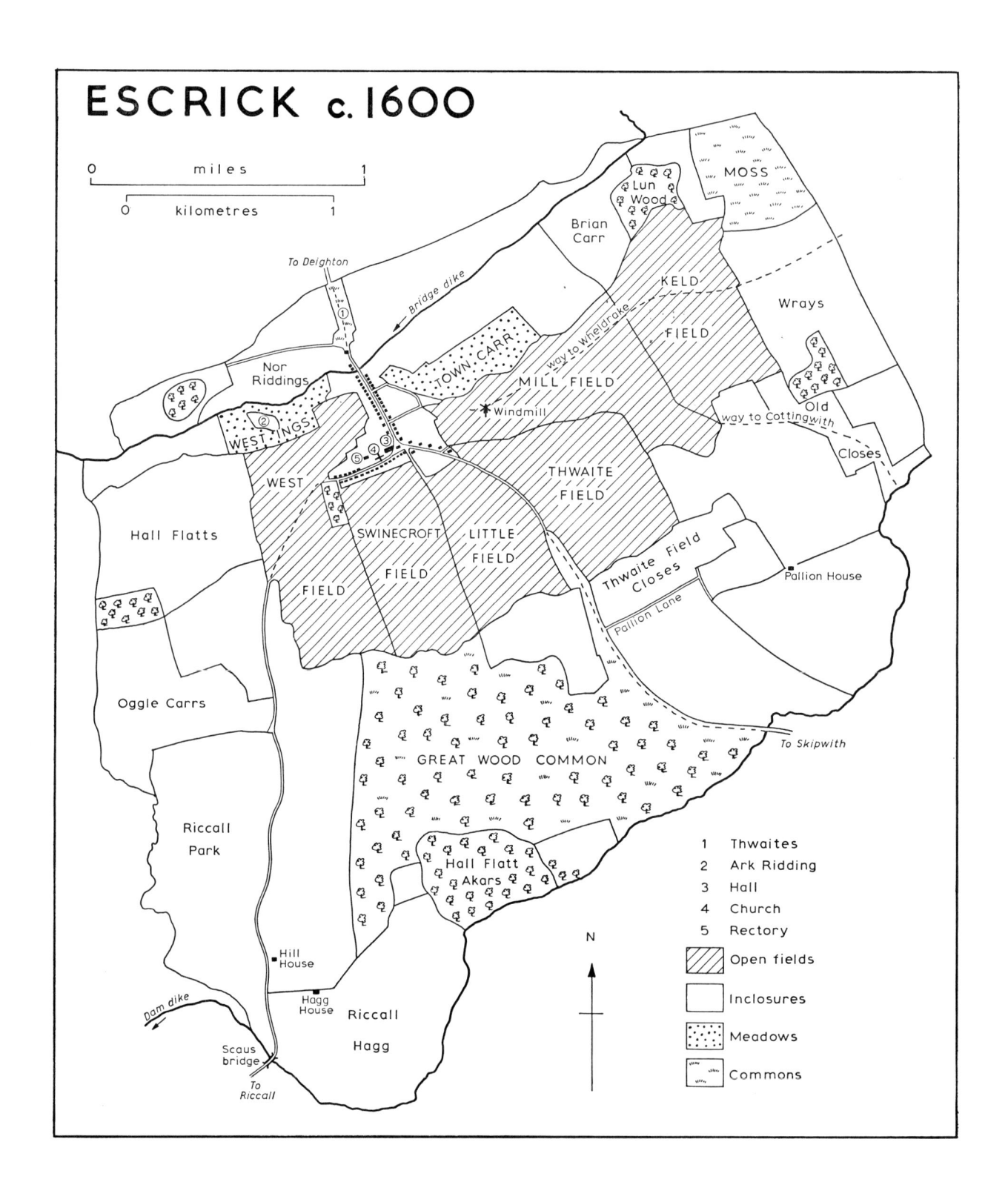

ESCRICK c. 1600

the 'many considerable improvements' which he proposed to make around the hall.[12]

During the next few years Beilby Thompson removed and rebuilt the church and Rectory on sites north of the village and by 1809 26 houses had been demolished: most of those that remained were in the main street formed by the York road, but there were still 9 on the Stillingfleet road.[13] The angle of the L was obliterated and the main street made into a cul-de-sac. From a point close to Bridge dike new roads were laid out to bypass the village and link up with the roads to Skipwith and Riccall. Trees were planted to screen the hall from view and a park was made on the former open-field land, incorporating an avenue of trees which appears to have been planted in the 1760s.[14] The Skipwith and Riccall roads were removed still further from the hall in or soon after 1825, when P. B. Thompson, Baron Wenlock, was authorized to make new roads to the east and west of the village. A third new road was to follow Bridge dike linking the other two.[15] By 1847 the remaining 9 houses on the Stillingfleet road had been demolished and the park had been extended as far as the new roads.[16] The park was said to contain about 450 a.[17] and it was stocked with deer, some 130 of them in 1820.[18] Also by the 1840s, and perhaps much earlier,[19] the village had been much enlarged by the building of houses beyond Bridge dike, extending the village street northwards to the new church.

In the older part of the village, south of Bridge dike, there are several houses of late-17th- or early-18th-century origin but they, like most of the early-19th-century houses, were remodelled in the early 1900s. Four of them are dated 1911. One of the altered houses is the village inn. There were three alehouses in Escrick from the 1750s to the 1770s. Subsequently there was only one,[20] known as the Spotted Bull in 1823 but later as the Bull and then the Black Bull.[21] North of Bridge dike stands the shop of the Escrick and District Co-operative Society, founded in 1872 and amalgamated with the York society in 1971;[22] the shop was formerly near the park gates.[23] Also north of Bridge dike is the village institute, later the Escrick and Deighton Club, built in 1908.[24] One body which perhaps used the institute was the agricultural society, established in 1881 and still mentioned in the 1920s.[25] At the junction of the village street and the Riccall road is an elaborate fountain, put up in 1897 to commemorate the queen's diamond jubilee.

Isolated in its own grounds at the north end of the village is the Villa, a large mid-19th-century house, given a distinctive appearance by bay windows rising through both storeys into a pediment above. Close to the village on the Skipwith road is a police station built in 1857–8.[26] Twentieth-century housing has greatly extended the village, besides filling some gaps in the main street. There are 16 council houses and several estates of privately built houses, some stone-faced and many of a 'superior' kind. Escrick had thus become to a large extent a dormitory village for York by 1972.

Apart from the main York road, the only roads in Deighton township are minor ones leading to Naburn and Wheldrake. Work to straighten the line of the main road, in Escrick as well as Deighton, was begun in the 1960s.[27] The village street of Deighton, where there were 30–40 houses in the 17th century,[28] is a cul-de-sac off the York road. Surviving 19th-century houses include two small two-storeyed cottages and an inn. There were two alehouses at Deighton from the 1750s to the 1770s, later only one;[29] it was known as the Swan in 1823 and became the White Swan in the 20th century.[30] Recent building includes eight council and several private houses.

The scattered farm-houses in Escrick township include Whinchat Hall, which has a pediment surmounting the three central bays of the main front. Mount Pleasant Farm, now demolished, was also pedimented.[31] Approach Farm has an ornamental façade facing one of the entrance drives into the park. The farm buildings at both Approach and Park Farms include wheelhouses. Escrick railway station stands by the York–Selby railway line, opened in 1871;[32] the station was closed for passengers in 1953 and goods in 1961.[33] At Deighton the scattered farms include Gravel Pit House, with farm buildings dated 1880. Deighton Grange has a big early-19th-century barn and a wheelhouse with a pyramidal roof. The houses that already stood away from both villages in the 17th century have all since been rebuilt.[34]

At the northern end of Deighton township is a small group of 19th- and 20th-century houses known as Crockey Hill. The name derives from 'Cockermire', mentioned in 1619; a 'great stone' in the road, near the parish boundary, was then said to mark the site of the former Cockermire cross.[35]

There were 135 poll-tax payers at Escrick in 1377.[36] In 1672 76 households, 19 of them exempt, were listed in the hearth-tax assessment. Of those taxed, apart from Escrick Hall, 39 had only one hearth each, 9 had 2, 6 had 3 or 4, and 2 had seven. There were 40 households at Deighton, 9 of them exempt; excluding Deighton Hall 22 had one hearth each, 6 had 2, and 2 had three.[37] In 1743 there were 71 families at Escrick and 27 at Deighton,[38] and still 98 in the whole parish in 1764.[39]

The population of Escrick township rose from

---

[12] Escrick Church Act, 21 Geo. III, c. 76.
[13] Escrick Park Estate Office, 1809 map.
[14] E.R.R.O., DDFA/37/28; T. Jefferys, Map of Yorks. (1772).
[15] E.R.R.O., HD/26–8.
[16] O.S. Map 6" (1851 edn.).
[17] Sheahan and Whellan, Hist. York & E.R. ii. 618.
[18] E.R.R.O., DDFA/5/19.
[19] The 1809 map does not show the area N. of Bridge dike.
[20] E.R.R.O., QDT/2/15.
[21] Baines, Hist. Yorks. (1823), ii. 202 and later directories.
[22] Ex inf. Secretary, York Co-operative Soc. Ltd., 1972.
[23] Local information.
[24] Kelly's Dir. N. & E.R. Yorks. (1909), 503.

[25] Bulmer, Dir. E. Yorks. (1892), 607 and later directories.
[26] E.R.R.O., QAP/5/12–20.
[27] E.R.C.C. Mins. passim.
[28] E 179/205/504; map and survey penes Mr. & Mrs. R.J. Perry, York Ho., Riccall, 1972.
[29] E.R.R.O., QDT/2/15.
[30] Baines, Hist. Yorks. (1823), ii. 193 and later directories.
[31] Local information.
[32] V.C.H. City of York, 478.
[33] Ex inf. Divisional Manager, Brit. Rlys. (Leeds), 1972.
[34] See pp. 23, 25.
[35] Map and survey penes Mr. and Mrs. Perry.
[36] E 179/202/58 m. 12.
[37] E 179/205/504.
[38] Herring's Visit. i. 182.
[39] B.I.H.R., Bp. V. 1764/Ret. 172.

406 in 1801 to 717 in 1831, declined to 589 in 1881, briefly recovered to 653 in 1891, and stood at 544 in 1901. It was 597 in 1911 and 1921, but thereafter fell to 443 in 1961, before the village began to be developed. In 1971 it stood at 950. Deighton did not experience such marked fluctuations. Its population was 172 in 1801, 200 in 1901, and 228 in 1971.[40]

MANORS AND OTHER ESTATES. In 1086 there were two estates at Escrick, each of 4 carucates, one of which comprised 'Chetelstorp'. Both were soke of the manor of Clifton (Yorks. N.R.) and belonged to Count Alan of Brittany; before the Conquest they had belonged to Morcar.[41] About 1100 Count Stephen gave 'Chetelstorp' and 2 carucates in Escrick to St. Mary's abbey, York,[42] and the other 2 carucates also passed to the abbey. The first 6 carucates were granted by St. Mary's to Picot de Lascelles between 1145 and 1161, and the other 2 to Roger de Lascelles between 1197 and 1219.[43] The Lascelles family, which had previously been the abbey's tenant at Escrick, thenceforth held the estate as part of the honor of Richmond and the liberty of St. Mary's.[44]

After the death of Roger de Lascelles c. 1300 the manor of ESCRICK was held in dower by his widow Isabel as the inheritance of his four daughters, Joan de Colewenne or Curwenne, Avice le Constable, Maud Tilliol, and Tiffany, widow of Ralph FitzRanulph. Isabel died in 1323. Tiffany's son Ralph, sometimes known as Ralph de Lascelles, was then heir to her share. Joan had granted the reversion of her part to Simon Ward and he to Roger Dammory, a rebel, and so it was seized by the Crown in 1323.[45] After Isabel's death the manor was divided between the Crown, Avice, Maud, and Ralph.[46] It was probably the last three shares which were consolidated in the hands of Ralph de Lascelles. He apparently had them by 1344,[47] and in 1362 he was described as lord of three-quarters of Escrick.[48] The Lascelles family retained the estate until the death of Roger Lascelles, whose daughter and heir Margaret (d. 1499) married James Pickering.[49] Margaret's grandson Christopher Pickering was succeeded in the early 16th century by his daughter Anne, who married Sir Henry Knyvett.[50] The Knyvetts thenceforth held the manor[51] and in 1607 Sir Thomas Knyvett (d. 1622) was created Baron Knyvett of Escrick. He was succeeded by his brother Sir Henry Knyvett, whose daughter and coheir Catherine married as her second husband Thomas Howard, earl of Suffolk, in or before 1583. Their son Edward was created Baron Howard of Escrick in 1628.[52] It was he who sold Escrick in 1668 to Sir Henry Thompson.[53]

The Thompsons held the manor until the death of Richard Thompson in 1820. His sister Jane had married Sir Robert Lawley, Bt., in 1764 and it was their son P. B. Lawley who succeeded to Escrick. He was created Baron Wenlock in 1839.[54] Beilby Lawley, the 3rd baron, died in 1912 and the estate passed to his daughter Irene, who in 1920 married C. G. Forbes Adam.[55] In 1920 the estate included 3,850 a. in Escrick township and in 1972 4,189 a.[56] It was still held by the Forbes Adam family in 1972. The hall and 34 a. of parkland were let in 1949 to the Woodard Society, which subsequently used the building to house Queen Margaret's School for Girls, formerly at Scarborough.[57]

Several holdings were merged with the chief estate in the 18th and 19th centuries. Property belonging to the Swann family was acquired in 1763 and 1805. On the latter occasion it comprised Park House farm, which John Swann had bought in 1748.[58] In 1737 Beilby Thompson (d. 1750) bought North House farm, which had belonged to Conan Aske in 1726,[59] and in 1736 he bought an estate which had been in the Wright family until a few years before.[60] Another farm was bought from Sir Ralph Milbank in 1764,[61] and Rush farm was acquired from W. H. Key in 1892.[62]

A manor-house at Escrick was mentioned in 1323,[63] and in 1557 it was called Escrick Hall.[64] The house had 17 hearths in 1672.[65] It was rebuilt by Henry Thompson (d. 1700) c. 1680–90. The new house was apparently similar to Bell Hall, Naburn; it was two storeys high with basement and attics, and the main front was seven bays long with a central entrance.[66] It was later refronted and raised to three storeys, perhaps in 1758, the date of surviving rainwater-heads which also bear the initials of Beilby Thompson (d. 1799). In 1763 John Carr of York was employed to design additions to the building.[67] Carr added a range which abuts the north front and extends beyond it to both east and west, more than doubling the length of the elevation, and a square stable block with four ranges around a central court on the north-east. He also remodelled the interior of the old house, and the main staircase and some ceilings and fire-places remain from these alterations.[68] The mid 19th century was another period of substan-

[40] *V.C.H. Yorks.* iii. 497; *Census,* 1911–71.
[41] *V.C.H. Yorks.* ii. 241, 322.
[42] *E.Y.C.* iv, p. 4.
[43] Ibid. pp. 132–3, 135–6.
[44] Ibid. v, pp. 183, 186; *Feud. Aids,* vi. 35. For a pedigree of the Lascelles family see *E.Y.C.* v, p. 184.
[45] *Cal. Inq. p.m.* vi, p. 251; *Yorks. Deeds,* v, p. 95; *Monastic Notes* (Y.A.S. Rec. Ser. xvii), 208–9; *Complete Peerage,* s.v. Lascelles.
[46] Details are given in *Cal. Close,* 1323–7, 28 sqq.
[47] E.R.R.O., DDCC/App. B/32; *Yorks. Fines, 1327–47,* pp. 29, 173; *Yorks. Deeds,* i, pp. 102–3; *Parl. Rep.* i (Y.A.S. Rec. Ser. xci), 98, 116.
[48] *Pub. Works in Med. Law,* ii. 240–1.
[49] C 142/12 no. 91; C.P. 40/960 m. 440; *Y.A.J.* xxvii. 151; *Visit. Yorks. 1584–5 and 1612,* ed. J. Foster, 120, 630.
[50] C 142/12 no. 91; *Complete Peerage,* s.v. Knyvett.
[51] *L. & P. Hen. VIII,* xviii (1), p. 262; *Cal. Pat. 1547–8,* 405; *Yorks. Fines,* i. 90, 108.
[52] *D.N.B.*; *Complete Peerage,* s.v. Howard.
[53] E.R.R.O., DDFA/5/133.
[54] J. Foster, *Pedigrees of . . . Yorks.* iii, s.v. Thompson of Escrick and Marston.
[55] *Complete Peerage,* s.v. Wenlock; Burke, *Peerage* (1970), 25.
[56] R.D.B., 227/13/11; ex inf. Escrick Park Estate Office, 1972.
[57] R.D.B., 826/277/237; *Yorks. Life Illus.* June 1961, 52–4.
[58] E.R.R.O., DDFA/10/7, 17; /20/1.
[59] Ibid. DDFA/3/1, 78, 83.
[60] Ibid. DDFA/3/31, 35, 37.
[61] Ibid. DDFA/3/7; /20/1.
[62] Ibid. DDFA/3/72.
[63] C 134/76 no. 14.
[64] Req. 2/23/48.
[65] E 179/205/504.
[66] E.R.R.O., DDFA/40/41.
[67] Carr's acct. was presented in 1763 and settled in 1765: E.R.R.O., DDFA/37/28.
[68] I. Hall, 'Escrick Park and John Carr', *York Georgian Soc. Ann. Rep. 1971,* 29–33.

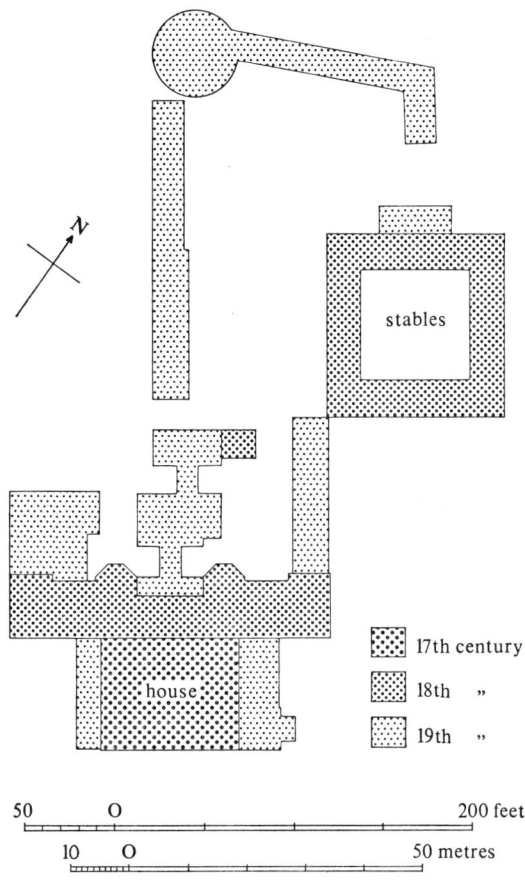

ESCRICK HALL: BLOCK PLAN SHOWING ITS DEVELOPMENT

tial building activity at Escrick. A north-west wing was added in 1846–8, and a north-eastern link to the stables was complete by 1850.[69] Plans to extend and remodel the south front in a Tudor style were not carried out, but a conservatory was added on the west and the east side was extended to provide a new entrance hall and an enlarged dining room. Many internal alterations were also carried out, among them the amalgamation of two rooms on the west front to form a library. To the north of the house several large subsidiary buildings, including a pump house, laundry, and dairies, were put up in the later 19th century. The conversion of the house for school use has resulted in some new building, notably a new laboratory block on the north-west, but much of the dormitory and classroom accommodation has been contrived within the old stables and secondary rooms, thus leaving the principal rooms intact.[70]

It was probably the Crown share of the manor in 1323 which was acquired by the Dammorys, though it had passed first to Avice le Constable. She in 1339 granted it to John Bardolf[71] and he conveyed it in 1340 to Nicholas Dammory, apparently for life.[72] Dammory was described in 1362 as lord of a quarter of Escrick.[73] The Bardolfs gave the name *BARDOL-GARTH* to the manor-house and so to the manor. In 1372 William Bardolf conveyed it to William Sandford,[74] and in 1530 Edmund Sandford sold it to George Gayle.[75] Bardolgarth passed from Robert Gayle to Sir Henry Knyvett in 1584[76] and subsequently descended with the capital manor.

Most of the small estates that existed in Escrick were eventually merged with the Thompsons' manor. They included a manor of *ESCRICK* which was held in the 14th century by William Marmyoun and was conveyed to William de Lyndlawe in 1341 and to John of Newton in 1347. It passed to the Dawnays, apparently in 1363, and about the same time they acquired 120 a. which William de Lascelles had granted to William of Grimsby in 1294. In 1402 John Dawnay thus had Escrick manor and a messuage called Grimsby's.[77] The Dawnays retained the property[78] until 1630, when John Dawnay's heir Mary married John Legard.[79] The Legards held it until Sir Thomas Legard sold it to Beilby Thompson in 1726.[80]

Deighton in 1086 consisted of a single 4-carucate estate, which was soke of Clifton and held by Count Alan.[81] Between 1158 and 1184 Eudes the marshal, son of the Breton, gave the lordship of Deighton to St. Mary's abbey, a gift confirmed by Alan son of Roald, constable of Richmond, who also gave whatever he himself had there.[82] Thus Deighton, like Escrick, was in the honor of Richmond and the liberty of St. Mary's. The estate was granted by the abbey between 1161 and 1184 to Duncan Darel,[83] who also received Geoffrey de Brettanby's land at Deighton and 2 bovates which Peter of Wheldrake had held of Thomas son of Erneis.[84] In 1202–3 Darel granted Deighton to Ralph de Mara, whose daughter and heir Mabel married Geoffrey de Nevill.[85] In 1273 it was given by Hugh de Nevill to the abbey,[86] which also received several smaller holdings in the township.[87] Thenceforth the manor of *DEIGHTON* was held in demesne by St. Mary's.

At the Dissolution the manor was worth about £26.[88] It was granted by the Crown in 1542 to John Aske[89] and was held by the Askes until 1596, when another John conveyed it to John Robinson.[90] The Robinson family retained Deighton until, after the death of Arthur Robinson, it was divided in 1713 between his daughters Grace Braithwaite and Elizabeth Denton.[91] Most of the Braithwaite share passed to the Thompsons in 1743 and 1758,[92] but some went to Thomas Eadon in 1741 and was acquired by Beilby Thompson in 1786.[93] It subsequently descended with Escrick capital manor.

[69] D. R. J. Neave, 'Escrick Hall and Park', ibid. 25–9.
[70] See plate facing p. 16.
[71] Yorks. Deeds, i, p. 103; ix, p. 65; Yorks. Fines, 1327–47, p. 140.
[72] Yorks. Fines, 1327–47, p. 139.
[73] Pub. Works in Med. Law, ii. 240–1.
[74] C.P. 25(1)/277/134 no. 1.
[75] E.R.R.O., DDFA/5/56; Yorks. Fines, i. 56.
[76] E.R.R.O., DDFA/5/29.
[77] Yorks. Deeds, ix, pp. 64–7, 69, 71, 75; Cal. Fine R. 1383–91, 358.
[78] e.g. Cal. Fine R. 1422–30, 143; Yorks. Fines, i. 80.
[79] cp. V.C.H. Yorks. E.R. ii. 211.
[80] E.R.R.O., DDFA/5/148–53.

[81] V.C.H. Yorks. ii. 241.
[82] E.Y.C. v, pp. 126–7.
[83] Ibid. pp. 222, 225.
[84] Ibid. p. 128; Yorks. Deeds, ii, p. 60.
[85] E.Y.C. v, pp. 128, 290–1.
[86] Yorks. Deeds, ii, p. 60; Dugdale, Mon. iii. 533.
[87] Yorks. Inq. ii, p. 122; Cal. Pat. 1301–7, 488; 1343–5, 253; Dugdale, Mon. iii. 533.
[88] Dugdale, Mon. iii. 572.
[89] E.R.R.O., DDBH/3/32.
[90] Yorks. Fines, iv. 57.
[91] E.R.R.O., DDFA/3/40.
[92] Ibid. DDFA/3/52, 57.
[93] Ibid. DDFA/10/28.

Various additions in Deighton were made to the estate, which comprised 1,262 a. in 1920 and 844 a. in 1972.[94]

The Denton half of the manor was divided in 1715 between Elizabeth's daughters Mary and Anne, who married John and Robert Bell respectively.[95] Anne succeeded to her sister's share, and her son J. T. Bell held half the manor until 1800, when it was bought by H. J. Baines.[96] The Baines family still had a small acreage in Deighton in 1971, but most of the estate was sold in 1953 and 1959 when about 470 a., including Deighton Hall farm, passed to Melville Fairburn and Anna Belsham.[97]

The manor-house was included in the Denton half of the manor at the partition of 1713. In 1619 it was described as 'fair and new built and moated round about', with a dovecot in its grounds,[98] and in 1672 it had 14 hearths.[99] Although the house now on the site incorporates two carved overmantels, some doors, a window, and some structural timbers of the early 17th century, it is a small square building and appears to have been erected in the earlier 18th century, perhaps soon after the partition of the estate, as a farm-house. The site is still moated.

A small estate in Escrick belonged to Thicket priory, which was granted 100 a. by Roger de Lascelles in 1291.[1] Its land was worth £1 16s. in 1535.[2] After the Dissolution the estate eventually passed to George Potts, who in 1666 granted it, described as a grange called Nun Pallions, to Henry Thompson.[3] Property in Escrick formerly belonging to Wilberfoss priory was sold by Francis Gayle to Christopher Allanson in 1606.[4]

ECONOMIC HISTORY. In 1086 there was woodland 2 leagues long and 2 broad in the soke of Clifton manor that lay in and around Escrick.[5] Pasture for 140 pigs in Escrick wood was mentioned c. 1146–61,[6] and in 1227 tenants of the manor each had common there for 10 cattle, 10 pigs, and 20 sheep.[7] Encroachments on the common woodland included those of the abbot of St. Mary's, York. In 1227 he was granted 130 a. of the wood by Picot de Lascelles in return for surrendering his rights in the rest of it, saving to the abbot's man at Escrick the same commonage as other tenants.[8] By 1276 the abbot had inclosed a park in Escrick,[9] most probably from the woodland granted to him. The bounds of the wood given by Picot show that it was the area in the south-west of Escrick known in the 17th century as Riccall Park.[10] It was separated from the remaining woodland by a track leading from Escrick to Riccall, and in 1362 the abbot and the lords of the manor were in dispute over the repair of the track.[11] The common wood that remained covered 260 a. in 1290–1, when it was known as 'Utewood'.[12] There are numerous references to timber being taken at Escrick in the 14th and 15th centuries,[13] and a man was surrendering rights of common in the abbot's park in 1456–7.[14]

As a result of reclamation from woodland and waste the manor had in 1290–1 a nucleus of common arable land amounting to 3 carucates of demesne and 93 bovates held by tenants. Some of it lay in various 'dales', situated in South, North, and Roger flats and elsewhere, and some in a *cultura* called Pavillon.[15] In addition there were 451½ a. of forland, said in 1323 to lie in 'divers fields and assarts'. This newer reclaimed land, which mostly seems to have been commonable, consisted of numerous plots, many of their names containing the significant elements 'ridding', 'thwaite', 'wood', 'hag', and 'hurst'. Other 14th-century assarts were held in severalty, among them Brynkar and the 26-acre Uggelker.[16] The demesne in 1323 included 10 a. of several pasture in Westker and 60 a. in the marsh called Estker, as well as 16½ a. of meadow land;[17] all these presumably lay near Bridge dike.

Escrick manor was worth about £103 in 1290–1 and 1323, and tenants' rents formed a large proportion. Five free tenants, holding 37 bovates, contributed about £1, 14 bondmen, holding 56 bovates, about £51, and 41 cottagers about £7.[18]

By 1548 the open-field land included about 46 bovates belonging to the Knyvett manor, only 8 of them held in demesne, but there is no indication of how the fields were arranged. East or Keld field was mentioned in 1542, however.[19] The medieval forland had mostly been converted to closes held in severalty by 1548, but there were still about 30 a. of 'forby land' in West sikes, North wood, the Tofts, and elsewhere. The closes included a dozen in demesne, among them Hall flats. Tenants held 37 closes, 28 of them containing a total of about 220 a.; most of them were of under 10 a., but Roger flat contained 20 a. and three-quarters of Riccall Hagg accounted for 100 a. Some tenants had small parcels in the common meadows, amounting to 26 a. in Carr ings and 18 a. in West ings.[20] The freehold lands in the 16th century similarly included both open-field and inclosed ground. The Dalbys, for example, in 1584 had 7 bovates in the fields and half a dozen closes, as well as the other quarter of Riccall Hagg.[21] Some of the closes seem still to have been held in common, however, for in 1592 the Knyvetts acquired 6 a. called Wetherlands, lying in a flat in the Old close.[22]

[94] R.D.B., 227/13/11; ex inf. Escrick Park Estate Office, 1972.
[95] E.R.R.O., DDBH/3/103, 105, 110.
[96] Ibid. DDBH/3/54, 123; R.D.B., CC/73/114. For the Baines fam. see pp. 77–8.
[97] R.D.B., 959/563/482; 1135/460/400; 1709/519/419.
[98] Survey *penes* Mr. and Mrs. Perry.
[99] E 179/205/504.
[1] *Cal. Pat. 1281–92*, 427.
[2] *Valor Eccl.* (Rec. Com.), v. 94.
[3] E.R.R.O., DDFA/5/122; /20/1.
[4] *Yorks. Fines, 1603–14*, 60.
[5] *V.C.H. Yorks.* ii. 241.
[6] *E.Y.C.* iv, p. 132.
[7] *Yorks. Fines, 1218–31*, pp. 111–12.
[8] Ibid.; *Monastic Notes*, i. 93.
[9] *Rot. Hund.* (Rec. Com.), i. 122, 129; *Plac. de Quo Warr.* (Rec. Com.), 201.
[10] Escrick Park Estate Office, undated map. See also *Yorks. Deeds*, ix, p. 64.
[11] *Pub. Works in Med. Law*, ii. 240, 247; *Yorks. Sess. of Peace* (Y.A.S. Rec. Ser. c), 38, 137–9.
[12] *Yorks. Inq.* ii, p. 133.
[13] e.g. *Cal. Pat. 1361–4*, 364; *Monastic Notes*, ii (Y.A.S. Rec. Ser. lxxxi), 65–6; *Fabric Rolls of York Minster* (Sur. Soc. xxxv), 62.
[14] *Y.A.J.* xii. 62.
[15] C 134/76 no. 14; *Yorks. Inq.* ii, p. 133; *Yorks. Deeds*, i, pp. 102–3.
[16] *Yorks. Deeds*, ix, pp. 64, 69, 75 n.
[17] C 134/76 no. 14.
[18] Ibid.; *Yorks. Inq.* ii, p. 133.
[19] E.R.R.O., DDPA/10/2.
[20] E 318/Box 31/1738.
[21] E.R.R.O., DDFA/5/76.
[22] Ibid. DDFA/5/68.

Several freeholders also had woodland near the common wood.[23] The tenants-at-will on the Knyvett manor in 1548 were 50 in number, 42 of them with houses in the village.[24] They enjoyed rights of intercommoning at that time on Wheldrake Moss, just as the inhabitants of Wheldrake were entitled to use the adjoining Escrick Moss.[25]

The common fields together contained 837 a. about 1600: there were 167 a. in West field, 163 a. in Thwaite field, 156 a. in Mill field, 152 a. in Keld field, 116 a. in Swinecroft field, and 83 a. in Little field. Tenants held 483 a. of the open-field land, 21 a. were glebe, and the rest were demesne. Around the fields were the extensive inclosed grounds: some 1,040 a. were demesne, 644 a. were held by tenants, and 945 a. belonged to freeholders. All of the tenants' closes were described as meadow and pasture, but the freeholders had 192 a. of arable. There were still 86 a. of common meadow land, in West ings and the Town carr, and 561 a. of common waste, of which the Great Wood common accounted for 493 a. and Escrick Moss for 64 a. Demesne and freehold woodland covered between 150 a. and 200 a. Tenants held 20 houses and 39 cottages and freeholders 8 houses and 6 cottages; all were in the village except for Pallion House in the south-east and Hill and Hag Houses towards Riccall. Around Pallion House was the 131-acre Nun Pallions, the former Thicket priory estate.[26] By 1639 this large close had been subdivided into six.[27]

The open fields had not been reduced in size by 1781, when Beilby Thompson was authorized by Act of Parliament to remove the old church and Rectory in order to improve the surroundings of Escrick Hall. It was declared that inclosure would be beneficial, and Thompson was given possession of the glebe land in the open fields and in West ings.[28] The common wood was presumably also involved in Thompson's scheme of improvement. Inclosure was probably soon accomplished and extensive parkland was laid out; certainly Thompson had by 1786 provided the rector with some ancient closes in lieu of his open-field land, as stipulated in the Act.[29] Both the common and the demesne woodland had continued to provide much timber until 1781; the Thompsons had sold 400 oaks from the common wood and 979 from Hollincars in 1719, for example.[30]

At Deighton the early reclamation of waste and woodland is indicated by *culture* called 'Pighel' and 'Rughtwayt' *c.* 1260–70, and by a reference to 'Northruhthwaite', 'Rathuatt', and 'Westthuait-ridinges'. An assart of 37½ a. was also mentioned in the later 13th century.[31] By 1276 the abbot of St. Mary's, York, had inclosed a park in Deighton,[32] lying south-west of the village towards Moreby. Timber from the remaining woodland was used in York in the 15th century.[33]

West and North fields were mentioned in 1422 and 1481 respectively,[34] and by 1539 the open-field land included 17 bovates belonging to the former St. Mary's abbey manor, all of it held by tenants. Also in the hands of tenants in 1539 were 18½ a. probably akin to the forland in Escrick. The demesnes comprised 141 a. of inclosed ground, including the 40-acre William Ridding and 80 a. in North closes. Tenants held some 30 closes, half of them with 'ridding' names, as well as another called West field which they all held jointly. At least one close, Marsh Ridding, was subject to commonage, for three tenants had a total of eight beast-gates there. The manor included woods called Deighton Spring, Deighton Park, and Rybton Shaw,[35] and there were said to be more oaks growing elsewhere. The tenants held 10 houses and 7 cottages, paid 1½d. each in lieu of 65 boon-works for stacking hay, and rendered many hens and eggs.[36]

There is no indication how the open-field land was arranged in 1539, but Old field and Mill field were mentioned in 1563 and strips or 'lands' there and in Padock Mire and Pescroft in 1585.[37] Part of West field was already inclosed by 1517 and was described as a close or pasture in 1538.[38] Beast-gates were enjoyed in it in 1557 and 1573.[39] Scattered trees outside the woodland were mentioned in 1539, and the value of trees growing in the closes is indicated by a lease of North closes in 1511 in which detailed conditions were laid down for the use of timber and underwood.[40] The demesne woods were separated from the manor after the Dissolution and let by the Crown in 1569 with instructions for their management and provision for the customary taking of wood by tenants.[41] Much timber was subsequently used from them.[42] The park with its surrounding ditch was mentioned in 1517,[43] and it, too, was later separated from the manor. At least one house was built away from the village during the 16th century for the 'Newhouse' in North closes was mentioned in 1558.[44]

The open fields covered about 212 a. in 1619, comprising 50 a. in Old field, 50 a. in West field, 54½ a. in Mill field, 36½ a. in Westergate field, and 20½ a. in Padomire field. Inclosure was apparently then contemplated, for the fields were shown in several parcels 'according as they are appointed to be divided'.[45] In the 1680s, however, all except West field were again mentioned[46] and the others were still called common fields in 1713. In the latter year the former West field, under its then alternative name Mill field,[47] was shown as lying in several closes, and Westergate and Padomire fields were each let to a single tenant.[48] If Old and Mill fields were indeed

---

[23] Ibid. DDFA/5/1.
[24] E 318/Box 31/1738.
[25] E.R.R.O., DDPA/10/2.
[26] Escrick Park Estate Office, undated map.
[27] E.R.R.O., DDFA/5/6, 120.
[28] 21 Geo. III, c. 76.
[29] B.I.H.R., TER. N. Escrick 1786.
[30] E.R.R.O., DDFA/5/11.
[31] Ibid. DDBH/3/63.
[32] *Rot. Hund.* i. 122, 129.
[33] *Fabric R. of York Minster*, 44, 75.
[34] E.R.R.O., DDBH/3/1.
[35] Later usually called Righton Shaw: e.g. ibid. DDFA/3/1.
[36] Ibid. DDBH/3/67.

[37] Ibid. DDBH/3/9, 15.
[38] E 303/26/Yorks./1121, 1123.
[39] E.R.R.O., DDBH/3/6, 10.
[40] E 303/26/Yorks./1120.
[41] *Cal. Pat.* 1566–9, p. 381.
[42] E 178/2771, 4839; C 3/366/7.
[43] E 303/26/Yorks./1123.
[44] E.R.R.O., DDBH/3/31. It was later called North house: ibid. DDFA/3/1.
[45] Survey and map *penes* Mr. and Mrs. Perry.
[46] E.R.R.O., DDBH/28/13.
[47] The alternative name was recorded as early as 1646: ibid. DDBH/3/97.
[48] Description and map for partition of the manor, 1712–13: ibid. DDBH/40, 168.

A HISTORY OF YORKSHIRE: EAST RIDING

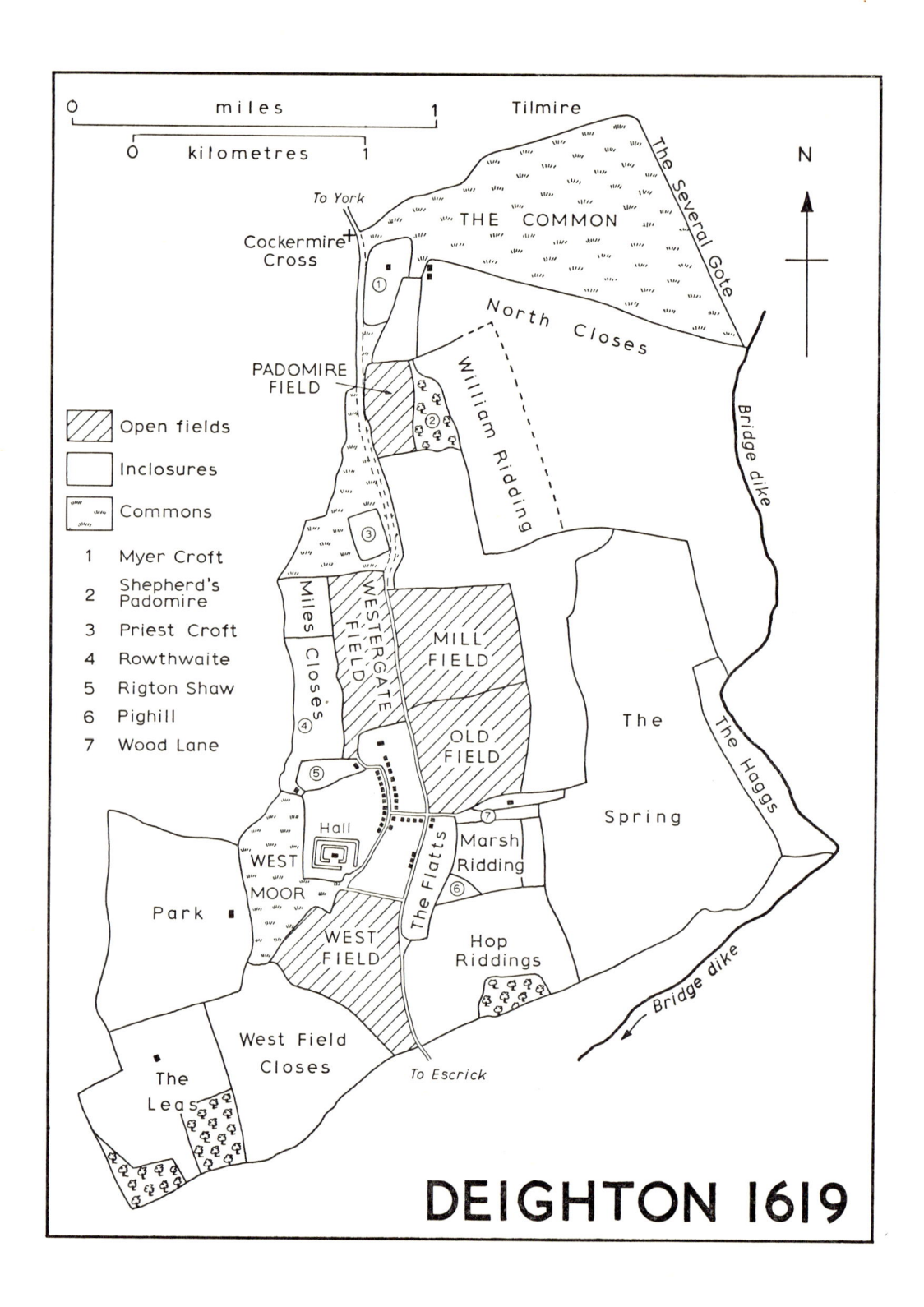

DEIGHTON 1619

used in common in 1713 their inclosure was apparently achieved soon after and they were not mentioned again.[49]

The inclosed grounds in 1619 included 26 small closes, totalling 161 a., held by tenants-at-will. Five tenants also had a total of 15 a. in the Flats, which may have been commonable, and several tenants had meadow in the Haggs, apparently held in severalty. The demesne land was entirely in closes, 350 a. all told. It included a dozen closes in the already inclosed part of West field, 97 a. altogether, four Miles closes, amounting to 36 a., ten closes making up Hopridings, 97 a. in all, and nine closes in the Leas, containing 98 a. The Leas had been described in 1606 as 'sometime part of Deighton West field'.[50] There were only four freeholders in 1619, among them Richard Aske, holding North closes, and Sir William Acklam, holding William Ridding and other closes. Most of the inclosed ground was used as meadow or pasture, but about 100 a. was arable. Demesne woodland covered about 40 a.[51]

The remaining waste grounds, in which the tenants had unstinted commonage, amounted to 274 a. in 1619. They comprised 173 a. in the north adjoining Fulford, 42 a. towards Naburn, 43 a. in the West moor, and 16 a. in Green Pool, which was shown laid in with Westgate field 'as it is appointed to be divided'. The largest area of common included part of Tilmire, which was said to be 'for the most part of the year overflown with water', and a rabbit warren called Myer Croft, then 'replenished with coneys'.[52] The inhabitants of Gate Fulford claimed the right to intercommon on Deighton Tilmire.[53] By 1681 'Deighton moor' was described as a close, which a tenant had entered to claim common against the lord of the manor,[54] but Tilmire and the adjoining wastes remained until 1717, when the lords of the moieties of the manor and the one interested freeholder agreed upon an inclosure.[55] It may have been carried out promptly and was certainly accomplished by 1743.[56]

Nineteen cottages and twelve houses were held by tenants-at-will in 1619. Most of them were in the village but there were several isolated houses, including one in the Leas, two in North closes, and another in the rabbit warren.[57] The house in the Leas already existed in 1606.[58] There was also a house in Deighton park in 1619, no longer part of the manor, and in 1727 it was described as Park House.[59]

In the 19th and 20th centuries woodland remained a prominent feature in the landscape of the parish, especially in Escrick where there were 533 a. in 1905.[60] At Deighton in 1804 there were 2,741 trees on a single farm,[61] though actual woodland amounted to only about 60 a. in 1843[62] and 1905.[63] Much of the land continued to be used as pasture. At Escrick there were 670 a. of meadow and pasture out of a total of 1,640 a. on ten farms in 1802,[64] and there were 1,926 a. of pasture compared with 1,622 a. of arable in the township in 1905. At Deighton in 1843 there were 704 a. of meadow and pasture and 1,175 a. of arable, and in 1905 430 a. of grass and 1,428 a. of arable.[65] In more recent years arable farming has become dominant and some land has been used for market-gardening, but a considerable acreage of pasture remained in Escrick township, especially near Bridge dike and on the low ground to the east and west of the park.[66]

The number of farmers in the 19th and 20th centuries was usually put at 12–15 in Escrick and 8–12 in Deighton,[67] but there were also many smallholders at Escrick. About a dozen of the Escrick farmers had more than 150 a. each in 1803, the 1850s, and the 1920s, and at Deighton 4 or 5 in the 1850s and about 10 in the 1920s.[68] Some of the smallholders had cottage allotments, the first in the East Riding and said to have been introduced by Lord Wenlock in 1834.[69]

Apart from estate work at Escrick Park there has been little non-agricultural employment in the parish. There was some brick-making at Deighton in the 17th century for Brick close was recorded in 1619[70] and Brick Kiln close in 1679.[71] There was a brickworks in Escrick, on the Riccall road, by 1851[72] and it was still in operation in 1972.[73]

A water-mill and a windmill at Escrick were mentioned as early as 1290–1.[74] The former was presumably on Bridge dike, and in 1348 flooding was said to have resulted from a failure to lower the mill and to enlarge its sluices.[75] The water-mill was not mentioned again, but the windmill remained and about 1600 and again in 1809 a post mill was shown standing on the moraine east of the village.[76] A miller was last mentioned in 1840.[77] At Deighton there was a windmill in 1447,[78] and presumably also in the later 16th century, when Mill field was first mentioned. It no doubt stood on the prominent mound known as the Plump, which was shown in Mill field in 1619[79] and still remained in 1972. The use of Mill field as an alternative name for West field in the 17th century and later suggests a second mill site, and the name Mill Hill survives in that area. On one or other of the sites stood a windmill said in the 1680s to have been 'erected within memory',[80] and repairs to a windmill were recorded in 1690.[81]

[49] An undated list of inclosures, probably made in the earlier 17th century, includes 'Deighton in Escrick': ibid. DDWR/1/60. [50] Ibid. DDBH/3/37.
[51] Survey and map penes Mr. and Mrs. Perry.
[52] Ibid.
[53] E.R.R.O., DDBH/3/4; /12/16.
[54] Ibid. DDBH/3/46; /12/10.
[55] Ibid. DDBH/3/104.
[56] Ibid. DDBH/3/59, 111.
[57] Map penes Mr. and Mrs. Perry.
[58] E.R.R.O., DDBH/3/37. [59] Ibid. DDFA/3/20.
[60] Acreage Returns, 1905.
[61] E.R.R.O., DDBH/3/56.
[62] B.I.H.R., TA. 76S. [63] Acreage Rets. 1905.
[64] A. Harris, *Rural Landscape of E.R. Yorks. 1700–1850*, 94.
[65] B.I.H.R., TA. 76S; Acreage Rets. 1905.
[66] [1st] Land Util. Surv. Map, sheets 27, 32; 2nd Land Util. Surv. Map, sheets 689 (SE 63–73), 699 (SE 64–74).

[67] Directories.
[68] E.R.R.O., DDFA/5/18; /41/3, 6; H.O. 107/2351; *Kelly's Dir. N. & E.R. Yorks.* (1921 and later edns.).
[69] *Jnl. of the Royal Agric. Soc.* ix (1848), 127 n.; Bulmer, *Dir. E. Yorks.* (1892), 605; O.S. Map 6" (1851 edn.).
[70] Map penes Mr. and Mrs. Perry.
[71] E.R.R.O., DDBH/3/132.
[72] H.O. 107/2351; O.S. Map 6" (1851 edn.).
[73] It was sold by the Escrick Park Estate to the operating company in 1953: R.D.B., 958/121/101.
[74] *Yorks. Inq.* ii, p. 133.
[75] *Pub. Works in Med. Law*, ii. 239.
[76] Escrick Park Estate Office, undated map; 1809 map.
[77] White, *Dir. N. & E.R. Yorks.* (1840), 327.
[78] Y.A.S., DD. 88/1.
[79] Map penes Mr. and Mrs. Perry; name from O.S. Map 6" (1851 edn.).
[80] E.R.R.O., DDBH/3/48.
[81] Ibid. DDBH/24/2.

In the 20th century corn was ground at a mill in Deighton worked by a portable steam engine and later by a paraffin engine;[82] the stones lay near by in 1972.

LOCAL GOVERNMENT. The appointment of officers by the court of St. Mary's abbey's manor of Deighton is recorded in court rolls surviving for eighteen scattered years in the period 1422–1602. A constable, a rent-collector, 2 bylawmen, 2 inspectors of carcases, and 2 aletasters were elected in 1447, and a constable, 2 aletasters, 2 affeerors, and 2 bylawmen in 1580. Lists of pains drawn up by the court survive from the period 1584–1638.[83]

The vestry appointed two men who served as constables as well as overseers at least from 1673 to 1812. The overseers' accounts survive from 1752 to 1816. Apart from rates some income was derived from putting out the town stock, which contained about £3 in 1752 and £12 in 1780. Besides weekly cash relief some payments were made in kind and a few boys were placed as apprentices. The poorhouses were first explicitly mentioned in 1788. Constables' expenses were included in the accounts for several years at the end of the period covered.[84]

In 1837 Escrick joined York poor-law union.[85] Escrick and Deighton both became part of Escrick rural district in 1894, Derwent rural district in 1935,[86] and the Selby district of North Yorkshire in 1974.

CHURCH. There was a church at Escrick in 1252.[87] The advowson of the rectory followed the descent of the manor, including the separation of a quarter of it from the rest c. 1340 until 1584.[88] Ralph Hall presented in 1564–5 by grant from Francis Gayle, lord of Bardolgarth manor,[89] and Edward Richardson and Richard Pagett presented in 1613 for unexplained reasons.[90] The patronage thereafter continued to descend with the manor,[91] although Henry Gale was said to be patron in 1794 and 1823.[92] After the death of Lord Wenlock in 1912 the patronage passed to his daughter Irene and she still held it in 1972.[93]

The church was valued at £30 in 1291[94] and about £24 in 1535.[95] In 1650 it was worth £120.[96] In 1829–31 the average net income was £530;[97] in 1884 it was £280 and in 1914 £382.[98]

Most of the income derived from tithes. Those of Escrick township were extinguished by an Act of 1781, which provided that Beilby Thompson, as sole lay landowner, should provide the rector with a rent-charge equal to the value of 353 bu. of wheat and with 85 a. of ancient closes.[99] The rent-charge was £100 in 1781, raised to £171 in 1802 but reduced to £145 in 1823 and £125 in 1862.[1] In Deighton a composition of 13s. 4d. was paid for the tithes of the hall and 314 a. of demesne closes by 1619,[2] and a composition of 3d. an acre for tithes of the Springs was first mentioned in 1727.[3] The former composition was frequently disputed by the rector in the 17th century,[4] but it was still being paid for 30 a. of closes in 1843, when another 260 a. were said to be tithe-free. The remaining tithes were commuted for £278 12s. 8d. that year.[5]

The glebe consisted in 1535 of 2 bovates of land in Escrick, a close in Deighton called Priest croft, and two tenements, besides the parsonage house.[6] By the Act of 1781 22 a. of glebe and two cottages were surrendered to Beilby Thompson and compensation was included in the tithe allotment. The Act also provided that Thompson should build a new Rectory in return for the site of the old one, which had stood close to the manor-house. The old house had five ground-floor rooms and four bedrooms in 1777.[7] The Rectory was duly rebuilt beside a new church to the north of the village and contained twelve rooms.[8] It was replaced by a larger house on the same site in 1848, designed by F. C. Penrose,[9] and an entrance lodge was added in 1853.[10] In 1949 the house, then known as Queen Margaret's Lodge, was let to the Woodard Society along with Escrick Hall.[11] A new Rectory was built close by in Deighton in 1951.[12]

There was apparently a chapel at Deighton in the 13th or early 14th century, for in 1306 the rector of Escrick was ordered to hand over to the abbot of St. Mary's, York, the bells, statues, window glass, and timber which had been removed from the chapel. The abbot was given authority to build a house in the close where the chapel had stood, but he was not to put up a new chapel within six years.[13] The building may have stood beside the Escrick road south of the village, where a cottage and garth in 1619 were described as 'at the old chapel'.[14] By 1914 there was a mission room at Deighton Grove[15] and it was used until 1959.[16] In 1972 the rector held services in Deighton Methodist chapel.

An obit and lights in Escrick church were supported by three lands in the open fields. Described

---

[82] Local information.
[83] E.R.R.O., DDBH/3/1–3; Y.A.S., DD. 88/1.
[84] E.R.R.O., DDFA/5/9.
[85] 3rd Rep. Poor Law Com. 171.
[86] Census.
[87] Reg. Gray, p. 111.
[88] E.R.R.O., DDCC/App. B/32; DDFA/5/29; Cal. Inq. p.m. vi, p. 252; Reg. Gray, p. 111; Reg. Wickwane, pp. 56, 127; Yorks. Fines, 1327–47, pp. 29, 173; 1347–77, p. 157; Yorks. Fines, i. 84; Cal. Inq. Misc. iii, p. 173.
[89] B.I.H.R., Inst. AB. 2, pt. 2, f. 32.
[90] Ibid. Inst. AB. 4, f. 73.
[91] Inst. Bks.; directories.
[92] B.I.H.R., Inst. AB. 16, p. 295; Baines, Hist. Yorks. (1823), ii. 202.
[93] York Dioc. Year Bk.
[94] Tax. Eccl. (Rec. Com.), 300.
[95] Valor Eccl. v. 95.
[96] C 94/3 f. 76.
[97] Rep. Com. Eccl. Revenues, 932.
[98] B.I.H.R., Bp. V. 1884/Ret.; Bp. V. 1914/Ret.

[99] 21 Geo. III, c. 76.
[1] B.I.H.R., TER. N. Escrick 1861, 1865.
[2] Survey penes Mr. and Mrs. Perry.
[3] B.I.H.R., TER. N. Escrick 1727 etc.
[4] Ibid. CP. H. 2319, 3672, 3691, 3897, 4114, 4419; D/C. CP. 10/73, 18/73, 25B/59; E.R.R.O., DDBH/3/72; /28/12–15; Cal. S. P. Dom. 1640, 453–4. For other disputes see B.I.H.R., CP. F. 19 (1402); G. 2304 (1587); H. 1408 (1619).
[5] B.I.H.R., TA. 76S.
[6] Valor Eccl. v. 95.
[7] B.I.H.R., TER. N. Escrick 1777.
[8] Ibid. 1786.
[9] Pevsner, Yorks. E.R. 224.
[10] B.I.H.R., TER. N. Escrick 1861.
[11] R.D.B., 827/342/292.
[12] Ibid. 895/373/315; ex inf. the rector, 1972.
[13] E.R.R.O., DDBA/3/63(56).
[14] Survey penes Mr. and Mrs. Perry.
[15] B.I.H.R., Bp. V. 1914/Ret.
[16] Ex inf. the rector, 1972.

as Lamplands, they were granted by the Crown in 1620 to Sir James Ouchterloney and Richard Gurney. The latter sold them to John Ward in 1640, he to John Foster in 1666, and he to the Thompsons in 1727.[17]

In 1301 and 1331 the living was held in plurality.[18] In the 15th and 16th centuries the cure was effectively served by a parochial chaplain.[19] The rector was non-resident in 1578[20] and resided on his living at Hooton Roberts (Yorks. W.R.) in 1764, employing a resident assistant curate at Escrick. The rector was also non-resident and had an assistant curate in 1868, but thereafter seems to have resided at Escrick.[21] Thomas Squire, rector 1613–63, was a Puritan.[22]

There were two services in the church each Sunday in 1743 and 1764 and Holy Communion was celebrated six times a year and received by 50–60 people.[23] Communion was held fourteen times a year in the 1860s, with about 30 communicants. In 1914 services were held once a week at Deighton, as well as twice at the church. In 1936 communion was celebrated weekly in the church and monthly in the mission room.[24] Services were held twice a week in 1972 but on alternate Sundays the evening service took place at Deighton Methodist chapel.

Little is known of the medieval church of *ST. HELEN.* Money and lead for its tower were bequeathed by Guy Roucliff, by will proved in 1460,[25] and the church was ordered to be repaired in 1663.[26] Provision was made in 1759 for the pulpit, reading desk, and pews to be renewed and for a gallery at the west end to be built to replace one at the east end.[27] In 1781, however, the site of the church, on the west side of Escrick Hall, was granted to Beilby Thompson to further his plans for improving the surroundings of the manor-house, on condition that he built a new church elsewhere.[28] The new building, designed in the Classical style and constructed of brick with stone quoins and dressings, was built beside the York road at the north end of the village and consecrated in 1783.[29] Faculties were granted in 1786 to make an archway in the north wall to accommodate a pew for the Thompson family and in 1803 to install a monument to Beilby Thompson.[30]

The brick church was replaced by a 'more seemly and commodious building of stone', designed by F. C. Penrose in the Decorated style and consecrated in 1857.[31] The cost was met by the Lawley family. The church consists of apsidal chancel, tower on the north side of the chancel, nave with north aisle, south porch with vestry above, and baptistery and chapel at the west end built over the Lawley vault. A choir vestry was added in 1896.[32] The church was gutted by fire in 1923 but it was fully restored and reopened in 1925.[33] It is one of the largest and most ambitious Victorian Gothic churches in the East Riding.

The wooden furnishings destroyed in 1923 included a communion table said in 1861 to have come from St. William's chapel, Ouse Bridge, York. The white marble font by Giovanni Tognoli,[34] consisting of a shallow bowl resting on the heads of two angels, survives, together with the effigy from a monument erected in 1876 to Caroline, Lady Wenlock (d. 1868), designed by Count Gleichen.[35] There is also part of the recumbent figure of a knight, said to commemorate Thomas Lascelles (d. 1324),[36] together with fragments of brasses comprising an inscription to John Paler (d. 1613) and shields of Arthur Robinson (c. 1636) and of Robinson and Garrard.[37] Monuments include those of Beilby Thompson (d. 1799), by Fisher of York, and Jane Thompson (d. 1816), by the Danish sculptor Thorwaldsen.[38] There were three bells in the church of 1783[39] but they were replaced in 1857 by five bells made by John Warner & Sons of London.[40] The restoration of the church completed in 1925 included the hanging of eight bells made the previous year.[41] The plate includes a silver service comprising cup, flagon, and salver given in 1794 by Beilby Thompson and his wife, together with an uninscribed paten. The service was made in London in 1792, probably by John Robins. Another silver service was given in 1863 by Lord Wenlock; it had originally been presented in 1682 to the Savoy chapel by Sir Edward Smythe. It comprises cup and paten made in London in 1681 and flagon made there in 1656.[42] The registers begin in 1617 and are complete except for the period 1688–1718.[43]

A new churchyard was consecrated with the church in 1783[44] and extended in 1857.[45]

NONCONFORMITY. In 1569 the rector and assistant curate of Escrick were found to be distributing seditious and papist literature.[46] There was a Roman Catholic and six protestant dissenters in the parish in 1676,[47] and a family of Roman Catholics was reported in 1743.[48] Houses were licensed for worship by protestant dissenters at Deighton in 1793 and Escrick in 1806, 1809 (two), 1820, 1822, and 1824.[49] A Methodist society was formed at

---

[17] E.R.R.O., DDFA/5/12, 85, 91.
[18] *Cal. Papal Regs.* i. 598; ii. 329.
[19] e.g. B.I.H.R., Prob. Reg. ii, f. 492; vi, f. 5.
[20] Ibid. V. 1578–9/CB. 1.
[21] Ibid. Bp. V. 1764/Ret. 172; V. 1868/Ret. 155.
[22] Marchant, *Puritans and the Ch. Courts in Dioc. York, 1560–1642,* 280–1.
[23] B.I.H.R., Bp. V. 1764/Ret. 172; *Herring's Visit.* i. 182.
[24] B.I.H.R., V. 1865/Ret. 168; V. 1868/Ret. 155; Bp. V. 1914/Ret.; Bp. V. 1936/Ret. 323.
[25] *Test. Ebor.* ii, p. 238.
[26] B.I.H.R., V. 1662–3/CB. 1.
[27] Ibid. Fac. Bk. i, p. 294.
[28] 21 Geo. III, c. 76.
[29] B.I.H.R., CD. 27; Sheahan and Whellan, *Hist. York & E.R.* ii. 618.
[30] B.I.H.R., Fac. Bk. ii, p. 356; iii, p. 345.
[31] Ibid. iv, p. 651; CD. 278; *Yorks. Gaz.* 4 July 1857. See above plate facing p. 17.
[32] *Kelly's Dir. N. & E.R. Yorks.* (1897), 452.
[33] B.I.H.R., Fac. Bk. x, p. 476; *Yorks. Gaz.* 10 Feb. 1923; *Yorks. Herald.* 16 Apr. 1927.
[34] B.I.H.R., TER. N. Escrick 1861.
[35] Bulmer, *Dir. E. Yorks.* (1892), 606; inscription on monument. A photograph in the church shows the monument before the fire.
[36] *Y.A.J.* xxix. 22.
[37] Ibid. xx. 295–6; xxvii. 150.
[38] Pevsner, *Yorks. E.R.* 224.
[39] B.I.H.R., TER. N. Escrick 1786 etc.
[40] Ibid. 1861; Boulter, 'Ch. Bells', 31.
[41] B.I.H.R., Fac. Bk. x, p. 476.
[42] *Yorks. Ch. Plate,* i. 245–7.
[43] B.I.H.R.
[44] Ibid. CD. 27.
[45] Ibid. TER. N. Escrick 1861.
[46] Aveling, *Post Reformation Catholicism,* 13.
[47] Bodl. MS. Tanner 150, ff. 27 sqq.
[48] *Herring's Visit.* i. 182.
[49] G.R.O. Worship Returns, Vol. v, nos. 909, 1998, 2309–10, 3450, 3880; B.I.H.R., DMH. Reg. 1, p. 455.

Deighton in 1807, and after 1850 meetings were held at Crockey Hill Farm.[50] In the 1860s and 1870s there were said to be 20–30 Wesleyan Methodists, who attended the parish church.[51] A chapel was, however, built at Deighton in 1880,[52] and there were 36 members in 1884.[53] The yellow-brick building was still used for services in 1972.

EDUCATION. A schoolmaster at Escrick was first mentioned in 1586, and others were recorded in 1715 and 1717.[54] In 1743 there was a school for ten pupils, who were taught to read and write and were instructed in Christian principles; the master's salary was paid by the rector.[55] There were 26 children at the school in 1764, when the master's stipend of £12 a year was paid by Beilby Thompson.[56] The north aisle of the church was used as a schoolroom in 1776.[57] By 1819 there were 60 pupils, twelve of whom were supported by the £12 received from the Thompsons.[58] New school buildings are said to have been erected by Lord Wenlock in 1825,[59] subsequently housing a National school which had been started in 1821 and an infants' school, begun in 1827; in 1835 about 240 children, including 90 infants, were on the roll. The schools were supported by school pence and by a subscription of £60 a year from Lord Wenlock, who also provided clothing for the children at the National school.[60] An annual parliamentary grant was received by 1849.[61]

In 1819 there was also said to be a school-house in Deighton, supported by a bequest of £5 a year. There was an infants' school there in 1835, begun in 1830 or 1831, with seven pupils paid for by Lord Wenlock.[62] A separate school was not mentioned again and Deighton children subsequently went to the Escrick schools.

The average attendance at the National school was 88 in 1871.[63] From 1908 until 1932 attendance was usually between 90 and 115, but it fell to 61 in 1938.[64] After the Second World War it increased along with housing development in the village and the number on the roll in April 1972 was 91.[65] The yellow-brick school stands in the main village street, not far from the hall. It is now used together with a new building near by, opened in 1973.[66]

An industrial school run by Lady Wenlock had 8 pupils in 1865, and it may have been the private school mentioned in 1871 with an attendance of sixteen.[67]

An evening school for farm lads was held in the winter in 1835, with about six boys attending for four months.[68] A similar school was held three times a week in winter in 1865, but by 1868 it was said that evening schools had been tried without success.[69]

CHARITIES FOR THE POOR. John Cooke and his wife at unknown date gave a rent-charge of £1 6s. a year out of 10 a. in Skipwith, to be distributed in bread to six poor people of Escrick. John Neville, also at unknown date, left £26, the interest to be given in bread to poor widows or spinsters of Escrick. In 1824 £1 6s. was received from each of these charities and a joint distribution in bread was made.[70]

In 1743 a small parcel of land devised to the poor of Escrick was said to yield a rent of £5 16s.[71] The Poor's Land in 1824 consisted of 3 a. in Fishergate, York, then let for £21 a year. The income was distributed to the poor in amounts varying from 2s. 6d. to 10s. and the poor of Deighton received a quarter of it.[72] The York land was sold in separate lots in 1894, 1900–1, and 1910.[73]

Frances, dowager Lady Howard of Escrick, by will proved in 1716, bequeathed £50 to provide coal for the poor of Escrick and several neighbouring villages. The bequest was not effective until 1862 when, after a lengthy suit in Chancery, an Order of the Master of the Rolls declared that interest on £550 stock held should be divided into seven and $\frac{2}{7}$ applied to Escrick.[74]

By a Scheme of 1902 all the above-mentioned charities were regulated as the Consolidated Poor's Charities. From the income £20 was to be used for the Escrick alms-houses, when built, £50 for help for the sick, and the rest for pensions and other payments. The income then comprised £3 rent from the Cooke and Neville charities, £4 interest on £157 stock from Lady Howard's, and £197 interest on £5,867 stock from the Poor's Land.[75]

Five alms-houses were built in 1904 by Lord Wenlock and members of his family.[76] By a Scheme of 1967 they and the Consolidated Poor's Charities were combined as the Escrick and Deighton Charities. Income then comprised £3 rent from land at Skipwith and interest on £3,815 stock. Apart from the upkeep of the alms-houses it was to be used for the relief of the poor, sick, and infirm.[77]

Escrick benefited from the charity of John Hodgson for parishes in York poor-law union.[78]

---

[50] J. Lyth, *Glimpses of Early Methodism in York and Dist.* 286.
[51] B.I.H.R., V. 1868/Ret. 155; V. 1877/Ret.
[52] Date on building.
[53] Lyth, *Glimpses*, 286.
[54] B.I.H.R., Schools index.
[55] *Herring's Visit.* i. 182.
[56] B.I.H.R., Bp. V. 1764/Ret. 172.
[57] Ex inf. Mr. D. R. J. Neave, Beverley, 1972.
[58] *Educ. of Poor Digest*, 1080.
[59] Ed. 7/135 no. 47.
[60] Ibid.; *Educ. Enquiry Abstract*, 1084.
[61] *Mins. of Educ. Cttee. of Council, 1849–50* [1215], p. cclv, H.C. (1850), xliii.
[62] *Educ. of Poor Digest*, 1080; *Educ. Enquiry Abstract*, 1084.
[63] *Returns relating to Elem. Educ.* 792.
[64] *Bd. of Educ. List 21* (H.M.S.O.).
[65] Ex inf. Chief Educ. Officer, County Hall, Beverley.
[66] Local information.
[67] B.I.H.R., V. 1865/Ret. 168; *Returns relating to Elem. Educ.* 792.
[68] *Educ. Enquiry Abstract*, 1084.
[69] B.I.H.R., V. 1865/Ret. 168; V. 1868/Ret. 155.
[70] *11th Rep. Com. Char.* 770–1.
[71] *Herring's Visit.* i. 182.
[72] *11th Rep. Com. Char.* 771.
[73] Char. Com. files.
[74] Ibid. (under Naburn).
[75] Ibid.
[76] Inscription on building.
[77] Char. Com. files.
[78] See p. 12.

FULFORD

THE PARISH of Fulford is well known as the site of the battle in 1066 at which Earl Tostig and Harold Hardrada defeated the English before going on to their own defeat at Stamford Bridge.[1] The village lies little more than a mile south of York and a substantial area of the parish has long possessed an entirely suburban character.[2] Gate Fulford village itself, sometimes known as Over Fulford, remained distinct in 1972, though increasingly hemmed in by further suburban development. It was an Anglian settlement, standing on a ridge of higher ground running parallel with the river Ouse; along the ridge the York–Selby road forms the main street, and at the southern end of the village Germany beck flows eastwards into the river. The road and a 'foul' crossing-point over either the beck or the river Ouse gave the village its name.[3] A little to the south, the hamlet of Water or Nether Fulford lies close to the Ouse. From the two townships the parish took the name Fulfords Ambo, first recorded in 1828.[4] The area of the elongated and irregularly-shaped ancient parish was 2,021 a. in 1890, of which 356 a. were in Water Fulford.[5] The boundaries of the ecclesiastical parish have not been altered but in 1884 536 a., including the suburban part of the parish, sometimes called New Fulford, were for civil purposes incorporated into the borough of York.[6] The remaining civil parish was given the name Water Fulford in 1895,[7] changed to plain 'Fulford' in 1935.[8]

Much of the parish is flat and featureless, lying at between 25 ft. and 50 ft. above sea-level, and in places the riverside ings are lower still. Parts of the ridge on which the village stands, however, exceed 50 ft., and in the north the parish extends to the crest of the York moraine at 75 ft. to 100 ft. Apart from alluvium beside the river, glacial and outwash sand and gravel cover most of the parish, with a small area of boulder clay on the moraine.[9] The open fields lay mainly on the higher ground, and extensive common moors occupied the lower areas in the east and south of the parish, including part of the watery Tilmire which stretched into Heslington, Grimston, and Deighton.[10] Open fields and commons were inclosed in 1759.

The entire western parish boundary is formed by the Ouse and sections of the boundary elsewhere follow streams or dikes. The straight eastern boundary apparently follows the line of a former Roman road running southwards from York.[11] In the north-east the boundary ran along a prehistoric earthwork known as Green Dykes, which lay across the moraine.[12] As the result of a dispute with the vicar of St. Lawrence's, York, the dikes themselves were in 1456 declared to be in Fulford.[13] The boundary between Gate Fulford and Water Fulford seems to have been uncertain in the mid 19th century. The Ordnance Survey showed the boundary on its map of 1853 but also indicated a more far-reaching boundary line 'claimed by the township of Water Fulford'.[14] A stone cross, still standing beside the main road from Fulford to York in 1972, apparently marked the boundary of York's rights of commonage in the parish.[15]

Apart from the main York–Selby road there are few roads in Fulford which date from before the period of suburban development. From Gate Fulford village Heslington Lane leads eastwards to Heslington, and in Water Fulford another road branches from the Selby road towards Naburn. A road from York to Heslington (Heslington Road) crosses the northern tip of the ancient parish. Church Lane (now St. Oswald's Road) leads from the main road towards the river Ouse, ending near the old church of St. Oswald standing remote from the village. It is possible that the church marks an older site of the village before it was moved to the main road.

The houses of the village line the York–Selby road, their crofts and garths running back to two lanes, that on the east called Back, later School, Lane and that on the west known as Fenwick's Lane from the mid 19th century.[16] The main street includes a great variety of houses, from small 18th- and 19th-century cottages to substantial farm-houses and elegant Georgian and Regency residences whose presence and style derive from the proximity of York. Among the larger 18th-century houses are the Old House, a three-storeyed brown-brick building, the White House, a stuccoed two-storeyed building with iron balconies to its first-floor windows, and Fulford House, which was acquired by William Richardson in 1751 and formerly belonged to a member of the Redman family.[17] It was enlarged in the mid and late 18th century, a water spout bearing the date 1785, and again after 1845,[18] when another William Richardson bought adjoining property to enlarge the site.[19] Fulford Park, a 19th-century stuccoed villa, has a later stable block in a French Gothic style.

Several 18th-century buildings also stand in the back lanes, and in St. Oswald's Road there is a single-storeyed cottage of that date with Gothic windows. In the western back lane stand two large early-19th-century houses in their own grounds, Delwood Croft and Gate Fulford Hall. The former, which was built before 1742 and enlarged before 1827,[20] has a three-storeyed garden front with canted bays rising through all the floors. The latter,

---

[1] See *V.C.H. City of York*, 16.
[2] This article was written in 1972. Help given by Miss I. H. Briddon of Fulford and Mrs. J. M. Pickering of Bishopthorpe is gratefully acknowledged.
[3] *P.N.E.R. Yorks.* (E.P.N.S.), 275; I. H. Briddon, *Brief Hist. of Fulford*, 3.
[4] *P.N.E.R. Yorks.* 275.
[5] O.S. Map 6" (1893 edn.).
[6] *V.C.H. City of York*, 321. Acreage calculated from O.S. Map 6" (1893, 1910 edns.).
[7] *Kelly's Dir. N. & E.R. Yorks.* (1897), 462.
[8] *Census*, 1931.
[9] Geol. Surv. Map 1", solid and drift, sheet 71 (1973 edn.).
[10] See pp. 32–3.
[11] *Roman York* (Royal Comm. on Hist. Monuments), 1; *Y.A.J.* xlii. 4.
[12] *Y.A.J.* xli. 587.
[13] *Cal. Papal Reg.* xi. 129, 389.
[14] O.S. Map 6", Yorks. (1853 edn.). The whole parish is covered by sheets 174 and 191.
[15] *V.C.H. City of York*, 316; see below pp. 32–3.
[16] See p. 30.
[17] R.D.B., U/394/748.
[18] Notes *penes* Mrs. B. Sandys-Renton, Fulford, 1972.
[19] R.D.B., GD/89/85.
[20] R.D.B., BP/585/974; EB/98/110; KL/277/371; *York Courant*, 19 Jan. 1742.

then known as Fulford Grove, was acquired by Robert Fenwick in 1862[21] and it was he who called it Gate Fulford Hall and gave his name to the back lane. In and adjoining the main street there are several 19th- and 20th-century rows of cottages, and more recent building has also taken place both in the main street, where it includes a block of flats, and in the back lanes. There are three inns in the main street, the Bay Horse, the Plough, and the Saddle, all of which existed by 1822–3. There had been 7–9 alehouses in the parish in the 1750s and 1760s, and 4 or 5 later in the century. Three others also existed in 1822–3, at least two, the Light Horseman and the Barrack Tavern, being in the York suburb.[22]

The two or three surviving houses in the hamlet of Water Fulford, besides the hall,[23] include Hall Farm, a long four-bay house of the 18th century.

Few houses isolated from the village are known before inclosure in 1759. One was Well House, next to St. Oswald's church and the river,[24] and nearer to York was Lady Well House, which was occupied by an innkeeper in 1745.[25] The latter house stood close to New Walk, a riverside promenade begun in 1732 by York corporation which leased ground in Fulford called Pickell or Pikeing for the purpose.[26] Inclosure released land for building and changes were taking place around the turn of the century in that part of the parish lying closest to the city. The first buildings of York cavalry barracks were put up in 1795–6,[27] for example. A 'mansion house' called Field House was built c. 1790 near the York road,[28] and by 1794 another large house, Fulford Grange, had been built near New Walk.[29] Close by, in the former Lady Well close, eight houses were built in New Walk Terrace c. 1836.[30] Other small houses were being built in the 1830s and 1840s[31] on the north side of the cemetery which was opened in 1837.[32] To the east of the cemetery The Retreat lunatic asylum was built in 1796,[33] and by 1840 houses called Garrow Hill and Belle Vue had appeared near by.[34] As a result of such developments the northern part of Fulford, though still largely open, contained by 1850 a scattering of large houses and other buildings, and several streets of modest dwellings. Two or three large nursery gardens had also been laid out along the York road, and a few houses had been built in Church Lane and on the main road at the north end of the village.[35]

By 1890 there were more houses on the main road close to the York boundary and several new streets had been built up near the river, including Frances Street, and north of the cemetery, on both sides of the York–Heslington road. Further building had also taken place in Church Lane.[36] In the same period the barracks were greatly extended and other military buildings erected, and a depot was built for the York–Fulford tramway that was opened in 1880.[37] Between 1890 and 1907 the most extensive new building was in more streets laid out between the York road and the river.[38] A pumping station was built near St. Oswald's church as part of York's new sewerage scheme, opened in 1895, and in Water Fulford the York City Asylum (now Naburn Hospital) was built in 1906.[39]

More rapid development took place between the two World Wars when, in addition to infilling nearer the city, a large area was built up around Broadway, between the barracks and Heslington Lane. The suburbs had thus reached the northern end of Gate Fulford village. After the 1940s the most noteworthy extension to the built-up area was eastwards along Broadway and Heslington Lane.[40] Twentieth-century additions to the buildings in the suburban area included more new barracks and several city schools.[41] The Sir J. J. Hunt Memorial Cottage Homes were built close to the village in 1954,[42] and near by in St. Oswald's Road a group of old people's homes called Connaught Court was built by the Royal Masonic Benevolent Institution in 1971.[43]

South of Gate Fulford village, in the rural part of the parish, a new cemetery was opened in 1915 to serve the city in general as well as Fulford, and it has several times been enlarged.[44] Beyond the cemetery much private and council housing has been built, especially since the Second World War, including council estates in Fordlands Road (formerly Dam Lands Lane). Two new hospitals were opened next to Naburn Hospital in 1954,[45] and for a time Fulford golf course lay near by: it was opened in 1906 but moved to Heslington in 1936.[46] A York bypass was being constructed across the southern part of the parish in 1974.

There were 112 poll-tax payers in Fulford in 1377, besides an unknown number in St. Peter's liberty in Water Fulford.[47] In 1672 there were 67 households, of which 13 were exempt from the hearth tax; of those that were chargeable 28 had one hearth each, 13 had 2, 6 had 3, 5 had 4 or 5, and 2 had nine.[48] In 1729 there were 18 houses and 42 cottages in Gate Fulford.[49] There were said to be 52 families in Fulford chapelry in 1743 and 50 in 1764.[50] The population of Gate Fulford was 642 in 1801; it rose throughout the century, reaching 1,939 in 1851 and 8,162 in 1901.[51] In 1911 the civil parish that remained after the extension of York's boundaries in 1884 had 1,408 inhabitants. The number rose to 1,707 in 1951, 2,339 in 1961, and 3,265 in 1971.[52] There are few separate figures for Water

[21] R.D.B., II/127/152.
[22] E.R.R.O., QDT/2/13, 15.
[23] See p. 31.
[24] Y.A.S., DD. 88/8 (undated map, probably 1767).
[25] E.R.R.O., QSF. Mich. 1745, B.1.
[26] B.I.H.R., TER. A. Fulford 1743 etc.; *V.C.H. City of York*, 207, 245.
[27] *V.C.H. City of York*, 541.
[28] R.D.B., ER/245/258. It has been demolished.
[29] H.U.L., DRA. 726.
[30] R.D.B., FA/223/243; FB/113/129–30; FC/307/313. Illus. in P. Nuttgens, *York*, 59.
[31] York City Archives, YL/D Acc. 46/56–7.
[32] *V.C.H. City of York*, 466.
[33] Ibid. 471.
[34] White, *Dir. E. & N.R. Yorks.* 328.
[35] O.S. Map 6″ (1853 edn.).
[36] Ibid. (1893 edn.).
[37] *V.C.H. City of York*, 477–8, 541–2.
[38] O.S. Map 6″ (1910 edn.).
[39] *V.C.H. City of York*, 465, 470.
[40] O.S. Map 6″ (1958, 1970–1 edns.).
[41] *V.C.H. City of York*, 445, 447, 542.
[42] Date on buildings.
[43] Ex inf. the matron, 1973.
[44] *V.C.H. City of York*, 466–7.
[45] Ibid. 471.
[46] *Yorks. Gaz.* 21 July, 22 Dec. 1933; ex inf. Fulford Golf Club, 1972.
[47] E 179/202/58 mm. 4, 10.
[48] E 179/205/504.
[49] Par. reg. 1700–1800 (in vestry).
[50] B.I.H.R., Bp. V. 1764/Ret. 201; *Herring's Visit.* i. 195.
[51] *V.C.H. Yorks.* iii. 498.
[52] *Census*.

Fulford. It had 7 houses in 1629, 4 houses and 2 cottages in 1729, and populations of 34 in 1811 and 55 in 1901.[53]

MANORS AND OTHER ESTATES. In 1086 Gate Fulford comprised a single estate of 10 carucates, held by Count Alan of Brittany, which had belonged before the Conquest to Morcar.[54] About 1100 it was given by Count Stephen of Brittany to St. Mary's abbey, York, along with a carucate and 3 bovates in Water Fulford.[55] The abbey retained the manor of GATE FULFORD until the Dissolution, when it was worth about £48.[56] Afterwards numerous Crown leases were made of lands in Fulford, but in 1600 the manor was granted in fee to Richard Burrell and John Ryder.[57] In 1615 the manor was conveyed by Richard and John Burrell to Thomas Marshall and James Godson,[58] and in 1654 Samuel and Arthur Marshall sold it to William Taylor.[59]

Taylor was succeeded by his son John, grandson Thomas, and great-grandson John.[60] In 1745 the manor was conveyed by John Taylor to Robert Oates subject to Taylor's own use for life.[61] At inclosure in 1759 Taylor, described as lord of the manor, was allotted 83 a. as part of his life estate.[62] Oates, who was himself allotted 101 a. in 1759, devised all his property to his cousin John Key by will proved in 1763,[63] and in 1773 Taylor conveyed his life interest in the manor, with 180 a. of old and new inclosures, to Key.[64]

By 1810–11 the Keys had 614 a., roughly equally divided between Gate and Water Fulford.[65] The estate descended in the family[66] until the death of R. E. Key in 1961,[67] and in 1964, when it comprised 647 a., it was sold to Key's nephew Mr. William Wormald.[68]

In 1086 Erneis de Burun held a carucate and 3 bovates in Water Fulford.[69] The land subsequently descended, like Burun's estate in West Cottingwith,[70] successively to Geoffrey son of Pain, William Trussebut, Hilary de Builers, and William de Ros.[71] In 1285 Robert de Ros had 8 bovates at Fulford.[72] Under the Ros family the manor of WATER FULFORD was apparently held in 1343 by Walter of Heslerton and in 1346 by Osbert of Spaldington.[73] After the attainder of Thomas, Lord Ros, in 1461 the estate in Fulford, including Ros Hall, was the subject of several grants for life by the Crown between 1464 and 1484.[74] On the accession of Henry VII the manor was restored to Edmund de Ros. Edmund's sister Eleanor married Sir Robert Manners and at Edmund's death in 1508 the manor passed to her son Sir George Manners. In 1525 Sir George's son Thomas Manners, Lord Ros, was created earl of Rutland.[75] Water Fulford was sold by Henry, earl of Rutland, to John Redmayne in 1553.[76]

The manor descended in the Redmayne or Redman family[77] to Thomas Redman (d. c. 1695), whose sisters Frances and Susannah married Noel Barton and Robert Clarke.[78] In 1702 the Bartons and the Clarkes sold it to Robert Oates; it then comprised Ros Hall and 11 bovates in Water Fulford.[79] It subsequently descended with Gate Fulford manor.[80]

The medieval manor-house was mentioned in 1343,[81] but the oldest part of the existing building is unlikely to be earlier than the 16th century. It was a timber-framed range of two storeys which is now completely enclosed by later work, and it probably does not represent the whole of the early house. It was extended to the south and east early in the 18th century and to the north in 1764. There were more additions on the north and east in 1851[82] and at about this time bays were added to the south-west room. The house has recently been reduced by the removal of some of the 19th-century kitchen buildings, and it has been subdivided into two residences, but most of the 18th-century fittings survive together with a quantity of reset 17th-century panelling. In the grounds are a stable range and a large dovecot.

In 1086 an estate at Water Fulford of a carucate and 3 bovates was soke of Clifton (Yorks. N.R.) and belonged to Count Alan of Brittany.[83] About 1100 it was given to St. Mary's abbey and subsequently it descended with Gate Fulford manor.[84]

The archbishop of York held a carucate and 2 bovates at Water Fulford in 1086.[85] The estate was assigned to Ampleforth prebend, presumably at its formation before 1219–34,[86] and c. 1295 the prebend had 12 bovates of land, 6 a. meadow, and a toft there.[87] Unspecified property in Fulford later descended with the prebend's manor of Heslington.[88] Part of the tithes of Water Fulford certainly belonged to the prebend,[89] but the only other reference to land is to 5 a. belonging to the prebend in 1844.[90]

Besides their interest in Gate Fulford manor the Taylor family had a substantial estate in the parish. About 200 a. of it, comprising Tilmire farm, were sold by John Taylor in 1769 to Timothy Mortimer.[91]

[53] York Pub. Libr., Parson's map of Dringhouses (1629); par. reg. 1700–1800 (in vestry); V.C.H. Yorks. iii. 498.
[54] V.C.H. Yorks. ii. 193.
[55] E.Y.C. iv, p. 4.
[56] Dugdale, Mon. iii. 572.
[57] E.R.R.O., DDX/148/2.
[58] Yorks. Fines, 1614–25, 25.
[59] C.P. 25(2)/614/1654 East. no. 11.
[60] E 134/9 Geo. I Hil./25.
[61] R.D.B., R/345/841; AS/405/675; Y.A.S., DD. 88/7/6.
[62] R.D.B., AC/265/12; 30 Geo. II, c. 36 (Priv. Act).
[63] Y.A.S., DD. 88/6.
[64] R.D.B., AS/405/675.
[65] E.R.R.O., DDX/148/13.
[66] Burke, Land. Gent. (1952), 1432.
[67] R.D.B., 1311/91/84.
[68] Ibid. 1386/193/176; E.R.R.O., DDX/225/13.
[69] V.C.H. Yorks. ii. 321.
[70] See p. 115.
[71] E.Y.C. x, pp. 23, 25.
[72] Yorks. Inq. ii, p. 34.
[73] Cal. Inq. p.m. viii, p. 335; Feud. Aids, vi. 223.
[74] Cal. Pat. 1461–7, 334, 467; 1467–77, 48; 1476–85, 13, 455.
[75] Complete Peerage, xi. 253; Burke, Dorm. & Ext. Peerages (1883), 460.
[76] Y.A.S., DD. 88.
[77] Visit. Yorks. 1584–5 and 1612, ed. J. Foster, 99.
[78] E 134/9 Geo. I Hil./25.
[79] Y.A.S., DD. 88/7/3.
[80] See above.
[81] C 135/71 no. 18.
[82] Dates on rainwater heads.
[83] V.C.H. Yorks. ii. 241.
[84] See above.
[85] V.C.H. Yorks. ii. 321.
[86] York Minster Fasti, i (Y.A.S. Rec. Ser. cxxiii), 60.
[87] Miscellanea, iv (Y.A.S. Rec. Ser. xciv), 25.
[88] See p. 70.
[89] See p. 32.
[90] B.I.H.R., TA. 545S.
[91] R.D.B., AL/462/820.

Charles Mortimer conveyed them to Henry Bland in 1815, and Bland's trustees to N. E. Yarburgh in 1838.[92] The farm descended with the capital manor of Heslington and was sold with it in 1964.[93]

Several York religious houses, in addition to St. Mary's abbey, had estates in the parish. Two houses and 12½ a. in Fulford were granted to St. Andrew's priory by Thomas Thurkill in 1395.[94] They were let to Ralph Prince in 1593.[95] St. Leonard's hospital had property in Fulford at the Dissolution, some of which descended with land in Naburn.[96] In the 12th century common rights in Fulford were granted to St. Nicholas's hospital by St. Mary's abbey.[97] The hospital's former property there and in York was granted by the Crown to John Somer and Thomas Kerry in 1564.[98] Between 1203 and 1241 Hilary de Builers gave a bovate, a toft and croft, and certain meadow in Fulford to Warter priory.[99] After the Dissolution the land in Fulford descended with Warter's property in Naburn.[1]

The tithes belonged to St. Mary's abbey until the Dissolution.[2] In 1613–14 those of Gate Fulford township were granted by the Crown to Francis Morrice and Francis Philips, having been in the tenure of John Redman.[3] There were disputes about their payment in 1598 and 1613.[4] Morrice and Philips apparently conveyed the tithes to Sir Thomas and Humphrey Smith, who sold them in 1615 to John Goodman the elder and younger.[5] In 1650, when they were worth £80, they were said to belong to Henry Belton.[6] In 1668 another John Goodman suffered a recovery of them,[7] and he or a namesake still had them in 1689[8] and 1708.[9] They passed to Francis Taylor in 1713 and to George Meeke in 1723.[10] At the inclosure of Gate Fulford in 1759 Francis Meeke was awarded £3,909, to be paid by the various proprietors for exemption from the tithes of both old and new inclosures in the township.[11] The payment of the curate's stipend devolved upon John Taylor and succeeding lords of the manor.[12]

The tithes of part of Water Fulford township, amounting to 167 a.,[13] apparently descended with those of Gate Fulford, and in 1759 Francis Meeke was awarded £210 for them.[14] The tithes of the rest of the township were divided into three equal parts. One, worth £33 in 1810–11, belonged to the lords of the manor,[15] the second, worth £5 in 1649, belonged to the prebend of Ampleforth,[16] and the third belonged to the rector of St. Martin's, Micklegate. Each was commuted for £28 a year in 1844.[17]

ECONOMIC HISTORY. In 1086 Morcar's estate at Gate Fulford had land for 10 ploughs; there were then, in fact, 2 ploughs on the demesne and 2 held by 6 villeins. There were also 20 a. of meadow. The estate had decreased in value from £1 in 1066 to 16s.[18] Little is known of the process of reclamation in the Middle Ages or of the arrangement of the common fields and meadows. Much of the southern half of the township was waste or moor, stretching out to the area known as Tilmire. There is mention of 7½ a. in an assart there called the new ridding.[19] The citizens of York were entitled to common pasture in Tilmire, a right which they maintained after a dispute with St. Leonard's hospital in 1401 and which was included in an agreement made with St. Mary's abbey in 1484.[20] The moor also included a turbary: in 1375, for example, the abbey granted a right to take turf there.[21] The unlicensed digging of turves was presented in the abbey's manorial court in 1447, as well as fishing and fowling in Tilmire, which was described as the abbey's demesne fishery.[22] The agreement made between York and St. Mary's in 1484 also confirmed the citizens' rights of pasturage in part of the open fields and meadows of Gate Fulford. The arable land included, in the extreme north-east, Seward How field. Some land in the fields already belonged to York men,[23] and that continued to be the case in later centuries.

During the 17th century there may have been attempts to grow new crops and improve upon old rotations in the open fields, reflected in a pain laid in 1695 forbidding the sowing of open-field land 'out of course of husbandry'.[24] More of the waste land was also being reclaimed. Closes called New fields were mentioned in 1642[25] and reference to open-field land called Breck butts in 1684[26] indicates that the near-by brecks already existed. In the mid 18th century the old inclosures of Gate Fulford included a large block of land in the south of the township, surrounded by the moors, comprising nearly 30 closes called New fields and about 20 called Intacks. More old inclosures, including the brecks, lay between the village and the moor, and other closes lay between the open fields and the moor.[27]

The remaining open fields and commons were inclosed in 1759[28] under an Act of 1756.[29] Allotments made totalled 907 a., comprising about 307 a. in Fulford field, lying between the village and York, 38 a. in Dam Lands field, south of the village, 54 a. in the riverside ings, and 508 a. in the commons.

[92] Ibid. CY/426/622; B.I.H.R., Yarburgh MSS., Estate papers.
[93] See pp. 69–70.
[94] Cal. Pat. 1391–6, 599.
[95] E 310/30/180 no. 22.
[96] See p. 78.
[97] E.Y.C. i, p. 251.
[98] E.R.R.O., DDKP/15/2; Cal. Pat. 1563–6, p. 11.
[99] E.Y.C. x, p. 44.
[1] See p. 78.
[2] Valor Eccl. (Rec. Com.), v. 8.
[3] C 66/1985 m. 1.
[4] B.I.H.R., CP. G. 3018, 3038, 3204–6; H. 822, 827, 911.
[5] Ibid. H. 4596.
[6] C 94/3 f. 76.
[7] C.P. 43/341 rot. 152.
[8] C.P. 25(2)/893/1 Wm. & Mary Mich. no. 37.
[9] R.D.B., A/81/108.
[10] Ibid. E/128/223; I/120/266.
[11] Ibid. AC/265/12.
[12] See p. 34.
[13] B.I.H.R., TA. 545S.
[14] R.D.B., AC/265/12.
[15] E.R.R.O., DDX/148/13.
[16] Lamb. Pal. Libr., COMM./XIIa/18/21.
[17] B.I.H.R., TA. 545S.
[18] V.C.H. Yorks. ii. 193, 241.
[19] Y.A.S., DD. 88/1 (calendar of St. Mary's deeds, p. 1, n.d.).
[20] V.C.H. City of York, 499.
[21] Yorks. Deeds, ii, p. 218.
[22] Y.A.S., DD. 88/1.
[23] York City Arch., E/30 f. 74; V.C.H. City of York, 498–9.
[24] Y.A.S., DD. 88/1.
[25] Y.A.J. vii. 104.
[26] E.R.R.O., DDFA/14/277.
[27] Y.A.S., DD. 88/8.
[28] R.D.B., AC/265/12. A working map and the final award map are in Y.A.S., DD. 88/8.
[29] 30 Geo. II, c. 36 (Priv. Act).

HEMINGBROUGH: the remains of Loftsome Bridge

WHELDRAKE: Ings Bridge, demolished in 1966

STAMFORD BRIDGE: the railway viaduct

CLIFFE: the former malting

DUNNINGTON: an old chicory kiln

The commons included approximately 50 a. in Low moor, 125 a. in East moor, 200 a. in West moor, and 125 a. in Tilmire. John Taylor was allotted 345 a. for manorial and other lands, Robert Oates received 101 a., and the citizens of York got 52 a. for their common rights. There were also 2 allotments of 30–50 a., 13 of 10–29 a., and 21 of under 10 a. Ten and a half cottages had common rights attached to them and these were replaced by £15 for each cottage, to be paid by those who were allotted land. The tithes of the township were commuted by the award for money payments.[30]

For Water Fulford no economic information was given in 1086. The Ros manor included 60 a. of arable and 14 a. of meadow in demesne in 1343,[31] and much the same in the early 16th century.[32] The prebendary of Ampleforth's estate c. 1295 contained 6 a. of meadow in demesne and 12 bovates held by 5 bondmen and one other tenant. The prebendary's tenants rendered money rent, hens, and eggs, mowed the lord's hay, and for each bovate provided five men to reap his corn. There was also one toft held by a cottar.[33]

The town fields of Water Fulford were mentioned in the early 18th century, together with parcels of meadow in the ings,[34] but inclosure took place about that time. About 1716 four closes were described as former open-field land, and inclosure by Robert Oates was mentioned.[35]

There were usually about ten farmers and market-gardeners in the whole parish in the 19th century, but the number later fell and there were four in the 1930s, only one of them having 150 a. or more.[36] Of the four farms on the Fulford Hall estate in 1964, one was of 209 a. and the others each about 130 a.[37] There were 468 a. under crops in 1801,[38] and in Water Fulford alone the tithable land in 1844 comprised 66 a. of arable and 192 a. of grassland.[39] In 1905 the parish included 721 a. of arable, 793 a. of permanent grass, and 48 a. of woods.[40] There has continued to be a substantial area under grass, especially near the Ouse and around Water Fulford.[41] The ings at Water Fulford were still in divided ownership in 1972 and more than a dozen boundary stones remained marking off the parcels.

The river Ouse has naturally always provided a means of transport for the parish, and a few Fulford men may have made a living by fishing. In 1744 Robert Oates and York corporation agreed to exercise concurrently the fishing rights that they both claimed.[42] At inclosure in 1759 all those who received allotments were said to enjoy the right to land goods from the river.[43] The chief wharf may have been that shown c. 1850 at the end of Landing Lane, between Gate and Water Fulford.[44] There was also some brick-making in the parish: a brickmaker was recorded in 1692, for example.[45] On a larger scale was the quarrying of gravel in the area north of Church Lane, and c. 1850 there were several pits from which rail tracks led down to riverside staiths.[46]

Siward mill hill, the site of a windmill, was mentioned in 1546,[47] and Siward How mill in 1587.[48] It stood on the moraine in the north-east of Gate Fulford[49] and was several times mentioned in the 18th century. It was then known as Lamel, Laming, or Lammon hill mill, and a new mill was apparently erected on the site between 1733 and 1758.[50] It was described as decayed in 1836.[51] A second windmill, called Fishergate mill in 1600,[52] is perhaps to be identified with White mill, recorded in 1767,[53] and with a mill shown next to the York road near Fishergate on maps of 1772.[54] A miller was last recorded in Fulford in 1823.[55]

LOCAL GOVERNMENT. For the manor of Gate Fulford there are transcripts of court rolls for several years between 1333 and 1400,[56] surviving rolls of 1447, 1483–4, and 1509,[57] extracts of rolls of 1637–43,[58] rolls of 1692–1703, together with several lists of pains, and a court book of 1771–1854, with some additional notes to 1877.[59] The records of St. Mary's abbey formerly included accounts of the steward of 'the manor of Sywardhow' for several years from 1327 to 1369,[60] but there is no other evidence that land in the north-east of Fulford comprised a separate manor.

All the courts were mainly concerned with domestic and agricultural business, but offences against the assize of ale were dealt with in the 15th century. A constable, 2 rent-collectors, 2 moor-reeves, 2 bylawmen, and 2 aletasters were elected in 1447, and a constable, 2 moor-reeves, a house-reeve, a cottage-reeve, 4 bylawmen, 2 aletasters, and a man described as *prepositus de manegreves* in 1483. In the 1690s a constable, 4 bylawmen, and a pinder were elected, and in the late 18th and earlier 19th centuries a constable and a pinder: the latter was still sworn as late as 1877.

Surviving parochial records include churchwardens' accounts for 1821–98 and vestry minutes for 1827–37. The former record the levying of rates for the churchwardens and for the constable. The select vestry in 1829 withdrew from an agreement made in 1820 for the use by Fulford of the workhouse at Holme upon Spalding Moor. Fulford had several poorhouses and in 1835 the occupant of one of them also had 'the prison house'.[61] Fulford

---

[30] See p. 32.
[31] C 135/71 no. 18 (partly illegible).
[32] Belvoir Castle MSS., Roos 976, 990.
[33] *Miscellanea*, iv. 25.
[34] R.D.B., E/227/398.
[35] B.I.H.R., PR. Y/MG. 37.
[36] Directories.
[37] E.R.R.O., DDX/225/13.
[38] 1801 Crop Returns.
[39] B.I.H.R., TA. 545S.
[40] Acreage Returns, 1905.
[41] [1st] Land Util. Surv. Map, sheet 27; 2nd Land Util. Surv. Map, sheet 699 (SE 64–74).
[42] Y.A.S., DD. 88/7/5.
[43] R.D.B., AC/265/12.
[44] O.S. Map 6" (1853 edn.); *Yorks. Gaz.* 9 July 1853.
[45] Y.A.S., DD. 88/1.
[46] O.S. Map 6" (1853 edn.).
[47] *L. & P. Hen. VIII*, xxi (1), p. 357.
[48] E 310/32/190 no. 4.
[49] Not in Heslington as on O.S. Map 6" (1853 and later edns.): see *Y.A.J.* xli. 584–7.
[50] Deeds *penes* Mrs. B. Sandys-Renton, Fulford, 1972.
[51] *Yorks. Gaz.* 7 May 1836.
[52] E.R.R.O., DDX/148/2.
[53] R.D.B., AL/5/9.
[54] T. Jefferys, *Map of Yorks.* Both mills are shown on J. Lund's map: York City Arch., D/Vv.
[55] Baines, *Hist. Yorks.* ii. 209.
[56] Y.A.S., DD. 88/2.
[57] Ibid. DD. 88/1.
[58] S.C. 2/211/162.
[59] Y.A.S., DD. 88/1.
[60] Ibid. DD. 88/2.
[61] Par. rec. in Vicarage, 1972.

joined York poor-law union in 1837.[62] It became part of Escrick rural district in 1894, Derwent rural district in 1935,[63] and the Selby district of North Yorkshire in 1974.

CHURCH. The surviving fabric of the 'old' church, which was replaced in the 19th century, shows that it was built *c.* 1150.[64] It was acquired by St. Mary's abbey, York, though it is not certain by what means. The right to the chapel may have derived from Count Stephen of Brittany's grant of Gate Fulford to the abbey *c.* 1100.[65] Alternatively it may have derived from Count Alan's grant of St. Olave's church, York, to the abbey before 1086,[66] and certainly after the Dissolution Fulford was dependent upon St. Olave's. Neither grant, however, mentions a chapel. In the Middle Ages both Fulford and St. Olave's were chapelries dependent upon the abbey.[67] Fulford chapel was first expressly mentioned in 1349, when it was dedicated and its yard licensed for burial while the plague lasted.[68] Gate Fulford burials otherwise took place at St. Olave's, a custom enforced by the abbey in 1398 after a man had been buried at Fulford.[69] After the Dissolution, however, the churchyard at Fulford was again used,[70] and at least by the mid 17th century baptisms and marriages also took place at Fulford.[71] It was nevertheless still described as a chapelry of St. Olave's in the earlier 18th century.[72] By the 19th century it was styled a perpetual curacy[73] and by 1872 a vicarage.[74]

The township of Water Fulford was equally divided between Gate Fulford chapelry and the parishes of St. Paul's, Heslington, and St. Martin's, Micklegate, in York.[75] The Heslington part corresponded to the prebendal estate and the St. Martin's part to the Ros fee. Hugh Annesley, by will proved in 1401, and Elizabeth Pindar, by will proved in 1558, asked to be buried respectively in the chancel of St. Peter's, Fulford, and in St. Paul's, Water Fulford;[76] it seems likely that these were references to Heslington church, which was formerly dedicated to St. Peter and St. Paul.[77] In 1585 John Redman, lord of Water Fulford, was licensed to use Gate Fulford chapel because of the great distance of St. Martin's church,[78] and several Redmans of Water Fulford were later buried in the chapel.[79] A later lord of the manor, Robert Oates, unsuccessfully disputed his liability to pay rates to St. Martin's in 1716–22,[80] and rates were also paid to Heslington in the 18th century.[81]

St. Olave's church was served by a chaplain from St. Mary's abbey,[82] and some provision was presumably made by the abbey for a chaplain to serve Fulford. After the Dissolution a grant of the 'advowson' of Fulford to the archbishop of York in 1558[83] presumably lapsed on the accession of Elizabeth I. Subsequently the impropriators provided curates at Fulford[84] and later presented to the vicarage. The advowson passed from the Key family to the archbishop in 1892.[85]

The stipend paid to the curate by the impropriator amounted to £6 13s. 4d. in 1650[86] and £4 in the 18th century. The curate also enjoyed the letting of certain headlands in the open fields, of ground called Pickell, and of the churchyard, which increased his income to £8 1s. 6d. in 1727. By 1743, moreover, he received a payment for each house and cottage in Fulford, as well as fees and offerings.[87] At inclosure in 1759 John Taylor, lord of the manor, was given an allotment in return for undertaking the payment of the curate's stipend, and he was to pay a further £2 a year for some of the glebe headlands, which had been incorporated in his allotments.[88] A payment of £2 2s. a year was received under the will of Mary Key, dated 1781, for preaching Good Friday and Ascension Day sermons.[89] The living was augmented from Queen Anne's Bounty in 1746, 1767, 1778, and 1808, each time with £200, on the two last occasions to meet like benefactions from John Key. In 1813 a parliamentary grant of £600 was given to meet a benefaction of £400 from the incumbent, Robert Sutton.[90] Bounty money was used to buy 7 a. in Southcoates (in Drypool), 14 a. in Fulford, 6 a. in East Cottingwith, and 9 a. in Huntington (Yorks. N.R.).[91] The average value of the living was £96 net a year in 1829–31.[92] In the early 19th century a payment of 5s. a year was made from Fulford to St. Olave's church for 'St. Olave's lights',[93] but it was stopped in 1873.[94] The gross value of the living in 1884 was about £100 and the net value in 1915 was £160.[95] Key's benefaction for sermons was still received in 1972–3.[96]

There was apparently no parsonage house until one was built in 1875[97] in Fulford Road, at what was later to be the corner of Derwent Road, £1,150 for it being given from the Common Fund.[98] It was replaced in 1960 by an existing house near the church in Fulford Road.[99]

In the 18th century the curate was non-resident, living in York in 1743 and at Walkington in 1764; in the latter year he had an assistant curate, who lived

---

[62] *3rd Rep. Poor Law Com.* 171.
[63] *Census.*
[64] See p. 35.
[65] See p. 31.
[66] *V.C.H. City of York,* 397.
[67] *Cal. Papal. Reg.* v. 2; xi. 129, 389.
[68] *Fabric Rolls of York Minster* (Sur. Soc. xxxv), 237.
[69] [T. Widdrington], *Analecta Eboracensia,* ed. C. Caine, 239–40; *Y.A.J.* xlii. 488.
[70] Minster Libr., Torre MS., 'Cleveland & E.R.', p. 630.
[71] Reg. (in vestry).
[72] B.I.H.R., TER. A. Fulford 1727; Bp. V. 1764/Ret. 201; *V.C.H. City of York,* 399.
[73] Lawton, *Rer. Eccl. Dioc. Ebor.* i. 43; *Rep. Com. Eccl. Revenues,* 936.
[74] *Kelly's Dir. N. & E.R. Yorks.* (1872), 367.
[75] O.S. Map 6" (1853 edn.).
[76] Minster Libr., Torre MS., 'Cleveland & E.R.', p. 628.
[77] See p. 73.
[78] B.I.H.R., Reg. 31, f. 58.
[79] Minster Libr., Torre MS., 'Cleveland & E.R.', p. 628.
[80] B.I.H.R., PR. Y/MG. 37; CP. I. 467.
[81] Ibid. PR. HES. 12.
[82] *V.C.H. City of York,* 397–8.
[83] *Cal. Pat.* 1557–8, 420.
[84] See p. 32.
[85] *Lond. Gaz.* 12 Feb. 1892, p. 761.
[86] C 94/3 f. 76.
[87] B.I.H.R., TER. A. Fulford 1727 etc.
[88] R.D.B., AC/265/12.
[89] *12th Rep. Com. Char.* 649.
[90] Hodgson, *Q.A.B.* 211, 449.
[91] B.I.H.R., TER. A. Fulford 1777, 1786, 1809, 1817.
[92] *Rep. Com. Eccl. Revenues,* 936.
[93] Lawton, *Rer. Eccl. Dioc. Ebor.* i. 43.
[94] Ex inf. Miss Briddon.
[95] B.I.H.R., Bp. V. 1884/Ret.; Bp. V. 1915/Ret.
[96] Char. Com. files.
[97] *Yorks. Gaz.* 6 Mar. 1875.
[98] *Lond. Gaz.* 14 Nov. 1873; 15 May 1874; 31 Mar. 1876.
[99] R.D.B., 1201/437/393; *Yorks. Eve. Press,* 3 Nov. 1960.

in York.[1] In 1835 he was also a prebendary at Ripon and rector of St. Michael, Spurriergate, in York.[2] From the 1860s the incumbent resided at Fulford and had no other living, though he was chaplain at the barracks; he usually had an assistant curate.[3]

A service was held each Sunday in 1743, with Holy Communion four times a year attended by 30–50 people.[4] By 1865 there were two weekly services and communion was held ten times a year. Communion was celebrated monthly by 1868, twice monthly by 1877, and weekly by 1884. In 1877 an additional weekly service was held on Wednesdays.[5] Three services were held each Sunday in 1972. After the building of the new church in 1866 the old one was used as a mortuary chapel from 1871.[6] Monthly services were held there in 1966,[7] but in 1973 it was declared redundant. Use was also made of an unlicensed chapel in Barrack Street in 1871, and a service was held each Sunday and Thursday at a mission room in 1884. The latter was perhaps St. Andrew's mission room, Frances Street, at which a Sunday and a weekday service, as well as twice-monthly communion, were held in 1894.[8] It was replaced by a new building in Alma Terrace in 1901,[9] which was used until 1955.[10]

The 'old' church of ST. OSWALD, in St. Oswald's Road, consists of chancel, nave, and west tower. It has been suggested that the nave was built c. 1150 and the chancel added c. 1180, the rubble masonry of the chancel being built up against the finer ashlar of the nave.[11] Two original windows survive in the north wall of the chancel and there is a plain 12th-century doorway in the nave. The chancel east window, of three lights, dates from the 14th century and two large square-headed windows in the nave south wall and a smaller one in the chancel south wall from the 17th. The north wall of the nave has been rebuilt without openings. The 'steeple' of the church was in decay in 1577[12] and the surviving brick tower is thought to have been built c. 1795,[13] when a faculty was obtained to erect a vestry beside the belfry and to insert a west gallery.[14] A faculty of 1809 authorized new pews to be provided and a new pulpit erected,[15] and the plastered ceilings are of the same period, although the roofs may be earlier. The church was roofed with fish-scale tiles c. 1870[16] and there is a lych-gate dated 1890. There is one bell.[17] The interior has been partly stripped of its fittings.

Burials under the church floor are mostly of members of manorial families, the earliest apparently being those of John Redman (n.d.) and John Taylor (d. 1705). The earliest headstone in the churchyard dates from 1740.[18]

A new church of ST. OSWALD was built on Fulford Road to replace the old one and was opened in 1866. It is of stone and consists of an aisled chancel, with north and south chapels, an aisled and clerestoried nave, transepts, and south-west tower, originally with a spire. The architect was J. P. Pritchett.[19] A vestry was added in 1875.[20] The church was burnt out in 1877 but restored and reopened early in 1878.[21] The unsafe spire was removed and the belfry stage of the tower rebuilt in 1924.[22] The 18th-century font was transferred from the old church.

The plate includes a brass alms-dish of 1708, a silver chalice and paten given by Ann Key in 1768, a silver flagon given by John Clifford in 1866,[23] and several later pieces. There is one bell, made by William Blews & Sons of Birmingham in 1869.[24] The registers date from 1653 but for the 17th century they are incomplete.[25]

The churchyard at the old church was closed in 1902[26] and since the new church had no burial ground burials subsequently took place at Fulford cemetery.[27] Edward Bowdler (d. 1906) left £600 to the churchwardens, £500 of it to be used to build a house for the keeper of 'the burial ground'. A dispute over where the house should be built was settled in 1910 when it was decided that the parish council should erect it at the new burial ground, on condition that the council should maintain the old churchyard. The other £100 was invested and the interest used for the upkeep of the Bowdler family's graves in the churchyard.[28] A church hall was built in the grounds of the new church and opened in 1960.[29]

NONCONFORMITY. In 1627 Thomas Metham and his wife were reported for recusancy. There was one family of Roman Catholics in the parish in the earlier 18th century and about ten individuals later in the century.[30]

There were 16 protestant dissenters in 1676[31] and a family of Quakers in 1743.[32] Houses were registered for worship by protestant dissenters in 1759[33] and 1777,[34] and a Methodist society was formed at Fulford in 1799.[35] Houses were registered in 1797, 1802, 1808, 1809, 1817, and 1825, and a room in 1829, most if not all for use by the Methodists.[36]

---

[1] B.I.H.R., Bp. V. 1764/Ret. 201; *Herring's Visit.* i. 195.
[2] *Rep. Com. Eccl. Revenues*, 936.
[3] B.I.H.R., V. 1865/Ret. 198; V. 1868/Ret. 180; V. 1871/Ret. 180; V. 1877/Ret.; Bp. V. 1884/Ret.; Bp. V. 1894/Ret.; Bp. V. 1900/Ret. 133; *Crockford*.
[4] *Herring's Visit.* i. 195.
[5] B.I.H.R., V. 1865/Ret. 198; V. 1868/Ret. 180; V. 1877/Ret.; Bp. V. 1884/Ret.
[6] Ibid. Fac. 1871/7.
[7] *Yorks. Eve. Press*, 1 Sept. 1966.
[8] B.I.H.R., V. 1871/Ret. 180; Bp. V. 1884/Ret.; Bp. V. 1894/Ret.
[9] Terrier and inventory, 1898 and 1925 (in vestry).
[10] Ex inf. Miss Briddon.
[11] *Church of St. Oswald* (guide bk. 1971).
[12] B.I.H.R., V. 1577–8/CB. 1.
[13] *Ch. of St. Oswald*.
[14] B.I.H.R., Fac. Bk. iii, pp. 79–80.
[15] Ibid. p. 494.
[16] *Ch. of St. Oswald*.
[17] Boulter, 'Ch. Bells', 31.
[18] *Ch. of St. Oswald*.
[19] *Illus. London News*, 21 Nov. 1868; *Yorks. Gaz.* 29 Dec. 1866.
[20] B.I.H.R., Fac. 1875/11.
[21] *Ch. of St. Oswald*; photographs in church.
[22] B.I.H.R., Fac. 1923/41; *Yorks. Gaz.* 12 Jan. 1924.
[23] *Yorks. Ch. Plate*, i. 252.
[24] Boulter, 'Ch. Bells', 31.
[25] In vestry.
[26] *Yorks. Gaz.* 10 May 1902.
[27] See p. 30.
[28] Briddon, *Hist. Fulford*, 36–7.
[29] *Yorks. Eve. Press*, 25 Feb. 1960.
[30] Aveling, *Post Reformation Catholicism*, 64.
[31] Bodl. MS. Tanner 150, ff. 27 sqq.
[32] *Herring's Visit.* i. 195.
[33] G.R.O. Worship Returns, Vol. v, no. 110.
[34] B.I.H.R., Fac. Bk. ii, p. 167.
[35] W. Camidge, *Methodism in Fulford*, 3.
[36] G.R.O. Worship Returns, Vol. v, nos. 1348, 1722, 2131, 2335, 3135, 3995, 4170; Camidge, op. cit. 4.

A Wesleyan Methodist chapel was built in 1820 in Back (later School) Lane, and the building still stood in 1972, when it was used as a farm building. It was replaced by a new chapel in the main street in 1845[37] and there were 34 members in 1885.[38] The chapel was rebuilt on the same site in 1896,[39] constructed of brick with stone dressings, in the Gothic style. It was still used in 1972. It was said in 1865 that few of the Wesleyans in the village failed also to attend the parish church but that in New Fulford, the suburban area, a third of the population were dissenters and a third attended no place of worship.[40]

EDUCATION. Thirty children were taught at a petty school in Fulford in 1743.[41] A free school was founded by John Key, by indenture of 1771; 20 pupils were supported by his endowment of a house and £9 12s. yearly rent-charge, and others were taught at their parents' expense. Mary Key, by will dated 1781, gave £100 for the school, from which the income in 1824 was £4.[42] In 1835 there were 26 boys and 6 girls at the school. There was also an unendowed school in the village in 1819, with 20 children, and two in 1835, one with 22 children and the other, which had started in 1831, with 20.[43]

The free school was held in the master's house, now no. 27 Main Street.[44] Schoolrooms for girls and for infants were built by Amelia Cholmley in 1844[45] and 1846[46] respectively, standing side by side in Back (later School) Lane, behind the old schoolhouse. The school was united with the National Society.[47] The boys remained in the original schoolhouse until 1865, when a mixed school was begun in the Back Lane buildings. By May 1866 attendance had risen from 28 to 44. An additional room was built later in 1866,[48] and the attendance was 111 in 1871.[49] An annual government grant was received by 1865,[50] and Miss Cholmley, by will proved in 1874, left stock to produce £10 a year for the school.[51] The buildings were extended in 1882[52] and there were 160 children on the roll in 1885.[53]

When Fishergate board school, in York, was opened in 1895 18 children were transferred there from Fulford school.[54] Many children from within the extended city boundary, however, still attended at Fulford, more than 50 in 1914, for example.[55] Attendance fell from 215 in 1908 to 170 in 1914 and 147 in 1919, but it later rose to 230 in 1922.[56] A new school was built near by in Heslington Lane in 1930,[57] and in 1938 the attendance was 290.[58] The buildings were extended in 1948 and 1954. The school also continued to use the old Back Lane buildings, part of which was converted to a social hall.[59] There were 286 pupils on the roll in April 1972.[60]

A county secondary school was built in Fulfordgate, Heslington Lane, and opened in 1963. It was renamed Fulford School in 1970 and became comprehensive.[61] There were 640 pupils on the roll in February 1972.[62]

CHARITIES FOR THE POOR. Mary Key, by will dated 1781, left £150 to provide £2 2s. a year for the minister and bread for the poor of the parish, as well as £100 for the school.[63] George Waite, by will proved in 1806, left £10 to provide bread. By 1824 these various legacies had been used to buy £436 stock. Catherine Key, at unknown date, left £100 for bread, represented by £104 stock in 1824. There was also in 1824 a benefaction fund of £100, made up of £45 given by John Redman, £10 by Eleanor Bailey, £5 by the Revd. Thomas Mosley, £35 by William Smith, and £5 from an unrecorded source, all at unknown dates but the first three before 1743.[64] The fund produced £5 a year interest in 1824, of which £1 15s. was distributed in cash as instructed by Smith and the rest in bread. Out of the total income for bread from all the above-mentioned charities a weekly distribution was made to 20 families.[65]

Anne Richardson (d. 1848) left £100 to provide coal,[66] T. W. Wilson, by will of 1856, bequeathed £50 for coal,[67] and John Smith, by will proved in 1875, left £100 for the poor of the parish.[68] No more is known of Richardson's bequest.

The charities of Mary and Catherine Key, John Smith, George Waite, and T. W. Wilson, as well as the benefaction fund, were later administered together. In 1972–3 the income was £18 from £137 stock, and doles of 50p. were given to 31 people.[69]

Fulford benefited from the charity of John Hodgson for parishes in York poor-law union,[70] and grants were made to four residents of Fulford in 1972.[71]

[37] H.O. 129/23/515.
[38] J. Lyth, *Glimpses of Early Methodism in York and District*, 288.
[39] Camidge, op. cit. 13.
[40] B.I.H.R., V. 1865/Ret. 198; V. 1868/Ret. 180.
[41] *Herring's Visit.* i. 195.
[42] *12th Rep. Com. Char.* 648–9.
[43] *Educ. of Poor Digest*, 1081; *Educ. Enquiry Abstract*, 1085.
[44] Inscribed stone from the house, now at the primary school.
[45] R.D.B., GA/116/150.
[46] Inscribed stone from the building, now at the primary school.
[47] O.S. Map 6" (1853 edn.).
[48] Ed. 49/8542; Elizabeth Ankers, 'Growth and Devt. of Fulford C. of E. Primary Sch. 1865–1930', TS. *penes* the headmaster, 1972, pp. 17–18, 20.
[49] *Returns relating to Elem. Educ.* 792.
[50] *Rep. of Educ. Cttee. of Council, 1865–6* [3666], p. 785, H.C. (1866), xxvii.
[51] Charity board in old church; Ed. 49/8542.
[52] Ankers, 'Growth and Devt.', p. 22.
[53] Briddon, *Hist. Fulford*, 45.
[54] Ibid.
[55] E.R. Educ. Cttee. *Mins.* 1914–15, 154.
[56] Bd. of Educ. List 21 (H.M.S.O.).
[57] E.R. Educ. Cttee. *Mins.* 1930–1, 40.
[58] List 21.
[59] Ankers, 'Growth and Devt.', pp. 52–3.
[60] Ex inf. Chief Educ. Officer, County Hall, Beverley, 1972.
[61] E.R. Educ. Cttee. *Mins.* 1963–4, 70; 1970–1, 35.
[62] Ex inf. Chief Educ. Officer.
[63] See p. 34 and above.
[64] *Herring's Visit.* i. 195.
[65] *12th Rep. Com. Char.* 649–50; charity boards in old church.
[66] Inscription in old church.
[67] Char. Com. files.
[68] Ibid.
[69] Ibid.
[70] See p. 12.
[71] Ex inf. Mr. A. R. Tunnah, Haxby, York, 1974.

HEMINGBROUGH

THE EXTENSIVE ancient parish of Hemingbrough occupies the southern end of the wapentake, bounded by the winding course of the Ouse on the south and west and by that of the Derwent on the east.[1] Its dimensions are in places five miles by four, and its total area in 1850 was 10,847 a.[2] The parish included a dozen villages and hamlets, one of which, Barlby in the extreme west, was a chapelry which achieved independence from the mother-church in the 18th century. In the 20th century part of Barlby has become in effect an industrial suburb of Selby, across the Ouse in the West Riding. Six of the hamlets are now so shrunken as to be virtually depopulated settlements, though none of them was ever very large. Since 1883 the parish has also included Newhay,[3] a former grange of Drax priory (Yorks. W.R.), which occupied ground that had lain south of the Ouse until the river changed its course in the early Middle Ages.

Most of the parish is covered by the typical outwash sand, gravel, and clay of the Vale of York, and it is on those deposits that its villages and hamlets are sited. It is nevertheless only in places, and especially towards the west of the parish, that the land exceeds 25 ft. above sea-level. Lying still lower is a belt of alluvium that stretches around the margins of the parish beside the Ouse and the Derwent.[4] Hemingbrough is thus devoid of marked natural topographical features, and the pattern of settlement and land utilization depends upon subtle variations in relief and soils.

The village of Hemingbrough and its various subordinate settlements were formed into seven civil parishes in the 19th century. This arrangement was, however, changed in 1935. Barlby and Osgodby civil parishes were then combined as Barlby civil parish; most of Cliffe with Lund and most of South Duffield civil parishes were combined as Cliffe civil parish; Hemingbrough and Brackenholme with Woodhall civil parishes, together with 29 a. from Cliffe with Lund and 130 a. from neighbouring Barmby on the Marsh, were combined as Hemingbrough civil parish; Menthorpe with Bowthorpe civil parish was added to neighbouring North Duffield; and 5 a. of South Duffield were transferred to neighbouring Wressle.[5] In this account Hemingbrough itself is described first, followed by the other townships according to the earlier arrangement of civil parishes.

HEMINGBROUGH

The village of Hemingbrough lies close to the river Ouse, about 13 miles south-east of York. The church and no doubt the rest of the early settlement stood on a small area of higher ground approaching the river bank, but the village later extended along a main street running parallel with the river. It was perhaps during the early Middle Ages that the Ouse cut a shorter course at this point across the neck of a wide meander. The old course was abandoned and Hemingbrough subsequently lost the advantages of a riverside site, the river now passing 500 yd. from the southern end of the village. Ancient use of the site is testified by the discovery of Romano-British remains,[6] and it was presumably the firm ground overlooking the river which attracted the later settlement, a 'stronghold' that may have been either Anglian or Scandinavian.[7] The township covered 1,141 a.[8]

Apart from the slightly higher ground at the village site, and an even smaller area just north of the village, the whole of the township lies at less than 25 ft. above sea-level. South of the village the belt of riverside alluvium broadens towards the confluence of the Ouse and the Derwent. The township boundary on the south and west follows the rivers, including the old course of the Ouse, but elsewhere it makes little use of natural features. The relatively small areas of open-field land lay close to the village, with meadows towards the river and extensive early inclosures from woodland in the north of the township. The remaining open fields were inclosed in 1844.

The chief roads in Hemingbrough are those leading north-westwards to Cliffe and eastwards towards Howden. Hagg Lane leads to South Duffield and another minor road to a former ferry crossing the Derwent to Barmby on the Marsh. In the 20th century the Cliffe and Howden roads, together with the streets of Hemingbrough village, became part of the Hull–Selby trunk road, and a bypass around the north-east side of the village was among the many alterations to the road made in the late 1920s.[9] The Derwent ferry, belonging to the prior of Durham as lord of the manor, was mentioned in 1330 and frequently in the 15th century.[10] It survived into the twentieth.[11] Another ferry, across the Ouse, was worked from a farm-house south of the village c. 1930.[12] In 1850 the old course of the Ouse was followed by a track known as Old Ways Lane,[13] but this has since ceased to exist. The Hull–Selby railway line, opened in 1840,[14] crosses the north of the township.

Most of the older village houses lie along the closely-built-up Town Street, their garths stretching back to the 'old' Ouse on the west and to Back and Garth Ends Lanes on the east. Town Street and the back lanes are connected at the north and south ends of the village and also in the centre, near the church,

---

[1] This article was written in 1973.
[2] O.S. Map 6" (1854 edn.).
[3] Bulmer, *Dir. E. Yorks.* (1892), 626.
[4] Geol. Surv. Map 1", solid and drift, sheet 71 (1973 edn.); drift, sheet 79 (1973 edn.).
[5] *Census*, 1931.
[6] *Y.A.J.* xli. 7.
[7] *P.N.E.R. Yorks.* (E.P.N.S.), 260–1.
[8] O.S. Map 6", Yorks. (1854 edn.). The whole township is on sheet 222.
[9] e.g. E.R.C.C. *Mins.* 1928–9, 237; 1929–30, 389; R.D.B., 358/563/459.
[10] Prior's Kitchen, Durham, D. & C. Muniments, 3. 2. Ebor. 42; chamberlains' accts., e.g. 1450–1(A).
[11] O.S. Map 6" (1958 edn.).
[12] Local information.
[13] O.S. Map 6" (1854 edn.).
[14] *V.C.H. Yorks. E.R.* i. 392.

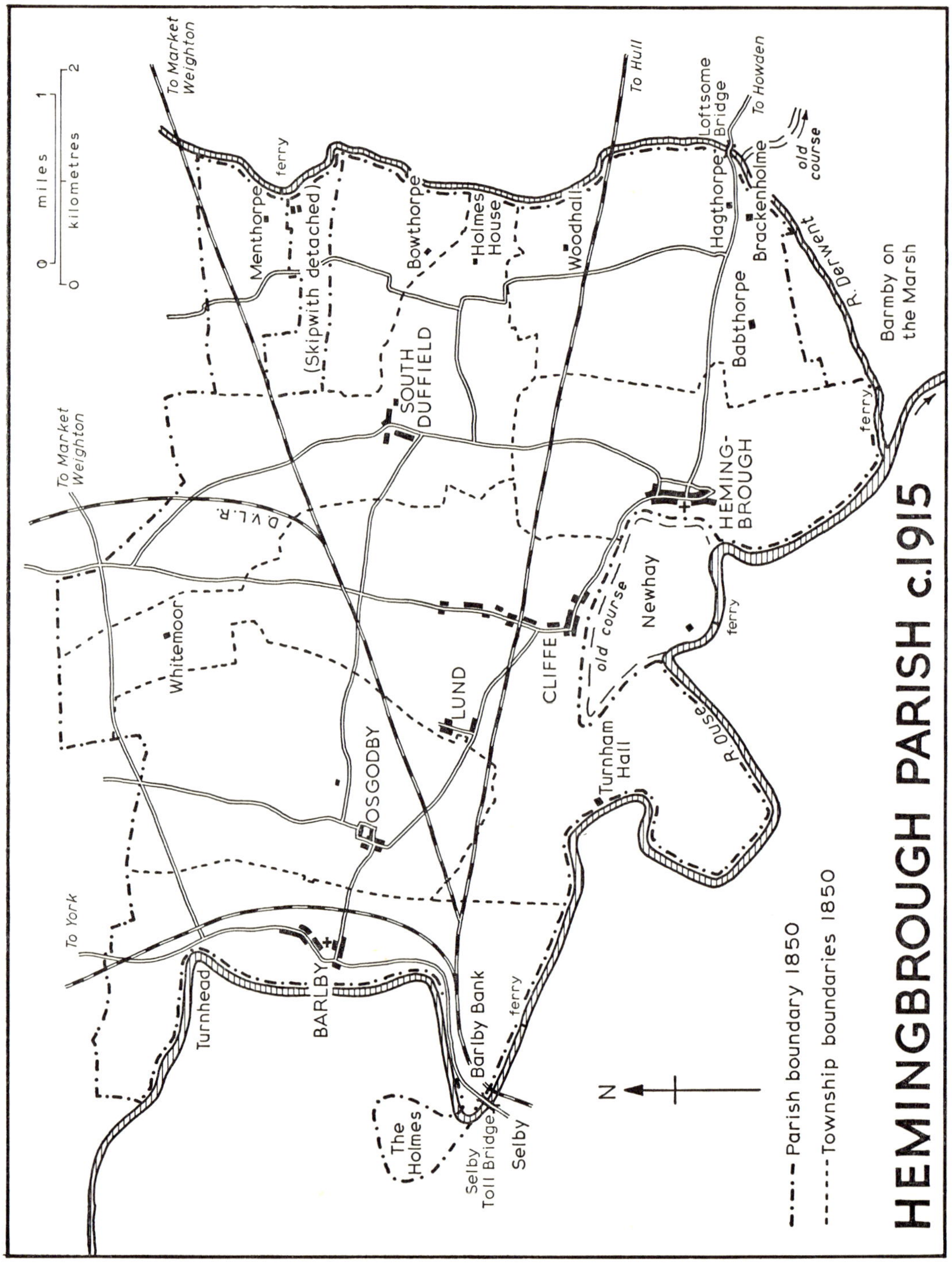
HEMINGBROUGH PARISH c.1915
Parish boundary 1850
Township boundaries 1850
miles
kilometres
To Market Weighton
To Hull
To Howden
Loftsome Bridge
old course
Hagthorpe
Brackenholme
R. Derwent
Barmby on the Marsh
Babthorpe
Woodhall
Holmes House
Bowthorpe
Menthorpe
ferry
(Skipwith detached)
SOUTH DUFFIELD
HEMING-BROUGH
D.V.L.R.
Newhay
Whitemoor
CLIFFE
LUND
OSGODBY
Turnham Hall
R. Ouse
To York
Turnhead
BARLBY
Barlby Bank
The Holmes
Selby Toll Bridge
Selby
N

by the old Howden road, known as Finkle Street where it leaves the village. Many of the houses in Town Street are 18th-century in date, most being of brown brick, two storeys high, and with marked plat bands, brick cornices, and projecting kneelers. Three are dated, the Hollies with 1763 inscribed on a keystone, Hoton House with 1751 on a kneeler, and a farm-house in the south of the village with wrought-iron tie-rod anchors for 1754. One later-18th-century house, sometimes known as the Old Hall, has a pretentious elevation with the centre bay recessed, raised an extra storey, and surmounted by a pediment. Most of the larger 19th-century houses are in the streets running east from Town Street; they include Manor Farm, which probably incorporates an earlier building, the Chase, the Cottage, the Villa, Hemingbrough Hall, and the former Vicarage.[15] Smaller 19th-century houses occur in Town Street but it was not until the present century that general development spread into the back lanes; in recent years there has been much new building, including 30 council houses, particularly towards the south and east. The few isolated farm-houses include Wood House in the north of the township and Hemingbrough Grange to the south of the village.

The house eventually known as Hemingbrough Hall was built in 1842 by John Ion, vicar (d. 1860), as his own residence; it was at first called Hemingbrough Villa.[16] The estate passed to Ion's daughter Jane, who married C. G. Tate, and the house was occupied by tenants, William Banks, owner of the Babthorpe estate, living there from 1874 until c. 1930.[17] It was sold to Fred Wright in 1938 and to George Carr in 1952.[18] It is a large red-brick house, designed in the Tudor style by Weightman & Hatfield of Sheffield.[19]

There were between three and five licensed alehouses in the village in the later 19th century,[20] and in 1823 the inns were known as the Britannia, the Dog, and the Half Moon.[21] The Dog became the Dog and Duck by 1840 and the Crown by 1872;[22] together with the Britannia it still existed in 1973. The Half Moon apparently closed c. 1910.[23]

In 1379 there were more than 150 poll-tax payers in Hemingbrough.[24] The villagers were granted relief in 1591 after a fire.[25] Fifty-nine households in the township were included in the hearth-tax return in 1672, six of them exempt. Of those chargeable, 26 had one hearth each, 17 had 2, 9 had 3 to 5, and one had nine.[26] In the whole parish there were about 300 families in 1743 and about 200 in 1764.[27] The population of Hemingbrough township in 1801 was 387; it fluctuated for the rest of the century, reaching a peak of 580 in 1871 and standing at 498 in 1901.[28]

Numbers increased to 531 in 1931 and, after the inclusion of Brackenholme with Woodhall in the civil parish,[29] to 647 in 1951 and 748 in 1971.[30]

MANOR AND OTHER ESTATES. Hemingbrough was at first described in Domesday as belonging to the king, but it was given by William I to the bishop of Durham in 1086–7[31] and the Domesday Summary showed it as the bishop's property. There were 3 carucates there in 1086, which Tosti had held before the Conquest.[32] The manor of *HEMINGBROUGH* was assigned by the bishop to Durham priory, and the manor and mill were worth about £39 just before the Dissolution. Land in Brackenholme, which had all along formed part of the manor, contributed some £2 to that total.[33]

For unexplained reasons Hemingbrough did not form part of the Durham chapter endowment after the dissolution of the priory, but was kept in hand until it was granted to Sir Arthur Ingram and Martin Freeman in 1614.[34] It belonged to the Ingrams until the death of another Arthur in 1742,[35] when it passed to his daughter Isabella, who married Col., later Gen., George Cary (d. 1792).[36] Hemingbrough passed to Gen. Cary's daughters Elizabeth, who married Sir Jeffery Amherst, and Catherine, later wife of Sir John Russell. They conveyed it in 1802 to Thomas Hartley, Richard Hobson, Thomas Smith, John Tweedy, and Thomas Wilson, who represented the York bankers Wilson & Tweedy.[37] In 1822 the manor was held in undivided twentieths, five by the devisees of Hartley, four by Smith's devisees, five by Tweedy, and six by Wilson.[38]

The Smith share belonged to T. R. Smith in 1897, when it was described as $\frac{8}{40}$, and it was subsequently held by trustees.[39] The Tweedy share, described as $\frac{15}{40}$ and including half of the Hartley share, passed to John's daughter Sophia, who married James Graham in 1843. They conveyed it that year to William and Joseph Earle, and in 1857 it passed to trustees, one of whom was H. J. Ware, a York solicitor.[40] The Wilson share, described as $\frac{17}{40}$ and including the other half of the Hartley share, belonged to T. W. Wilson in 1853.[41] It was sold in 1873 and five years later was acquired by H. J. Ware.[42] Ware died in 1902 and his trustees conveyed his $\frac{32}{40}$ of the manor in 1921 to William Ware (d. 1942).[43]

Before and after the Dissolution the lands in the manor had been held by copyholders and freeholders, and consequently no land was attached to the modern manor. None of the lesser estates has been very large.

[15] See p. 43.
[16] T. Burton, *Hist. Hemingbrough*, 124; Sheahan and Whellan, *Hist. York & E.R.* ii. 622.
[17] E.R.R.O., DDBH/9/2; H.U.L., DTT/1/38, 53–5, 60; directories; see p. 53.
[18] R.D.B., 589/254/199; 917/2/2.
[19] Burton, *Hemingbrough*, 124.
[20] E.R.R.O., QDT/2/15.
[21] Baines, *Hist. Yorks.* ii. 216–17.
[22] White, *Dir. E. & N.R. Yorks.* (1840), 331; *Kelly's Dir. N. & E.R. Yorks.* (1872), 374; O.S. Map 6" (1854 edn.).
[23] *Kelly's Dir. N. & E.R. Yorks.* (1909), 524; (1913), 545.
[24] *T.E.R.A.S.* xv. 33–5. There is no return for 1377.
[25] *Cal. S.P. Dom.* 1591–4, 147.
[26] E 179/205/504.
[27] B.I.H.R., Bp. V. 1764/Ret. 24; *Herring's Visit.* ii. 66.
[28] *V.C.H. Yorks.* iii. 498.

[29] The area added from Barmby had no population.
[30] *Census.*
[31] *E.Y.C.* ii, pp. 302–3, 316.
[32] *V.C.H. Yorks.* ii. 153, 196, 319.
[33] *Valor Eccl.* (Rec. Com.) v. 301.
[34] C 66/1985 no [1 from end].
[35] Burton, *Hemingbrough*, 154–5. For the Ingrams see J. Foster, *Pedigrees of ... Yorks.* i.
[36] Burton, *Hemingbrough*, 155–6.
[37] R.D.B., CC/442/662; CF/58/92.
[38] Burton, *Hemingbrough*, 157.
[39] R.D.B., 93/425/407 (1897); 214/368/308.
[40] Ibid. FU/292/328; FX/95/118; HQ/398/458; /399/459.
[41] Ibid. HC/302/379.
[42] Ibid. LE/92/133; MO/420/640; 60/538/484 (1900).
[43] Ibid. 43/164/148 (1902); 240/43/34; 768/362/307.

A small estate in Hemingbrough belonged to the guild of St. Christopher and St. George, York, and after the suppression was granted by the Crown to York corporation in 1549.[44]

From 1427 the income of Hemingbrough church, derived largely from tithes, belonged to the college established there that year.[45] The income subsequently fell,[46] and a new ordination of the college in 1479 reduced the stipends of the staff.[47] In 1535 the college was worth about £84 gross.[48] After the Dissolution various leases were made of rectorial tithes in the several townships, the chief being those to Christopher Salmon in 1548[49] and Sir William Babthorpe in 1571 and later.[50] In 1611 tithes in most of the townships were granted in fee to Francis Morrice and Francis Philips,[51] but they passed to the Ingrams before 1650 and thereafter descended with Hemingbrough manor. In 1650 the total value was £270, of which Hemingbrough township contributed £50.[52] Most of these tithes were still held with the manor when they were commuted in the early 19th century. Those in Hemingbrough township were commuted in 1841 for rent-charges totalling £295 payable to Thomas Wilson's devisees, John Tweedy, and Thomas Smith (d. 1841).[53]

The provosts of Hemingbrough college apparently lived after 1427 in a building later called Prior House, standing in Hall garth, on the south side of the church.[54] After the suppression of the college it was granted in 1554, along with 30 a. called 'the glebe lands', to Joan and John Constable.[55] The house eventually passed in 1662 to Sir Jeremiah Smith; it is said to have been demolished in 1697 and the materials used to rebuild Osgodby Hall.[56] It had nine hearths in 1672.[57] The Constables were also granted in 1554 the former bedern of the vicars of the college,[58] which perhaps stood near the provost's house.[59]

ECONOMIC HISTORY. In 1086 the 3 carucates comprising Hemingbrough afforded land for two ploughs worked by five villeins and three bordars. There were also 7 a. of meadow, and pasturable woodland ½ league in length and breadth. The value of the estate had fallen from £2 before the Conquest to 16s. at the time of the Survey.[60] It was later reckoned that, of the 3 carucates, 245 a. were 'old bovates' held in bondage (*antique bovate de antiquo bondagio*) and 115 a. were demesne bovates tilled by the same tenants. For all the land the bondmen paid rent of 2d. an acre and owed merchet, both before the Conquest to Tostig and afterwards to the king. After the manor was given to Durham priory, however, the bondmen's services were said to have been commuted; thereafter they paid 8d. or 1s. for each 'old bovate', together with 1d. in lieu of services, and 9d. or 1s. for each demesne bovate.[61]

The extent of the 'old' and demesne bovates together remained unchanged in the 14th and early 15th centuries, though in 1330 their respective acreages were given as 270 and 90.[62] They were presumably cultivated in common and formed the open-field land of the township, though no 'field' names were recorded until later. Beyond this old arable nucleus the priory had by 1330 reclaimed a further 400 a. of land. Of this about 250 a. lay in various named places and was described in 1430 as 'newly broken up'; several 'assarts' and 'riddings' were among the names. In 1330 the new land was held in small parcels by numerous tenants and some of it undoubtedly became part of the open fields in due course. Other parts of it, however, were eventually held in severalty and contributed to a large acreage of old inclosures in the township. The latter include the modern Haw closes,[63] which probably represent the 40-acre 'Hawe' of 1330. The assarted land was held at 8d. or 9d. an acre; in addition there still remained about 90 a. in Hemingbrough wood, also held in small parcels, but at a rent of 6d. an acre. A further 53 a. was held by the priest of the Waise chantry and was described in 1330 as waste.[64]

About 80 tenants were recorded in 1330, of whom 43 held 9 a. or less, 21 held 10–19 a., and 9 held 20 a. or more; the largest holding was about 45 a. Other tenants held the Derwent ferry, the mill, a stall or shop (*selda*), and the tolls on brewers.[65] There was no specific mention of fairs or a market, though in 1295 the priory had been granted a Thursday market and a fair on 14–21 August. The total rental of 1330 was over £34, together with nearly £1 from payments in lieu of 'works'.[66] The profits of the manor were accounted for at Durham by the chamberlain of the priory. In the later 14th century he was charged with rents of about £41 or £42 from Hemingbrough and Brackenholme, as well as over £1 for autumn works. In the 15th and early 16th centuries, however, the 'decay and waste' often amounted to £5 or £6 and included part or all of the rent due from the mill, ferry, and fisheries. The toll-house and a shop under it were several times mentioned in the chamberlains' accounts.[67]

In 1529, when John West's land in the township was used to endow a chantry,[68] the open-field land still lay in many different places. The first mention of fields reveals the existence of Water, Near Water, Uttermore Water, Chapel, Mill, and North fields, but West also had many parcels of land elsewhere.

---

[44] *Cal. Pat.* 1549–51, 31.
[45] See p. 42.
[46] Prior's Kitchen, D. & C. Muniments, M.C. 5701 (3–6), 6645 (provost's accts).
[47] *V.C.H. Yorks.* iii. 359.
[48] *Valor Eccl.* v. 139.
[49] Burton, *Hemingbrough*, 153.
[50] H.U.L., DRA/746; *Cal. Pat.* 1569–72, p. 173. For other leases see *Cal. Pat.* 1563–6, pp. 186–7; Burton, *Hemingbrough*, 153–4.
[51] C 66/1967 no. 2.
[52] C 94/3 f. 77.
[53] B.I.H.R., TA. 446S.
[54] Burton, *Hemingbrough*, 74; O.S. Map 6" (1854 edn.). There is no evidence to support Burton's suggestion that it had formerly been the rector's house.
[55] *Cal. Pat.* 1553–4, 146.
[56] Burton, *Hemingbrough*, 74–5; see below p. 65.
[57] E 179/205/504.
[58] For the bedern see Burton, *Hemingbrough*, 84–6.
[59] See pp. 42–3.
[60] *V.C.H. Yorks.* ii. 196.
[61] Prior's Kitchen, D. & C. Muniments, Cart. III f. 32v. (an 'extract of old muniments and rentals' compiled in 1430 by the chancellor of the priory). A transcript of the document in Burton, *Hemingbrough*, 388–9 contains some inaccuracies.
[62] Prior's Kitchen, D. & C. Muniments, 3. 2. Ebor. 42 (1330 rental); Cart. III f. 32v. (1430 extract).
[63] O.S. Map 6" (various edns.).
[64] See p. 43.
[65] *Cal. Chart. R.* 1257–1300, 457.
[66] Prior's Kitchen, D. & C. Muniments, 3. 2. Ebor. 42.
[67] Ibid. chamberlains' accts., *passim*. Some transcripts and extracts are printed in *Acct. Rolls of Abbey of Durham*, i (Sur. Soc. xcix), 168–97.
[68] See p. 43.

Some of the names, like Best plat, Grantacres, the Carrs, Worthorp, and Mortilcroft, had been in the list of assarted lands in 1330. Other arable parcels lay in Harstones in North field and in Somergangs, and there was meadow in Cow ings and 'between dikes'. There were 12 a. of inclosed pasture.[69] It is not clear whether all of the woodland had been cleared by the 16th century. John West had a small parcel 'in Hemingbrough wood', but among the former chantry property in 1553 was pasture called Hemingbrough wood.[70] Wood closes were mentioned in 1668.[71] The former wooded character of the north-east corner of the township is still recalled by the names Hagg Lane and Wood House.

There were apparently no large-scale changes in land use in the township during the 18th century and no revival of the medieval market and fair. A shop which may have been that forming part of the toll-house was granted away by the Crown, separately from the manor, in 1613–14. It may have been the building in the middle of the main street later used as a smithy which was ordered to be removed in 1780. The former fair was succeeded by a village feast, held at about the same time in August, but c. 1780 it was moved to the end of June to avoid harvest time.[72]

In 1841, just before final inclosure, the township comprised 867 a. of arable land, 173 a. of meadow and pasture, 35 a. of wood and waste, and 18 a. of orchards and gardens.[73] The remaining commonable lands were inclosed in 1844 under the general Inclosure Act of 1836.[74] There were found to be 540 a. to deal with, and allotments totalling 517 a. were made. The open fields and meadows were still much fragmented, comprising Chapel field (where allotments of 92 a. were made), Hawse field (13 a.), Mill field (36 a.), Myrtle Croft field (17 a.), Carr field (33 a.), Hearthstone field (7 a.), Between Dikes field (17 a.), Best Plot field (9 a.), North field (46 a.), Old Rudding field (57 a.), the Cringle (6 a.), Stork piece (2 a.), Common Wood field (18 a.), Far field (39 a.), Water field (32 a.), Hornham field (10 a.), Grant Acre field (18 a.), the Marsh (7 a.), and Little Toft field (5 a.); allotments totalling 50 a. were made from more than one area. The 'untilled slips or balks' in the fields had previously been used by the parish officers, who were accordingly allotted 3 a. of Ouse foreshore. There were 3 allotments of 50–99 a., 7 of 10–49 a., and 53 of under 10 a. After inclosure some roadside verges continued to be used in common by the inhabitants: in 1895 47 people were said to have 73 common rights in Hagg Lane, Old Ways, and elsewhere.[75]

By 1851 few larger farms had been created: there was then one of 200 a. and two of 100–200 a.[76] There were still only four farms of 150 a. or more c. 1930. The total number of farms in the later 19th and early 20th centuries was usually 12 to 15; in addition half-a-dozen market-gardeners were recorded from the 1870s onwards and a similar number of smallholders after 1920.[77] The smallholdings were the result of the acquisition of land for the purpose in Hemingbrough and Brackenholme by the East Riding county council.[78] Land use was still varied in character in the 1930s and later, though arable predominated in the south of the township and grassland in the north.[79]

In the Middle Ages the manor enjoyed a fishery in the Ouse which brought the priory into conflict with the city of York because fish garths obstructed navigation.[80] The fishery continued to be appurtenant to the manor after the Dissolution, and a few men made a livelihood from fishing in later centuries. Two Hemingbrough fishermen were mentioned in 1779,[81] for example, one in 1851,[82] and one in 1892.[83] There was a landing-place ½ mile south of the village by 1841[84] and 4 a. there were allotted for the purpose at inclosure in 1844. By a Scheme of 1955 it was constituted a charity for the general benefit of the inhabitants. The land was sold in 1956, and in 1972–3 the income of £10 from £181 stock was handed over to the parish council.[85]

Medieval river traffic may have given employment to a few Hemingbrough men: a mercer and a merchant were mentioned in 1379, for example, and there were also two weavers at that date.[86] Subsequently few men seem to have followed other than agricultural occupations or the usual village crafts and trades. A glover and a tanner were mentioned in 1624,[87] however, and a tanner in 1769.[88] Bricks have long been made at sites north of the village. A string of ponds along Hagg Lane in 1850 was probably the result of digging for clay, and a brick and tile yard already stood near the Cliffe road where it has been worked ever since;[89] only drainage tiles were being made in 1973.

The manorial windmill at Hemingbrough was mentioned in 1276–7[90] and repairs to it were frequently recorded in the Middle Ages.[91] It was granted away by the Crown separately from the manor in 1609–10 and was frequently recorded thereafter, often in the tenancy of the Howdell family who eventually bought it in 1730.[92] It was a post mill in 1892.[93] A miller was last mentioned in 1913[94] and the mill, which stood just to the south of the village, had been demolished by 1973.

LOCAL GOVERNMENT. Various disputes arose in the Middle Ages from the fact that Hemingbrough was deemed ancient demesne of the Crown. In 1291–2, for example, certain tenants alleged that the

[69] Prior's Kitchen, D. & C. Muniments, M.C. 6650.
[70] *Cal. Pat.* 1553, 22.
[71] E.R.R.O., DDHV/17/2.
[72] Burton, *Hemingbrough*, 149.
[73] B.I.H.R., TA. 410S.
[74] E.R.R.O., Enrolment Bk. H, pp. 57 sqq.
[75] Ibid. DDTR/Box 9 (uncalendared).
[76] H.O. 107/2358.
[77] Directories.
[78] e.g. see p. 53.
[79] [1st] Land Util. Surv. Map, sheet 32; 2nd Land Util. Surv. Map, sheet 689 (SE 63–73).
[80] Prior's Kitchen, D. & C. Muniments, chamberlains' accts., e.g. 1362–3, 1372–3.
[81] E.R.R.O., QSF. East. 1779, C. 20.
[82] H.O. 107/2358.
[83] Bulmer, *Dir. E. Yorks.* (1892), 633.
[84] e.g. B.I.H.R., TA. 446S; O.S. Map 6" (all edns.).
[85] Char. Com. files.
[86] *T.E.R.A.S.* xv. 33–5.
[87] Burton, *Hemingbrough*, 139.
[88] E.R.R.O., DDX/31/138.
[89] O.S. Map 6" (1854 edn.); directories.
[90] *Durham Annals and Documents of the 13th Cent.* (Sur. Soc. clv), 185.
[91] Prior's Kitchen, D. & C. Muniments, chamberlains' accts., e.g. 1372–3, 1521–2.
[92] Burton, *Hemingbrough*, 160–1.
[93] Bulmer, *Dir. E. Yorks.* (1892), 633.
[94] *Kelly's Dir. N. & E.R. Yorks.* (1913), 545.

prior of Durham, as lord of the manor, was not entitled to change their customs and services, as he had done.[95] In the same year the sheriff apparently upheld a claim that the prior owed suit to his tourns at York, despite the prior's claim that he enjoyed exemption because his own court at Hemingbrough was in ancient demesne.[96] In 1345 several tenants unsuccessfully contested that the prior should not have sued them in the 'assize' court at York but should have taken the matter to the manorial court, again because of the ancient demesne privileges. Prior and tenants were united in 1430 in opposing the practice of summoning Hemingbrough people to the bishop of Durham's court at Howden.[97] As tenants in ancient demesne the men of Hemingbrough considered themselves exempt from the payment of tolls, and in 1476 the sheriff was ordered not to distrain upon them for non-payment.[98] That and other privileges were confirmed to Hemingbrough by the king in 1626.[99]

Surviving court books for the period 1816–1935[1] are entirely concerned with surrenders and admissions.

There are surviving churchwardens' accounts for 1715–1878 which show that all the townships, including Barlby, were assessed to the Hemingbrough rates. There were commonly two churchwardens for Hemingbrough, two for Cliffe with Lund, and one each for Barlby, South Duffield, Osgodby, and Brackenholme, Woodhall, Menthorpe, and Bowthorpe combined.[2] Hemingbrough joined Howden poor-law union in 1837[3] and the nine former poorhouses in the main street were sold by the union in 1866.[4] The township became part of Howden rural district in 1894, Derwent rural district in 1935,[5] and the Selby district of North Yorkshire in 1974.

CHURCH. A church was recorded at Hemingbrough in 1086.[6] It was given with the manor to the bishop of Durham soon afterwards and assigned by him to Durham priory.[7] The rectory was a valuable one but the priory received from it only a pension of 5 marks.[8] Consequently attempts were made in the 14th century to appropriate the church, but papal sanction could not be obtained.[9] Instead the church was made collegiate in 1427, with a staff comprising a provost, having cure of souls in the parish, three prebendaries, six vicars, and six clerks.[10] A pension of 5 marks continued to be received by the priory.[11] Hemingbrough remained in the peculiar jurisdiction of the priory until the Dissolution.[12] The college was suppressed in 1545 and the church eventually became a vicarage.

The patronage of the rectory and the college belonged to Durham until the suppression,[13] and subsequently the Crown presented to the vicarage.[14] A grant of the advowson to the archbishop of York in 1558[15] presumably lapsed on the accession of Elizabeth I. In 1898 the advowson passed from the Crown to the archbishop by exchange.[16]

The living was said by the archbishop in 1290–1 to be worth £166 13s. 4d.[17] but the church was valued at £110 in the *Taxatio* of that year.[18] After 1427 part of the income may have been set aside for the college vicars serving the parish on the provost's behalf. Thus in 1442–3 the provost was discharged from accounting for sales of bread ('halibredesilver') because the parish priests claimed them;[19] and in 1535 the 'vicarage' was said to be worth £5 7s. 0½d. net.[20] Provision was later made for rectorial lessees to pay £6 13s. 4d. each to a vicar and two assistant curates.[21] A stipend of £20 a year was allowed to the minister by the impropriators in 1650[22] and later.[23] Parliamentary grants of £200 and £1,600 were received in 1810 and 1814, respectively,[24] and the average net income of the living in 1829–31 was £85 a year.[25] Hemingbrough was endowed from the Common Fund with £500 in 1862, £10 a year in 1881, and £13 6s. 8d. also in 1881.[26] The net income in 1914 was £178.[27]

Besides his stipend and fees and offerings the vicar in the 18th century received bequests for three anniversary sermons, left by Robert Allen, William Baxter, and Thomas Steele.[28] There was no glebe land until 1827, when the parliamentary grants were used to buy 37 a. in Hemingbrough;[29] they still belonged to the vicarage in 1973.[30]

A parsonage house may have existed in 1324.[31] The rector may for a time have lived in a house called the Stackgarth, which he rented from Durham priory in 1402–3.[32] The Stackgarth had in 1339 been assigned by the priory to the priests of the Cliffe chantry, then in course of foundation, and it lay opposite the church next to the Brackenholme road.[33] The chantry-priests apparently did not use it, however, and after the provost of the college assumed the duties of the former rectors in 1427 the

[95] Burton, *Hemingbrough*, 147–8.
[96] Ibid. 148.
[97] Ibid. 149–50.
[98] *Cal. Pat.* 1467–77, 600.
[99] B.I.H.R., PR. HEM. 39; E.R.R.O., DDX/31/397.
[1] B.I.H.R., Ware 1.
[2] Ibid. PR. HEM. 25–6.
[3] *3rd Rep. Poor Law Com.* 168.
[4] R.D.B., IY/167/238; O.S. Map 6" (1854 edn.).
[5] *Census.*
[6] *V.C.H. Yorks.* ii. 196.
[7] See p. 39.
[8] Prior's Kitchen, D. & C. Muniments, chamberlain's charty., f. 5; *Reg. Gray*, p. 154; *Tax. Eccl.* (Rec. Com.), 336.
[9] R. B. Dobson, *Durham Priory, 1400–1450*, 156–62.
[10] *V.C.H. Yorks.* iii. 359.
[11] Prior's Kitchen, D. & C. Muniments, chamberlains' accts., e.g. 1450–1 (A).
[12] *V.C.H. Yorks.* iii. 86.
[13] e.g. *Reg. Giffard*, i, pp. 30, 57; *Reg. Romeyn*, ii, p. 34; *Cal. Papal Regs.* iv. 222.
[14] e.g. Inst. Bks.
[15] *Cal. Pat.* 1557–8, 420.
[16] York Dioc. Regy., Order in Council 415.
[17] Burton, *Hemingbrough*, 49.
[18] *Tax. Eccl.* 302, 336.
[19] Prior's Kitchen, D. & C. Muniments, M.C. 6645.
[20] *Valor Eccl.* v. 145.
[21] Burton, *Hemingbrough*, 102.
[22] C 94/3 f. 77. For the descent of the rectory see p. 40.
[23] B.I.H.R., TER. N. Hemingbrough 1716 etc.
[24] Hodgson, *Q.A.B.* 442.
[25] *Rep. Com. Eccl. Revenues*, 940.
[26] *Lond. Gaz.* 5 Sept. 1862, p. 4366; 13 May 1881, p. 2499; 8 July 1881, p. 3407.
[27] B.I.H.R., Bp. V. 1914/Ret. There is no return to the visitation of 1884.
[28] Ibid. TER. N. Hemingbrough 1716, 1749; charity list in church; Burton, *Hemingbrough*, 140.
[29] B.I.H.R., TER. N. Hemingbrough 1853.
[30] Ex inf. the vicar, 1974.
[31] Burton, *Hemingbrough*, 74.
[32] Prior's Kitchen, D. & C. Muniments, chamberlain's acct.
[33] Ibid. chamberlain's charty., ff. 6d.–8v. For the chantry see below.

priory frequently had no tenants for the Stackgarth.[34] The suggestion that it was used as the bedern of the vicars of the college cannot be substantiated.[35] After the Dissolution nothing is known of the parish priests' place of residence until 1707, when the former Stackgarth was conveyed to trustees for the incumbent's benefit. It was enlarged at the vicar's expense in the mid 18th century but in 1786, when the vicar was non-resident, the house was let to the petty school master. It was partly rebuilt by the vicar in 1794 and repaired by his successor, John Ion, in 1826.[36] In 1842, however, Ion built Hemingbrough Villa for his own residence[37] and the need for a house belonging to the living was eventually met in 1862, when a large Vicarage was erected on the Howden road east of the village.[38] A new Vicarage was built on the Selby road in 1973,[39] when the 1862 house was known as the Hermitage.

The former Vicarage near the church provided income for the vicar after its disuse. Part of the site was sold in 1854 and the house itself in 1908, and the Old Vicarage Charity had £240 stock in 1938.[40]

There were four chantries in the church. The Waise chantry was founded by Robert de marisco, rector 1217–18 to 1258, and its establishment by his executors was confirmed by the archbishop in 1274. The endowments comprised a toft near the church, 13 a. of arable and 40 a. of waste in Hemingbrough, about 13 a. in Newhay, and a meadow called Mekelcroft. The chantry is said to have acquired its name from the fact that the toft lay near the Waise or old course of the Ouse.[41] The chantry was dedicated to St. Catherine. It was worth £6 13s. 4d. in 1535.[42] Much of the property of this and the other chantries was granted by the Crown in 1553 to John Witherington and Cuthbert Musgrave.[43]

The Cliffe chantry was founded by the executors of Henry of Cliffe (d. 1332), who devised the residue of his estate to support a chantry in Drax priory. It was nevertheless established, in 1345, in the parish church and was endowed with 2 houses, a mill, and 50 a. of land in Newhay and Rusholme (in Drax), and 7 cottages, 3½ bovates, and about 22 a. in Hemingbrough. There were to be two chantry-priests, and the chantry was to be at St. Mary's altar.[44] The chantry property, lying in Hemingbrough, Newhay, Lund, Woodhall, Brackenholme, and South Duffield, was worth £6 10s. in 1535.[45] The Babthorpe chantry, at the Trinity altar, is named after Thomas Babthorpe, who by will dated 1478 bequeathed a vestment to a chaplain who should celebrate there.[46] The West chantry was founded in 1529 by the executors of John West, incumbent of the Cliffe chantry, at St. Mary's altar.[47] Its property, lying in Hemingbrough, Newhay, Brackenholme, and Woodhall, was worth £7 6s. 8d. in 1535.[48]

Miracles were said to be wrought in the church in 1393, when penance for those attending at the Assumption was relaxed.[49] Statues in the church included those of St. Cuthbert (mentioned in 1348), St. Mary of Pity (1410), and St. Chad (1453).[50] A chapel of some kind apparently stood to the east of the village on the Howden road.[51] Chapel field, which took its name from it, was mentioned in 1529.[52] The chapel was perhaps suppressed in the 16th century and it was later used as a dwelling: a man 'of the chapel at the Chapel field' was mentioned in 1636.[53] Land was described in 1713 as 'abutting against the chapel'.[54]

The wealthy living was held by several eminent rectors before 1427, some of whom were non-resident and enjoyed other livings also.[55] Robert de marisco, rector 1217–18 to 1258, became dean of Lincoln in 1258. Richard of Middleton was the king's chancellor, and in 1270 he had a gift of fish from the royal fishpond of the Foss at York to stock his pond at Hemingbrough.[56] Hugh of Evesham, rector 1272–87, was a prebendary of York and a member of the Sacred College. Bogo of Clare (1287–94) was treasurer and prebendary at York, dean of Stafford, and the holder of many rich livings. John of Droxford (1294–1309) became bishop of Bath and Wells in 1309 and was chancellor of the Exchequer in 1307–16.[57] Stephen de Mauley (1309–17) was a prebendary of York and dean of Wimborne and Auckland. Joscelin d'Ossat (c. 1317–48) became cardinal bishop of Alba. Thomas of Walworth (1375–1409) was a prebendary of York and master of St. Nicholas's hospital there. John Rickinghall (1413–26) held offices at York minster, was chancellor of the university of Cambridge, and became bishop of Chichester in 1426.

After the suppression of the college at least two curates apparently served the cure together in the 16th and early 17th centuries. There seems to have been no regular incumbent during the Interregnum,[58] but the ministers at that time may have included Anthony Fido, who is said to have been ejected in 1662.[59] Thomas Revell, incumbent 1670–7, was described as vicar at his death.[60] In the 18th century several vicars held other livings. William Potter the younger, vicar 1769–79, for example, was also vicar of Brayton (Yorks. W.R.), and John Mallinson, vicar 1779–93, lived at Howden and held several curacies round about.[61] John Ion, vicar 1825–60, held Halsham vicarage.[62] The only

[34] Ibid. chamberlains' accts., 1475–6 etc.
[35] Burton, *Hemingbrough*, 86.
[36] B.I.H.R., PR. HEM. 25 (s.v. 1794); Burton, *Hemingbrough*, 86–7, 115–19, 122–3.
[37] See p. 39.
[38] B.I.H.R., TER. N. Hemingbrough 1865.
[39] Local information.
[40] Char. Com. files.
[41] Burton, *Hemingbrough*, 88–90.
[42] *Valor Eccl.* v. 139.
[43] *Cal. Pat.* 1553, 21–3.
[44] Prior's Kitchen, D. & C. Muniments, chamberlain's charty., ff. 6d.–8v.; 1. 2. Archiep. 1; Burton, *Hemingbrough*, 90–3.
[45] *Valor Eccl.* v. 139.
[46] Burton, *Hemingbrough*, 23.
[47] Prior's Kitchen, D. & C. Muniments, M.C. 6650; 3. 2. Ebor. 46; Burton, *Hemingbrough*, 93–4.
[48] *Valor Eccl.* v. 139.
[49] *Cal. Papal Regs.* iv. 454.
[50] Burton, *Hemingbrough*, 24.
[51] O.S. Map 6″ (various edns.).
[52] See p. 40.
[53] Burton, *Hemingbrough*, 129.
[54] E.R.R.O., DDTR/Box 3.
[55] This paragraph is largely based on Burton, *Hemingbrough*, 45–59.
[56] *Cal. Close*, 1268–72, 194.
[57] *Reg. Romeyn*, ii, p. 105 n.
[58] Burton, *Hemingbrough*, 108–9.
[59] *Calamy Revised*, ed. A. G. Matthews, 194.
[60] Burton, *Hemingbrough*, 37, 111.
[61] Ibid. 120.
[62] Ibid. 124; *Rep. Com. Eccl. Revenues*, 940.

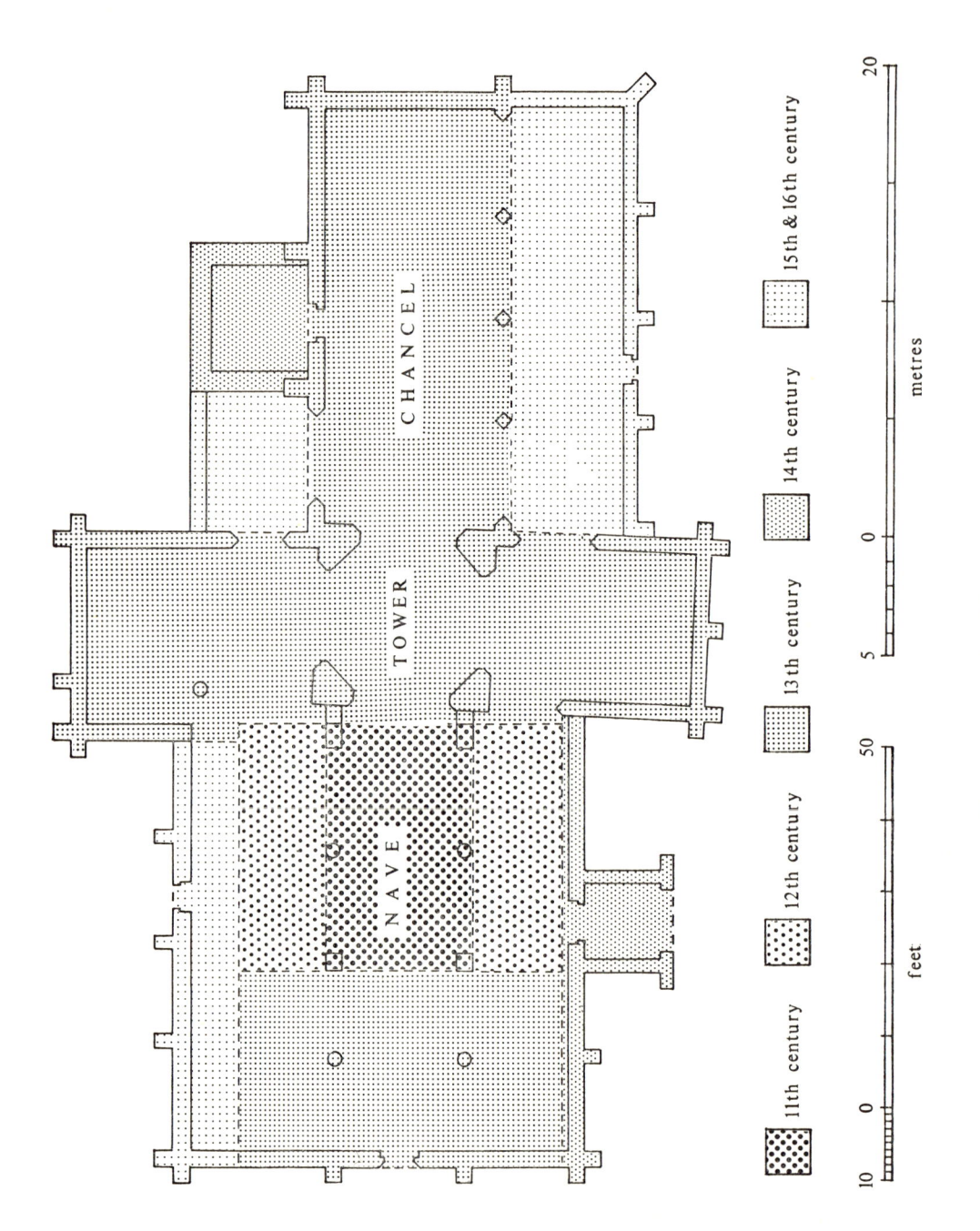

The church of St. Mary: block plan

references to an assistant curate are in 1852, when he received the whole income of the benefice,[63] and in 1865, when the vicar was non-resident.[64]

There was one service each Sunday in 1743 and 1764, and communion was received four times a year by about 100 people.[65] By 1851 there were two weekly services,[66] and in 1865 and later communion was celebrated monthly with about 20 communicants.[67] By 1914 communion was celebrated weekly.[68] There were three services each Sunday in 1973. A mission room was erected at Cliffe in 1908 and a weekly service and monthly communion were held there in 1914;[69] a service was still held there each Sunday in 1973.

The church of ST. MARY, mostly of limestone, has a chancel with north vestry and north and south chapels, a central tower with spire and transepts, and an aisled and clerestoried nave with south porch.[70]

The two eastern bays of both nave arcades are of the late 12th century but have been cut through the walls of an earlier building, of which all four corners can still be seen, which probably dates from the 11th century. Soon after 1200 the nave and aisles were extended westwards by two bays and a north transept, with a narrow aisle on its west side, was added. The latter suggests that the church was being enlarged to a cruciform plan which would involve an extensive reconstruction of the east end, but no evidence of this remains. The work may not have been completed, or there may have been some calamity like the fall of the crossing tower, for the south transept is of the late 13th century and the present crossing tower is only slightly later and is contemporary with an extensive reconstruction of the north transept and the building of the chancel. The lower storey of the vestry was built in the mid 14th century at about the time that the south aisle was widened and the south porch added. In 1410 £10 was bequeathed for the rebuilding of the 'north part' of the church;[71] possibly this was the north aisle but if so nothing survives as evidence that the work was done.

By 1426 the church was therefore already fairly large. It is not certain how much of the £171 said to have been spent by John of Wessington (prior 1416–46) on making it collegiate[72] was used for the domestic buildings, and how much for alterations about the church. The topmost part of the tower has Wessington's rebus and the spire is probably of his time. Collegiate use would also have made some refitting of the east end necessary but there is no longer any evidence of this. Several new windows were put in during the 15th century, the largest being at the west end of the nave and in the end walls of the transepts. The insertion of the new window in the south transept was part of a reconstruction that involved raising the roof and putting in a clerestory of three bays, the central one of which on each side being reused. The date of the nave clerestory may be nearer to 1500 and it appears to be contemporary with the north aisle.[73]

The transepts were used as chapels from an early date, and the original piscina and backing for a reredos remain in the south transept. The Babthorpe chantry chapel, between the north transept and the vestry, was probably built soon after the deaths of Thomas Babthorpe's father and brother in 1455[74] and the room over the vestry is contemporary with it. The south chapel, which is joined to the chancel by an arcade of four bays, was probably built at the expense of Anne Manners of Turnham Hall after 1513[75] and was used as a Lady chapel.

Many of the medieval fittings, including the rood screen and much stained glass, have gone, but among those that remain are the font of c. 1200, a single misericord of c. 1300, parts of stalls and much restored seating of the early 16th century, and the screens to the south chapel.

A gallery was put up and the pulpit was moved to beneath the south aisle in 1717.[76] During the following century box pews, using much of the timber of the old seating, were erected throughout the nave. The fabric was in frequent need of repair in the 18th century, but the major restorations of the nave and transepts were carried out between 1851 and 1858, apparently in part by J. L. Pearson,[77] of the chancel in 1882–3, directed by Ewan Christian,[78] and of the south chapel in 1884.[79]

There were four bells in 1552.[80] Five new bells were made by E. Seller of York in 1730,[81] and to those a sixth was added in 1907.[82] The plate includes a silver cup, made in 1617 by Francis Tempest of York, and two flagons and a pewter plate; one of the flagons is inscribed with the donor's name, John Allison of Lund, and the date 1719.[83] The registers begin in 1605 but have a gap between 1638 and 1653.[84]

Additions to the churchyard were consecrated in 1872[85] and 1915.[86]

NONCONFORMITY. Many recusants and non-communicants were reported in the parish in the later 16th and 17th centuries, the number sometimes reaching 50 or 60.[87] There was one Roman Catholic family in Hemingbrough in 1764.[88]

Two families of Presbyterians and one of Quakers were reported in the parish in 1743 and one family of unspecified dissenters in 1764.[89] Houses in

---

[63] Burton, Hemingbrough, 348.
[64] B.I.H.R., V. 1865/Ret. 236.
[65] Ibid. Bp. V. 1764/Ret. 24; Herring's Visit. ii. 66.
[66] H.O. 129/24/517.
[67] B.I.H.R., V. 1865/Ret. 236; V. 1868/Ret. 212; V. 1871/Ret. 211; V. 1877/Ret.
[68] Ibid. Bp. V. 1914/Ret.
[69] Ibid.
[70] See frontispiece.
[71] Burton, Hemingbrough, 17.
[72] Ibid. 18.
[73] Bequests for work on the nave were made in 1463 and 1508: B.I.H.R., Prob. Reg. 2, f. 588; N. Country Wills, i (Sur. Soc. cxvi), 272.
[74] Burton, Hemingbrough, 18.
[75] Ibid. 21.
[76] Ibid. 42.
[77] Ibid. 44–5; W. H. Wright, Restoration of Hemingbrough Ch.
[78] Y.A.J. xxiv. 142.
[79] Burton, Hemingbrough, 45.
[80] Inventories of Ch. Goods, 80.
[81] Boulter, 'Ch. Bells', 31.
[82] B.I.H.R., Fac. Bk. viii, p. 258.
[83] Yorks. Ch. Plate, i. 260.
[84] B.I.H.R., PR. HEM.
[85] Burton, Hemingbrough, 30.
[86] York Dioc. Regy., Consecration deed.
[87] Aveling, Post Reformation Catholicism, 63; Burton, Hemingbrough, 314–20.
[88] B.I.H.R., Bp. V. 1764/Ret. 24.
[89] Ibid.; Herring's Visit. ii. 66.

Hemingbrough township were registered for dissenting worship in 1787 and 1812.[90] A chapel was built there by the Wesleyan Methodists in 1836 and rebuilt in 1848,[91] and it was still used for worship in 1973. The Primitive Methodists replaced an earlier meeting-place[92] by a chapel built in 1857.[93] Its registration was cancelled in 1937[94] and it was used as a storehouse in 1973.

Methodists were numerous in the township and were said in 1865 to comprise about two-thirds of the population; in 1914 the vicar described them as strong but friendly and stated that most of them used the parish church for baptism, burial, and marriage.[95] A. J. Kelsey, by will proved in 1930, bequeathed £200 to be invested for the use of the Wesleyan Sunday school.[96]

EDUCATION. There are half-a-dozen instances of masters being licensed to teach a grammar school at Hemingbrough between 1619 and 1807,[97] but no more is known of the school. It may have been held in the church, where the chapel on the south side of the chancel was described as a schoolroom in 1750.[98] A petty school master was licensed in 1794;[99] he had also been mentioned in 1786.[1]

In 1835 there was reported to be a school at Hemingbrough, attended by 35 children and endowed with land worth £4 a year to teach 4 pupils free.[2] The endowment was also mentioned in 1823, when it was described as a 2-acre close in Barlby,[3] and it was presumably the land devised by Ralph Lodge, by will proved in 1661, for the education of poor children in Hemingbrough and Barlby.[4] The first known school-house is that built by Mary Carr on the corner of Finkle Street and the back lane in 1847.[5] There were said to be 70 children at a school in the township in 1868[6] and 24 children attending a school in 1871, but at the latter date there were two other schools for which details were not available.[7]

A school board was formed in 1875[8] and a school was built on the Howden road in 1877 and opened in January 1878.[9] Its initial income was about £55 from school pence and the average attendance in 1878 was 65 boys and girls and 20 infants.[10] An annual government grant, however, began to be received that year.[11] Mary Carr's schoolroom was subsequently used as a reading room[12] and in 1922 was acquired for a village institute.[13] It still stood in 1973, a small rectangular building of brick with stone dressings, wide overhanging eaves, and pointed wooden tracery in the windows. The charity close in Barlby was sold in 1896 and the proceeds invested in £72 stock; the income was used for payments to school children in accordance with a Scheme of 1880.[14]

The average attendance at the board school in 1903 was 69.[15] The school was enlarged by the county council in 1906–7 and its spire was removed in 1927.[16] In 1908–12 the average attendance was about 100 and in 1913–38 about 80–90.[17] Senior pupils were transferred to Barlby secondary school in 1960.[18] A new school at Hemingbrough, built on the same site, was opened in 1962, though part of the old building was retained.[19] There were 119 pupils on the roll in September 1973.[20] The charity income in 1973 was nearly £2, but no payments had been made for some years.[21]

CHARITIES FOR THE POOR. William Widdowes or Widhouse, by deed of 1624, gave a 5-acre close, the rent to be distributed to the poor at Hemingbrough. Before 1770 two unknown donors gave £1 a year and 10s. a year respectively from closes in the township. W. Sharrow, before 1770, left 7s. a year out of Barmby Sieve carr. All four gifts were reported to be distributed to the poor in 1823.[22] Known as the United Charities, they were regulated by a Scheme of 1918, when the endowments consisted of 5 a., rent-charges of £1 17s., and £22 stock. In 1972 the income was £18 and payments of over £1 were made to each of fifteen people.[23]

John Allanson or Allison, by will dated 1722, gave £2 from a house and land in Lund, to be distributed in bread to the poor of the parish. Joseph Underwood, in 1781, gave 12s. a year from 2 a. in Hemingbrough to be laid out in bread. These two bequests were used in 1823 to distribute weekly bread worth 1s.[24] Part of the rent-charge was being withheld in the early 20th century[25] and no more is known of the charity.

Thomas Steele, by will dated 1777 and codicil dated 1787, made a bequest to provide a threepenny loaf weekly for each of twelve poor women of the parish, as well as a guinea for the vicar for a sermon and 2s. 6d. for the parish clerk; any surplus income was to go to the church organist.[26] In 1816 it was decided to give the bread to 3 women in Hemingbrough, 3 in Cliffe with Lund, 2 in South Duffield,

---

[90] G.R.O. Worship Return, Vol. v, nos. 688, 2602.
[91] Stone on building.
[92] H.O. 129/24/517.
[93] Burton, *Hemingbrough*, 162. It was registered in 1860: G.R.O., Worship Reg. no. 9331.
[94] G.R.O. Worship Reg. no. 9331.
[95] B.I.H.R., V. 1865/Ret. 236; Bp. V. 1914/Ret.
[96] Ed. 49/8550.
[97] B.I.H.R., Schools index.
[98] Burton, *Hemingbrough*, 21.
[99] B.I.H.R., Schools index.
[1] See p. 43.
[2] *Educ. Enquiry Abstract*, 1086.
[3] *11th Rep. Com. Char.* 772.
[4] Burton, *Hemingbrough*, 141–2.
[5] Stone on building.
[6] B.I.H.R., V. 1868/Ret. 212.
[7] *Returns relating to Elem. Educ.* 796.
[8] *Lond. Gaz.* 26 Jan. 1875, p. 303.
[9] E.R.R.O., SBM. Hemingbrough, 1875–87.
[10] Ed. 7/135 no. 72.
[11] *Rep. of Educ. Cttee. of Council, 1878–9* [C. 2342–I], p. 1035, H.C. (1878–9), xxiii.
[12] B.I.H.R., Bp. V. 1894/Ret.; Ed. 49/8548.
[13] R.D.B., 244/265/226.
[14] Ed. 49/8549.
[15] E.R.R.O., SBM. Hemingbrough, 1887–1903.
[16] E.R. Educ. Cttee. *Mins.* 1906–7, 288; 1907–8, 61; 1926–7, 183; 1927–8, 181.
[17] *Bd. of Educ. List 21* (H.M.S.O.).
[18] E.R. Educ. Cttee. *Mins.* 1955–6, 151.
[19] Ibid. 1962–3, 110, 114.
[20] Ex inf. Chief Educ. Officer, County Hall, Beverley, 1973.
[21] Ex inf. the vicar, 1974.
[22] B.I.H.R., TER. N. Hemingbrough 1770; *11th Rep. Com. Char.* 772; list in church.
[23] Char. Com. files.
[24] *11th Rep. Com. Char.* 771–2; Burton, *Hemingbrough*, 139–40.
[25] Char. Com. files.
[26] Ibid.; Burton, *Hemingbrough*, 140–1.

2 in Menthorpe, Bowthorpe, Brackenholme, and Woodhall, one in Barlby, and one in Osgodby.[27] The income in 1972 was £9 from £300 stock; bread was given each week to one person and £4 was used for church purposes.[28]

William Pickup, by will proved in 1931, bequeathed £100 for the benefit of twelve widows in the township. In 1972 £100 stock produced over £3 income, distributed to twelve persons.[29]

BARLBY

The village of Barlby, probably an Anglian settlement, lies some 3 miles north-west of Hemingbrough, close to the river Ouse and on the edge of the higher ground which occupies the northern half of the township. Southwards more low-lying ground stretches as far as the Ouse and includes a large promontory formed by two sudden bends in the river. This promontory formerly stretched even further to the west, ending in land known as the Holmes lying within a meander of the river. It was perhaps in the early Middle Ages that the Ouse cut a new course across the neck of the Holmes, and in 1883 116 a. there were transferred for civil purposes to Selby (Yorks. W.R.).[30] In the 20th century residential and industrial development alongside the river in Barlby have created a virtual suburb to the town of Selby. Until 1883 Barlby township comprised 1,482 a.[31]

The higher ground in the township reaches little more than 25 ft. above sea-level. The alluvium of the lower ground occupies the southern part of the township, together with a narrow strip beside the Ouse on the west, widening in the north-west beyond another sharp bend in the river. The name Turnhead, recorded from the 14th century onwards, refers to the bend and to the promontory formed by it on the opposite bank.[32] Away from the river the township boundary partly follows drainage dikes on the lower ground. The small open fields of the township lay mainly on the higher ground but also extended to the south of the village; in the north Barlby common adjoined similar areas in Riccall and Osgodby. Common meadows and early inclosures occupied the low ground, including the Angrams near the river beyond Turnhead. The open fields and meadows were inclosed in 1846 and the common in 1858.

Flooding of the low ground was a problem from the Middle Ages onwards.[33] Several sluices or cloughs still discharge large quantities of water into the river, among them Angram clough which was rebuilt about 1858, when it was said to take water from 896 a. in Barlby and Riccall.[34]

Barlby village lies at the junction of roads leading northwards to Riccall and eventually York, southwards to Selby, and eastwards to Hemingbrough. From Turnhead another road leads eastwards towards Market Weighton, and at the inclosure of the common a road was set out running towards Skipwith, though this has been closed by the construction of Riccall airfield.[35] A ferry over the Ouse to Selby, belonging to the abbey there, was mentioned as early as 1260.[36] It was replaced by a wooden toll bridge in 1792, and in the following year the Selby to Market Weighton road was turnpiked.[37] About ¾ mile of the road approaching the bridge was realigned when the Selby–Hull railway line was constructed.[38] The toll bridge, still of timber, was rebuilt in 1969.[39] For a time in the 19th century there was a ferry for foot passengers about ½ mile east of the toll bridge.[40] In the 20th century several alterations have been made in the township to the trunk roads from Selby to York and Hull, notably the bypassing of Barlby village by the Hull road in the late 1920s[41] and of the Market Weighton junction on the York road near Turnhead soon after.[42] The railway line from Selby to Hull, passing through Barlby, was opened in 1840 with a lifting bridge over the Ouse not far from the road bridge; it was replaced in 1891 by a swing bridge.[43] The line to Market Weighton, opened in 1848, branches from the Hull line in Barlby, and the Selby–York line, opened in 1871, passes through the township.[44] The Market Weighton line was closed in 1965.[45]

Most of the older houses in Barlby village lie along the Riccall road but the church stands back from it and is approached by narrow lanes. There are a few 18th-century houses, including a farm-house close to the church and a long brick house further north where the vicar once lived.[46] The largest early-19th-century houses are the manor-house[47] and the Grove, the latter a stuccoed villa on the Riccall road with extensive outbuildings, including a dovecot. The former pinfold still stands near the manor-house. Much building has taken place in the 20th century, both before and after the Second World War, especially to the east and north of the village. At the north end there are more than 80 council houses. The chief outlying farm-house is Turnhead Lodge, close beside the Ouse.

The southern part of the township, towards Selby, was known as Selby Water Houses in the Middle Ages[48] and more often as Barlby Bank or New Barlby in later times. The name Bank Houses

---

[27] B.I.H.R., PR. HEM. 26.
[28] Char. Com. files.
[29] Ibid. (under Cliffe and Hemingbrough).
[30] Bulmer, *Dir. E. Yorks.* (1892), 546.
[31] O.S. Map 6", Yorks. (1854 edn.). Most of the township is covered by sheet 221, the rest by sheet 206.
[32] *P.N.E.R. Yorks.* (E.P.N.S.), 257.
[33] *Cal. Pat.* 1317–21, 479; 1343–5, 96, 182.
[34] E.R.R.O., DDFA/20/6.
[35] Ibid. QAH/1/26. See p. 83.
[36] *Selby Coucher Bk.* i (Y.A.S. Rec. Ser. x), 360; *Valor Eccl.* v. 12.
[37] K. A. MacMahon, *Roads and Turnpike Trusts in E. Yorks.* (E. Yorks. Loc. Hist. Ser. xviii), 32–3.
[38] B.I.H.R., TA. 642L; K. A. MacMahon, *Beginnings of E. Yorks. Rlys.* (E. Yorks. Loc. Hist. Ser. iii), 8.
[39] *Yorks. Eve. Press*, 30 Aug. 1969; 17 Jan. 1970.
[40] B. F. Duckham, *Yorks. Ouse*, 159.
[41] E.R.C.C. *Mins.* 1928–9, 237; 1929–30, 389; R.D.B., e.g. 348/138/116.
[42] E.R.C.C. *Mins.* 1929–30, 159; 1935–6, 245; R.D.B., 400/117/86.
[43] *V.C.H. Yorks. E.R.* i. 392; Duckham, *Yorks. Ouse*, 170.
[44] MacMahon, *Beginnings of E. Yorks. Rlys.* 14; *V.C.H. City of York*, 478.
[45] *Hull Daily Mail*, 12 June 1965.
[46] See p. 50.
[47] See p. 48.
[48] *Selby Coucher Bk.* i. 356.

occurs in 1675.[49] The buildings there included the still existing Bank Farm; others were added following the construction of the toll bridge and railway line. By 1841 there were three terraces of cottages facing the river near the bridges;[50] they had been demolished by 1973. More extensive development began in the late 19th century and continued apace in the twentieth. For about a mile from the toll bridge the main road is now lined with houses and mills.[51] The first 'village estate' of workers' housing was built by the Olympia Oil and Cake Co. soon after 1910, and by 1938 there were about 350 houses in such estates.[52] Other factories lie beside the river east of the bridges, together with the isolated Cherry Orchard Farm. Near the railway line from Selby to Market Weighton is a former powder magazine, built by the War Department in 1889.[53]

There were between one and three licensed alehouses in Barlby in the later 19th century.[54] In 1823 the inns were known as the Plough and the Bay Horse, but by 1826 the latter had been replaced by the Boot and Shoe,[55] which in turn had been replaced by the New Inn by 1872.[56] The Plough and the New Inn still existed in the old village in 1973. The only inn at Barlby Bank is the Olympia Hotel, opened by 1921;[57] it takes its name from the Olympia Mills and its sign shows seed-crushing machinery.

In 1379 there were 96 poll-tax payers at Barlby.[58] Fifty-four households were included in the hearth-tax return in 1672, twelve of them exempt. Of those chargeable 17 had only one hearth each, 19 had 2, 4 had 3–5, and 2 had eleven.[59] The population fluctuated in the 19th century but increased from 241 in 1801 to a maximum of 561 in 1901.[60] By 1911 it stood at 792 but during the next decade it rose sharply to 2,593; it was still only 2,627 in 1931. Barlby and Osgodby together had 3,329 inhabitants in 1951, but the number then decreased to 3,022 in 1971.[61]

MANOR AND OTHER ESTATES. In 1086 the bishop of Durham had 2 carucates in Barlby, one of which was soke of Howden manor.[62] The bishop's overlordship was still mentioned in 1580.[63]

The demesne lord of *BARLBY* manor in the mid 12th century was Gilbert of Barlby, holding 2 carucates of the bishop.[64] He was succeeded by his son William de Aton. Another William held it in 1284, and the heirs of Gilbert de Aton in 1302; it subsequently passed to another Gilbert (d. 1324) and to his son William (d. 1389).[65] William's heirs were his daughters Anastasia, who married Edward St. John, Catherine, who married Ralph Eure, and Elizabeth, who married first William Place and secondly Sir John Conyers.[66] The descent of Elizabeth's share has not been traced. Anastasia's daughter Margaret married Thomas Broomfleet, and their granddaughter married John, Lord Clifford.[67] The Cliffords held a share of the manor until 1553, when Henry Clifford, earl of Cumberland, sold it to Sir William Babthorpe.[68] In 1602 Ralph Babthorpe secured Catherine Aton's share from Ralph, Lord Eure,[69] and the Babthorpes probably then owned the whole manor.

Barlby was sold by another Sir William Babthorpe to Richard Bowes in 1621,[70] and c. 1665 the Bowes family conveyed it to James Strangeways (d. 1670). It apparently passed like Hagthorpe from Thomas Strangeways (d. 1702) to his son Thomas (later Thomas Robinson), and in 1707 it was sold to John Burdett.[71] The manor subsequently descended like Osgodby to Riley Briggs, who had only 16 a. in Barlby at his death in 1913.[72]

The medieval manor-house at Barlby, probably standing on a moated site later called the Island, apparently passed to the Lodge family in the early 16th century. In 1672 it had 11 hearths.[73] It was held by the Lodges until the death in 1717 of Ralph Lodge, who was succeeded by his sisters Eleanor Spofforth and Elizabeth Lacy.[74] In 1727 the Spofforths and Lacys conveyed the manor-house to John Denton, together with the adjoining 'new house', a garden called the Island, 'encompassed with a box hedge and a moat', and 100 a. of land.[75] The estate was sold by William Denton to Isaac Nurse in 1766, and by G. W. Nurse to John and Joseph Blanshard in 1785.[76] Susanna, Joseph's daughter, who married Joseph Stringer, is said to have rebuilt the house c. 1820.[77] The Stringers kept the estate until the death of J. B. Stringer in 1919, and his devisees sold the Hall and 12 a. the following year to J. W. R. Parker and J. F. Burn-Murdoch. They promptly conveyed it to the Selby Warehousing and Transport Co. Ltd.[78] It was sold in 1940 to the Olympia Oil and Cake Co. Ltd. and in 1959 to P. B. Flohil.[79] The early-19th-century red-brick house has a slated roof and a pediment over the centre of the entrance front.

The largest of the freehold estates in the township in the early 19th century was probably the Robinsons'.[80] After Mary Robinson's death in 1839 it was held in trust by her brother William's daughter Mary Carr (d. 1871). From her the trusteeship passed to her daughters Mary, wife of T. G. Parker, and Marian, wife of the Revd. J. M. Burn-

[49] E.R.R.O., DDCV/6/20.
[50] B.I.H.R., TA. 642L.
[51] For industry see p. 50.
[52] R.D.B., 172/568/488; 612/167/120.
[53] Bulmer, *Dir. E. Yorks.* (1892), 547.
[54] E.R.R.O., QDT/2/15.
[55] Ibid. QDT/2/13.
[56] *Kelly's Dir. N. & E.R. Yorks.* (1872), 313.
[57] Ibid. (1921), 437.
[58] *T.E.R.A.S.* xv. 53–4. There is no return for 1377.
[59] E 179/205/504. No separate figure for Barlby was given in 1743 and 1764: see p. 39.
[60] *V.C.H. Yorks.* iii. 498.
[61] Census.
[62] *V.C.H. Yorks.* ii. 217, 319.
[63] C 142/194 no. 22.
[64] *E.Y.C.* ii, p. 279.
[65] *Feud. Aids*, vi. 37, 138, 172, 224; *Yorks. Fines, 1347–77*, p. 94; *Cal. Chart. R. 1300–26*, 121; Burke, *Dorm. & Ext. Peerages* (1883), 15.
[66] *Cal. Close, 1385–9*, 580; *Feud. Aids*, vi. 543.
[67] *Yorks. Deeds*, ix, p. 117; Burton, *Hemingbrough*, 360.
[68] *Yorks. Fines*, i. 171; *Test. Ebor.* vi, p. 130.
[69] *Yorks. Fines*, iv. 194; *Test. Ebor.* vi, pp. 184, 187.
[70] C 2/B. 31/38.
[71] Burton, *Hemingbrough*, 361.
[72] R.D.B., ID/9/12.
[73] E 179/205/504.
[74] Burton, *Hemingbrough*, 361–3 and pedigree facing p. 363.
[75] R.D.B., I/457/978.
[76] Ibid. AI/49/103; BI/188/295.
[77] Burton, *Hemingbrough*, 364.
[78] R.D.B., 206/307/263; /308/264; 209/116/99; /118/101.
[79] Ibid. 641/573/478; 1128/321/280.
[80] E.R.R.O., Land Tax.

Murdoch.[81] The estate still contained 386 a. in Barlby in 1905[82] but subsequently it was gradually split up and sold.

In 1086 another carucate of land in Barlby was held by Ralph Paynel, having previously belonged to Merleswain.[83] Soon afterwards Paynel gave it to Holy Trinity priory, York, which he founded as a cell of Marmoutier abbey (Bas-Rhin).[84] The gift was confirmed on several occasions, the last in 1464.[85] The subsequent descent of the estate has not been traced.

Several small grants in Barlby were made by the Atons and others to Selby abbey.[86] After the Dissolution, however, grants of former abbey property in Barlby comprised free rents rather than land. Thus rents totalling over £5 were granted in 1558.[87] The rents apparently derived from land at Barlby Bank, close to Selby, which eventually passed, like Skipwith manor,[88] to Banastre Walton (d. 1784); his widow Jane sold 169 a. at Barlby Bank to Robert, Lord Petre, in 1785.[89] Laura M. Petre sold it, comprising 202 a., to Thomas Ashworth (d. 1870) in 1851.[90] Ashworth's trustees held it until 1913, when 177 a. were conveyed to the Selby Warehousing and Transport Co. Ltd.[91] In 1940 much of the estate was sold to the Olympia Oil and Cake Co. Ltd.,[92] and most of it still belonged to British Oil and Cake Mills Ltd. in 1973.

Most of the rectorial tithes of Barlby descended, like those of Hemingbrough township, with Hemingbrough manor.[93] They were worth £55 in 1650[94] and were commuted in 1841 for £367 payable to Wilson's devisees, Tweedy and Smith.[95] The tithes of pigs and poultry, however, descended with Babthorpe manor.[96] Together with those of Osgodby and Cliffe with Lund they were worth £3 in 1650 and those in Barlby were commuted in 1841 for £2 payable to C. T. Heathcote.[97]

ECONOMIC HISTORY. In 1086 there was land for ½ plough at Barlby, then said to be waste, together with 5 a. of meadow, and pasturable woodland measuring four furlongs by two.[98] Pasture for pigs in the wood was mentioned in the 13th century. At the same period other land was being brought into cultivation and the lower ground was being drained. There were references to open-field parcels in 'utfeld', in Barlby Waterhouses, and on the bank of the Ouse; an assart was mentioned; and named dikes included 'Brerflet', 'Rigdik', and Newdike. Meadow lay in Angram and in the Holmes, and c. 1300 mention was made of 40 a. of marsh and alder wood.[99] In the late 13th century rights in reclaimed land in the township were disputed between the Atons, as lords of the manor, and Selby abbey.[1]

By the 17th century open-field land was recorded as lying in several named 'fields': Bank field, High field, and the Outfield were all mentioned.[2] Parts of those fields were apparently being inclosed, however, about that time. A close in High field was described as 'lately inclosed' in 1632; closes 'formerly called Bank field' were mentioned in 1658; and New close in the Outfield was referred to in 1647.[3] Other assarted land was held in severalty, including Pippin and Wheat Riddings, and various closes in the carrs.[4] Part of the carrs had still been used in common in 1523, when bequests were made of horses running there.[5] There was meadow in 'Breenfleet', and the Outfield ings were mentioned.[6] Little is known of the tenants and their holdings, but in 1616 land in the township was conveyed by the Babthorpes, lords of the manor, to trustees so that the tenants might buy the freehold of their lands.[7]

More names of open-field areas may be identified in the 18th century: Morcar, High, Chapel, and Out fields, and High North croft, for example.[8] The fragmented character of the open fields and meadows is revealed by the tithe award map of 1841,[9] and when they were inclosed in 1846, under the general Inclosure Act of 1836,[10] there were a dozen areas to be dealt with comprising only 216 a. all told. Allotments were made from the Angrams, including 'Beenfleet' (totalling 57 a.), High field (50 a.), Barley Croft field (23 a.), Ing Roods field (16 a.), Long Moor carr (16 a.), Newland field (14 a.), Short Moor carr (11 a.), Fadeland field (9 a.), North Croft field (8 a.), Turnhead field (5 a.), and Scotch Croft field (3 a.). There were 25 allotments of under 10 a. each, 5 of 10–39 a., and one of over 40 a.

The tithable land in 1841 had consisted of 896 a. of arable, 240 a. of meadow or pasture, 80 a. of common, and 20 a. of woodland.[11] The common, mainly at the northern end of the township, remained until 1858, when it was inclosed under the general Inclosure Act of 1845.[12] A small area of common south of the village included Carr hill, near Barlby Bank. Allotments totalling 73 a. were made in lieu of 43 common rights. Nineteen people received under 10 a. each and the lord of the manor 14 a.

Until the early 20th century there were usually 12–15 farmers in Barlby,[13] only 5 of them having as many as 100–200 a. in 1851.[14] After the First World War, partly as a result of the increased use of land for industry, the number of farmers fell to half-

[81] R.D.B., FT/379/431; Burton, *Hemingbrough*, 159.
[82] R.D.B., 78/347/324; /350/325 (1905).
[83] *V.C.H. Yorks.* ii. 173, 270.
[84] *V.C.H. City of York*, 374; *E.Y.C.* vi, pp. 56, 66, 73.
[85] *Cal. Pat.* 1461–7, 375–6.
[86] *Selby Coucher Bk.* i. 350 sqq.; J. Burton, *Mon. Ebor.* 390.
[87] *Cal. Pat.* 1557–8, 286, 385–6.
[88] See p. 94.
[89] R.D.B., BF/599/1001; BI/23/39.
[90] Ibid. GW/323/417; 150/5/5.
[91] Ibid. 150/5/5.
[92] Ibid. 641/573/478.
[93] See p. 39.
[94] C 94/3 f. 77.
[95] B.I.H.R., TA. 642L.
[96] See p. 53.
[97] C 94/3 f. 77; B.I.H.R., TA. 642L.
[98] *V.C.H. Yorks.* ii. 270.

[99] *Selby Coucher Bk.* i. 350–1, 355–8, 361, 370, 374–5; *Yorks. Fines, 1232–46*, p. 70.
[1] *Selby Coucher Bk.* i. 360–1; Burton, *Hemingbrough*, 357–8.
[2] E.R.R.O., DDCV/6/2, 11.
[3] Ibid. DDCV/6/10, 12–13, 18; Burton, *Hemingbrough*, 362.
[4] E.R.R.O., DDCV/6/1, 5; DDBV/3/1; DDX/31/99.
[5] *Test. Ebor.* iv, p. 84 n.
[6] E.R.R.O., DDCV/6/1, 11.
[7] Ibid. DDCV/6/3.
[8] Ibid. DDFA/1/1; /14/110; B.I.H.R., TER. N. Barl. 1770.
[9] B.I.H.R., TA. 642L.
[10] E.R.R.O., Enrolment Bk. H, pp. 188 sqq.
[11] B.I.H.R., TA. 642L.
[12] E.R.R.O., IA. Barlby, including map.
[13] Directories.
[14] H.O. 107/2351.

a-dozen, together with a few market-gardeners. Two of the farms were of 150 a. or more in the 1920s and 1930s.[15] The acreage of arable land in 1905 was 861 and of meadow and pasture 350.[16] The predominance of arable farming has subsequently increased.[17]

From the Middle Ages onwards the Ouse at Barlby supported a fishery,[18] and there was doubtless some river traffic from the village. In 1341, for example, it was reported that wool was put aboard a ship at Turnhead to be sent to Hull.[19] A windmill was recorded in the 17th century[20] and there was a brickmaker in 1823,[21] but more diversified employment followed the development of Barlby Bank.

By the mid 19th century there were several agricultural and timber merchants, a few mariners, some railway and toll-bridge employees, and a flax spinner at Barlby Bank.[22] It was not until soon after 1900, however, that larger industrial firms became established there, mostly occupying land on either side of the Selby–Barlby road with frontages to the Ouse and the railway. Dent and Co., tar distillers, moved in c. 1905 and remained until 1957.[23] W. L. Kirby Ltd., steam flour millers, arrived in 1905 and their Imperial Mills were taken over by Joseph Rank Ltd. in 1967.[24] The Olympia Oil and Cake Co. Ltd. acquired sites in 1909–10; their buildings, which later dominated the road and river frontages, have been in the ownership of British Oil and Cake Mills Ltd. since 1952.[25] Fletcher's Sauce Co. Ltd. was established at Barlby in 1920 and remained in 1973 as part of Smedley–H.P. Foods Ltd.[26] The Yorkshire Sugar Co. Ltd., later part of the British Sugar Corporation Ltd., bought 69 a., stretching from the railway to the Ouse, in 1927; its riverside factory lies well away from the Selby–Barlby road.[27] Other 20th-century firms have included a cooper's, an agricultural marketing and supply company, and an engineer's.

LOCAL GOVERNMENT. No manorial records and no parochial records before 1835 are known. Barlby joined the Selby poor-law union in 1837,[28] and the site of four recently-demolished poorhouses was sold by the union in 1867.[29] Barlby became part of Riccall rural district in 1894, Derwent rural district in 1935,[30] and the Selby district of North Yorkshire in 1974.

CHURCH. A chapel dependent upon Hemingbrough church had existed at Barlby for some time before 1482, when the archbishop authorized services to be held there for three years in the customary way.[31] It was recommended in 1650 that Barlby, together with Osgodby, was fit to become a separate parish.[32] It eventually acquired parochial functions in the 18th century and was regarded as a perpetual curacy[33] until the late 19th century, when it became known as a vicarage.[34] By special arrangement New Barlby was served by the vicar of Selby after 1912, and in 1929 it and the Holmes were transferred to Selby for ecclesiastical purposes.[35] The advowson has always belonged to the vicar of Hemingbrough.[36]

The curate's income in 1716 comprised £4 contributed by the inhabitants and 10s. bequeathed by John Waud for a sermon; in 1727 it amounted to £16 from the town stock.[37] The income was augmented by £200 from Queen Anne's Bounty in 1726[38] to meet a benefaction of that amount given by John Vickers and Thomas Dalby.[39] Further augmentations of £200 Bounty money were received in 1759, 1786, and 1809.[40] The average net income in 1829–31 was £65.[41] Barlby was endowed from the Common Fund with £500 in 1863.[42] The net value of the living was £131 in 1884 and £197 in 1914.[43]

In 1736 Bounty money was used to buy 44 a. of glebe land in Babthorpe[44] and by 1743 14 a. had been acquired in Newhay. By 1770 6½ a. had been bought in Barlby, and in 1810 5 a. were bought in East Cottingwith. The total amount of glebe was put at 76½ a. in 1865,[45] and it still belonged to the vicarage in 1973.[46] In the late 19th century the vicar lived in a house on the Riccall road,[47] but there was no house belonging to the living until c. 1895, when the present Vicarage was built to the designs of C. H. Fowler.[48]

William Williamson, curate from 1625, was inhibited from preaching in 1632,[49] and subsequently Thomas Lecke, curate, was ejected.[50] In 1716 Thomas Froggott, vicar of Ricall, was curate,[51] and two vicars of Hemingbrough, Marmaduke Teasdale and William Potter the younger, both held Barlby as well later in the century. Robert Potter, curate 1761–8, was also vicar of Stillingfleet, and several 19th-century incumbents also held and resided upon other livings.[52] An assistant curate was employed during the incumbency of Thomas Braim

[15] Directories.
[16] Acreage Returns, 1905.
[17] [1st] Land Util. Surv. Map, sheet 32; 2nd Land Util. Surv. Map, sheet 689 (SE 63–73).
[18] e.g. E.R.R.O., DDFA/1/1; /14/262; *Public Works in Med. Law*, ii (Selden Soc. xl), 254, 267–8.
[19] *Cal. Inq. Misc.* ii, p. 438.
[20] e.g. E.R.R.O., DDCV/6/2.
[21] Baines, *Hist. Yorks.* ii. 152.
[22] H.O. 107/2351; White, *Dir. E. & N.R. Yorks.* (1840), 331–2.
[23] R.D.B., 100/330/303 (1907); 1064/457/407; *Kelly's Dir. N. & E.R. Yorks.* (1905), 417.
[24] R.D.B., 74/137/129; /138/130 (1905); 1513/91/82; *Kelly's Dir. N. & E.R. Yorks.* (1909), 429.
[25] R.D.B., 116/388/364; 126/304/274; H. W. Brace, *Hist. of Seed Crushing in Gt. Brit.* 154; *Kelly's Dir. N. & E.R. Yorks.* (1913), 445.
[26] R.D.B., 217/204/185; 286/564/482; 616/47/34; *Kelly's Dir. N. & E.R. Yorks.* (1921), 437.
[27] R.D.B., 348/205/159; *Kelly's Dir. N. & E.R. Yorks.* (1929), 443.
[28] *3rd Rep. Poor Law Com.* 178.
[29] R.D.B., KB/359/470.
[30] Census.
[31] Burton, *Hemingbrough*, 400–1.
[32] C 94/3 f. 77.
[33] e.g. B.I.H.R., TER. N. Barlby 1716 etc.; V. 1865/Ret. 34; *Rep. Com. Eccl. Revenues*, 916.
[34] *Kelly's Dir. N. & E.R. Yorks.* (1889), 324.
[35] *Lond. Gaz.* 30 Aug. 1929, pp. 5637–8.
[36] e.g. B.I.H.R., Bp. V. 1764/Ret. 24.
[37] Ibid. TER. N. Barlby 1716, 1727.
[38] Hodgson, *Q.A.B.* 433.
[39] Lawton, *Rer. Eccl. Dioc. Ebor.* ii. 443.
[40] Hodgson, *Q.A.B.* 433.
[41] *Rep. Com. Eccl. Revenues*, 916.
[42] *Lond. Gaz.* 28 July 1863, p. 3744.
[43] B.I.H.R., Bp. V. 1884/Ret.; Bp. V. 1914/Ret.
[44] Ibid. PR. BARL. 5.
[45] Ibid. TER. N. Barlby 1743, 1770, 1817, 1865.
[46] Ex inf. the vicar, 1974.
[47] O.S. Map 1/2,500, Yorks. CCXXI. 3 (1908 edn.); see p. 47.
[48] B.I.H.R., Bp. V. 1894/Ret.; E.R.R.O., DDX/234/1.
[49] R. A. Marchant, *Puritans and the Ch. Courts in Dioc. York, 1560–1642*, 292, 319.
[50] B. Dale, *Yorks. Puritanism and Early Nonconf.* 7.
[51] B.I.H.R., TER. N. Barlby 1716; Burton, *Hemingbrough*, 343.
[52] Burton, *Hemingbrough*, 343–8.

(1812–25),[53] again in 1835,[54] and probably on other occasions, too.

One service was held each Sunday in 1743 and 1764.[55] There was still only one weekly service in 1851[56] but two by 1865, and thereafter communion was celebrated about six times a year, with 12–20 communicants. By 1914 there was monthly communion.[57] There were three services each Sunday in 1973.

The present brick church of *ALL SAINTS*[58] consists of chancel with north vestry, nave, and west porch. When rebuilt in 1779–80 to replace the ruinous earlier chapel it comprised a simple rectangular building with an apsidal east end and a small octagonal bellcot.[59] Two small projections containing pews were later added to the north side, one about 1844 for the use of G. P. Dawson of Osgodby Hall and the other later for Robert Hubie,[60] but these were removed during the restoration of 1895. The vestry, also on the north side, was rebuilt in 1866.[61] A gallery across the west end of the church was built by the Hubie family in 1811.[62]

The church was enlarged and restored in 1895[63] to the designs of C. H. Fowler.[64] Besides the removal of the projections and the bricking up of the arches leading into them, a chancel, vestry, and west porch were added, all in a style matching that of the earlier work. The gallery was removed and the interior refitted.

There is one bell, dated 1704 and made by Samuel Smith of York.[65] The plate comprises silver chalice and paten, made in 1894, and pewter flagon.[66] The first known burial at Barlby was that of John Vickers in 1727[67] but registers of baptisms and burials do not begin until 1780.[68] The church was licensed for marriages in 1853.[69]

The churchyard was enlarged in 1872,[70] 1923–4, and 1943.[71]

NONCONFORMITY. A house in Barlby was registered for worship by Independents in 1772,[72] and other houses were registered by dissenters in 1818, 1822, and 1826.[73] The Wesleyan Methodists were said in 1851 to meet in a granary in summer and two houses in winter,[74] but soon afterwards they built a chapel, registered in 1857.[75] The chapel, standing on the Osgodby road, was replaced by a new one in 1961[76] and the old building was demolished in 1972.[77] The new chapel, on the same road midway between Barlby and Osgodby villages, was still in use in 1973.

EDUCATION. A grammar-school teacher was licensed at Barlby in 1585 and 1673.[78] There were two schools there in the early 19th century. One of them had 6 children in 1819 and 20 in 1835, and was said to have an endowment of 1 a. of land in the former year and £2 a year in the latter. The second school, entirely supported by parents' contributions, had about 40 and 25 pupils respectively in those years.[79] The endowment was that of Ralph Lodge, devised by will proved in 1661 for the education of poor children in the township.[80] The first known school-house was built in 1845,[81] and in 1871 35 children attended the National school.[82] It was rebuilt on a new site, east of the church, in 1875 and the average attendance was 27 the following year, when its income included 8s. 6d. from the endowment.[83] The school received an annual government grant by 1877–8.[84] There was also a Wesleyan day school in 1871, with 38 in attendance.[85] Mary Robinson (d. 1839) bequeathed £100 for the poor of Barlby, and her executors used it for the benefit of the National school; £105 stock was bought with it in 1877. Mary Hubie, by will dated 1836, gave £100 stock for the school, but the principal expired in 1859.[86]

A temporary building for infants was put up next to the school, apparently in 1909,[87] but in 1913 a new school was opened on the Selby road, just south of the village, with accommodation for 268.[88] The old school was subsequently used as a church hall[89] and still stood in 1973. The income of Lodge's and Robinson's charities was used for religious education after 1913.[90] The new school was enlarged in 1914,[91] when the average attendance rose from about 90 to 158; by 1919 there were 200 in attendance.[92] Many Barlby children, however, went to school in Selby: in 1920, for example, 270 attended the village school and 251 went to Selby.[93] A new school was provided for the area adjoining Selby in 1925 and in the same year a new infants' department was opened at the village school.[94] Attendance at the

[53] Ibid. 345–6.
[54] *Rep. Com. Eccl. Revenues*, 916.
[55] B.I.H.R., Bp. V. 1764/Ret. 24; *Herring's Visit.* ii. 66, 93.
[56] H.O. 129/24/513.
[57] B.I.H.R., V. 1865/Ret. 34; V. 1868/Ret. 34; V. 1871/Ret. 34; V. 1877/Ret.; Bp. V. 1884/Ret.; Bp. V. 1914/Ret.
[58] It was so dedicated in 1895: stone in building.
[59] B.I.H.R., Fac. Bk. ii, pp. 234–5; Burton, *Hemingbrough*, 338–9.
[60] B.I.H.R., How. 6, 1844; Burton, *Hemingbrough*, 329, 339–40, including illus.
[61] B.I.H.R., V. 1868/Ret. 34; Burton, *Hemingbrough*, 340.
[62] Burton, *Hemingbrough*, 340.
[63] B.I.H.R., Fac. Bk. vi, p. 1050; inscribed stone in building.
[64] E.R.R.O., DDX/234/1.
[65] Boulter, 'Ch. Bells', 30.
[66] *Yorks. Ch. Plate*, i. 212.
[67] Monument in church.
[68] B.I.H.R., PR. BARL. 1.
[69] Burton, *Hemingbrough*, 340. [70] Ibid.
[71] York Dioc. Regy., Consecration deeds; B.I.H.R., Fac. Bk. x, p. 352.
[72] B.I.H.R., Fac. Bk. ii, p. 98.
[73] G.R.O. Worship Returns, Vol. v, nos. 3170, 3676, 4052.
[74] H.O. 129/24/513.
[75] G.R.O. Worship Reg. no. 8097.
[76] Ibid. no. 68111. [77] Local information.
[78] B.I.H.R., Schools index.
[79] *Educ. of Poor Digest*, 1082; *Educ. Enquiry Abstract*, 1086.
[80] Burton, *Hemingbrough*, 141–2, 352; *10th Rep. Com. Char.* 667.
[81] Burton, *Hemingbrough*, 356.
[82] *Returns relating to Elem. Educ.* 790.
[83] Ed. 7/135 no. 8.
[84] *Rep. of Educ. Cttee. of Council, 1877–8* [C. 2048–I], p. 838, H.C. (1878), xxviii.
[85] *Rets. relating to Elem. Educ.* 790.
[86] Burton, *Hemingbrough*, 159, 352–3.
[87] Ed. 7/135 no. 8; E.R. Educ. Cttee. *Mins.* 1909–10, 226.
[88] Ed. 7/135 no. 8; E.R. Educ. Cttee. *Mins.* 1913–14, 331.
[89] B.I.H.R., Bp. V. 1914/Ret. [90] Ed. 49/8510.
[91] E.R. Educ. Cttee. *Mins.* 1914–15, 310.
[92] *Bd. of Educ. List 21* (H.M.S.O.).
[93] E.R. Educ. Cttee. *Mins.* 1920–1, 209.
[94] Ibid. 1925–6, 133.

village school remained at over 200 for some years, falling to 183 in 1938.[95] Prefabricated buildings were later added there,[96] and the number on the roll was 186 in September 1973.[97]

Barlby Bridge school, for the Selby 'suburb', was opened in 1925 with accommodation for 290 pupils.[98] The attendance was 217 in 1927 and 152 in 1938,[99] and the number on the roll was 95 in September 1973.[1]

A secondary school was opened at Barlby, on the Riccall road, in 1960 to serve about ten villages round about. The number on the roll was 458 in September 1972.[2]

CHARITIES FOR THE POOR. Caulem's dole comprised a garth and common right in South Duffield, the rent of which amounted to £1 10s. in 1823. Porritt's dole comprised an acre in Barlby producing £2 8s. rent in 1823; it was sold for £275 c. 1870 and used to buy 5 a. in Cliffe, producing £10 rent in the 1880s. Walker's dole comprised a rent-charge of 10s. from 1 a. in Barlby.[3] These three, along with an acre of land given in 1857, were brought together as the United Charities by a Scheme of 1912. The income in 1972 was £31 from £273 stock; nearly £1 each was given to 33 widows.[4]

Three other small charities have been lost: 3s. 4d. a year from ½ a. of meadow in Barlby, given by Thomas Nelson by will dated 1633; income from ¼ a. of meadow there, given by John Lodge by will proved in 1663; and 10s. a year from land in Barlby, given by Thomas Dalby by will dated 1719.[5]

Mary Robinson (d. 1839) gave £100 to provide for a weekly distribution of bread in Barlby. It was invested in £107 stock in 1868. Mary Hubie, by will proved in 1836, devised £233 stock to repair her family tomb in Barlby churchyard and to provide for a weekly distribution of bread worth 2s. 10d. to poor widows, one of them to be Mary Robinson, attending the church. The income was £7 in the 1880s.[6] These two charities were later administered as the United Bread Charity. The income in 1973 was £9 from £340 stock, and distribution was no longer made in bread but in cash.[7]

Robert Weddall, by will proved in 1841, directed his executors to pay £10 a year for the poor of Barlby. After his death £258 was invested for this purpose.[8] The income in 1973 was about £13.[9]

Mary Carr, by will proved in 1871, bequeathed £300 to provide coal for the poor of Barlby and South Duffield. It was invested in £323 stock in 1872, and in the 1880s ⅗ of the income was distributed to Barlby.[10] In 1972 the income was £5 but none was distributed.[11]

BRACKENHOLME WITH WOODHALL

Most of the land lying eastwards of Hemingbrough township and bounded by the river Derwent was occupied by the townships of Babthorpe, Brackenholme, Hagthorpe, and Woodhall; all four were comprised in the 19th-century civil parish of Brackenholme with Woodhall. Not included in the townships were 130 a. of land, lying between Babthorpe and the river, which were in Barmby on the Marsh until 1935.[12] Brackenholme was an Anglian settlement, but Babthorpe and Hagthorpe were Scandinavian, as presumably was Woodhall despite the late occurrence of its name: it was first recorded as Grimsthorpe in the 1130s but had acquired its alternative name by c. 1190 and thereafter was always known as Woodhall.[13] The area of Brackenholme, including Babthorpe and Hagthorpe, was 1,029 a. and of Woodhall 312 a.[14]

The whole of the civil parish lies at less than 25 ft. above sea-level. The four hamlets stood on the edge of the outwash deposits, close to the alluvium bordering the Derwent. The river now forms the eastern boundary of the townships, but it has changed its course in historic times, having previously flowed eastwards from the neighbourhood of Brackenholme to join the Ouse 4 miles away near Howden.[15] The 'old' Derwent was already mentioned in 959.[16] The new course broadly coincided with the boundary between the parishes of Hemingbrough and Barmby, but it isolated on the west bank an area of meadow and pasture belonging to the bishop of Durham's manor of Barmby. The ground is still known as Barmby pasture and Bishop's meadows. In the early 14th century Robert of Babthorpe and the bishop were in dispute about a watercourse near 'Bysshopcauce' (i.e. Bishop's causey), which lay between their demesne lands 'towards Babthorpe beyond Derwent';[17] the new course of the river was clearly well-established by that time.

The Hemingbrough–Howden road crosses the civil parish, and Brackenholme and Hagthorpe hamlets both lie beside it; Babthorpe stood just south of the road. From Brackenholme a minor road leads northwards towards North Duffield, passing through the hamlet of Woodhall. The Howden road led to a ferry over the Derwent, belonging to the bishop of Durham, which was mentioned in 1339.[18] It may have taken the place of a bridge, for timber for 'Barmby bridge' was taken from Brackenholme wood before 1228.[19] Loftsome ferry, as it was later called from the hamlet on the opposite bank,[20] was

[95] List 21.
[96] E.R. Educ. Cttee. Mins. 1950–1, 218.
[97] Ex inf. Chief Educ. Officer, County Hall, Beverley, 1973.
[98] Ed. 7/135 no. 212.
[99] List 21.
[1] Ex inf. Chief Educ. Officer.
[2] Ibid.
[3] 10th Rep. Com. Char. 667; Burton, Hemingbrough, 351–2.
[4] Char. Com. files.
[5] Burton, Hemingbrough, 352.
[6] Ibid. 159, 353; Char. Com. files.
[7] Char. Com. files; ex inf. the vicar, 1974.
[8] Char. Com. files; Burton, Hemingbrough, 353–4.

[9] Char. Com. files; ex inf. the vicar, 1974.
[10] Char. Com. files; Burton, Hemingbrough, 354.
[11] Char. Com. files.
[12] See p. 37.
[13] E.Y.C. ii, pp. 272, 322–3; P.N.E.R. Yorks. (E.P.N.S.), 258.
[14] O.S. Map 6", Yorks. (1854 edn.). The whole civil parish is covered by sheet 222.
[15] As shown on O.S. maps.
[16] E.Y.C. i, pp. 12–13.
[17] Reg. Pal. Dunelm. ii (Rolls Ser.), 1189–93, 1294.
[18] Prior's Kitchen, D. & C. Muniments, chamberlain's charty., f. 6d.
[19] Ibid. 2. 2. Ebor. 14.
[20] e.g. E.R.R.O., QSF. Mids. 1756, B.24.

replaced by a bridge in 1804, administered by a private company and having a toll-house at the Loftsome end.[21] The wooden bridge remained in use, still subject to tolls, until soon after 1930, when a new Loftsome bridge was built near by as part of the improvements to the Selby–Hull trunk road which were made about that time.[22] Parts of the old bridge still stand. There was a landing-place near by.[23] The Selby–Hull railway line, opened in 1840,[24] crosses Woodhall with a bridge over the Derwent about ½ mile north of Loftsome bridge.

The hamlet of Babthorpe was greatly shrunken long before 1850, when only a single house remained on the moated site of the manor-house. Later in the 19th century a lodge and two cottages were built on the main road, and after the estate was bought for smallholdings by the county council in 1920 a second house was built near the moated site and two others on the main road. Brackenholme had been reduced to two farm-houses by 1850. Five houses and cottages were later built at the end of the Woodhall road and a bungalow was added in the 20th century. On the opposite side of the main road stands the moated hall that was all that remained of Hagthorpe in 1850. One other house has been built in the present century. Woodhall consisted in 1850 of the mansion known as Wood Hall, the remains of its predecessor, and possibly two other houses.[25] Two or three more houses had been demolished since 1835 during improvements made to the surrounds of the hall by Robert Menzies, and at the same time the road was diverted away from the house.[26] The hall became derelict in the 20th century, but one new house has been built in the hamlet. Farm buildings at Babthorpe, Brackenholme, and Woodhall all include dovecots, and there is a wheelhouse at Woodhall.

There were 65 poll-tax payers in Brackenholme in 1379,[27] though the other hamlets may also have been included in that figure. Only 13 men were mustered at Brackenholme and Woodhall in 1539.[28] For the two places again 13 households were included in the hearth-tax return in 1672, two of them exempt. Of those chargeable 4 had only one hearth each, 5 had 2–3, and 2 had six.[29] The population fluctuated in the 19th century between 65 in 1801 and 115 in 1901.[30] It was 92 in 1931, before the civil parish was united with Hemingbrough.[31]

MANORS AND OTHER ESTATES. In 1086 2 bovates in Babthorpe formed a berewick of the bishop of Durham's manor of Howden, and 3 carucates and 2 bovates were soke of Howden.[32] The overlordship descended with Howden.[33] The demesne lords of BABTHORPE manor were a family taking their name from the township. The first member is thought to have been Ralph of Babthorpe (fl. c. 1190), who had earlier been known as Ralph of Hunsley.[34] The Babthorpes enjoyed unbroken ownership until the death of Sir Ralph Babthorpe in 1490; his daughter Isabel had married Sir John Hastings, who was in possession of the manor in 1492. Hastings died in 1504 and the estate passed to Isabel's cousin, another Isabel, wife of William Plumpton. At Isabel and William's marriage in 1496, however, it had been agreed that the manor should be assigned to William Babthorpe of Osgodby. Disputes over its ownership were not finally settled, in the Babthorpes' favour, until 1565.[35]

In 1621 the manor was conveyed by Sir William Babthorpe (d. 1635) to Richard Bowes,[36] whose family sold it c. 1665 to James Strangeways (d. 1670).[37] Babthorpe apparently passed like Hagthorpe from Thomas Strangeways (d. 1702) to his son Thomas (later Thomas Robinson), and in 1710 it was sold to Boynton Boynton.[38] At his death in 1725 Boynton's heirs were his daughters Elizabeth, who married Richard Langley, and Judith, who married John Twisleton (d. 1757).[39] Babthorpe evidently passed to the Twisletons and from them to John Twisleton's nephew Thomas Cockshutt, who took the surname Twisleton and died in 1764. From Josias Cockshutt Twisleton (d. 1823) Babthorpe passed to his nephew Bache Heathcote, and in 1843 C. T. Heathcote sold it to John Banks.[40] The Banks family retained it until 1920, when William Banks sold it, then comprising 276 a., to the East Riding county council, together with 17 a. in Hemingbrough and 13 a. in South Duffield.[41]

The medieval manor-house had a chapel in 1436–7 and licences to maintain it were granted later in the century;[42] there are still the remains of moats around the modern farm-house. A Gothic lodge stands on the main road at the entrance to the estate.

In 1086 a carucate and 6 bovates in Brackenholme, out of the 2 carucates and 5 bovates recorded in the township, were said to belong to the bishop of Durham's manor of Howden.[43] The overlordship descended with Howden.[44] By 1284 11 bovates in the township were held in demesne under the bishop by Ralph of Babthorpe.[45] This estate, comprising BRACKENHOLME manor, descended in the Babthorpe family until 1620, when it was sold by Sir William Babthorpe to George Wentworth.[46] At the death of Sir George Wentworth in 1660 the manor passed to his daughter

[21] 43 Geo. III, c. 49 (Local & Personal); E.R.R.O., DDTR/Box 8 (uncalendared), case for counsel's opinion, 1891 (giving date of building). See plate facing p. 32.
[22] E.R.C.C. Mins. 1929–30, 389; 1932–3, 136.
[23] O.S. Map 6″ (various edns.).
[24] V.C.H. Yorks. E.R. i. 392.
[25] O.S. Map 6″ (1854 edn.). For the manor-houses see pp. 54–5 and below.
[26] E.R.R.O., DDTR/plan 11.
[27] T.E.R.A.S. xv. 57–8. There is no return for 1377.
[28] L. & P. Hen. VIII, xiv (1), p. 308.
[29] E 179/205/504.
[30] V.C.H. Yorks. iii. 498.
[31] Census.
[32] V.C.H. Yorks. ii. 217. The Summary recorded only one carucate in Babthorpe: ibid. 319.
[33] See p. 57.
[34] For pedigrees see Burton, Hemingbrough, facing pp. 173, 311.
[35] Cal. Pat. 1494–1509, 481–2; Yorks. Fines, i. 315; Feud. Aids, vi. 36, 224, 271; Burton, Hemingbrough, 182–5; Select Cases in Counc. of Hen. VII (Selden Soc. lxxv), p. cxxxv.
[36] C 2/Jas. I/B 31/38.
[37] This paragraph is largely based on Burton, Hemingbrough, 186–9.
[38] R.D.B., A/371/531; /642/916.
[39] Ibid. K/347/720.
[40] Ibid. FW/129/132.
[41] Ibid. 225/2/2.
[42] Burton, Hemingbrough, 181–2.
[43] V.C.H. Yorks. ii. 319.
[44] See p. 57.
[45] Feud. Aids, vi. 36.
[46] Yorks. Fines, 1614–25, 163.

Anne, wife of William Osbaldeston,[47] and it subsequently descended like Hunmanby manor in the Osbaldeston and Osbaldeston-Mitford families.[48]

In 1856 it was sold, comprising 356 a., to John Banks (d. 1881),[49] and in 1882 William Banks sold it to Thomas Brearley.[50] It was acquired from Henry Brearley by C. E. Clark in 1899, and in 1907 he sold it to J. M. Jackson.[51] In 1911 Jackson bought another 92 a. from the devisees of Richard Jewitt, and in 1921 he sold the whole estate to Victor Greaves.[52] Most of it was conveyed to N. E. Hare in 1929,[53] and the Hares still owned it in 1973. The house known as Brackenholme is an ornate building of c. 1900, built of white brick and stone with red-brick dressings, and it has extensive earlier farm buildings.

In 1086 a carucate of land in Hagthorpe belonged to the bishop of Durham's manor of Howden,[54] with which the overlordship subsequently descended.[55] The demesne lords of HAGTHORPE manor were a family taking their name from the township: they held 6 bovates in 1284–5.[56] The first known member of the family is Robert of Hagthorpe (fl. c. 1190).[57] His successors held the manor until the death of Thomas Hagthorpe c. 1500, when it evidently passed to his daughter Joan, who married first Robert Proctor and secondly Thomas Newark. Joan was seised of Hagthorpe at her death in 1535. Land in Hagthorpe apparently passed to her son Geoffrey Proctor, for in 1536 he granted property there to William Babthorpe and others and in 1550 his remaining interest was acquired by Sir William Babthorpe.[58] The manor, however, went to the Newarks, and in 1584 John Newark's successors Thomas and Catherine Savile and Thomas and Catherine Hardwick sold it to Matthew Hutton, dean of York.[59]

In 1612 Matthew Hutton's son Sir Timothy sold the manor to Richard Bowes, the son of Matthew's wife Frances by a previous marriage.[60] The Bowes family[61] retained it until 1665, when Charles Bowes the younger sold it to James Strangeways. The profits of the manor were, however, enjoyed from 1668 to 1692 by Edward Kirlew and later by his son-in-law John Fenton, in satisfaction of the debts of Charles Bowes the elder (d. 1648).[62] When Thomas Strangeways died in 1702, Hagthorpe passed to his son Thomas, who later took the surname Robinson,[63] and in 1711 it was sold to Boynton Boynton.[64] At Boynton's death in 1725 the manor passed to his daughter Elizabeth, who married Richard Langley,[65] and in 1784 another Richard Langley sold it to John Watson.[66] In 1811 Watson's son John sold Hagthorpe to Jonathan Briggs the elder (d. 1840), the estate then comprising about 150 a.[67]

The manor was acquired from Briggs's son Jonathan in 1840 by J. F. Carr and his wife Mary,[68] who died in 1863 and 1871 respectively.[69] The estate was then held by trustees until 1946, when it was sold, comprising 167 a., to Annie Smith. In 1956 it was sold to Mary Parkin, in 1966 to J. H. Bacon, and in 1972 to M. A. Petit.[70] Hagthorpe Hall is a long later-18th-century farm-house, but parts of the moat of an earlier manor-house may still be seen. The house had a chapel in the early 16th century.[71] The outbuildings include several large brick barns and stables, contemporary with the present house.

Between 1133 and 1140 3 bovates in Grimsthorpe (later Woodhall) were given by the bishop of Durham to Durham priory,[72] and in 1158 the king confirmed a grant of a carucate of land there to the priory.[73] The carucate holding was given by the priory to Richard of Coldingham between 1186 and c. 1191,[74] and Thomas of Coldingham held it in 1284–5.[75] The manor of WOODHALL descended to Margery of Coldingham, and in 1313 her husband Walter de Paxton had it; by 1339, however, it apparently belonged to Richard Browne.[76] The estate seems subsequently to have been much divided.

In the 17th century a large holding was built up by the Kirlew family and sold c. 1674 by Thomas Kirlew to Joshua Colston. In 1700 Colston's heirs, three daughters, sold the manor of Woodhall to William Mason.[77] In 1717 Mason's daughter Frances Barker and her husband conveyed the manor to Mary Henson the elder,[78] whose trustees sold it in 1743 to John Burton, husband of her daughter Mary.[79] John Graham bought it from the Burtons in 1747[80] and his family held it until Maria Graham devized it in 1801 to John Reeves, the son of her servant Charles Reeves.[81] In 1835 another Charles Reeves sold the manor and 239 a. to Robert Menzies.[82] It was retained by the family until 1921, when Charlotte Menzies sold it to Richard Bramley.[83] The Bramleys still owned it in 1973.

An older house at Woodhall, mentioned in 1570,[84] was replaced by a new one in 1802, built by John Reeves.[85] That in turn was enlarged by Robert Menzies (d. 1839).[86] The square two-storeyed addition of the 1830s is in white brick, with a large

---

[47] Burton, *Hemingbrough*, 170.
[48] See *V.C.H. Yorks. E.R.* ii. 231–2.
[49] R.D.B., HL/65/83.
[50] Ibid. NL/306/450.
[51] Ibid. 10/105/101 (1899); 96/220/205 (1907).
[52] Ibid. 134/374/324; 236/318/255.
[53] Ibid. 384/237/183.
[54] *V.C.H. Yorks.* ii. 319.
[55] See p. 57.
[56] *Feud. Aids*, vi. 36.
[57] For pedigree see Burton, *Hemingbrough*, 190.
[58] Burton, op. cit. 192–3.
[59] *Yorks. Fines*, iii. 29.
[60] *Yorks. Fines, 1603–14*, 192; Burton, *Hemingbrough*, 193.
[61] For pedigree see Burton, *Hemingbrough*, facing p. 195.
[62] Burton, op. cit. 194–5.
[63] Ibid. facing p. 189.
[64] R.D.B., A/643/917; D/18/26; for Boynton see p. 53.
[65] Burton, *Hemingbrough*, facing p. 189.
[66] R.D.B., BH/443/757.
[67] Ibid. CS/388/549.
[68] Ibid. FO/117/113.
[69] Ibid. IL/113/138; KX/269/351.
[70] Ibid. 724/142/124; 1051/284/255; 1454/82/72; 1774/142/122.
[71] Burton, *Hemingbrough*, 191–2.
[72] *E.Y.C.* ii, p. 322.
[73] Ibid. p. 272.
[74] Ibid. p. 323.
[75] *Feud. Aids*. vi. 36.
[76] Ibid. 172; Burton, *Hemingbrough*, 201.
[77] Burton, *Hemingbrough*, 203–4.
[78] R.D.B., G/89/203.
[79] Ibid. S/133/309.
[80] Ibid. T/38/64.
[81] Ibid. CD/139/206; Burton, *Hemingbrough*, 207.
[82] R.D.B., EY/60/68; FA/15/20.
[83] Ibid. 229/356/316.
[84] E 164/38 f. 178.
[85] Date and initials on building.
[86] Burton, *Hemingbrough*, 209.

Venetian staircase window; its doorway probably remains from the house of 1802.[87] Wood Hall was derelict in 1973.

Among the lesser estates was that belonging in 1086 to Gilbert Tison, comprising 5 bovates in Brackenholme and 4 in Hagthorpe.[88] By 1228 it had passed to Eustace de Vescy,[89] and John de Vescy had it in 1284, when Robert of Menthorpe was the under-tenant.[90] The overlordship is said to have passed later to the Percy family and the estate to have been split up.[91] A further 2 bovates in Brackenholme belonged in 1086 to Ernuin[92] and had passed to Hugh de Collum by 1284.[93] Drax priory also had a smallholding in Brackenholme.[94]

Part of the rectorial tithes of Brackenholme and Babthorpe descended, like those of Hemingbrough township, with Hemingbrough manor.[95] The tithes of 73 a. were still held with that manor in 1842, when they were commuted for rent-charges of £10 payable to Wilson's devisees, Tweedy, and Smith.[96] Other tithes were separated from the manor in 1802, when Lady Amherst and Sir John Russell sold them to John Watson,[97] and most of them then descended with Hagthorpe manor to J. F. Carr in 1840.[98] Those on 106 a., however, were sold by Jonathan Briggs the elder to Robert Menzies and others,[99] and in 1842 they were commuted for £20 16s., of which £13 10s. was payable to Menzies.[1]

Another part of the tithes of Brackenholme and Babthorpe, as well as all of those of Woodhall, were granted separately by the Crown after the Dissolution. Those of Woodhall were sold to the Haddleseys and passed in 1637–8 to Edward Kirlew.[2] In 1650 the tithes of Woodhall and of 40 a. in Brackenholme were worth £12 to Kirlew, and others in Brackenholme, worth £15, were held by Charles Fenwick during the life of his wife, formerly the wife of the lord of Hagthorpe manor, Charles Bowes.[3] These various tithes later descended with Hagthorpe manor to J. F. Carr in 1840.[4] Thus Carr had the greater part of the tithes in these townships at commutation in 1842, and he was awarded rent-charges totalling £147 10s.[5]

ECONOMIC HISTORY. It is not clear whether the several hamlets were separate agricultural communities in the Middle Ages. There was certainly some open-field land at an early date, for eleven selions at Brackenholme, together with three tofts and meadow land, were mentioned in the 13th century;[6] and 8 copyholders had 7 houses and 10½ bovates in 1291–2.[7] Land in Bush field, Cow close, Wrang lands, Mowres, and Stainsby were mentioned at Brackenholme in 1529,[8] and in 1699 there were four closes known as Spring field and three as Stonesby.[9]

Land in 'the fields' of Woodhall was recorded in 1553,[10] but at least part of the open-field land there had been inclosed by 1616. At the latter date Woodhall pasture consisted of two adjoining parts, North field which lay in ridge-and-furrow and the Marsh running down to the Derwent; North field was stinted and the Marsh mown for hay. It was said in 1616 that a division between the two parts had been made with the help of a surveyor a few years earlier.[11] Middle field and Hither field closes at Woodhall, as well as the ings, were mentioned in 1667.[12]

Extensive woodland in Brackenholme belonged in 1228 to the bishop of Durham and was commoned by the tenants of the bishop, the prior of Durham, and the Vescys.[13] Part of the woodland area is occupied by modern closes called the Haggs.[14]

In the 19th and 20th centuries there have usually been only 4 or 5 large farms in the whole civil parish.[15]

LOCAL GOVERNMENT. No manorial records are known. Brackenholme with Woodhall joined Howden poor-law union in 1837;[16] it became part of Howden rural district in 1894, Derwent rural district in 1935,[17] and the Selby district of North Yorkshire in 1974.

CLIFFE WITH LUND

The village of Cliffe, lying a mile north-west of Hemingbrough, is strung out for about a mile along a single main street and was consequently sometimes known as Long Cliffe. At its southern end the village street runs from east to west along a ridge of elevated ground overlooking the former course of the river Ouse, and it was presumably the slope down to the river which gave the Anglian village its name.[18] Cliffe, like Hemingbrough, lost its riverside location in the early Middle Ages when the Ouse abandoned a circuitous meander for a new course further south. It was perhaps after that time that the village was extended northwards for the more convenient exploitation of the land in the township. The ground within the old meander of the river belonged to Newhay, a grange of Drax priory on the West Riding bank. The new course left Newhay on the north side of the river, but it was not until 1883

---

[87] Description and illus. in *E. Yorks. Georgian Soc. Trans.* iii (1), 41–6.
[88] *V.C.H. Yorks.* ii. 319.
[89] Prior's Kitchen, D. & C. Muniments, 2. 2. Ebor. 14.
[90] *Feud. Aids*, vi. 36.
[91] Burton, *Hemingbrough*, 168–9.
[92] *V.C.H. Yorks.* ii. 319.
[93] *Feud. Aids*, vi. 36.
[94] E.R.R.O., DDX/16/38; *Valor Eccl.* v. 15; *Cal. Pat. 1557–8*, 385–6.
[95] See p. 39.
[96] B.I.H.R., TA. 84S.
[97] R.D.B., CF/57/91.
[98] See p. 54.
[99] R.D.B., FO/117/113.
[1] B.I.H.R., TA. 84S.
[2] Burton, *Hemingbrough*, 154, which also mentions earlier leases.
[3] C 94/3 f. 77.
[4] See p. 54.
[5] B.I.H.R., TA. 84S.
[6] Hist. MSS. Com. 5, *6th Rep., Brummel*, p. 538.
[7] Burton, *Hemingbrough*, 167.
[8] Prior's Kitchen, D. & C. Muniments, M.C. 6650.
[9] E.R.R.O., DDSA/Box 1, uncalendared.
[10] *Cal. Pat. 1553*, 22.
[11] E 134/14 Jas. I East./6; Trin./2.
[12] Burton, *Hemingbrough*, 203.
[13] Prior's Kitchen, D. & C. Muniments, 2. 2. Ebor. 14 (printed in Burton, *Hemingbrough*, 144–5); *E.Y.C.* ii, p. 322.
[14] O.S. Map 6" (various edns.).
[15] Directories.
[16] *3rd Rep. Poor Law Com.* 168.
[17] Census.
[18] *P.N.E.R. Yorks.* (E.P.N.S.), 258.

that Newhay was transferred from Drax to Cliffe civil parish;[19] it contained 403 a.[20] The hamlet of Lund, a Scandinavian settlement, lies a mile north-west of Cliffe and almost as far from the river. The area of Cliffe with Lund, excluding Newhay, was 2,740 a. in 1850.[21]

The ridge of ground near the old course of the Ouse and large areas further north reach a little over 25 ft. above sea-level. Nevertheless, much of the eastern side of the civil parish as well as the flat land bordering the river are below that level. The open fields lay around Cliffe and Lund villages, not entirely on the higher ground. The riverside land included common meadows but also extensive early inclosures, many of them belonging to the manor of Turnham Hall, which stood on the banks of the Ouse. There were also extensive assarts north of the open-field land, including the medieval Whitemoor farm, but much of the northern part of Cliffe was occupied by commons. The open fields, meadows, and commons were inclosed only in 1863. The township boundaries apparently make little use of natural features apart from the river Ouse, but at several points they follow some of the many streams and drainage dikes on the lower ground.

At the southern end of Cliffe the village street continues eastwards to Hemingbrough and westwards as a minor road to the river at Turnham Hall. Northwards the street runs on towards Skipwith. Another road leads westwards from Cliffe village to Lund and on towards Barlby. The village street of Lund continues as a minor road along the parish boundary and joins another lane striking across the parish from Osgodby to South Duffield. The turnpike road from Selby to Market Weighton crosses the northern end of Cliffe. In the 20th century the Barlby and Hemingbrough roads became part of the Selby–Hull trunk road, and in the late 1920s they were straightened and the southern part of Cliffe village was bypassed.[22] The only ferry across the Ouse was that over the new course of the river at Newhay; it was mentioned in 1538[23] and last used c. 1930.[24]

The Selby–Hull railway line, opened in 1840,[25] crosses the parish, with a now disused station at Cliffe. The station was renamed 'Hemingbrough' in 1874; it was closed for goods traffic in 1964 and for passengers in 1967.[26] The line from Selby to Market Weighton, opened in 1848,[27] also crossed Cliffe, with a station called Cliffe Common north of the village. It was closed in 1965[28] and the line has been lifted. The Derwent Valley Light Railway, opened in 1912, ended beside the Market Weighton line at Cliffe Common, with its own station. It was closed for passengers in 1926[29] and goods in 1965,[30] and the line has been lifted.

The village street of Cliffe is more closely built up at its south end than elsewhere, but in general the 18th-century and later houses are loosely grouped along it. The buildings include several farm-houses with large barns and one with a dovecot. Recent buildings include nearly 30 council houses. A village institute was erected in 1923[31] to replace a hut acquired about five years earlier.[32] The hamlet of Lund contains farm-houses with a dovecot and a wheelhouse.[33] Newhay consists of two farms, both with wheelhouses, and two other houses, one of them at the former ferry; all the houses are close to the river bank. A stone at one farm is inscribed '1747 IFM', perhaps referring to John Middleton.[34] The extensive civil parish includes several outlying farm-houses. In addition to Turnham Hall, which originated in the Middle Ages,[35] they include four more standing beside the Ouse: Newland House, Cleek Hall, Barlow Lane Ends Farm, and Goole Hall. All probably had an early origin and at least three of them were mentioned in the 17th century, along with the later-demolished Micklehurst.[36] Farms to the north of the village include Whitemoor, which is medieval in origin.[37] In the extreme north of Cliffe there were still in 1973 numerous buildings connected with the former airfield at Riccall.[38]

There were 2–4 licensed alehouses at Cliffe with Lund in the later 18th century.[39] In 1823 the two inns were called the Queen's Head and the Plough and Ship, both standing in the south end of Cliffe village.[40] The Queen's Head, which was presumably the house called the Queen Charlotte in 1840,[41] was last mentioned in 1879. The Plough and Ship may have closed by the 1870s, though beer retailers were mentioned at that time. By 1879 the New Inn had been opened near the Selby–Hull railway line, and by 1889 the Station Inn had appeared at Cliffe Common. The latter, sometimes called the Railway Inn, apparently closed in the 1930s.[42]

There is no poll-tax return for Cliffe with Lund. In 1672 72 households were included in the hearth-tax return, 17 of them exempt. Of those chargeable 33 had only one hearth each, 15 had 2, 6 had 3–4, and one had seven.[43] The population in 1801 was 424. It fluctuated during the 19th century, reaching a maximum of 641 in 1881 and standing at 593 in 1901.[44] Numbers rose to 667 in 1921 but fell to 615 in 1931. After South Duffield was transferred to Cliffe civil parish in 1935 their combined population exceeded 700; in 1971 it was 718.[45]

---

[19] Bulmer, *Dir. E. Yorks.* (1892), 626. A small area around the ferry at Newhay was in Brayton (Yorks. W.R.), not Drax: O.S. Map 6" (1854 edn.).
[20] Sheahan and Whellan, *Hist. York & E.R.* ii. 622.
[21] O.S. Map 6", Yorks. (1854 edn.). Most of the civil parish is covered by sheets 221–2, the rest by sheets 206–7.
[22] E.R.C.C. *Mins.* 1928–9, 237; 1929–30, 389; R.D.B., e.g. 343/12/10.
[23] *Monastic Suppression Papers* (Y.A.S. Rec. Ser. xlviii), 99.
[24] Local information.
[25] *V.C.H. Yorks. E.R.* i. 392.
[26] Ex inf. Divisional Manager, Brit. Rlys. (Leeds), 1972.
[27] MacMahon, *Beginnings of E. Yorks. Rlys.* 14.
[28] *Hull Daily Mail,* 12 June 1965.
[29] *V.C.H. City of York,* 479.
[30] K. Hoole, *Regional Hist. of Rlys. of Gt. Brit.* iv (The North-East), 63.
[31] Date on building.
[32] Ex inf. Mr. T. A. Jacques, Cliffe, 1974.
[33] See plate facing p. 64.
[34] See p. 58.
[35] See p. 57.
[36] Burton, *Hemingbrough,* 284–5.
[37] See p. 57.
[38] See p. 83.
[39] E.R.R.O., QDT/2/15.
[40] Baines, *Hist. Yorks.* (1823), ii. 188; O.S. Map 6" (1854 edn.).
[41] White, *Dir. E. & N.R. Yorks.* (1840), 332.
[42] *Kelly's Dir. N. & E.R. Yorks.* (1879), 406, and later directories.
[43] E 179/205/504.
[44] *V.C.H. Yorks.* iii. 498.
[45] *Census.*

MANORS AND OTHER ESTATES. After the Conquest 3 carucates in Cliffe belonged to William Malet, but by 1086 they were in the possession of the count of Mortain and held of him by Niel Fossard; the whole estate was then soke of the bishop of Durham's manor of Howden.[46] The bishop's overlordship of Cliffe was still mentioned in 1415.[47]

Half the manor of *CLIFFE* was kept in demesne by the bishops of Durham[48] and passed in 1836, along with Howden, to the newly-created bishopric of Ripon.[49] At inclosure in 1863 the bishop received an allotment for his share of the ownership of the soil of the commons.[50] Much of the land was copyhold, eventually enfranchised.[51]

The rest of the manor passed from the Fossards to Joan, daughter of William Fossard, and her husband Robert of Turnham by 1199.[52] It descended c. 1220 from Robert's son, another Robert, to the latter's daughter Isabel, who married Peter de Mauley.[53] It was subsequently held like Turnham Hall[54] by the Mauley and Ros families.[55] At some time it was apparently held as under-tenants by the Malbis family and hence became known as the *MALVIS* manor. The estate was later subdivided. Part of it was held in the early 16th century by Thomas Beverley, and his son John bought a third of the manor from James Chaice in 1559 and other land from Anthony Mark in 1564.[56] John Beverley sold the manor to Brian Stapleton in 1589.[57] By 1658 it belonged to the Williamsons[58] and it subsequently descended with Turnham Hall.

A large part of the Turnham family's estate in the township was separate from Cliffe manor and was known as the manor of *TURNHAM HALL*. It was conveyed by Eleanor de Mauley, along with her half of Cliffe manor, to Hugh Despenser in 1323,[59] but the Despensers' estates were confiscated by the Crown in 1326[60] and the manor was granted to John de Ros in 1327.[61] It descended like Storwood until shortly before the death of William Cecil, Lord Ros, in 1618.[62] It was conveyed to William Ward in 1617 and sold in 1639 to Thomas Williamson.[63] The Williamsons sold it in 1689 to Cuthbert Harrison (d. 1699), whose daughter Lennox married George Smith.[64] The manor passed in 1706 to their son Jeremiah (d. 1714) and then to his widow Mary (d. 1743), who devised it to her sisters Anne, Elizabeth, and Jane Skinner.[65] The sisters were all dead by 1753 and the manor passed by a settlement made in 1750 to Elizabeth Bachelor (d. 1759), who devised it to her sister Mary. In 1769 it was sold to James Keighley.[66]

At Keighley's death in 1790 the estate passed to his daughter Elizabeth, wife of William Burton, and William was succeeded by his son Thomas (d. 1883), author of *The History and Antiquities of the Parish of Hemingbrough*.[67] The Burtons held Turnham Hall until 1919, when 763 a. were sold to the Olympia Agricultural Co. Ltd.[68] Most of this land comprised Newland House, Cottage, Cleek Hall, and Barlow Lane End farms. The estate was bought in 1923 by the Olympia Oil and Cake Co. Ltd.,[69] which in 1940 acquired the 126-acre Cherry Orchard farm,[70] part of which lay in Barlby. In 1951 the company sold all 878 a. of its estate to Mr. J. I. C. Dickinson.[71] In 1954 511 a., comprising Barlow Lane End, Cherry Orchard, and Cleek Hall farms, were sold to the University of Nottingham,[72] but the 94-acre Goole Hall farm was acquired by Mr. Dickinson in 1970.[73]

The manor-house of Turnham Hall was mentioned as early as 1327[74] and the 14th-century house included a chapel.[75] The present house is said to have been built by William Burton c. 1800.[76] It is a large square house of two storeys with contemporary outbuildings including a modest coach-house and stable block.

Of the freehold estates in Cliffe that which became known as Whitemoor may be traced back to the 13th century. It was granted to Emery de Eyville by the bishop of Durham in 1277, when it formed part of the waste called Blackwood.[77] It eventually passed to the Salvins and in 1580 Gerard Salvin sold it to Marmaduke Fawkes.[78] From Fawkes it passed to Maurice Blunt in 1594 and from Blunt to John Bewe in 1598. At the death of Josias Bewe in 1620 his heirs were William Bracebridge, son of his sister Mary, and Barbara, wife of Marmaduke Prickett.[79] A farm of 88 a. at Whitemoor was sold by Robert Prickett to Richard Seaton in 1678,[80] and by the Seatons to John Owram in 1700.[81] In 1792 Stephen Owram sold it to Richard Willbor,[82] who died by 1800 leaving as coheirs his daughters Anne, who married Thomas Tireman, and Mary, who married George Ellin.[83] It evidently passed to the Tiremans, who retained it until 1903, when Jemima Tireman sold it to A. F. Burton.[84] Another farm, of 79 a., was alternatively known as Swindlehurst. It was acquired by Burton from Annie Orr in 1912.[85] In

---

[46] V.C.H. Yorks. ii. 224.
[47] Yorks. Inq. Hen. IV–V, p. 108.
[48] e.g. Feud. Aids, vi. 36, 172.
[49] Univ. of Durham, Dept. of Palaeography, Durham Dioc. Rec., Orders in Council, 22 Dec. 1836 (Ripon).
[50] R.D.B., bound copy of award.
[51] e.g. ibid. 617/27/24.
[52] E.Y.C. ii, p. 329.
[53] Burton, Hemingbrough, 253.
[54] See below.
[55] e.g. Cal. Inq. p.m. ii, p. 172; viii, pp. 114–15; xiii, pp. 169–70.
[56] Yorks. Fines, i. 35, 231, 289.
[57] Ibid. iii. 111.
[58] Y.A.S., MD. 108.
[59] Burton, Hemingbrough, 269, 271.
[60] Cal. Inq. Misc. ii, p. 238.
[61] E.R.R.O., DDSC/18.
[62] e.g. Cal. Inq. p.m. viii, pp. 114–15; ix, pp. 192–3; x, pp. 34–5; xiii, pp. 169–70; for Ros see Complete Peerage; see below p. 183.
[63] Burton, Hemingbrough, 279–80.
[64] Ibid. 280–1.
[65] R.D.B., D/125/202; /302/499; Burton, Hemingbrough, 282. Manorial court records show Wm. Crowle as lord in 1708–14: Y.A.S., MD. 156; he was a trustee of Jeremiah Smith: Burton, Hemingbrough, 281–2.
[66] R.D.B., AM/74/116; /76/117–18; /77/119; /79/120; Burton, Hemingbrough, 282–3.
[67] R.D.B., BQ/214/321; Burton, Hemingbrough, 283.
[68] R.D.B., 192/185/170.
[69] Ibid. 259/139/118.
[70] Ibid. 641/573/478.
[71] Ibid. 894/28/21.
[72] Ibid. 989/202/180.
[73] Ibid. 1656/58/54.
[74] E 142/58 no. 8.
[75] Test. Ebor. iii, pp. 35, 316.
[76] Burton, Hemingbrough, 268.
[77] Ibid. 287.
[78] Yorks. Fines, ii. 159.
[79] E.R.R.O., DDHV/5/1.
[80] Burton, Hemingbrough, 290.
[81] E.R.R.O., DDHV/27/4.
[82] R.D.B., BQ/453/705.
[83] Ibid. CB/169/268.
[84] Ibid. 57/81/73 (1903).
[85] Ibid. 139/411/371.

1945 Burton's executors sold the 211-acre Whitemoor farm to G. H. Johnson, and he sold it to Mr. Wilfred Sails in 1947.[86] Beside the modern farmhouse there are traces of the moat which surrounded an earlier house.

In 1086 1½ carucate in Lund was soke of Wressle manor and belonged to Gilbert Tison.[87] Shortly before 1100 Gilbert gave a carucate of it to Selby abbey, and 7 bovates were subsequently held of the abbey by the Gunby family.[88] The descent of this land has not been traced.[89] Another religious house with land in the township was Thicket priory, which had a small estate in Cliffe.[90]

In 1086 Newhay belonged to Ralph Paynel, as lord of the manor of Drax (Yorks. W.R.),[91] and from the Paynels it was subsequently held by the Stanegrave family.[92] William Paynel founded Drax priory in the early 12th century,[93] and various gifts of land in Newhay were made to the priory by the Stanegraves and others.[94] In Edward I's time Drax had 2 carucates there of the Stanegrave fee[95] and it retained the estate until the Dissolution, when it was worth over £11.[96]

In 1543 the manor of NEWHAY, or Newhay Grange, was granted to William Babthorpe,[97] but soon afterwards it passed to the Salvins.[98] John Salvin apparently conveyed it to Edmund Latham in 1576,[99] but the Salvins still had property in Newhay in the early 17th century.[1]

The manor and estate were in 1738 sold by members of the Crowle family to John Middleton.[2] In 1806 they were bought by William Phillips, and c. 1820 by Thomas Preston.[3] Henry Preston had 196 a. there in 1837.[4] Newhay belonged to the Prestons, of Moreby,[5] until 1925, when Beatrice Preston sold it to A. H. and T. P. Jacques.[6] It was sold to William Higham in 1937 and to R. H. Falkingham in 1947,[7] and the Falkinghams still owned it in 1973.

The rectorial tithes of Cliffe with Lund descended like those of Barlby, most of them with Hemingbrough manor but those of pigs and poultry with Babthorpe manor.[8] The former were worth £80 and the latter, together with similar tithes in Barlby and Osgodby, £3 in 1650.[9] When they were commuted in 1841 rent-charges of £580 were awarded to Wilson's devisees, Tweedy, and Smith, and of £4 12s. to C. T. Heathcote.[10]

The tithes of Newhay belonged to John Morley in 1600.[11] They were sold by the Morleys to John Twisleton in 1612 and by Twisleton to Hugh Taylor in 1621.[12] Taylor still had them in 1650, when they were worth £10.[13] In 1838 the tithes belonged to Moffatt Palmer; those on his own estate were then merged, and the rest were commuted for £105.[14]

ECONOMIC HISTORY. There was land for two ploughs at Cliffe in 1086.[15] A large area was under cultivation in the 13th and 14th centuries, when there were also extensive low-lying meadows and pastures near the Ouse which were sometimes subject to flooding. It was probably part of the low ground, within a bend of the river, that was known as Ness in the 13th century.[16] In the north of the township was waste land that formed part of the woodland and moor of Blackwood, stretching into North and South Duffield; before 1280 the bishop of Durham granted 120 a. there to Emery de Eyvile, with licence to ditch, inclose, and sow it.[17]

The demesne arable land of the Mauley manor of Cliffe amounted to 172 a. in 1279;[18] Turnham Hall manor included 62 a. sown with corn and 140 a. of fallow arable in 1327;[19] and in 1349,[20] 1352,[21] and 1372[22] the Turnham Hall demesne included 4 carucates, said to contain 240 a., of arable land. Demesne meadow amounted to 24 a. in 1327 and 45 a. in 1349, and it was described in 1352 as lying in Swynale and the Haggs. Pasture covered 114 a. in 1349, and in 1352 it included the Carr, the Dayles when not flooded, and the Brend. Arable land was also said in 1352 to be frequently flooded, and an alder wood was worth nothing beyond the cost of repairing the river banks in 1327. The total value of the manor (probably always including Turnham Hall and half of Cliffe, as explicitly stated in 1372) was £20–30. To this the rents of unfree tenants contributed about £10, but both rents and court profits were said in 1349 and 1352 to have been reduced by poverty and 'the mortality'. Flooding was again mentioned in 1441, when the value of Turnham Hall manor was allegedly reduced following the destruction of the river banks.[23] In 1421–2 there was reference to Outer and Inner Newland, beside the river,[24] where Newland House still stands.

Newhay was first mentioned in the 12th century,[25] and it may have been colonized only after the Ouse had changed its course. In the early 14th century arable land, the 'utgang', and the Marsh all lay south of the old course of the river, and several dikes were mentioned.[26]

The low grounds towards the river may have been inclosed from an early date, but in 1773 'Cliffe ings

---

[86] R.D.B., 698/245/213; 751/368/308.
[87] V.C.H. Yorks. ii. 272.
[88] E.Y.C. xii, pp. 47, 50.
[89] For later landowners at Lund see Burton, Hemingbrough, 292.
[90] Valor Eccl. v. 94.
[91] V.C.H. Yorks. ii. 270.
[92] E.Y.C. vi, p. 119.
[93] V.C.H. Yorks. iii. 205.
[94] J. Burton, Mon. Ebor. 107–9.
[95] Burton, Hemingbrough, 295.
[96] Valor Eccl. v. 15.
[97] Parl. Rep. Yorks. ii (Y.A.S. Rec. Ser. xcvi), 10.
[98] Burton, Hemingbrough, 296.
[99] Yorks. Fines, ii. 96.
[1] e.g. Yorks. Fines, 1603–14, 119; 1614–25, 115.
[2] C.P. 43/623 rot. 249.
[3] Burton, Hemingbrough, 299.
[4] B.I.H.R., TA. 56L.
[5] See p. 106.
[6] R.D.B., 306/41/26.
[7] Ibid. 565/438/347; 773/509/442.
[8] See pp. 39, 53.
[9] C 94/3 f. 77.
[10] B.I.H.R., TA. 637L.
[11] West Sussex Co. Rec. Off., Chichester, Goodwood MSS., E4947.
[12] Yorks. Fines, 1614–25, 173, 178.
[13] C 94/3 f. 77.
[14] B.I.H.R., TA. 56L.
[15] V.C.H. Yorks. ii. 224.
[16] Abbrev. Plac. (Rec. Com.), 26; Cur. Reg. R. xi, pp. 129–30; E.Y.C. ii, p. 320.
[17] Cal. Chart. R. 1257–1300, 231.
[18] C 133/21 no. 14.
[19] E 142/58 no. 8.
[20] C 135/96 no. 21.
[21] C 135/117.
[22] C 135/229 no. 5.
[23] Cal. Fine R. 1437–45, 203–4.
[24] Belvoir Castle MSS., Roos 932.
[25] P.N.E.R. Yorks. (E.P.N.S.), 259.
[26] Cal. Pat. 1307–13, 348; Cal. Chart. R. 1300–26, 169–71.

and fields' adjoined the closes of Goole Hall farm and the 'old river Ouse warped up'.[27] Ings and Brocks there remained in common until the final inclosure of 1863. The long curving closes in which the former Ings still lie suggest that this land may indeed once have been in cultivation. The rest of the open-field land lay around Cliffe and Lund villages, some of it on the slightly higher ground. South field and 'Welecroke' field were mentioned in 1421–2[28] and Cadcroft field in 1776.[29] At inclosure in 1863 the open fields included 28¼ bovates and it was thought that the owners of those lands enjoyed rights of turbary in the common called Oxgangs, adjoining Skipwith. Another extensive common occupied much of the north of the township, and 91½ common rights were extinguished at inclosure. South of Lund village the Great (or Far) and Little Pastures were interlocked with land called Furlongs and they may represent open-field ground laid to grass.[30]

The remaining common lands were inclosed in 1863 under the general Inclosure Act of 1843.[31] Allotments were made totalling 1,180 a. The northern waste grounds accounted for 491 a. from Low common, 144 a. from Oxgangs, and 31 a. from Whitemoor common. Furlongs and Pastures, near Lund, made up 66 a., and Ings and Brocks, near the river, 94 a. Other allotments were made from Carr field (100 a.), Chantry field (77 a.), Cadcroft field (60 a.), Longland field (53 a.), Old Mill field (53 a), and Holmes field (11 a.). There were 55 allotments of under 10 a., 21 of 10–19 a., and 13 of 20–89 a. Only the Burtons, lords of Turnham Hall and Malvis manors, with 176 a. received more.

Before inclosure, in 1841, there had been 1,661 a. of arable land in the township, 325 a. of meadow or pasture, 66 a. of woodland, 24 a. of orchards and gardens, and 543 a. of commons, buildings, and roads.[32] In 1905 there were 2,049 a. of arable, 801 a. of grassland, and 53 a. of woodland.[33] Arable farming still predominated in the 1930s and later, though there was still a good deal of grassland in the north of the township and a notable development of market-gardening by the 1960s.[34] About 50 a. of woodland survived on the former commons.[35] In the later 19th century there were 30–40 farmers in Cliffe, and few of them had large farms; only 5 had more than 100 a. each in 1851.[36] By the 1920s there were fewer than 30 farmers, 5 or 6 having more than 150 a., but there had been 10–20 market-gardeners since the 1880s.[37]

Fishing in the Ouse, to the hindrance of navigation, was frequently mentioned in the 14th century.[38] There was still a fishery at Newhay in the 16th century[39] and later, and a fisherman was mentioned into the late 19th century.[40] Timber was used for staiths in the river at Turnham Hall in the 15th century,[41] and there was a common landing-place beside the Ouse near Goole Hall in the 18th and 19th centuries.[42] In the earlier 19th century clay was dug near Common End Farm to make bricks for the foundations of the road from Cliffe to Cliffe Common.[43]

A mill at Cliffe was mentioned in 1365[44] and the bishop of Durham's windmill was described as long totally waste in 1477–8.[45] There were windmills at both Cliffe and Lund in the early 19th century;[46] by 1841 a steam mill had been built near the Cliffe windmill and it had become a seed-crushing as well as a corn-milling business.[47] Besides the millers four men were occupied with flax, linseed, or oil in 1851.[48] All three mills still existed in 1863,[49] but the seed-crushing mill was up for sale in 1865–71[50] and neither of the Cliffe mills was mentioned again. There is no record of a miller after 1872,[51] though the Lund corn mill was still named as such in 1907.[52] All the mills have been demolished. By 1889 two large maltings had been built in the township, one beside the Hull–Selby railway line near Cliffe village and the other close to the line from Selby to Market Weighton at Cliffe Common station.[53] They were in use until c. 1960 and both still stood in 1973.[54]

LOCAL GOVERNMENT. The bishop of Durham's tenants at Cliffe owed suit to his court at Howden; as many as 68 tenants paid chevage there in 1609.[55] There are surviving court books for the manor of Turnham Hall for 1706–80[56] and 1885–1925,[57] and for the manor of Malvis for 1853–1925;[58] the courts were concerned solely with surrenders and admissions. John de Stanegrave claimed to enjoy the assize of ale in Newhay in 1293.[59]

No parochial records before 1835 are known. Cliffe joined Selby poor-law union in 1837,[60] and in 1841 nine parish poorhouses were sold.[61] The township became part of Riccall rural district in 1894, Derwent rural district in 1935,[62] and the Selby district of North Yorkshire in 1974.

NONCONFORMITY. Houses in Cliffe were registered for dissenting worship in 1787 and 1818.[63] A Wesleyan Methodist chapel on the Heming-

[27] E.R.R.O., DDSE(2)/2/5.
[28] Belvoir Castle MSS., Roos 932.
[29] H.U.L., DRA/674.
[30] R.D.B., bound original award with map.
[31] Ibid.   [32] B.I.H.R., TA. 637L.
[33] Acreage Returns, 1905.
[34] [1st] Land Util. Surv. Map, sheet 32; 2nd Land Util. Surv. Map, sheet 689 (SE 63–73).
[35] e.g. R.D.B., 410/407/323.
[36] H.O. 107/2351.
[37] Directories.
[38] E 142/58 no. 8; C 135/96 no. 21; C 135/117; C 135/229 no. 5; Pub. Works in Med. Law, ii. 251–5, 283–6.
[39] Monastic Suppression Papers, 99.
[40] E.R.R.O., DDCV/36/1; White, Dir. E. & N.R. Yorks. (1840), 332; Bulmer, Dir. E. Yorks. (1892), 634.
[41] Belvoir Castle MSS., Roos 932.
[42] E.R.R.O., DDSE(2)/2/5; O.S. Map 6" (1854 edn.).
[43] Ex inf. Mr. T. A. Jacques, Cliffe, 1974.
[44] C.P. 25(1)/276/127 no. 11.

[45] Univ. of Durham, Dept. of Palaeography, CC. 190240.
[46] E.R.R.O., DP/122; Baines, Hist. Yorks. (1823), ii. 188.
[47] B.I.H.R., TA. 637L; White, Dir. E. & N.R. Yorks. (1840), 332.   [48] H.O. 107/2351.
[49] R.D.B., bound inclosure award and map.
[50] Brace, Hist. of Seed Crushing in Gt. Brit. 154.
[51] Kelly's Dir. N. & E.R. Yorks. (1872), 374.
[52] O.S. Map 1/2,500, Yorks. CCXXI. 8 (1907 edn.).
[53] Kelly's Dir. N. & E.R. Yorks. (1889), 399.
[54] Local information. See plate facing p. 33.
[55] e.g. S.C. 2/211/62.   [56] Y.A.S., MD. 156.
[57] E.R.R.O., DDX/91/45.
[58] Ibid. DDX/91/42–3.
[59] Plac. de Quo Warr. (Rec. Com.), 220.
[60] 3rd Rep. Poor Law Com. 178.
[61] Ex inf. Mr. Jacques, Cliffe, 1974.
[62] Census.
[63] B.I.H.R., DMH. 419; DMH. Reg. 1, p. 57.

brough road was built in 1825.[64] It was closed in 1968[65] and had been demolished by 1973, though the adjoining Sunday school still stood. A Primitive Methodist chapel in the main street was built in 1842[66] and rebuilt in 1864.[67] It was deregistered in 1942[68] and was used as a storehouse in 1973.

EDUCATION. There was an unlicensed teacher at Cliffe in 1619.[69] By will proved in 1708 Mary Waud left £200 to establish a school and £20 to build a school-house. The house was duly built and £180 of the endowment was used to buy 15 a. at Knedlington.[70] The income was about £10 in 1743 and 1764, and at the latter date 20 children were taught free.[71] Benjamin Whittall bequeathed £100 to the school in 1791 and John Robinson £100 in 1832.[72] In 1819 the income was £25, in 1823 £41, and in 1835 £30, and there were 16, 30, and 29 free pupils respectively in those years. The total number of pupils in 1835 was 44.[73] The school-house was enlarged that year.[74]

The attendance was 80 in 1871,[75] when a new school was built on the same site. In 1873, when the average attendance was 58, the income included £35 from endowments.[76] An annual government grant was first received in 1875–6.[77] Elizabeth Burton, by will dated 1878, left £200 to the school.[78] The attendance was about 100 in 1908–14, but it fell thereafter and was 73 in 1938.[79] Senior pupils were transferred to Barlby secondary school in 1960,[80] but there were still 65 on the roll in September 1973.[81] In 1969–70 the endowment income from Waud's and Burton's charities was £106; nothing more is known of the Whittall and Robinson bequests.[82]

CHARITIES FOR THE POOR. The Poor's Lands included 3 a. at Cliffe, devised at an unknown date and producing £9 10s. rent in 1823, and 4 a. there, also of unknown origin, producing £11 19s. in 1823.[83] Until the late 1920s the charity trustees also had another 3-acre field on which stood two widows' cottages, but the land was sold in separate lots between then and 1966.[84] In 1973 the endowments were represented by 7 a. and £1,784 stock.[85]

Thomas Burton, by will proved in 1883, left an endowment for poor widows which was represented in 1973 by £90 stock. William Jacques, by will proved in 1919, provided for the distribution of coal in Cliffe and in 1973 the principal consisted of £429 stock. William Pickup, by will proved in 1931, bequeathed £100 for the benefit of twelve inhabitants of the township. In 1972 £100 stock produced over £3 income, distributed in seven doles of 50p each.[86]

All the above-mentioned charities were brought together as the Cliffe Relief in Need Charity by a Scheme of 1973. The income was to be used to provide money, goods, and services for the needy. The Scheme also regulated the Cliffe Parish Charity, which comprised an allotment of 3 a. made at inclosure in 1863 for the repair of roads. The income was to be used for the general benefit of the inhabitants.[87] The total income of both charities in 1973 was £55, excluding Pickup's bequest since the stock was not transferred to the charity trustees until 1974. Doles of £2–3 were given to 19 people and coal was distributed to 5 others.[88]

SOUTH DUFFIELD

The village of South Duffield lies 1½ mile north of Hemingbrough on ground rising slightly above the generally low land bordering the river Derwent. It was an Anglian settlement standing close to a stream now called Folly drain, one of several crossing the township and forming parts of its boundary. South Duffield also has a short frontage upon the Derwent. The township covered 1,686 a.[89]

Apart from the small 'islands' of higher ground around the village almost the whole of the township lies at less than 25 ft. above sea-level. The small open fields were situated north of the village, entirely on the lower ground, and much of the township was covered by early inclosures. High and Low Moors in the far north adjoined North Duffield, Osgodby, and Skipwith commons, and a small area of common pasture called the Dyon lay beside the stream on the township boundary towards the Derwent. The riverside alluvium was used for common meadow land. The final inclosure of the open fields, commons, and meadows took place in 1834.

The road forming the main village street of South Duffield leads northwards towards Skipwith and southwards to Hemingbrough. Other minor roads lead to Osgodby, Woodhall, and Bowthorpe, and the turnpike road from Selby to Market Weighton crosses the northern end of the township. South Duffield is also crossed by the railway from Selby to Market Weighton, opened in 1848[90] with a station north of the village. The station was closed in 1884[91] and the line in 1965.[92] The Derwent Valley Light Railway crossed the township as it approached Cliffe Common station.[93] South Duffield had a landing-place on the banks of the Derwent.[94]

---

[64] H.O. 129/24/513.
[65] Ex inf. Mr. Jacques, Cliffe, 1974.
[66] H.O. 129/24/513.
[67] Bulmer, *Dir. E. Yorks.* (1892), 634. It was registered in 1866: G.R.O. Worship Reg. no. 17555.
[68] G.R.O. Worship Reg. no. 17555.
[69] Burton, *Hemingbrough*, 263.
[70] *11th Rep. Com. Char.* 773.
[71] B.I.H.R., Bp. V. 1764/Ret. 24; *Herring's Visit.* ii. 66.
[72] Burton, *Hemingbrough*, 263.
[73] *Educ. of Poor Digest*, 1082; *11th Rep. Com. Char.* 773; *Educ. Enquiry Abstract*, 1086.
[74] Burton, *Hemingbrough*, 263.
[75] *Returns relating to Elem. Educ.* 790.
[76] Ed. 7/135 no. 32.
[77] *Rep. of Educ. Cttee. of Council, 1875–6* [C. 1513-I], p. 683, H.C. (1876), xxiii.
[78] Ex inf. Mr. T. A. Jacques, Cliffe, 1974.
[79] *Bd. of Educ. List 21* (H.M.S.O.).
[80] E.R. Educ. Cttee. *Mins.* 1955–6, 151.
[81] Ex inf. Chief Educ. Officer, County Hall, Beverley, 1973.
[82] Ex inf. Mr. Jacques, 1974.
[83] *11th Rep. Com. Char.* 772; board in church.
[84] Ex inf. Mr. Jacques, Cliffe, 1974. The cottages were shown on O.S. Map 6" (1854 edn.).
[85] Char. Com. files.   [86] Ibid.
[87] Ibid.   [88] Ex inf. Mr. Jacques, 1974.
[89] O.S. Map 6", Yorks. (1854 edn.). Most of the township is covered by sheet 222, a little by sheet 207.
[90] MacMahon, *Beginnings of E. Yorks. Rlys.* 14.
[91] Ex inf. Divisional Manager, Brit. Rlys. (Leeds), 1972.
[92] *Hull Daily Mail*, 12 June 1965.
[93] See p. 56.
[94] e.g. E.R.R.O., Enrolment Bk. G, p. 138; O.S. Map 6" (all edns.).

The most noteworthy houses in the village are South Duffield Hall, Manor House,[95] and the Knowle. The last-named is an 18th-century house, remodelled and stuccoed in 1913,[96] and it has a wheelhouse among its outbuildings. The few recent additions to the village include eight council houses. There were one or two licensed alehouses in South Duffield in the later 18th century.[97] The only inn mentioned in 1823 and later was the Cross Keys,[98] which apparently closed during the Second World War.[99] The outlying farm-houses include several which originated before final inclosure: Larabridge Farm, Lowmoor House, and North Toft House north of the village, and Dyon House and Holmes House to the east.[1] Holmes House is an outstanding 17th-century building.[2] A 'mansion house' in the North Toft was described as 'lately built' in 1709.[3]

There were 75 poll-tax payers at South Duffield in 1379.[4] Thirty-seven households were included in the hearth-tax return in 1672, 4 of them exempt. Of those chargeable 20 had one hearth each, 9 had 2, 2 had 3–4, one had 7, and one had eight.[5] The population was 160 in 1801; it subsequently fluctuated, reaching a maximum of 236 in 1861 and standing at 204 in 1901.[6] It fell to 159 in 1931 before South Duffield was united with Cliffe civil parish.[7]

MANORS AND OTHER ESTATES. An estate of 6 carucates at South Duffield belonged after the Conquest to William Malet and 2 carucates were said to belong to the king's manor of Pocklington. By 1086, however, 7 carucates and 5 bovates were held by Niel Fossard from the count of Mortain and 1½ carucate was soke of the bishop of Durham's manor of Howden.[8] By c. 1180 part of South Duffield belonged to William Esveillechien,[9] but by 1284–5 all 8 carucates there belonged to the bishop of Durham.[10] The overlordship subsequently descended with Howden, and the bishop was allotted 15 a. as lord of the manor at the inclosure of 1834.[11]

The demesne tenant under William Esveillechien c. 1180 was Alan Wastehose,[12] and by 1284–5 the Wastehose estate had passed by marriage to the Amcotes, Richard of Amcotes then holding 4 carucates.[13] By 1302–3 it had passed to Anthony Dealtry,[14] and the Bassett family held the manor of SOUTH DUFFIELD by the 1340s.[15] The estate was split up and sold by Alexander Amcotes in 1573–4, some of it passing to the Fawkes family.[16] The other 4 carucates in South Duffield were held in 1284–5 by Nicholas de Stapleton,[17] and in the 15th century the estate belonged to the Knight family as under-tenants.[18] In 1529 this manor of SOUTH DUFFIELD was conveyed by John Knight to William Maunsel,[19] and some of the land subsequently passed to the Laton and Fawkes families.[20]

Various holdings in South Duffield, including Laton and Fawkes property, were acquired in the late 16th and early 17th centuries by William Hildyard,[21] who in 1626 sold his estate to Matthew Topham. After the death of Arthur Topham in 1699, the chief house and 16 a. of land passed to his widow Elizabeth, and thence to John Preston in 1700 and to Richard Sawrey in 1701. Anne Sawrey married Bacon Morritt, who also bought other land in the township.[22] In 1777 J. S. Morritt sold 290 a. in South Duffield to Sir William Lowther.[23] A house and 106 a. were conveyed to Joseph Kirlew in 1805, and, known as South Duffield Hall, to Isaac Crowther in 1836 and William Haddlesey in 1867.[24] The property was bought by Jonathan Dunn in 1874 and James Thompson in 1893.[25] J. H. Thompson sold it in 1943 to Francis Tindall, and on the death of Nellie Tindall in 1965 it was sold by her executor to G. Holman & Sons,[26] the owners in 1973. The Topham's house had seven hearths in 1672.[27] The present South Duffield Hall is an 18th-century farm-house, enlarged in the 19th century, and it retains traces of a moat.

The largest estate in South Duffield built up from the land of the two former manors was that of the Barstows, a York family.[28] It included part of the Amcotes manor, and also Holmes House farm, which Michael Barstow is said to have acquired in 1663.[29] Thomas Barstow had 405 a. in the township in 1861.[30] The family retained the estate until 1925–6, when Sir George Barstow dispersed it; Holmes House farm went to Richard Bramley,[31] and the Bramleys still had it in 1973.

Holmes House has many of the features associated with the 'Artisan Mannerism' of the late 17th century and it was probably built by Michael Barstow. It has a central two-storeyed porch with pilasters, pediments, and a shaped gable, and the mullioned and transomed windows of the main front all have pediments. One end of the house retains its shaped gable.[32] There are traces of the moated site of an earlier house.

Another estate in the township belonged to the Robinson family. After Mary Robinson's death in 1839 it was held, like her land in Barlby, by trustees[33] and in 1890 they sold the 195-acre Manor

[95] See p. 62 and below.
[96] Date on building.
[97] E.R.R.O., QDT/2/15.
[98] Directories.
[99] Local information.
[1] E.R.R.O., IA. South Duffield.
[2] See below.
[3] R.D.B., A/224/320.
[4] T.E.R.A.S. xv. 51–2. There is no return for 1377.
[5] E 179/205/504.
[6] V.C.H. Yorks. iii. 498.
[7] Census.
[8] V.C.H. Yorks. ii. 224, 293.
[9] E.Y.C. ii, p. 317.
[10] Feud. Aids, vi. 37.
[11] E.R.R.O., Enrolment Bk. G, p. 141. See above p. 57.
[12] E.Y.C. ii, p. 317.
[13] Feud. Aids, vi. 37; Burton, Hemingbrough, 215; Cal. Close, 1259–61, 330.
[14] Feud. Aids, vi. 138.
[15] Ibid. 224; Yorks. Fines, 1347–77, p. 5; Cal. Chart. R. 1327–41, 471.
[16] Yorks. Fines, ii. 49; Burton, Hemingbrough, 215.
[17] Feud. Aids, vi. 37; Yorks. Fines, 1300–14, p. 76.
[18] Burton, Hemingbrough, 217.
[19] Yorks. Fines, i. 54, 65.
[20] Burton, Hemingbrough, 219–23.
[21] Yorks. Fines, iii. 142; iv. 186, 195; 1603–14, 9, 39, 158.
[22] Burton, Hemingbrough, 225–7.
[23] R.D.B., AZ/5/7.
[24] Ibid. CL/272/439; FA/380/391; KE/10/14.
[25] Ibid. LM/212/262; 61/257/248 (1893).
[26] Ibid. 659/136/115; 1396/86/80; 1400/238/210.
[27] E 179/205/504.
[28] E.R.R.O., Land Tax.
[29] Burton, Hemingbrough, 216–17, including pedigree.
[30] R.D.B., ID/110/147.
[31] Ibid. 316/525/434; 318/260/216; 328/359/273.
[32] See plate facing p. 129.
[33] See pp. 48–9.

House farm to William Wheldrick.[34] This may have been the house and land which Thomas Robinson bought from Harland Grainger in 1758.[35] The Wheldricks sold it to A. H. Blakey in 1959.[36] Manor House is an 18th-century building which was given a regular front seven bays long in the early 19th century. The extensive outbuildings include a dovecot.

Drax priory had a holding in the township, including a windmill.[37]

The rectorial tithes of South Duffield descended, like those of Hemingbrough township, with Hemingbrough manor.[38] They were worth £30 in 1650[39] and were commuted in 1834 for 293 a., awarded at the inclosure of the township to Thomas Wilson, John Tweedy, and the trustees of Thomas Smith (d. 1810).[40] In 1863 the estate, comprising Lodge Farm and 282 a., was sold to John Banks, who disposed of part of it the same year.[41] The house and remaining 108 a. were conveyed to Edward Morrell in 1886 and to Henry Ward in 1901.[42] Ward's trustees sold the farm, then of 138 a., to Mr. A. A. Robinson in 1956.[43]

ECONOMIC HISTORY. On the larger estate in 1086 there was land for four ploughs but only one plough, on the demesne, was then working. There was pasturable woodland two leagues long and half a league broad. The estate had decreased in value from £4 before the Conquest to £2 in 1086.[44] Woodland later lay in both the north and the south of the township. Adjoining the commons and woods of Skipwith and North Duffield in the north was Blackwood, belonging to the bishop of Durham, where Emme Wastehose had common rights in 1256.[45] In the south other woodland adjoined the woods of Hemingbrough and Brackenholme.

The medieval reclamation of woodland and waste is scantily recorded, though there was mention of Richard le Venur's assart 'towards the bridge of Bowthorpe' in 1311.[46] The 40-acre Eastwood was still in existence in the 1590s,[47] but Blackwood had apparently been inclosed by 1622.[48] The southern woods gave way to inclosures known as West Haye moors and Wood closes by the 19th century,[49] and there is still a small Haymoors wood.

The open-field land included Mill and West fields by 1606, Worm field by 1685,[50] and Townend and Far fields by the 18th century.[51] At final inclosure in 1834,[52] under an Act of 1820,[53] about 460 a. were dealt with, including the open fields, extensive commons occupying the former Blackwood area, a small stream-side common called Dyon, and meadow land near the Derwent. Allotments were made from High and Low Moor commons, totalling 258 a., Dyon common (15 a.), the ings (39 a.), Far field (39 a.), Worm field (30 a.), Mill field (18 a.), Townend field (16 a.), and Far North field (14 a.); a further 35 a. were in allotments made from more than one open field, together with small areas of roadside common. An allotment of 262 a. was awarded, along with 31 a. of old inclosures, to the impropriators in lieu of tithes. There were 2 allotments of 60–79 a., 2 of 10–19 a., and 15 of under 10 a.

There were usually 10–15 farmers in the 19th and 20th centuries. Seven of them had at least 100 a. in 1851[54] and 3 had 150 a. or more in the 1930s.[55] In the 20th century the southern part of the township has been largely arable, with much more grassland in the north and east.[56]

A linen weaver of South Duffield was recorded in 1685.[57] A windmill was mentioned in 1311[58] and in the 17th century.[59] A mill was worked throughout the 19th century and a miller was last mentioned in 1925.[60] The tower still stands, at the north-west end of the village.

LOCAL GOVERNMENT. No manorial records are known. South Duffield joined Selby poor-law union in 1837;[61] its poorhouses were still standing in 1850.[62] The township became part of Riccall rural district in 1894, Derwent rural district in 1935,[63] and the Selby district of North Yorkshire in 1974.

NONCONFORMITY. A house in South Duffield was registered for dissenting worship in 1808.[64] A Wesleyan Methodist chapel was built in 1824 at the expense of Jane Haddlesey.[65] It was closed in 1969[66] but still stood in 1973.

EDUCATION. In 1871 South Duffield children went to school at Hemingbrough and Skipwith,[67] and there is no mention of a school at South Duffield until one was built in 1881.[68] It was taken over by a school board in 1885.[69] In 1913 a temporary building was moved from Barlby to accommodate infants.[70] Attendance at the school was about 30–40 in 1908–38.[71] In 1960 senior pupils were transferred to Barlby secondary school, and South

---

[34] R.D.B., 37/211/195 (1890).
[35] Ibid. AA/14/14.
[36] Ibid. 1142/329/293.
[37] Cal. Chart. R. 1300–26, 180.
[38] See p. 39.
[39] C 94/3 f. 77.
[40] E.R.R.O. Enrolment Bk. G, pp. 138–41.
[41] R.D.B., IL/256/330; /259/331; /261/332.
[42] Ibid. 10/2/2 (1886); 32/48/46 (1901).
[43] Ibid. 1035/64/59.
[44] V.C.H. Yorks. ii. 224.
[45] Reg. Pal. Dunelm. ii. 1310–12.
[46] Cal. Chart. R. 1300–26, 180.
[47] E.R.R.O., DDLA/6/2–3.
[48] Ibid. DDHV/27/1.
[49] Burton, Hemingbrough, 212.
[50] Y.A.S., MD. 163.
[51] E.R.R.O., DDX/31/111, 120.
[52] Ibid. Enrolment Bk. G, pp. 129 sqq.; IA. South Duffield (map).
[53] 1 Geo. IV, c. 26 (Private).
[54] H.O. 107/2351.
[55] Directories.
[56] [1st] Land Util. Surv. Map, sheet 32; 2nd Land Util. Surv. Map, sheet 689 (SE 63–73).
[57] Y.A.S., MD. 163.
[58] Cal. Chart. R. 1300–26, 180.
[59] Yorks. Fines, 1603–14, 41.
[60] Kelly's Dir. N. & E.R. Yorks. (1925), 551 and other directories.
[61] 3rd Rep. Poor Law Com. 178.
[62] O.S. Map 6" (1854 edn.).
[63] Census.
[64] G.R.O. Worship Returns, Vol. v, no. 2129.
[65] Stone on building.
[66] B.I.H.R., Meth. Archives 2, S. Duffield.
[67] Returns relating to Elem. Educ. 790.
[68] Ed. 7/135 no. 169.
[69] Bulmer, Dir. E. Yorks. (1892), 633.
[70] E.R. Educ. Cttee. Mins. 1912–13, 323; 1913–14, 72.
[71] Bd. of Educ. List 21 (H.M.S.O.).

Duffield school was closed in 1962 and the pupils transferred to Hemingbrough.[72] The building still stood in 1973.

CHARITIES FOR THE POOR. An unknown donor at unknown date gave 7 a. at Hemingbrough for the poor of South Duffield and Osgodby. The rents were distributed in 1823.[73] No more is known of the charity.

South Duffield also benefited, with Barlby, from Mary Carr's charity.[74]

MENTHORPE WITH BOWTHORPE

The hamlets of Menthorpe and Bowthorpe lie respectively 3 and 2 miles north-east of Hemingbrough, the former beside the Derwent, the latter ¼ mile from the river and close to the stream that separates the township from South Duffield. Both were probably Scandinavian settlements. Bowthorpe township covered 457 a. and Menthorpe 638 a., but 197 a. of Menthorpe formed a detached part of Skipwith parish.[75]

The two townships nowhere reach 25 ft. above sea-level. They are crossed by a single road, linking Brackenholme with North Duffield, from which side lanes lead to the hamlets. The railway from Selby to Market Weighton, opened in 1848, crossed Menthorpe; a small station there was closed for passengers in 1953 and for goods in 1964, and the line was closed in 1965.[76] The remaining houses of Menthorpe stand around a small common, part of which beside the river had recently been inclosed in 1973. A ferry, mentioned in the 14th century,[77] crossed the river at this point to Breighton but was last used before the Second World War.[78] There were half-a-dozen houses at Menthorpe in the mid 19th century, along with a smithy,[79] but only three were occupied in 1973. Bowthorpe consists only of the Hall[80] and a few cottages. There was a licensed alehouse at Menthorpe c. 1750–70[81] and the Board inn was mentioned in 1823,[82] but there has never since been a public house there. Both hamlets had landing-places beside the Derwent.[83]

There were 32 poll-tax payers at Bowthorpe in 1379.[84] Ten men were mustered in the two hamlets in 1539,[85] and eleven households were included in the hearth-tax return in 1672, two of them exempt. Of those chargeable 5 had one or 2 hearths and 4 had 3 or four.[86] The population in 1801 was 61; it reached a maximum of 82 in 1841 and was only 51 in 1901.[87] After falling to 44 in 1911 numbers rose to about 70 in 1921–31 before the civil parish was joined to North Duffield.[88]

MANOR AND OTHER ESTATES. In 1086 Bowthorpe consisted of 4 carucates which were soke of the bishop of Durham's manor of Howden.[89] The bishop's overlordship was still mentioned in 1284–5.[90] In 1200 the bishop granted the estate to Richard d'Avranches,[91] whose family still had it in 1346.[92] By 1400–1 it had passed to the Skipwiths by the marriage of Catherine d'Avranches and William Skipwith,[93] but in 1428 it belonged to the Methams.[94] Property in Bowthorpe was conveyed by John Grendon and his wife Iseult, formerly wife of Richard de Metham, to John Portington and others in 1442.[95] The manor of BOWTHORPE was sold by Roger Portington to Sir William Babthorpe in 1576[96] and by the Babthorpes to Thomas Walmesley in 1604.[97] The Walmesleys conveyed the manor to Sir Godfrey Copley in 1678.[98]

In 1738 the Copleys sold the manor to Bacon Morritt,[99] and in 1777 J. S. Morritt sold it to Sir William Lowther; it comprised Bowthorpe Hall and 446 a.[1] It passed to Edward Weddall in 1807, to G. E. Dinsdale in 1810, and to Sir Thomas Plumer in 1812.[2] Plumer sold the manor to Richard Waterworth in 1820 and his devisees conveyed it to James Walker in 1833.[3] The Walkers retained it until 1924, when Sir Robert Walker sold it, with 452 a., to A. H. Blakey.[4] In 1969 T. O. Blakey sold the estate to the Flint Co. Ltd.[5] Bowthorpe Hall is a large greybrick house, built by Richard Waterworth.[6]

That part of Menthorpe lying in Hemingbrough parish belonged to the bishops of Durham and, like Barlby,[7] was held under them by the Atons and their descendants.[8] The demesne owners of some of the land, perhaps from as early as the 13th century, were the Freeman family.[9] On the death of Robert Freeman in 1717[10] the estate passed to his daughters Margaret, who married Thomas Champney, and Anne, later the wife of William Wilberfoss. In 1763 they conveyed it to Anne's son Robert,[11] whose son Thomas sold it in 1804 to William Chaplin: it then

---

[72] E.R. Educ. Cttee. Mins. 1955–6, 151; 1960–1, 98–9; 1962–3, 61.
[73] 11th Rep. Com. Char. 772.
[74] See p. 52.
[75] O.S. Map 6″, Yorks. (1854 edn.). The whole civil parish is covered by sheet 222.
[76] MacMahon, Beginnings of E. Yorks. Rlys. 14; Hoole, Regional Hist. of Rlys. of Gt. Brit. iv. 55; Hull Daily Mail, 12 June 1965.
[77] e.g. E.R.R.O., DDFA/5/38; Yorks. Deeds, ix, pp. 126, 161–2.
[78] Local information.
[79] B.I.H.R., TA. 339S; O.S. Map 6″ (1854 edn.).
[80] See below.
[81] E.R.R.O., QDT/2/15.
[82] Baines, Hist. Yorks. (1823), ii. 369. The Half Moon, recorded under Menthorpe in 1822 (E.R.R.O., QDT/2/13), is in Breighton.
[83] O.S. Map 6″ (various edns.).
[84] T.E.R.A.S. xv. 49–50.
[85] L. & P. Hen. VIII, xiv (1), p. 308.
[86] E 179/205/504.
[87] V.C.H. Yorks. iii. 498.
[88] Census.
[89] V.C.H. Yorks. ii. 319.
[90] Feud. Aids, vi. 36.
[91] Yorks. Fines, John (Sur. Soc. xciv), p. 3.
[92] Feud. Aids, vi. 36, 138, 172, 224.
[93] Burton, Hemingbrough, 244.
[94] Feud. Aids, vi. 272.
[95] C.P. 25(1)/280/159 no. 1.
[96] Yorks. Fines, ii. 94, 97; Burton, Hemingbrough, 246.
[97] Yorks. Fines, 1603–14, 15.
[98] E.R.R.O., DDCV/23/1–2.
[99] R.D.B., P/158/419.
[1] Ibid. AZ/5/7.
[2] Ibid. CR/256/322; /265/333; CT/54/98; E.R.R.O., Land Tax.
[3] R.D.B., DH/360/412; ET/56/64.
[4] Ibid. 285/576/481; for pedigree see Burke, Peerage (1925), 2282–3.
[5] R.D.B., 1600/211/185.
[6] Ibid. II/293/366.
[7] See p. 48.
[8] e.g. Feud. Aids, vi. 36, 138, 224, 272.
[9] Burton, Hemingbrough, 235.
[10] Ibid. 236.
[11] R.D.B., AE/292/567.

comprised a house, 105 a., and a share of the commons.[12] William's father Robert had acquired the rest of the former Aton fee from James Blanshard in 1752, when it consisted of a house and 117 a.[13] The Chaplins retained the estate until 1921, when Robert Chaplin sold 266 a. and common rights to Ernest and Palmer Holman.[14] Known as Hall farm, it was sold in 1938 to T. O. Blakey, and in 1969 to the Flint Co. Ltd.[15]

The rectorial tithes of Bowthorpe and of that part of Menthorpe lying in Hemingbrough parish descended, like those of Hemingbrough township, with Hemingbrough manor.[16] In 1650 the tithes of half of Menthorpe and those of Bowthorpe were worth £20.[17] The Menthorpe tithes were sold to John Chaplin in 1810,[18] and at commutation in 1839 he was awarded rent-charges of £66 for great tithes and £19 12s. 6d. for small.[19] The Bowthorpe tithes were sold to James Walker in 1838[20] and so were apparently merged with the manorial estate.

ECONOMIC HISTORY. There is little evidence of how the two hamlets were farmed before the 19th century. They were then entirely inclosed except for some 20 a. of common forming a 'green' near the river at Menthorpe and a strip called the Gale alongside the road leading to it.[21] The tithable land at Menthorpe comprised 465 a. of arable and 152 a. of meadow and pasture in 1839.[22] Grassland was predominant at both places in the 20th century.[23] There have usually been 2 or 3 farmers at Menthorpe and one at Bowthorpe in the 19th and 20th centuries, all of them having 150 a. or more in the 1930s.[24]

The lord of Menthorpe had a weir there for fishing in the 14th century,[25] and a fishery was mentioned in the 17th and 18th centuries.[26]

LOCAL GOVERNMENT. No manorial records are known. Menthorpe with Bowthorpe joined Howden poor-law union in 1837;[27] it became part of Howden rural district in 1894, Derwent rural district in 1935,[28] and the Selby district of North Yorkshire in 1974.

NONCONFORMITY. A house at Menthorpe was registered for dissenting worship in 1793.[29]

OSGODBY

The village of Osgodby lies 2½ miles north-west of Hemingbrough. The township nowhere reaches to the Ouse and it consists mostly of slightly elevated ground, exceeding 25 ft. above sea-level. In the south it includes a little of the flat land bordering the river, and a stream forms the township boundary there. Osgodby was a Scandinavian settlement. The area of the township was 1,559 a.[30] The open fields lay around the village, with common meadows further south; much of the land north of the village was occupied by early inclosures, including a park around the manor-house, but in the far north an extensive common adjoined similar land in Riccall and South Duffield. The open fields, meadows, and commons were inclosed in 1819.[31]

The village stands at the junction of roads leading to Barlby, Cliffe, South Duffield, and Skipwith, and the turnpike road from Selby to Market Weighton crosses the north of the township. The Barlby and Cliffe roads have been improved in the 20th century as part of the Selby–Hull trunk road, and a bypass south of the village was built in the 1920s.[32] The Selby–Hull railway line, opened in 1840,[33] and the line from Selby to Market Weighton, opened in 1848 and closed in 1965, both cross the south of the township.[34]

The older part of the village includes no noteworthy houses. There has been much new building in the 20th century, including eight council houses in the village centre. There are a few private houses on the South Duffield road near Osgodby Hall,[35] and many more on the bypass and both along and behind the Barlby road. A single alehouse in Osgodby was licensed in the 1750s and 1760s, but none later in the century.[36] The Half Moon was recorded in 1823[37] but thereafter only a beerhouse until 1879, when the Wadkin Arms was in existence.[38] It was still the only public house in 1973.

There is no poll-tax return for Osgodby. In 1672 25 households were included in the hearth-tax return, all of them chargeable. Fifteen had one hearth each, 6 had 2, and 4 had 3 to five.[39] In 1801 the population was 146; it reached a maximum of 225 in 1861 and 1881, but had fallen to 190 in 1901.[40] It rose to 294 in 1931 before Osgodby was united with Barlby civil parish.[41]

MANOR AND OTHER ESTATES. In 1086 2 carucates and 7½ bovates in Osgodby belonged to the count of Mortain and were held from him by Niel Fossard, who had succeeded William Malet. Of that total 3 bovates had been held before the Conquest by Norman and Tochi. The whole estate was

[12] R.D.B., CF/551/879.
[13] Ibid. W/75/165.
[14] Ibid. 239/537/454.
[15] Ibid. 595/7/5; 1600/211/185.
[16] See p. 39.
[17] C 94/3 f. 77.
[18] R.D.B., CR/124/153.
[19] B.I.H.R., TA. 339S.
[20] R.D.B., FH/242/249.
[21] O.S. Map 6" (1854 edn.); Burton, Hemingbrough, 232, 234.
[22] B.I.H.R., TA. 339S.
[23] [1st] Land Util. Surv. Map, sheet 32; 2nd Land Util. Surv. Map, sheet 689 (SE 63–73).
[24] Directories.
[25] Pub. Works in Med. Law, ii. 253.
[26] e.g. C.P. 43/503 rot. 106.
[27] 3rd Rep. Poor Law Com. 168.
[28] Census.
[29] B.I.H.R., Fac. Bk. iii, p. 11.
[30] O.S. Map 6", Yorks. (1854 edn.). Most of the township is covered by sheet 221, a little by sheets 206 and 222.
[31] R.D.B., DA/207/50 and plan.
[32] E.R.C.C. Mins. 1920–1, 194–5; 1928–9, 237; 1929–30, 389; R.D.B., 332/241/192.
[33] V.C.H. Yorks. E.R. i. 392.
[34] MacMahon, Beginnings of E. Yorks. Rlys. 14; Hull Daily Mail, 12 June 1965.
[35] See p. 65.
[36] E.R.R.O., QDT/2/15.
[37] Baines, Hist. Yorks. (1823), ii. 374.
[38] Directories.
[39] E 179/205/504.
[40] V.C.H. Yorks. iii. 498.
[41] Census.

THORGANBY: the coach-house and stables to the hall

KEXBY: Manor Farm

LUND: Oakwood Farm, showing the wheelhouse

DUNNINGTON: the old village, seen from the north-west, surrounded by recent housing

HESLINGTON, THE UNIVERSITY OF YORK
View from the south-east, showing Heslington Hall and church in the foreground

soke of the bishop of Durham's manor of Howden.[42] The bishop's overlordship was still mentioned in 1504.[43] From the Fossards the mesne lordship descended to Joan of Turnham and her husband Robert by 1204,[44] and to Isabel de Mauley and her husband Peter by 1223.[45]

In 1204 the manor of OSGODBY was held in demesne by Jordan de Hameldon, otherwise known as Jordan of Osgodby.[46] By 1223 it had passed to Jordan's daughter Denise, who married Sampson de la Pomeray,[47] and it subsequently passed to Adam of Osgodby.[48] In 1284–5 Robert of Osgodby held the manor[49] and he was followed by his son, another Robert. Its ownership was subsequently in dispute and a settlement was reached only in 1460, in favour of Thomas Babthorpe. The Babthorpes claimed that Robert of Osgodby the younger had two daughters, Emme, who married John Rabace, and Cecily, who married Hugh Turnyll, and that Hugh's son Ralph conveyed the manor to William Kettering. From Kettering it passed to the Babthorpes, apparently about 1440. The rival claim of the Hagthorpe family was that the manor passed to them by the marriage of Robert of Osgodby's sister to Thomas Hagthorpe.[50]

The Babthorpes retained Osgodby until 1622, when Sir William Babthorpe sold it to Sir Guy Palmes.[51] In 1668 William Palmes sold it to Sir Jeremiah Smith (d. 1675),[52] and in 1704 his grandson Jeremiah conveyed it to John Burdett.[53] On Richard Burdett's death in 1744 the manor passed to his daughter Elizabeth, who married first George Ridley and secondly, in 1778, T. F. Pritchard, who assumed the surname Burdett.[54] In 1785 T. F. Burdett sold the manor to George Dawson.[55] It was conveyed by G. P. Dawson to Riley Briggs in 1861, together with 1,125 a.[56]

Briggs died in 1913 and in 1919 his devisees sold the manor, with Osgodby Hall and 338 a., to A. G. Hopper.[57] The manor and hall, with 84 a. of land, were sold to Sir Charles H. Wilson (d. 1930) in 1927,[58] to L. S. Charlton in 1936, and to E. A. Whittaker in 1949, and, without most of the land, to M. S. Moorse in 1957 and to Mr. Oliver Adamson in 1969.[59] The sale to Hopper in 1919 included the 254-acre Home farm, most of which was sold to J. W. Johnson in 1924, to F. B. Lax in 1928, to J. W. Proctor in 1936, and to R. H. Simpson in 1945.[60] The Simpsons already had other property in the township, including the 161-acre White House farm, later called Osgodby Grange, which T. H. Simpson bought from Riley Briggs's devisees in 1920.[61]

The manor-house at Osgodby apparently contained a chapel in the 15th century.[62] In 1672 the largest house in the village, with five hearths, was occupied by Sir Jeremiah Smith,[63] who may thus already have been the tenant of the manor-house. There is a tradition that the Babthorpes' house was rebuilt c. 1700 and it is possible that it was an 18th-century house that passed to G. P. Dawson in 1844. Dawson employed Edmund Sharpe to enlarge and remodel the house in a Tudor style, providing a porch and entrance hall on the east and adding a tower in 1854.[64] His successor Riley Briggs made further alterations later in the century, notably by replacing many fire-places and refitting the entrance hall. After a fire c. 1956 the tower and central part of the house were demolished and the roof-line simplified.

The outline of the former park, with its drives, ponds, and planting, could still be traced in 1973, and the modern garden is in part bounded by a later-19th-century iron fence and incorporates an 18th-century dovecot and an icehouse. South-west of the house are the walls of an extensive early-19th-century kitchen garden and farmery. Large Victorian gate-piers from the former main entrance to the park have been re-erected at a new house east of the hall. Home Farm bears the date 1863 and the initials of Riley Briggs.

Drax priory,[65] Selby abbey,[66] and Thicket priory[67] all had small estates in Osgodby. The Knights Templars of Temple Hirst were given land there in the 13th century[68] and it was attached to the manor of Temple Hirst until the 20th century.[69]

The rectorial tithes of Osgodby descended like those of Barlby, most of them with Hemingbrough manor but those of pigs and poultry with Babthorpe manor.[70] The former were worth £35 and the latter, together with similar tithes in Barlby and Cliffe with Lund, £3 in 1650.[71] The former tithes were sold to George Dawson in 1812,[72] and they were commuted in 1841 for rent-charges of £71 18s. 6d. payable to G. P. Dawson. For the tithes of pigs and poultry £3 were awarded to C. T. Heathcote in 1841.[73]

ECONOMIC HISTORY. The larger of the two estates at Osgodby in 1086, containing 2 carucates and 4½ bovates, was said to have land for 2 ploughs.

---

[42] V.C.H. Yorks. ii. 224, 293.
[43] Cal. Inq. p.m. Hen. VII, ii, pp. 595–6.
[44] E.Y.C. ii, p. 329.
[45] Yorks. Fines, 1218–31, p. 54.
[46] E.Y.C. ii, p. 329.
[47] Yorks. Fines, 1218–31, p. 54.
[48] Burton, Hemingbrough, 305–6.
[49] Feud. Aids, vi. 37.
[50] E.R.R.O., DDX/16/230; Burton, Hemingbrough, 307–11; Feud. Aids, vi. 224, 271.
[51] Yorks. Fines, 1614–25, 188. For pedigree see Burton, Hemingbrough, facing p. 311.
[52] C.P. 25(2)/754/20 Chas. II Trin. no. [33 from end]. For pedigree of the Smiths see Burton, Hemingbrough, 324.
[53] R.D.B., F/15/30; Burton, Hemingbrough, 325.
[54] Burton, Hemingbrough, 326.
[55] R.D.B., BL/1/1.
[56] Ibid. ID/9/12.
[57] Ibid. 156/439/369; 206/164/139.
[58] Ibid. 355/196/146; 423/253/202.
[59] Ibid. 552/138/112; 837/541/447; 1086/502/455; 1635/17/12.
[60] Ibid. 280/513/447; 365/8/6; 547/466/375; 700/523/450.
[61] Ibid. 217/456/406.
[62] Prior's Kitchen, D. & C. Muniments, 2. 2. Ebor. 12; Burton, Hemingbrough, 330. There is no evidence that there was a chapel in Osgodby village, as on O.S. Map 6" (all edns.). A chantry mentioned in 1535 was at Osgodby (Yorks. N.R.): see V.C.H. Yorks. N.R. ii. 433–4.
[63] E 179/205/504.
[64] Burton, Hemingbrough, 329.
[65] Cal. Chart. R. 1300–26, 177–8; Valor Eccl. v. 15.
[66] Selby Coucher Bk. ii (Y.A.S. Rec. Ser. xiii), 1–4; Valor Eccl. v. 12.
[67] Valor Eccl. v. 94.
[68] B.L. Eg. Ch. 638; Toph. Ch. 40.
[69] R.D.B., DA/207/50; 169/449/371; Cal. Pat. 1553–4, 146.
[70] See pp. 39, 53.
[71] C 94/3 f. 77.
[72] R.D.B., CU/357/393.
[73] B.I.H.R., TA. 410S.

There were then, however, one plough on the demesne, 2 held by 9 villeins, and 2 more held by 6 sokemen, 4 villeins, and 2 bordars. The estate had decreased in value from £2 before the Conquest to £1 in 1086. The smaller estate, of 3 bovates, had one plough in demesne. There was 20 a. of meadow and pasturable woodland ½ league in length and breadth. The estate had fallen in value from 12s. to 5s.[74] The continued existence of waste and woodland in the 13th century is shown by references to common pasture for 200 sheep, common in the turbary, and pasture for pigs in the woodland. Much assarting was also taking place. Besides references to open-field land there was mention of an assart in Scouilacris, one under Stonihag, another belonging to William de Norais, and one called Swynhale; in addition 6 a. inclosed with a dike lay in an assart called Thinnewode. There was also meadow in the Outfield.[75]

A Wednesday market and a fair on 7–9 September were granted to Robert of Osgodby in 1302,[76] but are not mentioned later.

Old inclosures eventually covered much of the township. In 1819 they included 53 a. in Maw, Little Moor, Great Moor, and Gill Ruddings, and 28 a. in Little and Great Hall parks.[77] The latter were perhaps remnants of a medieval deer park; lands called Long flats within the park had been mentioned in 1591.[78] When the remaining open fields, meadows, and commons were inclosed in 1819,[79] under an Act of 1811,[80] they amounted to only 475 a. Allotments were made from the common, totalling 164 a., West field (46 a.), Mill field (30 a.), New Moors field (19 a.), Far field (17 a.), Teathill field (16 a.), and jointly from those fields and from the ings (177 a.). There were 7 allotments of under 10 a., 5 of 10–49 a., and one of 316 a. made to George Dawson, lord of the manor, which included 190 a. for rectorial tithes.

In 1841 there were 1,324 a. of arable land and 200 a. of meadow and pasture in the township.[81] A larger proportion of grassland was recorded in the 20th century, however, together with several large plantations.[82] The improvement of the estate by G. P. Dawson and Riley Briggs, successively lords of the manor, in the later 19th century apparently included the making of a new park, the construction of a large decoy lake, and the planting of woodland.[83] The park had been converted to farmland by 1973. There have usually been 10–15 farmers in the 19th and 20th centuries. Five of them had 100 a. or more in 1851[84] and 3 or 4 of them had 150 a. or more in the 1920s.[85] Since the 1930s there have also been several smallholders, working land acquired by the East Riding county council for the purpose.[86]

A windmill was worked at Osgodby throughout the 19th century[87] and a miller was last mentioned in 1905.[88] Part of the tower still stood in 1973, near the Cliffe road south-east of the village.

LOCAL GOVERNMENT. There are surviving call rolls and other court papers for Osgodby manor for a few years between 1824 and 1856.[89] The township had several poorhouses, still standing in 1841 on an island site at the junction of the Skipwith and South Duffield roads.[90]

Osgodby joined Selby poor-law union in 1837;[91] it became part of Riccall rural district in 1894, Derwent rural district in 1935,[92] and the Selby district of North Yorkshire in 1974.

NONCONFORMITY. The Babthorpe family were prominent Roman Catholics in the late 16th and early 17th centuries.[93] A house in Osgodby was registered for dissenting worship in 1819.[94] The Wesleyans had a meeting-place in 1851[95] and the Primitive Methodists another which had closed by 1914,[96] but there has never been a purpose-built chapel in the township.

EDUCATION. Osgodby children have always attended school at Barlby.

CHARITIES FOR THE POOR. The poor of Osgodby benefited from an unknown donor's gift at South Duffield.[97]

HESLINGTON

THE VILLAGE of Heslington, an Anglian settlement, lies little over a mile south-east of York, on the lower slopes of the York moraine.[1] Despite its proximity to the city the parish largely retained its rural aspect until the 1960s, when the estate of the lords Deramore, centred upon Heslington Hall, was split up and sold. Suburban housing development has begun along the northern margin of the parish, but the establishment of the University of York at Heslington has altered the landscape far more. Most of the ground lying between the village and the city boundary has been included in the university campus and by 1972 there were buildings catering for 2,600 students.[2]

[74] V.C.H. Yorks. ii. 224.
[75] Selby Coucher Bk. ii. 1–8; Cal. Chart. R. 1300–26, 177–8.
[76] Cal. Chart. R. 1300–26, 24.
[77] R.D.B., DA/207/50 and map.
[78] E.R.R.O., DDX/16/234.
[79] R.D.B., DA/207/50.
[80] 51 Geo. III, c. 98 (Local & Personal).
[81] B.I.H.R., TA. 410S.
[82] [1st] Land Util. Surv. Map, sheet 32; 2nd Land Util. Surv. Map, sheet 689 (SE 63–73).
[83] Burton, Hemingbrough, 328–9; O.S. Map 6" (1854 and later edns.).
[84] H.O. 107/2351.
[85] Directories.
[86] e.g. R.D.B., 515/80/68.
[87] e.g. E.R.R.O., DDBV/33/1; B.I.H.R., TA. 410S; H.O. 107/2351; directories.
[88] Kelly's Dir. N. & E.R. Yorks. (1905), 513.
[89] E.R.R.O., DDLO/17/1–3.
[90] B.I.H.R., TA. 410S.
[91] 3rd Rep. Poor Law Com. 178.
[92] Census.
[93] Aveling, Post Reformation Catholicism, 15, 26, 33, 35–6.
[94] G.R.O. Worship Returns, Vol. v, no. 3290.
[95] H.O. 129/24/513.
[96] B.I.H.R., Bp. V. 1914/Ret.
[97] See p. 63.
[1] This article was written in 1972, with some later additions.
[2] Univ. of York Prospectus, 1973–4, 22, 43. See above plate facing p. 65.

The parish of Heslington, roughly rectangular in shape, formerly covered 2,645 a., of which 1,401 a. were in the parish of St. Lawrence, York,[3] until 1869, when they were transferred to St. Paul's, Heslington.[4] The two parts remained separate civil parishes until they were united in 1884.[5] 'Heslington St. Paul' comprised the lands of the prebendal manor and 'Heslington St. Lawrence' those of the capital manor, and the boundary between them had cut the village in two. The open fields and commons were also divided between them.[6] Heslington civil parish was enlarged in 1935 by the transfer of Langwith township from Wheldrake,[7] but in 1968 153 a. in the north of Heslington were transferred to York.[8]

In the north of the parish the moraine lies mostly at 50 ft. or more above sea-level and in places exceeds 100 ft. To the south is a great expanse of lower ground, with only the modest Holme Hill in the south-east relieving the flatness of the landscape. The open fields lay partly on the boulder clay and glacial sand and gravel of the moraine but extended into the lower ground, which is entirely covered by outwash sand and clay.[9] A regular field pattern over much of the parish results from the inclosure of the open fields in 1857 and of much of the low-lying commons in 1762.[10] Part of the commons, however, in the south-western corner of Heslington, remained as open moor and scrub into the present century.[11] That section lying along the western parish boundary has been occupied by Fulford golf course since 1936, when the club moved from Water Fulford.[12] On the low ground much of the parish boundary is formed by dikes, and on the moraine it mostly follows the line of the former Roman road from Brough to York. Parts of the western boundary with Fulford follow the line of another Roman road and the prehistoric Green Dykes.[13]

From the northern end of the village roads lead westwards to Gate Fulford (now Heslington Lane), north-westwards towards York (now University Road), and north-eastwards to join the main road on the northern parish boundary (now Field Lane). Several other roads lead from the village into the fields. One short lane gives access to a surviving stretch of rough pasture known as the Out Gang; the lane was made in 1762, following the inclosure of the copyhold commons, for the benefit of the freeholders and replaced a lane running behind the garths on the west side of the village.[14]

Improvements were made to the lines of several of the roads by the Yarburgh family. The road to York was altered in 1798,[15] for example, and in 1855 the Fulford road and its continuation past the hall and church was realigned and straightened.[16] At the inclosure of the open fields in 1857 the line of the road running north-eastwards was confirmed and a branch from it northwards to the main road, largely on the line of a former field road past the windmill, was laid out.[17] The improvements of the 1850s took place at a time when Heslington Hall was being remodelled and its grounds improved. The gardens and park, with its fishpond, extended to the west of the hall as far as Spring Lane; the line of the lane was moved further away from the hall in 1865, enabling the park to be extended and a larger pond made.[18] The former Roman road along the northern boundary of Heslington has become the main York–Hull road. It was turnpiked in 1765 and the trust was renewed until 1872;[19] an old mile-stone survives. Field Lane was improved and given a new junction with the main road in the 1960s.[20] A York bypass was being constructed across the south and east of the parish in 1974.

The village lies for the most part along both sides of a long main street, with wide grass verges, which begins at the Fulford road near the hall and the church and ends to the south with a sharp turn into the winding Common Lane. The village pond, which formerly lay at the south end of the street, was filled in in 1855.[21] Behind the street to the east lies a back lane, now School Lane but known in 1857 as School House Road and Garth Ends Lane. A footpath, called School Lane in 1857, leads from the main street to the back lane.[22] Behind the garths to the west of the street runs a footpath known as Boss Lane,[23] on the line of the freeholders' former road to their commons.[24] Away from the main street a smaller section of the village lies along the Fulford road, beyond the hall grounds; it was entirely in the township of Heslington St. Lawrence, whereas the larger part of the main street was in St. Paul.

The older buildings are concentrated along the main street with only a few outliers along the Fulford road. There are several 17th- and early-18th-century houses, all of brown brick and low profile, and a few larger houses set back behind gardens. The latter include Little Hall, which has a plaster ceiling dated 1734, Moor Hall, which is mid-18th-century in date but was refronted with canted bays later in the century, and Manor House.[25] The built-up frontage also includes various 19th- and 20th-century houses and farm buildings.

There were three alehouses in the village in the mid 18th century, later generally only two,[26] known in 1823 as the Robin Hood and the Ship and in 1840 as the Bay Horse and the Fox.[27] The Bay Horse was

---

[3] O.S. Map 6″, Yorks. (1853 edn.). Most of the parish is covered by sheet 174, the rest by sheet 191.
[4] See p. 73.
[5] Kelly's Dir. N. & E.R. Yorks. (1889), 400.
[6] B.I.H.R., Yarburgh MSS., estate bks.; see map on p. 68 below.
[7] Census, 1931.
[8] Min. of Housing and Loc. Govt., The York Order, 1968. Acreage kindly supplied by York corp. planning dept., 1972.
[9] Geol. Surv. Map 1″, solid and drift, sheets 63 (1967 edn.), 71 (1973 edn.).
[10] See p. 72.
[11] O.S. Map 6″ (1853 edn.); 2nd Land. Util. Surv. Map, sheet 699 (SE 64–74).
[12] Ex inf. Fulford Golf Club, 1972.
[13] See p. 29.
[14] B.I.H.R., Yarburgh MSS., estate papers.
[15] E.R.R.O., QSF. East. 1798, D.3; Mids. 1798, D.3.
[16] Ibid. HD. 59.
[17] T. Jefferys, Map of Yorks. (1772); O.S. Map 6″ (1853 edn.).
[18] E.R.R.O., HD. 74; O.S. Map 6″ (1853 and later edns.).
[19] K. A. MacMahon, Roads and Turnpike Trusts in E. Yorks. (E. Yorks. Loc. Hist. Ser. xviii), 21–3, 70.
[20] E.R.C.C. Mins. 1967–8, 24; 1968–9, 109; 1969–70, 332.
[21] O.S. Map 6″ (1853 edn.); B.I.H.R., Yarburgh MSS., estate papers.
[22] E.R.R.O., DDGD/Box 1 (inclosure map).
[23] O.S. Map 6″ (1958 edn.). [24] See above.
[25] See p. 70. Little Hall was formerly called Croft Farm: ex inf. Nina, Lady Deramore, 1975.
[26] E.R.R.O., QDT/2/15.
[27] Baines, Hist. Yorks. (1823), ii. 217; White, Dir. E. & N.R. Yorks. (1840), 333.

A HISTORY OF YORKSHIRE: EAST RIDING

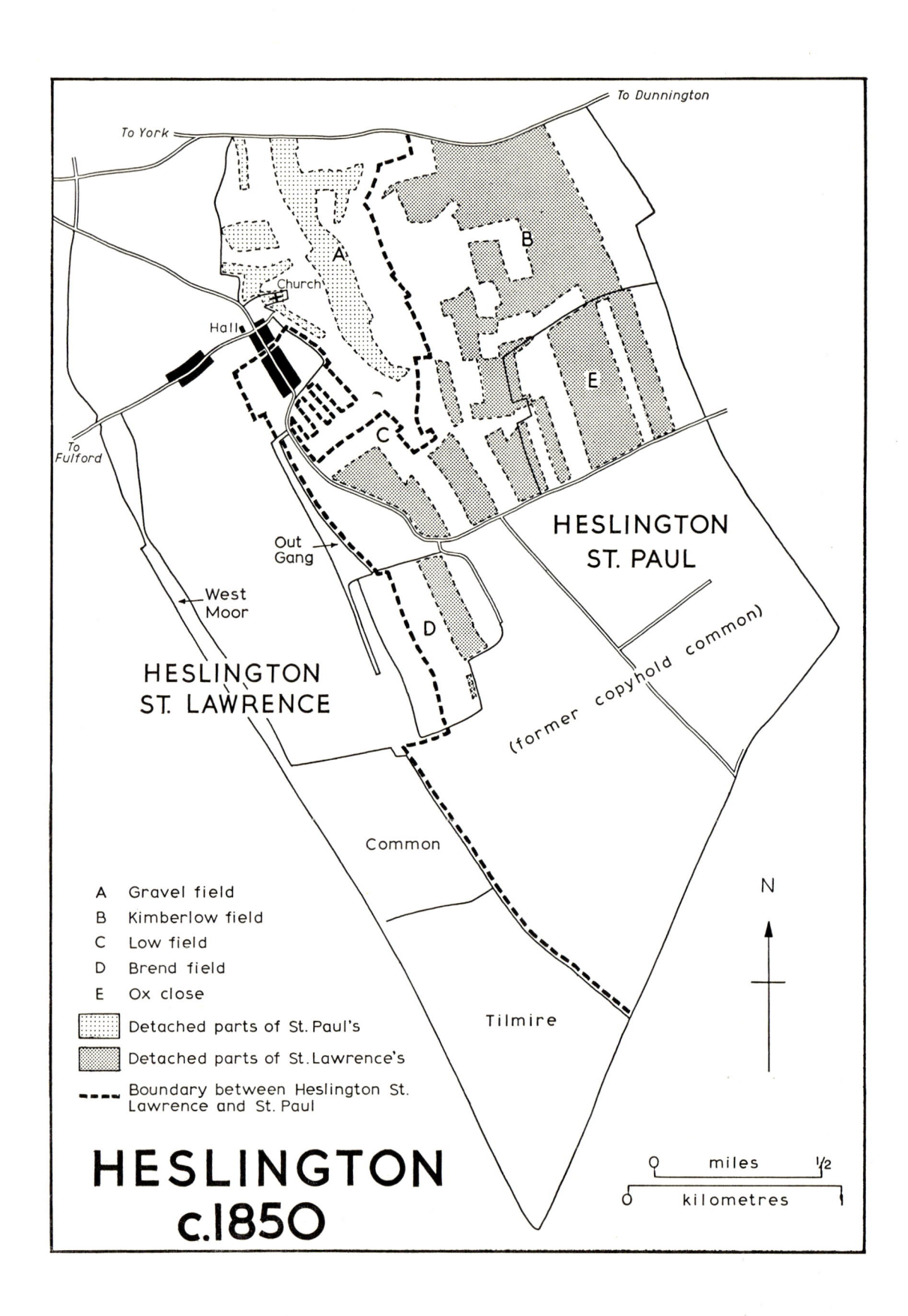

HESLINGTON c.1850

renamed the Charles XII after the winner of the 1839 St. Leger flat race, owned by N. E. Yarburgh.[28] By 1872 the second inn was called the Yarburgh Arms, and in 1967 it was renamed the Deramore Arms.[29] Apart from 32 council houses in and beyond School Lane and 4 council bungalows in Main Street, few additions were made to the buildings in the village until after the establishment of York University. A conservation area was established in 1969,[30] and by 1972 Main Street had still been little altered beyond the intrusion of several branch banks. On the Fulford road more than a dozen detached houses of traditional design have been built, as well as one or two, like Patch House (1968), in a more contemporary style. There is also a group of nearly 30 small brick and timber houses and flats (1968-9), and a 'neighbourhood development' of more than 100 red-brick houses and flats (1969-73), built for members of the university.[31]

The university was founded in 1960 and has a site of a little over 200 a., mostly lying between the Fulford and York roads. Heslington Hall forms its administrative headquarters. The old lake was greatly enlarged and many of the new buildings are situated around it. The architects were Robert Matthew, Johnson-Marshall and Partners, and most of the buildings are constructed in 'Clasp', an industrialized building system with a light steel frame and concrete cladding panels. The first two colleges were opened in 1965, and by 1972-3 there were six, together with laboratories, library, central hall, concert hall, and other buildings. Groups of houses are also included, some at Bleachfield and others near the old Spring Lane.[32]

By 1840 there was an inn, the Black Bull, on the main York–Hull road,[33] but the growth of the York suburbs into the parish did not begin until the 20th century. By c. 1940 there were 40–50 houses along the south side of Thief Lane, which forms the boundary of Heslington in the north-west, and a similar number near the Black Bull and in near-by Mill Lane.[34] Playing fields belonging to St. John's College, York, have been situated in Mill Lane since 1937.[35] In 1957 the York Waterworks Co. built a large water tower, a dominating castle-like structure, on the moraine at Heslington Hill[36] close to a prominent prehistoric barrow.[37] By 1972 there was a housing estate, known as Newland Park, south of Thief Lane, and a larger one, called Badger Hill, between the York–Hull road and Field Lane. Archbishop Holgate's Grammar School moved from York to a site near Badger Hill in 1963.[38]

There were 73 poll-tax payers in Heslington, excluding St. Peter's Liberty, in 1377.[39] In 1672 there were 59 households, of which 4 were discharged from the hearth tax; of those that were chargeable 40 had one hearth each, 8 had 2, 5 had 3 or 4, one had 6, and Heslington Hall had sixteen.[40] In Heslington St. Paul alone there were about 23 families in 1743 and 20 in 1764.[41] The population in 1801 was 416, of which 150 were in St. Paul's township. Heslington St. Lawrence was usually the more populous of the two in the 19th century. The total population rose to 513 in 1821 and 571 in 1861, but fell to 477 in 1881-91; in 1901 it was 506.[42] The number subsequently fell to 447 in 1931, but with the post-war expansion of the village it reached 882 in 1951, 1,223 in 1961, and 2,029 in 1971.[43]

Sydney Smith, the renowned canon of St. Paul's cathedral, lived in Heslington in 1809-14, in the house which later became the Vicarage.[44]

MANORS AND OTHER ESTATES. Of the three Domesday estates in Heslington one consisted of 5 carucates held by Count Alan of Brittany, and another of 3 carucates held by Hugh son of Baldric.[45] Hugh's holding later passed into the Mowbray fee. By 1148 a total of 5 carucates from the two fees had been given to St. Peter's (later St. Leonard's) hospital, York, by the under-tenant Robert son of Copsi.[46] At the Dissolution the hospital's property there was worth about £26.[47] It had been let to William Mennell in 1520.[48]

This manor of HESLINGTON comprised property that was often subsequently known as king's hold or freehold.[49] It was let by the Crown to Sir Thomas Eynns in 1557, and again in 1567 together with other parcels of former St. Leonard's property in Heslington.[50] In 1575-6 the manor-house was granted in fee to Christopher Hatton,[51] but he sold it soon after to Eynns's son, another Thomas (d. 1578).[52] In 1601 Richard Eynns conveyed it to Thomas Hesketh.[53] After the death of Eynns's widow the lease of the manor was sold in 1584 to Francis Nevill, and it later passed to Sir Richard Lewkenor and then to Thomas Wendy and Adrian Staughton.[54] In 1601, however, the manor was granted in fee to trustees[55] and conveyed by them to Thomas Hesketh later that year.[56]

Apparently in 1693 moieties of the manor were settled upon the daughters of Thomas Hesketh, namely Anne, who in 1692 had married James Yarburgh, and Mary, who in 1693 married Fairfax Norcliffe.[57] The manor was reunited in 1793 when Thomas Norcliffe Dalton, great-grandson of Mary and Fairfax Norcliffe, sold his share to Henry Yarburgh.[58] Heslington descended in the Yarburgh

[28] J. Fairfax-Blakeborough, *Northern Turf Hist.* ii. 330.
[29] *Kelly's Dir. N. & E.R. Yorks.* (1872), 375; *Yorks. Eve. Press,* 6 Feb. 1967.
[30] E.R.C.C. *Mins.* 1968-9, 259.
[31] P. Nuttgens, *York,* 88-92 (with illus.).
[32] Ibid. 80-3, 87; Pevsner, *Yorks. E.R.* 250-2; *Univ. of York Prospectus, 1972-3,* 22-5 (all with illus.). See plate facing p. 65 above.
[33] White, *Dir. E. & N.R. Yorks.* (1840), 333; O.S. Map 6" (1853 edn.).
[34] O.S. Map 6" (1958 edn.).
[35] R.D.B., 581/128/98.
[36] *V.C.H. City of York,* 461.
[37] Often mistakenly called Siward's Howe: see p. 33.
[38] York corp. *Mins.* 1962-3, 901.
[39] E 179/202/58 m. 16.
[40] E 179/205/504.
[41] B.I.H.R., Bp. V. 1764/Ret. 27; *Herring's Visit.* ii. 65.
[42] *V.C.H. Yorks.* iii. 498.
[43] Census.
[44] S. J. Reid, *Life and Times of Sydney Smith,* 142-3.
[45] *V.C.H. Yorks.* ii. 276, 321.
[46] *E.Y.C.* i, p. 150; v, pp. 63-7.
[47] *Valor Eccl.* (Rec. Com.), v. 17.
[48] *Cal. Pat.* 1557-8, 303.
[49] B.I.H.R., Yarburgh MSS., estate bks.
[50] *Cal. Pat.* 1566-9, p. 7; 1557-8, 303.
[51] C 66/1149 m. 1.
[52] *Y.A.J.* xviii. 23.
[53] C.P. 43/75 m. 7; *Yorks. Fines,* iv. 172.
[54] B.I.H.R., Yarburgh MSS., Eynns deeds.
[55] C 66/1550 m. 1.
[56] B.I.H.R., Yarburgh MSS., Heslington deeds.
[57] E.R.R.O., DDEL/41/10.
[58] R.D.B., BS/151/228; J. Foster, *Pedigrees of . . . Yorks.* iii.

family until the death of N. E. Yarburgh in 1852, when it passed to his nephew Yarburgh Greame.[59] The latter took the surname Yarburgh and died in 1856. He was in turn succeeded by his nephew G. J. Lloyd, who also assumed the surname Yarburgh, and in 1875 the manor passed to his daughter Mary and her husband G. W. Bateson (d. 1893). In 1876 Bateson took the additional surname de Yarburgh and in 1892 he changed his name from Bateson de Yarburgh to de Yarburgh-Bateson; he became the 2nd Baron Deramore in 1890.[60] Numerous small freehold and copyhold properties were added to the estate in the 18th and 19th centuries.[61]

After being put to military use during the Second World War Heslington Hall stood empty until it was sold, together with 17 a. around it, in 1956 to the Joseph Rowntree Social Service Trust Ltd. In 1962 the hall was acquired for the new University of York, 165 a. of the estate having been bought for the university site the previous year.[62] In 1964 the rest of the estate, comprising 2,076 a. in Heslington and 792 a. more in adjoining Deighton, Fulford, and Langwith, was sold to S. A. Spofforth and E. C. Bousfield.[63] The Deramores continued to live in Heslington, at Manor House, in Main Street, until 1968.[64]

Heslington Hall, a large brick house, was built between 1565 and 1568[65] for Sir Thomas Eynns, secretary to the Council in the North (1550–78).[66] It extends round three sides of a square courtyard. The central, western, range has a nearly symmetrical elevation to the court with a central doorway and two canted bay windows running the full height of the house. The original planning appears to have been conventional, with the two-storeyed hall and the principal room to the north of the entrance. After 1852 there were extensive alterations, designed by P. C. Hardwick.[67] The west, garden, front was extended by the addition of new rooms between the original projecting towers which terminated the elevation, the wings were remodelled and most of the windows enlarged, the roofline was decorated with new parapets, gables, and chimneys, and the interior was replanned. Further alterations, which may have included the addition of a south-west wing, were made in 1876. Early in the present century the interior was restored, much of the mid-19th-century panelling being removed and replaced by new work in late-16th-century style; minor alterations to the exterior included the removal of the steep 19th-century roofs of the towers. After 1960 further alterations were made when the house was converted to university use. To the west of the house there is a possibly contemporary walled garden, with much topiary work which is probably of 18th-century origin.[68] A gazebo and orangery are also of that date. The stable block was built after the straightening of the Fulford road in 1855.[69]

The third estate in Heslington in 1086 consisted of 4 carucates and belonged to the archbishop of York.[70] The chapter was said to have 5 carucates in 1284–5.[71] Four of these were assigned to Ampleforth prebend, presumably at its formation before 1219–34,[72] and c. 1295 the prebend had 32 bovates and other property there.[73] In the 16th century and later the prebendal estate, sometimes called the manor of *HESLINGTON*[74] and comprising land called Peter hold or copyhold,[75] was usually let along with that in Dunnington and Fulford. It was sold in 1649 by the parliamentary commissioners to Clement Baker,[76] but was recovered at the Restoration. In the 18th century the lessees were generally the Wickham family.[77] The estate was vested in the Ecclesiastical Commissioners in 1842, upon a voidance of the prebend,[78] and in 1851 it was sold by them to N. E. Yarburgh.[79] It subsequently descended with the capital manor.

The chief house on the prebendal estate may have been the large brick farm-house in the main street known since at least the 19th century as Manor House.[80] The Yarburghs held a house called Low Hall on the prebendal estate in 1747.[81]

The remaining carucate of the chapter's land was apparently assigned to Driffield prebend, which had been formed by 1166.[82] About 1295 the prebend had a toft and a carucate of land at Heslington.[83] In the 18th and 19th centuries the estate was known as the manor of *VERDENAL PLACE*,[84] no doubt after the Verdenel family, who held land in Heslington in the early 14th century.[85] In 1685 there were 8 houses and 8 bovates of this so-called Vernal hold land.[86] At least some of it later became part of the Yarburgh estate, for in 1785 3 houses and 4 bovates of it which had belonged to the Wightman family were sold to Charles Yarburgh.[87]

An estate in Heslington descended, like the capital manor of Fulford, in the Taylors, Oateses, and Keys in the 18th and 19th centuries.[88] Allotments of 168 a. and 58 a. were made at the inclosures of 1762 and 1857 respectively,[89] and they comprised practically the whole estate. It was merged with Lord

---

[59] For the Greames see *V.C.H. Yorks. E.R.* ii. 95.
[60] Foster, *Pedigrees of . . . Yorks.* ii; Burke, *Peerage* (1970), 772.
[61] B.I.H.R., Yarburgh MSS., Heslington title deeds.
[62] R.D.B., 1037/230/208; 1233/137/123; 1264/461/415.
[63] Ibid. 1376/52/50.
[64] *Yorks. Eve. Press*, 11 Mar. 1968.
[65] A stone on the W. front bears the date 1568 and the Eynns arms; *Country Life*, 19 July 1913; see below plate facing p. 113.
[66] R. R. Reid, *King's Council in the North*, 171.
[67] B.I.H.R., Yarburgh MSS., specifications, plans, and accts.; Pevsner, *Yorks. E.R.* 250–1. A stone on the S. front gives 1854 as the date of restoration and, no doubt wrongly, 1578 as the date of building.
[68] *Country Life*, 17 Nov. 1900.
[69] See p. 67.
[70] *V.C.H. Yorks.* ii. 321.
[71] *Feud. Aids*, vi. 34.
[72] *York Minster Fasti*, i (Y.A.S. Rec. Ser. cxxiii), 60.
[73] *Miscellanea*, iv (Y.A.S. Rec. Ser. xciv), 24.
[74] e.g. C 142/277 no. 258.
[75] B.I.H.R., Yarburgh MSS., estate bks.
[76] C 54/3447 no. 3.
[77] Minster Libr., D. & C. Archives, Wc. f. 23; Wm. p. 229; Torre MS., 'York Minster', p. 1085; Lamb. Pal. Libr., COMM./XIIa/18/23.
[78] B.I.H.R., Inst. AB. 21, p. 58; *Lond. Gaz.* 3 July 1848, p. 2500.
[79] R.D.B., GW/363/471.
[80] Directories.
[81] B.I.H.R., Yarburgh MSS., Hesketh deeds.
[82] *York Minster Fasti*, ii (Y.A.S. Rec. Ser. cxxiv), 20.
[83] *Miscellanea*, iv. 28.
[84] Minster Libr., D. & C. Archives, Wj. (26 Apr. 1774); Wm. p. 669.
[85] *Feud. Aids*, vi. 223; *Yorks. Lay Subsidy, 30 Edw. I* (Y.A.S. Rec. Ser. xxi), 105.
[86] B.I.H.R., CC. Ab. 10.
[87] R.D.B., BI/449/711; B.I.H.R., Yarburgh MSS., estate bks.
[88] e.g. E 134/9 Geo. I Hil./25; E.R.R.O., DDX/148/13.
[89] R.D.B., AC/139/5; E.R.R.O., Enrolment Bk. I, p. 69.

Deramore's estate in 1920, when the 241 a. comprising Tilmire and Grange farms were sold by W. H. Key.[90]

The tithes of Heslington St. Paul belonged to the prebend of Ampleforth and descended with the prebendal manor. In 1649 they were worth £30,[91] and in 1841 they were commuted for £190.[92] The rectory of St. Lawrence's, York, including the tithes of Heslington St. Lawrence, belonged to the chapter of York by the late 12th century.[93] The tithes on the prebend of Driffield's estate were, however, assigned to that prebend. The chapter's tithes were valued at £30 in 1649[94] and the Vernal tithes at £6 13s. 4d. in 1650.[95] They were commuted in 1841 for £215 payable to the chapter and £37 to the precentor of York,[96] to whose property the prebend of Driffield had been annexed since 1485.[97] The lessee of St. Lawrence's rectory leased a plot of ground beside St. Paul's churchyard from the prebendary of Ampleforth in 1299.[98] A tithe barn was later built on it and still stood in 1855.[99]

ECONOMIC HISTORY. No information is given in the Domesday Survey about the condition of the estates in Heslington. Subsequent assarting of waste land in the royal forest of Ouse and Derwent is reflected in a payment of 15s. by the township to the sheriff in 1187 for 30 a. of oats grown in the forest.[1] About 1295 the prebendary of Ampleforth had 8 bovates of land in demesne and 24 were held by 12 bondmen, each bovate including an acre of meadow. Another 1½ a. of meadow lay in Priest croft. There were also 4 cottars, each holding only a toft and croft. The bondmen and cottars rendered money-rents, hens, and eggs, and the bondmen also owed mowing and carting works and provided 5 reapers in autumn for each bovate that they held.[2] Besides the arable land and meadow revealed by the prebendal survey there were extensive common pastures in the southern half of the parish. The pasture and turbary belonging to St. Leonard's hospital there were mentioned in the 12th century and later,[3] and c. 1295 Ampleforth prebend had a pasture and turbary said to extend to Thursepole in the west, Langwith in the south, and Threkes in the east.[4] In the extreme south the commons included the wet area known as Tilmire, and dikes draining it were alleged in the 14th century to cause flooding in townships further south.[5] The value of the capital manor was said in 1364 to have been reduced by flooding.[6]

The open-field land in the 16th century apparently included Little field, mentioned in 1595, and the meadow land included West ings, adjoining York moor in Fulford. The brecks, also mentioned in 1595,[7] were presumably intakes from the waste. They were recorded as early as 1520, when St. Leonard's hospital's miller was entitled to summer pasture there for his horse and a cart-load of hay for winter feed.[8] Mill field was mentioned in the 17th century, and in 1633 there was open-field land in 'the Brend',[9] later called Brend field. The name Little field used for a close in 1696 suggests that there may have been some early inclosure of open-field land,[10] probably south-west of the village where 'Little field gate' gave access to the commons.[11] Other field land may have been inclosed north-west of the village, where 37 a. lay in five Fog closes, between Green Dykes and Mill field, in 1658.[12] Surviving ridge-and-furrow, both south-west and north-west of the village,[13] also indicates the former existence of open-field land. Other closes named in 1696 included Tile pits, Clover Grass close, and Whinny brecks.[14] By the later 18th century there were about 530 a. of closes in the capital manor, mostly north-west and south-west of the village in Heslington St. Lawrence.[15]

To the east of the village, adjoining Grimston township, was a stinted pasture called Ox close, first recorded in 1649.[16] It was inclosed and subdivided in 1698 by agreement between the 17 proprietors who enjoyed beast-gates there, 154⅓ gates in all. The close was said to contain 137 a. and allotments totalling 128¾ a. were made. Apparently in 1710 a Chancery decree was sought to confirm the agreement.[17] Within the commons one early inclosure was made in the extreme south-west, near Pool bridge; it was called Tilmire close in 1658 and was said to contain 100 a., together with a house.[18] In 1696 another 'great piece of ground' called 'the lord's several' was described as still uninclosed from the commons.[19]

The commons stretched right across the parish from Fulford in the west to Grimston, and extended from the open fields and early-inclosed lands southwards to the boundary with Langwith. A dike called Wade Gote crossed the commons and there were several ponds and watery areas. From the southern end of the village a wide 'outgang', with a branch on either side of Brend field, gave access to the commons, and a similar drove-way extended from the Fulford road west of the village alongside the parish boundary.[20] Both freeholders and copyholders shared the commons, but in 1754 the former claimed to have been deprived of their rights and agreed to sustain a law-suit against the copyholders.[21] It is not

[90] R.D.B., 208/248/215.
[91] Lamb. Pal. Libr., COMM./XIIa/18/21–2.
[92] B.I.H.R., TA. 11L.
[93] V.C.H. City of York, 385.
[94] Lamb. Pal. Libr., COMM./XIIa/18/117.
[95] Ibid. COMM./XIIa/17/166.
[96] B.I.H.R., TA. 776S; CC. Ab. 10.
[97] Lond. Gaz. 14 June 1853, p. 3549; V.C.H. Yorks. iii. 85.
[98] Reg. Romeyn, ii, p. 217.
[99] E.R.R.O., HD. 59. It is shown but not named on O.S. Map 6″ (1853 edn.).
[1] E.Y.C. i, p. 422.
[2] Miscellanea, iv. 24–5.
[3] E.Y.C. i, p. 244; Monastic Notes, i (Y.A.S. Rec. Ser. xvii), 247; Monastic Chancery Proc. (Y.A.S. Rec. Ser. lxxxviii), 163; Cal. Pat. 1370–4, 389.
[4] Miscellanea, iv. 24–5.
[5] Cal. Pat. 1343–5, 593; Public Works in Med. Law, ii (Selden Soc. xl), 239.
[6] Cal. Inq. Misc. iii, p. 202.
[7] B.I.H.R., Yarburgh MSS., court rolls.
[8] Cal. Pat. 1557–8, 303.
[9] B.I.H.R., Yarburgh MSS., Hesketh deeds.
[10] E.R.R.O., DDEL/41/10.
[11] B.I.H.R., Yarburgh MSS., undated map of the commons (perhaps 17th or early 18th century).
[12] Ibid. Hesketh deeds.
[13] Other ridge-and-furrow, now destroyed, is visible on air photographs: Humberside County Library, Beverley, 1974.
[14] E.R.R.O., DDEL/41/10.
[15] B.I.H.R., Yarburgh MSS., estate bks.
[16] C 54/3447 no. 3.
[17] B.I.H.R., Yarburgh MSS., estate papers.
[18] Ibid. Hesketh deeds; undated map of commons.
[19] E.R.R.O., DDEL/41/10.
[20] B.I.H.R., Yarburgh MSS., undated map of commons.
[21] Ibid. estate papers.

clear whether the two groups intercommoned over the whole of the commons or had separate areas within them, but an undated map, apparently earlier than 1754, shows the 'pretended division' between the King's hold (or freehold) and Peter hold (or copyhold) commons.[22] It was presumably the dispute of 1754 which led to the inclosure of the copyhold common in 1762,[23] under an Act of the previous year.[24] Altogether 786 a. were allotted, of which 172 a. went to Charles Yarburgh and 168 a. to Robert Oates; there were also 2 allotments of 50–100 a., 10 of 20–49 a., and 4 of under 20 a. In the outgang 32 a. were inclosed, leaving a much reduced outgang leading to the freehold common. An agreement of 1762 about a lane to the outgang[25] was signed by 13 copyholders and only 3 freeholders, who were copyholders as well.

The remaining open fields were known in the 18th century and probably before as Gravel, Low, Kimberlow, and Brend fields.[26] It was Gravel field which had earlier been known as Mill field. Inclosure of the fields took place in 1857, under the general Inclosure Act of 1836.[27] Allotments totalling 714 a. were made, including 230 a. from Kimberlow field, 214 a. from Gravel field, 173 a. from Low field, and 90 a. from Brend field. G. J. Yarburgh received 600 a., Samuel Key 58 a., and there were 17 allotments of under 15 a. each. There had already been some departure from customary crops and rotations in the fields, for turnips, potatoes, mustard, and flax were being grown in Heslington in the late 18th and early 19th centuries, and potatoes were said to replace a fallow in the open fields.[28] Chicory was also apparently grown in the parish, as in nearby Dunnington, for a pain laid in the manorial court in the early 20th century prohibited the washing of it in any watercourse.[29]

The number of farmers in the parish has decreased from more than 20 in the mid 19th century to about a dozen after 1900, and there have usually been one or two market-gardeners as well. About 1930 nearly half of the farmers had 150 a. or more.[30] The arable acreage remained relatively low until the inclosure of the open fields: in 1801, perhaps in Heslington St. Paul alone, there were only 340 a. under crops, mainly wheat and barley (213 a.),[31] and in 1839 St. Paul's included 438 a. of arable, 654 a. of meadow or pasture, and 6 a. of woodland.[32] By 1905, however, there were 1,626 a. of arable, compared with 575 a. of grassland and 56 a. of wood, in the whole parish.[33] A considerable area of common land has survived in the south of the parish. In 1856 there were 272 a. in Tilmire common and 11 a. in the Out Gang, and 6 men had 166 gates there, all but 14 of them belonging to G. J. Lloyd.[34] The Out Gang and much of the common remained in 1972, including the former drove-way beside the parish boundary, which had long been known as West Moor and which had become part of the golf course.[35] The pasture land in the 1930s and later included the area occupied by the University of York in 1972; most of the remaining farmland in the parish was arable.[36]

There was a gravel-dealer in Heslington in 1840 and gravel was sold from pits on the moraine.[37] A bleach works north-west of the village was described in 1804 as 'lately built'. It was used by Messrs. Stablers, linen cloth makers of York, and later by John Swale, who had a flax-mill in Lawrence Street in the near-by suburb. By 1857 the works were disused and the property was then bought by the Yarburghs.[38]

A windmill at Heslington is mentioned in 1530,[39] and it was called Stublowe mill in 1551.[40] Two windmills were shown north-east of the village, on the moraine, in 1787.[41] A new smock mill was built there in 1794–5,[42] later replaced by a brick tower mill; it is said to have lost its sails c. 1910 and a miller was last mentioned in 1913, but the stump was not demolished until 1941.[43]

LOCAL GOVERNMENT. Several fragmentary 16th-century court rolls survive, one of them for a court held by the farmer of the capital manor in 1595.[44] There are surviving call rolls for 1860–1925, and a court book and pains for 1900–25 which show that two bylawmen, a bailiff, and a pinder were elected.[45]

There are churchwarden's accounts for Heslington St. Paul for 1712–1883 and for Heslington St. Lawrence for 1753–1823.[46] Accounts of the constable of St. Paul's for 1754–1823 refer to the existence of a 'freehold constable' for St. Lawrence's.[47] There were similarly two copyhold and two freehold bylawmen, and the accounts of the former survive for 1748–1817; their sole income was from the letting of common balks in the open fields.[48] Heslington joined York poor-law union in 1837.[49] It became part of Escrick rural district in 1894, Derwent rural district in 1935,[50] and the Selby district of North Yorkshire in 1974.

CHURCH. The church of St. Paul, Heslington, was in the peculiar jurisdiction of the prebendary of Ampleforth,[51] who provided a curate to serve it. Though technically a chapel, it appears to have been

[22] B.I.H.R., Yarburgh MSS., estate papers.
[23] R.D.B., AC/139/5.
[24] 1 Geo. III, c. 38 (Priv. Act).
[25] See p. 67.
[26] e.g. R.D.B., A/97/136.
[27] E.R.R.O., Enrolment Bk. I, p. 69; DDGD/Box 1 (draft award and map).
[28] B.I.H.R., PR. HES. 19; PR. Y/L 26; Yarburgh MSS., estate papers.
[29] Ibid. Heslington manorial records.
[30] Directories.
[31] 1801 Crop Returns.
[32] B.I.H.R., TA. 11L.
[33] Acreage Returns, 1905.
[34] B.I.H.R., Yarburgh MSS., estate papers.
[35] E.R.R.O., DDX/225/14; O.S. Map 6" (1853 and later edns.).
[36] [1st] Land Util. Surv. Map, sheet 27; 2nd Land Util. Surv. Map, sheets 699 (SE 64–74), 709 (SE 65–75).
[37] B.I.H.R., PR. HES. 11; O.S. Map 6" (1853 edn.); White, *Dir. E. & N.R. Yorks.* (1840), 333.
[38] B.I.H.R., Yarburgh MSS., Heslington title deeds.
[39] E 303/26/Yorks./1204.
[40] *Cal. Pat.* 1566–9, p. 7.
[41] J. Tuke, *Map of Yorks.*
[42] B.I.H.R., Yarburgh MSS., Heslington title deeds.
[43] Directories; *Yorks. Gaz.* 4 July 1941.
[44] B.I.H.R., Yarburgh MSS., court rolls.
[45] Ibid. Heslington manorial records.
[46] Ibid. PR. HES. 8–10.
[47] Ibid. 12.
[48] Ibid. 11; Yarburgh MSS., estate papers. The accounts were made by 4 bylawmen in 1748–54.
[49] *3rd Rep. Poor Law Com.* 171.
[50] *Census.*
[51] *V.C.H. Yorks.* iii. 86.

fully parochial in the Middle Ages and was mentioned in 1299 together with its burial ground.[52] Part of Heslington, however, was in the parish of St. Lawrence, York, the church of which was near by in the city suburbs. It was separated from St. Lawrence's and united with St. Paul's in 1869.[53] St. Paul's, which had previously been styled a perpetual curacy, was thenceforth called a vicarage.[54] The township of Langwith was transferred from Wheldrake to Heslington ecclesiastical parish in 1971.[55]

Curates were nominated by the prebendary until 1842, when the prebend passed to the Ecclesiastical Commissioners and the advowson became vested in the archbishop of York.[56] He is still the patron. In 1650 and later the curate received a stipend of £5 from the prebendary's lessee.[57] The living was augmented from Queen Anne's Bounty in 1740, 1772, 1787, and 1795, each time with £200.[58] Bounty money was used to buy land and common rights at Grassington (in Linton, Yorks. W.R.), later represented by 18 a., together with 10½ a. at Newton upon Derwent and 17 a. in Holderness.[59] The average net value of the living in 1829–31 was £63.[60] Endowments totalling £228 a year were received from the Common Fund in 1870–1, of which £50 was to meet the gift of the Vicarage,[61] and in 1884 the net value of the living was £270; in 1914 it was £284.[62]

There was no parsonage house until 1871, when a large existing house in Heslington Lane was provided by the Yarburghs.[63] It was replaced by a new house in School Lane in 1965, together with an Anglican chaplaincy centre known as Bede House.[64]

The curate lived in York in 1764; he was also the vicar of St. Lawrence's, York, in 1743 and 1764, and in the former year held Huntington (Yorks. N.R.) as well.[65] In 1835 the curate was also a vicar-choral and sub-chanter at the minster, perpetual curate of a York living, and again vicar of Huntington.[66] In the 1860s, before the unification of Heslington as St. Paul's parish, the incumbent also held St. Crux's, York, but employed an assistant curate at Heslington.[67]

There was one service monthly and Holy Communion was administered three times a year in the 18th century, with about 15 communicants in 1743.[68] By 1851 there was a weekly service,[69] and between 1871 and 1894 there were two or three each Sunday, sometimes with a Wednesday service as well. Communion was celebrated four times a year in 1865, once a month in 1871, twice a month in 1877, and weekly in 1884.[70] In 1972, when the church was used jointly with the Methodists, there were three Anglican services each Sunday.

The old church of St. Peter and St. Paul consisted of chancel, nave with north aisle, and west tower; most of the fabric was said to be 'late and poor', but several windows were described as Norman.[71] The bylawmen paid £32 in 1769 'for building the church steeple etc.'.[72] A new church of *ST. PAUL* was erected on the same site in 1857–8, comprising chancel, nave, vestry, west tower with spire, and south porch. It is of stone, was designed by J. B. and W. Atkinson of York, in the Decorated style, and was paid for by G. J. and Alicia Lloyd. The two undated bells from the old church were retained.[73] Extensive alterations were made to the building in 1973, including the conversion of the chancel to a chapel, the removal of the high altar to an enlarged nave, and the addition of meeting rooms and vestries on the north side.

The plate formerly comprised a plated cup, paten, and flagon, the last dated 1861.[74] The chalice and paten were stolen in 1966,[75] but two new chalices and patens have been acquired.[76]

The registers begin in 1653 and are largely complete, the chief gaps being those in the marriages in 1656–64, 1703–16, and 1754–8.[77]

The churchyard was enlarged in 1862 and 1921.[78]

NONCONFORMITY. Methodism is said to have been introduced into Heslington in 1812,[79] and houses were licensed for dissenting worship in 1807,[80] 1816, 1820, 1826, 1829 (two), and 1846.[81] A chapel was opened by the Wesleyan Association in the 1830s and was still used in 1851, but no more is known of it. In the 1840s two more chapels were built, by the Wesleyan Methodists in 1844 on the west side of Main Street and by the Independent Methodists in 1847 on the east side.[82] The Wesleyans had fourteen members in 1884.[83] The Independent Methodist chapel was acquired by the Primitive Methodists and registered by them in 1887.[84]

The former Wesleyan chapel was closed in 1949[85] but the second Methodist chapel was used until 1971, when the Methodists and Anglicans arranged for the joint use of St. Paul's parish church.[86] A Methodist service was held in the church each Sunday in 1972. Both the former chapels still stood in 1972; the Wesleyan, then used as a meeting hall,

---

[52] *Reg. Romeyn*, ii, p. 217.
[53] York Dioc. Regy., Order in Council.
[54] *Rep. Com. Eccl. Revenues*, 940; Sheahan and Whellan, *Hist. York & E.R.* ii. 625; *Kelly's Dir. N. & E.R. Yorks.* (1872), 375.
[55] York. Dioc. Regy., Order in Council.
[56] Lawton, *Rer. Eccl. Dioc. Ebor.* ii. 443; *Clergy List* (1850); Ecclesiastical Commissioners Act, 3 & 4 Vic. c. 113, s. 41.
[57] C 94/3 f. 76; B.I.H.R., TER. N. Heslington St. Paul's 1727 etc.
[58] Hodgson, *Q.A.B.* 442.
[59] B.I.H.R., TER. N. Heslington St. Paul's 1749 etc.
[60] *Rep. Com. Eccl. Revenues*, 940.
[61] *Lond. Gaz.* 11 Feb. 1870, p. 805; 27 Jan. 1871, p. 299.
[62] B.I.H.R., Bp. V. 1884/Ret.; Bp. V. 1914/Ret.
[63] Ibid. V. 1871/Ret. 215; R.D.B., KS/288/382; Bulmer, *Dir. E. Yorks.* (1892), 636.
[64] Ex inf. the vicar, 1973.
[65] B.I.H.R., Bp. V. 1764/Ret. 27; *Herring's Visit.* ii. 65.
[66] *Rep. Com. Eccl. Revenues*, 940.
[67] B.I.H.R., V. 1865/Ret. 240; V. 1868/Ret. 216.
[68] Ibid. Bp. V. 1764/Ret. 27; *Herring's Visit.* ii. 66.
[69] H.O. 129/23/515.
[70] B.I.H.R., V. 1865/Ret. 240; V. 1871/Ret. 215; V. 1877/Ret.; Bp. V. 1884/Ret.; Bp. V. 1894/Ret.
[71] *Y.A.J.* xiv. 159–60.
[72] B.I.H.R., PR. HES. 11.
[73] Ibid. Fac. Bk. iv, pp. 668–9; *Yorks. Gaz.* 30 May 1857, 4 Sept. 1858; Boulter, 'Ch. Bells', 31.
[74] *Yorks. Ch. Plate*, i. 99–100.
[75] *Yorks. Eve. Press*, 8 Dec. 1966.
[76] Ex inf. the vicar, 1973.
[77] B.I.H.R.
[78] Ibid. CD. 331; York Dioc. Regy., Consecration deed.
[79] J. Lyth, *Glimpses of Early Methodism in York and District*, 290.
[80] B.I.H.R., Fac. Bk. iii, p. 451.
[81] G.R.O. Worship Returns, Vol. v, nos. 2996, 3354, 4031, 4162, 4190, 4645.
[82] H.O. 129/23/515.
[83] Lyth, op. cit. 290.
[84] G.R.O. Worship Reg. no. 30005; Bulmer, *Dir. E. Yorks.* (1892), 636.
[85] Ex inf. Mr. G. T. Gray, Heslington, 1973.
[86] *Yorks. Eve. Press*, 31 Mar. 1971.

is a brick and slate building with wide overhanging eaves and Tudor windows.

EDUCATION. The first school in Heslington was built in the back lane (now School Lane) in 1795, on ground given by Henry Yarburgh and at the expense of the township;[87] the bylawmen paid £4 towards the work that year.[88] In 1835 20 boys and 20 girls were taught there at their parents' expense.[89] A new school was projected by Yarburgh Yarburgh and built in 1856, after his death, by G. J. and Alicia Lloyd.[90] The earlier building, containing two ground-floor rooms and an attic, still stood in 1972. Yarburgh Yarburgh bequeathed £1,000 to the school and in 1858 £31 interest on it was received, as well as subscriptions and school pence. The average attendance was 54 in 1857,[91] and there were 72 in attendance in 1871.[92] The school was united with the National Society and it received an annual government grant by 1860.[93] The stock of Yarburgh's charity was sold to pay for the school's enlargement in 1907.[94] Attendance was about 90 in 1906–14, but it fell to 53 in 1938.[95] The buildings were again extended in 1957 and 1965, on the latter occasion to accommodate 280 pupils. The school had been reorganized in 1958 as an infants' and junior school, senior pupils being transferred to Fulford.[96] The number on the roll in September 1972 was 224.[97]

A county infants' school was built on the Badger Hill housing estate and opened in 1968.[98]

CHARITIES FOR THE POOR. Sir Thomas Hesketh (d. 1605) proposed to found a hospital at Heslington and it was built in 1608 by his widow dame Julia beside the York road, north of the hall.[99] The hospital was endowed by indenture of 1630 with £50 a year from Castle Mills, York. A master was to receive £6 13s. 4d. a year and eight other inmates, one a woman, were to get £5 each. A further endowment of £5 a year from land at Hutton Rudby (Yorks. N.R.) was probably given by another of the Heskeths.[1] The hospital was rebuilt on the Fulford road by Henry Yarburgh in 1795.[2] The two-storeyed brick building had a chapel in the pedimented centre, with terraces of four two-roomed apartments on either side for the men and a room behind for the woman. The hospital was repaired and modernized by Richard, Lord Deramore, in 1968.[3] In 1974 the endowment income was still £55, the former rent-charge on Castle Mills being paid by York corporation, and contributions were made by the inmates.[4]

Yarburgh Yarburgh, by will proved in 1856, bequeathed £1,000, three-tenths of the income from which was to go to the poor of Heslington. In 1972 Heslington's share of the income was £6.50, distributed in 50p doles to thirteen people.[5]

Robert, Lord Deramore, in 1903 built four almshouses for spinsters or widows at the south end of Main Street, in memory of his wife Lucy.[6] By an indenture of 1902 Lord Deramore endowed the charity with £1,125 stock and declared that the inmates were each to have £10 a year. In 1973 the income was £24 from £959 stock.[7]

Heslington benefited from the charity of John Hodgson for parishes in York poor-law union.[8]

NABURN

THE RIVERSIDE village of Naburn lies four miles south of York, at a point where the Ouse swings across its flood-plain against the firm ground to the east.[1] Most of the parish is only a little over 25 ft. above sea-level, but the extensive ings within the bends of the river are even lower.[2] The village houses are still for the most part confined to the main street alongside the river and there had by 1972 been no residential development of the kind that has taken place around other villages close to the city. The parish is roughly rectangular in shape and covers 2,636 a. Of this area 463 a. lay in the West Riding parish of Acaster Malbis, across the river, until the 1880s.[3]

Apart from the alluvium of the Ouse flood-plain and patches of glacial sand and gravel east of the village and in the north-west corner of the township, Naburn is entirely covered with outwash sand and clay.[4] The small open fields which lay around the village and a large common moor further east were not inclosed until 1768, but much of the township was occupied by early-inclosed assarts and woodland. Some woodland still exists in the south-east. Streams draining into the Ouse include Wood dike, which forms a short section of the southern parish boundary, and Howden dike, which joins the river at the north end of the village. It may have been the latter stream, rather than the river, which gave the village its Scandinavian name.[5] The Ouse forms the entire parish boundary on the west.

---

[87] Inscription on building.
[88] B.I.H.R., PR. HES. 11.
[89] Educ. Enquiry Abstract, 1086.
[90] Inscription on building.
[91] Ed. 7/135 no. 73. Yarburgh's will is given in B.I.H.R., PR. HES. 9 (at back of bk.).
[92] Returns relating to Elem. Educ. 792.
[93] Rep. of Educ. Cttee. of Council, 1859–60 [2681], H.C., p. 782 (1860), liv.
[94] Ed. 49/8551; Kelly's Dir. N. & E.R. Yorks. (1909), 526.
[95] Bd. of Educ. List 21 (H.M.S.O.).
[96] E.R. Educ. Cttee. Mins. 1955–6, 96; 1956–7, 96, 104; 1957–8, 50, 100; 1958–9, 123; 1964–5, 173; 1965–6, 163.
[97] Ex inf. Chief Educ. Officer, County Hall, Beverley, 1972.
[98] Ex inf. the headmistress, 1972.
[99] W. K. Jordan, Charities of Rural Eng. 266; O.S. Map 6″ (1853 edn.); inscription on later building.
[1] 12th Rep. Com. Char. 650–2.
[2] Inscription on building.   [3] Ibid.
[4] Ex inf. Messrs. Byron & Granger, York, 1974.
[5] Char. Com. files; ex inf. the vicar, 1972. The rest of the income was for the poor of Bridlington and Sewerby: see V.C.H. Yorks. E.R. ii. 82, 100.
[6] Inscription on building.
[7] Char. Com. files.
[8] See p. 12.
[1] This article was written in 1972.
[2] O.S. Map 6″, Yorks. (1851 edn.). The whole parish is covered by sheet 191.
[3] Census, 1881–91. For the detached parts of Acaster parish see O.S. Map 6″ (1851 edn.).
[4] Geol. Surv. Map 1″, solid and drift, sheet 71 (1973 edn.).
[5] P.N.E.R. Yorks. (E.P.N.S.), 274.

The road from York to Naburn and on towards Stillingfleet and Cawood follows the dry margin of the flood-plain. It crosses Wood and Howden dikes by small bridges, the latter known as Water-mill, Mill, or Great Mill bridge at least from 1642 until 1795,[6] and as Town End bridge in 1846–7.[7] It was rebuilt in brick and stone in 1741.[8] From the bridge Howden lane follows the dike eastwards towards Crockey Hill, in Deighton, and from a point south of the village Moor Lane leads to Deighton itself. The main village street is bypassed by the York–Stillingfleet road, which follows what was in effect the back lane of the village. There may have been a ferry across the Ouse at Naburn from early times and 'ferryman' occurs as a personal name there, for example in 1500.[9] In 1739 the ferry was situated just to the west of Naburn Hall,[10] but by the early 19th century a horse and foot road led from the village street past the hall and across the ings to a ferry close to Acaster Malbis village. The latter ferry is said to have been started by the Thompsons of Escrick after Beilby Thompson (d. 1750) married dame Sarah Dawes to provide a connexion with her estate at Acaster. When it became more widely used it proved a nuisance to the Palmes family at the hall,[11] and in 1824 the road was closed and the ferry moved to a point near the middle of the village.[12] The new ferry, for passengers and vehicles, was later worked by wheel and chain and was closed only in 1956.[13]

The Ouse itself was from early times an important highway for the trade of York, though perhaps little used by the inhabitants of Naburn. It was, however, within the parish that considerable improvements were made in the 18th and 19th centuries to overcome the difficulties created by shoals. A weir was made at Naburn, a mile downstream from the village, in 1741 and a 'dam' or weir and a lock were opened in 1757; the making of the lock cut created an island on which a water-mill was later built.[14] A banqueting house was built near the lock by the trustees of the river navigation in 1823.[15] A second, larger, lock was constructed beside the old one in 1888.[16] The original lock-keeper's house was rebuilt in 1823–4, and work done in 1888 included the building of a pair of lock-keepers' cottages.[17] North of the village the river is crossed by a large swing bridge carrying the York–Selby railway line, opened in 1871.[18] Naburn station, beside the York road, was closed for passengers in 1953 and goods in 1964.[19] There was formerly a gasworks at the station serving the signal lamps on the bridge.[20]

Most of the older houses of the village lie along the main street, with a few in the former back lane. An access way to the ferry and a short street connecting with the Stillingfleet road form a small crossroads with the main street, and near by a maypole was customarily erected from at least the early 18th until the later 19th centuries in connexion with the village feast on 12 May, 'old May Day'.[21] The most noteworthy of the 18th- and 19th-century houses are a one-and-a-half storeyed cottage which retains some timber framing inside,[22] and a contiguous pair of houses, one known as Marydale. The latter houses, perhaps of the early 18th century, are long and low, and each has a central as well as an end chimney. A few 20th-century houses have been built in the main street, and there are a dozen council houses near the church on the Stillingfleet road and about twenty more in Vicarage Lane, a cul-de-sac east of the main road. A village hall in Vicarage Lane stands on a site provided in 1947.[23] There were usually three alehouses in Naburn in the 1750s and 1760s, later reduced to one which by 1822 was called the Horse Shoe.[24] By 1872 it had acquired its present name, the Blacksmiths' Arms, and in 1889–1901 the publican was also a brewer.[25] The Yorkshire Ouse Sailing Club, begun in 1938, has a club house near the former ferry,[26] and at the north end of the village a marina was opened in 1970 on part of a 19-acre site acquired for the purpose in 1968.[27]

The outlying buildings include a fine 17th-century mansion at Bell Hall.[28] All the farm-houses date from the 18th and 19th centuries, though there was a house at Lingcroft by 1660[29] and at Gill Rudding in 1636–7.[30] The present Gill Rudding House is an imposing mid-19th-century building. Acres House was built in 1774.[31] Naburn Lodge has a wheel-house. Both Acres and Lodge farms belong to Naburn Hospital, the former York City Lunatic Asylum, for which they were acquired in 1899 and 1914 respectively,[32] but the hospital itself stands just within Fulford parish. A sewerage works for York covering about 20 a. was opened beside the river in Naburn in 1895 and has several times been extended.[33] Two large houses in the north-east of the parish near the York road are Lingcroft Lodge, a white-brick villa built c. 1860 for Edward Lloyd[34] and used since 1948 as a research centre by Armstrong's Patents Co. Ltd.,[35] and Deighton Grove, rebuilt on the site of an earlier house in 1847[36] and acquired for an annexe of York County Hospital in 1947.[37]

There were 74 poll-tax payers at Naburn in 1377.[38] Thirty-eight households were listed in the hearth-tax assessment of 1672. Of those that were chargeable, 11 had one hearth each, 10 had 2, 7 had

---

[6] E.R.R.O., DDPA/7/61; QSF. Mids. 1795, B.2.
[7] O.S. Map 6" (1851 edn.). For Moreby bridge over Wood dike see p. 102.
[8] B.I.H.R., PR. NAB. 9.
[9] E.R.R.O., DDPA/7/69.
[10] Map penes Cmdr. G. B. Palmes, Naburn Hall, 1972.
[11] W. Camidge, Ouse Bridge to Naburn Lock, 402–3.
[12] E.R.R.O., HD/24.
[13] Camidge, op. cit. 404; G.B. Wood, Ferries and Ferrymen, 10.
[14] See p. 80.
[15] V.C.H. City of York, 473 and facing plate.
[16] Ibid. 473–4; B. F. Duckham, Yorks. Ouse, 65, 70, 130.
[17] E.R.R.O., DDPA/7/381–3; Camidge, op. cit. 502, 506.
[18] V.C.H. City of York, 478.
[19] Ex inf. Divisional Manager, Brit. Rlys. (Leeds), 1972.
[20] Camidge, op. cit. 351.
[21] Ibid. 395 sqq.; W. M. Baines, Old Naburn, 95–7.
[22] Ex inf. Mrs. Vanessa Neave, Beverley, 1972.
[23] Char. Com. files.
[24] E.R.R.O., QDT/2/13, 15.
[25] Directories.
[26] Yorks. Ridings, Aug. 1967, 37.
[27] R.D.B., 1573/87/71; Yorks. Eve. Press, 15 July 1970.
[28] See p. 78.
[29] E.R.R.O., DDPA/7/134; see p. 78.
[30] C 142/498 no. 67.
[31] Bulmer, Dir. E. Yorks. (1892), 685.
[32] V.C.H. City of York, 470.
[33] Ibid. 465; Kelly's Dir. N. & E.R. Yorks. (1901), 528.
[34] The house bears his arms. He inherited in 1856 and died in 1869: Burke, Land. Gent. (1906), pp. 1029–30.
[35] R.D.B., 785/324/260.
[36] Ibid. GG/398/480.
[37] V.C.H. City of York, 468.
[38] E 179/202/58 m. 17.

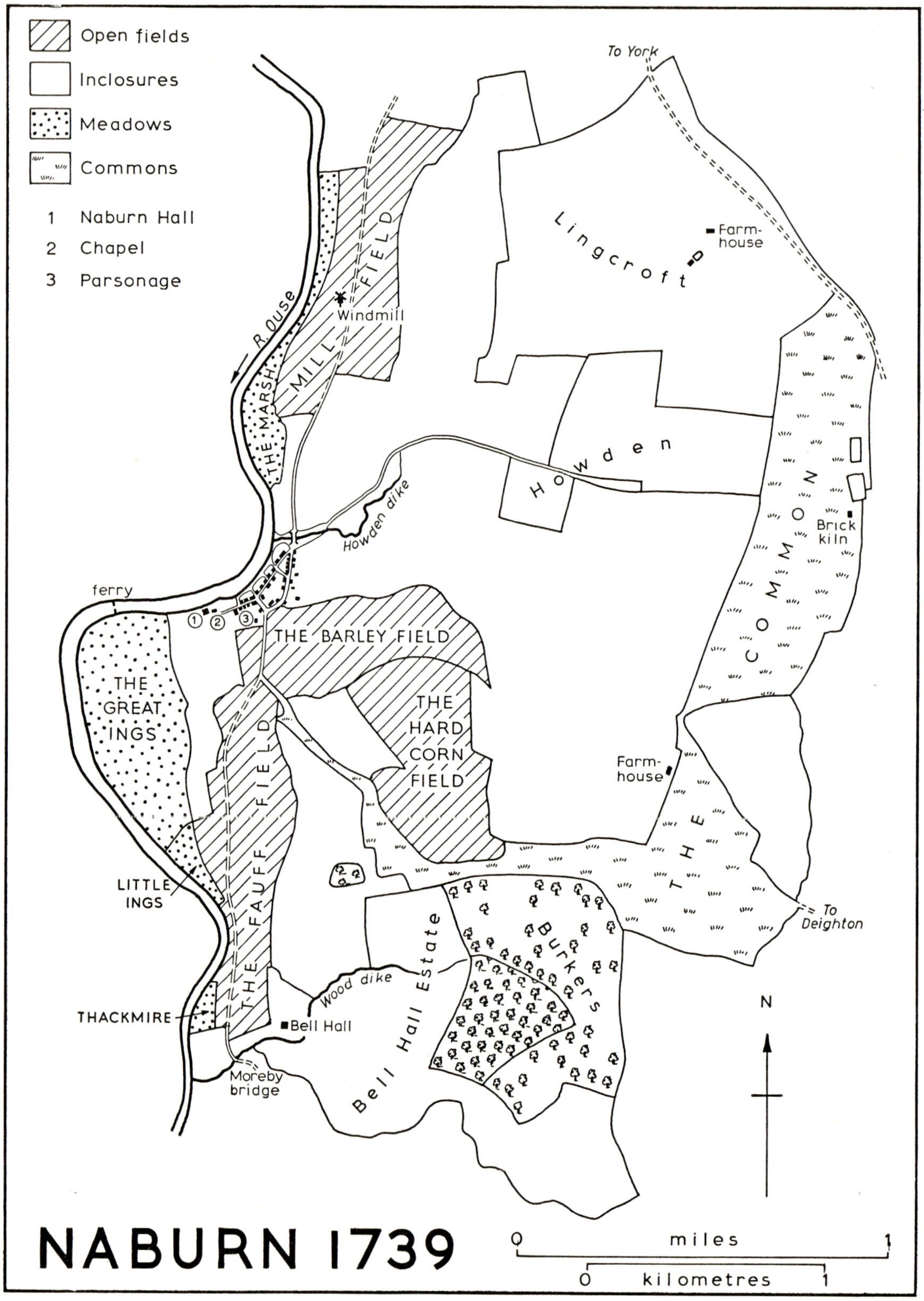
Open fields
Inclosures
Meadows
Commons
1 Naburn Hall
2 Chapel
3 Parsonage
To York
Lingcroft
Farm-house
R. Ouse
THE MARSH
MILL FIELD
Windmill
Howden
Howden dike
THE COMMON
Brick kiln
ferry
THE BARLEY FIELD
THE GREAT INGS
THE HARD CORN FIELD
THE FAUFF FIELD
Farm-house
THE
LITTLE INGS
To Deighton
Burkers
Bell Hall Estate
Wood dike
THACKMIRE
Bell Hall
Moreby bridge
N
NABURN 1739
0 miles 1
0 kilometres 1

3–5, and Naburn and Bell Halls had 8–9.[39] In 1743 there were 26 families in the township[40] and in 1764 30.[41] The population in 1801 was 363, steadily increasing to 574 in 1901; the largest inter-censal increase, 84, was in 1871–81.[42] The total had fallen to 537 by 1951, 473 by 1961, and 371 by 1971.[43]

MANOR AND OTHER ESTATES. There were two estates at Naburn in 1086, one of 4 carucates belonging to Robert de Todeni and the other of 2 carucates belonging to the king. The larger estate had been held in 1066 by Turgot; in 1086 Berenger de Todeni held it of his father.[44] Robert de Todeni's daughter Adelize married Roger Bigod and Naburn descended to their daughter Cecily de Belvoir and her husband William de Aubigny.[45] It was still held of the Aubignys in 1243[46] but by 1284–5 the overlordship had passed to Robert de Ros by his marriage with Isabel, daughter and heir of William de Aubigny.[47] The Ros interest was mentioned as late as 1434.[48]

About 1200 the Watervill family became lords of the manor of NABURN under the Aubignys. Richard de Watervill stated in 1231 that his grandfather Roger de Watervill had descended from Gunnore, sister and one of the coheirs of Ralph de Aubigny (d. 1191).[49] Richard de Watervill assigned the manor to William Palmes, who married Richard's sister Maud in, it is said, 1226.[50] The Watervills apparently retained a mesne lordship, for the heirs of Nicholas Palmes held Naburn of Reynold de Watervill in 1284–5, when it consisted of 2 carucates.[51] In 1346 and 1428 the mesne lordship belonged to the Malbis family.[52]

From 1226 the demesne lordship descended in the Palmes family.[53] William de Palmes held ¾ knight's fee there and in North Dalton in 1243,[54] and Nicholas de Palmes received a grant of free warren in Naburn in 1272.[55] For a period after 1351, when it was seized by the Crown following William Palmes's felony, the manor was held by the Malbises (1351–61), the Redemans (1361–3), John Herring (1363–4), and Walter Whitehorse (1364).[56] Part of the estate was in 1774 vested in trustees to be sold to meet the debts of George Palmes,[57] and over 800 a. were accordingly disposed of in 1775–9, more than half going to Emanuel Elam.[58] The estate comprised c. 1,100 a. in 1972, when it belonged to Cmdr. G. B. Palmes (d. 1974).[59]

The manor-house of the Palmeses was mentioned in 1345.[60] It had eight hearths in 1672.[61] A drawing of c. 1720 shows it as a two-storeyed house, three bays long, with attic windows in tall pointed gables.[62] The house was rebuilt in 1735,[63] but it was much altered in 1818[64] and restored and enlarged in 1870.[65] It consists of a three-storeyed square main block, with a two-storeyed later wing. The 18th-century coach-house has a clock turret and bellcot.

The smaller Domesday estate had belonged to Torchil in 1066. It later passed to Robert Malet, of whom it was held by Goisfrid de Beauchamp, but by 1086 Malet had surrendered it to the Crown.[66] It was subsequently attached to the honor of Eye (Suff.)[67] and by 1284–5 was held by Richard de Malbis as parcel of the earldom of Cornwall.[68] The demesne lords of this manor of NABURN in 1247 were the Maunsels[69] and they held a carucate from the Malbises in 1284–5 and from John of Hamerton in 1346.[70]

The Maunsel estate seems later to have passed to the Acklams of Moreby and to have been eventually split up. From it the Bell Hall estate was formed in the 16th century. In 1492 Richard Acklam acquired by exchange with Brian Palmes various closes in the south of the township, including 44 a. adjoining Naburn wood; Acklam already had other closes near by.[71] In 1543 John Acklam sold the 44 a. of closes to John North,[72] and in 1566 the property was settled on his granddaughter Jane upon her marriage with Richard Bell.[73] The Bells later acquired other Acklam land in the same area.[74] Richard Bell died in 1617 and was succeeded by his sisters Anne Haddlesey and Jane Greenbury, his nieces Susan Hutton and Faith Levett, and his nephew John Currance.[75] The Levetts had acquired the other shares by 1660,[76] and apparently in 1662 the estate was sold to Sir John Hewley.[77] About 80 a. of woodland were bought by Hewley from the Palmeses in 1663.[78]

Hewley died in 1697 and his widow in 1710, and the estate passed to Hewley Baines, grandson of Sir John's sister Margaret, who had married John Baines.[79] In 1719 the estate comprised nearly 180 a.[80] It descended in the Baines family[81] to W. M. Baines (d. 1912) and was later held in trust by H. M. Baines (d. 1945) and H. V. Baines (d. 1954), before

[39] E 179/205/504.
[40] *Herring's Visit.* i. 163.
[41] B.I.H.R., Bp. V. 1764/Ret. 159.
[42] *V.C.H. Yorks.* iii. 498.
[43] Census.
[44] *V.C.H. Yorks.* ii. 204, 241.
[45] Ibid. 160.
[46] *Bk. of Fees*, ii. 1101.
[47] *Feud. Aids*, vi. 34; *D.N.B.*
[48] *Cal. Close*, 1429–35, 275.
[49] *E.Y.C.* i, p. 462.
[50] E.R.R.O., DDBH/12/1; Burke, *Land. Gent.* (1965), i. 553.
[51] *Feud. Aids*, vi. 34.
[52] Ibid. 223, 271.
[53] For lineage see J. Foster, *Pedigrees of . . . Yorks.* iii; Burke, op. cit. i. 553.
[54] *Bk. of Fees*, ii. 1101.
[55] *Cal. Chart. R.* 1257–1300, 179.
[56] *Cal. Inq. Misc.* iii, pp. 197, 200; *Cal. Pat.* 1364–7, 18; *Cal. Fine R.* 1358–68, 281.
[57] 14 Geo. III, c. 66 (Priv. Act).
[58] R.D.B., espy. AU/295/468; AW/48/93; BC/146/212.
[59] Ex inf. Mr. J. Curtis, Naburn Grange, 1972; *Yorks. Eve. Press*, 11 Nov. 1974.

[60] C 135/76 no. 30.
[61] E 179/205/504.
[62] B.L. Lansd. MS. 914, f. 31.
[63] *Y.A.J.* xl. 449.
[64] Sheahan and Whellan, *Hist. York & E.R.* i. 648.
[65] Bulmer, *Dir. E. Yorks.* (1892), 685.
[66] *V.C.H. Yorks.* ii. 204, 292.
[67] Ibid. 168; *Plac. de Quo Warr.* (Rec. Com.), 189.
[68] *Feud. Aids*, vi. 34.
[69] *Yorks. Fines, 1246–72*, p. 4.
[70] *Feud. Aids*, vi. 34, 223.
[71] E.R.R.O., DDPA/7/62, 67.
[72] Ibid. DDBH/12/67.
[73] Ibid. DDBH/12/71.
[74] Ibid. DDBH/12/92–3.
[75] Ibid. DDBH/12/95.
[76] Ibid. DDBH/12/96, 98, 99, 119–20.
[77] Ibid. DDBH/12/122, 125, 131, 137, 153.
[78] Ibid. DDPA/7/97.
[79] Camidge, *Ouse Bridge to Naburn Lock*, 361; Baines, *Old Naburn*, 66.
[80] R.D.B., G/415/904; /416/905.
[81] For pedigree to late 19th cent. see Baines, *Old Naburn*, facing p. 64.

passing in 1956 to Mr. J. H. Baines, who still had c. 200 a. in Naburn in 1971.[82]

A house built on the estate by Richard Bell[83] had nine hearths in 1672.[84] It was replaced in 1680 by Sir John Hewley, though the new house subsequently retained the name Bell Hall. The only major addition was a service wing built in the 19th century and later demolished. The brick-built house with stone dressings is of two storeys with basement and attics, and is five bays long and three deep. There was originally a roof-top balustrade and lantern tower.[85] There are entrances approached by steps on the south and west. The house contains many contemporary fittings, as well as a reset early-17th-century fire-place and some panelling and a painted room of the 18th century.[86]

Several religious houses had small estates in Naburn. St. Andrew's priory, York, was granted a bovate there by Richard Maunsel in the 13th century.[87] It was let to Ralph Prince in 1593.[88] Property in Naburn belonging to the Corpus Christi guild, York, was in 1576 granted by the Crown to John and William Marsh, and in 1582 acquired by John Palmes.[89] The Knights Templars were given 221 a. and 94 a. by Richard Maunsel in 1240 and 1241 respectively.[90] In 1319 Thomas of Norfolk held a tenement in Naburn of the king because of the forfeiture of the Templars.[91] St. Leonard's hospital, York, had property in Naburn and Fulford worth £2 a year in 1535.[92] It included a few acres of meadow in Naburn ings, granted by the Crown to George Darcy in 1545 and acquired by Sir George Palmes in 1621.[93] St. Mary's abbey, York, already had property in Naburn in the 13th century, and it was granted 3 houses and 90 a. of land in Naburn and Deighton in 1334.[94] The property was granted to John Aske in 1542 along with Deighton manor.[95] Nun Monkton priory (Yorks. W.R.) was given an acre in Naburn in 1382.[96] Finally Warter priory had land there in 1292–3,[97] and in 1535 it had a reeve at Lingcroft and Wheldrake.[98] The property was granted by the Crown in 1541 to Thomas Manners, earl of Rutland, who sold it soon after to William Babthorpe. In 1597 Sir Ralph Babthorpe sold it to John and Sir George Palmes.[99] Lingcroft farm was among the lands sold under the Palmes Estates Act of 1774, but it was recovered by the Palmeses in 1918.[1] The present Lingcroft Farm was built in the early 18th century and existed in 1739.[2] Near by is a prominent moated site where an earlier house stood; pottery of c. 1600–1700 has been found there.[3]

St. George's church, York, to which Naburn chapel belonged, was appropriated to Nun Monkton priory and after the Dissolution the rectory was granted in 1538 to John Nevill, Lord Latimer.[4] In 1610 the rectory, including tithes in Naburn, was the subject of transactions by the coheirs of John, Lord Latimer,[5] and in 1621 one of them, Richard Fermor, conveyed the Naburn tithes to Guy Palmes and others.[6] These tithes were worth £10 in 1650.[7] They were commuted at inclosure in 1768, when compensation for them was included in George Palmes's allotment for his freehold estate; he was also allotted 22 a. for tithes from certain detached parts of Acaster Malbis.[8] The greater part of the rectorial tithes of the Acaster Malbis part of Naburn had been separated from those of St. George's parish. They were let by the Crown to Cuthbert Fairfax in 1567,[9] and granted in fee to Sir Thomas Fairfax in 1605.[10] In 1650 they were worth £15.[11] In 1750 Charles, Viscount Fairfax, sold them to Thomas, Viscount Fauconberg, and in 1769 they were acquired by George Palmes.[12] These tithes, arising from 320 a. mainly in Acaster parish, were commuted in 1848 for a rent-charge of £49 10s. payable to George Palmes. The owners of 1,499 a. were entitled to the tithes on their own lands, and those tithes were accordingly merged.[13]

ECONOMIC HISTORY. In 1086 Robert de Todeni's estate at Naburn had land for four ploughs, and there were three plough-oxen there. He had 30 a. of meadow, and underwood a league in length and breadth. The value of the estate had fallen from 10s. in 1066 to 7s. The king's estate had land for one plough.[14] Despite much reclamation, woodland long remained a notable feature of the township, mostly in the south-east towards Escrick, and there have always been extensive riverside ings, especially in the great bend of the Ouse south of the village.

Richard Maunsel was active in extending the cultivated land in the township in the earlier 13th century, and at least some of his assarts were from the first held in severalty. When he granted arable land, described as bovates, *culture*, and selions, to St. Andrew's priory, York, he denied the priory any share in the assarts which he had made or might make. A tenant of two bovates held from Maunsel similarly surrendered any claim to the assarts, in return for a grant of land in ground called Langthwaite.[15] Other reclamation was carried out by the Norfolks and the Palmeses. Martin of Norfolk granted cultivated land in a place called Fulmose to Richard Maunsel, but he excepted his 'great assart'

---

[82] R.D.B., 151/293/239; 955/535/474; 1058/133/112; 1709/519/419.
[83] E.R.R.O., DDBH/12/95.
[84] E 179/205/504.
[85] B.L. Lansd. MS. 914, f. 32.
[86] For description and illus. see *E. Yorks. Georgian Soc. Trans.* iii (2), 24–6; see also below plate facing p. 80. The date is over the main doorway.
[87] *Y.A.J.* xvii. 103.
[88] E 310/30/180 no. 22.
[89] E.R.R.O., DDPA/7/118.
[90] *Yorks. Fines, 1232–46*, pp. 82, 109–10.
[91] *Cal. Pat. 1317–21*, 396.
[92] *Valor Eccl.* (Rec. Com.), v. 17.
[93] E.R.R.O., DDPA/7/115, 129.
[94] *Cal. Close, 1227–31*, 300; *Monastic Notes*, i (Y.A.S. Rec. Ser. xvii), 233; *Cal. Pat. 1330–4*, 523; *1343–5*, 253.
[95] See p. 21.
[96] *Cal. Pat. 1381–5*, 212.
[97] *Abbrev. Rot. Orig.* (Rec. Com.), i. 79.
[98] *Valor Eccl.* v. 126.
[99] E.R.R.O., DDEV/50/13; DDPA/7/81; *Yorks. Fines*, i. 98.
[1] R.D.B., 183/172/147.
[2] Map *penes* Cmdr. Palmes, 1972.
[3] Ex inf. Mr. G. Rounthwaite, Lingcroft Farm, 1972.
[4] *V.C.H. City of York*, 381.
[5] *Yorks. Fines, 1603–14*, 125; Burke, *Peerage* (1970), 1544.
[6] *Yorks. Fines, 1614–25*, 172.
[7] C 94/3 f. 76.
[8] R.D.B., AH/378/16.
[9] *Cal. Pat. 1566–9*, p. 241.
[10] E.R.R.O., DDFA/10/5.
[11] C 94/3 f. 76.
[12] E.R.R.O., DDFA/10/5.
[13] B.I.H.R., TA, 518S.
[14] *V.C.H. Yorks.* ii. 204, 241.
[15] *Y.A.J.* xvii. 103.

there.[16] When Naburn wood was divided between William de Palmes and Richard Maunsel in the mid 13th century, reference was made to adjoining assarts and 'riddings', as well as Intack, Busk field, and Lincroft.[17] Intack was mentioned as early as 1232,[18] and arable land in Over and Nether Riddings was recorded in 1321.[19] William de Palmes had 90 a. of arable in demesne in 1345, a third of it lying fallow each year.[20]

North and South woods, in the south-east of the township, were mentioned in the 13th century,[21] and near by were the 'great moor' of Naburn and other areas in which the Palmeses and the Maunsels had rights of common.[22] In 1304 Nicholas of Norfolk upheld his right of common for 32 oxen, 8 horses, 30 cows, 200 sheep, and other beasts in 160 a. of wood and pasture in Naburn.[23] The moor of Fulmose belonged to the Maunsels and in 1300 Edmund Maunsel licensed a tenant to dig turf there.[24] Meadows near the Ouse, too, were mentioned in the 13th century, and in 1232 William de Palmes and the archbishop of York enjoyed common in each other's meadow land from mowing until Lammas, as in the other meadows in the township.[25] Thackmire, in the meadows, was recorded in 1291[26] and Ellers in 1361.[27] William de Palmes had 30 a. of demesne meadow in 1345.[28]

The survival of woodland and moor, as well as the existence of inclosed assarts, is clearly shown by an exchange arranged in 1486 between Brian Palmes and Richard Acklam. Palmes was to receive houses and unidentified arable and meadow land. In return he conveyed to Acklam 44 a. lying in seven closes adjoining Naburn wood; 18 a. adjoining a close of Acklam's and a moor called Birker Bushes; common for 12 cattle, 6 horses, 60 sheep, and 6 pigs in two moors adjoining certain riddings and closes and next to Birker and South wood; and meadow land in the ings. He was also to arrange for 10 a. in Gilridding to be conveyed by its owner to Acklam.[29] Gilridding had been mentioned as early as 1408.[30] Other grounds which were referred to in the 15th century include Owthen, Akkers, and the Marsh, and by 1476 Mill and South fields were in existence:[31] along with Busk field these were presumably the open fields of the township.[32]

The improvement of waste and woodland continued in the 16th and 17th centuries, as in the case of a 4-acre close taken from Naburn wood which Richard Bell was said in 1634 to have spent much on clearing and tilling.[33] The remaining woodland included the 50-acre Great wood, said to adjoin another 30 a. of inclosed wood in 1663.[34] Among the improved lands was a close called 'the Newfield', held by the Palmeses when first mentioned in 1632.[35] New field was later, however, one of the common fields of Naburn.

The meadows were known in the 16th century and later as Broad or Great ings and Little ings.[36] There is no evidence that Great ings had ever been subject to common rights by the inhabitants at large, and by the 18th century they apparently belonged entirely to the Palmeses, with the exception of a few acres of vicarial glebe. The numerous small parcels into which they were then divided[37] were evidently held by tenants, but the spring eatage or first bite and the 'fog' or aftermath belonged to the lords of the manor. In 1698 the Palmes rental included £43 for 42½ a. of 'letting meadow' and £17 for fog and eatage.[38] In 1768 the spring eatage and fog of the whole of Great ings, including the glebe, belonged to George Palmes.[39] In 1791 spring eatage and fog there were let for £36.[40]

The open fields were known in 1739 as Hard Corn, Barley, Mill, and 'Fauff' (i.e. fallow) fields.[41] The remaining common lands, amounting to 706 a., were inclosed in 1768[42] under an Act of 1766.[43] They comprised 101 a. in South field, 95 a. in Mill field, 87 a. in New field, 72 a. in Busk field, 11 a. in Little ing and Thackmire, 28 a. in the Marsh, and 313 a. in the Moor. The Great ings were specifically excluded from the inclosure. The bulk of the land allotted, 578 a., went to George Palmes in lieu of his freehold estate and tithes. The 'vicar' of Naburn received 29 a., Hewley Baines 16 a., and there were nine small allotments totalling 67 a. Woodland survived in the 18th century on both the manor and the Bell Hall estate. The wood at Bell Hall contained nearly 20 a., and it was arranged in 1720 to sell 616 trees there, as well as 330 in the hedgerows and near the hall.[44]

There have usually been a dozen farmers in the parish in the 19th and 20th centuries, half of them with 150 a. or more.[45] In 1848 the titheable land included about 1,000 a. of arable, 617 a. of meadow and pasture, and 120 a. of woodland,[46] and in 1905 there were 1,631 a. of arable, 718 a. of permanent grass, and 84 a. of woodland in the parish.[47] Arable has since remained predominant, with meadow and pasture near the river and around the village; by the 1960s there was also a little market-gardening.[48] The ings were no longer in divided ownership in 1972, but several former mere stones were then still in existence.[49] Timber continued to be sold from the woodland in the 19th century,[50] but in 1955 26 a. of Naburn wood were sold to the Ministry of Agri-

[16] Ibid. 104.
[17] E.R.R.O., DDBH/12/1.
[18] *Yorks. Fines, 1232–46*, pp. 2–3.
[19] *Y.A.J.* xvii. 106.
[20] C 135/76 no. 30.
[21] E.R.R.O., DDBH/12/1; *Y.A.J.* xvii. 103, 105.
[22] E.R.R.O., DDBH/12/1.
[23] *Abbrev. Plac.* (Rec. Com.), 251.
[24] *Y.A.J.* xvii. 106.
[25] Ibid. 103; *Yorks. Fines, 1232–46*, pp. 2–3.
[26] E.R.R.O., DDPA/7/8.
[27] *Y.A.J.* xvii. 107.
[28] C 135/76 no. 30.
[29] E.R.R.O., DDPA/7/62, 67–8.
[30] Ibid. DDPA/7/57.
[31] Ibid. DDPA/7/61.
[32] The East field of Naburn, mentioned in 1500 (ibid. DDPA/7/69), was probably an alternative designation for Busk field.
[33] Ibid. DDPA/7/92.
[34] Ibid. DDPA/7/97.
[35] Ibid. DDPA/7/88.
[36] e.g. ibid. DDPA/7/93, 102, 117.
[37] B.I.H.R., TER. A. Naburn 1764.
[38] E.R.R.O., DDPA/7/102.
[39] R.D.B., AH/378/16.
[40] E.R.R.O., DDPA/7/106.
[41] Map *penes* Cmdr. Palmes, 1972.
[42] R.D.B., AH/378/16.
[43] 6 Geo. III, c. 47 (Priv. Act).
[44] E.R.R.O., DDBH/12/5, 7, 8, 19.
[45] Directories; H.O. 107/2351.
[46] B.I.H.R., TA. 518S.
[47] Acreage Returns, 1905.
[48] [1st] Land Util. Surv. Map, sheet 27; 2nd Land Util. Surv. Map, sheets 698 (SE 44–54), 699 (SE 64–74).
[49] Ex inf. Mr. Curtis, 1972.
[50] E.R.R.O., DDBH/24/16; /26/5, 7, 13.

culture, Fisheries and Food by the Palmeses and in 1958 17 a. from the Bell Hall estate[51] to be managed by the Forestry Commission.

The river Ouse has played some small part in the economic life of Naburn. In the late 18th century landowners in the parish were entitled to use the 'common shore' or landing place,[52] where the ferry was later situated, and in 1791 this right was upheld by a man who had become a coal dealer.[53] Fishing rights in the river belonged to the lords of the manor and at inclosure in 1768 they were reserved to George Palmes on riverside land allotted to Hewley Baines.[54] One or two men as tenants of the Palmeses worked as salmon fishermen in the late 18th, 19th, and earlier 20th centuries.[55] There have been few other non-agricultural occupations in Naburn, but bricks were made in 1739, when there was a kiln near the boundary with Deighton.[56]

A water-mill at Naburn was mentioned in the 13th century;[57] it probably stood on Howden dike near its confluence with the Ouse, for in 1642 Water-mill bridge was in that locality.[58] A windmill was recorded in 1345.[59] Lingcroft mill, no doubt a windmill, was mentioned in 1354 and 1408;[60] it presumably stood in the north-east corner of the township. The name Mill field, mentioned in 1476, more likely referred to a mill nearer the village. A windmill belonged to the manor in 1552 and later,[61] and in 1697 a mill stood near the Naburn to Water Fulford road.[62] It still existed in 1772.[63]

By 1846–7 the only mill in the parish was that standing on the island near Naburn lock.[64] It was built between 1813 and 1817, and it made use of the head of water created by the weir and the lock.[65] It was at first a corn mill, but in the 1860s it was used to grind flint and stone for West Riding potteries, before reverting to corn. It was burnt down in 1877 but rebuilt. When it was reconstructed after another fire in 1913 a turbine was installed in place of the water-wheel. The mill went out of use c. 1955[66] and it was demolished in 1958.[67]

LOCAL GOVERNMENT. In 1293 Richard Malbis claimed to have gallows, infangthief, and amends of the assize of ale in Naburn.[68] There are surviving rolls of manorial courts held by the Palmeses in 1424, 1426, 1476, 1642, 1652, 1659, 1696, 1698–1700, and 1707–11. The business was largely concerned with agricultural offences but included infractions of the assize. In 1652 4 bylawmen, 2 surveyors of highways, 2 aletasters, a constable and deputy constable, and a pinder were appointed, and bylawmen, constable, and pinder were also sworn at the early-18th-century courts.[69]

Accounts of the 2 Naburn churchwardens, 2 overseers of the poor, and constable survive for 1735–72. There are also accounts of an additional churchwarden, who raised assessments in the Acaster Malbis part of the township to meet Naburn's share of the church expenses at Acaster.[70] It had been disputed in 1691 whether Naburn's share was a quarter or a third.[71] A poorhouse was first mentioned in 1736. Naburn joined York poor-law union in 1837.[72] It became part of Escrick rural district in 1894, Derwent rural district in 1935,[73] and the Selby district of North Yorkshire in 1974.

CHURCH. Most of Naburn township lay in the parish of St. George, York, but part was in Acaster Malbis parish (Yorks. W.R.) until the late 19th century.[74] A chapel at Naburn was first mentioned in 1353[75] and St. Nicholas's chapel was referred to in 1433.[76] In 1586 St. George's was united with St. Denys's, York, and the former church was allowed to become ruinous.[77] It is therefore not surprising that there were references to the 'vicarage' and the 'vicar' of Naburn in the 17th and 18th centuries. Naburn nevertheless remained a chapelry of St. Denys's with St. George's until 1842, when it was made a separate parish.[78] Naburn and Stillingfleet vicarages were united in 1951.[79]

From 1842 the advowson of the new living belonged to the Palmes family, who had been patrons of St. Denys's with St. George's. In 1911 the patronage passed to the archbishop of York,[80] and after 1951 he presented alternately to the united benefice.[81]

In 1535 the vicar of St. George's paid 13s. 4d. a year to a chantry-priest at Naburn,[82] presumably for the services he performed in the chapel. The 'vicarage' of Naburn was worth £13 6s. 8d. in 1650[83] and £15 in 1716.[84] In 1884 the living was valued at £90 net and in 1914 at £171 net.[85]

The vicarial income in 1727 included £1 10s. for tithe hay, and it was carefully laid down in the 18th century which parcels of meadow in the ings and elsewhere paid tithe to the vicar, and which to the impropriator.[86] At inclosure in 1768 the vicar was allotted 29 a. for tithes and glebe.[87] In 1770 vicarial tithes were still paid from certain detached parts of Acaster Malbis parish and by 1809 they were paid

---

[51] R.D.B., 1009/148/125; 1103/143/133.
[52] Ibid. AW/79/127 etc.
[53] E.R.R.O., DDBH/28/26.
[54] R.D.B., AH/378/16.
[55] E.R.R.O., DDPA/7/106; H.O. 107/2351; Camidge, *Ouse Bridge to Naburn Lock*, 411; directories.
[56] Map *penes* Cmdr. Palmes, 1972.
[57] *Y.A.J.* xvii. 104.
[58] E.R.R.O., DDPA/7/61; see p. 75.
[59] C 135/76 no. 30.
[60] E.R.R.O., DDPA/7/32, 51, 57.
[61] Ibid. DDPA/7/90; C 142/95 no. 48.
[62] E.R.R.O., DDPA/7/243.
[63] T. Jefferys, *Map of Yorks.* (1772).
[64] O.S. Map 6" (1851 edn.).
[65] E.R.R.O., DDFA/7/354, 365, 383.
[66] K. J. Allison, *E.R. Water-mills* (E. Yorks. Loc. Hist. Ser. no. xxvi), 45.
[67] York corp. *Mins.* 1958–9, 358.
[68] *Plac. de Quo Warr.* 207.

[69] E.R.R.O., DDPA/7/61.
[70] B.I.H.R., PR. NAB. 9.
[71] Ibid. CP. H. 4265.
[72] *3rd Rep. Poor Law Com.* 171.
[73] *Census.*
[74] See p. 74.
[75] *Cal. Pat.* 1350–4, 442.
[76] *Test. Ebor.* ii, p. 30.
[77] *V.C.H. City of York*, 381.
[78] York Dioc. Regy., Order in Council 20.
[79] Ibid. 706.
[80] *York Dioc. Cal.*
[81] *Crockford.*
[82] *Valor Eccl.* v. 22.
[83] C 94/3 f. 76.
[84] B.I.H.R., TER. A. Naburn 1716.
[85] Ibid. Bp. V. 1884/Ret.; Bp. V. 1914/Ret.
[86] Ibid. TER. A. Naburn 1727 and 1764; PR. NAB. 2.
[87] R.D.B., AH/378/16.

BELL HALL, NABURN: the south and west fronts

RICCALL: THE OLD VICARAGE
The house incorporates part of the former manor-house

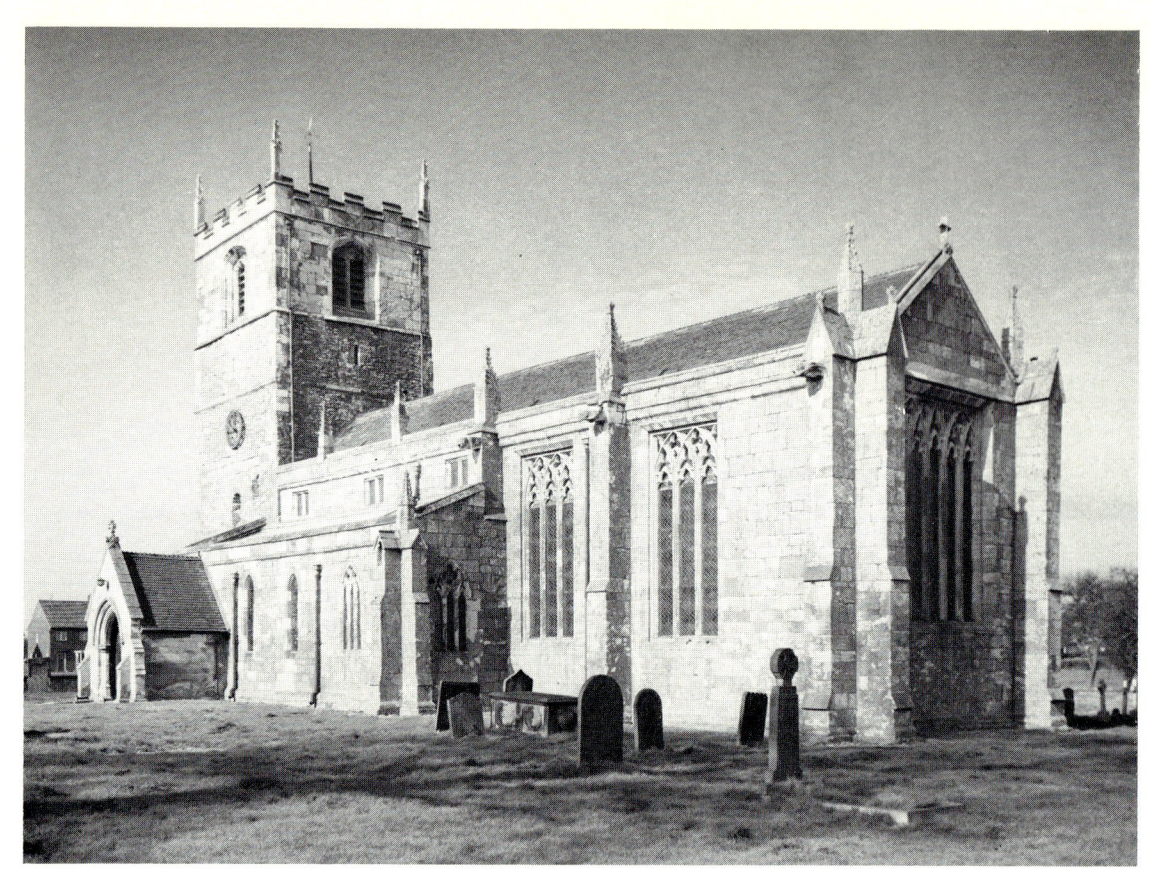

Skipwith Church from the south-east

Riccall Church before the 19th-century restoration

by composition.[88] In 1848 they were commuted for £13 1s. 6d.[89]

The vicar of St. George's enjoyed £2 rent from 14 a. of meadow in Naburn in 1535.[90] There were about 21 a. of glebe in the open fields and ings in the 18th century.[91] All the land allotted at inclosure in 1768 was sold in 1928.[92] There was a parsonage house in the village, near the old chapel, in 1739.[93] It was described in 1770 as mostly of brick with some half-timbering ('stooth and pannel'), and it was thatched; it had three ground-floor rooms, a back kitchen, and two bedrooms. By 1809 it was of brick and tile.[94] In 1812 it was exchanged with George Palmes for another house in Naburn.[95] A large new brick and slate Vicarage was built in 1877.[96] Since 1951 the vicar has lived at Stillingfleet.

A chantry was founded in Naburn chapel in 1353 by John of Barton, who endowed it with property in York and a house and bovate in Naburn.[97] It was united with a chantry at Stillingfleet in 1402 and the priest was required to say mass once a week at Naburn.[98] St. Catherine's chantry at Naburn was referred to in 1535, and in 1546 it enjoyed 13s. 4d. a year rent from 6 a. of land and 1 r. of meadow there.[99] In 1566 lands in Naburn, said to have belonged to St. Helen's chantry there and to have been given to support two services a week in the chapel, were granted by the Crown to Francis Barker and Thomas Blackway.[1]

The vicar of St. George's and later the rector of St. Denys's with St. George's no doubt usually lived in York before 1842. In 1590 Gabriel Squire was said to serve the cures of Acaster Malbis and Naburn,[2] but this may have referred to only the detached parts of Acaster parish, which included a section of Naburn village. In 1643 and 1743 the incumbent was also rector of St. Margaret, Walmgate, in York, and in the latter year he was curate of Stockton (Yorks. N.R.) as well.[3] Even after Naburn was made a parish in 1842 the incumbent sometimes lived in York. He did so in the 1860s, when he still also held St. Denys's, and in 1871.[4]

Thomas Lowry, described as curate at Naburn in 1636, was inhibited from preaching the following year.[5] George Liddell, 'vicar' of Naburn in 1643, was a Royalist delinquent.[6]

A service was held at Naburn once a fortnight in 1743 and Holy Communion was celebrated five times a year with about 50 communicants.[7] A weekly service was held in 1865 and communion was celebrated four times a year in the 1860s, about 30 persons receiving it. By 1871 there were two services every Sunday and communion was received monthly by about 15 persons. Communion was twice-monthly in 1884 and 1914.[8] There were still two services each Sunday in 1972.

The chapel of ST. NICHOLAS, in the grounds of Naburn Hall, was taken down and rebuilt c. 1870.[9] Little is known of the earlier building. The 'steeple' was out of repair in 1615, and work ordered in 1721 included repairs to the porch.[10] Also in 1721 Hewley Baines was licensed to erect a pew there.[11] A faculty was granted for a gallery across the west end in 1742.[12] The chancel was retained for use by the Palmes family when the new parish church was built in 1854.[13]

The new church of ST. MATTHEW consists of chancel, nave, north aisle, north-west tower and spire, and south porch. It was designed in the Decorated style by G. T. Andrews of York.[14] The pulpit was replaced in 1910.[15] There were two bells in 1764[16] but the new church had three: (i) 1849; (ii) 1709, Samuel Smith of York; (iii) 1854, C. & G. Mears of London.[17] They were replaced in 1879 by four bells given by Mrs. Rosabella Lloyd.[18] The plate, all silver-gilt, consists of a cup made in 1625 by Sem Casson of York, and two patens and a flagon made in London in 1864–5.[19] The registers begin in 1653 and are complete.[20]

Apart from the Palmes family, who used St. Nicholas's chapel, the inhabitants of Naburn were buried either in St. George's churchyard in York[21] or at Acaster Malbis. A churchyard was consecrated at Naburn in 1854[22] and extended in 1905.[23]

G. W. Reader, by will proved in 1936, devised Glebe House, Naburn, to Elizabeth Walker (d. by 1951) for life. After her death part of the income was to be used for the upkeep of his family graves and the rest for the benefit of the church. The house was sold in 1952 and the proceeds, £1,091, invested in stock.[24] The house had formed part of the glebe land until 1928.[25]

NONCONFORMITY. Members of the Palmes family were recorded as recusants or non-communicants from the 1570s onwards and the family remained Roman Catholics until the death of John Palmes in 1784. A group of servants and villagers followed their example, a dozen in 1582 for instance, 20 in 1633, and 15 in 1767.[26]

---

[88] B.I.H.R., TER. A. Naburn 1770 and 1809.
[89] Ibid. TA. 518S.
[90] *Valor Eccl.* v. 22.
[91] B.I.H.R., TER. A. Naburn 1716 etc.
[92] R.D.B., 366/525/423.
[93] Map *penes* Cmdr. Palmes, 1972.
[94] B.I.H.R., TER. A. Naburn 1716 etc.
[95] E.R.R.O., DDPA/7/353.
[96] Camidge, *Ouse Bridge to Naburn Lock*, 377.
[97] *Cal. Pat.* 1350–4, 442.
[98] Camidge, *Ouse Bridge to Naburn Lock*, 365–6; *Y.A.J.* xxxiii. 283; see below p. 110.
[99] *Valor Eccl.* v. 22; *Yorks. Chantry Surv.* i (Sur. Soc. xci), 47.
[1] *Cal. Pat.* 1563–6, p. 476.
[2] *Y.A.J.* xv. 224.
[3] *Miscellanea,* i (Y.A.S. Rec. Ser. lxi), 164–5; *Herring's Visit.* i. 105, 163, 168.
[4] B.I.H.R., V. 1865/Ret. 370; V. 1868/Ret. 328; V. 1871/Ret. 331.
[5] R. A. Marchant, *Puritans and Ch. Courts in Dioc. York, 1560–1642,* 260–1, 322.
[6] *Miscellanea,* i. 164–5.
[7] *Herring's Visit.* i. 163–4.
[8] B.I.H.R., V. 1865/Ret. 370; V. 1868/Ret. 328; V. 1871/Ret. 331; Bp. V. 1884/Ret.; Bp. V. 1914/Ret.
[9] Camidge, *Ouse Bridge to Naburn Lock*, 367; see above p. 77. It is identified on a map of 1824: E.R.R.O., HD/24.
[10] B.I.H.R., V. 1615/CB.; Y. V/Ret. 2, p. 3.
[11] E.R.R.O., DDBH/12/9.
[12] B.I.H.R., Fac. Bk. i, p. 72.
[13] Ibid. iv, p. 627.
[14] Sheahan and Whellan, *Hist. York & E.R.* i. 647.
[15] B.I.H.R., Fac. Bk. ix, p. 91.
[16] Ibid. TER. A. Naburn 1764.
[17] Boulter, 'Ch. Bells', 31.
[18] Camidge, *Ouse Bridge to Naburn Lock*, 373.
[19] *Yorks. Ch. Plate,* i. 293.
[20] B.I.H.R.
[21] Ibid. TER. A. Naburn 1770 etc.; Sheahan and Whellan, *Hist. York & E.R.* i. 647.
[22] B.I.H.R., CD. 248.
[23] York Dioc. Regy., Consecration deed.
[24] Char. Com. files.
[25] R.D.B., 367/302/268.
[26] Aveling, *Post Reformation Catholicism,* 64; T.B. Trappes-Lomax, 'Palmes family of Naburn and their contribution to the survival of Roman Catholicism', *Y.A.J.* xl. 443 sqq.

A house in Naburn was registered for worship by protestant dissenters in 1798,[27] the year in which Methodism is said to have been introduced into the township.[28] A Wesleyan Methodist chapel, in the back lane east of the village, was built in 1818[29] but replaced in 1857 by a larger chapel near the village centre.[30] In 1865 the Wesleyans were all said to attend the parish church also, and in 1877 the Wesleyan chapel was described as not well attended.[31] There were 20 members c. 1830 and 41 in 1885.[32] The chapel ceased to be used in 1970,[33] but still stood in 1972; it has a stone-built façade in the Gothic style.

A farm-house called Naburn Hill or White Cock Hall, beside the York road in the north-east of the parish, was used for Wesleyan Methodist worship in 1851 and was registered for the purpose in 1853; it had ceased to be so used by 1896.[34]

EDUCATION. A school was mentioned in 1743.[35] Edward Loftas, by will of 1784, left £100 for the education of ten children there. By 1809 the money had been invested in £138 stock and the income was about £6 a year; the free pupils were said in 1823 to be taught with other children at a school built by George Palmes.[36] There were 42 boys and girls at the school in 1835.[37] Thomas Dickinson, by will proved in 1843, left £100 to the school,[38] and by 1855 fifteen pupils were consequently taught free.[39] In the 1860s a boys' school was supported by the endowments, while the mistress of a girls' school was paid by 'a benevolent lady at the hall'.[40] The lady is said to have been Mrs. Lloyd, who was occupying Naburn Hall and provided a room for the girls.[41] The school was replaced by a National school, built near by in the back lane, in 1871–2[42] and enlarged in 1889.[43] It received an annual government grant from 1873.[44] The average attendance was 60–70 from 1906 until the 1920s and still exceeded 50 in the 1930s.[45] The number on the roll in April 1972 was 24.[46] By a Scheme of 1900 it was provided that the income from Loftas's endowment should be used for prizes;[47] in 1974 the income of £8 was used to buy books for the school. Dickinson's charity has been lost.[48]

CHARITIES FOR THE POOR. John Hebden at an unknown date gave £5 for the poor of Naburn and in 1823 the interest was distributed at Christmas.[49] No more is known of it.

Sir John Hewley at unknown date gave £10 to the poor and in 1770 the capital was held by Hewley Baines.[50] In 1823 H. J. Baines denied that the charity was chargeable on his estate[51] and no more is known of it.

Frances, dowager Lady Howard, by will proved in 1716, bequeathed money to provide coal for Escrick and other villages, including Naburn.[52] After 1862 Naburn received $\frac{1}{7}$ of the income; in 1972–3 it amounted to £2, which was not distributed that year.[53]

Emily Baines, in memory of her husband Henry (d. 1868), gave a share in the Hull & Selby Railway for the benefit of nine widows or the aged poor, the interest to be distributed in money or coal on St. Thomas's Day.[54]

Ambrose Walker in 1892 gave £100, the interest to be given to the poor on 13 December.[55]

C. H. C. Harrison, by will proved in 1935, left £90 for the poor.[56]

The three last-mentioned charities were later administered together. In 1965–6 £12 was distributed equally among eight widows, and in 1972–3, when the income was £15 from £210 stock, £1 was given to each of thirteen persons.[57]

Naburn benefited from the charity of John Hodgson for parishes in York poor-law union,[58] and one grant was made to a resident of Naburn in 1972.[59]

RICCALL

THE PARISH of Riccall lies about 8 miles south of York, on the east bank of the river Ouse.[1] Its name suggests that the village was an Anglian settlement, established on a ridge near a nook of land around which the river flowed.[2] The site of the village, more than 25 ft. above sea-level, is certainly surrounded on three sides by low-lying ground, and the Ouse at Riccall has one of the most prominent bends in its sinuous course. It was at Riccall that Earl Tostig and Harold Hardrada landed in 1066 before marching to battle at Fulford,[3] and about 50 skeletons found near the river, close to Riccall landing, in

---

[27] G.R.O. Worship Returns, Vol. v, no. 1450.
[28] J. Lyth, *Glimpses of Early Meth. in York and Dist.* 293.
[29] H.O. 129/23/515; O.S. Map 6" (1851 edn.).
[30] Lyth, *Glimpses*, 293.
[31] B.I.H.R., V. 1865/Ret. 370; V. 1877/Ret.
[32] Camidge, *Ouse Bridge to Naburn Lock*, 383; Lyth, *Glimpses*, 293.
[33] *Yorks. Eve. Press*, 24 Aug. 1971.
[34] H.O. 129/23/515; G.R.O. Worship Returns, Vol. v, no. 809.
[35] *Herring's Visit.* i. 163.
[36] B.I.H.R., TER. A. Naburn 1809; *10th Rep. Com. Char.* 667.
[37] *Educ. Enquiry Abstract*, 1092.
[38] Ed. 49/8576.
[39] Sheahan and Whellan, *Hist. York & E.R.* i. 648.
[40] B.I.H.R., V. 1865/Ret. 370; V. 1868/Ret. 328.
[41] Camidge, *Ouse Bridge to Naburn Lock*, 390.
[42] Ed. 7/135 no. 120.
[43] Camidge, op. cit. 393.
[44] *Rep. of Educ. Cttee. of Council, 1873–4* [C. 1019–I], p. 442, H.C. (1874), xviii.
[45] *Bd. of Educ. List 21* (H.M.S.O.).
[46] Ex inf. Chief Educ. Officer, County Hall, Beverley, 1972.
[47] Char. Com. files.
[48] Ex inf. the vicar, 1975.
[49] *10th Rep. Com. Char.* 667.
[50] B.I.H.R., TER. A. Naburn 1770; board in church.
[51] E.R.R.O., DDBH/26/1.
[52] See p. 28.
[53] Char. Com. files.
[54] Board in church.
[55] Ibid.
[56] Char. Com. files; ex inf. the vicar, 1975.
[57] Char. Com. files. [58] See p. 12.
[59] Ex inf. Mr. A. R. Tunnah, Haxby, 1974.
[1] This article was written in 1972–3.
[2] *P.N.E.R. Yorks.* (E.P.N.S.), 265.
[3] *V.C.H. Yorks.* iii. 396; see above p. 29.

1956–7 may be connected with the events of that year.[4] The parish, which is roughly triangular in shape, has an area of 2,667 a.[5]

Much of the east of the parish is more than 25 ft. above sea-level, and it is from this higher ground that the ridge forming the village site extends. These areas are largely composed of outwash sand and clay. North-east of the village is a tract of lower-lying clays, and alongside the Ouse there are large areas of alluvium.[6] The relatively small open fields of Riccall lay partly on the higher ground and partly between the village and the riverside ings. On both higher and lower ground there were extensive areas of early inclosures, and the eastern part of the parish was occupied by commons that continued into Skipwith and other neighbouring townships. Inclosure of open fields and commons did not take place until 1883.[7] An airfield was built on the former common for the Royal Air Force and opened in 1942; it was closed to flying in 1945[8] but derelict runways and buildings remained in 1972.

Streams and dikes form much of the northern and southern boundaries of Riccall. One of them, Dam dike, leaves the boundary with Escrick and flows across the north-west corner of the parish before joining the Ouse. Flooding was alleged in 1343 to have been caused by neglect of the banks along the dike, as well as of the sluice and river flood banks at its outfall into the Ouse.[9] Constant attention has always been necessary to maintain the banks and the sluices or cloughs.[10] In the 16th century, for example, frequent repairs were needed to several staiths, to the timber 'breastwork' along the river, and to the banks in the bishop of Durham's manor, and on at least one occasion the manor-house was flooded.[11] Water from eight parishes was said to be discharged at the Dam dike outfall in the 1850s, when a new clough was built there.[12] The Ouse forms the entire western parish boundary. The course of the river has at some time been straightened across a circuitous meander; the ground thus cut off from Riccall, known as the Nesses, remained in the parish until 1883, when it was transferred to Wistow (Yorks. W.R.).[13]

Riccall lies on the road from York to Selby. At the northern boundary the road crosses Dam dike by Scorce bridge, perhaps 'skew bridge', a name recorded as 'Scalewisbrigg' as early as 1227.[14] The bridge was rebuilt in brick and stone by the county in 1805,[15] and it was presumably this small single-arched structure that remained in 1972. One stretch of the Selby road, ½ mile south-east of the village, was straightened in 1801.[16] Apart from field roads only two other roads lead from Riccall village, one westwards to Kelfield and the other, King Rudding Lane, eastwards to the common, where it formerly continued towards Skipwith. The York–Selby railway line, opened in 1871,[17] passes under the main road south-east of the village and over it at a level-crossing north of the village. The station, on the road to the common, was closed for passengers in 1958 and for goods in 1964,[18] and it was used as a dwelling-house in 1972.

The large village of Riccall lies around the junction of the main York–Selby road with the road to Kelfield. Stretches of those roads are closely built up, and other houses stand in offshoots from them, namely North Field and Chapel Lanes, Church Street, Station Road, and Coppergate. At the road junction in the village centre is a triangular area, now partly built upon, two sides of which are known as Silver Street. It is possible that this was formerly a green and market-place, though there is no subsequent reference to the Wednesday market and fair on 19–21 July at Riccall granted in 1350.[19] Cross Hill House 'near the old cross', mentioned in 1732 and 1829,[20] may have stood thereabouts.

Apart from the former Vicarage, which incorporates the remains of the medieval prebendal manor-house,[21] the most noteworthy house in the village is Bangram Hill Farm, on the York road. It is timber-framed and probably 17th-century in date but was encased in brick in the 18th and early 19th centuries. A brick house in Church Street may have a similar origin. There are several other 18th-century brown-brick houses in the streets around the church and two substantial early-19th-century villas in Main Street, besides many smaller 19th-century houses. Part of the former pinfold stands on the York road, and there are several groups of farm buildings in the village, including a dovecot at Dam End Farm. Modern development, on all sides of the village, includes over 100 council houses and several estates of private houses.

There was a single licensed house in Riccall in the later 18th century,[22] but by 1823 there were four, the Greyhound, the Drovers' Inn, the Hare and Hounds, and the Shoulder of Mutton.[23] In 1842 there were five public houses[24] and in 1851 four,[25] the Gardeners' Arms replacing the Shoulder of Mutton among the names of 1823. Thereafter only the Greyhound, the Hare and Hounds, and the Drovers' Inn are recorded; the last-named apparently closed between 1913 and 1921,[26] but the others remained in 1972. Shops in the village include that of the Riccall Co-operative Society, founded in 1878[27] and occupying a prominent building of that time. An agricultural show was held at Riccall in 1879.[28] At inclosure in 1883 6 a. were allotted for a recreation ground,[29] which was opened

---

[4] Y.A.J. xl. 301–7.
[5] O.S. Map 6", Yorks. (1851 edn.). The whole of Riccall is covered by sheet 206.
[6] Geol. Surv. Map 1", solid and drift, sheet 71 (1973 edn.).
[7] See p. 85.
[8] Ex inf. Ministry of Defence, 1972.
[9] Cal. Pat. 1343–5, 96, 182; Cal. Inq. Misc. i, pp. 454–5.
[10] e.g. B.I.H.R., Bp. C. & P. XIX (1721); CC. Ab. 10 (1823–4); Cal. Pat. 1313–17, 492; see below p. 85.
[11] Univ. of Durham, Dept. of Palaeography, CC. 220920, 221641–3, 221672.
[12] E.R.R.O., DDFA/20/6.
[13] Kelly's Dir. N. & E.R. Yorks. (1889), 444.
[14] P.N.E.R. Yorks. 265–6.
[15] E.R.R.O., QAB/2/3.
[16] Ibid. HD/6.
[17] V.C.H. City of York, 478.
[18] Ex inf. Divisional Manager, Brit. Rlys. (Leeds), 1972.
[19] Cal. Chart. R. 1341–1417, 120.
[20] R.D.B., N/52/102; E.R.R.O., DDFA/13/193.
[21] See pp. 84, 87.
[22] E.R.R.O., QDT/2/15.
[23] Baines, Hist. Yorks. ii. 381.
[24] B.I.H.R., TA. 865VL.
[25] H.O. 107/2351.
[26] Directories.
[27] Ex inf. Mr. D. R. J. Neave, 1973; Kelly's Dir. N. & E.R. Yorks. (1879), 638.
[28] B.I.H.R., Rom. 62.
[29] E.R.R.O., Enrolment Bk. I, pp. 157 sqq.

two years later.[30] A village institute was built in 1927.[31]

There are several small farm-houses on the Selby road and the larger Riccall Grange stands in the east of the parish, towards Skipwith.

The number of poll-tax payers at Riccall is uncertain. There were 193 in St. Peter's liberty, the prebend of Riccall's manor, in 1377,[32] and 76 in St. Cuthbert's fee, the bishop of Durham's manor, in 1379.[33] There were more than 300 'housing people' in 1548.[34] In 1672 128 houses in the village were listed in the hearth-tax return, 24 of them exempt. Of those that were chargeable 69 had only one hearth each, 20 had 2, 9 had 3, 3 had 5, and 3 had 8 or nine.[35] In 1743 there were about 86 families[36] and in 1764 110.[37] The population in 1801 was 517. By 1821 it had risen to 599, by 1831 to 705, and by 1871 to 795, before falling to 702 in 1901.[38] It subsequently increased to 783 in 1961 and 1,029 in 1971.[39]

MANORS AND OTHER ESTATES. Two carucates of land in Riccall belonged to the archbishop of York in 1066, and the canons of the minster held it under him in 1086.[40] The estate was assigned to the prebend of Riccall, presumably at its formation (before 1217).[41] From 1612 almost continuously until the 19th century the lessees of the manor of *RICCALL* under the prebendary were the Wormley family.[42] The manor was sold by the parliamentary commissioners to William Consett in 1650 and he conveyed it to Henry Wormley the following year,[43] but it was recovered for the prebend at the Restoration. After the death of Christopher Wormley in 1800 his widow Jane (d. 1843) married Toft Richardson (d. 1827) in 1802, and they were succeeded by their son Wormley Edward Richardson.[44] The manor passed to the Ecclesiastical Commissioners in 1837 upon a voidance of the prebend,[45] and in 1856 they sold it, with 113 a. of land, to W. E. Richardson.[46] The manor and 158 a. were in 1858 sold by Richardson to B. R. Lawley, Baron Wenlock.[47] They thus became part of the Lawley family's already large estate in the parish.[48]

The prebendal manor-house was mentioned c. 1295, and licence to crenellate it was granted in 1350.[49] It passed with the manor to the Lawleys but in 1869 it was enlarged to serve as the Vicarage of Riccall.[50] The present house retains the eastern end of a 15th-century building, including a three-storeyed brick tower block, with projecting garderobe and stair turrets.[51] There are slight remains of the moat which once surrounded the house.

A second estate at Riccall in 1066, comprising a single carucate, belonged to the king. By 1086 it was soke of the bishop of Durham's manor of Howden,[52] and *RICCALL* manor, sometimes known as the manor of *WHEEL HALL*, subsequently belonged to the see of Durham until the 19th century. In 1322 the bishop let it for ten years to the Peruzzi of Florence.[53] After Edward VI's dissolution of the bishopric in 1553 Riccall manor was granted to Francis Jobson, but it was recovered the following year[54] when the bishopric was revived. Between the late 17th and early 19th centuries Wheel Hall was often let to the Mastermans.[55] The bishops of Durham retained the manor until 1836, when it was transferred, along with Howden, to the newly created bishopric of Ripon.[56] In 1850 the manor was let to F. B. Robinson, and in 1855 80 a. of it were sold to him.[57] The rest of the Ripon estate was vested in the Ecclesiastical Commissioners in 1857. In 1873 140 a., with the manor-house, were sold to Lord Wenlock[58] and were merged with his larger estate in Riccall.

The bishop of Durham's manor-house of Wheel Hall, 'the house by the river-deep', was mentioned in the early 14th century.[59] In the 16th century repairs were done to the hall, great chamber, chapel, stables, and other buildings, and to 'the drawdike about the manor'. The old gate house and water gate house were mentioned in 1662 and later.[60] The hall has been replaced by an 18th-century farmhouse but traces of the moat which surrounded it were still visible in 1972.

A holding in Riccall belonging to the Beckwith family was mentioned in 1538–9 and later.[61] It was conveyed by Newark and Leonard Beckwith to Edward Wormley in 1654,[62] and the chief house upon it apparently became the seat of the Wormleys. The house was said in 1776 to have formerly been called Beckwith's Hall and to have been rebuilt by Edward Wormley (d. 1787).[63] Known as Riccall Hall, it passed with the prebendal manor to the Lawleys in 1858 and additions and improvements were made to it by Lord Wenlock c. 1884.[64] The house was demolished in 1951–2[65] and in 1952 the site was sold to L. A. Winder,[66] who converted outbuildings and stable block into a house still known in 1972 as Riccall Hall.

The Lawley family's estate in Riccall was ap-

---

[30] B.I.H.R., Rom. 63.
[31] *Kelly's Dir. N. & E.R. Yorks.* (1929), 556.
[32] E 179/202/58 m. 2.
[33] *T.E.R.A.S.* xv. 61–2.
[34] *Yorks. Chantry Surv.* i (Sur. Soc. xci), 56.
[35] E 179/205/504.
[36] *Herring's Visit.* iii. 28.
[37] B.I.H.R., Bp. V. 1764/Ret. 210.
[38] *V.C.H. Yorks.* iii. 498.
[39] *Census.*
[40] *V.C.H. Yorks.* ii. 211.
[41] *York Minster Fasti,* ii (Y.A.S. Rec. Ser. cxxiv), 66.
[42] E.R.R.O., DDHV/29/29, 31, 39; Minster Libr., D. & C. Archives, L 2 (3) e, f. 15; S 1 (1) d. For pedigree see Y.A.S., MS. 530(b).
[43] E.R.R.O., DDSC/84; DDHV/29/36–7.
[44] Y.A.S., MS. 530(b).
[45] B.I.H.R., Inst. AB. 21, p. 2; *The Times,* 5 May 1837.
[46] R.D.B., HK/372/399.
[47] Ibid. HS/114/134.
[48] See p. 85 and below.
[49] *Miscellanea,* iv (Y.A.S. Rec. Ser. xciv), 1; *Cal. Chart. R. 1341–1417,* 120.
[50] See p. 87.
[51] See plate facing p. 80.
[52] *V.C.H. Yorks.* ii. 217.
[53] *Cal. Pat. 1321–4,* 401.
[54] Ibid. *1553,* 133; *1553–4,* 377–8.
[55] e.g. E 179/261/10; E.R.R.O., Land Tax; monument in church (Hen. Masterman, d. 1732); Univ. of Durham, Dept. of Palaeography, CC. 188447.
[56] Univ. of Durham, Dept. of Palaeography, Durham Dioc. Rec., Orders in Council, 22 Dec. 1836 (Ripon).
[57] R.D.B., MM/352/562.
[58] E.R.R.O., DDFA/13/215.
[59] *P.N.E.R. Yorks.* (E.P.N.S.), 265.
[60] Univ. of Durham, Dept. of Palaeography, CC. 188447, 220920, 221641–3; Cosin's Survey, 1662.
[61] C 142/403 no. 93; *Yorks. Fines,* i. 84, 148, 204, 206; *Yorks. Fines, 1614–25,* 90.
[62] E.R.R.O., DDSC/85.
[63] Ex inf. Mr. D. R. J. Neave, Beverley, 1973.
[64] R.D.B., NW/185/239.
[65] Ex inf. Escrick Park Estate Office, 1974.
[66] R.D.B., 910/196/159.

parently established by their predecessors the Thompsons in the earlier 18th century and it descended like the capital manor of Escrick.[67] By 1755 Beilby Thompson had 346 a. there.[68] Later acquisitions included 112 a. from the Hardwicks and 100 a. from the heirs of Gilbert Parker in 1766,[69] and in 1819 the estate comprised 635 a.[70] In 1829 125 a. formerly belonging to Henry Masterman were added.[71] By the 1850s the Lawleys had 961 a.[72] and by 1870 1,324 a.[73] At inclosure in 1883 Lord Wenlock was allotted 647 a. in lieu of open-field land and, as lord of both manors, for his share of the common land.[74] Irene, daughter of the 3rd Baron Wenlock (d. 1912), sold about 350 a. at Riccall in 1919 and some 750 a. in 1921,[75] and in 1972 the Forbes Adam estate comprised 335 a.[76]

The rectorial tithes of Riccall belonged to the prebendary and were worth £50 in 1650[77] and £65 in 1735.[78] They were commuted for £508 10s. a year in 1842.[79]

ECONOMIC HISTORY. On the estate belonging to the canons of the minster in 1086 there was land for 2 ploughs, but the canons then had 2 ploughs and 20 villeins had 4 more. There was meadow ½ league long and ½ league broad, and woodland a league long and ½ league broad. The estate had decreased in value from £5 before the Conquest to £1 10s. On the bishop of Durham's estate in 1086 2 sokemen, 3 villeins, and 2 bordars had 2 ploughs.[80]

There is little record of early assarting from woodland and waste, but Foulthwayt, Littelhurst, Thomashagh, and Huddridyng all existed by 1368.[81] The prebend still had 24 a. of woodland c. 1295, 4 a. called Aldergrove, at a place called Storhakenes, and the rest in Southwood. The prebendal demesne lands then included 46½ a. of arable, 14 a. of meadow, and 4 a. of pasture held in severalty. Among the tenants were 28 bondmen, holding 28½ bovates, who were liable to pay a special rent if they had any newly cleared land; they performed day-works at ploughing, harrowing, reaping, and mowing, carted wood, made malt, and repaired the lord's fences, and rendered hens and eggs. In addition 9 grassmen and 9 rentpayers held unspecified lands, for which they, too, owed works and services, and there were 35 cottars, who only gave hens and eggs. The prebendary's tenants and those of the bishop of Durham all had common rights in 60 a. of pasture at that time.[82] By c. 1400 the prebendary had 31 free tenants, holding 263 a. altogether, 24 bondmen, holding 12½ bovates and 104 a., and 27 cottagers, four of whom held 11½ a. between them and the rest only their houses.[83] The bishop's park at Riccall was mentioned in 1311,[84] and one of his closes near Wheel Hall was called the Park in the 16th century.[85]

In the 16th and 17th centuries the names were recorded of many closes assarted in the Middle Ages or later, among them Haver Thwaites, Long Ridding, which lay beside the Ouse, Brockhirst, Crose Rudding, and Southwood close.[86] A close called the Ness or Skurf was mentioned as early as 1558 and was no doubt the area in a bend of the Ouse later called the Nesses.[87] The open fields included East and West fields, named in the earlier 16th century,[88] and North field, mentioned in 1649.[89] Some of the riverside meadow and marsh was at least by the 17th century cultivated as part of the fields, for there was reference to arable land in Hither marsh in West field.[90] The extensive ings, in which many tenants held parcels, were also sometimes described as part of West field.[91] Throughout the 17th century, if not before, Hineing marsh was a stinted pasture in which many villagers had beastgates,[92] and Gosling marsh was described in 1698 as being let by the bylawmen as summer pasture to produce rents for the upkeep of the river flood banks.[93]

In the 18th century several new names were recorded for sections of the open fields, besides the older East, West, and North fields. Mill field, for example, mentioned in 1735,[94] may have been part of West field; Hornell and Crook Hornell[95] were part of North field; and King's Rudding[96] lay beyond East field. The great extent of early-inclosed land in the parish is illustrated by the Thompsons' estate, which in 1755 comprised 233 a. in closes and only 92 a. in the open fields and 21 a. in the meadows.[97] Although final inclosure was proposed in 1806,[98] open fields and commons in fact remained until 1883. Nearly 100 householders each had a common right in 1842,[99] but many common rights and marsh-gates were bought up by Lord Wenlock before inclosure.[1] The ings covered 117 a. in 1842.[2] The area inclosed in 1883 amounted to 1,156 a., lying in East field, West field, including the ings, Little North, Lower North, and Upper North fields, King's Rudding, the common moor, and a common called the Dam, alongside Dam dike. Lord Wenlock received 547 a., James Pratt 99 a., and Richard Moon 75 a. There were 19 allotments of 10–49 a. each and 27 of under 10 a., and 20 a. of allotment gardens were awarded to the parish officers for the poor.[3] A former boundary stone from

---

[67] See p. 20.
[68] E.R.R.O., DDFA/13/4.
[69] Ibid. DDFA/13/6, 139.   [70] Ibid. DDFA/41/4.
[71] Ibid. DDFA/13/152, 193.
[72] Ibid. DDFA/41/6.
[73] R.D.B., KS/282/377.
[74] E.R.R.O., Enrolment Bk. I, p. 157.
[75] R.D.B., 191/422/357; /523/447; 192/281/248; 228/414/353; 229/231/209; /233/210; 236/516/425; 242/342/275.
[76] Ex inf. Escrick Park Estate Office, 1972.
[77] C 94/3 f. 77.
[78] B.I.H.R., Bp. C. & P. XIX.
[79] Ibid. TA. 865VL.
[80] V.C.H. Yorks. ii. 211, 217.
[81] Cal. Fine R. 1356–68, 381.
[82] Miscellanea, iv. 1–3.
[83] Minster Libr., D. & C. Arch. M 2 (2) c.
[84] Reg. Pal. Dunelm. (Rolls Ser.), i. 19, 105.

[85] Univ. of Durham, Dept. of Palaeography, CC. 189550.
[86] E.R.R.O., DDHV/29/28; DDWB/15/63; DDSC/84.
[87] Ibid. DDHV/29/16; Y.A.J. xvii. 111 n.; see above p. 83.
[88] E.R.R.O., DDIIV/29/1.
[89] Lamb. Pal. Libr., COMM./XIIa/17/502.
[90] E.R.R.O., DDHV/29/34–5.
[91] e.g. Lamb. Pal. Libr., COMM./XIIa/17/502; B.I.H.R., TER. N. Riccall 1716.
[92] See p. 88.   [93] 10th Rep. Com. Char. 671.
[94] E.R.R.O., DDFA/13/1.   [95] Ibid. DDFA/13/4.
[96] R.D.B., T/282/517.
[97] E.R.R.O., DDFA/13/4.
[98] York Courant, 18 Aug. 1806.
[99] B.I.H.R., TA. 865VL.
[1] E.R.R.O., DDFA/13/241, 284, 342–62, 382.
[2] B.I.H.R., TA. 865VL.
[3] E.R.R.O., Enrolment Bk. I, pp. 157 sqq. and IA. Riccall (with map).

the ings, inscribed 'EW' (perhaps Edward Wormey), was at Dam End Farm in 1972, and another was at Bangram Hill Farm.

In 1842 there had been 1,269 a. of arable, 736 a. of meadow or pasture, and an estimated 1,000 a. of common waste in the parish.[4] The arable and grassland areas were similar in 1905, 1,303 a. and 661 a. respectively, when there was also 41 a. of woodland.[5] In the 1930s there was still much grassland alongside the Ouse and Dam dike, and several stretches of rough pasture remained on the former common. New plantations included a large one on the common. The most noteworthy change by the 1960s was the conversion to arable of much of the former grassland near the Ouse.[6]

There were 37 farmers in Riccall in 1823, and about 20 farmers and a market-gardener in the later 19th and 20th centuries.[7] In 1851 2 and in the 1930s 2–4 farms were of more than 150 a.[8] In 1921 278 a. were bought by the East Riding county council for smallholdings.[9] There were two large indoor poultry units near King Rudding Lane in 1972.

The Ouse was of some economic value to Riccall for fishing and transport. About 1295 there was a fishery there called Gedmer,[10] and the prebendal and episcopal manors long retained their fishing rights. Nets and weirs were mentioned in the mid 14th century, one at the Ness belonging to the prebendary and another at the Fleet to the bishop of Durham.[11] In 1477–8 three fisheries at Riccall belonging to the bishop were said to have been destroyed by the city of York because they obstructed navigation.[12] One or two men still made a livelihood from fishing in the mid 19th century.[13] A landing-place just south of the Dam dike clough[14] was said in 1856 to be used for bringing in such goods as potatoes and corn.[15] A coal merchant lived in the village in 1823, there were two boat owners in 1840, and a potato merchant and a corn merchant were listed in the 1870s and 1880s.[16] A new landing-place was provided at the end of Landing Lane, which was laid out across West field at inclosure in 1883. The Yorkshire Ouse and Hull River Authority had a works depot there in 1972.

Weavers were occasionally recorded at Riccall from the 16th to the early 19th century.[17] In 1851 there were altogether about 80 shopkeepers and tradesmen in this large village, among them a weaver, eight brickyard workers, and a flax-dresser.[18] The brickworks was in West field at that time, but was not mentioned again. A Tow dike was then situated on the common,[19] but later flax-dressers may have used the 20 or so 'old flax pits' which lay beside Dam dike in 1906.[20] In the 20th century main-road traffic attracted refreshment rooms, motor engineers, and haulage contractors, and there was also a cattle and poultry food manufacturer.[21] The Pratt family were timber merchants at least from 1859 until 1909, with a saw-mill in Station Road.[22]

The prebend had a water-mill on Dam dike which was said in 1343 to have been destroyed in Edward I's reign.[23] The name Watermill bridge was still used in the 19th century.[24] The site of the former mill was mentioned c. 1295, when the prebend also had a windmill and a horse-mill.[25] The prebend's windmill was mentioned in the 17th and 18th centuries, and it stood in West field,[26] probably on the site of the later West field mill. Another windmill, mentioned in the 15th century and later, belonged to the bishop's manor.[27] By 1803 it had gone and its site was marked by 'the old mill hill' in West field,[28] nearer to the river than the prebend's mill. In the 1840s there were two windmills, the older one in West field and another in East field.[29] West field mill had steam power by 1889; it later reverted to wind alone and was used until c. 1910. The tower still stood in 1972. The East field mill was not mentioned again, but it was replaced by a steam corn mill at the north end of the village, which apparently closed in the 1890s.[30] The building remained in 1972.

LOCAL GOVERNMENT. The bishop of Durham's manor came within the purview of his court at Howden, and there are presentments concerning Riccall in several court rolls of the early 17th century.[31] The prebendal manor of 'Riccall with Newbald and Cawthorpe' included property held by the prebend in North Newbald and Caythorpe (in Rudston).[32] Court rolls of the manor survive from 1559,[33] 1573,[34] and 82 years between 1621 and 1793,[35] and there is a court book for 1803–9.[36] Numerous court papers include extracts of surrenders and admissions for the 16th to 19th centuries,[37] a call roll for 1810–25,[38] and lists of pains for 1601, 1773, and 1877.[39] The bylawmen were mentioned in 1601, and there were six of them, together with a constable and a pinder, in 1756 and 1803–9.

There are no parochial records before 1835, but

[4] B.I.H.R., TA. 865VL.
[5] Acreage Returns, 1905.
[6] [1st] Land Util. Surv. Map, sheet 32; 2nd Land Util. Surv. Map, sheet 689 (SE 63–73).
[7] Directories.
[8] H.O. 107/2351; directories.
[9] R.D.B., 242/342/275.
[10] Miscellanea, iv. 3.
[11] Public Works in Med. Law, ii (Selden Soc. xl), 252–3, 301–2.
[12] Univ. of Durham, Dept. of Palaeography, CC. 190240.
[13] H.O. 107/2351; White, Dir. E. & N.R. Yorks. (1840), 335.
[14] O.S. Map 6" (1851 edn.).
[15] Sheahan and Whellan, Hist. York & E.R. ii. 627.
[16] Directories.
[17] E.R.R.O., DDFA/13/46, 76, 173; DDHV/29/3, 21; DDEL/32/1; QSF. Christ. 1733, C.14; East. 1767, B.1.
[18] H.O. 107/2351.
[19] O.S. Map 6" (1851 edn.).
[20] Ibid. 1/2,500, Yorks. CCVI. 11 (1908 edn.).
[21] Directories.
[22] E.R.R.O., DDFA/13/261; Kelly's Dir. N. & E.R. Yorks. (1909), 577; O.S. Map 1/2,500 (1908 edn.).
[23] Cal. Inq. Misc. i, pp. 454–5.
[24] O.S. Map 6" (1851 edn.).
[25] Miscellanea, iv. 1.
[26] E.R.R.O., DDHV/29/44; DDSC/84; B.I.H.R., Bp. C. & P. XIX.
[27] Univ. of Durham, Dept. of Palaeography, M. 80; CC. 18447, 189065, 189550, 190240, 220920.
[28] Ibid. Sundry Notitia, Bdle. 1, I, 42.
[29] O.S. Map 6" (1851 edn.).
[30] Ibid. 1/2,500 (1908 edn.); directories.
[31] S.C. 2/211/62.
[32] Miscellanea, iv. 3.
[33] Y.A.S., MD. 248 (a).
[34] B.I.H.R., Wenlock, court rolls.
[35] Ibid. except 1664 in Y.A.S., MD. 248 (a) and 1756 in B.I.H.R., Wenlock, court papers.
[36] B.I.H.R., Wenlock, minute book.
[37] Ibid. court papers; Y.A.S., MD. 248 (a).
[38] B.I.H.R., Wenlock, call roll.
[39] Ibid. misc. papers; court papers; Rom. 65, respectively.

the appointment of and instructions for an overseer of the poor survive from 1737, together with a specimen of the badge to be worn by those receiving relief.[40] Riccall joined Selby poor-law union in 1837,[41] and six former poorhouses were sold in 1869.[42] The parish became part of Riccall rural district in 1894, Derwent rural district in 1935,[43] and the Selby district of North Yorkshire in 1974.

CHURCH. Part of the surviving fabric of the church apparently dates from the 12th century. The church belonged to the prebendary of Riccall, and the parish was within his peculiar jurisdiction.[44] A vicarage was ordained in 1316,[45] and the constitution of the vicar's income was settled by the vicar and prebendary in 1360.[46] The prebendaries were also patrons.[47] When the prebend passed to the Ecclesiastical Commissioners in 1837 the advowson came to be vested in the archbishop of York, who presented in 1844.[48] He is still the patron.

The vicarage was valued at £6 net in 1535[49] and £13 6s. 8d. in 1650.[50] The living was augmented by £10 a year, given by a prebendary Marmaduke Cooke (d. 1684) and paid by the prebendal lessee.[51] A parliamentary grant of £1,000 was made in 1816,[52] and the average net income in 1829–31 was £95.[53] An endowment of £140 a year was given from the Common Fund in 1863,[54] and the net income was £300 in 1884 and £261 in 1914.[55] Tithes accounted for most of the income in 1535 and 1650. In 1716 and later those from a farm called Nesses were paid by a modus of 3s. 4d. a year.[56] The tithes were commuted in 1842 for a rent-charge of £140.[57] The only glebe land in 1649 was ½ a. of meadow and ½ a. of arable.[58] By 1849 20 a. had been bought at Hemingbrough[59] and in 1868 11 a. were given by Lord Wenlock.[60]

A vicarage house was mentioned in 1535,[61] and it was reported to be in decay in 1550 and 1600.[62] In 1649 it comprised hall, kitchen, parlour, and a bedroom,[63] and in 1764 the brick and tile building was said to contain study, kitchen, parlour, and outshot. The same house was apparently still used in 1825, and it stood beside the churchyard. By 1849 it had been replaced by a larger house of about ten rooms,[64] said to have been that later called the Villa, now no. 33 York Road.[65] The Vicarage was next moved to the old prebendal manor-house, which was included in Lord Wenlock's gift of land in 1868. The house was greatly enlarged for the purpose the following year;[66] it is in a Gothic style and contains a stained glass window from the old Vicarage incorporating a rebus of Thomas Elcock, vicar 1669–1704, and said to be the work of Gyles of York.[67] The cost of adapting the house was largely met by a grant of £1,400 from the Common Fund.[68] A new Vicarage was built in Church Street in 1967.[69]

A chantry at St. James's altar was founded by James Carleton, by will dated 1494. Another, at the altar of St. Nicholas, was said to have been founded by several inhabitants of Riccall.[70] It was probably that for which licence was granted to the vicar Richard Davy and others in 1483, when it was to be called Richard III's chantry.[71] Both chantries were worth about £3 net in 1535.[72] Grants of former chantry property after the suppression included one of a house, 3 cottages, 5 closes, and 23 a. of land in Riccall to Rowland Wandesford and Ralph Harrison in 1560.[73] Grants were also made of property formerly supporting obits in the church.[74]

The vicar of Riccall was allowed to be non-resident in 1306,[75] and Richard Davy was given permission in 1477 to hold another benefice.[76] John Newlove, vicar in 1620, was a Puritan.[77] Thomas Cooper, vicar 1721–46, left 'a considerable library' for the use of his successors.[78] The vicar in 1764 lived at Topcliffe (Yorks. N.R.), which he also served, but had a curate at Riccall.[79]

Two services were held each week in 1743 and communion was celebrated four times a year, with 130 communicants the previous Easter.[80] There was one weekly service and five celebrations a year in 1764. There were two Sunday services by 1851,[81] and from 1865 to the end of the century communion was received twelve times a year by about fifteen to 25 people. In 1914 communion was celebrated twice a month.[82] There were three services each Sunday in 1972.

The church of ST. MARY is of stone and consists of chancel, aisled and clerestoried nave with south porch, and west tower. The three westernmost bays of the nave may be mid- to late-12th-century in date, if the now reset north and south

[40] Ibid. Rom. 60.
[41] 3rd Rep. Poor Law Com. 178.
[42] R.D.B., KK/332/446–7.
[43] Census.
[44] V.C.H. Yorks. iii. 86.
[45] Minster Libr., D. & C. Arch., M 2 (4) g, f. 24v.
[46] E.R.R.O., DDSC/81.
[47] e.g. Lamb. Pal. Libr., COMM./XIIa/17/502; Y.A.J. xxv. 185; Rep. Com. Eccl. Revenues, 960.
[48] B.I.H.R., Inst. AB. 21, p. 65; Ecclesiastical Commissioners Act, 3 & 4 Vic. c. 113, s. 41.
[49] Valor Eccl. (Rec. Com.), v. 99.
[50] C 94/3 f. 77.
[51] B.I.H.R., TER. N. Riccall 1716; E. James, Par. Ch. of St. Mary, Riccall, 21–2.
[52] Hodgson, Q.A.B. 451.
[53] Rep. Com. Eccl. Revenues, 960.
[54] Lond. Gaz. 28 July 1863, p. 3735.
[55] B.I.H.R., Bp. V. 1884/Ret.; Bp. V. 1914/Ret.
[56] Ibid. TER. N. Riccall 1716 etc.
[57] Ibid. TA. 865VL.
[58] Lamb. Pal. Libr., COMM./XIIa/17/502.
[59] B.I.H.R., TER. N. Riccall 1849.
[60] Ibid. 1876; R.D.B., KF/71/93.
[61] Valor Eccl. v. 99.
[62] B.I.H.R., V. 1600/CB. 1; Fabric Rolls of York Minster (Sur. Soc. xxxv), 274.
[63] Lamb. Pal. Libr., COMM./XIIa/17/502.
[64] B.I.H.R., TER. N. Riccall 1764–1849.
[65] James, Ch. of St. Mary, 22.
[66] B.I.H.R., TER. N. Riccall 1876. See above plate facing p. 80.
[67] Pevsner, Yorks. E.R. 329; James, Ch. of St. Mary, 26, 31.
[68] Lond. Gaz. 18 Feb. 1868, p. 782.
[69] R.D.B., 1456/217/200; 1531/212/171.
[70] Yorks. Chantry Surv. i. 55–6.
[71] Cal. Pat. 1476–85, 464.
[72] Valor Eccl. v. 101.
[73] E.R.R.O., DDWB/15/63; Cal. Pat. 1553, 103, 295.
[74] Cal. Pat. 1553, 295; 1563–6, p. 475.
[75] Reg. Greenfield, i, pp. 3–4.
[76] Cal. Papal Regs. xiii(2), 593.
[77] Walker Revised, ed. A. G. Matthews, 396.
[78] B.I.H.R., TER. N. Riccall 1809; for his dates see Par. Reg. of Riccall, Yorks. 1669–1813 (Yorks. Par. Reg. Soc. cxxiv), 109, 142.
[79] B.I.H.R., Bp. V. 1764/Ret. 210.
[80] Herring's Visit. iii. 29.
[81] H.O. 129/23/513.
[82] B.I.H.R., Bp. V. 1764/Ret. 210; V. 1865/Ret. 423; V. 1877/Ret.; Bp. V. 1884/Ret.; Bp. V. 1894/Ret.; Bp. V. 1914/Ret.

doorways were original features of it, and the tower probably belongs to the last years of that century. Arcades were cut through both side walls early in the 13th century and narrow aisles built which also lapped the tower. A further bay was added on the east and the chancel was rebuilt, and presumably extended, and provided with a north chapel later in the century. After that there appears to have been no new work for some time, and in 1472 the chancel was reported to be in need of repair.[83] Between then and the Reformation much new work was carried out, including the heightening of the nave walls for clerestorys, the widening of the aisles, the introduction of a rood loft, and the addition of the porch and south chapel. The central pier of the tower arch was probably put in at this time. Early fittings include a 12th-century south door and a late-17th-century communion rail.

Extensive restoration, most if not all of it directed by J. L. Pearson, took place between 1862 and 1877. It included the rebuilding of some walls and much of the tower, which was heightened, and new roofs, porch, and east window.[84]

By an inquisition held in 1698, under a commission of charitable uses, it was found that Hineing marsh in Riccall had been given to the churchwardens so that 40 beast-gates should be held by 20 householders, each tenant to pay 10s. a year towards the repair of the church. The gates were subsequently enjoyed by the householders in the village in rotation.[85]

There are the remains of a brass to Maud Kelsey and her son Robert of c. 1500,[86] and monuments include those to Benjamin (d. 1707) and Henry Masterman (d. 1732), Robert (d. 1712) and Christopher Wormley (d. 1800), and Toft (d. 1827) and Jane Richardson (d. 1843). There are Royal Arms of 1792 and a large charity board of 1791.

New bells were mentioned in 1406,[87] and there were two bells in 1552.[88] One of the three bells was cracked in 1764.[89] There are three surviving bells: (i) 1765, Lester & Pack of London; (ii) undated; (iii) 1637.[90] The plate includes a silver cup and cover, given by Marmaduke Cooke (d. 1684), and a silver paten, made in London in 1722 by Nathaniel Gulliver.[91] The registers begin in 1669 and are complete, except for marriages in 1754–1812.[92] The volume covering the period before 1813 has been printed.[93]

The churchyard was enlarged by the addition of the old Vicarage site, including the Lady well, and other ground in 1867,[94] and another addition was made in 1921.[95] There is a medieval grave slab to a notary, inscribed with penner and inkhorn,[96] and the base and shaft of a cross.

NONCONFORMITY. A Riccall man was gaoled for recusancy in 1580–5[97] and another registered an estate as a papist in 1716–32.[98] There was one family of Roman Catholics in 1743 and 1764.[99]

A Methodist chapel had been built by 1798,[1] and a barn and two houses were registered for worship in 1819, 1820, and 1822.[2] The chapel, in Chapel Lane, was replaced in 1864[3] and subsequently demolished.[4] The new Wesleyan chapel, in the main street at the centre of the village, was still used in 1972. There was also a Primitive Methodist meeting-house by 1851,[5] and in 1857 a Primitive chapel was built[6] in the main street; it was last used in the late 1930s[7] but still stood in 1972.

EDUCATION. There was probably a school at Riccall soon after 1720, for Robert Turie, by will of that date, left £40 to teach six children to read.[8] The income was £2 a year and other children were taught at their own expense, about 30 pupils altogether attending the school in 1743, for example.[9] The money was subsequently paid to a school which was established in 1791 by subscription among the inhabitants. In 1818 £30 from the subscription, together with £40 given at unknown date by Susannah Wilkes to teach five girls,[10] was used to buy stock which in 1823 produced £3 18s. a year. About 1790 George Newsham gave £32 to the school, the income from which was £1 12s. in 1823.[11] The master's house and schoolroom were mentioned in 1819,[12] and in 1835 the attendance was 20 in autumn and 80 in winter. In the latter year there were also 5–25 children, mainly girls, attending another school in the village, and 10–30, also mainly girls, at a school begun in 1827; all were taught at their parents' expense.[13] The subscription school was held in a house at the corner of Common Lane and the main street.[14]

A new building for the subscription school had been erected by c. 1845 at the corner of Silver Street and the main street.[15] The school was united with the National Society,[16] and it was owned and chiefly supported by Lord Wenlock. Elizabeth Wilson, by will proved in 1862, bequeathed a third

---

[83] *Fabric R. of York Minster*, 255.
[84] B.I.H.R., V. 1868/Ret. 375; V. 1877/Ret.; Fac. Bk. v, pp. 81–3; tablet in church. For the church before restoration see above plate facing p. 81.
[85] *10th Rep. Com. Char.* 671. The inquisition is printed in *Par. Reg. of Riccall*, 173–4.
[86] *Y.A.J.* xx. 305.
[87] B.I.H.R., Prob. Reg. ii, f. 439.
[88] *Inventories of Ch. Goods*, 79.
[89] B.I.H.R., TER. N. Riccall 1764.
[90] Boulter, 'Ch. Bells', 32.
[91] *Yorks. Ch. Plate*, i. 302.
[92] B.I.H.R.
[93] *Par. Reg. of Riccall.*
[94] B.I.H.R., TER. N. Riccall 1876. For the well see W. Smith, *Ancient Springs and Streams of E.R.* 167–70.
[95] York Dioc. Regy., Consecration deeds.
[96] *Y.A.J.* xx. 223 and illus.
[97] Aveling, *Post Reformation Catholicism*, 64.
[98] E.R.R.O., QDB/2/(1).
[99] B.I.H.R., Bp. V. 1764/Ret. 210; *Herring's Visit.* iii. 28.

[1] B.I.H.R., Fac. Bk. iii, p. 214.
[2] G.R.O. Worship Returns, Vol. v, nos. 3339, 3372, 3673.
[3] Date on new chapel.
[4] A small house which stood behind it (shown on B.I.H.R., TA. 865VL) survived in 1972.
[5] H.O. 129/24/513.
[6] Bulmer, *Dir. E. Yorks.* (1892), 701.
[7] Ex inf. the Revd. M. J. Townsend, Barlby, 1975.
[8] *10th Rep. Com. Char.* 670.
[9] B.I.H.R., Bp. V. 1764/Ret. 210; *Herring's Visit.* iii. 28.
[10] The Wilkes bequest is included on a charity board in the church, dated 1791.
[11] *10th Rep. Com. Char.* 670.
[12] *Educ. of Poor Digest*, 1089.
[13] *Educ. Enquiry Abstract*, 1094.
[14] B.I.H.R., TA. 865VL.
[15] Ed. 7/135 no. 140 states that it was built c. 1839, but it was not shown on a map of 1842: B.I.H.R., TA. 865VL.
[16] O.S. Map 6" (1851 edn.).

of the income from £500 to the school.[17] The total income of about £71 in 1871 included nearly £11 from the endowments and £13 from school pence. Eighteen children were then taught free and the average attendance was 99 boys and girls and 21 infants.[18] There were still two other schools, each with about 20 children.[19]

Attendance at the school remained at 100–125 between 1907 and 1938.[20] The endowment income was still received until 1931, but by a Scheme of that year the income of £50 from 10 a. and £249 stock was directed to be used for general educational purposes, including education other than elementary.[21] The school was replaced by a new county school in Coppergate in 1931,[22] and the old building was used as a village hall in 1972. Senior pupils in 1937 and the remaining children in 1951 were transferred to Riccall from Kelfield school. In 1960, however, senior pupils from Riccall were transferred to Barlby secondary school.[23] The number on the roll in September 1972 was 185.[24] The charity income in 1973 was £97, and grants were made to fourteen children leaving Riccall primary school for secondary school.[25]

CHARITIES FOR THE POOR. Robert Foster in 1611 created a rent-charge of 5s. on 1 a. of meadow land, and Christopher Consett in 1614 created a charge of £1 on 2 a. of meadow.[26] Richard Stringer in 1617 gave two cottages and some land for the poor, and in 1685 Christopher Latham gave £20, which produced £1 income in 1791.[27] Ann Storey in 1695 created a charge of £1 4s. on a parcel of land, and Robert Fletcher before 1705 gave 6s. 8d. a year, charged upon Corney House. It was presumably the income from Stringer's and Latham's charities which was said in 1823 to be distributed in cash with that from Fletcher's and Foster's. The income from Consett's and Storey's gifts was then distributed jointly each week in bread.[28]

By an inquisition held in 1699, under a commission of charitable uses, it was found that Mary and Elizabeth Newsome had in 1684 created a rent-charge of £1 on a cottage, some gardens, and 1 a. of land for the benefit of the poor, and had in 1685 created a like charge on 3½ a. to set a poor child apprentice. It was also found that George Hudson had in 1662 created a charge of £1 10s. on various parcels of land. The Poor's Estate formed by these gifts produced £18 12s. rent in 1823, used for the poor and to bind apprentices. From the balance in hand nearly £8 had been paid to the parish school in 1821.[29] An unendowed almshouse, supported by the parish, mentioned in the 18th century[30] is probably to be identified with the four poor's cottages, said in 1823 to have been built by the parish on part of the Poor's Estate.[31] The cottages stood in the main street, east of the church, in 1842.[32]

Frances, dowager Lady Howard, by will proved in 1716, bequeathed money to provide coal for Escrick and other villages, including Riccall.[33] After 1862 Riccall received ⅐ of the income.

Elizabeth Wilson, by will proved in 1862, left £500, ⅔ of the income from which was to be distributed by the vicar, half in coal and clothing and the rest in bread.[34]

Foster's, Consett's, Storey's, Fletcher's, Howard's, and Wilson's, and probably also Stringer's and Latham's, charities, together with the Poor's Estate and the Gosling marsh charity for flood protection,[35] were all later administered together as the Riccall charities. In 1905 the endowment of the Poor's Estate and Howard's and Wilson's charities comprised £547 stock. In 1973 the income of the Riccall charities was £15 from stock and £81 from the rent of three parcels of land; doles of £2 were given to 52 old people.[36]

SKIPWITH

THE LARGE parish of Skipwith, including the township of North Duffield, lies about 9 miles south-east of York and stretches westwards from the river Derwent for 5 miles into the heart of the wapentake.[1] Part of the hamlet of Menthorpe, beside the Derwent, was also in the parish, the rest lying in Hemingbrough. The Anglian settlement of Skipwith, the 'sheep farm',[2] had extensive pastures, and the small village is still half surrounded by over 800 a. of common heath and woodland. The much larger village of North Duffield, also Anglian, which enjoyed a late-surviving market and fair, lies near the main road from Selby to Market Weighton and its ancient crossing place over the Derwent. The parish comprised 6,258 a., of which 3,417 a. were in North Duffield and 197 a. in Menthorpe.[3] The civil parish of North Duffield was enlarged in 1935 by the addition of Menthorpe with Bowthorpe civil parish.[4]

The whole parish is flat and low-lying without any prominent relief features. Much of it lies at more than 25 ft. above sea-level, but north-west of Skipwith village and south and east of North Duffield village large areas are lower still. Most of Skipwith

[17] See below.
[18] Ed. 7/135 no. 140.
[19] B.I.H.R., V. 1865/Ret. 423; *Returns relating to Elem. Educ.* 790; O.S. Map 6" (1851 edn.).
[20] *Bd. of Educ. List 21* (H.M.S.O.).
[21] Char. Com. files.
[22] *List 21*.
[23] E.R. Educ. Cttee. *Mins.* 1937–8, 179; 1950–1, 208; 1955–6, 151.
[24] Ex inf. Chief Educ. Officer, County Hall, Beverley, 1972.
[25] Ex inf. the vicar, 1974.
[26] *10th Rep. Com. Char.* 668.
[27] Board in church.
[28] *10th Rep. Com. Char.* 668. Fletcher's gift may have been to revive a like charge created by Rob. Corney in 1624 but not paid between 1677 and 1698: E.R.R.O., DDBV/36/1.
[29] *10th Rep. Com. Char.* 668–9. The inquisition is printed in *Par. Reg. of Riccall*, 168–70.
[30] B.I.H.R., Bp. V. 1764/Ret. 210; *Herring's Visit.* iii. 29.
[31] *10th Rep. Com. Char.* 670.
[32] B.I.H.R., TA. 865VL.
[33] See p. 28.
[34] Char. Com. files.
[35] See p. 85.
[36] Char. Com. files.
[1] This article was written in 1973.
[2] *P.N.E.R. Yorks.* (E.P.N.S.), 263.
[3] O.S. Map 6", Yorks. (1851 edn.). Most of the parish is covered by sheets 206 and 207, a small part by sheet 222.
[4] *Census*, 1931.

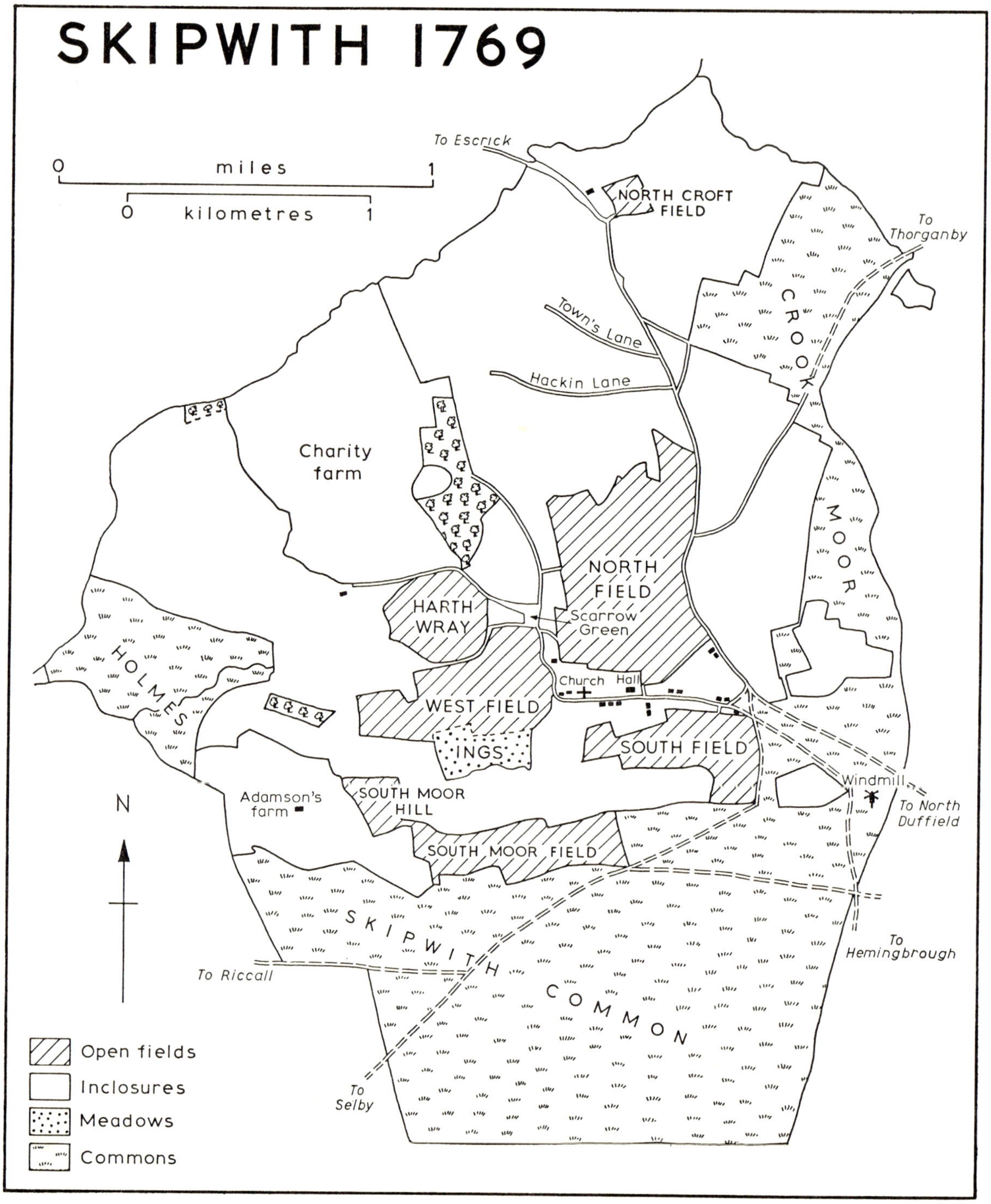
SKIPWITH 1769
0 miles 1
0 kilometres 1
To Escrick
NORTH CROFT FIELD
To Thorganby
Town's Lane
Hackin Lane
CROOK
Charity farm
MOOR
NORTH FIELD
HARTH WRAY
Scarrow Green
HOLMES
Church
Hall
WEST FIELD
INGS
SOUTH FIELD
Windmill
To North Duffield
Adamson's farm
SOUTH MOOR HILL
SOUTH MOOR FIELD
N
SKIPWITH COMMON
To Riccall
To Hemingbrough
To Selby
Open fields
Inclosures
Meadows
Commons

township and much of North Duffield are composed of outwash sand and clay, with some alluvium beside the Derwent.[5] The small open fields of Skipwith, which were not inclosed until 1904, lay largely above 25 ft., but those of North Duffield, inclosed in 1814,[6] stretched far into the lower ground. There were extensive areas of old-inclosed assarts in both townships. Carrs and ings lay beside the Derwent, and the surviving common land in Skipwith continued into North Duffield until inclosure in 1814.

Numerous dikes and streams drain into the Derwent or westwards towards the river Ouse. The entire northern boundary of Skipwith township is formed by a stream which becomes Dam dike in Riccall, further west, and another forms the northern boundary of North Duffield. The chief stream in Skipwith rises on the common and, as Holmes dike, joins Dam dike at the Riccall boundary. On the south the boundary with Cliffe and South Duffield formerly divided the commons and woodlands of Skipwith from those called Blackwood;[7] in 1280 Anvers, Burdun, and Moreby pits marked the boundary line.[8] The entire eastern parish boundary follows the Derwent. The riverside land has always been liable to flooding despite the maintenance of flood banks, described in 1760 as 'a rampart to defend the water out of the carrs, ings, etc.'.[9] In Skipwith the northern boundary stream flooded part of the township in the 14th century.[10]

Skipwith common or moor, including an area known as Crook moor, still covers 857 a.[11] Robert Aske ordered rebels to assemble there in 1536, during the Pilgrimage of Grace.[12] The common belonged to Skipwith manor and was sometimes called Lord's or Hall moor.[13] In part it consists of dry heathland, but there are many ponds and swampy places as well as extensive woods. The so-called Line ponds, near the village,[14] may have been used for flax-dressing. Three small plantations near the road across the common to Selby were said to have been established by J. P. Toulson[15] in the early 19th century, but much of the woodland is natural. There are many barrows, known as Danes' Hills, especially in the north and west of the common. When the open fields were inclosed in 1904 the common was left alone, but for its betterment a board of five conservators was established, one each to be appointed by the lord of the manor, the rural district council, and the parish meeting, and two by the commoners.[16] By-laws were subsequently made by the conservators.[17] The wartime airfield at Riccall extended into the common,[18] but a large area was in 1954 designated as a site of special scientific interest on account of the varied plant and animal life there and about 600 a. have been administered as a nature reserve since 1968.[19]

Skipwith village stands beside roads leading to Escrick and North Duffield which form part of the York–Howden road. Minor roads lead to Thorganby and Cliffe, but others running towards Selby and Riccall are in part only unsurfaced trackways on the common, and the Riccall road was blocked by the construction of Riccall airfield. From North Duffield village a minor road leads to Menthorpe and Hemingbrough, and others formerly led to South Duffield and Thorganby. The chief road in North Duffield, however, is that which now runs straight across the township, skirting the south end of the village, and forms part of the Selby to Market Weighton road. Until the late 18th century the road followed a circuitous course through the village.[20] It was turnpiked in 1793 and new sections were built to bypass the village and lead directly to the Derwent crossing; the old course from the Menthorpe road to the river has been lost. Several of the milestones erected by the trust still stand. The trust was discontinued in 1879.[21] The river crossing was also improved in 1793 by the building of a bridge to replace a ferry which had existed since at least the 13th century.[22] The bridge was owned not by the turnpike trust but by an independent company, and tolls continued to be collected at a house on the Duffield side of the river[23] until the bridge and toll rights were bought by the East Riding county council in 1936.[24] The stone bridge is of three arches with big round cutwaters, and the road approaches it on a causeway supported by seven brick arches.

The railway line from Selby to Market Weighton, opened in 1848,[25] crossed the south-east corner of North Duffield township, with a bridge over the Derwent; it was closed in 1965.[26] The line has been lifted but the bridge remains. The Derwent Valley Light Railway, opened in 1912, also crossed North Duffield, with a station near the boundary with Skipwith. It was closed for passengers in 1926[27] and goods in 1965;[28] the line has been lifted but the station remained in 1973.

Some of the houses of Skipwith village stand around the junction of the Escrick, North Duffield, Cliffe, and Selby roads, but most of them date only from the 19th and 20th centuries. In 1769 almost all the village houses were spread out along a road running westwards from that junction which eventually peters out as field and farm roads. This is still the main village street, and despite some recent infilling it remains only loosely built up. The church stands near one end of it. Apart from the hall and the Vicarage[29] there are few noteworthy houses; Red House Farm was built in 1908 by Lord Wenlock,[30] and there are sixteen council houses and bungalows. Beyond the village a few houses are known as Little Skipwith, and the road widens out into Scarrow

[5] Geol. Surv. Map 1", solid and drift, sheet 71 (1973 edn.).
[6] See pp. 97–8.
[7] See pp. 58, 62, 97.
[8] *Cal. Inq. Misc.* i, p. 35.
[9] E.R.R.O., DP/23, copy of map of 1760.
[10] *Cal. Inq. Misc.* i, pp. 454–5.
[11] L. D. Stamp and W. G. Hoskins, *Common Lands of Eng. and Wales*, 114.
[12] *L. & P. Hen. VIII*, xi, p. 249.
[13] E.R.R.O., DDFA/14/256 (undated sketch map of the common).
[14] O.S. Map 6" (1851 edn.).
[15] E.R.R.O., DDFA/14/256.
[16] Ibid. IA. Skipwith.
[17] Stamp and Hoskins, *Common Lands*, 114.
[18] See p. 83.
[19] Yorks. Naturalists' Trust, *Skipwith Common Nature Trail No. 1* and guide card.
[20] See map on p. 92.
[21] K. A. MacMahon, *Roads and Turnpike Trusts in E. Yorks.* (E. Yorks. Loc. Hist. Ser. xviii), 33, 70.
[22] *Selby Coucher Bk.* ii (Y.A.S. Rec. Ser. xiii), 13. Other early references to it are in C 134/64 no. 12 (1320); *Yorks. Fines, 1347–77*, p. 115 (1367); *Yorks. Deeds*, v, p. 32 (1407).
[23] Bulmer, *Dir. E. Yorks.* (1892), 713.
[24] E.R.C.C. *Mins.* 1935–6, 368.
[25] K. A. MacMahon, *Beginnings of E. Yorks. Rlys.* (E. Yorks. Loc. Hist. Ser. iii), 14.
[26] *Hull Daily Mail*, 12 June 1965.
[27] *V.C.H. City of York*, 479.
[28] K. Hoole, *Regional Hist. of Rlys. of Gt. Brit.* iv (*The North-East*), 63.
[29] See pp. 94, 99.
[30] It has the inscription 'W 1908'.

A HISTORY OF YORKSHIRE: EAST RIDING

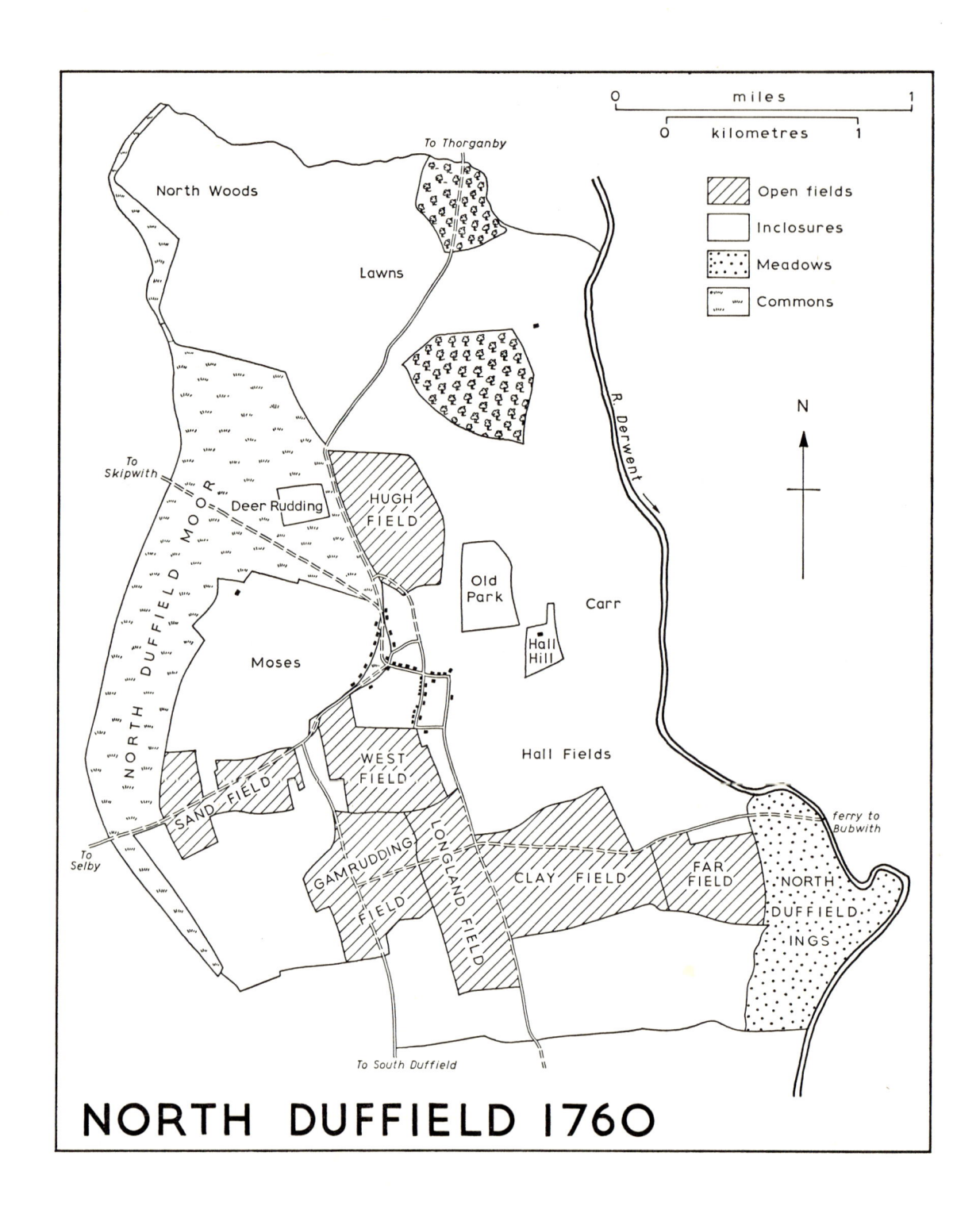

NORTH DUFFIELD 1760

Green before the farm roads begin. There are village ponds at the east end of the main street and at Scarrow Green. There were three licensed houses at Skipwith in the 1750s, only two later in the century.[31] The Hare and Hounds existed by 1822,[32] and by 1872 there was a second public house, the Drovers' Inn.[33] Both remained in 1973. A village institute was built in 1923.[34]

North Duffield is a large village, perhaps reflecting the success of the market and fair granted in the 13th century.[35] The closely built up main street is linked to a large green, partly surrounded by widely spaced houses. The green, with its pond, may have been laid out as a market-place and fair ground. It was reduced in size in 1814 by the inclosure of about 4 a. at the northern end. The main street is joined at both ends to a back lane, and a footpath called Priest Lane also runs between them. The village houses, dating from the 18th century onwards, include several 19th-century farm-houses, among them the Tudor-style Gothic Farm. In the 20th century several bungalows have been inserted around the green, a 'close' of private houses has been laid out off the main street, and 22 council houses and bungalows have been built, a dozen of them in the back lane. A village hall was opened in 1938.[36] Part of the pinfold wall stands by the roadside on the green.

There were two licensed houses at North Duffield in the 1750s but only one in the later 18th century.[37] The King's Arms and the Cart and Horses were in existence by 1822.[38] The former, near the green, still exists but the Cart and Horses, in the main street, closed c. 1950.[39]

By 1769 there were at least three outlying farmhouses in Skipwith, as well as the miller's house;[40] the farms were those known in 1973 as Bridge, Grange, and Peel Hall Farms, the last name deriving from Pithhill close, which adjoined the house in 1769. Another outlying house, in Hackings closes, mentioned in 1727[41] had apparently been demolished by 1760. The house later called Charity Farm seems to have existed by 1772, perhaps even by 1711 when the farm was sold together with its house.[42] Outlying buildings at North Duffield in 1760 were the miller's house, the hall,[43] and farmhouses now called North Duffield Lodge and Blackwood House.[44] A terrace of cottages called New Houses stands beside the road built to bypass the village, and Blackwood Hall was put up in the mid 19th century.[45] At Park House the farm buildings include a wheelhouse. The remains of a small motte, called Giant Hill, stand by the river opposite Aughton village.

There were 32 poll-tax payers at Skipwith in 1377, said to be 'of the geldable';[46] the bishop of Durham's fee was presumably excluded and there is no return for North Duffield. In 1379 there were 48 poll-tax payers at Skipwith and 136 at North Duffield.[47] There were 48 households at Skipwith in 1672, 7 of them exempt from the hearth tax; of those that were charged 29 had one hearth each, 7 had 2, 4 had 3 or 4, and one had seven. At North Duffield there were 59 households, 4 of them exempt; 43 had one hearth, 7 had 2, 4 had 3 or 4, and one had six.[48] There were 90 families in the parish in 1743 and 85 in 1764.[49]

The population of Skipwith was 247 in 1801. It reached 315 in 1821 but fell to 239 in 1901. The greatest number in the 20th century was 255 in 1911 and it stood at 202 in 1971.[50] North Duffield had 313 inhabitants in 1801. The number varied from 433 in 1821 to 344 in 1831, 470 in 1861, and 309 in 1901. It recovered to 349 in 1921 but fell to 317 in 1931, and even with Menthorpe and Bowthorpe included it was only 341 in 1971.[51]

MANORS AND OTHER ESTATES. In 1086 Skipwith consisted of 3 carucates belonging to Hugh son of Baldric, which before the Conquest had been held by Gam.[52] The bishop of Durham subsequently acquired 2 carucates there and in 1200 enfeoffed Richard d'Avranches of them.[53] The d'Avranches family held the estate until at least 1353,[54] but by 1400–1 it had passed to the Skipwith family, by the marriage of Catherine d'Avranches and William Skipwith.[55]

After 1086 a carucate in Skipwith passed to Robert de Stutville.[56] The overlordship descended to the Wakes by the marriage in or before 1229 of Joan de Stutville and Hugh Wake, and in 1325 Margaret Wake married Edmund, earl of Kent.[57] The heirs of the earl of Kent were recorded as overlords as late as 1418.[58] By 1166 Robert Murdac had succeeded Richard Murdac as tenant in demesne under the Stutvilles.[59] The estate subsequently passed to a family known alternatively as Thorpe or Skipwith.[60] They are first mentioned in the early 13th century, when Osbert of Skipwith had an interest there.[61] The name Skipwith prevailed, and in 1418 Sir Thomas Skipwith died seised of the whole manor of SKIPWITH, two-thirds held of the Durham fee and one-third of the Wake fee.[62]

The manor was held by the Skipwiths[63] until 1709, when Mary, widow of Willoughby Skipwith, sold it to Francis Annesley; besides rents it comprised only a farm of 63 a. Francis, the Revd.

[31] E.R.R.O., QDT/2/15.
[32] Ibid. QDT/2/13.
[33] Directories usually refer only to a beer retailer, but the house is named by Bulmer, *Dir. E. Yorks.* (1892), 713.
[34] *Kelly's Dir. N. & E.R. Yorks.* (1925), 617.
[35] See p. 98.
[36] Date on building.
[37] E.R.R.O., QDT/2/15.
[38] Ibid. QDT/2/13.
[39] R.D.B., 971/526/459.
[40] Map of 1769 at Escrick Park Estate Office.
[41] E.R.R.O., DDFA/14/92.
[42] R.D.B., A/666/949; T. Jefferys, *Map of Yorks.* (1772).
[43] See p. 95.
[44] E.R.R.O., DP/23; for Blackwood House see R.D.B., W/455/923.
[45] See p. 96.
[46] E 179/202/58 m. 1.
[47] *T.E.R.A.S.* xv. 52–3, 59.
[48] E 179/205/504.
[49] B.I.H.R., Bp. V. 1764/Ret. 38; *Herring's Visit.* ii. 105.
[50] *V.C.H. Yorks.* iii. 498; *Census,* 1911–71.
[51] Ibid. For Menthorpe and Bowthorpe see above p. 63.
[52] *V.C.H. Yorks.* ii. 277.
[53] *Yorks. Fines, John* (Sur. Soc. xciv), 3.
[54] *Feud. Aids,* vi. 35, 172, 224; *Cal. Inq. p.m.* x, p. 48.
[55] Burton, *Hist. Hemingbrough,* 244; for the Skipwiths see below.
[56] *E.Y.C.* ix, p. 74.
[57] *Complete Peerage,* s.v. Kent; *Cal. Inq. p.m.* ii, p. 261; ix, p. 206; x, p. 48.
[58] *Yorks. Inq. Hen. IV–V,* p. 130.
[59] *E.Y.C.* ix, p. 135.
[60] *Feud. Aids,* vi. 35, 173, 223; *Cal. Inq. p.m.* ii, p. 261; ix, p. 210.
[61] *E.Y.C.* ix, pp. 136, 138.
[62] *Yorks. Inq. Hen. IV–V,* p. 130.
[63] *Lincs. Pedigrees,* iii (Harl. Soc. lii), 895–6.

Francis, and Arthur Annesley sold it in 1801 to Thomas Bradford[64] and he the following year to J. P. Toulson.[65] Thus it was that Toulson was described as lord of the manor in 1802,[66] before he became entitled to the rest of the old manorial estate.

At least part of the manor was let by the Skipwiths to the Herberts, for in 1609 Rowland Herbert devised his lease of 'the demesnes' to his son Gilbert.[67] Elizabeth, widow of Richard Herbert (d. c. 1700), married George Toulson,[68] and it was to Toulson and his heirs that Richard Herbert's son Robert devised the manor-house and demesnes in 1706; they were said to be held on an 800-year lease.[69]

On the death of another George Toulson in 1766 the estate passed to his daughter Jane and her husband Banastre Walton (d. 1781).[70] Jane next married, in 1799, Robert Hudson and the manor was then settled successively on Hudson (d. 1808), Jane (d. 1819),[71] Jane's cousin John Parker, who had taken the surname Toulson (d. 1824),[72] and Toulson's son J. A. P. Toulson.[73] The Hudsons, as owners of the estate, lived at the hall but J. P. Toulson also lived in the parish and was, as has been seen, lord of the manor as early as 1802.[74] By 1827 J. A. P. Toulson was in possession,[75] and in 1840 his estate in Skipwith included 1,958 a.[76] After his death in 1889[77] his trustees sold the manor, with 1,864 a., to Lord Wenlock in 1898.[78] At inclosure in 1904 Wenlock was allotted 271 a. for open-field land and common rights.[79] The manor subsequently descended like Escrick,[80] and in 1972 the Forbes Adam family still had 2,511 a. in Skipwith.[81]

Before the acquisition of the manor the Wenlocks already had an estate in Skipwith, established by their predecessors the Thompsons. In 1789 Jane Walton settled some of the manorial lands upon her cousin John Parker.[82] She and her husband Robert Hudson nevertheless sold most of the property involved to Joseph Buckle in 1800.[83] The sale was disputed by Parker, who had in the mean time taken the name Toulson, and by an agreement of 1801 he was to receive the purchase money from Buckle.[84] The land was conveyed by the Buckles to Richard Thompson in 1819.[85] Thompson had already bought about 50 a. in the township in 1813,[86] and the Thompsons had 550 a. there c. 1857.[87]

The Skipwith family's manor-house probably stood on a large moated site which still existed, opposite the church, in 1973. It was presumably there that William Skipwith was allowed to have a portable altar in 1454.[88] The house appears to have survived until the 17th century, but in 1657 the manor-house or hall was described as 'prostrated and demolished'.[89] A cottage called Moat Hall stood there into the 20th century.[90] The site of the present house may have been occupied by the later 17th century. Richard Herbert had a house with seven hearths in 1672,[91] and a manor-house or hall-house was mentioned from at least 1705 onwards.[92] The service wing, in which there is a late-17th-century staircase, may have been part of this building. The main block of the house, facing south, appears to be of c. 1725 and is a plain three-storeyed building of red brick which retains its original staircase and some panelling and fire-places. Two-storeyed wings were added early in the 20th century, and there was some refitting at the time when the Forbes Adam family moved to Skipwith from Escrick.[93] One wall in the large walled gardens contains heating flues.

An estate of 7 carucates and 2 bovates at North Duffield belonged after the Conquest to William Malet, but he was disseised of it in 1069 and by 1086 it was held by Niel Fossard under the count of Mortain.[94] The soke of 2 bovates belonged to Howden.[95] Rival claims to Malet's possessions may explain disputes over the ownership of the estate in the 12th and early 13th centuries. It is said to have been acquired after 1086 by the bishop of Durham,[96] but it was also claimed by the Percys. As late as 1320, on the death of the demesne lord, it was first said to be held of Henry de Percy but in a later inquisition of the bishop of Durham,[97] and the bishop's overlordship was recorded as late as 1441.[98]

Under the Percys the estate was held by the Chamberlains, but in 1196 John Chamberlain was in dispute with Ralph Bardolf,[99] and in 1210 Robert Chamberlain upheld his claim against Roger Bardolf.[1] In the 1220s Robert was in dispute over North Duffield with the Mauleys, who claimed it by inheritance from the Fossards.[2] In 1251 Henry Chamberlain granted *NORTH DUFFIELD* manor to Roger of Thurkelby (d. 1260),[3] but the Chamberlains retained a mesne lordship under the bishops of Durham.[4] By 1280 the manor belonged to Robert Salvain, who claimed it as the inheritance of his wife Sibyl, niece of Roger of Thurkelby.[5] It was held by the Salvains[6] until 1486, when it was granted to John Hussey and Thomas Ballard during the minority of Anne, daughter and heir of Sir John Salvain.[7] By 1496 Anne was the wife of Sir William

[64] R.D.B., CD/223/333.
[65] Ibid. CD/278/416.
[66] See below.
[67] Y.A.S., MS. 530(d).
[68] Ibid.; R.D.B., A/666/949.
[69] E.R.R.O., DDFA/14/351.
[70] Ibid. DDFA/14/138, 262, 358.
[71] Monuments in church.
[72] R.D.B., DS/45/63.
[73] E.R.R.O., DDFA/42/19.
[74] Ibid. DDFA/14/264–5.
[75] Ibid. DDFA/14/200.
[76] B.I.H.R., TA. 3L.
[77] R.D.B., 33/320/295 (1889).
[78] Ibid. 7/327/299 (1898).
[79] E.R.R.O., IA. Skipwith.
[80] See p. 20.
[81] Ex inf. Escrick Park Estate Office, 1972.
[82] E.R.R.O., DDFA/14/359.
[83] Ibid. DDFA/14/362.
[84] Ibid. DDFA/14/179.
[85] Ibid. DDFA/14/368.
[86] Ibid. DDFA/14/281, 300.

[87] Ibid. DDFA/41/6.
[88] Cal. Papal Regs. x. 680.
[89] E.R.R.O., DDFA/14/19.
[90] Bulmer, Dir. E. Yorks. (1892), 711; O.S. Map 1/25,000, 44/63 (1947 edn.).
[91] E 179/205/504.
[92] E.R.R.O., DDFA/14/56, 245.
[93] Yorks. Life, July–Sept. 1953, 113–14.
[94] V.C.H. Yorks. ii. 224, 293.
[95] Ibid. 224 n., 225.
[96] Ibid. 153, 167.
[97] C 134/64 no. 12.
[98] C 139/102 no. 10.
[99] Cur. Reg. R. i. 25.
[1] Ibid. vi. 48, 309–10, 393.
[2] Ibid. viii. 140, 300–1; x. 141, 235, 281; xi, pp. 46, 255, 397, 537; xii, pp. 109, 174.
[3] Yorks. Fines, 1246–72, p. 29; D.N.B.
[4] e.g. Feud. Aids, vi. 36, 224, 271.
[5] Plac. de Quo Warr. (Rec. Com.), 196, 219; Cal. Chart. R. 1257–1300, 435.
[6] E.Y.C. xii, pp. 110–12.
[7] Cal. Pat. 1485–94, 87.

Hussey (d. 1530),[8] in whose family the manor subsequently descended. After William Hussey died seised of it in 1570 it passed to his brother John and then to John's daughter Anne, who married Sir Robert Constable.[9] In 1614 William Constable sold it to William Ingleby and others, and in 1624 they conveyed it to Peter Middleton.[10] Peter's son William held it in 1634,[11] and it belonged to John Middleton in 1673[12] and William Middleton in the late 18th century.[13]

In 1808 William and Peter Middleton sold the manor, with about 2,240 a., to John and William Scholfield, James Lister, and Robert Spofforth, the younger.[14] At inclosure in 1814 707 a. were allotted jointly to William Scholfield, Spofforth, and Lister.[15] Spofforth gave up his share to the others in 1823,[16] and in 1841 the estate was assigned by Scholfield and Lister to Robert Scholfield.[17] About 900 a. were sold soon after to Thomas Dunnington.[18] After Robert Scholfield's death in 1868 the rest of the estate passed successively to Edward Scholfield (d. 1869), to Robert's son R. S. Scholfield (d. 1913), and to E. P. Scholfield.[19] Most of it, some 1,350 a., was sold in separate lots in 1920–1,[20] and in 1922 the manor, with 29 a., was sold to C. H. (later Sir Charles) Wilson (d. 1930).[21]

The medieval manor-house of the Salvains, mentioned in 1320,[22] presumably stood on the site now occupied by a farm-house known as North Duffield Hall, which still has prominent earthworks around it. This is traditionally the site of a 'castle',[23] presumably the fortified manor-house.

The land bought by Thomas Dunnington in 1841[24] subsequently formed Lawns House, Lodge, and Redmoor House farms, and part of West Lodge farm in Thorganby. It was held by the Dunningtons and Dunnington-Jeffersons until 1953 and 1964, when 910 a. were sold in separate lots by Sir John Dunnington-Jefferson, Bt.[25]

That part of Menthorpe lying in Skipwith parish belonged, like Skipwith manor, to the Stutville fee. Some of the land was held by the Skipwith family in the Middle Ages.[26] The manor of MENTHORPE is said to have been sold by John Skipwith (d. 1680) about 1670 to Faith, widow of Robert Woodburne, vicar of Skipwith.[27] After the death of James Woodburne in 1717 the manor was sold by his trustees in the 1720s to the Robinson family. Richard Robinson, who married Anne Sandys, devised undivided shares in the manor to his five daughters, one of whom married Edwin Sandys Bain.[28] In 1838 and 1841 Bain acquired the other shares,[29] and in 1872 he conveyed the estate, comprising 197 a., to his daughter Frances and her husband E. W. Sandys.[30] Known as Hall farm, it was sold by W. B. R. Sandys to A. H. Blakey in 1919, and by T. O. Blakey to the Flint Co. Ltd. in 1969.[31]

Other land in the Stutville fee belonged in the 13th century to the Eyville family, apparently having been acquired by Emery d'Eyville from Walter of Bubwith in 1284.[32] It was conveyed by John d'Eyville to Thomas Dawnay in 1372,[33] and by Sir John Dawnay to Thomas Watkinson in 1572.[34] The Watkinsons also acquired land in Menthorpe from Marmaduke Fawkes in 1573[35] and William Babthorpe in 1619.[36] They sold the estate in 1668 to Christopher Adams, whose family retained it until the death of John Adams in 1791. It then passed to John's sister Frances, wife of Jocelyn Price, and at her death in 1816 she was succeeded by her daughters Lucy, who married a Capt. Willye, and Clara, who married Sir Charles Blois.[37] Clara and her husband granted their share of the estate, which comprised altogether 130 a., to Lucy's son Jocelyn in 1840.[38] Jocelyn Willye died in 1863 and the estate passed for life to his widow Frances (née Carus Wilson) (d. 1872).[39] It was sold to Martin Willans in 1874, then consisting of a house and 145 a.,[40] and after his death in 1887 it was held by trustees until sold in 1969 to the Flint Co. Ltd.[41]

In 1086 an estate of a carucate in North Duffield belonged to Gilbert Tison,[42] but before 1100 he confirmed the gift of it to Selby abbey (Yorks. W.R.) by his man Swane.[43] Some small additional gifts were made to the abbey in the 13th century.[44] Under the abbot as overlord the carucate of land was held by Gerard Salvain in 1320.[45] Some of the land of the Selby fee may have belonged to freeholders; in 1286 freeholders with at least 18 bovates did homage to the Salvains.[46] The descent of these holdings has not been traced.

Lands in Skipwith described as late of Gisborough priory were granted to Christopher Estofte and Thomas Doweman in 1553, when they were in the tenure of Rowland Herbert.[47] A hermitage at North Duffield belonging to the Knights Hospitallers was recorded between the 1190s and c. 1280.[48]

From 1279 the rectory of Skipwith belonged to

---

[8] E.Y.C. xii, p. 112; Yorks. Sta. Cha. Proc. iv (Y.A.S. Rec. Ser. lxx), 4–5.
[9] C 142/153 no. 39; Visit. Yorks. 1584–5 and 1612, ed. J. Foster, 92.
[10] Yorks. Fines, 1614–25, 13, 238.
[11] E.R.R.O., DDCC/133/101.
[12] C.P. 43/361 rot. 190.
[13] E.R.R.O., Land Tax; DDFA/11/9.
[14] R.D.B., CR/45/60.
[15] E.R.R.O., Enrolment Bk. G, pp. 64 sqq.
[16] Ibid. DDTR/Box 7.
[17] R.D.B., ED/327/361; FQ/321/333.
[18] See below.
[19] R.D.B., KF/341/466; KL/54/78; 167/392/333.
[20] Ibid. 225/321/269; /333/275; /335/276; /384/319; 226/53/45; /158/131; 228/575/499; 230/171/148; 238/253/216.
[21] Ibid. 248/395/323; 423/253/202.
[22] C 134/64 no. 12.
[23] Sheahan and Whellan, Hist. York & E.R. ii. 629; O.S. Map 6" (1851 edn.).
[24] R.D.B., FQ/340/336.
[25] Ibid. 937/56/51; 951/557/495; 952/416/371; 1349/244/220; see p. 114.
[26] Feud. Aids, vi. 36, 173, 223; Cal. Close, 1435–41, 476; see above p. 93.
[27] Burton, Hemingbrough, 241–2.
[28] Ibid. 242.
[29] R.D.B., FH/375/395; FP/381/404; FS/45/50.
[30] Ibid. LC/26/35.
[31] Ibid. 205/73/61; 1600/211/185.
[32] C.P. 25(1)/267/61 no. 45.
[33] C.P. 25(1)/277/140 no. 22.
[34] Yorks. Fines, ii. 18. [35] Ibid. 37
[36] Yorks. Fines, 1614–25, 131.
[37] R.D.B., BN/360/546; BU/479/728; FN/49/45; Burton, Hemingbrough, 239–40.
[38] R.D.B., FO/134/131.
[39] Burton, Hemingbrough, 240.
[40] R.D.B., LL/135/184.
[41] Ibid. 1497/414/354; 1600/210/184.
[42] V.C.H. Yorks. ii. 272. [43] E.Y.C. xii, p. 47.
[44] Selby Coucher Bk. ii. 8–11.
[45] Cal. Inq. p.m. vi, p. 133.
[46] Yorks. Deeds, v, p. 30. [47] Cal. Pat. 1553, 257–8.
[48] Cart. Antiq. Rolls 11–20 (P.R.S. N.S. xxxiii), p. 189; Cur. Reg. R. vi. 310; Yorks. Fines, 1218–31, pp. 19–20; Yorks. Deeds, v, p. 29.

Skipwith prebend in Howden college.[49] It was worth £33 6s. 8d. in 1291.[50] In 1535 the tithes produced £18, of which £10 13s. 4d. was from North Duffield, £5 6s. 8d. from Skipwith, and £2 from Menthorpe; the net value to the prebend was £13 6s. 8d. all told.[51] After the dissolution of the college the tithes were let by the Crown in 1568 to Thomas Mytton and others.[52] In 1594, when Nicholas Thompson was farmer of the rectory, it was found that the parsonage house, described as a 'cross house', had been demolished about sixteen years earlier.[53] Rowland Herbert devised a Crown lease of the tithes to his son Gilbert in 1609.[54] In the latter year the tithes were granted in fee to Francis Morrice and Francis Philips,[55] who conveyed them the same year to Gilbert Herbert.[56] In 1628 Philip Herbert conveyed the tithes of Skipwith to John Herbert and in 1629 those of North Duffield to Robert Marshall.[57] The value in 1650 was £80 to Rowland Herbert, £40 to Michael Marshall, and £13 to Thomas Watkinson,[58] the last-named enjoying the tithes of Menthorpe.[59]

Elizabeth Shilleto and Anne Marshall conveyed their tithes in Skipwith to George Toulson in 1747,[60] and they subsequently descended with Skipwith manor. In 1840 they were commuted for £113 payable to J. A. P. Toulson and 15s. to Matthew Kirk.[61]

The tithes of North Duffield were conveyed by John Herbert and others to Nathaniel Wilson and others in 1707.[62] Richard Wilson sold them in 1777 to John Raper and others, and they to Robert Spofforth, the elder, in 1796.[63] At inclosure in 1814 348 a. were awarded to Spofforth in lieu of tithes,[64] and this land subsequently formed part of Park farm and the Blackwood estate. Park farm, comprising 193 a., was sold by Samuel Spofforth to Charles Weddall in 1828,[65] and the Weddalls held it until 1918, when it was sold to the Bramley family.[66] The nucleus of the Blackwood estate, comprising the house and 56 a. of closes, was acquired by Spofforth in 1807[67] and to this most of the tithe allotment was added. The 382-acre Blackwood House farm was bought from Spofforth's trustees in 1835 by T. S. Benson and Sharon Turner in trust for the daughters and grandson of Henry Roxby (d. 1828).[68] Blackwood Hall was later built there by T. M. Roxby, who in 1868 mortgaged the estate to the Law Life Assurance Society.[69] The society's trustees sold the property to Annie and Eleanor Newsome in 1893,[70] and the Newsomes retained it until it was sold in separate lots in 1963 and 1967; the hall passed to Blackwood Hall Farms Ltd.[71]

The tithes of Menthorpe were evidently sold with the Watkinsons' land in the township to Christopher Adams in 1668 and subsequently descended with it. The Adams family were certainly the impropriators in the later 18th century.[72] When the tithes were commuted in 1839 rent-charges totalling £66 were allotted jointly to Sir Charles Blois and Lucy Willye.[73]

ECONOMIC HISTORY. At Skipwith in 1086 there was land for two ploughs, but Hugh son of Baldric had one plough and twelve villeins had three. There was woodland two leagues long and one broad. The estate had decreased in value from £2 before the Conquest to £1 in 1086.[74] Medieval assarting, though there is little record of it, produced a large area of early inclosed farm-land, as well no doubt as additions to the open field nucleus. Woodland and moor remained prominent, however, and were mentioned in the 13th and 14th centuries, when the Skipwith and d'Avranches families had shares in them.[75] In 1310 the 'parson' of Skipwith (either the prebendary or the vicar) surrendered to Richard d'Avranches his right to have wood, pasture, and turf in Skipwith wood, and in return was granted 5 a. of wood for his own use, common of pasture wherever Richard's free tenants had it, and fifteen loads of turf a year.[76] The value of wood, mostly taken from an area called Mapple wood, contributed £9 to the £53 at which Sir William Skipwith's manor was valued in 1536.[77]

The results of earlier assarting are to be seen in the names of numerous closes recorded in the early 17th century, several of them incorporating 'hurst' and 'ridding'.[78] By that time there was open-field land in Out, Inholme, West, South, and North fields, and in North Tofts, Southmoors, and Harthowrey.[79] South Ridding was also apparently held in strips,[80] though in 1769 it was a close adjoining South field and the common.[81] There was also common meadow land in the ings and pasture in the Holmes.[82] The villagers enjoyed rights on the common in the 17th century, taking pasture, turves, and whins; one man's rights, in 1642, were for 6 cattle, one horse, 80 sheep, 2 swine, ducks, and geese.[83]

The same areas of open-field land were all recorded in the earlier 18th century, though by 1769 Out and Inholme fields had been either inclosed or incorporated in the other fields. Most of the closes beyond the open fields were small and many were irregularly shaped, reflecting the process of early

[49] See p. 99.
[50] *Tax. Eccl.* (Rec. Com.), 302.
[51] *Valor Eccl.* (Rec. Com.), v. 138.
[52] *Cal. Pat.* 1566–9, p. 292.
[53] E 178/2755.
[54] Y.A.S., MS. 530(d).
[55] H.U.L., DP/80.
[56] E.R.R.O., DDFA/14/2.
[57] Ibid. DDFA/14/7, 10.
[58] C 94/3 f. 76.
[59] See below.
[60] R.D.B., T/53/100.
[61] B.I.H.R., TA. 3L.
[62] C.P. 25(2)/982/6 Anne Mich. no. 6.
[63] R.D.B., AY/207/314; BX/299/483.
[64] E.R.R.O., Enrolment Bk. G, pp. 64 sqq.
[65] R.D.B., EF/189/234.
[66] Ibid. 186/351/293.
[67] Ibid. CM/319/489.
[68] Ibid. FB/152/170; GM/195/249.
[69] Ibid. KH/97/103; Bulmer, *Dir. E. Yorks.* (1892), 712.
[70] R.D.B., 60/18/18 (1893).
[71] Ibid. 1312/213/186; 1337/516/459; 1515/532/471; 1531/268/212.
[72] B.I.H.R., TER. N. Skipwith 1764, 1786.
[73] B.I.H.R., TA. 339S. The lessees of the tithes in the early 19th century were apparently the Fliggs: ibid. TER. N. Skipwith 1809 etc.
[74] *V.C.H. Yorks.* ii. 277.
[75] *Yorks. Assize Rolls* (Y.A.S. Rec. Ser. xliv), 52; *Reg. Pal. Dunelm.* iii (Rolls Ser.), 169.
[76] *Cal. Pat.* 1307–13, 207.
[77] E.R.R.O., DDHA/12/1.
[78] Ibid. DDFA/14/4.
[79] Ibid. DDFA/14/4–6.
[80] Ibid. DDFA/14/11, 19.
[81] Map in Escrick Park Estate Office.
[82] E.R.R.O., DDFA/14/5–6.
[83] Ibid. DDFA/14/15, 270.

assarting; but in 1709 closes called Hughthwaite Carrs and the Wrays contained 30 a. and 50 a. respectively, though both had been subdivided by 1769.[84] An area of woodland belonging to the manor remained, north-west of the village, in 1769, and in 1776 Charity farm included Hollingwood, Holliker wood, and East wood.[85] The Holmes was now certainly a stinted pasture, in which various inhabitants had beast-gates, sometimes recorded as acreage equivalents;[86] 'acres' held in it in the early 17th century[87] may refer to a similar arrangement. Ten of the gates belonged to Charity farm.[88]

Throughout the 19th century the open fields remained, and common rights were still exercised on the common and in the Holmes. Payments were, however, exacted by the lord of the manor from those who held such rights. In 1807, for example, 14 people paid acknowledgements for 55¼ Holmes gates, 15 for rights on the common, and 11 for the use of lanes and balks.[89] Other payments were made to the lord of the manor in 1807–19 for turf, whins, ling, sand, and pasture taken on the common, in some cases by men of neighbouring villages.[90] In 1840 the manor owned 41 of the gates in the Holmes, Lord Wenlock 14, and another man 1¼;[91] the manor still had 41 gates in the Holmes in 1898, when it was computed at 94 a., as well as 26 of the 34 rights on the common, and money was still received for peat and sand.[92] By 1904 Lord Wenlock, then lord of the manor, had 28 of the rights on the common. The inclosure of that year did not affect the common,[93] but 319 a. of open-field land were inclosed: 271 a. were allotted to Lord Wenlock and there were seven small allotments.[94]

The general pattern of land-use in the township has apparently changed little in the 19th and 20th centuries. In 1840 there were 1,287 a. of arable and 258 a. of meadow and pasture,[95] and there were several woods around Charity, or Woodhall, Farm in the 1840s.[96] In 1905 there were 1,305 a. of arable, 427 a. of permanent grass, and 38 a. of woodland.[97] Most of the township, apart from the common, was under arable in the 1930s, with some grassland near the village and scattered elsewhere. There had been little alteration by the 1960s, though meadow and pasture had replaced rough grazing on much of the Holmes.[98] There were more than 20 farmers in Skipwith in the 19th and 20th centuries,[99] three of them having 150 a. or more in 1851.[1] The number dropped below 20 in the 1920s and 1930s, when from five to a dozen had 150 a. or more.[2]

Apart from the occasional mention of a weaver in the 18th century,[3] the only non-agricultural occupation in Skipwith was milling. A windmill was recorded in 1536 and later.[4] It was still a post mill in 1834[5] and it stood on the common, near the North Duffield road; there was also an 'old mill hill' in the 1840s.[6] A miller is last mentioned in 1851.[7]

At North Duffield the Mortain estate had land for four ploughs in 1086.[8] There were several early references to the reclamation of new land: assarts included one in the wood of Duffield, others called Hirst and Pichel,[9] another, in the late 12th century, containing 13 a. at the hermitage, where there were also eight houses,[10] and Ketelsriding, in Northwood, which existed by 1219.[11] The same process is indicated by a holding which in 1258 contained 2 bovates made up of 28 a. of old arable land and 5 a. newly broken up; 4½ a. of meadow; pasture held in severalty which had formerly been meadow in the carr; and rights of turbary and common pasture.[12] The manorial park was mentioned as early as 1260[13] and presumably lay near the hall, where a small group of closes was called Old park in 1760.[14] In the west of the township lay part of the woods and moor called Blackwood which extended into South Duffield and adjoined Skipwith moor; Blackwood was first referred to in the 13th century.[15] Immediately west of the village was an area of presumably wet ground called the Moss in 1258,[16] and still known as the Moses.

In the 13th century arable land belonging to Selby abbey comprised strips lying in numerous furlongs, which in many places were bounded by dikes made as the low-lying grounds were reclaimed. The abbey also had an intake called Munkebank and 12½ a. of land in a place called Fremanland, in Northwood, and there was mention of Newenge, near the Derwent. The absence of field names suggests that the arable land was not yet divided into large open fields, but furlongs called East and West Longlands may have been in the area later known as Longlands field. The name Birkdike also hints at the location of the later Birk field.[17] A similar pattern of furlongs and dikes is shown in a survey of 1407, which includes furlongs called Dawryddying, North Woderydding, Newmore, Newbrokes, and Thornebuskes, all indicative of assarted land. Newbroke may have been part of the later Broke field, and West field was actually named in the survey.[18]

Some indication of the number of tenants of the manor is given in 1320; there were then 160 a. of arable and 120 a. of meadow in demesne, 18 bondmen held as many bovates, and rents were paid by both free tenants and cottagers.[19]

The park was used as a stinted pasture by 1474,

---

[84] R.D.B., A/75/107; map in Escrick Park Estate Office.
[85] E.R.R.O., DDFA/45/10; map in Escrick Park Estate Office.
[86] E.R.R.O., DDFA/14/98, 100, 125, 136–7.
[87] Ibid. DDFA/14/5–6.
[88] R.D.B., A/666/949; see p. 100.
[89] E.R.R.O., DDFA/41/31. For similar lists of payments see ibid. /32–3 and /14/193, 213, 216, 221, 224.
[90] Ibid. DDFA/14/265.
[91] B.I.H.R., TA. 3L.
[92] R.D.B., 33/320/295 (1898).   [93] See p. 91.
[94] E.R.R.O., IA. Skipwith.
[95] B.I.H.R., TA. 3L.
[96] O.S. Map 6" (1851 edn.).
[97] Acreage Returns, 1905.
[98] [1st] Land Util. Surv. Map, sheet 32; 2nd Land Util. Surv. Map, sheet 689 (SE 63–73).
[99] Directories.
[1] H.O. 107/2351.   [2] Directories.
[3] E.R.R.O., QSF. Christ. 1722, C.15; DDFA/14/142.
[4] Ibid. DDHA/12/1 (1536); DDFA/14/181, 276; R.D.B., A/75/107; Yorks. Fines, i. 318.
[5] E.R.R.O., DDFA/14/210. See also map of 1769 in Escrick Park Estate Office.
[6] O.S. Map 6" (1851 edn.).
[7] H.O. 107/2351.
[8] V.C.H. Yorks. ii. 224.
[9] Selby Coucher Bk. ii. 8, 10, 15.
[10] Cart. Antiq. R. 189.
[11] Yorks. Fines, 1218–31, p. 20; Yorks. Deeds, v, p. 29.
[12] Yorks. Fines, 1246–72, p. 107.
[13] Yorks. Assize R. 96–7.
[14] E.R.R.O., DP/23.
[15] Feodarium Prioratus Dunelm. (Sur. Soc. lviii), 292. See above pp. 62, 91.
[16] Yorks. Fines, 1246–72, p. 107.
[17] Selby Coucher Bk. ii. 12–14.
[18] Yorks. Deeds, v, pp. 31–3.   [19] C 134/64 no. 12.

when the lord of the manor let two horse-gates and eight swine-gates, together with a 'cokshote', there.[20] By the 16th century the woodland of Blackwood was being inclosed and doubtless converted to pasture. Three closes called Blackwoods and the Brokes were mentioned in 1553,[21] and a 50-acre close called Blackwoods in 1598.[22] The Brokes was apparently known as the Brogs in 1622.[23] Further north there was a close called Norwood, where the digging of peat and turf was in dispute in 1534.[24] An intake from the common, called Deer Rudding, was divided into strips in 1760, held by the lord of the manor and a freeholder.[25]

By 1663 the open-field land of the vicarial glebe lay in West, Far, Broke, Sand, and Birk fields and in Mill Ridding. Longland field was added to these names in 1685, and the name Mill Ridding was replaced by Hugh field in 1764.[26] Clay field is mentioned in 1778,[27] and by 1809 Clay and Gam Rudding fields had taken the places of Birk and Broke fields.[28] The fields which remained to be inclosed in 1814,[29] under an Act of 1809,[30] were thus West, Far, Gam Rudding, Sand, Clay, Hugh, and Longland fields. The award also dealt with the ings and the common, and made exchanges involving about 240 a. of old-inclosed land. The acreage of the areas inclosed cannot be ascertained because allotments were frequently from two different areas. In all, 1,106 a. were inclosed. The lords of the manor, William Scholfield, James Lister, and Robert Spofforth, the younger, were allotted 707 a., the vicar received 182 a. for tithes and glebe, and Robert Spofforth, the elder, got 348 a. for the rectorial tithes. There was one allotment of 50 a., two of 10–20 a., and six of under 10 a.

In the 1840s there were extensive plantations on the former common,[31] but they were subsequently cleared. By 1905 there were 1,501 a. of arable, 1,424 a. of permanent grass, and 23 a. of woodland in the township.[32] The low-lying areas in the south and east remained as meadow or pasture in the 1930s and 1960s.[33] The number of farmers in the 19th and 20th centuries has usually been 15–20;[34] in 1851 8,[35] and in the 1920s and 1930s between 8 and 17, farmers had 150 a. or more.[36]

By the 13th century there was a fishery in the river Derwent at North Duffield,[37] and Gerard Salvain's weir was said to obstruct boats in the mid 14th century.[38] There was a fisherman among the inhabitants in 1379.[39] The fishery continued to be recorded until the 18th century.[40] A landing-place near the Market Weighton road was alloted at inclosure in 1814;[41] a small cut beside it, which was in existence by 1850, has been filled in.[42]

Other men employed in non-agricultural work at North Duffield included an occasional weaver, like one mentioned in 1748,[43] and three brick-makers and a millwright in 1851.[44] The brickworks, beside the Skipwith road,[45] were not recorded again. A mill was mentioned in the 13th century,[46] and there were two windmills and a horse-mill in 1320.[47] A windmill was referred to in the 15th and 17th centuries,[48] and in 1772 it stood on the common north-west of the village.[49] By 1839 the 'old windmill' had been replaced by another to the north of the green,[50] but there is no mention of mill or miller after 1872.[51]

A Wednesday market and a fair on 9–11 August were granted to Roger of Thurkelby by Henry III, and again to Gerard Salvain in 1294.[52] The fair dates were changed to 24–26 July in 1313.[53] In 1363 the earlier grant was confirmed to another Gerard Salvain with the clause *licet*, whereupon perhaps the grant of 1313 lapsed.[54] The 1294 charter was exemplified at the request of William Hussey in 1555.[55] A market and fair were mentioned in 1624,[56] and a cattle and sheep fair was held on 4 May in 1770[57] and in the later 19th century.[58]

LOCAL GOVERNMENT. Tumbril, pillory, and amends of the assize of bread at North Duffield were claimed by Gerard Salvain in 1294 as appurtenant to the market and fair which he was granted that year. The claim was disallowed by the Crown, apparently because the privileges contained in the 1294 charter had not yet been used. Salvain also claimed amends of the assize of ale as the common custom of the district, and enquiry was ordered as to this.[59] The Skipwith manor court appointed bylawmen, of whom there were three in the earlier 19th century.[60]

Accounts of an overseer of the poor for Skipwith township survive for 1747–1837. Income included rent from the 'poor land'. Payments were made in money and in kind, and poorhouses were first mentioned in 1783, when they were extensively repaired.[61] They may have been the four 'almshouses' that were maintained by the parish in 1743.[62] The 'town's houses' later stood beside the Cliffe road, and there were others at North Duffield

---

[20] *Yorks. Deeds*, v, p. 35.
[21] E.R.R.O., DDEV/18/1.
[22] Ibid. DDLA/6/3.
[23] Ibid. DDHV/27/1.
[24] *Yorks. Sta. Cha. Proc.* iv. 73.
[25] E.R.R.O., DP/23.
[26] B.I.H.R., TER. N. Skipwith 1663 etc.
[27] E.R.R.O., QSF. Mich. 1778, B.1.
[28] B.I.H.R., TER. N. Skipwith 1809.
[29] E.R.R.O., Enrolment Bk. G, pp. 64 sqq.
[30] 49 Geo. III, c. 83 (Local and Personal, not printed).
[31] O.S. Map 6" (1851 edn.).
[32] Acreage Returns, 1905.
[33] [1st] Land Util. Surv. Map, sheet 32; 2nd Land Util. Surv. Map, sheet 689 (SE 63–73).
[34] Directories.
[35] H.O. 107/2351.
[36] Directories.
[37] *Selby Coucher Bk.* ii. 11.
[38] *Cal. Inq. Misc.* ii, pp. 320–1; *Public Works in Med. Law*, ii (Selden Soc. xl), 276.
[39] *T.E.R.A.S.* xv. 52–3.
[40] e.g. C.P. 43/642 rot. 146; *Yorks. Fines, 1614–25*, 109.
[41] E.R.R.O., Enrolment Bk. G, pp. 65 sqq.
[42] O.S. Map 6" (1851 and later edns.).
[43] H.U.L., DX/58/37.
[44] H.O. 107/2351.
[45] O.S. Map 6" (1851 edn.).
[46] *Selby Coucher Bk.* ii. 14.
[47] C 134/64 no. 12.
[48] E.R.R.O., DDCC/133/101; *Yorks. Deeds*, v, p. 36.
[49] Jefferys, *Map Yorks.*
[50] E.R.R.O., DDTR/Box 7; O.S. Map 6" (1851 edn.).
[51] H.O. 107/2351; *Kelly's Dir. N. & E.R. Yorks.* (1872), 546.
[52] *Cal. Chart. R. 1257–1300*, 435.
[53] Ibid. 1300–26, 221.
[54] Ibid. 1341–1417, 178.
[55] *Cal. Pat. 1555–7*, 160–1.
[56] *Yorks. Fines, 1614–25*, 109.
[57] *Yorks. Fairs and Mkts.* (Thoresby Soc. xxxix), 175.
[58] Sheahan and Whellan, *Hist. York & E.R.* ii. 629; Bulmer, *Dir. E. Yorks.* (1892), 712.
[59] *Plac. de Quo Warr.* (Rec. Com.), 219–20.
[60] E.R.R.O., DDFA/14/193; /41/31–3.
[61] *Penes* Selby district council, 1975.
[62] *Herring's Visit.* ii. 105.

at the north end of the green.[63] After 1820 Skipwith was a member of the Holme upon Spalding Moor union and made payments to the workhouse there.[64] Both villages joined Selby poor-law union in 1837,[65] and in 1855 six former poorhouses at North Duffield were sold by the union.[66] The parish became part of iccall rural district in 1894, Derwent rural district in 1935,[67] and the Selby district of North Yorkshire in 1974.

CHURCH. Skipwith church was first mentioned in 1084, when the king gave it to the bishop of Durham.[68] In the 1120s the bishop granted it to Durham priory,[69] and it long remained in the peculiar jurisdiction of the priory.[70] The priory's church at Howden was made collegiate in 1267,[71] and when Skipwith prebend was established in the college in 1280 it was endowed with Skipwith church, and a vicarage was ordained.[72] The living was united with Thorganby vicarage in 1967.[73] There was a subordinate chapel at North Duffield in the Middle Ages.[74]

The patronage was presumably given to Durham priory along with the church, and it was confirmed to the priory in 1154–6;[75] the priory presented until the Dissolution.[76] A grant of the advowson to the archbishop of York in 1558[77] presumably lapsed on the accession of Elizabeth I. The advowson has since been retained by the Crown[78] and exercised by the Lord Chancellor.[79]

In 1291 the living was valued at £8[80] and in 1535 at £10 11s. 2½d. net.[81] It was worth £40 in 1650[82] and £42 10s. in 1764.[83] The average net income in 1829–31 was £300 a year,[84] and the living was worth £300 net in 1884 and £201 net in 1914.[85]

At ordination in 1280 the vicar was assigned the small tithes and tithe hay throughout the parish, together with 2 bovates of glebe in North Duffield;[86] these were presumably the 2 bovates which had belonged to the church since at least the mid 12th century.[87] In 1685 the glebe was accounted at 28 a., but by 1716 a further 78 a., comprising closes called Great and Little Northwoods, had been given in lieu of the small tithes of land adjoining North Duffield Hall.[88] The vicarial tithes of Skipwith township were commuted for £150 in 1840[89] and those of that part of Menthorpe belonging to Skipwith for £19 12s. 6d. in 1839.[90] At the inclosure of North Duffield in 1814 182 a. were allotted in lieu of tithes and glebe in the township.[91] The remaining glebe land, 161 a., was sold in 1914.[92]

In 1226 the minister (*serviens*) lived on a toft near the church,[93] and in 1280 the prebendary was required to provide a site for a parsonage.[94] The house was last mentioned in 1727[95] and it was not until 1865 that a new Vicarage was built, designed by Joseph Fawcett of Sheffield.[96] It was sold in 1958 and a new house built on an adjoining site in 1968.[97]

The chapel at North Duffield was served by the incumbent of Skipwith. In the 1260s the prior of Durham ordered, after complaint had been made, that the rector should continue to maintain due service at the chapel,[98] and in 1280 the vicar was required to do so.[99] The chapel may not have survived the suppression of the chantries, and in 1577, under the name of St. James's chapel, it was granted by the Crown to John Farnham.[1] There is no record of a chantry at North Duffield, but in 1333 Richard d'Avranches was licensed to grant land, rent, and turf to a chaplain to celebrate at St. Mary's altar in the parish church.[2] There was a chaplain at Skipwith in 1535.[3]

After the decay of the Vicarage in the early 18th century the vicar was not always resident at Skipwith. He resided in 1743, but not in 1764, when he had a curate who himself lived at Escrick. Before the new house was ready the vicar was also non-resident in 1865.[4] From 1954 onwards the vicar also held Thorganby and lived there until 1967.[5]

Two services were held each Sunday in 1743 and communion was celebrated six times a year, with 60 communicants the previous Easter.[6] There was only one weekly service and five celebrations a year in 1764.[7] By 1851 there were again two weekly services[8] and in the later 19th century communion was received six times a year by about twenty people.[9] By 1894 the schoolroom at North Duffield was licensed for a weekly service[10] and it continued to be so used until the 1930s.[11] In 1973 there was one service at the church every week, with two on alternate Sundays.

[63] O.S. Map 6" (1851 edn.).
[64] Overseer's accts.
[65] *3rd Rep. Poor Law Com.* 178.
[66] E.R.R.O., DDTR/Box 7.
[67] *Census.*
[68] *V.C.H. Yorks.* ii. 153.
[69] Prior's Kitchen, Durham, D. & C. Muniments, 1. 1. Archiep. 7a.
[70] *V.C.H. Yorks.* iii. 86.
[71] Ibid. 361.
[72] *Reg. Wickwane*, pp. 229–30.
[73] York Dioc. Regy., Order in Council 800.
[74] See below.
[75] Prior's Kitchen, D. & C. Muniments, 1. 1. Archiep. 19; *E.Y.C.* ii, p. 276.
[76] e.g. *Reg. Gray*, p. 93; *Reg. Greenfield*, v, p. 148; *Y.A.J.* xxv. 209.
[77] *Cal. Pat.* 1557–8, 420.
[78] e.g. Inst. Bks.; *Cal. Pat.* 1569–72, p. 192; *Rep. Com. Eccl. Revenues*, 968.
[79] *Crockford*; directories.
[80] *Tax. Eccl.* 302.
[81] *Valor Eccl.* v. 137.
[82] C 94/3 f. 76.
[83] B.I.H.R., Bp. V. 1764/Ret. 38.
[84] *Rep. Com. Eccl. Revenues*, 968.
[85] B.I.H.R., Bp. V. 1884/Ret.; Bp. V 1914/Ret.
[86] *Reg. Wickwane*, pp. 230–1.
[87] *E.Y.C.* ii, p. 272.
[88] B.I.H.R., TER. N. Skipwith 1685, 1716, 1777.
[89] Ibid. TA. 3L.
[90] Ibid. TA. 339S.
[91] E.R.R.O., Enrolment Bk. G, pp. 64 sqq.
[92] R.D.B., 164/406/346.
[93] *Reg. Gray*, p. 6.
[94] *Reg. Wickwane*, p. 231.
[95] B.I.H.R., TER. N. Skipwith 1727.
[96] Ibid. MGA. 1864/5; Bulmer, *Dir. E. Yorks.* (1892), 712.
[97] R.D.B., 1123/340/314; 1498/8/3; ex inf. the vicar, 1972.
[98] *Durham Annals and Documents* (Sur. Soc. clv), 137.
[99] *Reg. Wickwane*, p. 231.
[1] C 66/1157 m. 16.
[2] *Cal. Pat.* 1330–4, 401.
[3] *Valor Eccl.* v. 137.
[4] B.I.H.R., Bp. V. 1764/Ret. 38; V. 1865/Ret. 497; *Herring's Visit.* iii. 105.
[5] Ex inf. the vicar, 1972.
[6] *Herring's Visit.* iii. 106.
[7] B.I.H.R., Bp. V. 1764/Ret. 38.
[8] H.O. 129/24/513.
[9] B.I.H.R., V. 1865/Ret. 497; V. 1868/Ret. 453; V. 1871/Ret. 459; V. 1877/Ret.; Bp. V. 1884/Ret.
[10] Ibid. Bp. V. 1894/Ret.
[11] Directories.

The church of ST. HELEN is built of coursed rubble and ashlar and has a chancel, aisled and clerestoried nave with south porch, and west tower.[12] It is of special interest in that there are two phases of development before the Conquest.[13] Of the first, perhaps of the 10th century, there still remain two units, a short nave and a square building of the same width which may have been a porch. Presumably the early church also had a chancel. In the 11th century a chamber was built over the porch to form a low western tower. This church seems to have sufficed until the late 12th century, when the side walls of the nave were broken through to form two-bayed arcades to new aisles, first on the north and then on the south side. Late in the 13th century the aisles were extended one bay to the east and this immediately preceded the erection of a new chancel of notable size and quality. The east window contains the arms of Anthony Bek, bishop of Durham (d. 1311).[14] A rood screen was put in during the 15th century and a belfry stage was added to the tower. In the earlier 16th century new windows were inserted into the old north aisle and the clerestorey.

By 1582 the chancel was in decay,[15] most of the stained glass had gone, and the fittings were missing or dilapidated. In 1761 a gallery was built[16] and in 1821–2 a south porch,[17] but both were removed during a major restoration under the direction of J. L. Pearson in 1876–7. He built a new porch, refitted the interior, and repaired the roofs.[18]

There were two bells in 1552[19] and three in 1764[20] and 1875: (i) n.d.; (ii) 1684, Samuel Smith of York; (iii) 1700, also Samuel Smith.[21] The third was recast in 1891, and all three were rehung in 1929. Three additional bells were provided in 1934.[22] The plate includes two silver cups, one made in York in 1570 and the other in London by Joseph Ward in 1713, one of them with a cover.[23] The second cup was given, along with the cover, by Marmaduke Fothergill, vicar (d. 1731).[24] Fothergill also offered his organ and books to serve as a clerical library for the district, all of which were in London at his death,[25] but the offer was apparently not accepted. The registers date from 1670 and are complete.[26]

The churchyard was extended in 1867[27] and 1891.[28] Part of the churchyard wall has coping formed out of medieval grave slabs.

NONCONFORMITY. Half-a-dozen recusants and non-communicants were reported at North Duffield in the later 16th and 17th centuries, including William Hussey in the 1560s.[29] The Watkinsons of Menthorpe were also prominent Roman Catholics at that time.[30] There may already have been Quakers living at Skipworth by 1734, when a house and 15 a. of land there were bought under the terms of the will of Edward Leppington of Bridlington to provide money to distribute to poor Quakers at the winter Quarterly Meeting at York.[31] There were certainly three Quaker families at Skipwith in 1743 and one in 1764.[32] A Quaker burial ground, near the hall, was disused by the 1840s[33] and was sold in 1873.[34]

In 1764 there were two Methodist families in the parish[35] and in 1788 29 Methodists at 'Duffield'.[36] Houses were licensed for worship at Skipwith in 1764, 1796, and 1815,[37] and at North Duffield in 1794, 1817, and 1819.[38] A Primitive Methodist chapel was built at North Duffield in 1821,[39] near the south end of the main street, and was apparently used until the 1920s.[40] It was used as a dwelling-house in 1973. A Wesleyan Methodist chapel was built close by on the road from Selby to Market Weighton in 1833.[41] This small plain building was replaced in 1876[42] by a larger chapel on an adjoining site, built of brick with stone dressings in the Gothic style. The vicar of Skipwith alleged that there were 300 or 400 Methodists at North Duffield in the 1860s.[43] The earlier building remained in 1973, when the later was still in use. At Skipwith a Primitive Methodist chapel was built in 1868[44] and was still used in 1973.

EDUCATION. A school at Skipwith was founded by Dorothy Wilson (d. 1717), who by will dated 1713 devised £5 a year from ten cattle-gates in the Holmes in Skipwith to teach ten poor children.[45] The school was run by the parish clerk in 1743.[46] The cattle-gates were attached to an estate in Skipwith which Mrs. Wilson devised for the upkeep of a hospital in York; part of the estate was let to the Thompson family in the later 18th and early 19th centuries, and in 1829 it comprised about 230 a. in Skipwith and 40 a. in Riccall.[47] The school also benefited from a bequest of £400 by Joseph Nelson, vicar, by will proved in 1817, for the teaching of Skipwith children. By 1824 £14 interest on £451 stock provided for thirteen additional pupils.[48] By 1835 there were 45 pupils[49] and in 1851 eleven were boarders.[50] The attendance was put at 54 in 1871[51] but an average of only about 30 in 1872. The income

[12] See plate facing p. 81.
[13] H. M. and Joan Taylor, *Anglo-Saxon Architecture*, ii. 550–4.
[14] *Y.A.J.* xxvii. 160–1.
[15] B.I.H.R., V. 1582/CB.
[16] Ibid. PR. SKIP. 13.
[17] Ibid. 9, 13.
[18] Ibid. Fac. Bk. vi, pp. 158–60; *Yorks. Gaz.* 28 Apr. 1877.
[19] *Inventories of Ch. Goods*, 81.
[20] B.I.H.R., TER. N. Skipwith 1764.
[21] Boulter, 'Ch. Bells', 32.
[22] B.I.H.R., Fac. Bk. xi, p. 394; notice in church.
[23] *Yorks. Ch. Plate*, i. 314–15.
[24] B.I.H.R., TER. N. Skipwith 1764.
[25] Ibid. Bp. C. & P. III.
[26] B.I.H.R.
[27] Ibid. PR. SKIP. 13.
[28] Bulmer, *Dir. E. Yorks.* (1892), 711.
[29] Aveling, *Post Reformation Catholicism*, 64.
[30] Ibid. 22, 34.
[31] E.R.R.O., DDFA/14/105, 107.
[32] B.I.H.R., Bp. V. 1764/Ret. 38; *Herring's Visit.* iii. 105.
[33] O.S. Map 6" (1851 edn.).
[34] E.R.R.O., DDFA/14/222.
[35] B.I.H.R., Bp. V. 1764/Ret. 38.
[36] E.R.R.O., MRP/1/7.
[37] G.R.O. Worship Returns, Vol. v, nos. 219, 1249, 2873.
[38] Ibid. nos. 943, 3039, 3329.
[39] H.O. 129/24/513.
[40] Directories.
[41] Date on building.
[42] Date on building.
[43] B.I.H.R., V. 1865/Ret. 497; V. 1868/Ret. 453.
[44] Date on building.
[45] *4th Rep. Com. Char.* H.C. 312, pp. 381–3 (1820), v.
[46] *Herring's Visit.* iii. 105.
[47] E.R.R.O., DDFA/5/51; /13/9; /45/10; R.D.B., EM/65/68; *4th Rep. Com. Char.* 483–4.
[48] *10th Rep. Com. Char.* 672–3; *Educ. of Poor Digest*, 1093.
[49] *Educ. Enquiry Abstract*, 1095.
[50] H.O. 107/2351.
[51] *Returns relating to Elem. Educ.* 790.

of about £56 then included £34 from the endowments, the rest from school pence. The school was still held in the house provided by Mrs. Wilson, but the boys' room was said to have been much improved and a girls' room added a few years before.[52] By Schemes of 1923 the charity income was directed to be used for general educational purposes, including education other than elementary. The income from Nelson's charity was then £20 a year from a principal of £788.[53] From 1907 until the 1930s the attendance was usually 30–40; in 1938 it was 26.[54] In 1957 Skipwith school was closed and the pupils transferred to Thorganby.[55] Since 1959 the building has been used as a village hall;[56] in 1973 it still bore the inscription, 'The gift of Mrs. Dorothy Wilson of York 1714'. The income from it was £156 in 1974 and grants were made to children attending Thorganby school.[57]

At North Duffield there were two schools in 1835 and 40–60 children were taught at their parents' expense.[58] In 1871 17 children attended a school there.[59] A large new building, in the Tudor style, was built in 1872[60] by R. S. Scholfield, and in 1873 the average attendance was 54.[61] The building was bought by the East Riding county council in 1921.[62] Attendance was about 50 in 1907–14 and more then 60 in the 1920s; in 1938 it was 43.[63] After 1960 senior pupils went to Barlby secondary school.[64] The number on the roll in January 1973 was 43.[65]

CHARITIES FOR THE POOR. In 1824 there were found to be three rent-charges, of unknown origin, for the benefit of the poor of Skipwith: £1 was paid out of a 3-acre close belonging to John Dunnington-Jefferson, 4s. from a cottage, and 4s. from 'the poor land' of 1 or 2 roods. The money was distributed in coal. In addition the payment of £1 to the poor of North Duffield by the gift of William Andrie, which was recorded in 1786, was found to have ended c. 1800.[66]

Frances, dowager Lady Howard, by will proved in 1716, bequeathed money to provide coal for Escrick and other villages, including Skipwith.[67] After 1862 Skipwith received $\frac{1}{7}$ of the income.

In 1973 the income of the Poor's Estate was £22 and of Howard's charity £4; it was distributed in provisions to 16 people, but gifts of coal are normally still made as well.[68]

STILLINGFLEET

THE VILLAGE of Stillingfleet is situated on the northern edge of the Escrick moraine, near the east bank of the river Ouse, some 7 miles south of York.[1] It lies on either side of Stillingfleet beck, a stream which flows alongside the moraine to the Ouse, and most of the houses are strung out along the dry margins of the valley. The intervening ground, which is still regularly flooded, was formerly known as Town greens[2] and continued to be common land in 1972. It was probably the beck, which was known as 'the fleet' in the 13th century[3] and Fleet dike in the 16th century,[4] rather than the river which gave the village its Anglian name.[5] Further south the Ouse swings to the east and the Anglian settlement of Kelfield lies on the firm northern bank. Moreby Hall and its park occupy the north-western corner of the parish on the site of the depopulated village of Moreby, the Scandinavian 'farmstead on the marsh'.[6] Until 1850 the irregularly-shaped parish included the West Riding township of Acaster Selby, across the river;[7] the history of Acaster is, however, reserved for treatment elsewhere. The East Riding part of the parish covered 4,440 a., of which 1,835 a. lay in Kelfield and 681 a. in Moreby.[8]

South of the beck the moraine, composed of boulder clay and glacial sand and gravel, in places exceeds 50 ft. above sea-level. Other large areas of boulder clay lie north of the beck, and the rest of the parish is mostly covered by outwash sand and clay, all lying at 25 ft.–50 ft.[9] Lying still lower are the areas of alluvium beside the river and streams, where the ings were formerly situated. The entire western and southern parish boundary is formed by the Ouse, and elsewhere the boundary mostly follows some of the many streams and dikes which drain the parish. The open fields of Stillingfleet township lay for the most part on the moraine. North of the village there were extensive old inclosures and to the south the commons. The open fields and commons were inclosed in 1756 and the resulting regular field pattern contrasts with the irregular fields of the early-inclosed areas. Kelfield's open fields presumably lay immediately north of the village. In the north-west of the township the field pattern is less regular and the moor lay in the north-east. The open fields and moor were inclosed in 1740 and the remaining commons and ings in 1812.

The low grounds have always been liable to flooding. Frequent floods, which hindered access to the parish church, were the reason for the grant of a private oratory to the lady of Kelfield manor c. 1300.[10] In 1345 failure to cleanse a dike, probably Stillingfleet beck, and maintain its banks was

[52] Ed. 7/135 no. 162.
[53] Char. Com. files.
[54] Bd. of Educ. List 21 (H.M.S.O.).
[55] E.R. Educ. Cttee. Mins. 1956–7, 14, 210.
[56] R.D.B., 1160/50/45.
[57] Ex inf. Messrs. Byron & Granger, York, 1974.
[58] Educ. Enquiry Abstract, 1095.
[59] Returns rel. Elem. Educ. 790.
[60] Date on building.
[61] Ed. 7/135 no. 125.
[62] R.D.B., 233/532/428.
[63] List 21.
[64] E.R. Educ. Cttee. Mins. 1955–6, 151.
[65] Ex inf. Chief Educ. Officer, County Hall, Beverley, 1973.
[66] 10th Rep. Com. Char. 672–3.
[67] See p. 28.
[68] Char. Com. files; ex inf. Mr. G. Britain, Skipwith, 1974.
[1] This article was written in 1972.
[2] E.R.R.O., DDFA/15/91. See plate facing p. 112.
[3] Selby Coucher Bk. i (Y.A.S. Rec. Ser. xi), 338.
[4] Sta. Cha. 2/4/36.
[5] P.N.E.R. Yorks. (E.P.N.S.), 267.   [6] Ibid.
[7] Lond. Gaz. 15 Nov. 1850, p. 2991.
[8] O.S. Map 6", Yorks. (1851 edn.). Most of the parish is covered by sheet 206 and the remainder by sheet 191.
[9] Geol. Surv. Map 1", solid and drift, sheet 71 (1973 edn.).
[10] See p. 105.

alleged to have caused flooding at Stillingfleet and elsewhere.[11] Three public drains were set out at the inclosure of Stillingfleet in 1756, and 6 a. were awarded in lieu of meadow called the common grass, the rent of which had long been used to repair the gates and rails over the outfall sluices or cloughs in the township.[12] The principal clough at the outfall of the beck into the Ouse was rebuilt in brick by the township in 1815.[13] It was repaired and improved in 1858, when it took water from eight neighbouring parishes,[14] and again in the 20th century. Long stretches of the beck have been straightened. At the inclosure of Kelfield in 1812 one public drain was set out and it was ordered that an embankment beside the river should be maintained by the owners and occupiers of adjoining land.[15] The land allotted at Stillingfleet in 1756 was known as the Bylaw field. By a Scheme of 1971 it was directed that the income from the field, then containing 11 a., was to be used for the general benefit of the inhabitants. In 1972–3 income was £110 and expenditure included payments for drainage and rabbit clearance; £4 was given to the Poor's Land charity.[16]

The road from York through Stillingfleet to Cawood (Yorks. W.R.) crosses the dike which forms the northern parish boundary by the small Moreby bridge. The bridge was reported to be in disrepair in 1371 and c. 1394, when the townships of Moreby and Naburn were responsible for its upkeep.[17] From the early 19th century it was maintained by the county.[18] South of the bridge the road was diverted in 1829 to the east away from Moreby Hall,[19] and in 1844 a shorter section was diverted further eastwards around the edge of the park.[20] In 1926 the road was widened near the park entrance.[21] It continues southwards, as York Road, into Stillingfleet village, where it is carried over the beck by Stillingfleet bridge. The existence of a bridge there by 1301–2 is suggested by the name of an inhabitant, Thomas 'at the bridge'.[22] In 1818 the bridge was said to be narrow and in disrepair.[23] It was rebuilt in stone in 1820[24] and has one semicircular arch and long approaches across the Town greens. In 1902 the parish council erected two small cast-iron lamps on the end piers.[25]

From Stillingfleet bridge Church Hill climbs the moraine to join the road from Escrick, which follows the crest of the moraine almost to the Ouse. The latter road continues as Cawood Road by a circuitous route to Kelfield, where it forms the main street. About ¾ mile west of Kelfield, however, a road leads south-westwards from it and is carried over the river to Cawood by an iron swing-bridge built in 1872. Until 1882, when it was taken over by the county, it was a toll-bridge.[26] Before the bridge was built a ferry, described in 1772 as a horse ferry,[27] crossed the river at this point. Until 1812 a road led to the ferry across the ings from the west end of Kelfield village, but it was liable to flooding and at the inclosure of that year it was replaced by a new road further north.[28] The new road, also subject to flooding, had not been completed by 1814, when it was itself replaced by the present road to the bridge.[29] From the east end of Kelfield village other roads lead to Stillingfleet and Riccall.

From Stillingfleet village Stewart Lane leads westwards and formerly gave access to a ferry, first mentioned in 1734, over the river to Acaster Selby.[30] The road was liable to flooding and at inclosure in 1756 a new road to the ferry was laid out.[31] It was described as a bridle road in the mid 19th century.[32] The ferry, at the north end of Acaster village, apparently ceased between 1892 and 1906.[33]

Most of the houses in Stillingfleet village stand along side-lanes bordering Town greens, one of them called the Gale or Gale Lane.[34] In addition to Stillingfleet bridge, paths carried over the beck by foot-bridges link the two halves of the village. The church stands near the north end of the bridge. Most of the houses date from the 18th and 19th centuries but Swallow House may be of the 17th century or earlier. It has a ground floor of brick but a timber-framed upper storey. Later-18th-century houses include Rose Villa, in Stewart Lane. The 19th-century Crab Tree Farm has a wheelhouse. A few 20th-century houses and bungalows have been built in the village and there are ten council houses near York Road and six in Cawood Road. A village institute opposite the church was built in 1927.[35] The Cross Keys inn stands in the south of the village. There were usually three alehouses in Stillingfleet in the 1750s, two in the 1760s and 1770s, and one in the 1780s and 1790s.[36] By 1822 there were again two, the Plough and the White Swan.[37] The former had closed by 1840[38] and the Cross Keys is first mentioned in 1889.[39] A clothing club existed in the 1860s[40] and a parish library and reading room from the 1870s until at least 1914.[41]

Most of the houses and cottages in Kelfield village, all dating from the 18th century and later, lie along the main street. To the north, however, a cluster of mostly 19th-century houses has grown up at Moor End on the Stillingfleet road. Manor Farm, at the west end of the village, is a large 18th- or

---

[11] *Cal. Pat.* 1343–5, 593.
[12] R.D.B., Y/49/15.
[13] Inscribed stone on clough.
[14] E.R.R.O., DDFA/20/6.
[15] R.D.B., CQ/189/9.
[16] Char. Com. files.
[17] *Public Works in Med. Law*, ii (Selden Soc. xl), 241.
[18] E.R.R.O., QAB/2/3.
[19] Ibid. HD/33.
[20] Ibid. HD/51.
[21] E.R.C.C. *Mins.* 1926–7, 258.
[22] *Yorks. Lay Subsidy, 30 Edw. I* (Y.A.S. Rec. Ser. xxi), 104.
[23] E.R.R.O., QAB/1/6.
[24] Sheahan and Whellan, *Hist. York & E.R.* ii. 630.
[25] E.R.C.C. *Mins.* 1902–3, 302.
[26] Bulmer, *Dir. E. Yorks.* (1892), 716; Cawood Bridge Act, 33 & 34 Vic. c. 65 (Local).
[27] T. Jefferys, *Map of Yorks.*
[28] 46 Geo. III, c. 71 (Local and Personal, not printed); R.D.B., CQ/189/9; E.R.R.O., IA. Kelfield.
[29] 54 Geo. III, c. 32 (Local and Personal, not printed).
[30] E.R.R.O., QSF. Mids. 1734, B.4.
[31] R.D.B., Y/49/15.
[32] O.S. Map 6" (1851 edn.).
[33] Ibid. (1892 and 1906 edns.).
[34] R.D.B., Y/49/15; O.S. Map 6" (1958 edn.).
[35] Date on building.
[36] E.R.R.O., QDT/2/15.
[37] Ibid. QDT/2/13.
[38] White, *Dir. E. & N.R. Yorks.* (1840), 338.
[39] *Kelly's Dir. N. & E.R. Yorks.* (1889), 460.
[40] E.R.R.O., SLB. Log Bk. 1863–95.
[41] B.I.H.R., V. 1877/Ret.; Bp. V. 1884/Ret.; Bp. V. 1894/Ret.; Bp. V. 1914/Ret.

early-19th-century house and its outbuildings include a brick dovecot. Among the few 20th-century buildings in the village are eight council houses, and four others stand in Kelfield Lane. There were usually one or two alehouses in the later 18th century[42] and in 1822 there was one, the Boot.[43] It was known as the Boot and Shoe by 1840, when there was also another inn, the Black Swan.[44] By 1872 they had been replaced by the Grey Horse,[45] which still existed in 1972.

Apart from Moreby Hall the most noteworthy of the outlying buildings in the parish is Stillingfleet House.[46] By the late 16th century there were apparently two or more houses standing near the Ouse towards Riccall. The 'Wele houses' were mentioned in 1598, 'Weilhouse' close in 1604, and a messuage called the 'Wheildhouse' in the 1660s. The name, like that of near-by Wheel Hall in Riccall, refers to a deep part of the river.[47] The other isolated farm-houses all date from after the 18th- and early-19th-century inclosures. Hill Farm, in Stillingfleet, has a wheelhouse. An inn was built in 1827 beside the ferry in Kelfield.[48] It was known in 1840 as the Cawood Ferry[49] and in 1847 as the Ferry Boat.[50] In 1851 the innkeeper was also the ferryman.[51] It had probably closed by the 1870s.[52]

There were 120 poll-tax payers at Stillingfleet with Moreby in 1377.[53] In 1672 49 households in the two townships were recorded in the hearth-tax assessment. Three were discharged from paying; of the remainder 36 had one hearth, 4 had 2, one had 3, 3 had 4, and one each had 7 and ten.[54] Kelfield had 85 poll-tax payers in 1377[55] and 30 households were recorded in 1672. One was discharged from paying the tax, 16 had one hearth, 7 had 2, 2 had 3, 2 had 6, and one each had 7 and nine.[56] In 1743 there were 101 families in the whole parish[57] and in 1764 103.[58] The population of Stillingfleet with Moreby was 304 in 1801 and it increased steadily to a peak of 422 in 1861, before decreasing to 302 in 1901. The population has remained stable in the 20th century and was 294 in 1971. In 1801 the population of Kelfield was 175, but it increased rapidly to 421 in 1851, the largest intercensal increase, 106, occurring in 1841–51. It subsequently decreased to 288 by 1901 before rising to 346 in 1961; it stood at 314 in 1971.[59]

MANORS AND OTHER ESTATES. In 1086 an estate of 1½ carucate in Stillingfleet, which had been held before the Conquest by Ranchil, was in the possession of Hugh son of Baldric.[60] It apparently passed soon after, with the rest of Hugh's Yorkshire estates, to Robert de Stutville (fl. 1089),[61] in whose family it descended until it passed to Hugh Wake on his marriage with Joan, daughter of Nicholas de Stutville (d. 1233).[62] In 1284–5 the heirs of Baldwin Wake were overlords of 3 carucates in the township.[63] The overlordship subsequently descended like Buttercrambe manor (Yorks. N.R.), passing to Edmund of Woodstock, earl of Kent, whose wife Margaret was sister of Thomas Wake (d. 1349), and later to John de Neville, whose wife Elizabeth was the sister-in-law of Thomas, earl of Kent (d. 1397).[64] It was probably forfeited to the Crown on the attainder in 1569 of Charles Neville, earl of Westmorland.[65]

A mesne lordship in one carucate was held in 1284–5 by Jordan Foliot, nephew of Robert de Stutville (d. before 1275),[66] and the heir of that or another Jordan Foliot held property of the earl of Kent in 1353.[67] Nothing more is known of it.

In 1240 Robert de Grey acquired a carucate in Stillingfleet from Henry son of Ellis, and in 1244 Robert's brother Walter, archbishop of York, granted him his temporal estate. The latter included 12 bovates in Stillingfleet given to Walter in 1234 by Norman of Heslerton,[68] and other land there given by William Daubeney, Robert Trussebut, William de Ros, Ralph of Thorpe, the vicar of Stillingfleet, William de Stutville, and William Fairfax.[69] In 1284–5 Robert de Grey was demesne lord of 2 carucates of the Wake fee as well as lord of the Trussebut fee.[70] The remaining carucate of the Wake fee was then held by Gilbert de Luthe but by 1346 it had passed to John de Grey.[71] The manor of STILLINGFLEET descended in the Grey family[72] until the death of Robert, Lord Grey of Rotherfield, in 1388, when it passed to his daughter Joan, wife of John Deincourt.[73] Her son William died without issue in 1422–3 and his widow Elizabeth married Sir Richard Hastings (d. 1437).[74] In 1428 the manor, consisting of 8 carucates, was held by Edward Hastings.[75] By 1431, however, it had passed to Margaret, sister of William Deincourt (d. 1422–3) and wife of Ralph, Lord Cromwell,[76] and on her death in 1454 it passed to her sister Alice, wife of William, Lord Lovell.[77] On Alice's death in 1474 the manor passed to her grandson Francis, Lord Lovell,[78] on whose attainder in 1485 it was forfeited to the Crown.[79]

---

[42] E.R.R.O., QDT/2/15.
[43] Ibid. QDT/2/13.
[44] White, *Dir. E. & N.R. Yorks.* (1840), 338.
[45] *Kelly's Dir. N. & E.R. Yorks.* (1872), 549.
[46] See pp. 104, 106.
[47] E.R.R.O., DDPR, uncalendared. See p. 84.
[48] Date on building.
[49] White, *Dir. E. & N.R. Yorks.* (1840), 338.
[50] O.S. Map 6" (1851 edn.).
[51] H.O. 107/2351.
[52] Directories.
[53] E 179/202/58 m. 6.
[54] E 179/205/504.
[55] E 179/202/58 m. 3.
[56] E 179/205/504.
[57] *Herring's Visit.* iii. 91.
[58] B.I.H.R., Bp. V. 1764/Ret. 56.
[59] *V.C.H. Yorks.* iii. 498; *Census*, 1911–61.
[60] *V.C.H. Yorks.* ii. 277.
[61] *E.Y.C.* ix, p. 1.
[62] Ibid. pp. 35–7; *V.C.H. Yorks. N.R.* i. 513.
[63] *Feud. Aids*, vi. 35.
[64] C 138/253 no. 51; C 142/78 no. 95; *V.C.H. Yorks. N.R.* i. 513; *Cal. Inq. p.m.* ix, p. 206; x, p. 48; *Hen. VII*, i, p. 275; *Complete Peerage*, s.v. Kent.
[65] *V.C.H. Yorks. N.R.* i. 513.
[66] *Feud. Aids*, vi. 35; *E.Y.C.* ix, p. 37.
[67] *Cal. Inq. p.m.* x, p. 48.
[68] *Yorks. Fines, 1232–46*, pp. 18, 87.
[69] F. Drake, *Eboracum*, App. pp. lxiv–lxv; a confirmation of this deed is in *Cal. Chart. R. 1226–57*, 387–8.
[70] *Feud. Aids*, vi. 35; see below p. 106.
[71] *Feud. Aids*, vi. 223.
[72] *Cal. Inq. p.m.* x, p. 408; xiv, p. 135. For pedigree see *Complete Peerage*, s.v. Grey of Rotherfield.
[73] *Yorks. Inq. Hen. IV–V*, p. 78.
[74] J. W. Clay, *Ext. and Dorm. Peerages of N. Cos. of Eng.* 93, 100.
[75] *Feud. Aids*, vi. 271.
[76] C.P. 25(1)/292/67 no. 116.
[77] C 139/159 no. 34.
[78] C 140/526 no. 64.
[79] Clay, op. cit. 94; *Cal. Pat. 1485–94*, 100.

The manor was granted in 1552 to Leonard Beckwith, who was apparently the lessee as early as 1535,[80] and in 1579 Roger Beckwith sold it to Ralph Ellerker.[81] It was successively held by Edward (d. by 1587), Randolph, Sir Ralph (d. c. 1640), and James Ellerker.[82] Upon the death of John Ellerker in 1655 it passed to his daughter Dorothy, wife of Sir James Bradshaw.[83] The latter's son Ellerker Bradshaw (d. 1742) devised the manor to Eaton Mainwaring, who assumed the additional name of Ellerker,[84] and at the inclosure of 1756 he was awarded 1,008 a.[85]

After the death of R. M. Ellerker in 1775 the manor passed to his four sisters, and in 1789 their trustees sold it to Robert Cave.[86] In 1809 Robert's widow Catherine Cave sold it to James Wood.[87] Wood split up the estate in 1811, selling the manor and 810 a. to Richard Thompson, about 500 a. to Barnard Clarkson, and 116 a. to John Crosdill.[88] In 1818 Crosdill sold his property to Thompson.[89] The manorial estate subsequently descended like Escrick in the Thompson family, later barons Wenlock, and it was increased between 1814 and 1839 by purchases from Barnard Clarkson, George Burnell, John Turner, and the trustees of Francis Sledge.[90] About 1857 the estate comprised 1,190 a.[91] In 1919 some 300 a. were sold[92] and in 1972 the Forbes Adam family held 876 a. in Stillingfleet township.[93] Leonard Beckwith had a manor-house at Stillingfleet in 1535,[94] and the estate still included a manor-house in 1789.[95]

The holding bought by Barnard Clarkson in 1811 was sold to Joshua Ingham in 1820 and by him to Henry Preston in 1827.[96] It subsequently descended with the Preston family's manors of Kelfield and Moreby and was sold by Beatrice Preston in separate lots in 1956.[97] A mansion house on this holding, described in 1820 as newly erected, is apparently that now known as Stillingfleet House; now a farm-house, it stands on rising ground near the Ouse, west of the village. It is a square yellow-brick house with pedimented fronts.

Another manor of STILLINGFLEET, first mentioned in 1475, when it was held by Ralph Crathorne of the earl of Westmorland,[98] may have arisen from a reorganization of the estates of Alice Lovell after her death in 1474.[99] Ralph died by 1490 and was succeeded in turn by his son Thomas (d. 1509) and grandson Ralph (d. by 1517).[1] Ralph's brother James died by 1543 and was succeeded by his son Thomas (d. 1568), whose heir was his son Ralph.[2] The Crathornes sold property in the township to William Oglethorpe in 1579[3] and to four men, including William Oglethorpe and Nicholas Heslington, in 1615.[4] At least some of the property was sold by another Nicholas Heslington to Ellerker Bradshaw in 1710[5] and subsequently descended with the capital manor.

An estate of 2¼ carucates at Kelfield in 1086, which had formerly been a manor, was soke of Count Alan of Brittany's manor of Clifton (Yorks. N.R.).[6] The overlordship descended in the earls of Richmond until after 1346,[7] when it apparently passed to Selby abbey. It was last mentioned in 1534.[8] Count Alan apparently enfeoffed Hermer (fl. 1089–1114) of the estate[9] and he gave it Selby abbey before 1145.[10] The abbey held a mesne lordship in 1284–5 and 1343.[11]

The demesne lordship descended from Hermer's family to Henry son of Conan (fl. 1201–4), sometimes described as of Kelfield.[12] It descended to Henry's son Conan and then to his grandson Henry (d. c. 1285), who was succeeded in turn by his son Conan and, by 1311, his grandson Henry.[13] Henry son of Conan held it in 1346,[14] and in 1440 it belonged to John FitzHenry, whose heir was his son Henry.[15] The family held KELFIELD manor until the death of another John FitzHenry by 1496.[16] His heirs were two daughters, one of whom may have married John Stillington, who was in possession of the manor at his death in 1534.[17]

It was probably John's son Thomas who was succeeded at his death in 1591 by his son William.[18] Another John Stillington held it in the early 17th century.[19] At the inclosure of 1740 Joseph Stillington (d. 1746) received about 570 a.[20] He was succeeded by his three daughters, two of whom were dead by 1755 when the third, Mary, came of age. Mary died in 1769 and was succeeded by her aunt Dorothy Peirse, whose daughter Mary married the Revd. Edward Stillingfleet. Mary (d. 1804) devised the manor to trustees,[21] and the estate was split up in 1812; the manor and 384 a. were sold to Barnard Clarkson, 261 a. to Samuel Hague, 201 a. to Robert Brown, and 195 a. to Thomas Mitchell.[22] Clarkson sold 186 a. the same year to the Revd. Thomas Preston[23] and the manor and 88 a. to Samuel Hague in 1814.[24] Preston bought 85 a. from the Revd. C. D.

[80] *Cal. Pat. 1550–3*, 357; *Yorks. Sta. Cha. Proc.* ii (Y.A.S. Rec. Ser. xlv), 124.
[81] C.P. 25(2)/260/21 Eliz. I East. [no. 20].
[82] C 142/213 no. 122; C 142/496 no. 109.
[83] E.R.R.O., DDKE/10/1. For pedigree of the Ellerkers see G. Oliver, *Hist. Beverley*, 508.
[84] E.R.R.O., DDFA/15/19.
[85] R.D.B., Y/49/15.
[86] E.R.R.O., DDFA/15/60; DDPR, uncalendared.
[87] Ibid. DDFA/15/66.
[88] R.D.B., CS/217/337; /258/381; E.R.R.O., DDFA/15/70.
[89] E.R.R.O., DDFA/15/73.
[90] Ibid. DDFA/5/51.
[91] Ibid. DDFA/41/6.
[92] Ibid. DDFA/20/7.
[93] Ex inf. Escrick Park Estate Office, 1972.
[94] *Yorks. Sta. Cha. Proc.* ii. 124–5; see below p. 106.
[95] E.R.R.O., DDPR, uncalendared.
[96] R.D.B., DG/396/504; EC/228/258.
[97] Ibid. 1039/382/345; 1040/545/486; 1044/70/68.
[98] *Cal. Inq. p.m. Hen. VII*, i, p. 275.
[99] C 140/526 no. 64.
[1] C 142/65 no. 30; C 142/78 no. 95; *Cal. Inq. p.m. Hen. VII*, i, p. 275.
[2] C 142/65 no. 68; C 142/149 no. 150.
[3] *Yorks. Fines*, ii. 146.
[4] Ibid. *1614–25*, 48.
[5] R.D.B., A/300/434.
[6] *V.C.H. Yorks.* ii. 241; in the Summary the estate is said to comprise 2 carucates and one bovate: ibid. 321
[7] *Feud. Aids*, vi. 34, 210.
[8] C 142/56 no. 39.
[9] *E.Y.C.* iv, pp. 3–4; v, p. 53.
[10] Ibid. iv, p. 18.
[11] *Feud. Aids*, vi. 34; *Selby Coucher Bk.* i. 342.
[12] *E.Y.C.* v, p. 53; for an acct. of the family see *Guisborough Charty.* ii (Sur. Soc. lxxxix), 183 n.
[13] *Feud. Aids*, vi. 34; *Yorks. Inq.* ii, p. 92 n.; *Cal. Chart. R. 1327–41*, 303; *Y.A.J.* xviii. 417.
[14] *Feud. Aids*, vi. 210.
[15] *Test. Ebor.* ii, p. 217.
[16] *Cal. Inq. p.m. Hen. VII*, iii, pp. 476–7.
[17] C 142/56 no. 39.
[18] C 142/231 no. 104.
[19] C 3/380/3; *Miscellanea*, i (Y.A.S. Rec. Ser. lxi), 107.
[20] E.R.R.O., DDFA/7/4.
[21] Ibid. DDFA/7/5; DDPR, uncalendared.
[22] R.D.B., CT/421/629; /426/632; /429/633; CU/83/81.
[23] Ibid. CT/389/591.
[24] Ibid. CX/301/371.

Wray in 1825[25] and his son Henry Preston bought the manor and 302 a. from Barnard Hague in 1828.[26] Other purchases by Henry Preston included 144 a. from Lorenzo Moore, 85 a. from P. B. Thompson, 142 a. from Thomas Mitchell, 42 a. from Barnard Clarkson, and 57 a. from Mary Cock's devisees, all in the 1830s.[27] The Prestons retained the estate, comprising about 1,320 a. in 1930,[28] until Beatrice Preston sold it in various lots in 1956–8 and 1966.[29]

A moated site in the north of Kelfield village may represent the site of the manor-house which Henry of Kelfield held in 1290–1.[30] The horseshoe-shaped moat, still partly filled with water in 1972, encloses a mound and the small mid-19th-century Manor House. Several depressions, which may have been medieval fish-ponds, lie near by.[31]

In the late 13th or early 14th century an oratory in her manor-house at Kelfield was granted to Parnel, widow of Conan son of Henry, and by 1303–4 property in the township had been given by her family to support a chantry there.[32] The former chantry property was granted in 1570 to Hugh Counsell and Robert Pistor.[33]

The Stillington family occupied a house of 10 hearths in 1672.[34] This was probably Kelfield Hall, which was mentioned in 1598 and stood beside the river in the south of the village.[35] In 1839 the hall was a two-storeyed building with basement and attics, and the irregular main front was four bays long. The second bay from the west end of the front contained the entrance, with a round-headed window above, and the projecting fourth bay had rusticated quoins. This arrangement suggests an old house of medieval plan. A small building with a pyramidal roof surmounted by a ball finial stood close to the house and survived in 1972, at one corner of a level area partly surrounded by an 18th-century brick wall with central and terminal gate piers. The hall itself was demolished by the Prestons c. 1840.[36] An adjacent moated site may represent an earlier site of the manor-house.

In 1086 an estate of one carucate and 7 bovates at Kelfield, held before the Conquest by Game, was in the hands of Hugh son of Baldric.[37] Like Hugh's Stillingfleet estate[38] it passed soon after the Survey to the Stutvilles and was apparently included in the land given in wardship during the minority of Eustace de Stutville to Saer, earl of Winchester, and after Saer's death to his son Roger de Quincy in 1220.[39] The overlordship of one carucate of the estate thereafter descended in the Quincy family and is last mentioned in 1346.[40] In 1284–5 an intermediate lordship in the Quincy estate was held by Roger of St. Andrew.[41] Nothing more is known of it.

The demesne lord of the one-carucate holding in 1219 was Henry son of Walter.[42] In 1284–5 it was held by Henry of Kelfield, presumably the Henry son of Conan who was demesne lord of the Richmond fee,[43] Robert the long, and Henry son of Thomas.[44] In 1343–4 the holding was granted by John Percy to William Aldborough,[45] and, described as the manor of KELFIELD, it passed on William's death about 1388 to his son William.[46] The latter was dead by 1392, when the manor passed to his sisters Sibyl, wife of William of Ryther, and Elizabeth, wife of Brian Stapleton.[47] In 1402 Sibyl and William granted their half of the manor to Nicholas Gascoigne[48] and in 1417 Elizabeth and her then husband Richard Redeman granted the other half to William Gascoigne (d. 1422).[49] In 1449 another William Gascoigne granted the manor to Henry Vavasour.[50] It was later held by William (d. 1500), John (d. 1524), and William (d. by 1566) Vavasour,[51] and in 1577 John Vavasour sold it to Thomas Stillington.[52] It subsequently descended with the capital manor.[53]

In 1591 the manor-house of the Vavasour manor was known as Auburn Hall.[54]

Eustace de Stutville died in 1241 and by 1244 his widow Nichole had married William de Percy.[55] The overlordship of the remaining land of the former Stutville estate, sometimes said to be 6 and sometimes 7 bovates, subsequently descended in the Percy family of Kildale (Yorks. N.R.) and was last mentioned in 1392.[56] The demesne lord was Geoffrey de Basinges in 1240,[57] and John of Stonegrave and Stephen 'le Tuler' in 1284–5.[58] Stonegrave's daughter Isabel married Simon de Pateshull, who in 1296 held 4 bovates.[59] By 1346 the estate, then comprising 7 bovates, was held by Henry Laurence.[60] Nothing more is known of it.

An estate of one carucate at Moreby in 1086, which had formerly been a manor, was soke of Count Alan of Brittany's manor of Clifton.[61] The overlordship was held by the earl of Richmond in 1284–5[62] but by 1295 it had passed to the heirs of Robert Greathead[63] and nothing more is known of it.

---

[25] Ibid. DU/238/296.
[26] Ibid. ED/285/331; /288/332.
[27] Ibid. EO/357/347; ER/220/230; /221/231; /398/437; EX/270/306.
[28] Ibid. 411/85/70.
[29] Ibid. 1039/437/399; /491/450; 1041/12/10; /216/192; 1046/395/352; 1050/290/263; 1101/272/241; 1104/386/351; 1473/384/331.
[30] *Abbrev. Plac.* (Rec. Com), 223.
[31] O.S. Map 6″ (1851 edn.).
[32] *Reg. Greenfield*, iii (Sur. Soc. cli), 17; *Abbrev. Plac.* 249.
[33] *Cal. Pat.* 1569–72, p. 38.
[34] E 179/205/504. The house was recorded under Stillingfleet but it was presumably Kelfield manor-house.
[35] E.R.R.O., DDPR, uncalendared; Jefferys, *Map Yorks.*
[36] Y.A.S., MS. 530(c), sketch of hall 1839, letter 1895.
[37] *V.C.H. Yorks.* ii. 277.
[38] See p. 103.
[39] *E.Y.C.* ix, pp. 17–18.
[40] *Feud. Aids*, vi. 34–5, 223.
[41] Ibid. 35.
[42] *Yorks. Fines, 1218–31*, p. 16.
[43] See p. 104.
[44] *Feud. Aids*, vi. 34–5.
[45] *Whitby Charty.* ii (Sur. Soc. lxxii), 702 n.; in 1346 it was said to be held by Nich. of Moreby: *Feud. Aids*, vi. 223.
[46] *Cal. Close*, 1385–9, 512.
[47] C 136/69 nos. 2, 3.
[48] C.P. 25(1)/279/149 no. 32.
[49] B.L. Harl. Chart. 112 C.30; *Parl. Rep.* i (Y.A.S. Rec. Ser. xci), 180.
[50] C.P. 25(1)/281/160 no. 63.
[51] C 142/118 no. 42; C 142/135 no. 144; *Cal. Inq. p.m. Hen. VII*, ii, p. 259.
[52] *Yorks. Fines*, ii. 104.
[53] C 142/231 no. 104; see p. 104.
[54] C 142/231 no. 104.
[55] *E.Y.C.* ix, pp. 17–18.
[56] C 136/69 nos. 2, 3; *Bk. of Fees*, ii. 1476; *Feud. Aids*, vi. 34.
[57] *Yorks. Fines, 1232–46*, p. 85.
[58] *Feud. Aids*, vi. 34.
[59] *Yorks. Inq.* iii, pp. 25–6; *Cal. Inq. p.m.* iii, p. 233.
[60] *Feud. Aids*, vi. 223.
[61] *V.C.H. Yorks.* ii. 241.
[62] *Feud. Aids*, vi. 34.
[63] *Cal. Inq. p.m.* iii, p. 182.

In 1244 archbishop Walter de Grey granted to his brother Robert his Moreby estate, including land which he had acquired from Agnes de Moreville, Nicholas Palmer, and William Fairfax.[64] In 1284–5 Robert de Grey was demesne lord of the estates,[65] which passed like Stillingfleet to the Crown in 1485.[66] The Crown granted the Moreby land to John Wellisburne in 1528 and he sold it in 1529 to Leonard Beckwith.[67] Roger Beckwith sold *MOREBY* manor, consisting of about 300 a., to Edward Talbot, probably c. 1580,[68] and by 1596 it had passed to George Harvy and Henry Slingsby.[69] In 1604 Slingsby sold it to George Lawson,[70] who was succeeded by his son George in 1638.[71] In 1762 it passed on the death of Marmaduke Lawson to his cousin William Preston.[72] The estate, comprising 632 a. in 1842,[73] subsequently descended in the Preston family. In 1956–8 Beatrice Preston sold about 600 a.,[74] but the hall and its 90-acre park were retained[75] and in 1964 Mr. A. T. Preston repurchased the 139-acre Woodlands farm.[76]

The Lawson family occupied a house of seven hearths in 1672.[77] In the early 18th century the house was a two-storeyed building with attics and had a front seven bays long with a central pediment over three bays.[78] This was the house, known as Moreby Hall and owned by William Preston, which in 1772 stood in a park near the river in the north of the township.[79] The present large stone-built hall, in a Tudor style, was erected on the same site in 1827–32 by Anthony Salvin for Henry Preston.[80] There is still a large park.

Another estate of one carucate at Moreby had been held before the Conquest by Fulchri and in 1086 was in the possession of Hugh son of Baldric.[81] Like his Stillingfleet estate it passed to Robert de Stutville, who granted land there between c. 1089 and 1106 to St. Mary's abbey, York.[82] The Stutvilles retained property in Moreby until at least 1227[83] but by 1284–5 the earl of Richmond was overlord of the whole carucate.[84] By 1346 it had become part of the Marmion fee.[85] Nothing more is known of the overlordship. A mesne lordship was held of the earl of Richmond by Thomas of Merston in 1284–5.[86]

The demesne lord in 1240 was John of Wistow, who in that year granted the estate to William de Belkerthorpe.[87] By 1284–5 it was held by William of Moreby.[88] It passed to the Acklam family on the marriage of Mary, daughter of Henry Moreby, with William Acklam c. 1370.[89] The manor of *MOREBY*, known in the 16th and 17th centuries as *MOREBY HALL*, was held by John Acklam (d. 1551), William Acklam (d. 1567), and Sir William Acklam (fl. 1619).[90] It passed to Sir William Milbanke (d. 1680) on his marriage in 1659 to Elizabeth, daughter of John Acklam (d. 1643).[91] In 1787 Ralph Milbanke sold his Moreby estate to William Preston[92] and it was merged with the capital manor.

The Acklam family had a manor-house, containing a chapel, at Moreby in 1493[93] and the house was known as Moreby Hall in 1552.[94] It still existed in 1612[95] but it is not mentioned again, and it was perhaps demolished when the Milbankes succeeded to the estate.[96] It may have stood near Home Farm, where a field called Old Acklam was mentioned in 1906.[97]

In 1066 Grim held 2 carucates in Stillingfleet, which in 1086 were held by Hunfrid, Erneis de Burun's man.[98] The estate evidently passed, like West Cottingwith, successively to Geoffrey son of Pain, William Trussebut, Hilary de Builers, and William de Ros.[99] The overlordship descended in the Ros family[1] and was last mentioned in 1454.[2]

In 1284–5 Robert de Grey was demesne lord of 1½ carucate of the Ros fee.[3] The estate subsequently descended with the capital manor.[4]

An estate of 2 bovates at Stillingfleet in 1086 was soke of Count Alan of Brittany's manor of Gate Fulford.[5] In 1284–5 the overlordship was held by the earl of Richmond, and two mesne lordships were held by Robert the long and Henry son of Conan. Robert of Fiskgate and Thomas son of John held the estate in demesne.[6] Nothing more is known of it.

Another Domesday estate, also of 2 bovates, was held by the king.[7] It had apparently passed by the early 12th century to St. Peter's (later St. Leonard's) hospital, York, which granted it to Henry son of William.[8] Henry granted it to John son of Daniel, who gave a bovate to Selby abbey.[9] In 1284–5 the abbey and Warin the calfherd each held a bovate of St. Leonard's hospital.[10]

[64] Drake, *Hist. York*, App. pp. lxiv–lxv.
[65] *Feud. Aids*, vi. 34.
[66] C 142/80 no. 151; *Cal. Inq. p.m.* iii, p. 182; *Yorks. Inq. Hen. IV–V*, pp. 4–5; see above p. 103.
[67] *L. & P. Hen. VIII*, iv (1), p. 2079; (3), p. 2349.
[68] *Cal. Proc. Chanc. Eliz. I* (Rec. Com.), iii. 143; *Yorks. Fines*, ii. 149.
[69] *Yorks. Fines*, iv. 39.
[70] Ibid. *1603–14*, 8.
[71] C 142/490 no. 6.
[72] R.D.B., AD/501/1001; Susanna Preston (d. 1711) married Marm. Lawson: J. Foster, *Pedigrees of . . . Yorks.* s.v. Preston of Flasby and Moreby.
[73] B.I.H.R., TA 46S.
[74] R.D.B., 1037/155/146; /351/318; etc.
[75] Ibid. 1107/198/187.
[76] Ibid. 1353/292/269.
[77] E 179/205/504.
[78] B.L. Lansd. MS. 914 f. 33.
[79] Jefferys, *Map Yorks.*
[80] *Country Life*, 16 Feb. 1907; date 1832 on rainwater heads; see above plate facing p. 16.
[81] *V.C.H. Yorks.* ii. 277.
[82] *E.Y.C.* ix, pp. 1, 84.
[83] *Yorks. Fines, 1218–31*, p. 104.
[84] *Feud. Aids*, vi. 34.
[85] Ibid. 223. Avice (fl. 1280), daughter and heir of Jernegan son of Hugh, a descendant of Hugh, the earl of Richmond's steward in 1138–45, married Rob. Marmion, and another Avice, daughter of John Marmion (d. 1335–6), married John de Grey: *E.Y.C.* v, pp. 41–4; Clay, *Ext. and Dorm. Peerages of N. Cos.* 132.
[86] *Feud. Aids*, vi. 34.
[87] *Yorks. Fines, 1232–46*, p. 72.
[88] *Feud. Aids*, vi. 34.
[89] *Visit. Yorks. 1584–5 and 1612*, ed. J. Foster, 109.
[90] E.R.R.O., DDBH/3/78; /12/92; C 142/537 no. 53.
[91] C 142/537 no. 53; B.I.H.R., PR. STILL. 3; Foster, *Pedigrees of . . . Yorks.* s.v. Milbanke of Halnaby.
[92] R.D.B., BM/244/402.
[93] *Test. Ebor.* iii, p. 358.
[94] E.R.R.O., DDBH/3/78.
[95] C 142/337 no. 114.
[96] See above.
[97] O.S. Map 6" (1906 edn.).
[98] *V.C.H. Yorks.* ii. 279–80.
[99] See p. 115.
[1] *Feud. Aids*, vi. 35; *Cal. Inq. p.m.* viii, p. 346; x, p. 39.
[2] C 139/159 no. 34.
[3] *Feud. Aids*, vi. 35.   [4] See p. 103.
[5] *V.C.H. Yorks.* ii. 241, 321.
[6] *Feud. Aids*, vi. 35.
[7] *V.C.H. Yorks.* ii. 204, 321.
[8] *Selby Coucher Bk.* i. 339.
[9] Ibid. 338.
[10] *Feud. Aids*, vi. 35.

Selby abbey acquired other land in both Stillingfleet and Kelfield. In 1205–10 Durand the clerk granted 3 bovates and 28 a. in Stillingfleet to the abbey,[11] and Richard son of Adam gave unspecified land there, probably also in the 13th century.[12] In Kelfield Henry son of Conan granted a bovate probably c. 1200.[13] In 1535 the abbey's property in Stillingfleet was included in its manor of Acaster Selby[14] and ten years later was granted with it to Sir George Darcy.[15] Its Kelfield estate was then worth 13s. 4d.[16] and it was granted in 1557 to James Lambarte and George Cotton,[17] from whom it apparently passed the same year to Leonard Vavasour.[18] In 1353 John of Ness and Peter of Crakehall granted a house and an acre to St. Mary's abbey, York,[19] and in 1557 the abbey's former estate there passed, with that of Selby, to Lambarte and Cotton, and then to Vavasour.[20] In 1584 3 a. in Moreby, which had formerly belonged to a chantry in St. John's church, Ouse Bridge, York, was let by the Crown to John Johnson.[21]

The Thompsons of Escrick acquired an estate at Kelfield in the earlier 19th century by purchases of 106 a. from Philip Akam in 1817 and 238 a. from John Eadon in 1839.[22] It descended with Escrick and in 1972 the Forbes Adam family held 278 a. in the township.[23]

Stillingfleet rectory was held by St. Mary's hospital, Bootham, near York, from 1318 until 1557.[24] It was worth £40 in 1291.[25] In 1535 it was worth £33 13s. 4d., of which tithes accounted for over £31.[26] In 1557 the chapter of York obtained it and applied it for the support of St. Peter's School, York.[27] In 1562 it was reported that 10 a. of meadow in Kelfield had long been assigned to the rector in lieu of hay tithes.[28] In 1650 the rectory was worth £130[29] and in 1698 £183.[30] It was let to the Moyser family for much of the later 17th and 18th centuries.[31] At the inclosure of Stillingfleet in 1756 E. M. Ellerker, as sub-lessee of James Moyser for the tithes of Stillingfleet and Moreby townships, was awarded 78 a., together with a rent-charge of £92 10s. a year.[32] In 1838 the Kelfield tithes were commuted for £320 payable to the dean and chapter,[33] and in 1842 those remaining in Moreby for £80.[34] The rectorial estate subsequently passed to the governors of St. Peter's School and in 1907 they sold 94 a. to Lord Wenlock.[35]

ECONOMIC HISTORY. In 1086 the Stillingfleet estate of Hugh son of Baldric had land for one plough, but Hugh had half a plough and seven villeins had two more. Both before and after the Conquest the estate was worth 10s. Erneis de Burun's estate had land for two ploughs and Hunfrid his man had two ploughs. Two villeins and one bordar were also recorded. The estate had increased in value from 10s. before the Conquest to 15s.[36]

Some reclamation of the township's waste had taken place before 1205–10, when assarts made by William Trussebut amounted to 18 a., including one in meadow land called 'Hehinge'.[37] Reclamation evidently continued throughout the 13th century and there were references to land reckoned in acres, presumably assarted, in 1231,[38] an area of assarts called Green Rudding in 1244, and two assarts near the beck.[39] In 1244 the archbishop of York granted to his brother Robert de Gray his wood in Stillingfleet and 2½ a. of waste there,[40] and Stillingfleet waste was mentioned in 1322.[41] Some reclaimed land became part of the open fields, areas of which were known as Clerkridding and Sleghtholmes in 1399.[42] The extent of medieval reclamation is indicated by the many 17th-century and later names of open-field land and closes which include the elements 'ridding' or 'intake'.[43]

The common fields were first named in the late 17th century as Garth End, Clow, Mill, and Far fields.[44] Rape was grown in Stillingfleet, evidently as a new crop, in 1697.[45] Meadow land called North marsh and West ings, and commons known as Longlands and Banks, were first recorded in 1716.[46]

The open fields, meadows, and commons were mostly inclosed in 1756,[47] under an Act of the previous year.[48] In all, 1,382 a. were allotted. The open-field land comprised 125 a. in Clow field, 139 a. in Garth End field, 198 a. in Far field, 195 a. in Mill field, 21 a. in Gawtrees field, and 10 a. in Thistle Barf field. There were then stinted pastures, Longlands containing 270 a., Keys Banks 40 a., and Woody pasture 33 a. Of the 52 'commons' or gates in these pastures 45 belonged to the lord of the manor. Three areas of meadow land lay beside the river and the owners of open-field land had 'distinct and known parts' in them. They were Ings meadow or South ings[49] containing 57 a., Twings marsh 4 a., and North marsh 15 a. There were also five moors or greens in which all the inhabitants of the township had unstinted pasturage. Town greens were not inclosed[50] and continued to be

[11] *Selby Coucher Bk.* i. 334–5; *Yorks. Fines, 1218–31,* p. 142.
[12] *Selby Coucher Bk.* i. 339.
[13] Ibid. 341.
[14] *Valor Eccl.* (Rec. Com.), v. 12.
[15] E 318/Box 9/350.
[16] Dugdale, *Mon.* iii. 508.
[17] *Cal. Pat.* 1557–8, 273.
[18] B.L. Harl. MS. 606 no. 127.
[19] *Cal. Pat.* 1350–4, 531.
[20] B.L. Harl. MS. 606 no. 127; *Cal. Pat.* 1557–8, 273.
[21] E 310/33/202 no. 89.
[22] R.D.B., DC/358/486; FL/274/238.
[23] Ex inf. Escrick Park Estate Office, 1972; see p. 20.
[24] *V.C.H. Yorks.* i. 422.
[25] *Tax. Eccl.* (Rec. Com.), 300.
[26] *Valor Eccl.* v. 31.
[27] *V.C.H. Yorks.* i. 422.
[28] B.I.H.R., CP. G. 1081.
[29] C 94/3 f. 77. The value was given as £180 in Lamb. Pal. Libr., COMM. XIIa/17/309.
[30] B.I.H.R., Bp. C. & P. I.
[31] E.R.R.O., DDX/103/1; DDFA/15/44.
[32] R.D.B., Y/49/15.
[33] B.I.H.R., PR. STIL. 19.
[34] Ibid. TA. 46S.
[35] E.R.R.O., DDFA/15/94.
[36] *V.C.H. Yorks.* ii. 277, 279–80.
[37] *Selby Coucher Bk.* i. 334–5.
[38] *Yorks. Fines, 1218–31,* p. 142; see below p. 124.
[39] *Selby Coucher Bk.* i. 338; Drake, *Eboracum,* App. p. lxv.
[40] Drake, *Eboracum,* App. pp. lxiv–lxv.
[41] *Yorks. Deeds,* ix, p. 64.
[42] E.R.R.O., DC/45/26.
[43] Ibid. DX/137; DDFA/15/3, 75; B.I.H.R., TER. N. Stillingfleet n.d. (17th cent.); CP. H. 4504.
[44] B.I.H.R., TER. N. Stillingfleet n.d. (17th cent.).
[45] Ibid. CP. H. 4504.
[46] Ibid. TER. N. Stillingfleet 1716.
[47] R.D.B., Y/49/15; E.R.R.O., DDFA/15/91 is a copy of a map made in 1778, itself apparently a copy of the inclosure map.
[48] 28 Geo. II, c. 22 (Priv. Act).
[49] E.R.R.O., DDFA/15/91.
[50] Ibid.

used for common grazing until the earlier 20th century, when small-scale milk production became impracticable.[51] Large moor comprised 196 a., Little moor 70 a., and Lyer green 9 a.; the acreage of Clow green cannot be determined. E. M. Ellerker was awarded 1,008 a. as lord of the manor and 78 a. as lessee of the rectory. The vicar received 75 a. There were 2 allotments of 50–100 a., 4 of 10–49 a., and 2 of less than 10 a.

In 1086 the estate of Hugh son of Baldric at Kelfield had land for one plough and four villeins had a plough there. There was woodland a league long and half a league broad and 8 a. of meadow. In both 1066 and 1086 the estate was worth £1.[52] Reclamation was taking place in 1210, when Henry son of Conan was licensed to assart part of his wood in the township. The wood was separated from the townships of Stillingfleet and Kelfield by two fields.[53] In 1219 3 a. of reclaimed land lay in areas called Waltef ridding, Calfhay, and Drihurst.[54] The last-named was presumably the area called Dryesses, which lay in closes in 1708.[55] In 1276 a holding included 24½ a. of land which may have been reclaimed.[56] In 1311 Henry son of Conan was licensed to hold his woodland inclosed and emparked as his ancestors had done,[57] and Kelfield wood was mentioned in 1322.[58]

Three open fields, East, North, and West or Thwaites fields, were named in the mid 16th century, and by 1600 there was a fourth, Calfhay field.[59] The common pastures in the 16th and 17th centuries were the moor and the riverside banks, in both of which beast-gates were enjoyed. Meadow land lay in the marsh and the ings.[60] Many closes were named in the same period, including Robert Ridding, the Haggs, the town's intake, Hall Warm closes, and the Flaggs, beside the Ouse.[61]

The open fields and the moor were inclosed by agreement in 1740. Joseph Stillington, as lord of the manor, was allotted 570 a. and two others received 76 a. and 15 a.[62] Acts of 1746 and 1747 confirmed the inclosure and empowered the Stillingtons to raise money for it.[63] The remaining meadows, commons, and wastes were inclosed in 1812[64] under an Act of 1806.[65] In all, 233 a. were allotted. Allotments totalling 35 a. were made from the ings, 5 a. from the banks, and 181 a. from both; in addition 5½ a. were awarded from Goose green, 4½ a. from beside the township's lanes, 1 a. from the carr, and 1 a. from waste in the village.

In 1086 the estate of Hugh son of Baldric at Moreby had land for half a plough, but four villeins had one plough there. There was woodland one league long and half a league broad and 20 a. of meadow. The estate had fallen in value from 5s. before the Conquest to 3s.[66] An early example of reclamation was that carried out in 1227 by St. Mary's abbey, which was granted 8 a. from Moreby meadow and a plot of land 'towards the fields', together with sufficient fencing material from Moreby wood to inclose them.[67] In 1295 a holding included 30 a. of assarted land and 10 a. of meadow.[68]

Moreby village was apparently never large enough to appear separately in tax assessments.[69] In 1529 the Beckwith estate there was wholly inclosed but there were still four houses and tofts. Three closes were called Bridgefield, Shawfield, and Southfield, possibly the names of the former open fields. A field called Armetpark and a wood called Southgaile were also mentioned.[70] The Acklam estate, too, had been inclosed by 1552, although 19½ a. in the Great ings and herbage of the wood were mentioned. The hall was then surrounded by a park. A large number of close names on both estates incorporated the elements 'ridding', 'shaw', or 'hurst'.[71] There were 160 a. of grassland and 120 a. of arable on the former Beckwith estate c. 1580.[72] Stinted common rights were still held in the ings in 1747[73] and it is not known when they were extinguished. Between 1847 and 1891 the ings became part of the park.[74]

In 1801 1,321 a., i.e. nearly a third, of the whole parish were under crops, mainly wheat (296 a.), beans (271 a.), and oats (250 a.).[75] In Kelfield township in 1838 there were 1,386 a. of arable, 250 a. of permanent grass, and 24 a. of woodland.[76] The township was said in 1856 to be noted for potatoes, rape, mustard, and flax.[77] In Moreby in 1842 there were 302 a. of arable, 190 a. of grass, and 111 a. of woodland.[78] In Stillingfleet and Moreby in 1905 there were 1,205 a. of arable, 1,119 a. of permanent grass, and 160 a. of woodland, and in Kelfield 1,143 a. of arable, 429 a. of grass, and 50 a. of woodland.[79] In the 1930s and 1960s the parish was still largely under arable, but there was much grassland around Moreby Hall in the north-east of the parish, beside the river, and around both villages.[80] Some woodland remained in Moreby park in 1972, and the Forestry Commission has managed 60 a. of woodland in Stillingfleet township and 35 a. in Kelfield since 1954.[81]

In the 19th and 20th centuries there have usually been 9–12 farmers in both Stillingfleet and Kelfield and 2–4 in Moreby, and in addition in the 20th century 5–7 market-gardeners at Kelfield.[82] Of the

---

[51] Local information.
[52] V.C.H. Yorks. ii. 277.
[53] Pipe R. 1210 (P.R.S. N.S. xxvi), 40.
[54] Yorks. Fines, 1218–31, p. 16. Waltef derives from the Anglian personal name Waltheof: P.N.E.R. Yorks. 266.
[55] E.R.R.O., DDDA/19/1.
[56] Yorks. Fines, 1272–1300, p. 9.
[57] Cal. Pat. 1307–13, 356.
[58] Yorks. Deeds, ix, p. 64.
[59] E.R.R.O., DDPR, uncalendared; DDDA/19/1. Forms of the name Calfhay included Cawsay, Cawfa, Cawferr, and Calf Forth.
[60] E.R.R.O., DDBH/19/32; DDFA/15/7; DDPR, uncalendared.
[61] Ibid. DDPR, uncalendared.
[62] Ibid. DDFA/7/4.
[63] 19 Geo. II, c. 10 (Priv. Act); 20 Geo. II, c. 29 (Priv. Act).
[64] R.D.B., CQ/189/9.
[65] 46 Geo. III, c. 71 (Local and Personal, not printed); E.R.R.O., DDFA/4/31.
[66] V.C.H. Yorks. ii. 277.
[67] Yorks. Fines, 1218–31, p. 104.
[68] Cal. Inq. p.m. iii, p. 182.
[69] See p. 103.
[70] Cat. Anct. D. i, A 1360.
[71] E.R.R.O., DDBH/3/78.
[72] Cal. Proc. Chanc. Eliz. I, iii. 143.
[73] R.D.B., T/96/191.
[74] O.S. Map 6" (1851 and 1893 edns.).
[75] 1801 Crop Returns.
[76] B.I.H.R., PR. STIL. 19.
[77] Sheahan and Whellan, Hist. York & E.R. ii. 630.
[78] B.I.H.R., TA. 46S.
[79] Acreage Returns, 1905.
[80] [1st] Land Util. Surv. Map, sheets 27, 32; 2nd Land Util. Surv. Map, sheets 689 (SE 63–73), 698 (SE 44–54), 699 (SE 64–74).
[81] Ex inf. Forestry Com., York, 1972.
[82] Directories.

Kelfield farmers in 1851 3 held over 200 a., 4 held 100–199 a., and 7 held under 100 a.,[83] and of those at Stillingfleet c. 1857 one held over 200 a., 6 held 100–199 a., and 4 held under 100 a.[84] In 1937 5 farmers at Stillingfleet, 7 at Kelfield, and one at Moreby held 150 a. or more.[85]

The river Ouse has long played a significant part in the economy of the parish. In 1362 two stakes in the river at Kelfield belonging to the lord of the manor and the archbishop of York, and which presumably facilitated either fishing or navigation, were said to have existed from time immemorial.[86] Fishing rights belonged to Kelfield manor in 1598.[87] A fisherman was mentioned at Stillingfleet in 1728[88] and at Moreby in 1840.[89] In the early 19th century the lord of Kelfield manor enjoyed fishing rights in the river.[90] In 1698 the principal inhabitants of Stillingfleet were associated with a petition against the Aire and Calder Navigation Bill, which they feared would lead to the decline of river traffic on the Ouse.[91] In 1778 a landing-place in Stillingfleet lay near the mouth of the beck[92] and in 1812 another at the west end of Kelfield village.[93] In 1829 Henry Preston had a 'carriage boat' at Moreby.[94] Stillingfleet landing still existed in the mid 19th century, together with another south of Moreby Hall.[95]

Weavers were recorded at Moreby in 1394–5,[96] and a Brick Kiln close was mentioned at Moreby in 1728[97] and at Stillingfleet in 1811.[98] A brickworks may have stood to the west of Stillingfleet village, where in 1847 two ponds and a pump were situated.[99] By 1840 there were two brickworks in Kelfield, beside the river east of the village,[1] and in 1851 one of them employed seven men.[2] Brick-making apparently ceased there between 1901 and 1905,[3] and in 1972 ponds, outbuildings, and a row of four cottages marked the sites.

There was a windmill at Stillingfleet in 1244[4] and in the late 16th and early 17th centuries.[5] A miller was recorded in the township in 1823[6] and in 1847 a post mill stood south of the village beside the Escrick road.[7] Milling apparently ceased in the 1870s[8] and the mill was subsequently demolished. A mill may have also stood on Mill hill, south-east of Kelfield village.[9]

LOCAL GOVERNMENT. Court rolls for the manor of Stillingfleet survive for the years 1756–68 and 1772–6, call rolls for 1775–8, and surrenders and admissions for several years between 1758 and 1817.[10] The court mostly dealt with land transfers, agricultural offences, and petty misdemeanours, and the officers usually appointed were four bylawmen, two affeerors, and a constable. Court rolls for Kelfield manor in 1660–72 mention bylawmen, a constable, and a pinder.[11]

No parochial records before 1835 are known. Stillingfleet township joined York poor-law union and Kelfield Selby union in 1837.[12] Seven former parish poorhouses were sold in 1876.[13] Stillingfleet became part of Escrick rural district and Kelfield part of Riccall rural district in 1894. Both joined Derwent rural district in 1935[14] and the Selby district of North Yorkshire in 1974.

CHURCH. The existing fabric reveals that there was a church at Stillingfleet in the Norman period. It was first mentioned in 1244, when it was served by a vicar.[15] There was, however, also a sinecure rector, who in 1250, with archiepiscopal sanction, leased the rectory to a clerk.[16] In 1292 the vicarage was consolidated with the rectory,[17] but in 1318 the church was appropriated to St. Mary's hospital, Bootham, York, and a vicarage was ordained.[18] In 1951 the livings of Stillingfleet and Naburn were united.[19]

The patron in 1275 was Robert de Stutville[20] and in 1287 Gilbert de Luthe.[21] In 1311 Gilbert's son Nicholas quitclaimed the advowson to the dean of York,[22] who that year disputed it with Margaret, widow of Jordan Foliot.[23] The dean evidently established his right and in 1318 his successor granted the advowson to the master of St. Mary's hospital, Bootham, which he had founded.[24] It was held by the master until 1557, when it apparently passed with the rectory to the chapter of York.[25] Since 1951 the chapter and the archbishop of York, as patron of Naburn, have presented alternately.[26]

The vicarage was valued at £9 7s. 6d. net in 1535.[27] It was worth £20 in 1650.[28] In 1652 an augmentation of £50 a year was ordered to be paid out of North Cave rectory.[29] The augmentation, if it was ever paid, evidently lapsed at the Restoration. Before 1716 the income from £60 was given by Joseph Stillington to augment the benefice, and from 1716 until at least 1849 interest of £3 a year was paid to the vicar.[30] In 1734 the living was further aug-

[83] H.O. 107/2351.
[84] E.R.R.O., DDFA/41/6.
[85] Kelly's Dir. N. & E.R. Yorks. (1937), 536.
[86] Public Works in Med. Law, ii (Selden Soc. xl), 294.
[87] E.R.R.O., DDPR, uncalendared.
[88] B.I.H.R., PR. STIL. 4.
[89] White, Dir. E. & N.R. Yorks. (1840), 338.
[90] E.R.R.O., DDFA/4/34.
[91] Ho. of Lords Papers, 1697–9 (N.S. iii, in continuation of Hist. MSS. Com.), 211.
[92] E.R.R.O., DDFA/15/91.
[93] R.D.B., CQ/189/9.
[94] York Herald, 26 Sept. 1829.
[95] O.S. Map 6" (1851 edn.).
[96] V.C.H. Yorks. ii. 409.
[97] R.D.B., N/153/336.
[98] E.R.R.O., DDFA/15/75.
[99] O.S. Map 6" (1851 edn.).
[1] Ibid.; White, Dir. E. & N.R. Yorks. (1840), 338.
[2] H.O. 107/2351.
[3] Kelly's Dir. N. & E.R. Yorks. (1901), 564; (1905), 584.
[4] Drake, Eboracum, App. p. lxv.
[5] Yorks. Fines, ii. 104; 1603–14, 156.
[6] Baines, Hist. Yorks. ii. 392.
[7] O.S. Map 6" (1851 edn.).
[8] Directories.
[9] O.S. Map 6" (1851 and 1958 edns.).
[10] E.R.R.O., DDFA/15/27–30, 43, 48.
[11] Ibid. DDPR, uncalendared.
[12] 3rd Rep. Poor Law Com. 171, 178.
[13] E.R.R.O., DDFA/15/6.
[14] Census.
[15] Drake, Eboracum, App. p. lxiv.
[16] Reg. Gray, pp. 265, 270.
[17] Reg. Romeyn, i, pp. 172–3.
[18] Cal. Pat. 1317–21, 259–60.
[19] York Dioc. Regy., Order in Council 706.
[20] Reg. Giffard, p. 253.
[21] Reg. Romeyn, i, pp. 63–4.
[22] Yorks. Fines, 1300–14, p. 89.
[23] Reg. Greenfield, iii, p. 66.
[24] C.P. 25(1)/270/92 no. 14.
[25] V.C.H. Yorks. i. 422.
[26] Inst. Bks.; Crockford.
[27] Valor Eccl. v. 101.
[28] C 94/3 f. 77.
[29] Cal. Cttee. for Compounding, iii. 2040.
[30] B.I.H.R., TER. N. Stillingfleet 1716–1849.

mented with £200 from Queen Anne's Bounty.[31] In 1829–31 the average net income was £412 a year,[32] in 1884 £447, and in 1914 £328.[33]

Tithes provided most of the income in 1535.[34] Their payment was disputed in the 1560s, 1590s, 1602, and 1697.[35] At the inclosure of Stillingfleet in 1756 the vicar was awarded 61 a. for tithes.[36] In 1838 the vicarial tithes of Kelfield township were commuted for a rent-charge of £143,[37] and in 1842 those of Moreby for £48.[38]

At the ordination of the vicarage in 1330 the vicar was given ½ bovate of glebe at Stillingfleet.[39] In the late 17th and early 18th centuries it was said to comprise 8 a., and the vicar also had an acre of meadow land.[40] In 1734 15 a. of common land in Stillingfleet and 18 a. in Kelfield were added to the living by the parish and a year later Bounty money was used to buy 11 a. in Osgodby and 2 a. in Cliffe (both in Hemingbrough).[41] At the inclosure of 1756 the vicar was awarded 14 a. for glebe.[42] In 1920 the glebe, comprising 111 a., was sold.[43]

The house in which the vicars had lived before 1292 was assigned to the vicar in 1330.[44] A vicarage house was mentioned in 1535 and in the late 17th century.[45] In 1764 it was of brick and tile and consisted of three main ground-floor rooms, together with kitchens, and six upper rooms.[46] In 1768 it was uninhabitable, but it was repaired in 1770 and a new wing built, consisting of three rooms on the ground floor and three upstairs.[47] The house, which adjoined the church on the north, was rebuilt in the 1950s.[48] The cost of the new house was partly met from a trust fund of £10,000 set up in 1947 by Sir Owen W. Wightman for that purpose and to augment the incumbent's stipend.[49]

About 1336 Nicholas of Moreby built a chantry chapel dedicated to St. Mary in Stillingfleet church and gave property in the parish and elsewhere to support the priest, who was to reside continuously and assist the vicar.[50] In 1535 the chantry-priest had a house and ½ bovate of land worth about £4 a year.[51] In 1549 the former chantry property was granted to Thomas Gargrave and William Adam.[52] The owners of the former Acklam estate at Moreby were responsible for repairing the chantry chapel until at least 1688.[53]

Probably in the 14th century Henry of Acklam founded a chantry at the altar of St. Anne in Stillingfleet church and endowed a priest to celebrate there. In 1402 the chantry was united with one at Naburn and the priest was ordered to celebrate weekly at Naburn and only on great festivals at Stillingfleet.[54] Before 1244 1d. a year was given for a light in the church.[55] Property in Stillingfleet and Acaster Selby given for two lights was granted in 1566 to Francis Barker and Thomas Blackway.[56]

In 1527, in addition to the vicar and a chantry-priest, four parochial chaplains were recorded, each receiving between £2 and £5 6s. 8d.[57]

In 1291 the rector also held the living of Langton (Lincs.) and a canonry in Southwell minster.[58] John of Sandale, rector in 1313, held eleven other benefices and the treasurership of Lichfield cathedral.[59] In 1662 the vicar Thomas Gilbert, a Puritan, was ejected.[60] In 1757 the vicar was also schoolmaster at Acaster Selby,[61] in 1764 he was also curate of Barlby,[62] and in 1835 he was a canon of St. George's chapel, Windsor.[63] An assistant curate was employed in the early 17th century and in the 1860s and early 1870s.[64]

Two services were held each Sunday in 1743 and Holy Communion was celebrated five times a year. About 100 people were said to receive at Easter.[65] By 1764 communion was celebrated four times a year, but by 1865 monthly celebrations were held with 15–30 communicants. In 1884 there were 20 celebrations a year and in 1914 they were fortnightly. A service was held each Sunday in Kelfield school from at least 1865 until 1914.[66] In 1972 a weekly service was held at the church.

Matthew Johnson, by will dated 1849, left £50, from the interest on which 15s. was to be given to the vicar for an annual sermon on Ascension Day to the Kelfield Sunday school children, 5s. to the schoolmaster for taking them to church, and the rest to the children who attended church that day.[67] By a Scheme of 1953 the charity was applied to Stillingfleet Sunday school, that at Kelfield having closed. The endowment then amounted to £56 stock and £6 cash.[68] In 1974, when the income was £3, no sermon was given because the children attended a service for the deanery at Riccall on that day.[69]

The church of *ST. HELEN* is of ashlar and consists of chancel with north chapel, nave with north aisle and south chapel, and west tower.[70] The

---

[31] Hodgson, *Q.A.B.* 454.
[32] *Rep. Com. Eccl. Revenues*, 968.
[33] B.I.H.R., Bp. V. 1884/Ret.; Bp. V. 1914/Ret.
[34] *Valor Eccl.* v. 101.
[35] B.I.H.R., CP. G. 976, 1052, 1081, 2992, 3031; CP. H. 101, 4504.
[36] R.D.B., Y/49/15.
[37] B.I.H.R., PR. STIL. 18–19.   [38] Ibid. TA. 46S.
[39] Minster Libr., Torre MS., 'Cleveland & E.R.', p. 391.
[40] B.I.H.R., TER. N. Stillingfleet n.d. (17th cent.), 1716, 1727.
[41] Ibid. 1743, 1760.
[42] R.D.B., Y/49/15.
[43] B.I.H.R., PR. STIL. 20 (10).
[44] Minster Libr., Torre MS., 'Cleveland & E.R.', p. 391.
[45] B.I.H.R., TER. N. Stillingfleet n.d. (17th cent.); *Valor Eccl.* v. 101.
[46] B.I.H.R., TER. N. Stillingfleet 1764.
[47] Ibid. 1777; PR. STIL. 8.
[48] Ex inf. the vicar, 1975.
[49] Char. Com. files.
[50] *Cal. Pat.* 1330–4, 372; *Yorks. Chantry Surv.* i (Sur. Soc. xci), 85.
[51] *Valor Eccl.* v. 101; *Yorks. Chantry Surv.* i. 85.
[52] *Cal. Pat.* 1548–9, 198.
[53] B.I.H.R., CP. H. 4441.
[54] Minster Libr., Torre MS., 'Cleveland & E.R.', p. 393; *Y.A.J.* xxxiii. 283; see above p. 81. Two other chantries were wrongly ascribed to Stillingfleet in *Yorks. Chantry Surv.* ii (Sur. Soc. xcii), 378–9; they were, in fact, in Rotherham church (Yorks. W.R.): E 301/64/8.
[55] Drake, *Hist. York*, App. p. lxv.
[56] *Cal. Pat.* 1563–6, p. 476.
[57] *Y.A.J.* xxi. 248.
[58] *Cal. Papal Regs.* i. 535.   [59] Ibid. ii. 119.
[60] *Calamy Revised*, ed. A. G. Matthews, 481.
[61] B.I.H.R., Fac. Bk. i, p. 256.
[62] Ibid. Bp. V. 1764/Ret. 56.
[63] *Rep. Com. Eccl. Revenues*, 968.
[64] B.I.H.R., V. 1865/Ret. 516; V. 1868/Ret. 470; V. 1871/Ret. 476; *V.C.H. Yorks.* i. 454.
[65] *Herring's Visit.* iii. 91.
[66] B.I.H.R., V. 1865/Ret. 516; V. 1868/Ret. 470; V. 1871/Ret. 476; V. 1877/Ret.; Bp. V. 1884/Ret.; Bp. V. 1894/Ret.; Bp. V. 1914/Ret.
[67] Bulmer, *Dir. E. Yorks.* (1892), 716.
[68] Char. Com. files.
[69] Ex inf. the vicar, 1975.
[70] The church is described in detail in Assoc. Archit. Soc. *Rep. & Papers*, xiv. 73–9.

nave and chancel appear to be the full extent of the church in the later 12th century, when for its size it was notably well decorated with a carved string-course and a south doorway of five orders.[71] The door is decorated with ironwork which is stylistically a century earlier.[72] The north doorway was reset in the earlier 13th century when the north aisle and chapel were built. The former has an arcade of three bays, the latter one of two bays, and they may have been undivided. The tower was added at about the same time. New windows were inserted in the south and east walls of the chancel in the earlier 14th century, and the south chapel appears to be that to St. Mary which was built c. 1336.[73] The chapel has an arcade of two bays to the nave, and there may also at this time have been a porch in the angle between the chapel and the south doorway.

Bequests of about £50 were made for work in the church in 1520[74] and this may be the date of a number of alterations, including the play of new windows in the north aisle, the removal of the chancel arch, and the addition of the upper part of the tower. The chancel was in decay in 1567[75] and some repairs may have been carried out in the later 17th century.[76] The nave was reroofed in 1828.[77] In 1864 the vicar reported that restoration was needed,[78] and in 1877 a major restoration was carried out by C. H. Fowler. The north and east walls of the chancel aisle were rebuilt, a new Decorated-style east window inserted, and the windows in the south wall of the chancel restored. The south doorway was repaired, the gable above it rebuilt, and two two-light windows inserted over it. A doorway was inserted in the south wall of the Moreby chapel and an arch between the chancel and nave aisles and a new chancel arch built. A gallery was removed and the church reroofed and repewed.[79]

In the Moreby chapel is a knight's effigy, bearing on a shield the arms of Moreby. It apparently represents Robert of Moreby (d. c. 1337).[80] Above it is an alabaster and marble wall monument with kneeling figures of two men and two women, erected in 1613 in memory of John Acklam (d. 1611). A window in the chancel aisle has coloured glass containing the arms of Stillington impaling Bigod and an inscription recording that the glass was inserted in 1520 and renewed in 1698 by Henry Gyles of York.[81] There is a floor slab with brass inscriptions to Cuthbert Harrison of Acaster Selby (d. 1699) and his wife Lennox (d. 1658).

The font was given by Elizabeth Dure in 1832. The Moreby chapel contains two wooden screens, said to have been made from 17th-century pews and communion rails in 1877.[82]

There were three bells in 1552 and 1764[83] and there are three still: (i) 1626; (ii) 1747, E. Seller of York; (iii) 1626.[84] The plate includes two silver cups, one made in London in 1639 and the other in Newcastle by John Langlands in 1770 and given by Grace Lawson in that year. There are two silver patens, one made in York by John Plummer in 1657 and given by Ursula Gill in 1726, and the other made in London in 1759, probably by Ebenezer Coker, and given by Grace Lawson in 1770. A flagon was made in London in 1787 and given by the vicar George Hustler in 1874.[85] The marriage and burial registers begin in 1598 and those of baptisms in 1603. They are complete except for burials in 1623–52 and all entries in 1697–9.[86]

The churchyard contains a monument to eleven members of the church choir who were drowned in 1833 when crossing the river from Acaster Selby. An additional burial ground opposite the church was consecrated in 1917.[87]

The private oratory in Kelfield manor-house[88] had apparently become known as Kelfield chapel and was used by all the inhabitants by the earlier 16th century. In the reign of Henry VIII the vicar used the income from ground called Vicar ing to provide a priest to celebrate there weekly.[89] In 1572 it was reported that the 'chapel' priest had also been supported by contributions from all the inhabitants.[90] A room in the possibly medieval Kelfield Hall was known as the 'chapel' as late as 1805.[91]

NONCONFORMITY. In 1569 the vicar of Stillingfleet was found to be distributing seditious and papist literature.[92] Two families, the Acklams of Moreby and the Stillingtons of Kelfield, were Roman Catholics in the later 16th and early 17th centuries and six Roman Catholics were reported in 1676 and one in 1743.[93] There was one family and a single Quaker in the parish in 1743.[94]

Methodism was introduced into the parish in 1769[95] and houses were registered for dissenting worship in 1774, 1787, 1797, 1809, 1811, and 1812, and a barn in 1813.[96] A room known as the 'chapel' in Kelfield Hall was registered in 1805.[97] The first chapel in the parish was built by the Wesleyan Methodists in Kelfield in 1815.[98] A chapel at Stillingfleet was registered in 1819[99] and in 1884 the Wesleyans had 18 members there.[1] Both chapels were still used in 1972. The Primitive Methodists built a chapel at Kelfield in 1852[2] but worship

[71] See plate facing p. 177.
[72] It is pre-Conquest in style, if not in date: Y.A.J. xxi. 254–5; Pevsner, Yorks. E.R. 16, 350–1.
[73] See p. 110.
[74] W. K. Jordan, Chars. of Rural Eng. 1480–1660, 391. The date also appears in a window in the north chancel aisle.
[75] B.I.H.R., V. 1567–8/CB. 2.
[76] Assoc. Archit. Soc. Rep. & Papers, xiv. 73.
[77] White, Dir. E. & N.R. Yorks. (1840), 337.
[78] B.I.H.R., V. 1865/Ret. 516.
[79] Ibid. Fac. 1877/13; Assoc. Archit. Soc. Rep. & Papers, xiv. 73–9.
[80] Y.A.J. xxix. 52.
[81] Ibid. xxvii. 161.
[82] Ibid. xxiv. 168.
[83] B.I.H.R., TER. N. Stillingfleet 1764; Inventories of Ch. Goods, 83.
[84] Boulter, 'Ch. Bells', 32.
[85] Yorks. Ch. Plate, i. 319–20.
[86] B.I.H.R., PR. STIL. 1–13. The later registers remain in the church.
[87] York Dioc. Regy. Consecration deeds.
[88] See p. 105.
[89] E 134/14 Eliz. I Hil./1.
[90] E 134/14 & 15 Eliz. I Mich./11.
[91] See p. 105 and below.
[92] Aveling, Post Reformation Catholicism, 13.
[93] Bodl. MS. Tanner 150, ff. 27 sqq.; Aveling, Post Reformation Catholicism, 64; Herring's Visit. iii. 91.
[94] Herring's Visit. iii. 91.
[95] J. Lyth, Glimpses of Early Methodism in York and Dist. 297.
[96] G.R.O. Worship Returns, Vol. v, nos. 404, 692, 1352, 2280, 2531, 2671, 2761.
[97] B.I.H.R., Fac. Bk. iii, p. 388.
[98] G.R.O. Worship Returns, Vol. v, no. 2916.
[99] Ibid. no. 3312.
[1] Lyth, op. cit. 297.
[2] Sheahan and Whellan, Hist. York. & E.R. ii. 630.

had ceased there by 1894.[3] It was used as a storeroom in 1972.

EDUCATION. Children from Stillingfleet and Kelfield townships may have been taught at Acaster Selby grammar school from the 15th to the 18th centuries.[4]

In 1743 the vicar reported that £1 6s. a year had been left for teaching four children in Kelfield.[5] The donor was later said to be 'the Revd. Mr. Turey'.[6] Mary Stillingfleet, by will dated 1802, bequeathed £400, the interest to be used for teaching Kelfield children,[7] and in 1819 20 poor children were taught free and a further 20–30 paid fees.[8] The school's annual income was over £21 in 1823,[9] and in 1835 there were 30 pupils.[10]

A new school was built in 1849[11] and in 1871 there were 46 pupils.[12] In 1880, when the average attendance was 38, most of the income came from voluntary contributions and school pence.[13] The school first received an annual government grant in 1881.[14] From 1906 until 1936 attendance varied only between 41 and 65, but in 1937 the senior children were transferred to Riccall and in 1938 there were only 26 pupils.[15] In 1951 the school was closed and the remaining pupils transferred to Riccall.[16] The school had been converted to a house by 1972.

There was a school at Stillingfleet in 1819 with 40–50 pupils, supported by subscriptions and fees.[17] In 1835 there were 70 pupils, 16 of whom were supported by subscription, 12 by assessment, and the rest by fees.[18] By 1840 the school, which still stands in the south of the village, was united with the National Society.[19] A new school was built in the centre of Stillingfleet in 1855 and in 1858 most of its income came from voluntary contributions.[20] An annual government grant was first received in 1859.[21] In 1871 there were 41 pupils[22] and in 1906 57. Thereafter until 1938 attendance varied between 29 and 60.[23] The village hall was used as a classroom in the 1950s.[24] In 1961 the senior children were transferred to Barlby secondary school[25] and in 1963 the school was closed and the remaining pupils transferred to Riccall.[26] Both buildings survived in 1972, the later one converted to a house.

In 1865 the vicar reported having taken evening classes for several years, but that attendance was irregular.[27]

CHARITIES FOR THE POOR. Elizabeth Stott, by deed dated 1693, gave 2 a. in Stillingfleet, the rent of which was to be distributed annually in bread to the poor of the township, and ½ a. in Kelfield, the rent of which was to be equally divided between the poor of Stillingfleet and Kelfield.[28] Before 1735 Francis Wilkinson gave £8 and William Cowling £5 to the poor of Stillingfleet. In that year it was agreed that the three bequests, together with 5s. a year left by Eleanor Wray at an unknown date, should be distributed jointly. Bread worth 10d. was to be given each week and the vicar was to contribute about 15s. to make up the cost. In 1766 it was agreed that the deficiency should be met from church offerings.[29] In 1823 £4 rent from the 2 a. given by Elizabeth Stott was still distributed weekly in bread, but 16s. from the ½ a. was distributed in cash. It was reported that Wilkinson's and Cowling's gifts had apparently been lost c. 1784. The poor of Kelfield benefited in 1823 from land worth 4s. a year given by a Mr. Newstead.[30]

Frances, dowager Lady Howard, by will proved in 1716, bequeathed money to provide coal for Escrick and other villages, including Stillingfleet.[31] After 1862 Stillingfleet received ¼ of the income.

By a Scheme of 1971 it was provided that the income from the Poor's Land and Howard's charity should be used jointly for payments to the needy. The endowments were then 2 a. for the Poor's Land and £79 stock for Howard's charity. In 1972–3 the joint income was £6; none was distributed and there was a cash balance of £23.[32]

Stillingfleet benefited from the charity of John Hodgson for parishes in York poor-law union.[33]

THORGANBY

THE COMPACT parish of Thorganby lies about 8 miles south-east of York on the west bank of the Derwent, and the houses of the village and its hamlet of West Cottingwith are strung out along the dry margin of the flood-plain of the river.[1] Thorganby was probably a Scandinavian settlement but West Cottingwith was Anglian.[2] The parish covers 2,938 a., of which West Cottingwith accounts for 1,494 a.[3] A vill called Crossum was mentioned, usually in association with West Cottingwith, from

---

[3] B.I.H.R., Bp. V. 1894/Ret.
[4] V.C.H. Yorks. i. 452–4.
[5] Herring's Visit. iii. 91.
[6] 10th Rep. Com. Char. 673.
[7] Ibid. 673–4.
[8] Educ. of Poor Digest, 1094.
[9] Baines, Hist. Yorks. ii. 359.
[10] Educ. Enquiry Abstract, 1096.
[11] Ed. 7/135 no. 89.
[12] Returns relating to Elem. Educ. 790.
[13] Ed. 7/135 no. 89.
[14] Rep. of Educ. Cttee. of Council, 1881–2 [C. 3312–I], p. 778, H.C. (1882), xxiii.
[15] Bd. of Educ. List 21 (H.M.S.O.); E.R. Educ. Cttee. Mins. 1937–8, 179.
[16] E.R. Educ. Cttee. Mins. 1950–1, 208.
[17] Educ. of Poor Digest, 1094.
[18] Educ. Enquiry Abstract, 1096.
[19] White, Dir. E. & N.R. Yorks. (1840), 337; O.S. Map 6" (1851 edn.).
[20] Ed. 7/135 no. 173.
[21] Rep. of Educ. Cttee. of Council, 1859–60 [2681], p. 793, H.C. (1860), liv.
[22] Returns relating to Elem. Educ. 792.
[23] List 21.
[24] E.R. Educ. Cttee. Mins. 1951–2, 162; 1956–7, 16.
[25] Ibid. 1960–1, 98.
[26] Ibid. 1962–3, 4, 194; 1963–4, 158.
[27] B.I.H.R., V. 1865/Ret. 516.
[28] 10th Rep. Com. Char. 673.
[29] B.I.H.R., PR. STIL. 5.
[30] 10th Rep. Com. Char. 673.
[31] See p. 28.
[32] Char. Com. files.
[33] See p. 12.
[1] This article was written in 1972.
[2] P.N.E.R. Yorks. (E.P.N.S.), 263–4.
[3] O.S. Map 6", Yorks. (1854 edn.). The whole of Thorganby and part of West Cottingwith are covered by sheet 207 and the remainder of the parish by sheet 192.

STILLINGFLEET: the church, bridge, and Town greens

ALLERTHORPE: the village street

THICKET PRIORY
One of Edward Blore's design drawings

HESLINGTON HALL
The north-east front before restoration

the late 12th to the early 14th century, and, as 'Gressone', in 1452.[4] Its location is not known but it may have given its name to Crossholmes close, mentioned in 1671.[5]

Thorganby lies just to the south of the Escrick moraine and is mostly composed of outwash sand and clay.[6] Much of the parish, including the area west of the villages where the small open fields were situated, lies at a height of only 25 ft. to 50 ft. above sea-level. Around the margins of the parish, particularly in the north and near the Derwent in the east, large areas are lower still. Ings on the riverside alluvium and commons in the west of the parish formerly occupied much of the lower ground. Most of the eastern parish boundary is formed by the Derwent; a small part of the parish projects beyond the present course of the river as far as the old course further east. Elsewhere the parish and township boundaries mostly follow dikes, notably Keldcarrs drain on the north and west.

Flooding from the river and the dikes has always threatened the lower parts of the parish. Failure to repair and cleanse dikes allegedly caused flooding at Thorganby in 1343[7] and on the road to Escrick in 1371.[8] The parish maintained the dikes in the 18th and 19th centuries, repairing banks and bridges, including Seam bridge in the village street, and regulating sluices which let drainage water into the river.[9] At inclosure in 1817 eight drains were laid out, to be cleansed twice a year by the constables at the expense of landowners and occupiers.[10]

The road on which the two villages lie runs northwards to Wheldrake and southwards to Skipwith. From West Cottingwith village Ings Lane led to the riverside meadows and Ferry Lane down to a crossing place providing a link with East Cottingwith. The ferry was mentioned in 1706[11] and remained in use until the 1950s.[12] North Hills bridge, leading to Thorganby's extension beyond the new course of the river, was first mentioned in 1691.[13] A wooden drawbridge was replaced by a fixed bridge c. 1960.[14] Several minor roads lead into the fields, one of them, now Southmoor Road, formerly continuing to Escrick. The Derwent Valley Light Railway, established in 1912, ran across the parish and there were two stations, about ¾ mile west of the villages.[15] The line was closed for passenger traffic in 1926[16] and for goods in 1965,[17] and the track has been lifted.

The houses and cottages of both villages are all of brick and date mostly from the late 18th and 19th centuries. There are few 20th-century buildings apart from six council houses. The hall and the church stand in the centre of Thorganby. In the south of the village is Hedley House, an ornate building of red brick with stone quoins and dressings, dated 1845. Three or four alehouses were licensed in the parish in the 1750s and two later.[18] The Hare and Hounds inn stood in the centre of Thorganby village in the 1840s and 1850s but had closed by 1872.[19] A building for a village institute was given by Sir John Dunnington-Jefferson, Bt., in 1921 and used until c. 1970, when farm buildings were converted into a village hall by Mr. J. B. Eastwood.[20]

West Cottingwith is larger and more densely built-up, but it has few buildings of note. The Old Hall stands in Ings Lane. The Ferry House or Ferry Boat inn existed by 1823 and stands near the river.[21] The Smith's Arms, in the village street, was so-called in the 1840s and 1850s, but had become the Jefferson's Arms by 1872.[22]

The isolated farm-houses in the parish apparently all date from after the inclosure of 1817, although there were already five outlying houses in Thorganby township in that year, four of them on the sites of present farms.[23] Common, Grange East, and Woodfield Farms all have wheelhouses. Thicket Priory, with its extensive parkland, occupies the north-eastern corner of the parish.[24] The remains of a small motte, known as Giant Hill, stand near the river in the south of the parish, opposite Ellerton village.

In 1829 48 inhabitants formed the Thorganby with West Cottingwith Association for the Prosecution of Felons. It existed until 1843, when it was merged with a similar York-based society.[25]

In 1379 there were 88 poll-tax payers in Thorganby and West Cottingwith.[26] In 1672 76 households were recorded in the hearth-tax assessment, of which 26 were discharged from paying. Of the 20 chargeable households in Thorganby 14 had one hearth, 3 had 2, and the others had 3, 4, and 11 hearths, the last presumably the manor-house. Thirty households paid the tax in West Cottingwith, of which 20 had one hearth, 8 had 2, and the others had 3 and 10 hearths, the last again the manor-house.[27] There were 65 families in the parish in 1743[28] and about 60 in 1764.[29] During the 19th century the population fluctuated. It rose from 201 in 1801 to 403 in 1811, but fell to 342 in 1831, rose to 407 in 1861, and fell to 345 by 1901.[30] There were 358 inhabitants in 1931, 278 in both 1951 and 1961, and 237 in 1971.[31]

MANORS AND OTHER ESTATES. In 1086 there was one estate of 3 carucates at Thorganby held by Ralph Paynel. It had been held before the

---

[4] E 179/202/127; *E.Y.C.* ii, pp. 423–4; J. Burton, *Mon. Ebor.* 260; *Lay Subsidy, 30 Edw. I* (Y.A.S. Rec. Ser. xxi), 104.
[5] E.R.R.O., DDJ/14/37.
[6] Geol. Surv. Map 1″, solid and drift, sheet 71 (1973 edn.).
[7] *Cal. Inq. Misc.* i, pp. 454–5.
[8] *Public Works in Med. Law,* ii (Selden Soc. xl), 241.
[9] E.R.R.O., PR. 2–3, 10–12.
[10] Ibid. DDJ/14/395.
[11] Ibid. DDJ/14/353.
[12] Local information.
[13] E.R.R.O., DDJ/14/57.
[14] Ex inf. N. Area Manager, Yorks. Water Authority, York, 1974. For illus. of the former bridge see Derwent R.D.C., *Official Guide* (n.d., 2nd edn.).
[15] See plate facing p. 161.
[16] *V.C.H. City of York,* 479.
[17] K. Hoole, *Regional Hist. of Rlys of Gt. Brit.* iv (*The North-East*), 63.
[18] E.R.R.O., QDT/2/15.
[19] White, *Dir. E. & N.R. Yorks.* (1840), 339; *Kelly's Dir. N. & E.R. Yorks.* (1872), 552; O.S. Map 6″ (1854 edn.).
[20] Char. Com. files.
[21] E.R.R.O., DDJ/14/395; Baines, *Hist. Yorks.* (1823), ii. 394, and later directories; O.S. Map 6″ (1854 edn.).
[22] White, *Dir. E. & N.R. Yorks.* (1840), 339; *Kelly's Dir. N. & E.R. Yorks.* (1872), 552; O.S. Map 6″ (1854 edn.).
[23] E.R.R.O., DDJ/14/395.
[24] See p. 115.
[25] E.R.R.O., DDJ/14/34–5.
[26] *T.E.R.A.S.* xv. 65–6.
[27] E 179/205/504.
[28] *Herring's Visit.* iii. 167.
[29] B.I.H.R., Bp. V. 1764/Ret. 74.
[30] *V.C.H. Yorks.* iii. 498.
[31] *Census.*

Conquest by Merleswain.[32] The overlordship may have passed to William de Vescy by 1166[33] and in 1284–5 John de Vescy was overlord of all but 2 bovates.[34] By 1329, however, the overlordship had passed to Geoffrey Lutterell[35] and in 1346 18 bovates were held of the Lutterell fee.[36] Nothing more is known of the overlordship. A mesne lordship may have been held by Simon of Stonegrave in John's reign,[37] and in 1284–5 'the heirs of Stonegrave' were mesne lords. Another mesne lordship was held by the Playce family. In 1284–5 'the heirs of W. Playce' held an intermediate lordship between Vescy and Stonegrave,[38] and in 1329 it was held by William de Playce.[39] Neither of the mesne lordships has been traced further.

The demesne lord in 1228 may have been Robert de Meynell, who then claimed the advowson.[40] He was apparently succeeded by Hubert de Vaux. Hubert's daughter Maud married Thomas de Multon who, in the mid 13th century, granted THORGANBY manor to William de Breuse.[41] Richard de Breuse was in dispute over the manor in 1267–8[42] and held rights of free warren in Thorganby in 1275–6.[43] Thomas de Multon's widow Maud was nevertheless in possession of 22 bovates in 1284–5[44] and her son, another Thomas, died seised of the manor in 1295.[45] It may have been his son, also Thomas, who before 1309 enfeoffed Ralph of Maunby of the manor,[46] and in 1316 Ralph was returned as lord of the township.[47]

The manor passed to the Saltmarsh family in 1336 on the marriage of Ellen, daughter and heir of Thomas of Maunby, with Edward of Saltmarsh.[48] In 1346 the Saltmarshes held 14 bovates in Thorganby.[49] Edward Saltmarsh (d. 1482) was succeeded by his son John, and another Edward Saltmarsh (d. 1548) by his grandson Thomas. From Robert (d. 1603) son of Thomas Saltmarsh the manor passed to Robert's son Thomas,[50] and it was sold in 1616 by Philip Saltmarsh to Sir James Altham, William Austin, and others.[51] It was subsequently divided and in 1641–2 Arthur Annesley, later Viscount Valentia, bought half from Richard Vaughan, earl of Carbury, and half from Richard Taylor and John White.[52] It was held by the Annesleys[53] until Arthur Annesley sold it to Thomas Bradford in 1801, when it comprised 1,039 a.[54]

Bradford sold the manorial estate in separate lots between 1802 and 1810.[55] The largest holding, of 243 a., went in 1802 to John Dunnington,[56] whose family had held a small estate in Thorganby since, it is said, 1685.[57] The manorial rights and 69 a. went to Thomas Kendall in 1810[58] and he sold them in 1815 to John Dunnington,[59] who had taken the additional name Jefferson in 1812 on inheriting the property of a distant relative, Robert Jefferson (d. 1811).[60] The Dunnington-Jeffersons subsequently increased their holding in Thorganby,[61] and retained it until 1964, when Sir John Dunnington-Jefferson, Bt., sold it, then comprising 3,080 a. in Thorganby and West Cottingwith, to Mr. J. B. Eastwood,[62] who was the owner in 1972.

The Saltmarsh family had a manor-house at Thorganby in the mid 16th century[63] and in 1672 a house there had eleven hearths.[64] Both the Old Hall in West Cottingwith and Thorganby Hall opposite the church existed in 1772.[65] The Old Hall, a square two-storeyed brick building of early-18th-century date, may have passed to John Dunnington, the owner in 1817, when he inherited the Jefferson estates in 1812.[66] Thorganby Hall was probably the manor-house of the Annesleys and it may have been the 'hall house' sold in 1802 by Thomas Bradford to John Dunnington,[67] whose son owned it in 1817.[68] The present house was built in 1822, a date which appears on both the north and south fronts, together with the arms of the Dunnington and Jefferson families. The hall, built of grey brick, has a front of three bays, the central one surmounted by a pediment. Outbuildings, which belonged to the earlier house, include stables and a coach-house incorporating a dovecot,[69] and among the farm buildings are a large barn[70] and a wheelhouse. After the 1840s, when Thicket Priory became the manor-house,[71] the hall was usually let to private residents or occupied by the estate steward.[72]

The largest estate at West Cottingwith in 1086, of 2¾ carucates, was soke of Aughton manor and was held by Niel Fossard of the count of Mortain.[73] It apparently passed to the Mauleys on the marriage of Isabel of Turnham, granddaughter of Joan Fossard and Robert of Turnham, with Peter de Mauley in the early 13th century;[74] in 1284–5 the overlordship of the estate was held by another Peter de Mauley.[75] The Mauley overlordship was last mentioned in 1319.[76] A mesne lordship was held throughout the

---

[32] *V.C.H. Yorks.* ii. 270.
[33] *E.Y.C.* vi, p. 142.
[34] *Feud. Aids*, vi. 35.
[35] *Cal. Inq. Misc.* ii, pp. 261–2.
[36] *Feud. Aids*, vi. 223.
[37] *E.Y.C.* vi, p. 119.
[38] *Feud. Aids*, vi. 35.
[39] *Cal. Inq. Misc.* ii, pp. 261–2.
[40] See p. 118.
[41] C.P. 40/55 rot. 19; G. Wrottesley, *Ped. from Plea Rolls, 1200–1500*, 537.
[42] *E.Y.C.* vi, p. 119.
[43] *Rot. Hund.* (Rec. Com.), i. 122.
[44] *Feud. Aids*, vi. 35; *E.Y.C.* vi, p. 142.
[45] *Yorks. Inq.* iii, p. 8.
[46] *Cal. Pat.* 1307–13, 173.
[47] *Feud. Aids*, vi. 173.
[48] *Yorks. Fines, 1327–47*, p. 96; *T.E.R.A.S.* xx. 31.
[49] *Feud. Aids*, vi. 223.
[50] e.g. C 140/561 no. 9; C 142/86 no. 49; C 142/284 no. 57; *Test. Ebor.* vi, p. 265.
[51] *Yorks. Fines, 1614–25*, 53.
[52] C.P. 25(2)/525/18 Chas. I East. no. 67; C.P. 25(2)/528/16 Chas. I Hil. no. 3.
[53] E.R.R.O., DDFA/5/118; /20/2; DDJ/30/33; *Complete Peerage*, s.v. Valentia.
[54] E.R.R.O., DDJ/14/241–2.
[55] R.D.B., CD/470/729; /587/869; /588/870; CE/296/434; /312/460; /597/903.
[56] Ibid. CD/521/796.
[57] Burke, *Peerage* (1970), 1442.
[58] R.D.B., CR/485/666.
[59] Ibid. CZ/209/322.
[60] E.R.R.O., unsorted MS.; Burke, *Peerage* (1970), 1442; see below p. 115.
[61] E.R.R.O., DDJ/14/260, 264; R.D.B., DB/243/367; FW/189/188.
[62] R.D.B., 1349/244/220; E.R.R.O., DDX/225/12.
[63] *Test. Ebor.* vi, p. 265.
[64] E 179/205/504.
[65] T. Jefferys, *Map of Yorks.*
[66] E.R.R.O., DDJ/14/395; see above.
[67] R.D.B., CD/521/796.
[68] E.R.R.O., DDJ/14/395.
[69] See plate facing p. 64.
[70] Described as a tithe-barn in 1850: O.S. Map 6" (1854 edn.).
[71] See p. 115.
[72] Directories.
[73] *V.C.H. Yorks.* ii. 224. West Cottingwith is there erroneously said to be in Aughton parish and East Cottingwith in Thorganby.
[74] *E.Y.C.* ii, pp. 327–8.
[75] *Feud. Aids*, vi. 33.
[76] *Monastic Notes*, ii (Y.A.S. Rec. Ser. lxxxi), 44–5.

13th century by the Hay family,[77] and this was also last mentioned in 1319.[78]

Early demesne tenants of this fee were Roger son of Roger, who founded Thicket priory for Benedictine nuns and endowed it with 4 bovates in Richard I's reign, and Thomas son of Roger, who before 1190 granted a further 4 bovates to the priory. Other gifts to Thicket of a bovate by Picot and of an assart of waste by Geoffrey of Fitling and Hugh of Bolton, together with a toft in Crossum, were confirmed in 1204.[79] In 1231 and 1284–5 the priory held 10 bovates of the Mauley fee.[80] Other land was granted to the priory from the Vescy fee in 1319,[81] and in 1535 Thicket's estate in West Cottingwith was worth nearly £5. It also had an estate worth £1 in Thorganby.[82] At its dissolution the priory included a church, chapter-house, cloisters, hall, two parlours, bakehouse, buttery, kitchen, and various chambers.[83]

The priory's former estate in Thorganby and West Cottingwith was let by the Crown to William Wytham in 1540,[84] before being granted in fee to John Aske in 1542. At the same time Aske acquired the former Ellerton priory estate.[85] In 1596 another John Aske sold his West Cottingwith estate to John Robinson.[86] Before his death in 1601 Robinson sold the estate to his younger sons Arthur and Henry.[87] The latter sold it in 1622, part to Robert Ducy and the rest to Humphrey Robinson,[88] who was the son of John, the eldest son of John Robinson (d. 1601).[89] Humphrey (d. 1626) was succeeded by his son Richard[90] and Sir William Ducy sold his father's part to Richard in 1659.[91] The estate was conveyed to Richard's son, another Richard, the same year[92] and was held by Humphrey Robinson in the 1680s and in 1718.[93] It was sometimes described as a grange.[94] In 1752 Nicholas Robinson (d. 1754) left it to his daughter Sarah, who had married Henry Waite in 1752,[95] and Waite adopted the additional surname Robinson. In 1760 he sold WEST COTTINGWITH manor and about 450 a. to Emanuel Jefferson.[96] In 1801 the Revd. Nicholas Waite Robinson sold 23 a. to Robert Jefferson[97] and in 1803 the remainder of the estate, comprising 220 a., to Joseph Dunnington.[98] In 1812 John Dunnington succeeded to the Jefferson estates and the land subsequently descended with Thorganby manor.[99]

A manor-house may have been built by the Robinsons on the site of the former Thicket priory in the earlier 17th century. The capital house of Thicket was mentioned in 1656[1] and in 1672 Richard Robinson occupied a house with ten hearths.[2] About 1720 it was a plain square building with mullioned and transomed windows.[3] The house was apparently known as Thicket Hall in the later 18th century[4] and as Thicket Priory in 1803, when it was sold to Joseph Dunnington.[5] The present Thicket Priory, a rambling red-brick mansion in the Tudor style, was built near by in 1845 by Edward Blore for the Revd. Joseph Dunnington-Jefferson.[6] It was sold by Sir John Dunnington-Jefferson to the Carmelites in 1955[7] and has since been a nunnery.

In 1086 a carucate in West Cottingwith, which had been held before the Conquest by Grim, was in the hands of Erneis de Burun.[8] The estate evidently passed by 1115–18, like most of Burun's holdings, to Geoffrey son of Pain, and after 1153 to William Trussebut.[9] After the death of William's son Robert the estate was divided in 1194 between his three sisters, the lands in West Cottingwith passing to Hilary de Builers.[10] On her death in 1241 the property passed to William de Ros, grandson of Rose, another of the sisters, who was the wife of Everard de Ros.[11] In 1284–5 Robert de Ros was overlord.[12] The Ros family was last mentioned in connexion with West Cottingwith in 1309.[13] An intermediate lordship was held by Simon at the bridge in 1284–5, but nothing more is known of it.

The demesne tenant of the whole carucate in 1284–5 was Ellerton priory, which also held 3 bovates of the Mauley fee and 2 of the Vescy fee.[14] The prior was returned as lord of the township in 1316[15] and in 1535 Ellerton's estate there was worth about £7. The priory also held land in Thorganby worth £1 6s.[16] Both holdings subsequently descended with the former Thicket priory estate.[17]

A third Domesday estate in West Cottingwith was a berewick of Thorganby and consisted of 10 bovates, held in 1086 by Ralph Paynel.[18] The overlordship of 5 bovates descended, like Thorganby, to John de Vescy and in 1284–5 mesne lordships were held under him by Maud de Vaux (referred to as 'de Multon'), the heirs of Stonegrave, and the heirs of Playce. John of Allerthorpe was demesne lord of these 5 bovates, although one of them had been held since c. 1235 by St. Mary's abbey, York, with whom John was disputing the title.[19] John's son Thomas granted 2 bovates to Thicket priory in 1319.[20]

The overlordship of the other 5 bovates had passed

[77] E.Y.C. ii, pp. 423–4; Yorks. Fines, 1246–72, pp. 76–7; Feud. Aids, vi. 33.
[78] Mon. Notes, ii. 44–5.
[79] E.Y.C. ii, pp. 423–4; V.C.H. Yorks. iii. 124.
[80] Yorks. Fines, 1218–31, p. 135; Feud. Aids, vi. 33.
[81] See below.
[82] Valor Eccl. (Rec. Com.), v. 6, 94.
[83] L. & P. Hen. VIII, xv, p. 551; xvi, p. 30; Y.A.J. ix. 201–4.
[84] L. & P. Hen. VIII, xv, p. 563.
[85] E 318/Box 2/49; L. & P. Hen. VIII, xvii, p. 158.
[86] Yorks. Fines, iv. 57.
[87] C 142/514 no. 21; N. Country Wills, ii (Sur. Soc. cxxi), 185.
[88] Yorks. Fines, 1614–25, 186, 204.
[89] Monastic Suppression Papers (Y.A.S. Rec. Ser. xlviii), 162; Cal. Proc. Chanc. Eliz. I (Rec. Com.), ii. 400.
[90] C 142/429 no. 148.
[91] H.U.L., DRA/570.
[92] Ibid. /571.
[93] Ibid. /6, 8; E.R.R.O., PR. 10.
[94] E.R.R.O., DDBH/3/79; H.U.L., DRA/563.
[95] E.R.R.O., DDJ/14/338; Mon. Suppression Papers, 162.
[96] R.D.B., AD/437/906.
[97] Ibid. CD/89/125.
[98] Ibid. CG/81/138.
[99] See p. 114.
[1] H.U.L., DRA/5.
[2] E 179/205/504.
[3] B.L. Lansd. MS. 914 no. 35.
[4] E.R.R.O., DDJ/14/271, 328; Jefferys, Map Yorks.
[5] R.D.B., CG/81/138.
[6] B.L. Add. MSS. 42023 f. 20; 42027 f. 68; 42028 ff. 98–100; 42029 ff. 71–2, 110; date on rainwater heads.
[7] R.D.B., 1027/251/208.
[8] V.C.H. Yorks. ii. 279.
[9] E.Y.C. x, pp. 8–9, 23–4, 32–3.
[10] Ibid. p. 25; Abbrev. Plac. (Rec. Com.), 97.
[11] E.Y.C. x, p. 25.
[12] Feud. Aids, vi. 33.
[13] Fountains Charty. ed. W. T. Lancaster, ii. 831.
[14] Feud. Aids, vi. 33; see below p. 116.
[15] Feud. Aids, vi. 173.
[16] Valor Eccl. v. 128.
[17] See above.
[18] V.C.H. Yorks. ii. 270.
[19] Feud. Aids, vi. 34; E.Y.C. ii, p. 425; see above p. 114.
[20] Mon. Notes, ii. 44–5.

to Robert de Percy by 1284–5, when the demesne lord was Thomas in the willows (*in Sallicibus*). Ellerton priory, however, had held 2 of Thomas's 5 bovates since c. 1275[21] and it may later have acquired the remainder.

St. Mary's abbey held 3 bovates in West Cottingwith in 1284–5.[22] They were retained until the Dissolution[23] and in 1582 the Crown let a bovate of former abbey land to Edward Batley.[24] In 1586 Robert Atkinson held former abbey property there and in Thorganby.[25] In 1284–5 a bovate in West Cottingwith was held by the chapter of York.[26] Nunburnholme priory had land in West Cottingwith worth about 1s. in 1535.[27] It was let by the Crown on several occasions in the later 16th century, the last being 1587, when it went to Christopher Ridley.[28] Nothing more is known of these three estates.

The tithes were held by Ellerton priory from 1351 until the Dissolution.[29] The priory let tithes in West Cottingwith to William Gibson in 1505 and in Thorganby to Edward Saltmarsh in 1533.[30] The tithes were let by the Crown on several occasions in the later 16th and early 17th centuries,[31] but by 1609 they were held in fee by George Stable. He sold them that year to Dakins Constable,[32] who in turn sold them in 1616 to Sir James Altham, William Austin, and others,[33] and they subsequently descended with Thorganby manor.[34]

The impropriators let the great tithes of Thorganby, together with a tithe barn, to Edward Saltmarsh in 1621.[35] The tithes of the whole parish were worth £80 in 1650.[36] For much of the 18th century the impropriators were members of the Baldwin family, apparently as lessees of the Annesleys.[37] By 1801 many tithes in Thorganby had been commuted for a total rent-charge of about £21,[38] and in 1802–10 the tithes of the manorial estate were extinguished.[39] In 1785 and 1801 the West Cottingwith tithes were held at lease by John Dunnington, in the latter year for £110,[40] and at inclosure in 1817 his son received 269 a. for them. Part of Thicket Hall farm, as former demesne of Thicket priory, was tithe-free in 1817.[41]

ECONOMIC HISTORY. Thorganby township had land for two ploughs in 1086, when Ralph Paynel had one plough and four villeins had another. There was woodland a league long and half a league broad. The estate had decreased in value from £1 before the Conquest to 12s.[42] Reclamation of woodland and waste doubtless went on in the 12th and 13th centuries. Some of the reclaimed land was reckoned in acres rather than bovates and amounted to 45 a. in 1295, all held by free tenants.[43] Other assarted land took the form of *culture*, some of which later became part of the open fields while others remained separate. A large area of irregularly shaped closes, called Dunstalls in 1548,[44] in the north-west of the township and a smaller area called Hall closes in the south-east may have originated as *culture*. So may other grounds which in 1624 were distinguished from the open fields although apparently divided into strips.[45] The name Finkle Rudding also suggests an early assart.[46]

The manor was worth £42 in 1283–4.[47] In addition to field land and assarts the demesne in 1295 included a small amount of woodland, 19 a. of several pasture, and other pasture called Smithfield. There were also 7 a. of demesne meadow and a tenant held another 5½ a. Rents of bond tenants accounted for nearly £14 and of cottagers for nearly £7. There were also eight freeholders holding 7 bovates and other property for a total rent of about £2 10s. Boon works and renders of hens and eggs were also mentioned.[48] Services formerly owed to Thicket priory are indicated by rents paid in lieu of two 'sickle boons' in the later 16th century.[49]

The common fields were first mentioned in 1624, when they were called Wood, Mill, and Middle fields.[50] Between 1691 and 1785 Middle came to be known as Mickleland field[51] and in 1802 Wood was alternatively called Little field.[52] Further inclosures may have been made from the waste in the 17th or 18th century, resulting in a wide belt of regularly-shaped closes which adjoined the common and extended along the western township boundary in 1817.[53]

Thorganby ings are first mentioned in 1548, together with the Side and Gilde ings.[54] Meadow land called Hall Bank had been inclosed by 1548[55] and in 1817 three closes of that name covered a large area to the north of the ings. Other meadow closes called Pains Bank, adjoining the ings on the south, were mentioned in 1704.[56] Much attention was paid to the upkeep of the river banks in the ings in the 18th and early 19th centuries.[57] Stinted pasturage at the rate of one or two beasts to the acre was allowed on the aftermath there in the 18th century.[58]

The remaining open fields, meadows, and commons in Thorganby, amounting to over 300 a., were inclosed in 1817[59] under an Act of 1810.[60] Allotments totalling 57 a. were made from Mill field, 43 a. from

---

[21] *Feud. Aids*, vi. 33.   [22] Ibid. 33–4.
[23] It is not possible to distinguish the abbey's land in West Cottingwith from its larger holding in East Cottingwith in 1535: *Valor Eccl.* v. 6–8.
[24] E 310/27/163 no. 49.
[25] C 142/277 no. 43.
[26] *Feud. Aids*, vi. 33.
[27] *Valor Eccl.* v. 129.
[28] E 310/27/158 no. 40; E 310/29/171 no. 81; E 310/31/186 no. 77.
[29] See p. 118.
[30] E 303/22/Yorks./180, 182, 185–6, 188.
[31] e.g. E 310/32/190 no. 3; *Cal. Pat. 1566–9*, pp. 52–3.
[32] *Yorks. Fines, 1603–14*, 109.
[33] Ibid. *1614–25*, 72, 76.
[34] See p. 114.
[35] E.R.R.O., DDFA/20/2.
[36] C 94/3 f. 76.
[37] B.I.H.R., TER. N. Thorganby 1727–70.
[38] E.R.R.O., DDJ/14/242.
[39] See p. 114.
[40] E.R.R.O., DDJ/14/242.   [41] Ibid. DDJ/14/395.
[42] *V.C.H. Yorks.* ii. 270.
[43] *Yorks. Inq.* iii, p. 8.
[44] *Cal. Pat. 1547–8*, 406.
[45] H.U.L., DRA/503.
[46] E.R.R.O., DDJ/14/241.
[47] C.P. 40/55 rot. 19.
[48] *Yorks. Inq.* iii, p. 8.
[49] E 310/28/164 no. 27; E 310/31/188 no. 34.
[50] H.U.L., DRA/503.
[51] E.R.R.O., DDJ/14/175, 241.
[52] Ibid. DDJ/14/188.
[53] Ibid. DDJ/14/395.
[54] *Test. Ebor.* vi, p. 265.
[55] Ibid. p. 264.
[56] E.R.R.O., DDFA/5/118; DDJ/14/395.
[57] Ibid. PR. 2.   [58] Ibid. PR. 3.
[59] Ibid. DDJ/14/395 (with map).
[60] 50 Geo. III, c. 69 (Local and Personal, not printed).

Mickleland field, 37 a. from Wood field, 96 a. from the common, 63 a. from the ings, and 33 a. from more than one area. John Dunnington-Jefferson, lord of the manor, received 140 a. and there were 3 allotments of 20–40 a., 6 of 10–19 a., and 13 of under 10 a.

Of the three estates at West Cottingwith in 1086 two, those of Ralph Paynel and Erneis de Burun, were waste. They had land for a plough and half a plough respectively and Burun's estate contained woodland two furlongs long and two broad. The count of Mortain's estate had land for five ploughs, although six sokemen and one bordar had only one plough there.[61]

Reclamation of the waste had begun by 1204, when the king confirmed a grant to Thicket priory of an assart in the township.[62] In the 13th century a *cultura* divided into strips lay in West field and another in single ownership lay in or near Dale field;[63] 'Setecoppe' in West field, 'Skelmerplat', and Lundcroft were other arable plots containing strips.[64] A 14-acre close called 'Alleridding', mentioned in 1542,[65] and a piece of open-field land called 'wadgh rudding' in 1652[66] also indicate early reclamation. There was apparently also some reclaimed land of the kind usually reckoned in acres, and known as forland, for the former Ellerton priory estate included 'forby land' in 1542.[67] A 2-acre holding in the 13th century carried pasture rights for 20 sheep in the remaining waste.[68]

Most of the woodland had apparently been cleared by 1542, when the grant of the Thicket priory estate to John Aske included £2 for the repair of buildings because of the scarcity of trees in the neighbourhood. The open-field area by then included Westow, later West How, field. Much of the reclaimed land was then held in severalty; about 100 a. of the former priory's demesne lay in pasture closes of 2–14 a. each.[69] Meadow in North Hills was first mentioned in 1540[70] and two years later the Thicket estate also included meadow in Little marsh.[71]

In 1541 the rents of tenants-at-will on the former Thicket estate amounted to about £5 and those of freeholders to about £2.[72] Much of the former Ellerton priory estate in 1542 was held at lease but two freeholders held a total of 4 bovates.[73] Former holdings of Thicket priory each paid rents in lieu of four 'sickle boons' in the later 16th century.[74]

Strips in Scarn Flat were mentioned in the 1650s[75] and Scarn Flatt field was first recorded in 1665.[76] The arable area in the 17th century also included closes divided into strips. Such were Park close, which in 1639 contained 'broad lands called Park lands',[77] and the Open Hacker and Westow close, which both contained strips in 1653.[78] Communal farming in the closes had ceased by 1817, when they consisted of smaller closes held in severalty. Thus there were then two Park closes, four Hackin closes, and about a dozen West How closes.[79] Surviving waste land included the common, which was stinted by 1676, when a holding included 3½ beast-gates in it.[80] In 1777 23 people held a total of 130 gates there.[81] North and South moors, adjoining the common, were first mentioned in 1715.[82] A low-lying area called Segg carr in the south-west of the township had been partly inclosed by 1677, when a close there was mentioned,[83] but 20 'lands' within it were sold in 1688.[84] By 1817 most of the carr had been divided into half-a-dozen closes.[85]

A survey of a 468-acre estate in 1777 shows that farms were generally small, only one of the eleven tenants holding over 100 a. Inclosed land accounted for 268 a. There were 150 a. of open-field land, and 52 a. of meadow land, of which 33 a. lay in the ings and 19 a. in North Hills. Seven of the tenants held a total of 53 gates on the common, apparently with no correlation between the size of a holding and the number of gates.[86]

In 1714 four bylawmen were appointed to regulate the common fields and ings of West Cottingwith.[87] Their duties continued until 1817, when the remaining common lands were inclosed[88] under an Act of 1810.[89] In all, 812 a. were dealt with. Allotments of 47 a. were made from Scarn Flatt field, 107 a. from West field, 48 a. from Dale field, 2 a. from Ling Croft field, 210 a. from the common, 96 a. from North Hills, 60 a. from the ings, 14 a. from South moor, and 4 a. from Segg carr. In addition 233 a. were awarded from two or more areas, and allotments made from West How field and North moor cannot be distinguished. John Dunnington-Jefferson received 250 a. as lord of the manor and 269 a. as impropriator. One man received 70 a. and there were 5 allotments of 20–50 a., 2 of 10–19 a., and 11 of under 10 a.

In 1801 683 a. of the whole parish were under crops, mainly wheat (222 a.), beans (205 a.), and oats (181 a.).[90] There have usually been 15–20 farmers in the parish in the 19th and 20th centuries.[91] Of the 20 in 1851 10 held 100–200 a.,[92] and of the same number on the Dunnington-Jefferson estate in 1964 6 held 100–200 a. and 4 over 200 a.[93] In 1905 there were 1,450 a. of arable and 1,375 a. of grassland,[94] and in 1965 grassland still covered about half the area of the parish, mostly in the east and north.[95] There was little woodland in the mid 19th century, apart from a large plantation which

---

[61] *V.C.H. Yorks.* ii. 224, 270, 279.
[62] *E.Y.C.* ii, p. 423.
[63] H.U.L., DRA/549.
[64] Ibid.; Dugdale, *Mon.* iv. 386.
[65] E 318/Box 2/49.
[66] E.R.R.O., DDJ/14/9.
[67] E 318/Box 2/49.
[68] H.U.L., DRA/549.
[69] E 318/Box 2/49.
[70] *L. & P. Hen. VIII*, xv, p. 289.
[71] E 318/Box 2/49; E.R.R.O., DDJ/14/203.
[72] E.R.R.O., DDJ/14/396.
[73] E 318/Box 2/49.
[74] E 310/27/163 no. 117; E 310/31/188 no. 34; E 310/32/193 no. 34.
[75] E.R.R.O., DDJ/14/8, 9, 12.
[76] B.I.H.R., CP. H. 5090.
[77] H.U.L., DRA/564.
[78] E.R.R.O., DDJ/14/10.
[79] Ibid. DDJ/14/395.
[80] Ibid. DDJ/14/76.
[81] Ibid. DDJ/14/387.
[82] Ibid. PR. 10.
[83] H.U.L., DRA/575.
[84] Ibid. DRA/585.
[85] E.R.R.O., DDJ/14/395.
[86] Ibid. DDJ/14/387.
[87] Ibid. PR. 10.
[88] Ibid. DDJ/14/395 (with map).
[89] 50 Geo. III, c. 69.
[90] 1801 Crop Returns.
[91] Directories.
[92] H.O. 107/2351.
[93] E.R.R.O., DDX/225/12.
[94] Acreage Returns, 1905.
[95] [1st] Land Util. Surv. Map, sheets 27, 32; 2nd Land Util. Surv. Map, sheet 699 (SE 64–74).

covered the former Thorganby common;[96] after the plantation had been cleared there were only 89 a. of woodland in 1905.[97]

In 1086 there were eight fisheries at Thorganby.[98] Thicket priory had a weir at West Cottingwith in 1332, presumably for fishing; along with others it was said to obstruct boats and cause flooding.[99] In 1337 it was ordered that Thomas of Maunby's weir at Thorganby should be diminished.[1]

There was a weaver in the parish in 1379.[2] A brick-maker lived at West Cottingwith in 1718,[3] but brick-making had apparently ended by the 19th century, when Brick croft (later field) lay west of the village.[4] At Thorganby Brick close lay north of the church in 1817.[5] A horse-mill was mentioned at Thorganby in 1295.[6] There was a windmill on the former Thicket priory estate in 1542[7] and a miller lived at West Cottingwith in 1688.[8] A windmill stood in West field in 1707[9] and in Common Lane in 1850.[10] Between 1889 and 1893 it was converted to steam power,[11] but milling apparently ended in the 1920s[12] and the mill has been demolished. The probable site of a windmill in Thorganby is indicated by a mound near the village called Mill hill.[13]

LOCAL GOVERNMENT. Except for overseers of the poor each township had its own officers in the 18th and 19th centuries who kept separate accounts. Both Thorganby and West Cottingwith thus had a churchwarden, a constable, and two surveyors of highways. For Thorganby township churchwardens' accounts survive for 1707–18, and 1826–62, constables' accounts for 1706–1816, and surveyors' accounts for 1833–64.[14] The constable accounted for expenditure on the upkeep of drains, bridges, sluices, and roads. Before 1833 the surveyors' expenses were regularly entered in the constables' accounts; after that date most of the surveyors' expenditure was for gravel, 60–70 tons a year in the 1830s and 1840s and twice as much in the 1850s and 1860s. For West Cottingwith churchwardens' accounts survive for 1715–61, 1769–1806, and 1846–64, constables' accounts for 1709–61, 1777–1807, and 1846–64, and surveyors' accounts for ten separate years between 1720 and 1746 and for 1856–8.[15]

Overseers' accounts survive for 1718–71 and 1825–71, when there were two such officers for the whole parish.[16] In the 18th century no poor-rates were levied, the rent of the poor's estate providing the only income.[17] Poorhouses were first mentioned in 1738 and there were three of them in 1764, each divided into two apartments.[18] A select vestry was formed in 1836 but apparently ceased the following year; its minutes survive.[19] It had 20 members, met twice a month, and was concerned solely with poor-relief. In 1837 the parish joined York poor-law union[20] and the four cottages then comprising the poorhouses were sold in 1845.[21] It became part of Escrick rural district in 1894, Derwent rural district in 1935,[22] and the Selby district of North Yorkshire in 1974.

CHURCH. A church at Thorganby is mentioned in 1228, when Robert de Meynell claimed the advowson.[23] Presentations to it were made by Richard de Breuse, lord of the manor, in 1268 and 1271.[24] By 1312, however, Thorganby had come to be regarded as a chapelry of Aughton and in that year the patron of Aughton successfully resisted Ralph of Maunby's claim to present to Thorganby.[25] Aughton church was appropriated by Ellerton priory by 1351[26] and the priory presumably arranged for the cure of Thorganby to be served. In 1442 the inhabitants of Thorganby disputed their liability to contribute towards the repair of the nave at Aughton,[27] but Thorganby apparently remained a chapelry until the Dissolution. By the later 16th century it was regarded as a separate curacy,[28] and it so remained until the later 19th century. It was first described as a vicarage in 1872.[29] In 1967 the benefices of Thorganby and Skipwith were united.[30]

A grant of the 'advowson' to the archbishop of York in 1558[31] can have had little meaning, and in any case it presumably lapsed on the accession of Elizabeth I. The impropriator in 1567 was bound to find a priest at Thorganby[32] and subsequently the appointment of curates belonged to the impropriators.[33] After 1872 the advowson of the vicarage belonged to the Dunnington-Jeffersons, and since 1967 they and the Lord Chancellor, as patron of Skipwith, have had alternate turns.[34]

The chaplain of Thorganby received £4 a year in 1527,[35] and in 1650 the curate received a stipend of £15 a year from the impropriator.[36] In 1657 £25 a year was granted to Thorganby by the parliamentary trustees,[37] but this apparently lapsed at the Restoration and in 1716 and 1727 the £15 stipend was again the sole income.[38] The stipend was increased to about £26 by 1743, £30 by 1760, and £35 by

---

[96] O.S. Map 6" (1854 edn.).
[97] Acreage Returns, 1905.
[98] V.C.H. Yorks. ii. 270.
[99] Cal. Inq. Misc. ii, pp. 320–1.
[1] Pub. Works in Med. Law, ii. 276.
[2] Y.A.J. ix. 158–9.
[3] E.R.R.O., DDJ/14/89.
[4] Ibid. DDJ/14/395; O.S. Map 6" (1854 edn.).
[5] E.R.R.O., DDJ/14/395.
[6] Yorks. Inq. iii, p. 8.
[7] E 318/Box 2/49.
[8] E.R.R.O., DDJ/14/20.
[9] Ibid. DDJ/14/101.
[10] O.S. Map 6" (1854 edn.).
[11] Kelly's Dir. N. & E.R. Yorks. (1889), 463–4; (1893), 497.
[12] Directories.
[13] O.S. Map 6" (1854 edn.).
[14] E.R.R.O., PR. 2–4, 8–9.
[15] Ibid. PR 10–13.
[16] Ibid. PR. 6–7.
[17] See p. 120.
[18] B.I.H.R., Bp. V. 1764/Ret. 74.
[19] E.R.R.O., PR. 5.
[20] 3rd Rep. Poor Law Com. 171.
[21] E.R.R.O., DDJ/14/399.
[22] Census.
[23] Yorks. Fines, 1218–31, p. 118.
[24] Reg. Giffard, pp. 50, 57.
[25] Year Bk. 5 Edw. II (Selden Soc. xxxi), pp. xxii–xxiii
[26] Cal. Pat. 1350–4, 134, 136.
[27] Cal. Papal Regs. ix. 254.
[28] Cal. Pat. 1557–8, 420; 1566–9, pp. 52–3.
[29] Kelly's Dir. N. & E.R. Yorks. (1872), 552.
[30] York Dioc. Regy., Order in Council.
[31] Cal. Pat. 1557–8, 420.
[32] Ibid. 1566–9, pp. 52–3.
[33] See p. 116.
[34] Directories; Crockford.
[35] Y.A.J. xxi. 249.
[36] C 94/3 f. 76.
[37] Cal. S.P. Dom. 1656–7, 356.
[38] B.I.H.R., TER. N. Thorganby 1716, 1727.

1770, and that last sum continued to be paid until at least 1865.[39] The living was augmented with £200 from Queen Anne's Bounty in 1799 and again in 1827, and by a parliamentary grant of £200 in 1817.[40] The average yearly net income was £53 in 1829–31.[41] The benefice was further augmented with £50 a year in both 1867 and 1869,[42] and in 1914 the net income was £253.[43]

Chaplains before the Dissolution and curates afterwards may have lived in 'the priest house' at Thorganby, which was let with the rectorial estate in 1582.[44] In 1743, and probably also in 1764, the curate lived in the school-house.[45] A parsonage house had been built by 1835[46] but in 1839 the curate, Joseph Dunnington-Jefferson, was licensed to live at Thicket Priory,[47] and he continued to do so until his death in 1880.[48] The 'old Vicarage', in West Cottingwith, became a private house.[49] After 1880 the vicar lived first at Thorganby House, a large red-brick 'Tudor' building, and from 1926 until 1967 at Hedley House. Since 1968 the vicar has lived at Skipwith.[50]

A guild of St. Helen existed in the church and lands formerly belonging to it were granted by the Crown to Francis Barker and Thomas Blackway in 1566.[51] Other land in Thorganby 'given for a priest in the church there' was granted in 1570 to Hugh Counsell and Robert Pistor.[52] An obit was established by Edward Saltmarsh in 1531[53] and grants of land which formerly supported an obit and three lights were made by the Crown in 1563 and 1566.[54]

In 1743 Holy Communion was administered four times a year to 40–50 people.[55] In 1764 there were two services on Sundays and communion was celebrated five times a year.[56] In 1851 there was an additional service, held in a lecture room.[57] An assistant curate was employed in the 1860s and 1870s. From 1876 communion was administered at least twelve times a year, generally with about 30 communicants. In 1884, when there were two communion services each month, only about eleven people received. There were then four services each Sunday but by 1894 there were again only two. Communion was administered every Sunday in 1914,[58] and in 1972 there was always one and sometimes two services each week.

The church of ST. HELEN consists of chancel with north vestry, nave with south porch, and west tower. Except for the tower and chancel arch, the church was entirely rebuilt in the early 18th century.[59] Little is known of the medieval building. The chancel arch may date from the 14th century. In 1481 Edward Saltmarsh left about £13, together with bricks and tiles, to be used for the fabric.[60] The embattled stone tower, probably of 15th-century date, is of three stages. There are four square-headed two-light belfry windows, with perpendicular tracery, and a similar window in the first stage. The plain octagonal font may also be medieval.

The nave and south porch were rebuilt by Francis Annesley, lord of the manor, in 1710 and the chancel in 1719,[61] all of orange-red brick with stone quoins and other dressings. The east window contains Perpendicular-style tracery. The six round-headed windows, four in the nave and two in the chancel, contain leaded glass inserted in 1929.[62] The porch and north doors are also round-headed, as is a blocked door on the south side of the chancel. A brick plinth capped with stone runs around the nave and a stone one around the chancel. There is a stone string-course a little below the eaves of both nave and chancel. The vestry was probably added in the earlier 19th century and the church was restored c. 1955.[63] There are Royal Arms of Victoria. A medieval slab in the chancel commemorates Alice, widow of Edward 'Saltuiche', perhaps a member of the Saltmarsh family.

There were three bells in 1770[64] and there are three still: (i) 1738, E. Seller of York; (ii) n.d.; (iii) 1666.[65] The plate consists of a silver flagon, cup, paten, and basin, said to have been given by Francis Annesley about 1719, and a pewter cup.[66] The registers begin in 1653 and, except for baptisms and burials for the period 1792–1812, are complete.[67]

The churchyard was extended in 1897 and 1966.[68]

NONCONFORMITY. The Saltmarshes were recusants in the late 16th and early 17th centuries, and two or three Roman Catholics were recorded at Thorganby in the 1620s and 1630s and after 1666.[69] There were nine protestant dissenters in the parish in 1676.[70] One Quaker was reported in 1743.[71] In the 1790s the Methodists usually had 6–10 members at Thorganby and 12–20 at West Cottingwith.[72] Houses at Thorganby were licensed for worship in 1788 and 1790,[73] and at West Cottingwith in 1794, 1798 (two), and 1820; a barn at West Cottingwith was licensed in 1819.[74]

A chapel was built by the Wesleyan Methodists at Thorganby in 1815.[75] It was rebuilt on the same site

[39] Ibid. 1743–1865.
[40] Hodgson, *Q.A.B.* 454; Lawton, *Rer. Eccl. Dioc. Ebor.* 467.
[41] *Rep. Com. Eccl. Revenues*, 972.
[42] *Lond. Gaz.* 25 June 1867, p. 3559; 16 July 1869, p. 4011.
[43] B.I.H.R., Bp. V. 1914/Ret.
[44] E 310/32/191 no. 47.
[45] B.I.H.R., Bp. V. 1764/Ret. 74; *Herring's Visit.* iii. 167.
[46] *Rep. Com. Eccl. Revenues*, 972.
[47] E.R.R.O., DDJ/14/398.
[48] B.I.H.R., V. 1865/Ret. 535; V. 1868/Ret. 489; V. 1871/Ret. 495; V. 1877/Ret.; Bp. V. 1884/Ret.; Burke, *Peerage* (1970), 1442.
[49] *Kelly's Dir. N. & E.R. Yorks.* (1893), 497.
[50] Ex inf. the vicar; see p. 113.
[51] *Cal. Pat.* 1563–6, pp. 474–5.
[52] Ibid. 1569–72, p. 38.
[53] *Test. Ebor.* vi, p. 16.
[54] *Cal. Pat.* 1563–6, pp. 53, 474–5.
[55] *Herring's Visit.* iii. 168.
[56] B.I.H.R., Bp. V. 1764/Ret. 74.
[57] H.O. 129/23/515.
[58] B.I.H.R., V. 1865/Ret. 535; V. 1868/Ret. 489; V. 1871/Ret. 495; V. 1877/Ret.; Bp. V. 1884/Ret.; Bp. V. 1894/Ret.; Bp. V. 1914/Ret.
[59] See plate facing p. 128.
[60] *T.E.R.A.S.* xx. 32.
[61] *Letters to Ralph Thoresby* (Thoresby Soc. xxi), 252. Not 1690 as in Pevsner, *Yorks. E.R.* 355.
[62] B.I.H.R., Fac. Bk. xi, p. 37.
[63] Notes in vestry.
[64] B.I.H.R., TER. N. Thorganby 1770.
[65] Boulter, 'Ch. Bells', 32.
[66] B.I.H.R., TER. N. Thorganby 1770; *Yorks. Ch. Plate*, i. 324; ex inf. the vicar, 1972.
[67] B.I.H.R.
[68] Ibid. CD. 555; York Dioc. Regy., Consecration deeds.
[69] Aveling, *Post Reformation Catholicism*, 64.
[70] Bodl. MS. Tanner 150, ff. 27 sqq.
[71] *Herring's Visit.* iii. 167.
[72] E.R.R.O., MRP/1/7.
[73] G.R.O. Worship Returns, Vol. v, nos. 699, 769.
[74] Ibid. nos. 978, 1402, 1446, 3303, 3443.
[75] Ibid. no. 2902; H.O. 129/23/515; O.S. Map 6" (1854 edn.).

in 1861[76] and 1909,[77] and was still used for worship in 1972.

EDUCATION. In 1733 Thomas Dunnington devised a house for a school in West Cottingwith and a rent-charge of £2 a year to support a schoolmaster.[78] In 1743 the schoolmaster was also the curate; there were 12 free pupils, some of them apparently supported by a £2 rent-charge left by Richard Blythe before 1718 to educate poor children, and 18 paid fees.[79] In 1764 the schoolmaster, again the curate, stated that since 1754 Emanuel Jefferson, owner of the land from which the rent-charge was due, had refused to pay it.[80] The school-house was repaired, partly at the cost of the parish, in 1768.[81]

Additional endowments were subsequently provided. A rent-charge of £2 a year was left to the school by Thomas Bradford, probably in the period 1801–10, and Robert Jefferson by will dated 1803 left £10 10s. a year to the schoolmaster to teach 8 children of his tenants.[82]

In 1819 the school contained 50–60 children, 18 of whom were taught free.[83] The school was rebuilt in 1820 by John Dunnington-Jefferson at the corner of Hab Lane, in West Cottingwith.[84] In 1835 there were 27 boys and 14 girls in attendance; the total endowment of £16 10s. was used to teach 20 free pupils.[85] The school first received an annual government grant in 1856.[86] By 1865 all the pupils received free instruction, the extra cost of £70 a year being met by Joseph Dunnington-Jefferson, perpetual curate.[87] In 1871, when it was described as a National school, it had 47 pupils.[88] By a Scheme of 1879 ⅔ of the income of the Poor's Estate were assigned to educational purposes, along with the proceeds of Dunnington's, Blythe's, Bradford's, and Jefferson's charities. Apart from the education of poor children, the objects of the charities were to include the provision of a reading room and books.[89]

The building was found to be unfit for use in 1903 and a new school was built near by the following year.[90] The old school still stood in 1972. Between 1908 and 1938 the attendance varied only between 41 and 58.[91] On the closure of Skipwith school in 1956 its pupils were transferred to Thorganby, but after 1960 the senior pupils went to Barlby secondary school.[92] In April 1972 there were 42 on the roll.[93]

CHARITIES FOR THE POOR. The Poor's Estate was founded by Thomas Saltmarsh, who gave a house, a cottage, and land in Thorganby and West Cottingwith in 1598.[94] In 1743 the estate was managed by the principal inhabitants,[95] and in 1764 the income of about £13 a year was distributed by the overseers.[96] In 1824 the estate comprised 23 a. in West Cottingwith and 8 a. in Thorganby, and the income was about £61.[97] By a Scheme of 1879 ⅔ of the income of the charity were assigned to educational purposes; the poor's share was to be used for gifts of money and goods and for subscriptions and donations for the benefit of the poor of Thorganby.[98]

Robert Jefferson by will dated 1803 left a rent-charge of £6 a year to be distributed in coal to the poor of West Cottingwith who did not receive regular relief.[99] By the Scheme of 1879 the income was to be used in the same way as the eleemosynary part of the Poor's Estate, but for the poor of West Cottingwith.

The Poor's Estate and Jefferson's charity, together with the educational charity, were later administered together as the Thorganby and West Cottingwith charity. The total income in 1971 was £148, and the poor's share was distributed in money and goods.[1]

Thorganby benefited from the charity of John Hodgson for parishes in York poor-law union.[2]

WHELDRAKE

THE VILLAGE of Wheldrake, an Anglian settlement, lies on the Escrick moraine near the east bank of the river Derwent, some 6 miles south-east of York.[1] The main street runs along the top of the ridge, and the element 'ric' in the place-name may refer to the moraine; the first element in the name may be an allusion to the wells or springs that occur at the site.[2] A now deserted hamlet known as Waterhouses was situated on the banks of the Derwent in the Middle Ages. The parish extends for nearly 3 miles across the low ground north of the moraine, where it formerly included the township of Langwith. In 1935, however, Langwith was combined with Heslington civil parish.[3] The irregularly-shaped parish of Wheldrake formerly covered 5,310 a., of which 793 a. lay in Langwith.[4]

The boulder clay of the moraine is topped by a narrow strip of sand and gravel, in places exceeding

[76] G.R.O. Worship Reg. no. 13825.
[77] Date on building.
[78] E.R.R.O., DDJ/35/14.
[79] Ibid. PR. 6; Char. Com. files; *Herring's Visit.* iii. 167.
[80] B.I.H.R., Bp. V. 1764/Ret. 74.
[81] E.R.R.O., PR. 6.
[82] *10th Rep. Com. Char.* 674–5; see above pp. 114–15.
[83] *Educ. of Poor Digest*, 1095.
[84] Sheahan and Whellan, *Hist. York & E.R.* ii. 631; O.S. Map 6" (1854 edn.).
[85] *Educ. Enquiry Abstract*, 1097.
[86] *Mins. of Educ. Cttee. of Council, 1856–7* [2237], p. 192, H.C. (1857 Sess. 2), xxxiii.
[87] B.I.H.R., V. 1865/Ret. 535.
[88] *Returns relating to Elem. Educ.* 464–5.
[89] Char. Com. files.
[90] E.R. Educ. Cttee. *Mins.* 1903–4, 321; 1904–5, 51.

[91] *Bd. of Educ. List 21* (H.M.S.O.).
[92] E.R. Educ. Cttee. *Mins.* 1955–6, 151; 1956–7, 14.
[93] Ex inf. Chief Educ. Officer, County Hall, Beverley, 1972.
[94] H.U.L., DRA/576.   [95] *Herring's Visit.* iii. 167.
[96] B.I.H.R., Bp. V. 1764/Ret. 74.
[97] *10th Rep. Com. Char.* 674, in which it was erroneously stated that the land had been given by Lord Valentia c. 1580.
[98] Char. Com. files.   [99] *10th Rep. Com. Char.* 675.
[1] Char. Com. files.   [2] See p. 12.
[1] This article was written in 1972, with some amendment in 1974.
[2] *P.N.E.R. Yorks.* (E.P.N.S.), 269–70. See above p. 17.
[3] *Census*, 1931.
[4] O.S. Map 6", Yorks. (1851–4 edn.). Most of the parish is covered by sheet 192, some by sheets 174, 175, and 191.

50 ft. above sea-level.[5] Elsewhere the outwash sand, gravel, and clay lie mostly at between 25 ft. and 50 ft., occasionally lower still. Except where it crosses the moraine south-west of the village, the parish boundary largely follows some of the numerous streams and dikes that drain these low grounds. The relatively small open fields of Wheldrake lay partly on the moraine, but extended into the lower ground north and south of the village. Beyond the open fields were assarts made from waste and woods, and in the north-west of the parish extensive commons. Open fields and commons were inclosed in 1773 and the resulting regular field pattern contrasts with that of some of the areas of old assarts.

Alluvium beside the Derwent was occupied by common meadows, especially the ings which stretched beyond the present course of the river to its old course further east. The old course forms the parish boundary around the ings and another loop of the older river forms the boundary around Bank island, this time to the west of the present course. The ings are still regularly flooded and provide a winter refuge for swans and other wildfowl; nearly 300 a., together with an adjoining 100 a. in Thorganby, were designated a nature reserve in 1971–2.[6]

There seems never to have been a village community at Langwith, unless the place-name 'Thorp', recorded there in 1086, testifies to one in early times.[7] Langwith was a forest hay or clearing in the 13th century, and its assarts and commons later belonged to a handful of isolated farm-houses. A new runway built at Elvington airfield in 1956 extends across the township.[8]

The main street of Wheldrake is continued to the south-west as a road leading along the moraine to Escrick. Near the parish boundary it appears to have been diverted away from Grange Farm, perhaps soon after inclosure in 1773.[9] Eastwards from the village the main street continues towards the Derwent as New Lane, before leading southwards to Thorganby. New Lane dates from c. 1300, when it was diverted from a more southerly course[10] which perhaps lay close to the grange which Fountains abbey established in the 13th century.[11] Also from the east end of the village Greengales Lane leads northwards to Elvington, and from the Escrick road another minor road leads north-westwards towards Fulford, crossing Bridge dike at the parish boundary by Pool bridge, which was mentioned in 1374–5.[12] Field roads include Broad Highway and Heeling Lane, to the north of the village, and Leonard Scales Lane, to the south-west. Broad Highway probably led to the common in Langwith, and both it and Leonard Scales Lane have names of 13th-century origin.[13]

Almost all the older houses of the village lie along the closely built-up Main Street and its continuation Church Lane. Back lanes run behind the garths to north and south, the latter still only a field road. Dalton Hill links the north back lane with Main Street. The regular layout of the village results from a replanning which may have been carried out in the late Dark Ages or following William I's harrying of 1069–70. The village as then laid out may have consisted of eight tofts on either side of the street.[14] The growth of the village up to c. 1850 was achieved almost solely by the subdivision of those original tofts, and only more recently has development extended beyond the back lanes.

Westwards of the parish church the main street is almost continuously flanked by houses, which are set back behind a grass verge. No. 53 has exposed timber framing, probably of the 17th century, and fragments of framing have been found inside other houses, notably nos. 3–5 and 51. In addition several houses of brick, including nos. 13, 16, 20, and 23, have a three-roomed plan and axial stack which suggest a 17th-century origin.[15] Most of the brick houses are, however, of the 18th and 19th centuries, as are the numerous brick barns and outbuildings which occupy much of the ground immediately behind the street frontage. The largest house is no. 52, an 18th-century building with added bays, behind which there is a stable range with central dovecot and a group of farm buildings which include a wheelhouse. No. 71 also has a dovecot.

A little infilling of houses has occurred in the main street, but the 20th-century expansion of Wheldrake as a dormitory for York has been taking place mainly around the north side of the village, beyond the back lane, where there are estates of new houses and bungalows. Beyond the east end of the old village street there are about 30 council houses. At the west end the former railway station remained in 1972 but the lines had been lifted. The Derwent Valley Light Railway was opened through the parish in 1912; it was closed for passengers in 1926[16] and for goods in 1965 southwards from Wheldrake and in 1968 northwards.[17] There were two inns in the village in 1972, the Wenlock Arms and the Alice Hawthorn, the latter named after a racehorse of the 1840s.[18] There were five licensed alehouses in the 1750s and 1760s, later in the century only three,[19] which by 1823 were known as the Red Lion, the Blacksmith's Arms, and the County Hospital;[20] the last was presumably named after the hospital in York. All three were replaced by the large Wenlock Arms, built in 1856,[21] but beer retailers were also mentioned in the late 19th and earlier 20th centuries.[22] There was a clothing club in the village in the later 19th century and a branch of the Order of Foresters in the early 20th.[23]

---

[5] Geol. Surv. Map 1", solid and drift, sheet 71 (1973 edn.).
[6] R.D.B., 1739/263/234; 1770/242/196; *Wheldrake: Aspects of a Yorks. Village* (Wheldrake Loc. Hist. Soc. 1971), 28–9.
[7] See p. 123.
[8] See p. 13.
[9] T. Jefferys, *Map of Yorks.* (1772); O.S. Map 6" (1851–4 edn.).
[10] *Fountains Charty.* ed. W. T. Lancaster, ii. 828; *Monastic Notes*, i (Y.A.S. Rec. Ser. xvii), 65; June A. Sheppard, 'Pre-enclosure Field and Settlement Patterns in an Eng. Township: Wheldrake, near York', *Geografiska Annaler*, xlviii (Series B), 67.
[11] See p. 123. There is no evidence for the location of the grange but it is likely to have been at the manor-house site.
[12] *V.C.H. City of York*, 316.
[13] *Fountains Charty.* ii. 816, 835.
[14] Sheppard, 'Wheldrake', 72–3.
[15] *Wheldrake: Aspects*, 8–11, 44. See below plate facing p. 129.
[16] *V.C.H. City of York*, 479.
[17] *Wheldrake: Aspects*, 41.
[18] J. Fairfax-Blakeborough, *Northern Turf Hist.* i. 98–101.
[19] E.R.R.O., QDT/2/15.
[20] Baines, *Hist. Yorks.* ii. 399.
[21] *Wheldrake: Aspects*, 11.
[22] Directories.
[23] B.I.H.R., PR. 86, 158–9.

The hamlet of Waterhouses, first mentioned in the 13th century,[24] lay between the Thorganby road and the Derwent where there are still fields known as Waterhouse Garths. Its inhabitants may have been largely concerned with fishing and other activities along the river.[25] It apparently declined after the Black Death and there was certainly one waste tenement there in 1361. It has been suggested that the hamlet belonged to the Darels and that it was not repopulated after their estate was acquired by Fountains abbey in 1383.[26] There was at least one house there in the 16th century[27] and the Water House remained until the 20th century.[28] In 1972, after part of Waterhouse Garths had been ploughed, pottery of c. 1500 to c. 1700 was picked up from the surface.[29]

Alongside Waterhouse Garths, Ings Lane leads down to a bridge over the Derwent giving access to the ings. The 'hay bridge' was mentioned in the 14th century,[30] and in 1606 its role in the harvesting of hay was mentioned to justify its recent rebuilding with timber from Crown woods in Wheldrake.[31] A drawbridge there was in 1966 replaced by a fixed bridge.[32]

Most of the numerous scattered farms in the parish were no doubt built after the inclosure of Wheldrake in 1773. Wiggenholme Farm (now Wigman Hall), however, certainly existed by 1696[33] and probably by 1609.[34] Grange Farm is also pre-inclosure in date.[35] The farm-houses at Langwith, where inclosure was earlier, also had an older origin.[36] There is the remnant of a moat at Langwith Lodge.

There were about 69 households at Wheldrake in 1316, 84 in 1348, 73 in 1361, and 56 in 1394.[37] There were 216 poll-tax payers in 1377.[38] The village was given no tax relief in 1354, but its quota was reduced by a quarter in 1452.[39] There were at least 65 houses in 1609.[40] In 1672 115 households were included in the hearth-tax return, 15 of them exempt. Of those chargeable 81 had only one hearth each, 17 had 2 to 4, one had 6, and one had nine.[41] There were about 84 families in 1743[42] and 100 in 1764.[43] The population of Wheldrake township in 1801 was 493; it increased to a maximum of 689 in 1851 but fell to 518 in 1901. It had dropped below 500 by 1921 and stood at 451 in 1961. With the development of housing estates in the village numbers rose to 936 in 1971. There is no indication of the population of Langwith township until 1801, when it was 29; it reached a maximum of 57 in 1901 and was 45 in 1931.[44]

MANOR AND OTHER ESTATES. In 1066 Wheldrake comprised 6 carucates and 6 bovates, and was held by Norman. After the Conquest it passed to William Malet, but by 1086 it belonged to William de Percy and was held from him by William Colevile.[45]

In 1166 Thomas Darel held Wheldrake under the Percys and at the division of William de Percy's estates in 1175 it was assigned to the share of the earl of Warwick. Maud de Percy, countess of Warwick, between c. 1180 and c. 1200 gave her nephew Richard Malbis the service of Thomas Darel's heirs, and the Malbis family thus became immediate lords of WHELDRAKE with the Darels as under-tenants.[46] After the death of Thomas Darel's son Geoffrey before 1185, Wheldrake was held from Richard Malbis by Geoffrey's daughters Beatrice of Fitling and Cecily of Bolton. Beatrice's son Geoffrey took the name Darel.[47]

In the late 12th century several gifts of land at Wheldrake were made to Holy Trinity priory, York, and Richard Malbis confirmed gifts totalling 7 bovates.[48] All this was subsequently granted by the priory to Fountains abbey, and Fountains got 2 more bovates from Kirkham priory.[49] Richard Malbis (d. 1210) moreover granted all his property at Wheldrake to the abbey.[50] Fountains held 30¼ bovates in 1316[51] and the manor was worth £104 16s. 6d. in 1535.[52]

After the Dissolution various Crown leases were made of former Fountains property in Wheldrake, including those of the manor to Humphrey Boland in 1543, Thomas Powle in 1558,[53] and Thomas Knyvett, later Baron Knyvett of Escrick, in 1597.[54] In 1612 Lord Knyvett conveyed his interest in the manor to Thomas Howard, earl of Suffolk, and his son Theophilus[55] and in 1625 the manor was granted in fee by the Crown to Sir Edward Howard,[56] later Baron Howard of Escrick.

In 1706 the manor was sold by Charles, Lord Howard, to Sir William Scawen,[57] and in 1761 the latter's great-nephew Thomas sold it to Sarah Thompson.[58] It subsequently descended like Escrick.[59] Additional land was acquired by the Thompsons until they held most of the township. Sales by the Forbes Adam family from the 1920s onwards included nearly 1,000 a. in 1949,[60] but 720 a. still formed part of the Escrick Park estate in 1972.[61]

The lord of Wheldrake built a small castle there before 1149, when the king authorized the citizens of York to destroy it.[62] In 1200 Richard Malbis was

---

[24] *Fountains Charty.* 824.
[25] See p. 125.
[26] Sheppard, 'Wheldrake', 69, where the number of waste tofts in 1361 is wrongly given as nine. For the Darel manor see below p. 123.
[27] *Select 16th Cent. Causes in Tithe* (Y.A.S. Rec. Ser. cxiv), 62; *Yorks. Deeds*, ii, p. 130 n.
[28] O.S. Map 6" (1851–4 edn.); 1/2,500, Yorks. CXCII. 10 (1910 edn.).
[29] *Penes* K. J. Allison, 1974.
[30] B.L. Add. MS. 40010, f. 158d.
[31] E 178/2771.
[32] Ex inf. Northern Area Manager, Yorks. Water Authority, York, 1974. See plate facing p. 32.
[33] E.R.R.O., DDFA/18/48.
[34] L.R. 2/230 f. 294.
[35] Jefferys, *Map Yorks.*
[36] e.g. B.I.H.R., CC. D/C 11. 17 (1772 map).
[37] Sheppard, 'Wheldrake', 69, calculated from B.L. Add. MS. 40010.
[38] E 179/202/58 m. 9.
[39] E 179/202/53, 127.
[40] L.R. 2/230.
[41] E 179/205/504.
[42] *Herring's Visit.* iii. 202.
[43] B.I.H.R., Bp. V. 1764/Ret. 124.
[44] *V.C.H. Yorks.* iii. 498; *Census*, 1911–71.
[45] *V.C.H. Yorks.* ii. 167, 262, 293.
[46] *E.Y.C.* xi, pp. 62, 186–9.
[47] Ibid. p. 189.
[48] *Fountains Charty.* ii. 808–11.
[49] Ibid. 812–13.
[50] Ibid. 818–19. For his date of death see *E.Y.C.* ix, p. 187.
[51] Sheppard, 'Wheldrake', 76.
[52] *Valor Eccl.* (Rec. Com.), v. 253.
[53] *L. & P. Hen. VIII*, xviii (1), p. 552; *Cal. Pat.* 1557–8, 457–8.
[54] *Cal. S.P. Dom.* 1595–7, 380.
[55] E.R.R.O., DDFA/5/40.
[56] Ibid. DDFA/18/1.
[57] Ibid. DDFA/18/59.
[58] Ibid. DDFA/18/6.
[59] See p. 20.
[60] R.D.B., 809/332/273; /595/482; 810/360/298; 811/304/256; 817/401/325; /405/328; /409/329.
[61] Ex inf. Escrick Park Estate Office, 1972.
[62] *V.C.H. City of York*, 26.

licensed to fortify a castle that he was building, but its completion was prevented, again at the instance of York.[63] The castle probably stood on a spur of higher ground near the flood-plain of the Derwent, in a position to command the river.[64] It is possible that a manor-house stood at this site after 1200 and it may have belonged to the Darels, who as undertenants of Fountains abbey had a manor-house in 1361.[65] The manor-house of the capital manor probably lay at the east end of the village and it seems likely that it became the site of the abbey's grange. Little is known of the house that was built on the site after the Dissolution. A bed of tulips there attracted visitors from York in 1738.[66] Christopher Sykes, of the Sledmere family, lived at the hall in the 1770s, when he also leased part of the glebe and established a nursery.[67] The house is said to have been demolished c. 1820.[68] It probably lay a few yards to the south-east of the present farm-house, which is entirely of the 19th century, close to the centre of walled enclosures totalling nearly 8 a. and approached from the road through a formal gateway. Some of the surviving farm buildings, including a dovecot above a tall entrance arch, are of the 18th century. There may at some time have been a park south of the house, where the names 'the Parks' and 'Lawn closes' occur.[69]

After the capital manor was granted to Fountains abbey by Richard Malbis the Darels remained undertenants of one carucate, and their estate was sometimes referred to as the manor of WHELDRAKE. William Darel conveyed it to feoffees in 1368 and their successors conveyed it to Fountains in 1383.[70] These transactions also involved the acquisition by St. Leonard's hospital, York, of a rent-charge upon Fountains abbey's estate in Wheldrake. The hospital was apparently enjoying the profits of William Darel's manor in 1364, in return for giving hospitality to Darel and his wife,[71] and in 1383 it was assigned 16 marks to be paid by the abbey.[72] The hospital's estate there was worth £10 in 1535[73] but no more is known of it.

At Langwith 1½ carucate belonged to Morcar in 1066 and to Count Alan of Brittany in 1086, when it was soke of Clifton (Yorks. N.R.). Half a carucate at Thorp, in Langwith, belonged to Hugh son of Baldric in 1086.[74] Count Alan subsequently acquired the smaller estate also. The gift by Count Stephen (d. 1135–6) of the 2 carucates to St. Peter's (later St. Leonard's) hospital, York, was confirmed by his son between 1136 and 1145.[75] Langwith later passed to the Crown and was used as a forest hay; in the 13th century it was in the keepership of the Cawood family.[76]

The hay was given by the Crown in 1270 as part of the foundation endowment of Darnhall abbey (Ches.).[77] The abbey granted it in 1276 to Warter priory, and Warter in 1279 to the chapter of York.[78] In the late 13th and early 14th centuries it was let to the archbishop.[79] About 430 a. there were sold by the parliamentary commissioners in 1652[80] but were recovered at the Restoration. In 1852 the chapter's property was vested in the Ecclesiastical Commissioners,[81] and they sold 267 a. to Jane Baillie in 1854[82] and 516 a. to G. J. Yarburgh in 1859.[83] The Yarburghs, later lords Deramore, subsequently enlarged their estate there and retained it until 147 a. were sold to the Air Ministry in 1956 and 511 a. to S. A. Spofforth and E. C. Bousfield in 1964.[84]

Several small estates in Wheldrake were held by religious houses. Thicket priory had 5 bovates, given by Geoffrey of Fitling and others.[85] A house, two closes, and 8 a. of land formerly belonging to the priory were granted to Sir Edward Howard in 1625, along with the capital manor.[86] Other land descended with the site of the priory to the Askes, Robinsons, and Jeffersons.[87] In 1888 J. J. Dunnington-Jefferson exchanged 50 a. with Lord Wenlock for other land in Wheldrake.[88]

Warter priory obtained a carucate in Wheldrake,[89] worth nearly £10 after the Dissolution.[90] It was granted to Thomas, earl of Rutland, in tail in 1536 and in fee in 1541.[91] Henry, earl of Rutland, conveyed it to Thomas Hussey and William Sygrave in 1562–3.[92] Its descent has not been traced further.

Nunburnholme priory had land in Wheldrake worth 7s. in 1535.[93] In the early 16th century Roland Herbert claimed to hold a house and 82 a. on lease from the priory,[94] and a cottage formerly Nunburnholme's was granted to Sir Edward Howard in 1625.[95] Kirkham priory was granted 2 bovates there by William Darel but they were released to Fountains abbey in 1246.[96] Property in Wheldrake belonging to Wilberfoss priory was sold by Francis Gayle to Christopher Allanson in 1606.[97]

ECONOMIC HISTORY. The Domesday estate at Wheldrake had land for four ploughs, but in 1086 William Colevile had one plough and three villeins and three bordars had another. There was woodland a league and a half long and a league broad, 20 a. of meadow, and three fisheries rendering 2,000 eels. Both before and after the Conquest the estate was worth 20s.[98]

[63] *Chron. of Roger of Howden* (Rolls Ser.), iv. 117.
[64] *E.Y.C.* xi, p. 192.
[65] B.L. Add. MS. 40010, f. 191d. For the Darel manor see below. [66] *Y.A.J.* iii. 44.
[67] E.R.R.O., DDSY/73/1; *Wheldrake: Aspects*, 22–3.
[68] T. Allen, *Hist. Co. York*, iv. 145.
[69] O.S. Map 6″ (1851–4 edn.).
[70] *Feud. Aids*, vi. 222; *Fountains Charty.* ii. 836–8.
[71] *Cal. Inq. Misc.* iii, p. 202.
[72] *Fountains Charty.* ii. 837–9.
[73] *Valor Eccl.* v. 17.
[74] *V.C.H. Yorks.* ii. 241, 276, 321; *E.Y.C.* iv, pp. 131–2.
[75] *E.Y.C.* iv, pp. 16–17, 84.
[76] *Yorks. Inq.* ii, pp. 105, 111–12, 215.
[77] Dugdale, *Mon.* v. 709.
[78] B.L. Harl. Ch. 53 H. 24–5.
[79] Ibid.; *Yorks. Inq.* iii, pp. 38–9; *Reg. Corbridge*, ii, p. 1.
[80] C 54/3659 no. 31.

[81] *Lond. Gaz.* 10 Sept. 1852, pp. 2436, 2446–7, which mentions about 360 a. in Langwith closes. The wood presumably passed to the commissioners soon after. See below p. 125. [82] R.D.B., HQ/203/256.
[83] Ibid. HZ/275/348. [84] Ibid. 1051/97/92; 1376/52/50.
[85] J. Burton, *Mon. Ebor.* 280.
[86] E.R.R.O., DDFA/18/1. [87] See p. 115.
[88] E.R.R.O., DDFA/18/20.
[89] *Fountains Charty.* ii. 815–16.
[90] Dugdale, *Mon.* v. 314.
[91] *L. & P. Hen. VIII*, xi, p. 207; xvi, p. 325.
[92] *Cal. Pat.* 1560–3, 616; *Yorks. Fines*, i. 272.
[93] *Valor Eccl.* v. 129.
[94] *Yorks. Sta. Cha. Proc.* iv (Y.A.S. Rec. Ser. lxx), 101.
[95] E.R.R.O., DDFA/18/1.
[96] *Cal. Chart. R.* 1327–41, 367; *Fountains Charty.* ii. 813.
[97] *Yorks. Fines, 1603–14*, 60.
[98] *V.C.H. Yorks.* ii. 262.

It has been suggested[99] that a nucleus of some 350 a. of arable land lying around the 11th-century village was surrounded by a turf bank, continued by a stream called Wilgesic flowing towards the river Derwent. This nucleus included land called the Flats and Toft Acres. Assarting of new land beyond the bank and stream may not have begun until the mid 12th century, but during the following 100 years more than twenty such clearings were made. Several bore names with the suffix 'ridding', or clearing, and all were apparently made and enjoyed by individual villagers. The only larger assarts at this period were those which Richard Malbis had royal licence to make c. 1200.[1] After Fountains abbey had acquired a large part of Wheldrake, and established a grange there,[2] it took the lead in the extensive assarting that was carried on in the mid and later 13th century. Arrangements were made between the abbey and other landowners about their share of reclaimed land. Some assarts were divided between all freeholders in proportion to their share of older arable land in the township,[3] and on other occasions assarting by one landowner or his tenants gave other freeholders the right to make corresponding assarts in proportion to their holdings.[4] Most of the 13th-century assarts lay north and south of the village, with some in the west of the parish beyond the unreclaimed wastes. They were divided into closes in which tenants held strips and over which they enjoyed limited rights of grazing.[5]

By the end of the 13th century the older arable land within the ring of new assarts consisted of fragmented holdings, sometimes described as bovates, sometimes as lying in *culture*. Some of the *culture*, however, were in single ownership.[6] There is no evidence how the older arable was farmed, but it was later to become the open fields of the township. Beside the Derwent there were large areas of meadow, especially within the great loop of the river beyond its modern course. Part of the ings was divided between the villagers, but by 1218 Fountains abbey had secured sole rights over the easternmost part, known as Alemar.[7] The common pastures consisted of sandy stretches known as North and Roxhall moors, and wetter areas called Moze or Moss and Horse marsh. Moze was intercommoned by Wheldrake and Escrick, together with the adjacent common of Escrick.[8] The woodland c. 1300 included North and South woods, lying within the area of 13th-century assarts.

The township of Langwith was mostly woodland and pasture. In the early 12th century it was described as a dairy farm belonging to the count of Brittany[9] and later in the century it was a hay or forest inclosure, which was retained for hunting after the forest of Ouse and Derwent was dis-afforested in 1234. In 1270 the hay was estimated to contain 400 a. 'in covert' and 100 a. 'in plain', but exact measurement was impossible because of flooding; there were thought to be 4,000 oaks in the covert.[10]

The greater part of Wheldrake lay within Fountains abbey's estate. Apart from the Darels and Warter priory there were only 6 freeholders in 1316, with a total of 7 bovates. The abbey had 9 tenants at will, 27 tenants in bondage, and 25 cottagers. By 1361 the grange was farmed out.[11]

During the 14th century the older arable land in Wheldrake, the bovates and *culture*, was reorganized as four open fields. They were named in the early 15th century as West, North-west, North, and East fields. Most of the first three contained normal open-field holdings, measured in bovates. But much of East field, together with the Flats and most of the area of 13th-century assarts, was now called forland, measured in acres. The fields were doubtless subject to a fixed rotation, while the forland or 'extra land' was not.[12] In the 15th and 16th centuries much of the forland was converted to pasture. The former assarts in the west of the township, beyond the common, became pasture closes; they included Wiggenholmes close, which was the subject of several leases after the dissolution of Fountains abbey.[13] Extensive commons remained in the 16th century, and in 1546 the inhabitants of Wheldrake and Escrick agreed to continue to intercommon on Wheldrake moor and Escrick Moss.[14]

The abbot supplied oaks from Wheldrake in 1527–8,[15] and after the Dissolution woods called Wiggenholme Spring, Darel Hagg, and the Park were let by the Crown.[16] Large quantities of timber were removed in the 16th and early 17th centuries.[17]

By 1609 the forland in East field and the Flats had been added to the open fields, which otherwise remained much as before. The rest of the forland had been divided into pasture closes, some held in severalty and others shared by several inhabitants holding beast-gates. There were then 13 freeholders and 58 leaseholders on the manor, holding 65 houses. Fifty of those holdings included open-field land, but 25 of them had only 10 a. or less; 12 contained 11–20 a. and 13 21–44 a. each. Meadow land was included in 36 holdings, all but one having only 1–3 a., and 27 holdings had beast-gates, varying from 3 to 34 in number. One man had 120 a. of several pasture. Fifteen tenants, including a weaver and a miller, held only their houses.[18]

By the later 17th century North field had become known as Dovecot field and North-west as Well field, and by the early 18th century West field was called Mill field.[19] Probably in the 1720s some consolidation of the scattered strips of the open-

[99] The land-use history of the township has been examined in detail in Sheppard, 'Wheldrake'. Much of this section is based on Miss Sheppard's article, but the more useful primary sources are appended.
[1] Variously given as 24 a. and 80 a. in *E.Y.C.* xi, p. 187 and *Fountains Charty.* ii. 817, which presumably refer to the same licence.
[2] See p. 123. The grange is mentioned in *Fountains Charty.* ii. 823.
[3] *Fountains Charty.* ii. 816, 826.
[4] Ibid. 815–16, 834–5; *Year Bk. 16 Edw. III* (Rolls Ser.), (1), 182–6; *Cal. Pat.* 1338–40, 424.
[5] *Fountains Charty.* ii. 814, 816, 825, 831–5.
[6] Ibid. 810, 814, 821, 827.
[7] Ibid. 829–30; *Cur. Reg. R.* vii. 257–8.
[8] *Fountains Charty.* ii. 833–5.
[9] *E.Y.C.* iv, pp. 16–17.
[10] *Yorks. Inq.* i, pp. 111–12. For venison from it in 1251 see *Cal. Lib.* 1251–60, 8.
[11] B.L. Add. MS. 40010, ff. 70–1d, 191d.
[12] Forland was sometimes called forby land.
[13] *L. & P. Hen. VIII*, xxi (1), p. 784; *Cal. Pat.* 1557–8, 24.
[14] E.R.R.O., DDPA/10/2.
[15] *Fabric Rolls of York Minster* (Sur. Soc. xxxv), 102; *Y.A.J.* xxix. 193.
[16] E.R.R.O., DDFA/18/1.
[17] E 178/2771, 4839.
[18] L.R. 2/230 ff. 273–95.
[19] B.I.H.R., TER. N. Wheldrake n.d. (17th cent.), 1727. A dovecot in Dovecot field was mentioned in 1659: E.R.R.O., DDJ/15/1.

field holdings was carried out.[20] In 1769 the open fields, commons, and ings amounted to nearly 2,000 a., compared with over 2,400 a. of ancient inclosures. About 2,000 a. of the latter belonged to Beilby Thompson, lord of the manor, and included about 1,120 a. of pasture, 330 a. of meadow, 440 a. of arable, and 60 a. of wood.[21] The remaining commonable lands were inclosed in 1773[22] under an Act of 1769.[23] Allotments totalling 221 a. were made from Mill field, 157 a. from Well field, 109 a. from Dovecot field, and 104 a. from East field, the last perhaps including the Flats. The ings comprised 210 a. and allotments from the commons totalled 1,175 a., of which 84 a. lay in Horse Course, the former Horse marsh. A few small closes were allotted as part of exchanges. Beilby Thompson received 1,484 a., the rector 210 a. for glebe and tithes, and there were 2 allotments of over 30 a. each, 10 of 10–29 a., and 11 of under 10 a.

The woods and pastures of Langwith were inclosed at an early date. About 360 a. in Langwith closes were let by the chapter of York as two or three farms from the early 16th century onwards.[24] The woods were in the charge of a keeper in the 16th century,[25] but later they too were let.[26] Timber was frequently sent to York during the 14th to 16th centuries.[27] In 1769 the inhabitants of Wheldrake still enjoyed a right of stray on a narrow strip of land, in the nature of a droveway, running around Langwith. By the award of 1773 that right was extinguished and the occupiers of Langwith paid a total of £15 to be distributed in compensation.[28]

In the earlier 19th century there were 30–40 farmers in Wheldrake and 2–3 in Langwith, though only about 10 of them had 150 a. or more.[29] There have since usually been 20–30, about 10 of them having 150 a. or more in the 1920s.[30] There were 20 farms in Wheldrake in 1971 with an average size of 157 a.[31] In 1801 only 638 a. were returned as under crops, chiefly oats (245 a.), peas, and turnips or rape.[32] At Langwith in 1841 there were 327 a. of arable, 200 a. of grass, 23 a. of wood, and 168 a. of waste.[33] By 1905 Wheldrake contained 2,835 a. of arable, 1,642 a. of pasture, and 269 a. of wood.[34] The arable land lay mostly on the moraine and in the north of the parish in the 1930s and later, and there was much meadow and pasture along the sides of the moraine and near the Derwent.[35] In 1971 there were 2,221 a. of arable in Wheldrake township, including 1,245 a. of barley, and 912 a. were in permanent pasture or leys; there were over 800 cattle and about 440 sheep.[36] About 370 a. of woodland have been managed by the Forestry Commission since 1949.[37]

In the 13th century and later, Fountains abbey enjoyed fisheries in both the Derwent and in Alemar, the 'eel pond', which lay in the ings. A ditch was made separating Alemar from the rest of the ings. Fishermen were occasionally mentioned and weirs were built in the river.[38] In the 14th century the abbot's weirs were alleged to obstruct the passage of boats.[39] Wheldrake may also have made some use of river traffic in later times. In 1722 an inhabitant left money for the lord of the manor to make a roadway to the river 'for a watering place to the old staith',[40] and there was a landing-place beside the hay bridge.[41]

Weavers were recorded at Wheldrake in 1609[42] and in the earlier 18th century,[43] and a brick-maker in 1782;[44] there was an old brick field in the 1850s.[45] In the 19th and 20th centuries the large number of shopkeepers and tradesmen at Wheldrake mark it as one of the leading villages of the district.[46] There was a water-mill in the 13th century,[47] perhaps situated on Wilgesic near ground still called Mill hill, and two windmills and a water-mill in the early 14th century.[48] A windmill and a horse-mill existed in 1609.[49] The 17th-century windmill may have stood west of the village, where West field later became known as Mill field.[50] The mill there was first explicitly mentioned in 1719.[51] It was repaired in 1835[52] but no longer existed in 1850.[53]

LOCAL GOVERNMENT. A manor court for the recovery of small debts was said to be held in 1823 and Lord Wenlock held a court twice a year in 1840.[54]

There are surviving accounts of the churchwardens for 1740–1881, constables for 1745–1837, surveyors for 1791–1811, and overseers for 1765–1820, as well as overseers' assessments for 1717–1807. Another book contains a summary of the officers' accounts for 1760–1882.[55] There were always two of each of the officers, and bylawmen were mentioned by the constables in 1747. The surveyors recorded an annual list of the inhabitants and their quota of day-work or compositions.

The overseers of the poor maintained poorhouses which were first mentioned in 1743; in 1764 there were eight of them.[56] Wheldrake joined York poor-

---

[20] E.R.R.O., DDFA/45/5–9 (undated maps of the fields, in the case of Dovecot and Well fields showing the situation before and after consolidation).
[21] Ibid. DDFA/18/245.
[22] R.D.B., AT/3/2.
[23] 8 & 9 Geo. III, Sess. 2, c. 23 (Priv. Act).
[24] Minster Libr., D. & C. Archives, Wa. ff. 29, 92 (16th cent.) to Wm. pp. 471–2, 639, 735 (19th cent.).
[25] Ibid. Wa. ff. 28, 46; Wb. ff. 125, 281.
[26] Ibid. We. ff. 5, 19 (17th cent.) to Wm. p. 639 (19th cent.).
[27] *Fabric R. of York Minster*, 56, 58, 69, 115, 117, 124, 130–2, 200; *Cal. Pat.* 1374–7, 227.
[28] R.D.B., AT/3/2.
[29] E.R.R.O., DDFA/41/3, 6; H.O. 107/2351; Baines, *Hist. Yorks.* (1823), ii. 399; White, *Dir. E. & N.R. Yorks.* (1840), 339–40.
[30] Directories.
[31] *Wheldrake: Aspects*, 36.
[32] 1801 Crop Returns.
[33] B.I.H.R., TA. 187S.
[34] Acreage Returns, 1905.
[35] [1st] Land Util. Surv. Map, sheet 27; 2nd Land Util. Surv. Map, sheet 699 (SE 64–74).
[36] *Wheldrake: Aspects*, 36.
[37] Ex inf. Forestry Com., York, 1972.
[38] *Fountains Charty.* ii. 825–6, 829–31.
[39] *Monastic Notes*, i. 68; *Cal. Inq. Misc.* ii, pp. 320–1.
[40] E.R.R.O., DDFA/18/26.
[41] O.S. Map 1/2,500, Yorks. CXCII. 10 (1910 edn.).
[42] L.R. 2/230 f. 285.
[43] E.R.R.O., DDFA/18/122, 159, 214.
[44] Ibid. QSF. Christ. 1782, C.1.
[45] O.S. Map 6" (1851–4 edn.).
[46] Directories.
[47] *Fountains Charty.* ii. 818, 827.
[48] B.L. Add. MS. 40010, f. 83d.
[49] L.R. 2/230 f. 293.
[50] See p. 124.
[51] E.R.R.O., DDFA/18/4.
[52] *Wheldrake: Aspects*, 13.
[53] O.S. Map 6" (1851–4 edn.).
[54] Baines, *Hist. Yorks.* (1823), ii. 399; White, *Dir. E. & N.R. Yorks.* (1840), 339.
[55] B.I.H.R., PR. WHEL. 13–18.
[56] Ibid. Bp. V. 1764/Ret. 124; *Herring's Visit.* iii. 202.

law union in 1837,[57] and the poorhouses were sold by the union in 1867.[58] The parish became part of Escrick rural district in 1894, Derwent rural district in 1935,[59] and the Selby district of North Yorkshire in 1974.

CHURCH. There was a church at Wheldrake in 1086.[60] The archbishop's servants at Langwith were ordered in 1294–5 to attend church at Wheldrake and pay tithes to the rector,[61] and there is no evidence of a chapel at Langwith at any time. In 1971 Langwith was transferred to Heslington parish.[62]

The gift of the church by the Darel family to Warter priory was confirmed between c. 1170 and 1181;[63] it presumably involved only the advowson, and that was surrendered by the priory to the archbishop in 1268.[64] The patronage has since belonged to the archbishop, though the Crown has presented on several occasions. Thus Crown presentations were recorded in 1304,[65] 1397, when the see was apparently vacant, and 1398,[66] and in 1568 the Crown empowered the dean of Westminster to present for one turn.[67] The Crown also presented in 1576,[68] 1628,[69] and 1641.[70]

The church was valued at £20 in 1291 and £25 18s. 2d. net in 1535.[71] In 1650 it was worth £140,[72] and the tithes and glebe were let for between £125 and £150 a year in the 18th century.[73] The average net income in 1829–31 was £474,[74] but although the gross income remained over £400 the net value was only £221 in 1884 and £338 in 1914.[75] Tithes had earlier provided most of the income. There were disputes over their payment in 1407, 1613, and 1691.[76] At the inclosure of Wheldrake in 1773 the rector was awarded 210 a. for tithes and glebe, besides rents of £135 6s. 6d. for the tithes of ancient inclosures and meadows. There was then also a modus of 5s. from the 8-acre Far closes.[77] The tithes of Langwith township were commuted for about £53 in 1840.[78] Glebe at Wheldrake was mentioned as early as 1245–6,[79] and in the 17th and 18th centuries it consisted of about 17 a.[80] Ninety-one acres of glebe were sold in 1903[81] and 133 a. in 1920.[82]

A parsonage house was mentioned in 1535[83] and it had nine hearths in 1672.[84] In the 18th century the south front was said to be wholly of brick, the rest partly of timber and plaster; two gabled bays projected from the south front. In 1764 the house had four main ground-floor rooms, besides service rooms, and there were nine rooms upstairs;[85] it was enlarged soon after 1825.[86] The older part was demolished in the 1930s.[87] A new Rectory was built in 1969[88] and the earlier house was in 1972 known as Woodlands.

In 1381 Adam of Thorp gave property in Wheldrake and elsewhere for a chaplain to celebrate at St. Mary's altar.[89] James Butler, citizen of London, by will proved in 1527, provided for a priest to celebrate at Wheldrake, his birth-place.[90]

On several occasions the archbishop used the living to reward Church officials, and Lamplugh and Harcourt both presented their sons.[91] Non-resident and pluralist incumbents included the rector in 1362, who was a canon at York. In 1435 the rector was a canon at Wells and rector of Heversham (Westmld.), in 1514–34 he was vicar of Middleham (Yorks. N.R.), in 1628–c. 1641 he was rector of Bolton Percy (Yorks. W.R.), in 1743 he was vicar of Wakefield (Yorks. W.R.), in 1750–80 he was dean of Ely, and in 1835 he was a canon at York and rector of both Etton and Kirby in Cleveland (Yorks. N.R.). An assistant curate was employed at Wheldrake in 1743, 1835, and 1865.[92]

Peter du Moulin, rector in 1641, was ejected in 1645[93] and Henry Byard, rector in 1650, in 1662.[94] Later rectors included William Palmer, divine (1577–1605), and Charles Blake, divine and poet (1719–30).[95] W. V. Harcourt, rector 1824–34, amateur scientist, played a leading part in organizing the first meeting of the British Association for the Advancement of Science at York in 1831.[96]

In 1580 many parishioners were cited for not attending church.[97] Two services were held each Sunday in 1743 and Holy Communion was administered four times a year to 45–50 people.[98] By 1764 communion was celebrated six times a year, by 1868 once a month, by 1884 twice a month, and by 1914 every week; there were 20–25 communicants in the 1860s, about 12 in the 1870s. In 1871 a room at Langwith was used for worship in summer, and farm-house services were occasionally held there in 1914.[99] Two services were held each Sunday at Wheldrake in 1972.

The church of ST. HELEN consisted of sanctuary, nave, west tower, and vestry. Only the ashlar tower survives from the medieval building. The lower stage is of the early 14th century, but the upper stage is a hundred or more years later and at

---

[57] *3rd Rep. Poor Law Com.* 171.
[58] York City Archives, Acc. 2, 1560–7.
[59] *Census.*   [60] *V.C.H. Yorks.* ii. 262.
[61] *Reg. Romeyn,* i, pp. 180, 183.
[62] York Dioc. Regy., Order in Council.
[63] *E.Y.C.* x, pp. 118–19.
[64] *Reg. Giffard,* pp. 50–1.
[65] *Reg. Corbridge,* ii, p. 172.
[66] *Cal. Pat.* 1396–9, 66, 293, 317.
[67] Ibid. 1566–9, p. 319.
[68] Minster Libr., Torre MS., 'Cleveland & E.R.', p. 407.
[69] *Cal. S.P. Dom.* 1628–9, 182.
[70] Inst. Bks.
[71] *Tax. Eccl.* (Rec. Com.), 300; *Valor Eccl.* v. 97.
[72] C 94/3 f. 76.
[73] B.I.H.R., TER. N. Wheldrake 1727, 1743, 1760.
[74] *Rep. Com. Eccl. Revenues,* 978.
[75] B.I.H.R., Bp. V. 1884/Ret.; Bp. V. 1914/Ret.
[76] Ibid. CP. F. 29–30; H. 887, 4280.
[77] R.D.B., AT/3/2; 8 & 9 Geo. III, Sess. 2, c. 23 (Priv. Act).
[78] B.I.H.R., TA. 187S.
[79] J.I. 1/1045 m. 9.
[80] B.I.H.R., TER. N. Wheldrake n.d., 1727, etc.
[81] R.D.B., 55/23/23 (1903).
[82] Ibid. 221/26/24.
[83] *Valor Eccl.* v. 97.   [84] E 179/205/504.
[85] B.I.H.R., TER. N. Wheldrake 1727, 1764.
[86] Ibid. 1849; PR. 91; MGA. 1825/2.
[87] *Wheldrake: Aspects,* 16.
[88] Ex inf. the rector, 1972.
[89] *Cal. Pat.* 1381–5, 19.
[90] *N. Country Wills,* i (Sur. Soc. cxvi), 279.
[91] *Wheldrake: Aspects,* 14.
[92] B.I.H.R., V. 1865/Ret. 583; *Cal. Papal Pets.* i. 388; *Cal. Papal Regs.* viii. 522; *Herring's Visit.* iii. 202; *Rep. Com. Eccl. Revenues,* 978; *Wheldrake: Aspects,* 14.
[93] *Walker Revised,* ed. A. G. Matthews, 392; *D.N.B.*
[94] C 94/3 f. 76; *Calamy Revised,* ed. A. G. Matthews, 96.
[95] *D.N.B.*
[96] Ibid.; *Wheldrake: Aspects,* 16.
[97] J. S. Purvis, *Tudor Par. Doc. of Dioc. York,* 76–7.
[98] *Herring's Visit.* iii. 202.
[99] B.I.H.R., Bp. V. 1764/Ret. 124; V. 1865/Ret. 583; V. 1868/Ret. 536; V. 1871/Ret. 542; V. 1877/Ret.; Bp. V. 1884/Ret.; Bp. V. 1914/Ret.

about the same time a west doorway was inserted. Dilapidations were reported in 1578, 1628–30, and 1745,[1] and repair work was done in 1741–2.[2] Apart from the tower the building dates from a rebuilding of 1778–9.[3]

The big rectangular nave and the five-sided sanctuary are built of pale red brick with darker brick and stone dressings. The stonework includes eaves cornice, stringcourse, and plinth. The windows and doorways are round-headed, except for circular windows over the doorways. Only the vestry window retains the original glazing bars, and inside only the cornice survives of the original plaster ceiling, as the result of an extensive restoration of 1873. The plaster decorations were replaced by a square design of wooden slats, but these were removed when the roof timbers and ceiling were renovated in 1972. Other changes in 1873 included the removal of a west gallery and the provision of new seating, floors, and font.[4] The redecoration of the church in 1972 marked the beginning of a process of restoring its 18th-century character, and in 1973 the sanctuary windows were reglazed.[5]

Two large marble tablets in the sanctuary commemorate Charles Blake, rector 1719–30, one bearing his own modest words and the other the praises of his friends.[6] There is a Royal Arms of 1779 and a charity board of 1780. An octagonal font of *c.* 1300 was restored to the church in 1974.[7] A stone pedestal for a sun-dial stands in the churchyard.

The three bells from the old church were retained in 1778: (i) 1640; (ii) 1676; (iii) 1677, the last two by Samuel Smith the younger of York.[8] Three more bells were added in 1920.[9] The plate comprises silver cup and paten and plated flagon; the cup was made in York in 1642 by Thomas Harrington.[10] The registers of baptisms and marriages begin in 1603 and of burials in 1653; they are complete except for baptisms in 1658–69 and marriages in 1648–53.[11]

The churchyard was extended in 1824,[12] 1908, and 1957.[13]

NONCONFORMITY. In 1569 the assistant curate of Wheldrake was found to be distributing seditious and papist literature, and one or two recusants were discovered in 1586 and in the early 17th century.[14] One family of Roman Catholics was reported in 1764.[15] There were four protestant dissenters in the parish in 1676.[16] Houses and other buildings were licensed for dissenting worship in 1762, 1801, 1808, 1809, 1813, and 1815,[17] that in 1801 for Methodists.[18] The Wesleyans built a chapel in 1816,[19] and in 1823 there was said to be also a meeting-place of the 'new connexion'.[20] The latter may refer to the Primitive Methodists, who held two meetings at Wheldrake in 1819.[21] The Wesleyan chapel was rebuilt in 1863,[22] enlarged by a schoolroom in 1894, and used until 1970.[23] It was subsequently converted into a private house. In 1865 the Wesleyans were said to have twelve members and many other attenders, and in 1894 the rector reported a 'strong tendency to dissent'.[24]

EDUCATION. A schoolmaster was mentioned in 1623.[25] A master received a salary of £5 a year to teach 10 children in 1743,[26] and the school-house was repaired that year.[27] The mud-walled and thatched structure may have been rebuilt in the 1750s,[28] and in 1768 it was enlarged.[29] By the 1820s the master's salary was £12 8s. Of this sum £5 was received from the lord of the manor, under a benefaction made by Thomas and James Scawen in 1761 for the education of 10 children; £2 8s., to provide for 4 children, was received from Silvester Walker's charity; and £5 interest derived from Thomas Clingand's bequest of £100, by will dated 1820, to provide for 5 boys.[30]

The school was united with the National Society in 1828. By 1835 it was attended by 62 boys and 27 girls, and in addition to the endowments it was supported by subscriptions and school pence. A lending library was then attached to it. An infants' school was also started in 1828, with 10 boys and 17 girls attending in 1835, when school pence and a subscription by the rector's wife provided the mistress's salary. At another school, started in 1826, 15 girls were taught at their parents' expense.[31]

Both the main and the infants' schools were extensively repaired in 1867 and 1869,[32] and the main school rebuilt in 1871. The average attendance in 1873 was 61, including 21 infants.[33] Under a Scheme of 1869 the educational charities were administered with those for the poor and two-thirds of the income went to the school.[34] In 1871 the endowment income amounted to £39; subscriptions included those of Lord Wenlock and the rector, and 8s. was received under the will of John Raimes (d. 1858), who left £100 for the school.[35] An annual government grant was received by 1874.[36] The infants' department was rebuilt in 1892, and the

---

[1] Ibid. V. 1578–9/CB. 1; D/C. CP. (1628–30); C. V/CB. 9.
[2] Ibid. PR. WHEL. 13.
[3] Building accts., plans, etc. are printed in J. Howat, *Documents concerning the Rebuilding of Wheldrake Church, 1778* (priv. print. 1971). See below plate facing p. 128.
[4] B.I.H.R., PR. WHEL. 24; *Yorks. Gaz.* 10 Jan. 1874; *Wheldrake: Aspects*, 7.
[5] Ex inf. the rector, 1974.
[6] For details see *Wheldrake: Aspects*, 15.
[7] Ex inf. the rector, 1974.
[8] Boulter, 'Ch. Bells', 32.
[9] B.I.H.R., Fac. Bk. x, p. 78.
[10] *Yorks. Ch. Plate*, i. 333.
[11] B.I.H.R.
[12] Ibid. CD. 111.
[13] York Dioc. Regy., Consecration deeds.
[14] Aveling, *Post Reformation Catholicism*, 13, 64.
[15] B.I.H.R., Bp. V. 1764/Ret. 124.
[16] Bodl. MS. Tanner 150, ff. 27 sqq.
[17] G.R.O. Worship Returns, Vol. v, nos. 155, 1643, 2133, 2308, 2773, 2870, 2993.
[18] B.I.H.R., Fac. Bk. iii, p. 275.
[19] G.R.O. Worship Returns, Vol. v, no. 2993.
[20] Baines, *Hist. Yorks.* ii. 399.
[21] *Wheldrake: Aspects*, 17.
[22] G.R.O. Worship Reg. no. 15685.
[23] *Wheldrake: Aspects*, 17.
[24] B.I.H.R., V. 1865/Rct. 583; Bp. V. 1894/Rct.
[25] B.I.H.R., Schools index.
[26] *Herring's Visit.* iii. 202.
[27] B.I.H.R., PR. WHEL. 13.
[28] *Wheldrake: Aspects*, 23.
[29] B.I.H.R., TER. N. Wheldrake 1777.
[30] *12th Rep. Com. Char.* 652–3; see below p. 128.
[31] *Educ. Enquiry Abstract*, 1099.
[32] *Wheldrake: Aspects*, 24; Bulmer, *Dir. E. Yorks.* (1892), 728.
[33] Ed. 7/135 no. 200.
[34] See p. 128.
[35] B.I.H.R., PR. 66; plaque in church.
[36] *Rep. of Educ. Cttee. of Council, 1874–5* [C. 1265-I], p. 449, H.C. (1875), xxiv.

school was enlarged in 1914.[37] From 1908 until 1914 the attendance was about 90–110; after the First World War it varied between 88 in 1927 and 53 in 1938.[38] The number on the roll in April 1972 was 124.[39] A new school, in the back lane, was opened in 1973.[40] In addition to income from the poor's charities, over £2 was received from Raimes's charity in 1973.[41]

An evening school was held in the 1860s and 1880s.[42]

CHARITIES FOR THE POOR. George Haxby, by will dated 1625, devised a stable in York to the poor of Wheldrake.[43] In the later 18th century a rent of 16s. a year was received from it.[44] The premises were subsequently surrendered for the sum of £50, which produced £5 a year interest in 1784 and £2 10s. in 1824.[45]

George Parish, rector, by will dated 1681, gave £100, the interest to be used to put out a boy or two girls as apprentices.[46] Samuel Terrick, rector, by will dated 1718, left £30 for the poor.[47] Richard Morris, by will dated 1720, similarly left £20.[48] Charles Blake, rector, by will dated 1728, left £50 to be used with the three previous endowments to buy land.[49] Another £33 was borrowed and about 35 a. were bought at Brackenholme (in Hemingbrough) in 1731.[50] In 1764 the rent of the estate produced £10[51] and in 1824 £18 a year, of which £8 16s. was used for apprenticing and the rest was distributed to the poor.[52] The land was usually known as the Hemingbrough or Woodhall charity estate.

Frances, dowager Lady Howard, by will proved in 1716, bequeathed money to provide coal in Escrick and other villages, including Wheldrake.[53] After 1862 Wheldrake received ¼ of the income.

Silvester Walker gave £200, which was used in 1775 to buy an annuity of £7 charged upon 16 a. in Wheldrake then belonging to Beilby Thompson. It was provided in a deed of that year that £2 12s. should be distributed in bread to widows, £2 given in clothes to three men, and £2 8s. given to the schoolmaster.[54]

All the above-mentioned charities were regulated by a charity commissioners' Scheme of 1869. It was provided that a third of the total income should be distributed to the poor in money or goods and that two-thirds should go to Wheldrake school.[55] The charities' assets in 1896 comprised £481 stock, producing £13 interest, the Hemingbrough estate, producing £20 rent, rent-charges of £12 from land in Wheldrake, and the school site and buildings.[56] The Hemingbrough estate was sold in 1911.[57] A Scheme of 1923 allowed a wide range of uses for the educational part of the income, including grants for education other than elementary.[58] In 1924 and 1931 the income from stock was £37 and from rents £12.[59]

In 1972 the combined charities, including Howard's, had an income of £61 from £1,047 stock, and the proceeds were divided in accordance with the 1869 Scheme except that the whole income of Howard's charity went to the poor. By a Scheme of 1973 the charities were to be administered together as the Wheldrake Relief in Need charity to provide gifts of money and goods.[60]

George Davison (d. 1888) left £400 for orphan boys of Wheldrake.[61] The income was £9 in 1890 and £13 in 1917, and it was used for orphans' clothes and school fees.[62] The income was £12 in 1965–6, when there was an accumulated balance of £200, and a grant of £20 was made.[63] In 1973 nearly £17 was received and no disbursements were made.[64]

Wheldrake benefited from the charity of John Hodgson for parishes in York poor-law union,[65] and one grant was made to a resident of Wheldrake in 1972.[66]

---

[37] *Wheldrake: Aspects*, 25.
[38] *Bd. of Educ. List 21* (H.M.S.O.).
[39] Ex inf. Chief Educ. Officer, County Hall, Beverley, 1972.
[40] E.R. Educ. Cttee. *Mins.* 1972–3, 171.
[41] Ex inf. the rector, 1974.
[42] B.I.H.R., V. 1865/Ret. 583; V. 1868/Ret. 536; Bp. V. 1884/Ret.
[43] B.I.H.R., PR. WHEL. 52–3.
[44] Ibid. TER. N. Wheldrake 1809; Bp. V. 1764/Ret. 124.
[45] Ibid. PR. WHEL. 65; *12th Rep. Com. Char.* 653–4.
[46] B.I.H.R., PR. WHEL. 54–5.
[47] Ibid. 58.
[48] Ibid. 31.
[49] Ibid. 34.
[50] *12th Rep. Com. Char.* 653.
[51] B.I.H.R., Bp. V. 1764/Ret. 124.
[52] *12th Rep. Com. Char.* 653.
[53] See p. 28.
[54] *12th Rep. Com. Char.* 653; see above p. 127.
[55] B.I.H.R., PR. WHEL. 127.
[56] Ibid. 128.
[57] Ibid. 131, 143.
[58] Ibid. 118.
[59] Ibid. 140.
[60] Char. Com. files.
[61] Plaque in church.
[62] B.I.H.R., PR. WHEL. 68.
[63] Char. Com. files.
[64] Ex inf. the rector, 1974.
[65] See p. 12.
[66] Ex inf. Mr. A. R. Tunnah, Haxby, 1974.

Thorganby Church from the south-east

Wheldrake Church from the south-east

SOUTH DUFFIELD: Holmes House

BARMBY MOOR: Barmby Manor

WHELDRAKE: no. 51 Main Street

BARMBY MOOR: Barmby Moor House, formerly an inn

HARTHILL WAPENTAKE

THE WAPENTAKE, the largest in the East Riding, extends from the river Hull in the east to the river Derwent in the west, and in places reaches the Humber in the south. A great variety of landscape is consequently contained in it, ranging from the low-lying ground of the Vale of York and the Hull valley to the higher country of the Yorkshire Wolds and the Jurassic hills. All areas are still largely rural and agricultural, but the proximity of Beverley and, more especially, of Kingston upon Hull has brought changes to the surrounding countryside.

In the Vale of York much of the land lies at about 25 ft. above sea-level and, as in Ouse and Derwent wapentake, consists of drift deposits of clay, sand, and silt. The most noticeable relief features are the Escrick moraine, which continues into the wapentake from the west side of the Derwent, and Church hill at Holme upon Spalding Moor. The boulder clay and gravel of the moraine reach 50 ft. and more above sea-level, while the Keuper marl outcrop at Holme hill exceeds 150 ft. The name Jurassic hills is applied to a stretch of undulating country, up to 2 miles wide, along the eastern side of the Vale of York. Formed in part of limestone, they reach about 50 ft.–200 ft. and their most prominent feature is a small escarpment which gives its name to the villages of North and South Cliffe. Behind the Jurassic hills rises the altogether more impressive escarpment of the wolds. Close to the escarpment the chalk hills in places exceed 500 ft. above sea-level, and on the northern boundary of the wapentake, at Bishop Wilton, they reach 800 ft., the highest point in the riding. In Harthill as elsewhere the wolds are dissected by numerous steep-sided dry valleys. Boulder clay covers the chalk on the lower eastern slopes of the wolds, down which numerous streams flow towards the river Hull. The flat silt- and peat-covered floor of the Hull valley, nowhere exceeding 25 ft. above sea-level, occupies the last 2 or 3 miles before the eastern boundary of the wapentake is reached.[1]

Most of the villages in the Vale of York stand on ground rising only slightly above the generally low level. In the Jurassic hills streams flowing from the wolds escarpment provided sites for many of the settlements, while a line of villages is strung out beneath the escarpment itself. On the higher parts of the wolds villages are few and mostly confined to sheltered valleys, but the lower slopes are densely settled, with many villages placed near the upper and lower margins of the boulder clay. The few old settlements in the Hull valley were sited, as in the Vale of York, on 'islands' of drier ground.

Much of the wolds was occupied here, as in Dickering wapentake,[2] by open-field arable land and sheepwalks until the 18th and early 19th centuries, when the agricultural landscape was transformed by parliamentary inclosure. In contrast parts of the Vale of York experienced a more varied agricultural development, already noted in Ouse and Derwent wapentake,[3] and in both the Vale of York and the Hull valley the draining of marshland has been of special significance. Building materials in the wapentake are equally varied. Limestone houses are still common in the Jurassic hills, but on the wolds chalk is now generally confined to farm buildings, and both there and in the Vale of York the brick-built houses mostly date from the 18th century and later.

---

[1] *E. Yorks. and Lincs.* (Brit. Regional Geol.) (H.M.S.O.), 6 sqq.; Geol. Surv. Map 1″, solid and drift, sheets 63 (1967 edn.), 64 (1954 edn.), 71 (1973 edn.); drift, sheets 72 (1960 edn.), 79 (1973 edn.).
[2] See *V.C.H. Yorks. E.R.* ii, *passim.*
[3] See p. 1.

A HISTORY OF YORKSHIRE: EAST RIDING

The wapentake includes three small market towns, Pocklington and Market Weighton in the Vale of York and Great Driffield on the eastern slopes of the wolds. From the 18th century onwards several of the villages in the south-east of the wapentake have gradually expanded as dormitories for Hull, and in the present century similar but more rapid growth has taken place around both Hull and Beverley. Some industrial development has occurred there, too, as well as in the market towns and in several villages where rivers, canals, and railways have provided facilities for transport.

The Domesday hundreds in the East Riding were transformed into wapentakes during the 12th century.[4] Harthill wapentake, first mentioned in 1166,[5] was made up of Driffield, Hessle, and Weighton hundreds, and parts of Cave, Pocklington, Sneculfcros, Warter, and Welton hundreds.

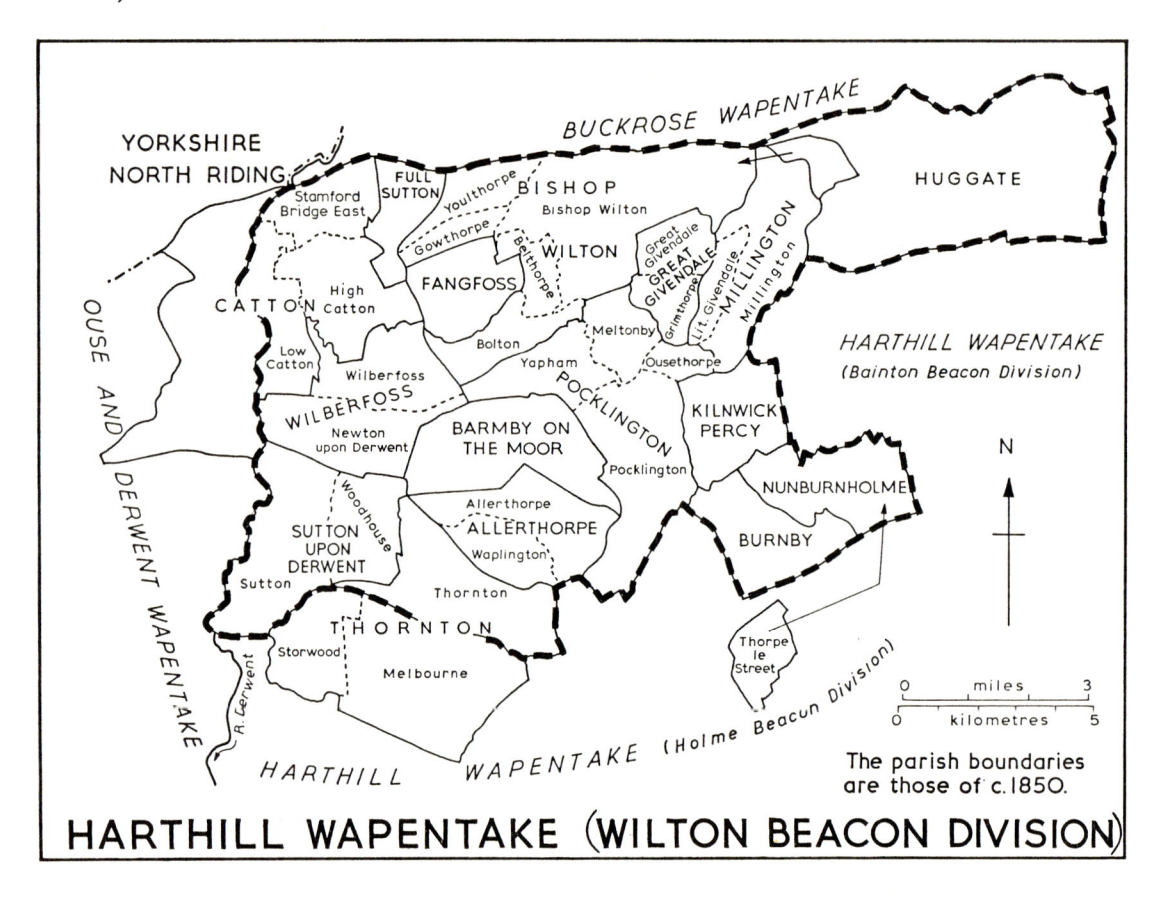

HARTHILL WAPENTAKE (WILTON BEACON DIVISION)

From Driffield hundred the wapentake drew the townships of Bainton, 'Cheldale' (in Driffield), Cranswick, Great and Little Driffield, Eastburn, part of Elmswell, Hutton, Kelleythorpe, Kirkburn, Neswick, Rotsea, Skerne, Southburn, Sunderlandwick, Tibthorpe, and 'Torp'.[6] The rest of Elmswell, which lay in Turbar hundred in 1086, later became part of Harthill wapentake.[7] The hundred meeting-place may have been near Spellow Farm, Elmswell, a name deriving from 'speech mound'.[8] Hessle hundred contributed to the wapentake the townships of Anlaby, Breighton, Bubwith, 'Crachetorp' (possibly Tranby), Kirk Ella, North Ferriby, Gunby, Hessle, Newsholme, Myton, Riplingham, 'Siwarbi' (possibly Loftsome), Spaldington, 'Totfled', part of Wauldby, Willerby, Willitoft, Wolfreton, and Wressle.[9]

From Weighton hundred the wapentake took the townships of Bishop Burton,

[4] See p. 3.
[5] *Pipe R.* 1166 (P.R.S. ix), 48.
[6] *V.C.H. Yorks.* ii. 320–1.
[7] See *V.C.H. Yorks. E.R.* ii. 3.

[8] O. S. Anderson, *English Hundred-Names*, 15, which also suggests Moot Hill, Driffield. The latter, however, appears to be the motte of a small castle.
[9] *V.C.H. Yorks.* ii. 318.

130

Cleaving, North Cliffe, Easthorpe, Goodmanham, Harswell, Holme upon Spalding Moor, Houghton, Kiplingcotes, Londesborough, Sancton, Shipton, Thorpe, Towthorpe, and Market Weighton.[10] Welton hundred contributed Bentley, part of Brantingham, Cottingham, Elloughton, Lund, 'Pileford' (in Cottingham), Risby, Skidby, part of Walkington, the rest of Wauldby, and Little Weighton.[11]

From Cave hundred the wapentake drew the townships of Aughton, North and South Cave, 'Chetelstorp' (probably in Storwood), South Cliffe, East Cottingwith, Drewton, Ellerton, Everthorpe, Foggathorpe, Gribthorpe, Hotham, Hunsley, Kettlethorpe, Laytham, Melbourne, Newbald, Seaton Ross, and Thornton.[12] From Pocklington hundred it drew the townships of Allerthorpe, Barmby Moor, Beilby, Belthorpe, Bolton, Burnby, Catton, Everingham, Fangfoss, Gowthorpe, Greenwick, Hayton, Pocklington, Sutton upon Derwent, Thorpe le Street, Waplington, Bishop Wilton, and Youlthorpe.[13] Sneculfcros contributed Aike, Beswick, Bracken, Cherry Burton, South Dalton, Etton, Gardham, Holme on the Wolds, Kilnwick, Leconfield, Lockington, Middleton on the Wolds, Newsham (possibly in Leconfield), Newton (in Cherry Burton), 'Persene' (perhaps in Scorborough), Raventhorpe, Scorborough, 'Steintorp' and 'Torp' (both possibly in Etton), and Watton.[14] The hundred meeting-place was presumably at Sneculf's cross, the location of which is unknown.[15] Finally, Warter hundred contributed to the wapentake the townships of North Dalton, Great and Little Givendale, Grimthorpe, Hawold, Huggate, Kilnwick Percy, Meltonby, Millington, Nunburnholme, Ousethorpe, Warter, and Yapham.[16]

Among the places not mentioned in 1086 but which later lay within the wapentake were Arram, Arras, Brind, Broomfleet, Brough, Bursea, Faxfleet, Harlthorpe, Hundburton, Newton (in Cottingham), Newton upon Derwent, Rowley, Sculcoates, Stamford Bridge, Storwood, Full Sutton, Swanland, Wholsea, and Wilberfoss, all recorded from the 12th or 13th centuries. The wapentake also includes New Village, which has existed only since the late 18th century.[17]

The uncertain early relationship between Howdenshire and the wapentakes of Harthill and Ouse and Derwent has been discussed above.[18] Howdenshire emerged as a distinct wapentake by the mid 14th century. It comprised a large block around Howden itself, together with Ellerker, Melton, Welton, large parts of Brantingham and Walkington, and smaller parts of several other townships, all lying detached within Harthill wapentake. The whole of Brantingham and Walkington are reserved for treatment under Howdenshire.

The area of Harthill wapentake was reduced in 1299 by the creation of the borough of Kingston upon Hull, and again in 1440 when Hull was erected into a county of its own and the township of Myton was included in it. The enlargement of the county of Hull in 1447 involved the further removal from Harthill of the parishes of Hessle, with

[10] Ibid. 319–20.
[11] Ibid. 318.
[12] Ibid. 318–19.
[13] Ibid. 321–2.
[14] Ibid. 320.
[15] *P.N.E.R. Yorks.* (E.P.N.S.), 153.
[16] *V.C.H. Yorks.* ii. 321.
[17] *P.N.E.R. Yorks.* passim.
[18] See p. 3.

its township of Tranby, North Ferriby, with the township of Swanland, and Kirk Ella, with the townships of Anlaby, West Ella, Willerby, and Wolfreton. Haltemprice priory, which occupied the site of the former township of Newton, in Cottingham, was also included in the county of Hull in 1447. The county's boundaries thereafter remained unchanged until 1835, when they were reduced to become coextensive with those of the borough.[19] The former outlying parts of the county are reserved for treatment elsewhere.

Extensions to the boundaries of the borough in the 19th and 20th centuries have taken in the whole of Sculcoates parish and part of Cottingham. The history of Sculcoates was accordingly dealt with along with that of the rest of the city of Hull.[20] Most of Cottingham, including the village itself, remains outside the city and the history of the whole parish will be treated under Harthill wapentake.

The wapentake remained with the Crown until at least the 17th century. The office of wapentake bailiff was granted for life to successive holders in 1542, 1552, and 1567.[21] A new bailiff was appointed in 1619–20.[22]

The meeting-place of the wapentake was presumably Hart hill; its site is not known but it may have been in the neighbourhood of Market Weighton.[23] At least some of the townships paid a share of the wapentake fine and owed suit at the court.[24] The sheriff accounted for 53 marks from the wapentake in 1399–1400,[25] and in the 16th and 17th centuries he received nearly £6 in blanch farm from Harthill.[26]

The four divisions of the wapentake, namely Bainton Beacon, Holme Beacon, Hunsley Beacon, and Wilton Beacon, first appear in Elizabeth I's reign.[27] They were probably created as areas of assessment for the maintenance of the beacons that stood at Bainton, Holme upon Spalding Moor, Hunsley, and Bishop Wilton.[28] There was a beacon at Hunsley by 1537.[29] Part of Wilton Beacon division is dealt with in this volume.

[19] *V.C.H. Yorks. E.R.* i. 2, 4–5, 12–13.
[20] See *V.C.H. Yorks. E.R.* i, *passim*.
[21] *L. & P. Hen. VIII*, xvii, p. 33; *Cal. Pat. 1550–3*, 295; 1566–9, p. 82.
[22] E 199/51/33.
[23] *P.N.E.R. Yorks.* 152.
[24] *Plac. de Quo Warr.* (Rec. Com.), 188–9, 196.
[25] E 370/6/27.
[26] E 370/6/28; /13/217; /15/28, 43, 57, 60.
[27] E 179/204/354, 376–7.
[28] J. Nicholson, *Beacons of E. Yorks.* 9.
[29] *L. & P. Hen. VIII*, xii (1), p. 184.

WILTON BEACON DIVISION

(Western part)

ALLERTHORPE

THE VILLAGE of Allerthorpe lies about 13 miles east of York, just south of the main York–Hull road.[1] The largely depopulated village of Waplington is less than a mile to the south-west of Allerthorpe and close to Stone beck. Allerthorpe's name suggests a subsidiary Scandinavian settlement, but Waplington was apparently Anglian.[2] The parish, which is roughly lozenge-shaped, has an area of 2,391 a., of which Waplington accounts for 812 a.[3] In 1935 the civil parishes of Allerthorpe and Waplington were united.[4]

The more southerly parts of the parish lie at less than 50 ft. above sea-level, but the ground rises to 75 ft. at the northern parish boundary. Allerthorpe village is on the higher ground, and Waplington was probably similarly located. The soils of the parish are based upon sand and gravel deposits.[5] Allerthorpe's open fields lay on the higher ground around the village, where narrow curving closes still reflect their inclosure by agreement in 1640.[6] Waplington apparently had its own open fields until the inclosure of 1774, but their location is obscure. Much of the outlying western part of the parish, including some of the higher ground, has always been uncultivated; this waste land was encroached upon in both townships, and virtually disappeared at Waplington in the late 18th century.[7] Nevertheless, over 400 a. of 'bare land and felled woodland' survived into the 1960s in Allerthorpe,[8] when it was replanted by the Forestry Commission. A 15-acre nature reserve was established there in 1965.[9] Only 23 a. beside a former outgang leading from the village remained as common land in 1974.[10] The meadow land of the parish lay alongside Pocklington beck.

Drainage has long been a problem in the more low-lying parts of the parish. In 1415 frequent flooding, presumably on the road through Allerthorpe and Waplington to the mother-church of Pocklington, was held to justify the granting of burial rights to Thornton.[11] The streams and dikes of the parish formerly drained into Pocklington beck, which constituted the eastern boundary, but in 1818 the Pocklington canal was completed along the beck's course.[12] Part of the canal and one of its locks lie just within the parish boundary.

Allerthorpe is situated on a minor road which branches from the York–Hull road and crosses the parish in a south-westerly direction towards Thornton and Melbourne. In the west of the parish two minor roads cross the common. The York–Hull road, which runs along the north-eastern parish boundary and gives access to the neighbouring parishes of Pocklington and Barmby Moor, follows the course of a Roman road. Its repair between Barmby and Hayton was one of the objects of an indulgence granted in 1480.[13] It was turnpiked in 1764 and the trust was renewed until 1881;[14] two milestones from this period no longer survive. The road was widened and realigned in the 1950s and 1960s.[15]

Pocklington airfield[16] extended across the main road into Allerthorpe. The land and buildings adjoining the road have been used for commercial purposes in recent years,[17] and other airfield buildings have been converted to farm uses or demolished.

Allerthorpe village street is flanked by wide grass verges which virtually constitute a small green.[18] The church stands at one end, and at the other the street turns abruptly to become the Melbourne road. A back lane behind the garths on the north side of the village joins the street at both ends. The village consists mainly of small 18th- and 19th-century houses, but it also includes the larger Gables farm-house and a Victorian parsonage. Since the Second World War houses have been built beyond the church, in the back lane, and alongside the Melbourne road, among them eight council houses. There were two licensed alehouses in Allerthorpe in 1755 but later only one.[19] The Plough was mentioned from 1823[20] and is still the only public house in the village.

The former Allerthorpe Hall, a large brick and slate house of three storeys, stands in its own grounds in the angle between the village street and the Melbourne road. The present house was largely built between 1802 and 1809 by Charles Stanley on the

---

[1] This article was written in 1973.
[2] *P.N.E.R. Yorks.* (E.P.N.S.), 182, 184.
[3] O.S. Map 6″, Yorks. (1855 edn.). Most of Allerthorpe appears on sheet 193, the rest on sheet 176.
[4] *Census.*
[5] Geol. Surv. Map 1″, solid and drift, sheet 71 (1973 edn.).
[6] These closes are best seen on O.S. Map 6″ (1855 edn.).
[7] See p. 137.
[8] R.D.B., 1217/507/450; 1546/592/483.
[9] Ibid. 1442/432/371.
[10] Ex inf. Clerk to the Council, County Hall, Beverley, 1973.
[11] Minster Libr., Torre MS., 'Peculiars', p. 718.
[12] B. F. Duckham, *Inland Waterways of E. Yorks. 1700–1900* (E. Yorks. Loc. Hist. Ser. xxix), 64.
[13] *Fabric Rolls of York Minster* (Sur. Soc. xxxv), 241.
[14] K. A. MacMahon, *Roads and Turnpike Trusts in E. Yorks.* (E. Yorks. Loc. Hist. Ser. xviii), 7, 23, 70.
[15] e.g. R.D.B., 1518/481/431; 1573/309/264; 1598/579/484; E.R.C.C. *Mins.* 1955–6, 499; 1966–7, 20; 1967–8, 128, 131.
[16] See p. 140.
[17] See p. 138.
[18] See plate facing p. 112.
[19] E.R.R.O., QDT/2/15.
[20] Directories.

site of an 18th-century house[21] and was substantially enlarged to the east and west during the 19th century. It was known as the Lodge until c. 1850.[22] It was used as a boarding school in the 1870s,[23] and T. W. Calverley-Rudston lived there from 1878 to 1915.[24] It was divided into a number of dwellings in the 1950s.[25]

A small estate in Allerthorpe belonged to the Prickett family,[26] who were also rectorial lessees,[27] and in 1672 they had the largest house in the village, with seven hearths.[28] The house was apparently that now known as the Gables. It originated as a 17th-century brick building with a main range and a cross-wing extending towards the street at the east end. In the 18th century a similar cross-wing was added at the west end. New windows were put into the street front and there was some internal remodelling in the early 19th century, but much of this was swept away in major alterations in the 1880s,[29] when the garden front was rebuilt and the roof on that side heightened. The house was bought in 1947 by James O'Gram, who later purchased the manor.[30]

The few outlying houses in Allerthorpe include Manor Farm to the west of the village, Low, formerly Home, Farm, which was part of the Waplington Hall estate,[31] and Chicory Farm, where that crop was presumably grown. A few scattered houses have been built near the York–Hull road at different times.

Apart from Waplington Hall[32] only Manor Farm and a lodge remain at the probable site of Waplington village. The present Manor Farm is a mid-19th-century building; an earlier house stands near by and was disused in 1973. Warren House and a few cottages lie at some distance from the hall.

Fifty-nine people in Allerthorpe paid the poll tax of 1377.[33] The hearth-tax assessment of 1672 listed 31 households in the township; of the 27 that were chargeable 19 had only a single hearth, 6 had 2 or 3, and the other 2 had 5 and 7 hearths.[34] There were 27 families in the parish in 1743 and 1764.[35] In 1801 the population of Allerthorpe township was 125; it fluctuated during the rest of the century, rising to 172 in 1871, and stood at 117 in 1901.[36] It had risen to 163 by 1921 but fell to 137 in 1931. In 1951 Allerthorpe and Waplington together had a population of 240, and there were 178 inhabitants in 1971.[37]

Waplington had 15 poll-tax payers in 1377.[38] The township was apparently badly hit by the Black Death, for its tax assessment was reduced by about 40 per cent in 1354; in 1446 the reduction stood at 25 per cent.[39] In 1584 7 men attended the muster from Waplington.[40] There were 13 households in 1672, of which 4 were exempt from the hearth tax and the rest had one hearth each.[41] The population increased from 11 in 1801 to 58 in 1861, but fell to 30 in 1901.[42] There were 63 inhabitants in 1921 and 49 in 1931.[43]

William Dewsbury (1621–88), Quaker preacher and author, was born at Allerthorpe.[44]

MANORS AND OTHER ESTATES. In 1086 the king had 6 carucates at Allerthorpe as soke of his manor of Pocklington.[45] By 1185 the estate had been granted by Richard de Moreville to the Knights Templars,[46] and by 1250 the order had also acquired 6 bovates in Waplington by the gift of William son of Roger of Waplington and Simon the archer.[47] Following the Templars' suppression in 1312 the manor of *ALLERTHORPE*, together with the Waplington holding, was transferred to the Knights Hospitallers.[48]

On the eve of the Dissolution the order leased the manor to John Manners for 30 years.[49] The Hospitallers briefly regained the property from the Crown in 1558.[50] For much of Elizabeth I's reign Allerthorpe was in the hands of lessees.[51] In 1587 the property, consisting of 12 bovates, 2 closes, and some meadow, was let to Robert Myers.[52] Despite a grant to Edmund Downing and Roger Rante in 1590[53] the manor had passed by 1608 to Robert Myers. From 1625 Thomas Myers held it, described as the manor of Allerthorpe with Waplington in 1629. It was perhaps another Thomas Myers who was lord in the 1650s and a third of the same name whose guardians held the property in the 1670s.[54] The last-mentioned may have been the Thomas Myers who was lord of the manor from 1696 to 1717; he was succeeded by his son Jeremiah by 1719.[55]

By his will dated 1723 Jeremiah devised the manor to John Idle and William Cookson in trust;[56] the surviving Myers heir released her rights to Frances Idle, sister of John, in 1766.[57] Frances died the following year, whereupon the Idle inheritance passed to the Revd. Zachary Suger, son of Frances's cousin Anne Idle. In 1770 Zachary was succeeded by his sisters Martha Suger (d. c. 1773), Elizabeth

---

[21] E.R.R.O., DDPY/3/2 pp. 99, 156.
[22] Ibid. DDPY/3/3 p. 138; Sheahan and Whellan, *Hist. York & E.R.* ii. 554.
[23] *Kelly's Dir. N. & E.R. Yorks.* (1872), 311.
[24] E.R.R.O., DDPY/3/3 pp. 347–52; R.D.B., 171/105/88.
[25] R.D.B., 1018/285/260; 1061/408/368; 1093/138/119; 1141/466/394.
[26] Deeds *penes* Mr. T. O'Gram, 1974. For the Pricketts see F. F. Prickett, *Pricketts of Allerthorpe*.
[27] See p. 136.
[28] E 179/205/504.
[29] Builder's bill, 1884, *penes* Mr. O'Gram.
[30] R.D.B., 757/496/413; see p. 135.
[31] O.S. Map 6" (1855 edn.); E.R.R.O., DDX/159/2.
[32] See p. 136.
[33] E 179/202/59 m. 25.
[34] E 179/205/504.
[35] B.I.H.R., Bp. V. 1764/Ret. 16; *Herring's Visit.* i. 39.
[36] *V.C.H. Yorks.* iii. 492.
[37] *Census*.
[38] E 179/202/59 m. 77.
[39] E 179/202/53, 120.
[40] *Miscellanea*, v (Y.A.S. Rec. Ser. cxvi), 91.
[41] E 179/205/504.
[42] *V.C.H. Yorks.* iii. 492.
[43] *Census*.
[44] *D.N.B.*
[45] *V.C.H. Yorks.* ii. 197.
[46] *Rec. of Templars in Eng. in Twelfth Cent.* ed. B. A. Lees, pp. ccxi, 123.
[47] *Bk. of Fees*, ii. 1202; *Plac. de Quo Warr.* (Rec. Com.), 191.
[48] *Cal. Inq. Misc.* ii, p. 476; *Cal. Close, 1346–9*, 188; *Knights Hospitallers in Eng.* (Camd. Soc. [1st ser.], lxv), 141.
[49] *Cal. Pat.* 1560–3, 182.
[50] Ibid. 1557–8, 318–19.
[51] C 66/1287 m. 14; *Cal. Pat.* 1560–3, 182; 1569–72, p. 131.
[52] C 66/1287 m. 14.
[53] C 66/1349 m. 11.
[54] E.R.R.O., DDKP/2/1–4; B.I.H.R., CP. H. 2543.
[55] E.R.R.O., DDPY/3/1; R.D.B., F/336/724.
[56] Ibid. DDPY/3/1 p. 118; R.D.B., H/619/1254.
[57] E.R.R.O., DDPY/3/1 p. 55 (2nd part); R.D.B., AG/429/819.

Suger (d. c. 1782), and Jane Wilmer (d. 1806).[58] Jane passed the manor to her son-in-law Joshua Field in 1792.[59] Field's son John Wilmer Field died in 1837 seised of the manor and was succeeded by his daughter Delia and her husband Arthur Duncombe.[60]

In 1841 the manor consisted of 938 a., including the common.[61] In 1844 135 a. were sold to Robert Denison,[62] and a further 100 a. were disposed of in 1897.[63] Arthur Duncombe (d. 1889) was succeeded by his son C. W. Duncombe,[64] whose brother G. A. Duncombe was lord in 1913.[65] In 1919 B. A. C. Duncombe sold Manor farm, comprising 250 a., to H. E. Stubbins, and the manor and Allerthorpe common, amounting to 403 a., to Henry Whitworth.[66] Manor farm was still held by the Stubbins family in 1973. The manor and common were sold by H. P. Whitworth to James O'Gram in 1954.[67] In 1961 the Ministry of Agriculture, Fisheries and Food bought 371 a. of the common.[68]

Although a manor-house was referred to in the 16th-century grants[69] and a house formed part of the Hospitallers' estate,[70] its location is unknown. The five-hearth house occupied by Henry Johnson, husband of the widowed Judith Myers, in 1672 was possibly the manor-house,[71] and Manor Farm may stand on its site.

The relationship of the main estate at Allerthorpe with that held of the Mowbray family is not clear. By the early 13th century Robert de Maluvel held 3 carucates in Allerthorpe as tenant of Niel de Mowbray.[72] John de Mowbray, returned as lord of Allerthorpe and Waplington in 1316,[73] died c. 1327, when his lands included *ALLERTHORPE* manor as ¼ knight's fee; his heir was his son John. The site of a manor-house was mentioned c. 1327.[74]

The king had 2 carucates at Waplington in 1086 as soke of Pocklington manor,[75] but by 1198 John le Poer had been granted 2½ carucates there, which he held with land elsewhere by the service of providing an archer for the defence of York castle.[76] Thenceforth the estate descended, like another at Barmby Moor,[77] in the Poer, Chamberlain, Crepping, and Stodowe families.[78]

Poer's Waplington holding was divided in the late 12th and early 13th centuries.[79] The largest part, comprising 12 bovates, was granted by John le Poer to John son of Henry of Fishergate, and he or another of his family conveyed it to Drax priory (Yorks. W.R.), to be held of Poer and his heirs.[80] In 1275–6 the prior was paying 2s. rent to Robert de Crepping.[81] About 1339 John of Hook granted the house a further 2 bovates in Waplington, held of John de Mowbray.[82] Drax retained its estate until at least the 1370s, when the prior took action against the lessee for waste;[83] the house's connection with Waplington was apparently severed before the Dissolution.

The Drax estate probably passed to the Percy family: in 1389 Henry Percy, created earl of Northumberland, was holding 2 carucates in Waplington of Denise Stodowe, and the custody of Robert Stodowe's inheritance in the township and elsewhere was subsequently granted to Henry Percy, the earl's son.[84] Waplington was forfeited to the Crown by the Percys in 1405 but restored to them in 1416.[85] In 1455 Henry Percy's lands included *WAPLINGTON* manor.[86] The estate, held in chief by 1489,[87] was conveyed to the Crown by Henry Percy, earl of Northumberland (d. 1537), along with his other northern estates, in 1537.[88]

The descent thereafter is confused. As a member of Pocklington manor Waplington was allegedly granted to Thomas Bishop during Henry VIII's reign.[89] After July 1553 Bishop complained of dispossession by his erstwhile steward Thomas Doweman, who with Christopher Estofte certainly secured a royal grant of the property in that month.[90] The Doweman, or Dolman, and Bishop families were apparently intermittently in dispute over Waplington for the rest of the century,[91] and c. 1590 Thomas Dolman was taking the issues of property in Waplington which was held to belong to the Crown by Thomas Bishop's attainder.[92] A licence for another Thomas Bishop to grant rents there to Marmaduke Dolman in 1628 may represent the end of the affair.[93] Sir Robert Dolman was dealing in the manor in 1625.[94] The Crown later seized part of it for Thomas Dolman's recusancy but let the property to him from 1629.[95] The manor was sequestrated by the Commonwealth and sold in 1653 to Edward Tooke,[96] but it was apparently regained by the Dolmans shortly afterwards.[97]

Under the terms of an Act of 1765,[98] which

[58] E.R.R.O., DDPY/3/1 pp. 122, 135, 146, 174; DDKP/17/4.
[59] Ibid. DDPY/3/2 pp. 7–8.
[60] Ibid. DDPY/3/10.
[61] R.D.B., FO/13/16.
[62] Ibid. GC/195/233.
[63] Ibid. 88/485/464 (1897).
[64] J. Foster, *Pedigrees of . . . Yorks.* iii; *Kelly's Dir. N. & E.R. Yorks.* (1893), 356–7.
[65] *Kelly's Dir. N. & E.R. Yorks.* (1913), 442–3.
[66] R.D.B., 206/246/209; /478/416.
[67] Ibid. 963/266/239.
[68] Ibid. 1217/507/450.
[69] e.g. *Cal. Pat.* 1560–3, 182.
[70] *Knights Hospitallers*, 141.
[71] E 179/205/504; B.I.H.R., CP. H. 2982.
[72] *Bk. of Fees*, ii. 1461.
[73] *Feud. Aids*, vi. 167.
[74] *Cal. Inq. p.m.* vii, pp. 53–4.
[75] *V.C.H. Yorks.* ii. 197.
[76] *V.C.H. City of York*, 521; *Bk. of Fees*, i. 4–5; ii. 1354.
[77] See p. 142.
[78] C 136/64 no. 4; *Bk. of Fees*, ii. 1202; *Cal. Fine R.* 1347–56, 248; 1383–91, 339; *Cal. Inq. p.m.* ii, p. 199.
[79] *Bk. of Fees*, ii. 1202; *Cur. Reg. R.* i. 365; *Plac. de Quo Warr.* 191.
[80] C 145/178 no. 17; *E.Y.C.* i, pp. 344–5; *Bk. of Fees*, ii. 1202. A 14th-cent. inspeximus suggests that Poer's grant was made directly to Drax: *Cal. Chart. R.* 1300–26, 180.
[81] *Rot. Hund.* (Rec. Com.), i. 104.
[82] C 145/178 no. 17; *Cal. Pat.* 1338–40, 243.
[83] *Monastic Notes*, i (Y.A.S. Rec. Ser. xvii), 42.
[84] C 136/64 no. 4; *Cal. Fine R.* 1383–91, 339; 1391–9, 69; *Rot. Hund.* i. 104.
[85] J. M. W. Bean, *Estates of Percy Family, 1416–1537*, 159; see below p. 151.
[86] C 139/160 no. 20.
[87] C 142/5 no. 14.
[88] Bean, *Percy Estates*, 154. For Percy pedigree see *Complete Peerage*, s.v. Northumberland.
[89] E 318/Box 6/222.
[90] C 1/1492 no. 67; E 318/Box 28/1599; *Cal. Pat.* 1553, 257. For Dolman pedigree see Foster, *Pedigrees of . . . Yorks.* iii.
[91] *Cal. Pat.* 1560–3, 394; *Yorks. Fines*, i. 271; ii. 148, 174.
[92] E 178/3018.
[93] E.R.R.O., DDPY/19/6.
[94] C.P. 25(2)/518 pt. 2/1 Chas. I East. no. 3.
[95] C 66/2689 no. 8.
[96] E.R.R.O., DDPY/19/7; *Cal. Cttee. for Compounding*, iv. 2642; *Royalist Composition Papers*, iii (Y.A.S. Rec. Ser. xx), 22.
[97] C.P. 25(2)/615 no. 9.
[98] 5 Geo. III, c. 91 (Priv. Act).

enabled some of Robert Dolman's estates to be sold to clear the family's debts and provide for its younger members, Waplington manor was conveyed to George Ewbank and Samuel Waud in 1769; Ewbank sold his interest to Waud in 1772. In 1775 the property passed to Henry Egerton and in 1776 to Samuel Crompton. The latter sold it to Thomas Chatterton and John Ball in 1788, and the manor was consequently divided into moieties in 1790. Purchases of 1804 reunited the property in the hands of Charles Stanley, who sold it to Robert Cockburn in 1831. Cockburn's tenure was short, ending in 1837 with a sale to Robert Denison of Kilnwick Percy,[99] who retained the property until at least 1856.[1] The manor was subsequently held by the Haffenden family,[2] before its acquisition by George Walker in 1882.[3]

In 1914 Walker's trustees sold Waplington to Walter Cliff.[4] A. F. Burton acquired the manor, Waplington Hall, and three farms, in all comprising 914 a. in Waplington and Allerthorpe, from Cliff's executors in 1920.[5] The property has since been divided. The hall was sold by A. C. Burton in 1950 and thereafter converted into separate dwellings.[6] In 1972 Burton sold the 334-acre Manor farm to John Huxtable, but in 1973 his trustees still retained over 500 a.[7]

A house on the Drax estate was referred to in the 1370s.[8] No large house at Waplington was mentioned in the hearth-tax assessment of 1672.[9] A map of 1839 shows no house, but Stonehouse croft lay close to a garth on the site of the later hall.[10] In 1846 Waplington Manor was described as a large mansion about four years old.[11] The house, which had been renamed Waplington Hall by 1856,[12] was surrounded by a park with a large lake.[13] It is a large and irregular building of brick and slate.

Wilberfoss priory held 2 bovates in Waplington by serjeanty in 1250.[14] A 2-bovate estate in Allerthorpe, held by Thicket priory of the Hospitallers at the Dissolution, was granted by the Crown to Henry Jones c. 1560.[15]

After 1252 Allerthorpe rectory belonged to the dean of York.[16] The tithes of corn and hay in Allerthorpe township were let to George Hall, farmer of the manor, in 1560 for 43 years, and his successors as lords of the manor leased them for lives from 1596.[17] They were worth £51 a year in 1650, when the wool and lamb tithes yielded about £13.[18] The tithes were commuted in 1839 for £185, including £30 for those of wool and lambs.[19] The 2-bovate rectorial glebe, first mentioned in 1593, was apparently let separately in the late 16th and early 17th centuries,[20] but from 1616 onwards it was usually included in the lease of the Waplington tithes. Leases for lives were adopted in the mid 17th century, and the Prickett family farmed these properties in the 17th and early 18th centuries.[21] They were followed as impropriators in the 1730s by the Revd. Leonard Ash.[22] In 1759 the lease passed to the Clark family, as relatives of Elizabeth Ash,[23] and the Clark trustees were still farming the tithes in 1839.[24] The corn and hay tithes of Waplington were worth £14 a year in 1650, the wool and lamb tithes £3 10s.[25] In 1839 the dean was awarded £61 for the Waplington tithes.[26] The rectory was vested in the Ecclesiastical Commissioners in 1844.[27]

ECONOMIC HISTORY. By 1185 the Templars had let 5 of the 6 carucates they held at Allerthorpe.[28] Their tenants' obligations included carrying services to the order's properties at York, Faxfleet, and Weedley.[29] In 1327 the demesne lands of the Mowbray manor of Allerthorpe consisted of 16 a. sown with 'winter seed' and 19 a. with 'summer seed', as well as some fallow land and 6 a. of meadow. There were few tenants on the manor; 4 bondsmen paid 6s. for 4 bovates of land, and about 10s. was received from free tenants and 4 tenants-at-will.[30] The Hospitallers' manor had 310 a. of demesne in 1338, and its tenants' rents were valued at about £9, including 4s. for works.[31] The demesne was farmed out in 1363.[32] In 1539–40 the Hospitallers' estate in Allerthorpe and Waplington comprised about 40 bovates, excluding the demesne and some inclosed and waste land. Several individual strips or 'ridges' of land were rented by tenants, including two in Ox field. Of a total charge of £22 the rents of the tenants of 15 houses, 18 cottages, and land accounted for about £15; the residue represented the bailiff's farm of the demesne.[33]

At the beginning of the 17th century Allerthorpe had three open fields: Kirk field to the east of the village, North field towards the Hull–York road, and

---

[99] E.R.R.O., DDKP/15/17, abstract of title of Rob. Denison, 1765–1841.
[1] Sheahan and Whellan, *Hist. York & E.R.* ii. 554.
[2] R.B.D., HX/94/117; IB/204/261; LQ/304/428; NB/262/429; *Kelly's Dir. N. & E.R. Yorks.* (1872), 311; (1879), 338.
[3] R.D.B., NM/206/334.
[4] Ibid. 53/162/153 (1892); 164/53/46; *Kelly's Dir. N. & E.R. Yorks.* (1893), 356; (1897), 385; (1901), 403; (1913), 442.
[5] R.D.B., 181/291/245; 209/398/337.
[6] Ibid. 866/9/9; 953/24/23; 962/1/1; 984/440/396.
[7] Ibid. 1201/555/498; 1787/208/169.
[8] *Monastic Notes*, i. 42.   [9] E 179/205/504.
[10] B.I.H.R., TA. 441S.
[11] White, *Dir. Hull & York* (1846), 469.
[12] Sheahan and Whellan, *Hist. York & E.R.* ii. 554.
[13] O.S. Map 6" (1855 edn.).
[14] *Bk. of Fees*, ii. 1202.
[15] E 318/Box 44/2402; *Valor Eccl.* (Rec. Com.), v. 94.
[16] See p. 187.
[17] Minster Libr., Torre MS., 'York Minster', p. 542; D. & C. Archives, S 3 (5) a, f. 1; S 3 (5) c, ff. 1–2; W 2 (1788); E.R.R.O., DDDA/32/3; R.D.B., D/166/274; F/360/772; FD/324/369; Lamb. Pal. Libr., COMM./ XIIa/17/374–5; B.I.H.R., CC. DY. Allerthorpe; *Y.A.J.* xiv. 122.
[18] Lamb. Pal. Libr., COMM./XIIa/17/374–5; *Y.A.J.* xiv. 122.
[19] B.I.H.R., TA. 317M.
[20] Minster Libr., Torre MS., 'York Minster', pp. 542–3.
[21] Ibid. D. & C. Arch., S 1 (2) f, ff. 5, 15; S 3 (5) a, f. 14; S 3 (5) b, pp. 87–9; Lamb. Pal. Libr., COMM./XIIa/17/374–5; *Y.A.J.* xiv. 122; see above p. 134.
[22] Minster Libr., D. & C. Arch., S 3 (5) a, f. 14; S 3 (5) c, f. 65; R.D.B., N/200/449; /392/859.
[23] R.D.B., AB/115/257; Minster Libr., D. & C. Arch., S 3 (5) c, f. 65; W 2 (1783, 1785).
[24] R.D.B., FD/139/155; Minster Libr., D. & C. Arch., S 1 (1) e, f. 38d.
[25] Lamb. Pal. Libr., COMM./XIIa/17/374–5; *Y.A.J.* xiv. 122.
[26] B.I.H.R., TA. 441S.
[27] *Lond. Gaz.* 19 July 1844, p. 2499.
[28] *Y.A.J.* xxix. 380.
[29] *Rec. Templars*, 123.
[30] C 135/5 no. 5.
[31] *Knights Hospitallers*, 141.
[32] *Yorks. Sess. of Peace* (Y.A.S. Rec. Ser. c), 60.
[33] *Miscellanea*, iv (Y.A.S. Rec. Ser. xciv), 100.

South field between the village and Waplington.[34] The township also had land in closes, some of which lay within the confines of the open fields.[35] Meadow land, including the Great ings, lay alongside the beck on the south-eastern boundary of the township.[36]

To the west of the village, and connected with it by an outgang, lay the common, where householders were entitled to agist their cattle, to cut turves once a year, and to take whins and wood for repairs.[37] These rights were extinguished by agreement in 1961.[38] Encroachment on the waste is suggested by 'Moresickeclose', which was mentioned in 1628, and by the New intack in Barmby Butts of 1633.[39] The common was similarly diminished in the 18th century. By 1741 another close called Intack had been made from High moor,[40] and this may be the inclosure called New Piece in 1839.[41]

Some of the land reclaimed from the common was used as stinted pasture. The manorial court regulated the fencing and grazing of Cow Hold, west of the village, where tenants had beast-gates, from the 17th to the 19th century.[42] The Reas, or Old Hold,[43] towards Barmby may also have been used in common. Other common pastures probably lay in the north and east of the township; there were gates in Prick moor and the Pearts in the 17th and 18th centuries,[44] and a close called Ox Hold was mentioned from 1612.[45]

By 'the exchange and new inclosure' of 1640 the open fields were divided and allotted in unspecified amounts to about 20 tenants.[46] Meadow land was probably apportioned at about the same time, and in 1656 reference was made to inclosed land in the ings. One of the new closes was still 'inclosed, stooped and railed' in 1657, although its lessee was empowered to remove these temporary divisions and had agreed to hedge one of its sides.[47] In the 1780s the seigneurial estate of 448 a. was held by 9 tenants, and 26 freeholders and tenants had a further 504 a. in the parish.[48]

At Waplington the estate of Drax priory was worth about £1 a year in 1359[49] and had been farmed out by the 1370s, when Thomas of Waplington was accused of wasting the property. The buildings included cow- and sheep-houses, stables, and granaries, as well as the house itself.[50] The Percy estate in Waplington was said in 1455 to be worth only £1 net because of neglect there,[51] but by the late 15th and mid 16th centuries its annual value had risen to nearly £4.[52]

Waplington had its own open fields, mentioned in 1563[53] and named in 1774 as North, South, and Leys fields. In the latter year the lord and the two other proprietors of the township agreed to consolidate their holdings, and in 1777 the same two owners ceded their rights in the 169-acre common to the lord. Closes mentioned in the 18th century included some like Moor Syke which had almost certainly been made by encroachment on the common.[54]

The common was apparently used as a warren. Between 1777 and 1839 all but 40 a. was inclosed, some of the closes being named after the warren.[55] By the 1850s Warren farm had been established on the former common.[56] Two other fields described as warren in 1839 were later taken into the grounds of Waplington Hall.[57]

In the 19th and 20th centuries there were generally 6 to 8 farmers in Allerthorpe, 2 of whom had over 150 a. in the 1930s. Waplington was farmed by one to 3 farmers over the same period; in the 1930s the township's two farms were under one management.[58]

In 1786 at Allerthorpe there were 525 a. of pasture, 294 a. of meadow, 83 a. of corn, and 49 a. of fallow and turnips.[59] Only 77 a. were returned as under crops in 1801.[60] There were 700 a. of arable, 421 a. of grassland, and 450 a. of common at Allerthorpe in 1839. In that year Waplington had 647 a. of arable, 53 a. of grassland, 40 a. of common, and 50 a. of woodland.[61] By 1905 Allerthorpe and Waplington together had 942 a. of arable, 522 a. of permanent grass, and 127 a. of woodland.[62] Land use in the two townships changed little from the 1930s onwards; woodland covered a considerable area of the parish, notably on the common, and arable was more significant than grassland.[63] Since 1961 the Forestry Commission has managed about 350 a. of Allerthorpe common.[64]

The name Hempdike close, mentioned in the 17th century, suggests the retting of hemp, as do the hemp pits which lay to the west of the village in 1851. There was a saw-mill in Waplington in the same year; it was presumably steam-operated for close by was a tank, from which Tank plantation and Tank cottages were named.[65] A brickyard had been established in Waplington by 1840, but was not mentioned again.[66] Brickpit plantation is situated near Warren House in the south-west of the township and Brickpond plantation close to Waplington Hall.[67] Gravel was being extracted commercially from a pit near Chicory Farm in 1973. In 1960 land and buildings in Allerthorpe which had been part of

[34] E.R.R.O., DDKP 2/1 (1610, 1611).
[35] Ibid. (1609).
[36] Ibid. DDPY/3/1 (1700); B.I.H.R., TA. 317M.
[37] B.I.H.R., TA. 317M; E.R.R.O., DDPY/3/9 (1834), 11.
[38] R.D.B., 1217/510/451.
[39] E.R.R.O., DDKP/2/2.
[40] R.D.B., R/45/105.
[41] B.I.H.R., TA. 317M.
[42] E.R.R.O., DDKP/2/3 (1653); DDPY/3/9 (1843).
[43] Ibid. DDPY/3/6 (1725).
[44] Ibid. DDKP/2/3 (1654); DDPY/3/1 (1700).
[45] Ibid. DDKP/2/1.
[46] Ibid. DDKP/2/2. There is no inclosure award as such, but the manorial court roll contains the surrenders and admissions by which the inclosure was effected. No details of the lord's part in the inclosure are given.
[47] Ibid. DDKP/2/2 (1635); /2/3.
[48] B.I.H.R., CC. DY. Allerthorpe.
[49] C 145/178 no. 17.
[50] *Monastic Notes*, i. 42.
[51] C 139/160 no. 20.
[52] C 142/5 no. 14; S.C. 6/ Hen. VIII /4283–91.
[53] Castle Howard MS., Box 24, Survey of Estates, 1563.
[54] E.R.R.O., DDKP/1/3.
[55] B.I.H.R., TA. 441S; R.D.B., CS/530/745.
[56] Sheahan and Whellan, *Hist. York & E.R.* ii. 554.
[57] B.I.H.R., TA. 441S; O.S. Map 6″ (1855 edn.).
[58] Directories.
[59] B.I.H.R., CC. DY. Allerthorpe.
[60] 1801 Crop Returns.
[61] B.I.H.R., TA. 317M, 441S.
[62] Acreage Returns, 1905.
[63] [1st] Land Util. Surv. Map, sheet 27; 2nd Land Util. Surv. Map, sheet 699 (SE 64–74).
[64] See p. 135.
[65] E.R.R.O., DDPY/3/1 (1697); O.S. Map 6″ (1855 edn.).
[66] White, *Dir. E. & N.R. Yorks.* (1840), 232.
[67] O.S. Map 6″, SE 74 NE. (1958 edn.).

Pocklington airfield were sold by the Air Ministry,[68] and they have since been used by a timber products firm[69] and agricultural trading companies.[70]

A windmill was mentioned at Allerthorpe as early as 1327, and there were possibly two in the township by 1338.[71] In the 16th century George Hall, farmer of the manor, rebuilt a windmill;[72] the mill may have stood to the north-west of the village, in or near the field called Mill Doors, and was last mentioned in 1791.[73]

LOCAL GOVERNMENT. Drax priory claimed amends of the assize of ale at Waplington in 1293.[74] Court rolls of the manor of Allerthorpe with Waplington survive for 1608–47, 1653–61, and 1669–79.[75] The series is continued by court books covering 1696–1941.[76] There are also surrenders and admissions from 1576 to 1786,[77] a minute book and call roll for the period 1860–99,[78] and a book of pains for 1812–99.[79]

In 1609 the manorial officers included a greave, a constable, a pinder, 4 bylawmen, 2 aletasters, and 2 overseers of highways.[80] Two affeerors were mentioned in the 18th century.[81] In 1653 2 of the bylawmen were for the husbandmen and 2 for the grassmen.[82] There were only 2 bylawmen at Allerthorpe after the inclosure of the open fields;[83] in 1758 one was responsible for Low and the other for High moor.[84] The bylawmen were said to supervise the taking of wood from the common as late as 1870.[85] By the 19th century there were 2 constables and 2 pinders, and the officers in 1899 still included 2 affeerors, a bylawman, and 2 pinders.[86]

No parochial records survive before 1835. There were 2 overseers of the poor at Allerthorpe by 1814, when they opposed the fiscal demands of the Pocklington overseers.[87] Allerthorpe and Waplington joined Pocklington poor-law union in 1836[88] and Pocklington rural district in 1894.[89] They became part of the North Wolds district of Humberside in 1974.

CHURCH. The early history of Allerthorpe church is the same as that of Thornton, except that Allerthorpe was not concerned in the confirmation of 1225. The curacy of Allerthorpe was usually held by the vicar of Thornton from the 17th century, and in 1973 the two places still constituted a united vicarage.[90]

In 1525–6 a chaplain serving Allerthorpe received £4 a year.[91] Allerthorpe was worth c. £76 in 1818,[92] and in 1835 the curate's stipend was £60.[93]

Small tithes in Allerthorpe contributed to the income of the joint living. At the ordination of 1252 the tithes of gardens, flax, and hemp, as well as a share of the altarage, were assigned to the vicarage.[94] The small tithes were worth £3 in 1650.[95] By 1684 the inhabitants of Allerthorpe and Waplington were paying a composition of £5 a year for tithes and surplice fees,[96] and in 1839 rent-charges of £60 were awarded to the vicar of Thornton and Allerthorpe in lieu of the Allerthorpe tithes and £13 12s. for those of Waplington.[97]

In the late 17th century the glebe in Allerthorpe consisted of two gates in the Cow Hold, the right to two loads of turf and whins from the common, and 2 a. in Yorkgate close;[98] by 1726 1 a. in Prick Moor close had also been acquired.[99] A small house and garth belonged to the church in 1684 and were possibly intended for the curate's use. In the 17th and 18th centuries, however, the incumbent of the joint living resided at Thornton.[1] By 1809 the vicar had moved to Allerthorpe and occupied a brick-built house containing two parlours, a kitchen, a back kitchen, and seven bedrooms.[2] The Vicarage was replaced in the 1860s, when adjoining land was bought and a large brick house built on the enlarged site with a grant from the Common Fund.[3]

In the 18th and early 19th centuries the incumbent also held the vicarage of Barmby Moor and Fangfoss.[4] Allerthorpe and Waplington marriages often took place at Thornton in the 18th century.[5] In 1743 there was a service at Allerthorpe once a fortnight; Holy Communion was celebrated four times a year and about 45 people communicated at Easter.[6] By 1851 services were weekly,[7] but the average number of communicants was only about 15 by 1865.[8] Between 1877 and 1915 two services a week were generally held.[9] There were weekly celebrations of Holy Communion in 1915; at Easter 1914 there were 19 communicants.[10] In 1973 there were three services a month in the church, two of which were held with the Methodists, and a further united service was held in the Methodist chapel.

The original church of *ST. BOTOLPH* was small, and consisted of chancel and nave with pedi-

---

[68] R.D.B., 1180/6/5; 1195/509/452; /511/453.
[69] Ibid. 1205/299/273.
[70] Ibid. 1368/509/454; 1540/163/151.
[71] C 135/5 no. 5; *Knights Hospitallers*, 141.
[72] Lamb. Pal. Libr., COMM./XIIa/17/473.
[73] Minster Libr., D. & C. Arch., W 2 (1784, 1791); Torre MS., 'York Minster', p. 542; E.R.R.O., DDFA/9/5, 8, 10, 11.
[74] *Plac. de Quo Warr.* 191.
[75] E.R.R.O., DDKP/2/1–4.
[76] Ibid. DDPY/3/1–3, 15.
[77] Ibid. DDPY/3/5; DDKP/2/5.
[78] Ibid. DDPY/3/4.
[79] Ibid. DDPY/3/9.
[80] Ibid. DDKP/2/1.
[81] Ibid. DDPY/3/1 (1727).
[82] Ibid. DDKP/2/3.
[83] Ibid. DDKP/2/3 (1660); DDPY/3/1 (1697).
[84] Ibid. DDPY/3/1.
[85] Ibid. DDPY/3/11.
[86] Ibid. DDPY/3/9 (1813, 1879, 1899).
[87] Ibid. DDPY/3/9.
[88] *3rd Rep. Poor Law Com.* 169.
[89] *Census.*
[90] See pp. 187–8.
[91] *Y.A.J.* xxiv. 72.
[92] Lawton, *Rer. Eccl. Dioc. Ebor.* 316.
[93] *Rep. Com. Eccl. Revenues*, 972.
[94] *Reg. Gray*, pp. 212–13.
[95] Lamb. Pal. Libr., COMM./XIIa/17/373.
[96] B.I.H.R., TER. I. Allerthorpe 1684.
[97] Ibid. TA. 317M, 441S.
[98] Ibid. TER. I. Allerthorpe 1684.
[99] Ibid. TER. I. Allerthorpe 1726.
[1] Ibid. TER. I. Thornton 1716, 1786; CP. H. 1783; *Herring's Visit.* i. 39.
[2] B.I.H.R., TER. I. Allerthorpe 1809.
[3] Ibid. TER. I. Allerthorpe 1865; R.D.B., JO/270/390; JT/287/403; *Lond. Gaz.* 5 Apr. 1867, p. 2126.
[4] B.I.H.R., Bp. V. 1764/Ret. 16, 45, 82, 178; TER. I. Barmby Moor and Thornton 1716, 1726, 1781, 1809, 1825; *Herring's Visit.* i. 39.
[5] B.I.H.R., PR. THORN. 3.
[6] *Herring's Visit.* i. 39.
[7] H.O. 129/23/516.
[8] B.I.H.R., V. 1865/Ret. 540.
[9] Ibid. V. 1877/Ret.; Bp. V. 1884/Ret.; Bp. V. 1894/Ret.; Bp. V. 1915/Ret.
[10] Ibid. Bp. V. 1915/Ret.

mented bellcot and south porch.[11] It was in decay in 1615.[12] In the early 19th century a vestry was added to the north of the chancel.[13] It was rebuilt in 1876, by Arthur Duncombe,[14] of limestone rubble with ashlar dressings, in a mixture of 14th- and 15th-century styles; it comprises chancel with north vestry and nave with bellcot and south door. The bellcot is supported by a large corbelled buttress.

The church has two bells as it had in 1552.[15] There was one chalice in 1552, a second having been stolen.[16] The plate includes a silver communion cup, made in York in 1570, and a pewter flagon and paten. In 1876 a silver service consisting of a chalice, paten, and flagon was presented by Charlotte Sykes, Arthur Duncombe's daughter.[17]

The registers begin in 1616, with no entries for baptisms in 1674–81 or marriages in 1674–95, and burial entries cease in 1695.[18]

Despite the grant of burial rights to Allerthorpe in 1360, and the entries in the Allerthorpe register, many Allerthorpe burials took place at Pocklington from the early 17th century[19] and there were also some at Thornton in the 18th century.[20] The churchyard at Allerthorpe, described as the 'ancient' one, was, however, consecrated in 1828[21] and used thereafter.

NONCONFORMITY. There were three Roman Catholics at Allerthorpe between 1637 and 1640.[22] Members of the Dolman family, lords of Waplington manor, were punished for recusancy in the 17th and 18th centuries.[23]

In 1814 the Methodists had seven members at Allerthorpe,[24] and a house was registered for dissenting, presumably Methodist, worship in 1824.[25] Wesleyan Methodists met in a house in 1851,[26] but a chapel was built in 1869–70 and was still used in 1973.[27] There was also a Primitive Methodist 'preaching-house' at Allerthorpe between 1861 and 1866.[28]

EDUCATION. An old woman taught at Allerthorpe in 1743,[29] and in 1819 12 children attended an unendowed school there.[30] By 1835 the school drew a yearly income of £9 from a bequest of £200 under John Hart's will, dated 1818; 9 of the 23 pupils were then taught free.[31] In 1865 c. 30 pupils attended what was described as an unendowed church school.[32] It was later united with the National Society. There were 17 pupils in 1871, only one a fee-payer.[33] A new building was provided in 1874;[34] its income in 1876 came entirely from the fees of the 22 pupils.[35] By a Scheme of 1875 the school was allotted half the income from the Poor's Houses, Poor's Land, and Westoby's charities, and the whole of that from Hart's.[36] From 1878 the school received an annual government grant.[37]

Between 1907 and 1927 30–40 children attended the school, but by 1938 only nineteen.[38] In 1956 the senior pupils were transferred to Pocklington, and in 1958 the school was closed, the junior pupils similarly transferred,[39] and Hart's charity vested in the Diocesan Board of Finance. Since 1960 the former school has been used as a village hall.[40]

CHARITIES FOR THE POOR. Thomas Wood, by will dated 1568, devised a rent-charge of £10 from an estate at Kilnwick Percy for the benefit of Allerthorpe, Waplington, and many other townships. In 1824 3s. 6d. was distributed in Allerthorpe and 1s. 8d. in Waplington.[41] Henry Frederick, Baron Hotham, owner of the Kilnwick Percy estate, redeemed the rent-charge in 1961 and £7 stock was subsequently assigned to Allerthorpe and £3 to Waplington.[42]

William Westoby's charity had been established by 1659,[43] and in the late 17th century its net annual value was £4.[44] In 1813, when the trustees held c. 8 a. in Allerthorpe, the bulk of the income of £15 was distributed in doles of £2 to £6 to unrelieved inhabitants.[45]

At the inclosure of the open fields in 1640 two selions were assigned to the poor of the township,[46] and in 1777 the income of £2 from the Poor's Land, an acre in Prick Moor close, was administered by the Westoby trustees.

The Poor's Houses charity originated in 1765, when William Bell gave a house for the poor. By 1813 there were 2 houses divided into 3 dwellings. Of the 5 dwellings of 1824 2 were occupied rent-free by widows receiving pensions from the Poor's Land charity and one by a man supported by the parish.[47] The houses were sold before 1875.[48]

By a Scheme of 1875 the Westoby, Poor's Land, and Poor's Houses charities were consolidated and half of the net income applied to education. The poor's share of the income was applied mainly to gifts of money and goods. The charity lands were sold in the 1950s and 1960s. In 1973 the income,

---

[11] T. Allen, *Hist. Co. York*, iii. 416; Sheahan and Whellan, *Hist. York & E.R.* ii. 554.
[12] B.I.H.R., V. 1615/CB. f. 188.
[13] Sheahan and Whellan, *Hist. York & E.R.* ii. 554.
[14] *Yorks. Ch. Plate*, i. 211; *Kelly's Dir. N. & E.R. Yorks.* (1879), 338.
[15] B.I.H.R., TER. I. Allerthorpe 1770; Boulter, 'Ch. Bells', 26; *Inventories of Ch. Goods*, 75.
[16] *Inventories of Ch. Goods*, 75.
[17] *Yorks. Ch. Plate*, i. 211.
[18] B.I.H.R.
[19] Pocklington par. reg., *penes* the vicar.
[20] B.I.H.R., PR. THORN. 3.
[21] Ibid. CD. 148.
[22] Aveling, *Post Reformation Catholicism*, 59.
[23] E.R.R.O., QDR/2/21–2; see p. 135.
[24] E.R.R.O., MRP/1/7.
[25] B.I.H.R., DMH. Reg. 1, p. 460; G.R.O. Worship Returns, Vol. v, no. 3890.
[26] H.O. 129/23/516.
[27] G.R.O. Worship Reg. no. 19779; E.R.R.O., MRP/1/70, 94.
[28] G.R.O. Worship Reg. no. 13740.
[29] *Herring's Visit.* i. 39.
[30] *Educ. of Poor Digest*, 1075.
[31] *Educ. Enquiry Abstract*, 1078; Char. Com. files.
[32] B.I.H.R., V. 1865/Ret. 540.
[33] *Returns relating to Elem. Educ.* 794.
[34] Char. Com. files.
[35] Ed. 7/135 no. 3.
[36] Ed. 49/8507; see below.
[37] *Rep. of Educ. Cttee. of Council, 1877–8* [C. 2048-I], p. 838, H.C. (1878), xxviii.
[38] *Bd. of Educ. List 21* (H.M.S.O.).
[39] E.R. Educ. Cttee. *Mins.* 1955–6, 152; 1957–8, 196.
[40] Ex inf. Secy., York Dioc. Bd. of Finance, 1974; see p. 140.
[41] *11th Rep. Com. Char.* 721–2, 735.
[42] Ex inf. Char. Com., Liverpool, 1974.
[43] E.R.R.O., DDKP/2/3.
[44] Ibid. DDBV/2/1.
[45] *11th Rep. Com. Char.* 721–2.
[46] E.R.R.O., DDKP/2/2.
[47] *11th Rep. Com. Char.* 721–2.
[48] Char. Com. files.

together with that from Wood's charity, was £59 from £1,258 stock; grants of over £4 each were made to seven persons. The educational part of the income was in 1973 vested in the Diocesan Board of Finance.[49]

BARMBY MOOR

THE PARISH of Barmby Moor lies 11 miles east of York astride the York–Hull trunk road and close to the market-town of Pocklington.[1] The village was probably a Scandinavian settlement, 'Barne's farm'; it was not until the late 13th century that Barmby was used as an alternative spelling to Barnby. The suffix 'by Pocklington' was used in the 14th century,[2] when 'in' or 'upon the Moor', perhaps a reference to Spalding moor, also appeared.[3] Though the parish was occasionally called simply Barnby Moor in the 18th century,[4] it was not until 1935 that the shortened form was officially adopted.[5] The irregularly-shaped parish covered 2,578 a. in 1851.[6] In 1901 50 a. were transferred to Pocklington civil parish,[7] and in 1960 the boundaries of the civil and ecclesiastical parishes of Barmby were brought into conformity.[8]

From below 50 ft. above sea-level in the western part of the parish the ground rises to over 100 ft. in the north-east. The village was established just to the north of the junction of the Roman roads from York and Stamford Bridge to Brough, beside a beck running from Keld, or Skel,[9] spring. The northern and western parish boundaries are largely formed by Black dike, which flows southwards towards the Beck in Thornton. The parish is almost entirely covered with outwash sand and gravel, but Keuper marl and sandstone, glacial sand and gravel, and alluvium form a small area in the north.[10] The open fields lay north and east of the village on the sand and gravel, and an extensive common was situated on the low-lying sandy area in the west and south of the parish. The open fields and other common lands were inclosed in 1783. A large area to the east of the village was used by the Royal Air Force for Pocklington airfield, opened in 1941. The airfield ceased to be operational in 1946 and closed in 1965.[11] Part of it was later converted to industrial and recreational uses, and much has been reclaimed for agriculture.[12]

The Roman road from Brough formed part of Barmby's southern boundary before it entered the parish near the village. The precise course of the branch to Stamford Bridge is now lost. The course of the York branch is, however, still followed by the main York–Hull road. The road was turnpiked in 1764 and the trust renewed until 1881.[13] A toll-bar was situated ½ mile west of the village near the house known in 1974 as Bar Farm; two mile-stones erected by the trust survive.[14] The road was straightened south of the village in the late 1960s and in the west of the parish in 1974.[15]

A branch from the main road passes through the village and continues towards Pocklington; it was known as Barmby Row from the 15th century.[16] Another branch from the main road leads to Yapham and crosses the Pocklington road on the outskirts of the village. Other minor roads lead from the York road to Sutton upon Derwent and Stamford Bridge, and in the east of the parish Hodsow Lane connects the main road with Pocklington. In 1348 a hermit of Stamford Bridge chapel was seeking alms for the repair of a road across Barmby moor,[17] possibly the road from Stamford Bridge which crossed the common to enter the village from the west until it was diverted to the York road at inclosure.[18] The railway from York to Market Weighton, opened in 1847, passed through the parish.[19] The line was closed in 1965[20] and the track has been lifted; a former gatehouse stands beside the Yapham road.

The church and the moated manor-house site stand together at the village centre. Further west many houses formerly stood along the margins of the common and its two wedge-shaped projections into the village.[21] The personal names *de* and *super viridi* and 'of the green', used by eight inhabitants c. 1295,[22] perhaps referred to the common. After the inclosure of the common in 1783 the projections were left as 'greens', one alongside the main street and the other around a parallel street beside the beck. The two streets are connected by short cross lanes on either side of the manor-house site, one of which was called Hall Spout in the mid 19th century,[23] and by a third lane at the western end of the village along the former common edge.

In addition to the two greens there are wide grass verges beside other streets in the village. By 1772 the beckside green already contained an island garth,[24] later occupied by the 19th-century Kimberley House and other buildings. Further encroachment occurred in the later 19th century; in 1863, for example, a tenant rented from the lord a piece of land inclosed from the village waste in front of his

---

[49] Char. Com. files; see p. 139; ex inf. the vicar, 1974.
[1] This article was written in 1974.
[2] *Cal. Pat.* 1343–5, 310; 1345–8, 192; *Cal. Fine R.* 1383–91, 155.
[3] *P.N.E.R. Yorks.* (E.P.N.S.), 184–5.
[4] e.g. B.I.H.R., TER. I. Barmby Moor 1726, 1743, 1749.
[5] *Census*, 1931.
[6] O.S. Map 6″, Yorks. (1854–5 edn.). Most of the parish appears on sheet 176 and the rest on sheets 175, 192–3.
[7] E.R.R.O., CCO. 92.
[8] *Lond. Gaz.* 15 Apr. 1960, p. 2720.
[9] E.R.R.O., DDPY/5/2 pp. 117–213; O.S. Map 6″ (1854–5 edn.).
[10] Geol. Surv. Map 1″, solid and drift, sheet 71 (1973 edn.).
[11] Ex inf. Ministry of Defence, 1972.
[12] For industry see p. 144.

[13] K. A. MacMahon, *Roads and Turnpike Trusts in E. Yorks.* (E. Yorks. Loc. Hist. Ser. xviii), 70.
[14] O.S. Map 6″ (1854–5 and later edns.).
[15] e.g. R.D.B., 1195/155/132; 1573/309/264; E.R.C.C. Mins. 1966–7, 223; 1967–8, 131; 1970–1, 31, 99; 1972–3, 128, 131.
[16] H.U.L., DDLA/1/1–3; O.S. Map 6″ (1854–5 edn.).
[17] *Cal. Pat.* 1345–8, 447.
[18] E.R.R.O., DDPY/5/2 (inclosure map); T. Jefferys, *Map of Yorks.* (1772).
[19] K. A. MacMahon, *Beginnings of E. Yorks. Rlys.* (E. Yorks. Loc. Hist. Ser. iii), 14.
[20] *Yorks. Eve. Press*, 20 Oct. 1965.
[21] E.R.R.O., DDPY/5/2 (inclosure map); Jefferys, *Map Yorks.* [22] *Miscellanea*, iv (Y.A.S. Rec. Ser. xciv), 19.
[23] E.R.R.O., DDSY/2/1; O.S. Map 6″ (1854–5 edn.).
[24] Jefferys, *Map Yorks.*

house.[25] In 1974 the beckside green was still used for the parish feast, held in July. Most of the village is only loosely built-up. The older houses date from the 18th and 19th centuries, and some of them have recently been renovated with Barmby's increasing popularity as a residential village. Extensive new building includes about 90 council houses, flats, and bungalows, many of them in an estate south of the beckside street. A village institute was built in the 1930s.[26]

'The George' was referred to in the later 17th century,[27] and an inn, kept by the occupant of Barmby Moor House, stood on the main road south of the village by 1770.[28] A new inn is said to have been built on the site by Thomas Heard (d. 1824):[29] it was sometimes known as Barmby Moor House or Inn, alternatively as the Bunch of Grapes and later the Wilmer Arms.[30] It closed after 1851.[31] It is an elegant building with a central pediment, bow windows, and a canopied porch.[32] The Boot and Slipper, in the centre of the village, has existed since at least 1823, when it was called the Boot and Shoe. By 1840 the New Inn had been built beside the main road 1½ mile west of the village;[33] it was renamed the Squirrels in 1974.

Outlying buildings include a dozen farm-houses, mostly built in the late 18th and 19th centuries after inclosure. One of them, Barmby Grange, now stands among the industrial buildings on the former airfield. A small estate of bungalows has grown up on the Sutton road, where there is also a turkey farm. Scattered bungalows and houses lie beside the trunk road in the west of the parish.

In that part of the parish transferred to Pocklington in 1901 Wilberforce Lodge, St. John's Lodge, and Dolman House were built by Pocklington School in the 1850s.[34] The suburbs of Pocklington have spread into the area in the present century.

There were 91 poll-tax payers in Barmby in 1377.[35] Of the 79 households listed in the hearth-tax return of 1672 17 were exempt; of those that were chargeable 55 had a single hearth, 3 had 2, 2 had 3, and one each had 4 and 7 hearths.[36] There were about 60 families in the parish in 1743 and 75 in 1764.[37] From 321 in 1801 the population rose to 537 in 1861, but fell to 437 in 1881.[38] After the transfer of part of the civil parish to Pocklington in 1901, Barmby's population was 442.[39] Numbers increased from 455 to 548 in 1921–31. The increase to 787 in 1951 and decrease to 502 in 1961 presumably reflected the changing status of the airfield. Residential development resulted in an increase to 768 in 1971.[40]

MANOR AND OTHER ESTATES. Ulf, the son of Torall a prince of Deira, gave Barmby to York minster[41] before 1066, and 7 carucates and 2 bovates there were held by the archbishop in 1086.[42] The estate was assigned to the prebend of Barmby, presumably at its formation before 1233.[43] The prebendal manor of *BARMBY UPON THE MOOR* was apparently in hand in 1479 and for much of the 16th century, but it was usually let from the 1570s.[44] Short-term leases in the 16th and 17th centuries[45] were succeeded in the 18th and 19th by leases for lives. The Beaumont family held the property in the early 17th century.[46] It was sold by the Commonwealth in 1649 to Tempest Milner and Thomas Hassell.[47] In 1658 Thomas Geere was dealing in the manor,[48] which was, however, returned to the prebendary at the Restoration. The Johnson family were lessees from 1661 to 1751.[49] John Idle was lessee in 1752, but his sister Frances succeeded him before 1758.[50] The leasehold interest subsequently descended, like Allerthorpe manor, in the Suger, Field, and Duncombe families.[51] In 1783 Jane Wilmer (née Suger) had about 350 a. in Barmby, of which 145 a. were held as the prebendary's lessee.[52]

The manor passed to the Ecclesiastical Commissioners in 1847 upon a voidance of the prebend[53] and was sold to Arthur Duncombe in 1853, along with 149 a. of land.[54] It subsequently descended like Allerthorpe in the Duncombe family.[55] Other 19th-century purchases by the Fields and Duncombes included over 100 a. of copyhold and 70 a. of freehold land from the Denison family *c.* 1860.[56] In 1902 C. W. Duncombe sold the 203-acre Barmby Moor House farm to T. B. Martin,[57] but the family still had 392 a. in Barmby in 1916.[58] B. A. C. Duncombe sold the manor to Henry Whitworth in 1919[59] and over 300 a. in three lots in 1920, including 240 a. in Barmby Grange farm to Robert Jack.[60] In 1944 the manor was vested in H. P. Whitworth, who sold it in 1955 to Henry Frederick, Baron Hotham.[61] Lord Hotham died in 1967 and was succeeded by his son Henry Durand Hotham, the 8th baron.[62]

The manor-house passed with the rest of the

[25] E.R.R.O., DDPY/5/8.
[26] Char. Com. files.
[27] Hist. MSS. Com. 29, *13th Rep. II, Portland*, ii, p. 313.
[28] E.R.R.O., QSF. East. 1770, S. 1.
[29] Ibid. DDPY/5/7 p. 431; W. D. Wood Rees, *Hist. of Barmby Moor* (Pocklington, priv. print. 1911), 28.
[30] Directories; Wood Rees, *Barmby*, 25–8.
[31] O.S. Map 6" (1854–5 edn.).
[32] See plate facing p. 129.
[33] Directories.
[34] P. C. Sandys and C. M. Haworth, *Hist. of Pocklington Sch., E. Yorks. 1514–1950*, 204–5, 209–10.
[35] E 179/202/59 m. 130.
[36] E 179/205/504.
[37] B.I.H.R., Bp. V. 1764/Ret. 45; *Herring's Visit.* i. 116.
[38] *V.C.H. Yorks.* iii. 493.
[39] *Census*, 1911.
[40] *Census*.
[41] Minster Libr., Torre MS., 'York Minster', pp. 349, 905; *Feud. Aids*, vi. 51; *V.C.H. Yorks.* iii. 11.
[42] *V.C.H. Yorks.* ii. 211, 322.
[43] *Reg. Gray*, p. 59.
[44] H.U.L., DDLA/1/1; E.R.R.O., DDKP/3/1.

[45] Minster Libr., Torre MS., 'York Minster', p. 906; E.R.R.O., DDKP/3/8.
[46] C 54/3510 m. 1; E.R.R.O., DDKP/3/1, k–q.
[47] C 54/3510 m. 1.
[48] C.P. 25(2)/615 no. 73.
[49] E.R.R.O., DDKP/3/8–9, 12; /4/1; DDPY/5/1 pp. 39, 79.
[50] Ibid. DDPY/5/1 pp. 89, 92.
[51] Ibid. DDPY/5/15; B.I.H.R., CC. P. Barnby; see pp. 134–5.
[52] E.R.R.O., DDPY/5/2 pp. 136–7, 188–93.
[53] *Lond. Gaz.* 7 Dec. 1847, p. 4519.
[54] R.D.B., HB/202/263.
[55] See p. 135.
[56] R.D.B., HY/40/63; E.R.R.O., DDPY/5/5 pp. 281, 286, 303. For their other purchases see E.R.R.O., DDPY/5/3 p. 334; /5/5 pp. 203, 340; /5/6 p. 39; R.D.B., HR/350/424; KP/352/463.
[57] R.D.B., 45/412/394 (1902).
[58] Ibid. 173/500/426.
[59] Ibid. 206/246/209.
[60] Ibid. 206/482/420; 208/109/98; 209/407/344.
[61] Ibid. 673/601/500; 1005/405/348.
[62] *Debrett's Peerage* (1973–4), 590–2.

estate to Arthur Duncombe in 1853,[63] and Sir Tatton Sykes bought the house and 36 a. in 1861.[64] The property was apparently acquired by exchange by the executors of the Revd. Frederick Gruggen in 1875,[65] and they sold the house to Hannah Burland in 1878.[66] In 1908 Margaret Wanstall sold it to Mary Dunn and she in 1950 to Cecily Tryon.[67] H. D. Crawford bought the house in 1954 and sold it to Mrs. E. L. L. Elmhirst in 1960.[68]

The house was mentioned c. 1295[69] and the prebendary had a fishpond in the 1340s,[70] perhaps a reference to the moat which surrounded the house. The present house, now called Barmby Manor, was mentioned in 1649[71] and apparently had seven hearths in 1672.[72] The main range probably represents the complete house of the early 17th century and the kitchen wing an addition made late in the century, at which time the west front was rebuilt with brick pilasters and an enriched doorcase.[73] Further alterations took place in the early 19th century, when part of the main chimney stack was removed to create an entrance hall and the main range was increased in depth to provide for a staircase. Later in the century much 17th- and 18th-century panelling was introduced, at least some of it coming from the old church.[74]

The demesne occupied only a small part of the parish and in 1783 1,678 a. was copyhold. This land was occupied by many tenants, only three of whom had over 100 a., one of them also the lessee of the manor.[75] Between 1859 and 1926 at least 699 a. were enfranchised and a further 369 a. after the Law of Property Act came into force in 1926.[76]

The king had 6 bovates in Barmby as soke of his manor of Pocklington in 1086,[77] but by 1198 John le Poer had been granted the estate, which he held with land elsewhere by the service of providing an archer for the defence of York castle.[78] William le Poer quitclaimed some Barmby property to Henry of Helium in 1235.[79] By 1250 Walter le Poer had been succeeded as tenant of 2 carucates at Barmby and elsewhere by John Chamberlain.[80] Robert de Crepping, who held rent in Barmby of Robert Chamberlain by archery service, died c. 1280 leaving his son John as heir.[81] Unspecified property in Barmby was settled on Robert Crepping in 1310,[82] and in 1346 Catherine, widow of Remigius Crepping, held a house and 4 bovates there.[83] The estate passed to Robert Crepping's daughter Denise Stodowe in 1386, when its serjeanty tenure was mentioned for the last time.[84] Denise died in 1389, when her heir was Robert Stodowe, grandson of her husband Robert.[85] Robert granted his Barmby property to Richard Berwyse in 1414,[86] and it was later held successively by Thomas Couper, his brother William, and John and Joan Hambald, the last of whom were seised of it in 1444.[87] Its subsequent descent has not been traced.

Pocklington Grammar School acquired 30 a. at Barmby by exchange in 1824.[88] In 1863 60 a. of former rectorial land was sold to the school by the Swanns,[89] and by the later 19th century the estate had been much enlarged.[90] It comprised in 1910 the 183-acre Greenland farm, received in exchange for property at Duggleby, and 200 a. in Newland and Field House farms.[91] The school sold the three farms to Sydney, Alfred, Gilbert, and Hubert Richardson in 1919.[92]

From 1252 the rectory belonged to the dean of York.[93] The corn and hay tithes were leased for short terms from 1538[94] and were held by the Johnson family from 1679 until at least 1738.[95] They were worth £63 in 1650[96] and were commuted for 298 a. of land and rent-charges of £10 9s. 1d. at inclosure in 1783.[97] The rectorial estate was vested in the Ecclesiastical Commissioners in 1844,[98] and in 1853 John and George Swann, tenants under a lease of 1842, purchased the reversion of 269 a. from the commissioners.[99] The Swanns sold 157 a. to Frederick Bardwell[1] and 88 a. to Sir George Strickland in 1862.[2] Bardwell conveyed his part to his son T. N. F. Bardwell in 1889,[3] and the latter divided and sold it in 1919.[4]

ECONOMIC HISTORY. At the Conquest the 7¼-carucate archiepiscopal estate at Barmby was held with 3 carucates at Millington as one manor. There was land for 6 ploughs in 1086, and 15 villeins had 9 ploughs there. The estate was worth £5 in 1066 but only £2 in 1086.[5]

The prebendary of Barmby had 6 bovates, together with three flats containing 28 a., in demesne c. 1295. Five free tenants paid nominal rents and 5s. for five tofts and 4 a. Thirty-one villeins held 60 bovates, paying £7 10s. rent and rendering poultry and eggs at Christmas and Easter, generally at the rate of 2 cocks or hens and 23 eggs to the bovate; they also owed hay-making and hay-carting works, the duty of carting the lord's fuel and timber 'within

---

[63] See p. 141.
[64] R.D.B., JE/364/490; JP/381/497.
[65] Ibid. MT/147/215.
[66] Ibid. MP/415/611.
[67] Ibid. 106/196/176; 861/90/83.
[68] Ibid. 973/193/176; 1195/521/462.
[69] *Miscellanea*, iv. 19.
[70] *Cal. Pat.* 1348–50, 166, 171–2.
[71] C 54/3510 m. 1.
[72] E 179/205/504.
[73] See plate facing p. 129.
[74] See p. 145.
[75] E.R.R.O., DDPY/5/2 pp. 117–213.
[76] Ibid. DDPY/5/5–7, 16; R.D.B., 173/499/425.
[77] *V.C.H. Yorks.* ii. 197, 322.
[78] *Bk. of Fees*, i. 4–5; ii. 1354; *V.C.H. City of York*, 521.
[79] *Yorks. Fines, 1232–46*, p. 34.
[80] *Bk. of Fees*, ii. 1202.
[81] *Yorks. Inq.* i, p. 207; *Cal. Inq. p.m.* ii, p. 199.
[82] *Yorks. Fines, 1300–14*, p. 83.
[83] *Cal. Pat.* 1345–8, 192.
[84] *Cal. Fine R.* 1347–56, 248; 1383–91, 155; *Cal. Close, 1385–9*, 178.
[85] C 136/64 no. 4; *Cal. Fine R.* 1391–9, 69.
[86] *Cal. Pat.* 1413–16, 182.
[87] Ibid. 1441–6, 320–1.
[88] *19th Rep. Com. Char.* H.C. 374, p. 543 (1828), xi (1).
[89] R.D.B., JO/257/371.
[90] Directories.
[91] Sandys and Haworth, *Pocklington Sch.* 85, 213.
[92] R.D.B., 191/482/411.
[93] See p. 144.
[94] Minster Libr., D. & C. Archives, S 3 (5) a, f. 2; E.R.R.O., DC/3451, 3453, 3458, 3461, 3463; C 94/3 f. 55.
[95] E.R.R.O., DDKP/3/10–11; B.I.H.R., CC. DY. Barmby Moor.
[96] C 94/3 f. 55.
[97] E.R.R.O., DDPY/5/2 pp. 137–9, 198–201.
[98] *Lond. Gaz.* 19 July 1844, p. 2499.
[99] R.D.B., HB/401/484; HC/25/33; B.I.H.R., CC. DY. Barmby Moor.
[1] R.D.B., JG/145/207.
[2] Ibid. JK/154/192.
[3] Ibid. 31/252/244 (1889).
[4] Ibid. 202/17/14; /422/364.
[5] *V.C.H. Yorks.* ii. 211; iii. 11

Derwent', and arbitrary relief and merchet. Twenty-seven cottars held 32 tofts, a croft, and 3½ a. for about £1 10s., as well as poultry and eggs, usually giving 23 eggs for each toft. They also owed haymaking service and a day's work at harvest-time, worth 1d., and were bound to work for the lord from Michaelmas to Lammas for 1d. a day.[6] A day-work was referred to in 1667,[7] and as late as the 1850s payments were made for 'boons'.[8] In 1649 the demesne comprised 6 bovates, or 60 a., in the town fields, a 5-acre flat in South field, 20 a. in closes, and 6 beast-gates. Its value was then about £52.[9]

No open field is named until 1479, when South field was mentioned; it then included land called the Sandholmes.[10] By 1690 South field had apparently been renamed Great field, which included a 'long sandome'.[11] It was, however, more commonly known as Hodsow field by the 1780s, when it occupied most of the parish to the south of the Barmby–Pocklington road. East and West fields were mentioned in 1649[12] but were called Broat and Furland fields by 1690. In the 1770s Broat field lay north-east and Furland, later Farland, field north-west of the village.[13]

The moor or common of Barmby was estimated in 1691 to comprise about 1,000 a. and to support 400 horses, several hundred sheep, and other 'beasts' in summer; the pasture was then unstinted.[14] From 1655 part of the common was let by the lord as a rabbit warren. By a draft lease of 1718 the lord agreed to build a warrener's house, to stock the warren with 600 pairs of rabbits, and to bear the cost of restocking up to 300 pairs in the event of any 'general rot'.[15] A warrener was mentioned in 1738,[16] and Greenland Warren survives as a place-name in the south of the parish. Parts of the common may have been temporarily cultivated in the 18th century, when rape was being grown on pared and burnt ground, and sainfoin in closes.[17] On the eve of inclosure 45 tenants had 74 common rights in the common, which included all the parish south of the York road and west of the present Stamford Bridge road, and also extended to the east of the latter road. Beast-gates mentioned in the 17th century were enjoyed in the stinted Ox pasture.[18] Great and Keld spring common pastures lay respectively north-west and north-east of the village in the 18th century.[19]

Some land had already been inclosed by the 17th century. Banbery or Kell spring close was mentioned in 1641, an arable close on the edge of West field in 1649,[20] Northland close in 1673, and Town end close or Gilman garths in 1691.[21] A grassland close called Hodsow close, referred to from 1649, may have been taken from Hodsow field.[22] At final inclosure in 1783 Barmby included about 110 a. of ancient inclosures, situated around the village and in the east of the parish; the tenants of the latter closes included several inhabitants of Pocklington.[23]

The open fields and other common lands were inclosed in 1783[24] under an Act of 1777.[25] Seventy-two bovates were held by 26 tenants on the eve of inclosure, and many other tenants had only common rights. A total of 2,273 a. was allotted, including 410 a. in Hodsow field and at least 1,031 a. lying in the common, 229 a. in Broat field, and 71 a. in Furland field. Allotments made jointly from Great pasture and the common accounted for 149 a., those from Furland field and Great pasture for 193 a., and those from all three areas for 27 a. A further 163 a. consisted of joint allotments from Broat and Furland fields and Skel spring pasture. The prebendary of Barmby received 145 a. for his land, a common right, and manorial rights in the waste; the dean of York 298 a. and the vicar 23 a. for their tithes; and Jane Wilmer 206 a. for her freehold and copyhold estate. Of the other allotments 4 were of 100–190 a., 6 of 50–99 a., 12 of 20–49 a., and 36 of under 20 a. In the case of the prebendary, dean, and vicar the costs of inclosure were met by the deduction and sale of a proportion of their allotments;[26] Jane Wilmer's 206 a. thus included a 28-acre purchase of lands originally allotted to the prebendary. Other proprietors apparently opted to pay their shares of the costs in cash. Several Pocklington tradesmen were among those receiving small allotments.

In the 19th and early 20th centuries there were generally 20–30 farmers in Barmby, of whom 4–6 had 150 a. or more in the 1920s and 1930s.[27] In 1801 only 233 a. in Barmby were returned as under crops.[28] By the mid 19th century parts of the former common had been afforested and were known as Elston and Gray's plantations.[29] Other parts were still unimproved, and in 1824 75 a. of heath land was valued chiefly for its rabbits and turves.[30] A farmer and warrener at Barmby was mentioned as late as 1840.[31] In 1836 43 a. of common, allotted to the lord in 1783, were still unimproved, and another 55-acre allotment was partly covered with furze.[32] By the late 19th century Barmby was noted for the cultivation of carrots,[33] and there was a carrot and potato dealer there from then until at least 1937.[34] In 1905 there were 1,678 a. of arable, 501 a. of grass, and 127 a. of woodland.[35] Arable was still predominant in the 1930s and later, but some waste land remains in the west of the parish and on the former airfield.[36]

Barmby reputedly had a weekly market before 1823, when an annual fair was still held.[37]

[6] *Miscellanea*, iv. 19.
[7] E.R.R.O., DDKP/4/1.
[8] Ibid. DDKP/18/6.
[9] C 54/3510 m. 1.
[10] H.U.L., DDLA/1/1.
[11] E.R.R.O., DDKP/4/1.
[12] C 54/3510 m. 1.
[13] E.R.R.O., DDPY/5/2 pp. 117–213.
[14] B.I.H.R., CP. H. 4250.
[15] E.R.R.O., DDKP/3/12.
[16] Ibid. QSF. Christ. 1738, C. 33.
[17] A. Harris, 'Pre-inclosure Agric. Systems in E. Yorks.' (London Univ. M.A. thesis, 1951), 106.
[18] Minster Libr., D. & C. Arch., S 1 (2) f, f. 34; C 54/3510 m. 1.
[19] E.R.R.O., DDPY/5/2 pp. 117–213.
[20] C 54/3510 m. 1.
[21] E.R.R.O., DDKP/3/7; /4/1.
[22] Ibid. DDBC/15/391, 396, 406; C 54/3510 m. 1.
[23] E.R.R.O., DDPY/5/2 pp. 117–213.
[24] Ibid.
[25] 17 Geo. III, c. 111 (Priv. Act).
[26] See p. 187.
[27] Directories.
[28] 1801 Crop Returns.
[29] O.S. Map 6" (1854–5 edn.).
[30] *11th Rep. Com. Char.* 723.
[31] White, *Dir. E. & N.R. Yorks.* (1840), 232–3.
[32] B.I.H.R., CC. P. Barnby.
[33] Bulmer, *Dir. E. Yorks.* (1892), 550–2; *Kelly's Dir. N. & E.R. Yorks.* (1925), 456.
[34] Directories.
[35] Acreage Returns, 1905.
[36] [1st] Land Util. Surv. Map, sheet 27; 2nd Land Util. Surv. Map, sheets 699 (SE 64–74), 709 (SE 65–75).
[37] Baines, *Hist. Yorks.* (1823), ii. 153–4; Bulmer, *Dir. E. Yorks.* (1892), 550–2.

Weavers at Barmby were mentioned in the 1390s[38] and in the late 18th and early 19th centuries.[39] In the mid 19th century hemp pits on the former common were used for retting flax for a Pocklington mill.[40] In the 1920s and 1930s the repairing of agricultural machinery provided employment, and one or two garages and a refreshment room were opened beside the trunk road. There were gravel pits in the north-east of the parish in the mid 19th century, and the farmer at Barmby Grange extracted sand and gravel commercially in the early 20th century. There was a building firm in Barmby by 1929.[41] The former airfield was developed as an industrial estate during the 1960s,[42] and existing and new buildings were used by about 15 firms in 1974 for light and civil engineering, warehousing, and fuel storage.

There was a windmill at Barmby c. 1295.[43]

LOCAL GOVERNMENT. Surviving manorial court records consist of rolls for the period 1666–1941,[44] surrenders and admissions for 1479–1900,[45] minute books for 1860–99,[46] and various other papers, mostly of the 19th century.[47] A constable was mentioned in 1662 and 1711, and two affeerors in 1726.[48] In the mid 18th century the officers included 2 constables, 3 bylawmen, and 2 pinders and moormen.[49] Two affeerors and a pinder were referred to a century later.[50]

There are churchwardens' accounts from 1822 onwards and accounts of the two highway surveyors for 1817–48.[51] Barmby joined Pocklington poor-law union in 1836,[52] and in 1852 eight poorhouses were sold by the guardians.[53] The parish became part of Pocklington rural district in 1894[54] and the North Wolds district of Humberside in 1974.

CHURCH. Although not named, Barmby Moor, like Fangfoss, was one of the chapels given by the king between 1100 and 1108, along with their mother-church of Pocklington, to the archbishop of York and York minster. They were apparently assigned by the archbishop to the dean, and between c. 1119 and 1129 the king confirmed the assignment.[55] Barmby was subsequently within the dean's peculiar jurisdiction. In 1252 a vicarage was ordained jointly at Barmby and Fangfoss, with provision that a minister be found for each church.[56] Thereafter Barmby was a vicarage and Fangfoss a curacy. There were separate ministers in 1525–6, but from 1568 the vicarage and curacy were apparently always held by one man.[57] Barmby and Fangfoss still constituted a united vicarage in 1974.

The advowson presumably belonged to the dean of York in the Middle Ages and later. In 1650 the Commonwealth held it,[58] but the patronage was subsequently restored to the dean.[59] When the rectory passed to the Ecclesiastical Commissioners in 1844 the advowson was automatically vested in the archbishop of York,[60] who was still the patron in 1974.

The vicar's income was £7 in 1525–6,[61] and the living was valued at £5 6s. 8d. net in 1535.[62] In 1650 the vicarage was worth £6.[63] During the Interregnum £12 10s. rent, formerly received by the dean for the great tithes, was diverted to the living.[64] The income was augmented by £200 from Queen Anne's Bounty in 1777 and 1799.[65] The average net income of the joint living in 1829–31 was £50 a year.[66] The living was endowed with a rent-charge of £1 6s. 2d., formerly belonging to the dean, in 1860, and with annual payments from the Common Fund of £24 and £166 in 1860 and 1862 respectively.[67] The net value of the living was £270 in 1884 and £338 in 1915.[68]

In 1252 the vicarage was assigned the small tithes.[69] At inclosure in 1783 the vicar was awarded 23 a. and rent-charges of £2 1s. 2d. in lieu of tithes.[70] Before inclosure the only glebe was a common right belonging to a house in Barmby.[71] Between 1809 and 1817 Bounty money was used to buy 23 a. at Misson (Notts.).[72] In 1860 the Ecclesiastical Commissioners transferred to the vicarage 9 a. formerly belonging to Barmby prebend[73] and in 1863 39 a. formerly part of the rectory.[74] In 1868 11 a. in Barmby were bought against the Common Fund annual grant, which was consequently reduced to £179.[75] Seventy-three acres in Barmby were sold in 1920, 2 a. in 1964, and 7 a. in 1971.[76] The glebe at Misson had also been sold by 1974.[77]

The vicarage house at Barmby was in decay in the

---

[38] Cal. Inq. Misc. vi, p. 247.
[39] E.R.R.O., DDPY/5/2 pp. 117–213; Wood Rees, Barmby, 103.
[40] Wood Rees, Barmby, 87; O.S. Map 6″ (1854–5 edn.).
[41] O.S. Map 6″ (1854–5 edn.); directories.
[42] e.g. R.D.B., 1180/242/216; 1201/168/153; 1209/302/273; 1245/127/115.
[43] Miscellanea, iv. 19.
[44] E.R.R.O., DDKP/4/1; DDPY/5/1–7, 16.
[45] Ibid. DDKP/3/1; DDPY/5/10; H.U.L., DDLA/1/1–3.
[46] E.R.R.O., DDPY/5/8–9.
[47] Ibid. DDPY/5/8, 11–15.
[48] Ibid. DDKP/4/1; QSF. Mids. 1711, B. 6–7; Cal. S.P. Dom. Add. 1660–85, 60.
[49] E.R.R.O., DDPY/5/1 (1758–9).
[50] Ibid. DDPY/5/6 (1873), 8.
[51] Par. rec. penes the vicar, 1974.
[52] 3rd Rep. Poor Law Com. 169.
[53] R.D.B., HA/13/17.
[54] Census.
[55] E.Y.C. i, pp. 333–7.
[56] Reg. Gray, pp. 212–13.
[57] B.I.H.R., TER. I. Barmby and Fangfoss 1684, 1726, 1743, 1777, 1817, 1853; Y.A.J. xviii. 210; xxiv. 64, 72; Herring's Visit. i. 116, 220.
[58] C 94/3 f. 55.
[59] Rep. Com. Eccl. Revenues, 916.
[60] Eccl. Comrs. Act, 3 & 4 Vic. c. 113, s. 41; Lond. Gaz. 19 July 1844, p. 2499.
[61] Y.A.J. xxiv. 64.
[62] Valor Eccl. (Rec. Com.), v. 141.
[63] C 94/3 f. 55.
[64] Lamb. Pal. Libr., COMM./VIa/7.
[65] Hodgson, Q.A.B. 433.
[66] Rep. Com. Eccl. Revenues, 916.
[67] B.I.H.R., TER. I. Barmby Moor 1865; Lond. Gaz. 30 Oct. 1860, p. 3913; 5 Sept. 1862, p. 4345.
[68] B.I.H.R., Bp. V. 1884/Ret.; Bp. V. 1915/Ret.
[69] Reg. Gray, pp. 212–13.
[70] E.R.R.O., DDPY/5/2 pp. 139–40, 201–2; B.I.H.R., TER. I. Barmby Moor 1786. The former source undervalues the tithe rents by 3d.
[71] B.I.H.R., TER. I. Barmby Moor 1777.
[72] Ibid. TER. I. Barmby Moor 1809, 1817, 1849.
[73] Lond. Gaz. 30 Oct. 1860, p. 3913. The terriers refer to only 6 a., excluding the 3-acre site of the Vicarage: B.I.H.R., TER. I. Barmby Moor 1849, 1861.
[74] B.I.H.R., TER. I. Barmby Moor 1865; Lond. Gaz. 20 Nov. 1863, p. 5563.
[75] B.I.H.R., TER. I. Barmby Moor 1877; R.D.B., KJ/180/237; KL/173/227.
[76] R.D.B., 215/335/286; 223/250/205; 1375/203/179; 1702/193/170.
[77] Ex inf. the vicar.

1590s.[78] It was possibly rebuilt in the mid 17th century,[79] but was ruinous again in 1684 and 1693, and by 1716 no longer existed.[80] The house may have adjoined the churchyard where a glebe frontstead and garth lay in the mid 18th century:[81] in the 19th century the site was called the 'little churchyard'.[82] In 1845 a grant was received from the Common Fund towards a residence, and a house was built in 1847 to the north of the village.[83] It was enlarged in 1871.[84] In 1971 a new Vicarage was built in the grounds of the old one,[85] which was called Northwood House in 1974.

There may have been a chantry in the church, for land in Barmby granted by the Crown in 1571 to Francis Barker and Thomas Browne included a chapel garth,[86] and it was presumably the same garth which was sold in 1593 along with seven 'St. Catherine's headlands'.[87]

Besides the vicar there was a chaplain receiving £2 a year in 1525–6.[88] Thereafter Barmby was probably often without a resident minister until the mid 19th century. The vicar was non-resident in the 1590s and in 1650.[89] The church was being served by a stipendiary priest in 1691,[90] and during the 18th and early 19th centuries the incumbent also held the vicarage of Thornton with Allerthorpe and resided in one of the latter villages.[91] Barmby marriages consequently often took place at Thornton in the 18th century.[92] The vicar of Barmby also held Pocklington with Yapham in 1835.[93] Robert Taylor, vicar 1840–85, engaged the vicar of Pocklington to assist him in 1868 and was helped by the Revd. Frederick Gruggen, headmaster of Pocklington Grammar School, in 1871.[94] Taylor, by will dated 1875, devised £400 to establish a trust for religious education.[95] An assistant curate was appointed by 1877 but was not mentioned after 1894, when he was possibly responsible for Fangfoss.[96]

There was a service once a fortnight in 1743, and Holy Communion was celebrated four times a year with about 56 communicants at Easter.[97] A service was held weekly by 1851,[98] and by 1865 there was an additional service on alternate Sundays. Communion was celebrated monthly in 1865, but the number of communicants on feast days had fallen to about 20.[99] In 1894 there were two services a week,[1] and communion was celebrated at least weekly in 1915.[2] In 1974 there was one service every Sunday and two once a month.

The repair of *ST. CATHERINE'S* church was one of the objects of an indulgence granted in 1480, and a church at 'Barnby' was decayed in the late 15th and early 16th centuries.[3] The church was again in disrepair in 1570 and 1687.[4] It was reroofed *c.* 1787 and repewed in 1828.[5] In 1831 it consisted of chancel, nave with south porch, and west tower with spire, and had two Norman windows in the nave.[6] The chancel door and a north door also had plain semicircular heads prior to rebuilding.[7] A choir loft was repaired in the 1830s.[8]

The church was largely rebuilt in 1850–2 by R. D. Chantrell.[9] The old tower, with its stone spire, was, however, retained; it has a 15th-century upper stage and west window, but the unbuttressed lower stage is probably earlier. The new church of stone consists of an undivided chancel and nave, with north vestry and south porch; it is 14th-century in style with an elaborate timber roof. It is paved with tiles given by Herbert Minton of Stoke-upon-Trent, Robert Taylor's brother-in-law,[10] and has a tiled Royal Arms above the vestry door. The fittings include an octagonal stone font given by Delia Duncombe in 1852.[11] A stoup in the tower stood near the south door until *c.* 1840 and later in the Vicarage garden.[12] There is an ornate brass lectern in memory of the Revd. Frederick Gruggen (d. 1872), and a plain mural tablet by Fisher of York.

In 1874 a cottage, garth, and blacksmith's shop were bought by Robert Taylor and settled upon trustees to provide income for repairs to the church. St. Catherine's House was built on the site shortly afterwards.[13] It was sold in 1953, and the following year the fund had £1,628 stock.[14]

The church had four bells in 1552[15] and three in 1770.[16] There are still three: (i) 1880, Mears & Stainbank of London; (ii) 1598; (iii) 1670.[17] The plate includes a silver cup, made in York in 1698 by William Busfield, a plated cup, paten, and flagon, and a pewter paten and flagon dated 1783, the last bearing the name George Hudson.[18] The registers begin in 1720; those of baptisms and burials are complete, but the marriage registers lack entries for 1811–13.[19] A worn rectangular stone erected near the south door may be a medieval gravestone, and

---

[78] *Y.A.J.* xviii. 318, 320.
[79] E.R.R.O., DDKP/20/7.
[80] B.I.H.R., TER. I. Barmby Moor 1684, 1716; V. 1693/CB.
[81] Ibid. TER. I. Barmby Moor 1770.
[82] Wood Rees, *Barmby*, 46.
[83] B.I.H.R., TER. I. Barmby Moor 1849; R.D.B., GD/203/232; *Lond. Gaz.* 3 Oct. 1845, p. 2985.
[84] B.I.H.R., TER. I. Barmby Moor 1877.
[85] Ex inf. the vicar, 1974.
[86] *Cal. Pat.* 1569–72, p. 236.
[87] E.R.R.O., DDKP/3/3.
[88] *Y.A.J.* xxiv. 72.
[89] C 94/3 f. 55; *Y.A.J.* xviii. 224, 317.
[90] B.I.H.R., CP. H. 4250.
[91] See p. 188.
[92] B.I.H.R., PR. THORN. 3.
[93] *Rep. Com. Eccl. Revenues*, 916.
[94] B.I.H.R., V. 1868/Ret. 36; V. 1871/Ret. 36; Wood Rees, *Barmby*, 49.
[95] Barley, *Par. Doc. of Archd. of E.R., an Inventory* (Y.A.S. Rec. Ser. xcix), pp. 8–9.
[96] B.I.H.R., V. 1877/Ret.; Bp. V. 1884/Ret.; Bp. V. 1894/Ret.; see p. 169.
[97] *Herring's Visit.* i. 116.
[98] H.O. 129/23/516.
[99] B.I.H.R., V. 1865/Ret. 37.

[1] Ibid. Bp. V. 1894/Ret.   [2] Ibid. Bp. V. 1915/Ret.
[3] *Fabric Rolls of York Minster* (Sur. Soc. xxxv), 241, 261, 270.
[4] B.I.H.R., CP. H. 3770; *Y.A.J.* xviii. 214.
[5] White, *Dir. E. & N.R. Yorks.* (1840), 232–3; Wood Rees, *Barmby*, 30–1.
[6] T. Allen, *Hist. Co. York*, iii. 409–10.
[7] *Yorks. Gaz.* 17 Apr. 1852.
[8] Board in church.
[9] B.I.H.R., Ch. Ret.; *Yorks. Gaz.* 17 Apr. 1852. J. B. Atkinson made the dilapidation report (Wood Rees, *Barmby*, 30–1) and was not the architect for the rebuilding as in Pevsner, *Yorks. E.R.* 166.
[10] *Kelly's Dir. N. & E.R. Yorks.* (1872), 313; Wood Rees, *Barmby*, 35.
[11] Date on font.
[12] Wood Rees, *Barmby*, 47, with illus.
[13] B.I.H.R., PR. BARM. 1; TER. I. Barmby Moor 1877.
[14] Char. Com. files.
[15] *Inventories of Ch. Goods*, 82.
[16] B.I.H.R., TER. I. Barmby Moor 1770, 1777, 1849.
[17] Boulter, 'Ch. Bells', 26; Wood Rees, *Barmby*, 35–6.
[18] *Yorks. Ch. Plate*, i. 213.
[19] *Penes* the vicar, 1974. There are a few baptismal entries of 1700–6 on the cover of the 1720 register. A register of 1682–1729, mentioned in 1939 (Barley, *Par. Doc.* 8–9), was missing in 1974.

NONCONFORMITY. In 1664 five recusants from Barmby were mentioned.[20] A Quaker meeting-house was licensed in 1707[21] and in 1743 there was a Quaker family in the parish.[22] In 1779 an Independent meeting-house was registered.[23] The Methodists had 12 members at Barmby in 1787 and 9–26 in 1788–1818.[24] A Wesleyan Methodist chapel was registered in 1807[25] and rebuilt on an enlarged site in 1869.[26] It was still in use in 1974.

Houses registered for dissenting worship in 1812 and 1820, and a building licensed for use as a chapel in 1825, may have been Primitive Methodist meeting-places;[27] a Primitive Methodist 'chapel' certainly existed in 1831.[28] It was presumably a new chapel which was registered in 1834.[29] It closed in the 1930s[30] and was used as a dwelling-house in 1974.

EDUCATION. In 1743 there was a school at Barmby in which the parish clerk gave religious instruction.[31] Twenty children were taught in an unendowed school in 1819.[32] A schoolmaster teaching reading, writing, and accounts to 8–12 children was employed in 1824 by the trustees of the Poor's Land charity, who also provided coal, stationery, and books.[33] In 1835 there were two schools in which 38 pupils were taught at their parents' expense.[34] There were two dame schools and a private school conducted by a master at Barmby in 1844.[35] In 1845 a National school and master's house were built on a site given by Arthur Duncombe, who also contributed £180 towards the cost.[36] By 1850 the school received an annual government grant. It was enlarged c. 1859;[37] the average attendance was 44 in 1850,[38] 73 in 1867, and 54 in 1871.[39] The Poor's Land charity continued to support it during the 19th century;[40] in the 1890s the school received £20 a year from the charity and about 17 pupils were taught free.[41] By a Scheme of 1908 a separate Poor's Land Educational Foundation was created.[42]

Between 1906 and 1938 attendance was usually about 70, though it fell to 55 in 1918 and rose to 87 in 1931.[43] The school was enlarged to accommodate 140 children in 1934. In 1955 the senior pupils were transferred to Pocklington and the school was reorganized as a junior and infants' school. The first part of a new school on a site in the north of the village was opened in 1974, when the old building was also still used.[44] There were 84 pupils on the roll in January 1974.[45] By a Scheme of 1965 the income of the Poor's Land Educational Foundation was to be used for exhibitions, financial or other help to those entering employment, and the general promotion of education; in 1973 the income of £21 and money in hand was spent on a school trip and a pre-school play group.[46]

CHARITIES FOR THE POOR. Thomas Wood, by will dated 1568, devised a rent-charge of £10 a year from an estate at Kilnwick Percy for the benefit of Barmby Moor and many other townships, and in 1824 Barmby received 5s.[47] Henry Frederick, Baron Hotham, owner of the Kilnwick Percy estate, redeemed the rent-charge in 1961 and £10 stock was subsequently assigned to Barmby.[48] In 1973 26p were received and distributed with the income of the Poor's Land charity.[49]

The Barmby poor were entitled to 5s. a year from the charity of William Westoby of Allerthorpe, which was founded before 1659. In 1824 the charity was administered with those of Wood, Layton, and Johnson,[50] but Westoby's was not subsequently mentioned.

Robert Appleton, by will proved in 1658, left £13 for the purchase of a house for the poor.[51] The house had been bought by 1666[52] and was rented for £1 4s. in 1743 and £1 10s. in 1764. A Dr. Johnson paid 12s. a year to the overseers in 1743 and had left £1 a year for the poor by 1764.[53] He was probably Henry Johnson, lessee of the manor and a York physician (d. 1744).[54] No more is heard of either of these charities.

William Layton gave ⅓ bovate to the poor in 1722, and John Johnson surrendered a messuage and a cottage to the poor's trustees in 1744. At inclosure in 1783 the trustees were awarded 82 a. for the land and common rights of both charities. In 1824, when the charities were apparently being administered jointly, the cottages and land were let for about £38; this

---

[20] *Depositions from York Castle* (Sur. Soc. xl), 122.
[21] E.R.R.O., QSP/154.
[22] *Herring's Visit.* i. 116.
[23] B.I.H.R., Fac. Bk. ii, p. 229; G.R.O. Worship Returns, Vol. v, no. 557.
[24] E.R.R.O., MRP/1/7.
[25] G.R.O. Worship Returns, Vol. v, no. 2060.
[26] Ibid. Worship Reg. no. 19347; E.R.R.O., MRP/1/68.
[27] G.R.O. Worship Returns, Vol. v, nos. 2562, 3368, 3955; B.I.H.R., DMH. Reg. 1, pp. 491–2.
[28] Allen, *Hist. Co. York*, iii. 410.
[29] G.R.O. Worship Returns, Vol. v, no. 4324.
[30] R.D.B., 611/411/308; *Kelly's Dir. N. & E.R. Yorks.* (1929), 444; (1933), 412.
[31] *Herring's Visit.* i. 116.   [32] *Educ. of Poor Digest*, 1076.
[33] *11th Rep. Com. Char.* 722–4.
[34] *Educ. Enquiry Abstract*, 1079.
[35] National Soc. application form, 1844, *penes* the vicar, 1974.
[36] B.I.H.R., Ch. Ret.; White, *Dir. Hull & York* (1846), 469; date on building. A beckside house known as Old School in 1911 is illus. in Wood Rees, *Barmby*, 94.
[37] E.R.R.O., SGP. 3.
[38] *Mins. of Educ. Cttee. of Council, 1849–50* [1215], p. cclii, H.C. (1850), xliii.
[39] *1st Rep. Com. on Employment of Children, Young Persons, and Women in Agric., Appendix, Pt. II* [4068-I], p. 377, H.C. (1867–8), xvii; *Returns relating to Elem. Educ.* 794.
[40] White, *Dir. E. & N.R. Yorks.* (1840), 232–3; White, *Dir. Hull & York* (1846), 469; Sheahan and Whellan, *Hist. York & E.R.* ii. 555–6.
[41] B.I.H.R., Bp. V. 1894/Ret.; Bulmer, *Dir. E. Yorks.* (1892), 550–2.
[42] Char. Com. files.
[43] *Bd. of Educ. List 21* (H.M.S.O.).
[44] R.D.B., 1375/203/179; E.R. Educ. Cttee. *Mins.* 1934–5, 191; 1955–6, 152; 1963–4, 117; 1971–2, 216; 1972–3, 92, 198.
[45] Ex inf. Chief Educ. Officer, County Hall, Beverley, 1974.
[46] Char. Com. files.
[47] *11th Rep. Com. Char.* 723–4.
[48] Ex inf. Char. Com., Liverpool, 1974.
[49] Char. Com. files.
[50] *11th Rep. Com. Char.* 724; see above p. 139.
[51] E.R.R.O., DDKP/20/7.   [52] Ibid. DDKP/4/1.
[53] B.I.H.R., Bp. V. 1764/Ret. 45; *Herring's Visit.* i. 116.
[54] R.D.B., R/280/681.

income was partly distributed in sums of from 5s. to £2 2s. and partly spent on education.[55] The poor's allotment in 1783 included 76 a. of common, and this land was called California, or Calley, in the 19th century; the two charities have since sometimes been referred to as the Calley Trust. Part of California was brought into cultivation in the mid 19th century and let in small plots to villagers.[56] The charities had an average net income of about £43 a year in 1857–61,[57] and they were jointly administered by a Scheme of 1876, which also adopted Poor's Land charity as an alternative name for Layton's and Johnson's charities. By a Scheme of 1908 £20 of the £63 income was assigned to a separate Poor's Land Educational Foundation. A subscription to a clothing club was being made in 1915.[58] In 1954 and 1962 the land was sold,[59] and in 1965 the charity had £2,420 stock, a house, and two cottages. The cottages were sold in 1969.[60] By a Scheme of 1965 the income was to be used for gifts, cash grants, and subscriptions, and in 1973 £184 was distributed in coal, £57 in other goods, and £34 in cash from an income of £256 and money in hand.[61]

In 1830 Catherine Straw bequeathed £10 to provide bread for eight poor widows, but the capital was spent on church repairs.[62]

CATTON

THE ANCIENT parish of Catton lies on both banks of the river Derwent, partly in Ouse and Derwent wapentake and partly in the Wilton Beacon division of Harthill wapentake.[1] In places the irregularly-shaped parish measures five miles by four, and its total area in 1850 was 8,002 a.[2] On the east bank of the river, in the Wilton Beacon division, it included the townships of High and Low Catton and Stamford Bridge East. Part of Stamford Bridge comprised the manor of Hundburton and there may at one time have been a distinct hamlet of that name. West of the river, in Ouse and Derwent wapentake, lie the townships of Kexby, which was made a separate parish in 1853, Scoreby, and Stamford Bridge West. Scoreby became depopulated during the Middle Ages.

Though it lies close to the edge of the Vale of York, most of the parish west of the Derwent and much of it to the east is covered by typical deposits of outwash sand, silt, and clay, with a narrow belt of alluvium along the river valley. Both the York and the Escrick moraines, however, end in the neighbourhood. The Escrick moraine forms a prominent ridge of boulder clay and glacial sand and gravel which runs northwards through the Cattons, before turning north-eastwards towards Full Sutton. It provides an elevated site for High Catton village, whereas Low Catton stands close beside the Derwent. A smaller area of glacial sand and gravel forms a capping to an outcrop of Keuper marl in Stamford Bridge East township. The York moraine skirts the northern margin of Scoreby and Stamford Bridge West townships. Stamford Bridge village stands at a natural crossing point on the Derwent, and both Scoreby and Kexby were also sited close to the river.[3]

High Catton and Low Catton were separate civil parishes until 1935, when they were combined as 'Catton'. Stamford Bridge East civil parish was enlarged by the transfer of 25 a. from Stamford Bridge West and Scoreby in 1935, and was renamed Stamford Bridge civil parish. The rest of Stamford Bridge West and Scoreby civil parish was transferred to Kexby civil parish that year.[4] In the following account the Cattons and Stamford Bridge East, whose histories were closely connected, are treated together, as are the townships west of the river.

HIGH AND LOW CATTON AND STAMFORD BRIDGE EAST

The village of Low Catton, with the parish church, stands 6 miles east of York on firm ground 100 yd.–200 yd. from the bank of the river Derwent. Mill Sike beck, which rises in Stamford Bridge, formerly entered the Derwent close to the church,[5] though it was later diverted to a more northerly junction. High Catton, ¾ mile further east, stands on the lower slopes of the Escrick moraine, which forms a prominent ridge behind the village. Throwmires beck passes close to the village, running roughly parallel to the Derwent before joining it well to the south. Both places were Anglian settlements. The Cattons stand quietly apart from the large and busy village of Stamford Bridge, a mile to the north. An outcrop of Keuper sandstone provides a ford in the Derwent upon which several Roman roads converged and which later attracted the Anglian settlement at 'the stone-paved ford'.[6] A bridge built near by was mentioned in accounts of the battle of 1066, when King Harold defeated Earl Tostig and Harold Hardrada before marching to Hastings.[7] Stamford Bridge was a meeting-place for quarter sessions in the 14th century,[8] and the east–west road crossing the river there became one of the main routes from York to the East Riding and the coast. The village has also grown in recent years as a dormitory for

[55] 11th Rep. Com. Char. 723; see above p. 146.
[56] Char. Com. files; E.R.R.O., DDPY/5/2 (inclosure map); O.S. Map 6", SE 74 NE (1973 edn.); Wood Rees, Barmby, 86–7; Yorks. Gaz. 29 July 1911.
[57] E.R.R.O., DDPY/5/13.
[58] B.I.H.R., Bp. V. 1915/Ret.
[59] R.D.B., 976/310/276; 1263/30/26; 1264/413/369.
[60] Ibid. 1610/287/256; 1611/442/392.
[61] Char. Com. files.
[62] Board in church.
[1] This article was written in 1973–4.

[2] O.S. Map 6" Yorks. (1854 edn.).
[3] Geol. Surv. Map 1", solid and drift, sheet 71 (1973 edn.).
[4] Census, 1931.
[5] Petworth House Archives, no. 3072.
[6] P.N.E.R. Yorks. (E.P.N.S.), 186–8.
[7] See F. W. Brooks, Battle of Stamford Bridge (E. Yorks. Loc. Hist. Ser. vi), passim.
[8] Proc. before J.P.s in the 14th and 15th Cent. ed. B. H. Putnam (Ames Foundn.), 30; Yorks. Sessions of the Peace, 1361–4 (Y.A.S. Rec. Ser. c), 143.

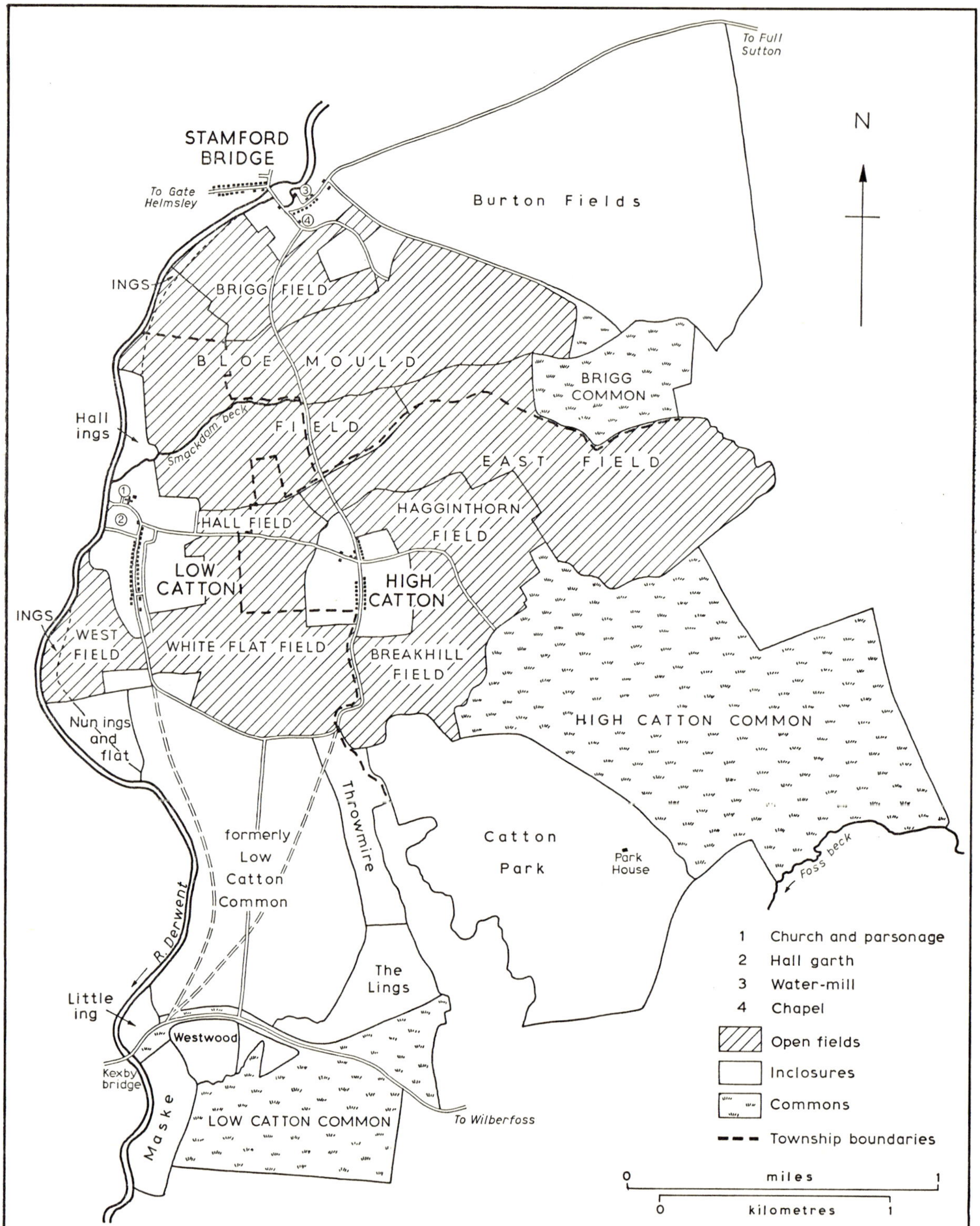

CATTON AND STAMFORD BRIDGE 1616

York. The name Burton Fields for the eastern part of the township suggests the location of the manor, and possibly hamlet, of Hundburton. In 1850 the area of Low Catton was 1,346 a., of High Catton 1,697 a., and of Stamford Bridge East 1,122 a.[9]

Much of Stamford Bridge township and the northern part of the Cattons lie at more than 50 ft. above sea-level, though lower ground borders both the Derwent and Mill Sike beck. The higher ground is continued southwards through the Cattons by the Escrick moraine, which forms a narrow ridge in places more than 100 ft. high. On either side of the moraine large areas of High and Low Catton lie at only 25–50 ft. above sea-level. The extensive open fields lay mainly on the higher ground and were inclosed in 1766. The deer park of the lords of Catton manor lay partly on the moraine but included much adjoining low ground. The rest of the low ground, on either side of the park, was occupied by High and Low Catton commons, the former inclosed with the open fields but much of the latter c. 1600.

Only limited areas of alluvium lie within the bends of the Derwent and both common and demesne meadow land was of small extent. The river formed almost the whole of the western boundary of the townships, but Stamford Bridge East township included about 2 a. of Mill ings on the west bank of the river[10] which belonged, with much of the township, to Catton manor.[11] The northern boundary of the parish follows the Roman road running eastwards from Stamford Bridge.

Most of the roads in the Cattons and Stamford Bridge are narrow winding lanes connecting the three villages or leading to neighbouring Fangfoss, Full Sutton, and Wilberfoss. Conspicuously straight roads cross the late-inclosed commons. Thus Long Lane, with its wide verges, dates from the inclosure of Low Catton common c. 1600; it replaced two roads running obliquely across the common from Kexby bridge.[12] Long Lane joins the road from Kexby to Wilberfoss, which crosses the south of Low Catton township and now forms part of the York–Hull trunk road. The latter road crosses Throwmires beck by Arnull bridge, mentioned in 1752,[13] and as it approached the Derwent it apparently crossed the stone-built 'Kexby Little Bridge', mentioned in the early 18th century.[14] The road was turnpiked in 1764 and the trust was continued until 1881; a toll bar near Kexby bridge was replaced in 1827 by one at the end of Long Lane.[15] The road was widened and straightened in the 1960s and 1970s.[16]

At Stamford Bridge the main road east of the village lies on the line of the Roman road which led directly down to the ford in the Derwent. The Roman road from York approached the ford in Stamford Bridge West. The ford was also on the line of Roman roads from the north-east and south-east, the latter running from Brough (*Petuaria*). The line of the south-easterly road is not followed by any modern roads in High Catton or Stamford Bridge townships. There is no evidence that the Romans replaced the ford with a bridge.[17]

It was presumably the Anglians who first built a bridge and the vill was referred to as Stamford Bridge in the Anglo-Saxon Chronicle in the description of the battle of 1066.[18] The apparently narrow timber bridge of 1066 may have been near the ford or alternatively some 150 yd. downstream, on the site of the later medieval bridge. The movement of the river crossing was perhaps due to the construction of a weir to work the water-mills and the consequent deepening of the river above the mills and creation of a pond below them.[19] It was presumably a bridge on the new site which was in need of repair in 1280 and 1282.[20] When it was in disrepair in 1362 Henry Percy, lord of Catton and Stamford Bridge, was held not to be responsible for its upkeep.[21] A bequest was made towards the repair of the bridge in 1385,[22] and grants of pontage were made for three years each in 1384 and 1391.[23] Another bequest was made in 1491.[24] The bridge had become the responsibility of the county by 1581, when townships in Buckrose wapentake were assessed to its repair.[25] It is said to have been built of timber with stone piers. It was replaced by another bridge a further 150 yd. downstream, the new site perhaps being chosen because the river was narrower there. It was completed in 1727 at the expense of the East Riding to the designs of William Etty of York.[26] It was regularly repaired by the county thereafter,[27] and in 1966–7 a steel footbridge was erected alongside.[28] The bridge, of stone, has a central segmental arch, flanked by two semicircular arches which are normally dry.

The main road crossing the bridge was turnpiked in 1765 and the trust was continued until 1872.[29] In 1812 a toll bar was situated in the village, between the bridge and the mill.[30] The road is now part of the main York–Bridlington road.

The Derwent was navigable up to Stamford Bridge in the Middle Ages but at least from 1602, when a new weir was built, the water-mill there may have prevented boats from passing further upstream.[31] The river was made navigable under an Act of 1702.[32] By the early 1720s a cut with a lock had been made on the west bank, bypassing the mill, the lock itself lying in Stamford Bridge West township. The river carried mainly coal, lime, corn,

[9] O.S. Map 6" Yorks. (1854 edn.). The Cattons are covered by sheet 175, Stamford Bridge by sheets 158 and 175.
[10] O.S. Map 6" (1854 edn.). Acreage from O.S. Map 1/2,500, Yorks. CLVIII. 15 (1893 edn.).
[11] Boundary descriptions in surveys of 1577 and 1616: Petworth Ho. Arch., nos. 1417, 3072.
[12] Ibid. no. 3072; see p. 148.
[13] As Arnell bridge: E.R.R.O., QSF. Mich. 1752, B. 18.
[14] E.R.R.O., QAB/2/1; QSF. East. 1737, B. 2.
[15] K. A. MacMahon, *Roads and Turnpike Trusts in E. Yorks.* (E. Yorks. Loc. Hist. Ser. xviii), 46, 70.
[16] e.g. E.R.C.C. *Mins.*, 1962–3, 22; 1966–7, 126.
[17] H. G. Ramm, 'The Derwent Crossing at Stamford Bridge', *Y.A.J.* xli. 368–76.
[18] *A.-S. Chron.* ed. Dorothy Whitelock (1961), 141–2, 144.
[19] For the mills see p. 154.
[20] *Reg. Wickwane*, p. 325.
[21] *Public Works in Med. Law*, ii (Selden Soc. xl), 328.
[22] *Y.A.J.* xxii. 281.
[23] *Cal. Pat.* 1381–5, 366; 1391–6, 8.
[24] *Test. Ebor.* iv, p. 54.
[25] B.I.H.R., CP. G. 2579/3.
[26] Ramm, 'Derwent Crossing', *passim*; Brooks, *Battle of Stamford Bridge*, 17–19. The work was done under an Act of 1725: 11 Geo I, c. 19.
[27] e.g. E.R.R.O., QAB/2/1–3.
[28] E.R.C.C. *Mins.* 1966–7, 22, 217.
[29] MacMahon, *Roads and Turnpike Trusts*, 23, 70.
[30] Petworth Ho. Arch., no. 669.
[31] See p. 154.
[32] 1 Anne, c. 20.

and flour, and there were stables, a warehouse, and a coalyard at Stamford Bridge, as well as a lock-keeper's house. Until 1854, when they sold it to the North Eastern Railway, the navigation belonged to the Wentworths, earls FitzWilliam, as lords of the manor of Malton. It was less used thereafter and traffic ended c. 1900; the lock and cut were described as no longer usable in 1939.[33]

The railway line from Market Weighton to York, opened in 1847,[34] crosses Stamford Bridge and High Catton townships. It was closed in 1965[35] and the track has been lifted. The station and station master's house at Stamford Bridge, of brick with a stone portico, still stood in 1974, together with an engine shed. Near by a high viaduct across the Derwent valley consists of 15 brick arches and an iron span above the river.[36]

Low Catton village stands along a single street roughly parallel with the Derwent. From its northern end a lane runs towards the river and the church. On the other side of the manor-house site Wath Lane formerly led to the river bank where there was once a ford;[37] the lane was overgrown in 1974. The 18th- and 19th-century houses and cottages are not noteworthy, except for the former Rectory.[38] Cast-iron lamp standards beside the lane to the church commemorate the Diamond Jubilee. There are six council houses and a few other recent dwellings. An alehouse at Low Catton was licensed in the later 18th century[39] and a victualler was mentioned in 1840. The Gold Cup inn was recorded from 1851 onwards[40] and still exists. The village street of High Catton, bordered by wide grass verges, contains mainly 19th-century houses, with four council houses. There were two licensed alehouses there in the 1750s and one later in the century.[41] The Woodpecker Lass was mentioned from 1823 but apparently closed c. 1880.[42] Just south of the village one house survives at a place called Land of Nod, where poorhouses formerly stood.

The main village street of Stamford Bridge by-passes the site of the early ford and runs down to the Derwent between high-banked verges; it approaches the site of the medieval bridge before turning abruptly towards the 18th-century bridge. The layout of the approach roads and the form of the village street thus clearly reflect the successive movements of the river crossing. The former watermill still dominates the centre of the village, though part of the mill pond, known as the Shallows, has in recent years been filled and 'landscaped'. Outstanding among a variety of 18th- and 19th-century houses is that called Ashburnholme, a large two-storeyed early-18th-century building with a decorative eaves course and stringcourse and a hood over the doorway. Several buildings in the village incorporate some local Jurassic stone.

There were two or three licensed houses in Stamford Bridge in the later 18th century.[43] The Three Tuns, recorded in 1823, was not mentioned again but the Bay Horse and the New Inn, recorded in 1823 and 1840 respectively, still exist; the New Inn was renamed the Swordsman in 1974. The Jolly Sailors, mentioned in 1840, was perhaps the house known as the Hope and Anchor by 1851 and last recorded in 1892; it stood near the cut west of the river but in Stamford Bridge East township.[44] A girls' boarding school was held in the village from 1840 until the 1890s, when it was accommodated in Vine House.[45] A reading room, recorded from 1872 until 1937 and known as St. John's Room,[46] was used as a shop in 1974.

Buildings began to be erected away from the old village centre in the later 19th century. A chapel-of-ease to the parish church was consecrated in 1868 on the Catton road,[47] and further south, beyond the railway station, a red-brick and slate Gothic-style mansion called Derwent Hill was built by Frederick Wright c. 1880.[48] Stamford Bridge House, on the Full Sutton road, was built c. 1900.[49] Since the Second World War extensive private and council house estates have been built south of the village and other houses were going up in 1974. Stamford Bridge House was used as an emergency isolation hospital during the same war and Derwent Hill became a county council old people's home in 1952;[50] a new home was built in its grounds in 1974. A village hall was built near by in 1957.[51] A stone commemorating the battle was put up at the centre of the village in 1956.[52] By 1974 ground beside the cut on the west side of the river was used as a caravan site.

The dozen outlying farms in High and Low Catton all post-date the 1766 inclosure except Catton Park, on the site of a keeper's lodge in the former deer park.[53] At Primrose Hill four bungalows have been built near the farm. The outlying houses in Stamford Bridge East include Burtonfield Hall,[54] a few farms, and a group of cottages near the former brickworks.

There were 111 poll-tax payers in 'Catton' in 1377,[55] exclusive of Stamford Bridge. About 30 houses stood in each of the Cattons in the early 17th century,[56] and 31 households in each were included in the hearth-tax return in 1672, 13 altogether being exempt. Of the chargeable households in 1672 41 had one hearth each, 4 had 2 or 3, 3 had 4, and one had six.[57] There were 94 families in Catton, presumably including Stamford Bridge, in 1743[58] and c. 100 in 1764.[59] The population of Low Catton was

---

[33] B. F. Duckham, *Inland Waterways of E. Yorks.* (E. Yorks. Loc. Hist. Ser. xxix), 46–58; C. Hadfield, *Canals of Yorks. and N.E. Eng.* 96–100, 316–25, 440–4.
[34] K. A. MacMahon, *Beginnings of E. Yorks. Rlys.* (E. Yorks. Loc. Hist. Ser. iii), 14.
[35] *Yorks. Eve. Press*, 20 Oct. 1965.
[36] See plate facing p. 33.
[37] Petworth Ho. Arch., no. 3072; O.S. Map 6" (1854 edn.). The name derives from Scand. *vað*, a ford: *P.N.E.R. Yorks.* 186.
[38] See pp. 155–6.
[39] E.R.R.O., QDT/2/15.
[40] Directories; O.S. Map 6" (1854 edn.).
[41] E.R.R.O., QDT/2/15.
[42] Directories.
[43] E.R.R.O., QDT/2/15.
[44] Directories; O.S. Map 6" (1854 edn.).
[45] Directories; Bulmer, *Dir. E. Yorks.* (1892), 575, names the house.
[46] Directories; R.D.B., 236/284/226; O.S. Map 1/2,500, Yorks. CLVIII. 15 (1893 edn.).
[47] See p. 157.
[48] R.D.B., MM/420/655; MW/277/425; 18/20/20 (1887).
[49] Directories.
[50] E.R.C.C. *Mins.* 1940–1, 171; 1951–2, 294; 1952–3, 105.
[51] *Dalesman*, Nov. 1965, 627.
[52] Inscription.
[53] See p. 153.
[54] See pp. 151–2.
[55] E 179/202/59 m. 70.
[56] Petworth Ho. Arch., nos. 1416, 3072.
[57] E 179/205/504.
[58] *Herring's Visit.* i. 148.
[59] B.I.H.R., Bp. V. 1764/Ret. 118.

147 in 1801; it rose to 193 in 1891 but was only 135 in 1901 and 85 in 1931. High Catton had 181 inhabitants in 1801, rising to a maximum of 221 in 1831, but falling to 146 in 1901. In 1931 there were 174. The combined population of the two villages was 277 in 1951 and 266 in 1971.[60]

At Stamford Bridge East and Hundburton 62 people paid the poll tax in 1377.[61] In 1604–5 27 deaths occurred from the plague.[62] There were about 15 houses in the early 17th century[63] and 18 households in 1672, 4 of them exempt from hearth tax; of those chargeable 8 had one hearth each and 6 had 2 or three.[64] The population was 170 in 1801, rising to 298 in 1821 and a maximum of 417 in 1861, and standing at 394 in 1901. After falling to 315 in 1921 it rose to 395 in 1931. After Stamford Bridge was enlarged by the transfer of part of Stamford Bridge West, with 32 inhabitants in 1931, the population rose to 577 in 1951, 674 in 1961, and 1,206 in 1971.[65]

MANORS AND OTHER ESTATES. In 1066 the manor of Catton together with its extensive soke comprised 40 carucates, of which possibly 12 were in Catton itself and Stamford Bridge. It then belonged to Earl Harold and in 1086 it was held by William de Percy of Hugh, earl of Chester.[66] CATTON manor was subsequently held by the Percies in chief, as of the honor of Chester.[67]

The Percies' enjoyment of the manor was interrupted by the forfeiture for rebellion of the possessions of Henry Percy, created earl of Northumberland,[68] and Catton was consequently granted in 1405 to the king's son John.[69] In 1416, however, the property was restored to Henry Percy, earl of Northumberland (d. 1455)[70] and retained by the family until 1537, when Henry Percy, earl of Northumberland (d. 1537) surrendered it to the Crown with the rest of his northern estates.[71] In 1555 the manor was granted for life to Mary, the same earl's widow, and two years later a reversionary grant of the property was made to Thomas Percy, earl of Northumberland (d. 1572).[72]

The manor descended in the family until the death of Joceline Percy, earl of Northumberland, in 1670, when it passed to his daughter Elizabeth; she in 1682 married Charles Seymour, duke of Somerset (d. 1748). On the death of Algernon Seymour, duke of Somerset, in 1750 his unentailed estates, together with the titles earl of Egremont and Baron Cockermouth, passed to his nephew Sir Charles Wyndham. When George Wyndham died in 1837 his East Riding estates passed to his illegitimate son George, who was created Baron Leconfield in 1859.[73] The Catton and Stamford Bridge estate comprised about 2,000 a. in 1897.[74] It was split up and sold in separate lots by Charles Henry Wyndham, Lord Leconfield, mainly in 1920–1.[75] The manorial rights in Stamford Bridge were sold to John Hetherton in 1923.[76]

The manor-house, which stood immediately south of the church at Low Catton, was apparently moated in 1258–9.[77] It was mentioned in 1315 and 1352,[78] but in 1577 it was described as 'so utterly ruinated . . . that [it] hardly can be judged where [it] hath stood'. A house 'in the side' of Hall garth was said to be used as the court house.[79] There is no later mention of a manor-house but some traces of earthworks remain.

That part of Stamford Bridge East sometimes called Hundburton and later Burton Fields was held separately under the Percys. In 1284–5 3 carucates at 'Burton' were held by Thomas Burdon, or Burton, lord of Kexby,[80] and in 1316 Brian Burdon and Eleanor Percy were lords of Hundburton.[81] Until the 17th century the descent is obscure. Hundburton apparently belonged, like Scoreby, to the Nevilles. The manor of 'Burtonfield' was referred to after the death of Richard Neville in 1460,[82] and Edmund Neville conveyed HUNDBURTON manor to William Watkinson the elder and his sons in 1611.[83] At his death in 1614 William Watkinson the younger devised the estate to his wife for life and then to his daughter Anne, wife of Edward Payler.[84] It later passed to Sir W. P. Payler, to his son Watkinson Payler, and then to Watkinson's daughter Mary. In 1758 Mary Payler's trustees conveyed Burton Fields to H. B. Darley, who promptly sold it to Robert Bewlay; it then comprised Burton House and 509 a. of closes.[85]

At Bewlay's death in 1781 the estate passed to one of his executors, Timothy Mortimer.[86] By 1810 it belonged to Charles Mortimer, and in 1833 it was bought by Henry Darley.[87] By 1840 it had passed to C. A. Darley (d. 1887), whose trustees in 1889 sold 169 a., later called Hill farm, to Thomas Coates and 283 a., called Burtonfields farm, to John Kirby.[88] Coates acquired Kirby's farm in 1895, and the Coates family sold all 452 a. to John Sherbourne in 1922.[89] The farms were sold in separate lots by Ronald Sherbourne in 1965.[90]

In 1840 the estate included Burtonfield House 'lately erected' by C. A. Darley.[91] The house, then known as Burtonfield Hall, and 64 a. were sold by William Darley to W. M. Harrison in 1896, and in

---

[60] V.C.H. Yorks. iii. 493; Census, 1911–71.
[61] E 179/202/59 m. 135.
[62] B.I.H.R., PRT. Stam. Bridge 1604.
[63] Petworth Ho. Arch., nos. 1416, 3072.
[64] E 179/205/504.
[65] V.C.H. Yorks. iii. 493; Census, 1911–71.
[66] V.C.H. Yorks. ii. 219.
[67] e.g. Cal. Close, 1396–9, 484; Cal. Inq. p.m. xii, p. 40; Cal. Inq. p.m. Hen. VII, i, pp. 202–3.
[68] D.N.B.
[69] Cal. Pat. 1405–8, 40.
[70] D.N.B.
[71] Yorks. Fines, i. 77; J. M. W. Bean, Estates of Percy Family, 1416–1537, 154. For pedigrees see Complete Peerage, s.v. Northumberland; Visit. Yorks. 1563 and 1564, ed. C. B. Norcliffe, 241–4.
[72] Cal. Pat. 1555–7, 168; 1557–8, 186–7.
[73] D.N.B.; J. T. Ward, E. Yorks. Landed Estates in the 19th Cent. (E. Yorks. Loc. Hist. Ser. xxiii), 29–30.
[74] R.D.B., 3/170/163 (1898).
[75] Ibid. e.g. 225/439/366; 226/65/55; /73/59; 228/209/170; 230/484/401; 335/590/499; /592/500; 241/540/458.
[76] Ibid. 273/379/326.
[77] C 132/23 no. 7.
[78] C 134/41 no. 1; C 135/116 no. 1.
[79] Petworth Ho. Arch., no. 1417; see p. 155.
[80] Feud. Aids, vi. 47.
[81] Ibid. 168.
[82] Cal. Pat. 1452–61, 578; see below p. 160.
[83] Yorks. Fines, 1603–14, 165.
[84] C 142/514 no. 88.
[85] R.D.B., H/18/37; Z/424/984; /498/1145; /499/1146.
[86] Ibid. BD/24/41; E.R.R.O., Land Tax 1783.
[87] R.D.B., EU /377/381; E.R.R.O., Land Tax 1810.
[88] R.D.B., FO/42/43; 28/217/205; /218/206 (1889).
[89] Ibid. 73/177/168 (1895); 253/291/251.
[90] Ibid. 1403/208/184; /363/325.
[91] Ibid. FO/42/43.

1917 Harrison devised them to George Laver and Reginald Bush.[92] The Bush family still owned them in 1973. The house is a large and irregularly-planned villa standing in a small park.

A little land in Catton was, like Scoreby, Stamford Bridge West, and Hundburton, in the king's hands in the 1490s and was accounted for along with Sheriff Hutton.[93] It was perhaps this land which comprised the 37 a. said c. 1602 to have been lately bought by the Percies from the 'duchy of York',[94] presumably property enjoyed by a royal duke of the 15th century.

Several small estates at Catton belonged to religious houses. Nun Appleton priory had 2 bovates in 1284–5.[95] Byland abbey was given 60 a. and more, together with pasture for 400 sheep, by William de Percy;[96] the former Byland holding amounted to about 120 a. c. 1602.[97] The Knights Templars had a carucate in Catton in 1284–5[98] and the Knights Hospitallers a bovate;[99] the Hospitallers' property was briefly restored to them in 1558,[1] and it was in the hands of the Crown c. 1602, when it comprised about 30 a.[2] Sawley abbey was given a carucate in Catton by Maud de Percy c. 1180.[3] St. Peter's hospital, York, had 2 bovates in the parish,[4] and Wilberfoss priory had a like amount in 1284–5.[5] In 1539 the former Wilberfoss estate comprised a house and about 40 a. in Catton and a house in Stamford Bridge.[6]

ECONOMIC HISTORY. Catton itself cannot be separated from its extensive soke in the Domesday Survey. The whole soke contained land for 24 ploughs, and in 1086 there was one plough in demesne, perhaps in Catton, and 17 ploughs held by 32 villeins and 6 sokemen. With a mill and woodland two leagues long and one wide the estate had been worth £28 in 1066; in 1086 its value was only £5.[7]

Subsequent reclamation from waste and wood may be glimpsed in the early mention of a tenant's assart[8] and in the 77 a. of forland belonging to the manor in 1315. Medieval extents of the manor of Catton apparently included the soke in Stamford Bridge and in the adjoining townships of Full Sutton, Newton, and Wilberfoss, all on the east side of the Derwent. On the west bank, however, Kexby, Scoreby, and Stamford Bridge West were all held separately from Catton. The Catton demesnes included 227 a. of land in 1258–9,[9] 132 a. in 1315,[10] and 120 a. in 1352,[11] together with about 30 a. of meadow on each occasion. In 1258–9 there were 180 a. of woodland, and pasture in the woods was recorded in 1315; it was probably there that the Percies made their park, first expressly mentioned in 1352 with its beasts, herbage, and underwood. The making of the park may perhaps be seen in an agreement made between Richard de Percy and various inhabitants in the 13th century whereby the latter gave up their claim to common in 'Lund subtus Brek',[12] that is the wood lying below the breck (later Breakhill field).

Much land was held by tenants. In 1258–9 free tenants held 39 bovates and two tofts, cottagers 23 tofts and 6 a. of land, and bondmen 14 bovates; their rents totalled about £12. In 1315 rents amounted to £19, and the holdings in bondage were described as 196 a. of land and 6 a. of meadow; villeins' works were then worth £2. Rents were valued at a similar figure in 1352, but the total value of the manor had fallen from £50–55 at the earlier dates to about £40, and a further indication of the decline perhaps resulting from the Black Death was the lack of tenants which left 18 bovates lying waste.

Catton manor and soke were worth about £66 in the 15th century[13] and £72 in 1539–40.[14] At the latter date, and no doubt much earlier, the demesnes were farmed out and accounted for £15 of the bailiff's charge. Tenants' rents made up about £30, commuted works were worth £2, and Stamford Bridge mills[15] were let for £24. The herbage of the park was farmed, too, but 3 a. of meadow were reserved for the upkeep of the beasts there and the park lodge was repaired that year.

By the later 16th and early 17th centuries[16] there were over 1,200 a. lying in the open fields around the villages of High and Low Catton and Stamford Bridge. Individual field names were mentioned in 1577, and in 1616 there were 44 a. in Hall field, 175 a. in White Flat field, 88 a. in West field, 107 a. in Breakhill field, 94 a. in Hagginthorn field, 318 a. in East field, 356 a. in Bloe Mould field, and 89 a. in Brigg field. Piecemeal inclosure of open-field land was recorded in 1577, when freeholders were alleged to keep small parcels amounting to about 18 a. inclosed, and the field acreages of 1616 included 105 a. of closes. Brigg field lay entirely in Stamford Bridge, Bloe Mould and East fields partly there and partly in the Cattons, and the other fields entirely in High and Low Catton. It is not known how the fields were divided for the purposes of rotation, but c. 1602 a parcel of meadow and a small close were said to lie in the fallow field every third year. Small areas of meadow near the Derwent were reckoned as part of the open fields: they amounted to 13 a. in West, 7 a. in Bloe Mould, and 9 a. in Brigg fields in 1616. About 150 a. of open-field land were in demesne, comprising almost all of Hall field and 50–60 a. each in White Flat and Bloe Mould fields, where some of it formed whole flats, or furlongs.

[92] R.D.B., 86/7/7 (1896); 184/294/247.
[93] D.L. 29/650/10510.
[94] Petworth Ho. Arch., no. 1416.
[95] Feud. Aids, vi. 47.
[96] J. Burton, Mon. Ebor. 331. And see Percy Charty. (Sur. Soc. cxvii), 93; E.Y.C. xi, p. 80; Cal. Inq. p.m. v, p. 320.
[97] Petworth Ho. Arch., no. 1416.
[98] Feud. Aids, vi. 47. And see Percy Charty. 474; Y.A.J. xxix. 381.
[99] Feud. Aids, vi. 47. And see Percy Charty. 474; Miscellanea, iv (Y.A.S. Rec. Ser. xciv), 104.
[1] Cal. Pat. 1557–8, 319.
[2] Petworth Ho. Arch., no. 1416.
[3] E.Y.C. xi, pp. 54–5. And see Percy Charty. 90, 474.
[4] Percy Charty. 463.
[5] Feud. Aids, vi. 47. And see Percy Charty. 474; Cal. Pat. 1461–7, 342.
[6] S.C. 6/Hen. VIII/4522.
[7] V.C.H. Yorks. ii. 219.
[8] Percy Charty. 107.
[9] C 132/23 no. 7.
[10] C 134/41 no. 1.
[11] C 135/116 no. 1.
[12] Percy Charty. 99.
[13] Bean, Estates of Percy Family, 38.
[14] S.C. 6/Hen. VIII/4283.
[15] See p. 154.
[16] Unless otherwise stated the following 5 paragraphs are based on surveys and rentals of 1570 (E 164/37 ff. 259–69), 1577 (Petworth Ho. Arch., no. 1417), c. 1602 (ibid. no. 1416), and 1616 (ibid. no. 3072), and maps of 1616 (ibid.) and n.d., c. 1616 (ibid. no. 3428).

Beyond the open fields lay common pastures said in 1577 to amount to about 1,000 a., equally divided between West and East moors or commons. The inhabitants of neighbouring villages were granted rights in the commons by Richard de Percy in the 13th century in return for giving up a claim to common in 'Lund subtus Brek', but Wilberfoss men were exceeding those rights in the later 16th century.[17] In 1616 East moor apparently comprised 536 a., including Full Sutton common; within it were Brigg Doles or common (93 a.), mainly in Stamford Bridge, and Whinberry Hills (64 a.), partly in Wilberfoss. High Catton had sole right of common in 185 a., Wilberfoss shared Whinberry Hills, and High Catton, Stamford Bridge, and Full Sutton intercommoned in the rest. A small part of East moor was set aside as the Cow Hold. Much of West moor appears to have been inclosed in the early 17th century and only about 170 a. remained in 1616. It was used chiefly by Low Catton, but Newton upon Derwent had rights in about half of the remaining common. The area recently inclosed comprised about 440 a. in 1616, apparently including grounds known as Throwmire and the Lings. Other grounds, once part of West Moor, were already inclosed by 1570: they included the Maske or Marsh (38 a.) and Little ing (10 a.), beside the Derwent, and Westwood (22 a.); all were held in demesne, as was Hall ing (16 a.), beside the river near Low Catton village. In addition, Old Hagg was a 40-acre old inclosure which had been restored to the common.

The Percies' park lay between East and West moors and contained over 350 a. In 1577 it included seven groves and there was still a keeper's lodge, but the pale was greatly decayed; only 24 deer were left in it and the herbage was let. Between 1577 and 1601 1,055 oaks and much smaller timber were taken from the park and from Westwood, and either sold or used for repairs to Stamford Bridge and Thornton mills, the court house at Catton,[18] and the park lodge and pale. One of the former groves was converted to an arable close in 1602 on condition that the tenant should plant the pale and other inclosures in the park with quickwood. By 1616 the park was divided into a dozen closes and the lodge was known as Park House.

In the late 16th century freeholders formed a large group of tenants in High and Low Catton and Stamford Bridge, holding 13 houses in 1570 and 25 houses and cottages in 1577. At the latter date the largest freeholds were one of 6 bovates and one of 78 a. There were also 25 customary tenants and 11 cottagers in 1570, and 36 tenants-at-will in 1577. Twenty-two of the tenants-at-will had under 10 a. each, 4 had 10–19 a., and 10 had 20 a. or more, the largest holding amounting to 39 a. Most of the holdings consisted of open-field arable land, small parcels of meadow, garths and crofts, and a common right. Former labour services were represented by the payment of 'boon silver' by 36 tenants.

By c. 1602 freeholders in the two Cattons and Stamford Bridge held 26 houses and cottages and 555 a. of land, including the rectorial glebe. Tenants-at-will held 42 houses and 522 a.; 25 of them had holdings of under 10 a. each, 4 had 10–19 a., and 13 had 20 a. or more. In 1616 there were 22 freeholders with 658 a. of land, 9 of them holding under 10 a. each, 3 with 10–19 a., 3 with 20–29 a., and 7 with more. The largest freeholds were one of 90 a., belonging to Christopher Beamond,[19] and another of 133 a. In the same year there were 38 tenants-at-will with 573 a. of land, 21 holding under 9 a. each, 2 with 10–19 a., 4 with 20–29 a., and 11 with more, the largest holdings comprising 40 a. and 43 a. Most of the holdings included arable land in two or more of the open fields and some had small parcels of meadow as well.

Besides the open fields and commons which were shared with the other townships in the soke, Stamford Bridge included the lands of the manor of Hundburton. There is no evidence to show whether a village community ever existed there, but it is possible that the Burton fields or Burton closes referred to from the late 16th century[20] onwards occupied the former open fields of Hundburton. Burton closes comprised about 500 a.[21] To the west of them lay Ox close, which covered 76 a. in 1758 when it was still used as a stinted pasture by the occupiers of lands in both Burton fields and Skirpenbeck.[22]

The remaining open fields and commons within the soke of Catton were inclosed in 1766,[23] under an Act of 1760.[24] Allotments were made totalling 1,416 a. from fields and commons, and a further 1,261 a. of old inclosures were also allotted. The earlier open fields had by then been subdivided, several of the new names having been already used in the early 17th century for parts of the fields. Allotments were made from the following fields: Furlong (156 a.), Far (113 a.), Blow Mould (75 a.), Reckon Dale (30 a.), Hagginthorn (27 a.), Breckhill (23 a.), Merrill Thorn (22 a.), Dock Flat (18 a.), Brigg (14 a.), Angram (10 a.), Half Acre (9 a.), and Cross Lands (7 a.). Allotments comprising 591 a. were made from High Catton common (i.e. East moor), 215 a. from Low Catton common (i.e. West moor), and 100 a. from Stamford Bridge common, together with 6 a. in Cow Lane, the outgang which had led to the common from Stamford Bridge village.

While some men received allotments consisting entirely of land from the open fields and commons, others had their former open-field and common rights satisfied wholly or partly by the allotment of old inclosures. Thirty-two men received allotments of one kind or another. The largest allotment, of 1,507 a., went to the earl of Egremont, and the rector received 270 a. for glebe and tithes. There were 4 allotments of 100–150 a., 2 of 50–99 a., 3 of 20–49 a., 5 of 10–19 a., and 16 of under 10 a. The inclosure commissioners were not concerned with that part of Stamford Bridge lying outside the soke of Catton, but probably the only man with a considerable holding there was the owner of Burton Fields.

The Egremont estate in Catton and in the adjoining townships of the soke comprised 2,870 a. in 1797 and there were 60 tenants, large and small. Only 10 tenants had 100 a. or more, and 12 had 50–99 a.[25] In 1851 17 farmers in the Cattons and

---

[17] Petworth Ho. Arch., no. 1416; *Percy Charty.* 99; see above p. 152.
[18] See p. 155.
[19] For the Beamonds or Beamonts see C 142/250 no. 33; C 142/338 no. 84; *Yorks. Fines, 1603–14,* 137.
[20] Petworth Ho. Arch., no. 1417; E 164/37 ff. 259–64.
[21] See p. 151.
[22] R.D.B., Z/499/1146.
[23] Ibid. AH/177/5.
[24] 33 Geo. II, c. 43 (Priv. Act).
[25] Petworth Ho. Arch., no. 3075.

Stamford Bridge had 100 a. or more.[26] The total number of farmers there was usually 20–30 in the 19th and 20th centuries, a dozen of whom had 150 a. or more in the 1920s and 1930s.[27] Garden allotments for the poor of Stamford Bridge were provided by C. A. Darley c. 1840.[28] There was much grassland in some parts of these townships after inclosure. Thus at Stamford Bridge in 1795 there were 363 a. of arable and 737 a. of grassland,[29] and in 1905 751 a. of arable, 384 a. of grassland, and 4 a. of woodland. In the Cattons in 1905 there were 1,802 a. of arable, 953 a. of grassland, and 76 a. of woodland.[30] Grass was still plentiful in the Burton Fields area of Stamford Bridge and alongside the Derwent in the Cattons in the 1930s and later.[31] There were two large turkey farms at Catton in 1974. The chief area of woodland is the 43-acre Black plantation, in High Catton, which has been managed by the Forestry Commission since 1959.[32]

A fishery in the Derwent was frequently mentioned as an appurtenance of Catton manor from 1258–9[33] onwards. Fishing there was said to obstruct the passage of boats up to Stamford Bridge in the 14th century.[34] There was a landing-place near the church at Low Catton in 1616,[35] and the improvement of the Derwent in the 18th century[36] was doubtless of benefit to both Catton and Stamford Bridge. At the latter there was a 'mariner' in 1840 and a waterman in 1851.[37]

The growth of Stamford Bridge in the 19th century led to an increase in the numbers of shopkeepers and tradesmen there, and garages and refreshment rooms have appeared in the 20th century.[38] Otherwise, the chief non-agricultural employment has been provided by brick-making, quarrying, and milling. Brick-making in Catton, near the present Moorfield (formerly Brickworks) Farm, was recorded from 1840 and at Stamford Bridge, near Beechwood House, from 1823, in each case until the 1870s.[39] Gravel pits were worked commercially in High Catton, close to the village street, in the 1930s and later, and at Stamford Bridge, in the Burton Fields area, from the 1920s.[40] All were disused in 1973. In 1850[41] there was a chicory kiln near the brickyard at Stamford Bridge, still standing in 1973, and a warehouse and maltkiln in Catton, demolished when Kexby bridge was rebuilt in the 1960s.

The mill recorded under Catton in 1086[42] may have been at Stamford Bridge. There was, however, a small water-mill in Catton itself, apparently that described in 1258–9 as 'sometimes grinding in winter'.[43] It was probably the fulling mill called Beck mill that was mentioned in 1474.[44] It stood in Smackdam close, on Mill Sike beck north of Low Catton village,[45] and had been demolished by c. 1602.[46] Mills certainly existed at Stamford Bridge by c. 1130–5,[47] and they consisted of 'seven mills on one pond in the Derwent' in 1258.[48] A new fulling mill was mentioned in 1331,[49] and in 1352 the mills comprised three corn and two fulling mills.[50] Both corn and fulling mills were frequently recorded thereafter[51] and the various 'mills' may have been housed from the first in buildings on both banks of the river. In the later 16th century there were two corn mills and one fulling mill on each bank, but in 1602 they were taken down and rebuilt on the south-east bank and at the same time a stone dam or weir was built.[52] Soon afterwards they were described as five corn and two fulling mills 'all under a roof'.[53] In 1797 the mills contained three water-wheels and five pairs of stones for corn, and one water-wheel in an attached fulling mill; a second, adjoining, fulling mill was in a different tenancy.[54] The second fulling mill was apparently that belonging to a dyer who was in dispute with the corn-miller in 1715;[55] a dye-house near the bridge was recorded in 1724.[56] The mills were burnt in 1749 but repaired the following year.[57] When the York to Garrowby Hill turnpike trust was renewed in 1807 the earl of Egremont and his tenants were exempted from toll on traffic to and from the mills,[58] though their exemption was in dispute in 1812.[59] A small bleaching or 'beetling' mill (presumably the former separate fulling mill) stood near the mills in 1812.[60] Nearly £1,000 was spent on the mills in 1847–50,[61] and it was perhaps then that the building was enlarged. There were subsequently two water-wheels and seven pairs of stones, and the mill was worked until 1964; it was converted into a restaurant in 1967, but some of the machinery remains.[62] The building consists of an 18th-century block with steep-pitched roof and an adjoining five-storeyed 19th-century block, with a lower projection towards the west.[63]

LOCAL GOVERNMENT. The profits of manorial courts at Catton were recorded from 1258–9 onwards,[64] and there are many surviving court rolls for

---

[26] H.O. 107/2351. [27] Directories.
[28] 1st Rep. Com. on Employment of Children, Young Persons, and Women in Agric., Appendix, Pt. II [4068–I], p. 386, H.C. (1867–8), xvii.
[29] E.R.R.O., DPX/84.
[30] Acreage Returns, 1905.
[31] [1st] Land Util. Surv. Map, sheet 27; 2nd Land Util. Surv. Map, sheet 709 (SE 65–75).
[32] Ex inf. Forestry Commission, York, 1972.
[33] C 132/23 no. 7.
[34] Cal. Pat. 1330–4, 290; 1340–3, 312; 1388–92, 266, 351; Cal. Inq. Misc. ii, pp. 320–1; Pub. Works in Med. Law, 276.
[35] Petworth Ho. Arch., no. 3072.
[36] See p. 149.
[37] H.O. 107/2351; White, Dir. E. & N.R. Yorks. (1840), 237.
[38] H.O. 107/2351; directories.
[39] Directories.
[40] Ibid.; O.S. Map 6", SE 75 SW. (1958, 1971 edns.); R.D.B., 659/397/337; 1147/159/149.
[41] O.S. Map 6" (1854 edn.).
[42] V.C.H. Yorks. ii. 219. [43] C 132/23 no. 7.
[44] Petworth Ho. Arch., Yorks. MCR/9.
[45] For medieval references to 'Smackedik' and 'Milnesyk' see Percy Charty. 94, 115.
[46] Petworth Ho. Arch., no. 1416.
[47] E.Y.C. xi, p. 23.
[48] C 132/23 no. 7.
[49] Percy Charty. 169. [50] C 135/116 no. 1.
[51] e.g. S.C. 6/Hen. VIII/4283; E 134/28 Eliz. I Trin./13; E 164/37; Cal. Inq. Misc. vi, p. 247; Bean, Estates of Percy Family, 39, 48.
[52] Petworth Ho. Arch., no. 1416.
[53] Ibid. nos. 1416, 3072. [54] Ibid. no. 3075.
[55] E.R.R.O., QSF. Mids. 1715, C.1 and D.1.
[56] Brooks, Battle of Stamford Bridge, 18.
[57] E.R.R.O., QSF. East. 1750, A.(ii)–(iv).
[58] MacMahon, Roads and Turnpike Trusts in E. Yorks. 51.
[59] Petworth Ho. Arch., nos. 669, 1095.
[60] Ibid. no. 669. [61] Ibid. no. 1095.
[62] K. J. Allison, E.R. Water-mills (E. Yorks. Loc. Hist. Ser. xxvi), 49–50.
[63] See plate facing p. 176.
[64] C 132/23 no. 7; C 134/41 no. 1; C 135/116 no. 1; S.C. 6/Hen. VIII/4283.

the manor and soke from the late 15th to the late 17th century,[65] as well as court books and call rolls for the period 1806-72.[66] The bailiffs at Stamford Bridge, presumably acting for the lord of Catton, claimed the right to take tolls and measurage in 1275-6.[67] Liberties claimed as appurtenant to the manor in 1616 included the right to take waifs, strays, escheats, and forfeitures, and the goods of felons, fugitives, and outlaws.[68] A house 'in the side' of Hall Garth was used as the court house in 1616.[69] This, the so-called 'Hall House', later became the Rectory.[70]

Officers elected in the 1470s were a constable for each of High and Low Catton, Stamford Bridge, Hundburton, and Kexby Bridge, and an aletaster for each of the Cattons and Stamford Bridge.[71] In the 1660s a constable was elected for each of the Cattons, and a constable and a bylawman for Stamford Bridge.[72] In the 19th century a constable, deputy constable, four bylawmen, and a pinder were appointed for each of High Catton, Low Catton, and Stamford Bridge townships.[73]

No parochial records before 1835 are known. There were parish poorhouses at Stamford Bridge[74] and at a place called Land of Nod, south of High Catton village.[75] The Cattons and Stamford Bridge joined Pocklington poor-law union in 1836[76] and Pocklington rural district in 1894.[77] They became part of the North Wolds district of Humberside in 1974.

CHURCH. Catton church was mentioned in the early 13th century, when parochial rights were granted to its dependent chapel at Full Sutton.[78] There were also chapels at Kexby and Stamford Bridge, both of which may have been suppressed as chantry chapels in the 16th century. Churches were built there in the 19th century and Kexby became a separate parish in 1853.[79]

The Percies presented to Catton rectory in 1268[80] and the advowson descended with the manor until the 17th century.[81] It was said in 1577 to belong to William Stanley, Lord Monteagle,[82] and the Crown presented, presumably by lapse, in 1578 and 1592.[83] There were unexplained presentations in 1678 by Sir William Pierrepont and Sir Orlando Gee and in 1685 by Gee alone.[84] By an exchange of 1692-3 the advowson passed from the duke of Somerset to the Crown,[85] which presented in 1739 and 1755.[86] The earls of Egremont later laid claim to the advowson by virtue of a settlement of 1687 whereby it was to pass to the heirs of Elizabeth, duchess of Somerset. They successfully disputed the Crown's right of presentation in 1786-7 and 1814.[87] Thereafter the advowson descended with the manor and in 1972 belonged to Lord Leconfield's trustees.[88]

The church was worth £40 in 1291,[89] £21 12s. 8d. net in 1535,[90] and £116 16s. 8d. net in 1650.[91] The average net value was £410 in 1829-31,[92] and the income was £500 in 1884 and £390 in 1915.[93] Tithes provided £21 of the gross income in 1535, £8 coming from Kexby and Scoreby.[94] There were several disputes over their payment in the 16th and 17th centuries.[95] In 1650 moduses of over £10 were paid in lieu of tithes in the townships,[96] and in 1716 moduses totalled over £15, comprising over £4 from Kexby, about £2 10s. from Scoreby, £1 10s. from Burton Fields, nearly £2 from Scoreby Grange, over £1 from Stamford Bridge mills, nearly £2 from certain ancient inclosures in Catton, and £1 13s. 4d. from the rector of Full Sutton.[97] At the inclosure of Catton in 1766 the rector received allotments of 270 a. for his glebe and tithes, but most of the moduses remained payable.[98] The moduses from Scoreby and Scoreby Grange were apportioned as rent-charges in 1841 and those from Catton, Kexby, and the mills in 1843.[99]

Glebe land contributed £1 to the gross income in 1535.[1] In the 17th century the rector had about 60 a. of open-field land, two parcels of meadow, and a 20-acre close, making a total of 87 a. in 1728.[2] The land allotted at inclosure in lieu of glebe and tithes comprised White House and Glebe farms; the two farms, amounting to 266 a., were sold in 1920.[3]

A house belonging to the rector was said in 1539 to have been let to the countess of Northumberland.[4] It stood close to the church in 1616,[5] and was recorded among the property of the rectory from 1663 onwards.[6] During the rector's non-residence the curate lived in the 'parsonage' in 1743.[7] The house was described as ruinous but about to be rebuilt in 1818[8] and as unfit for residence in 1835.[9] It was presumably the present Glebe Farm, of which part of the south front and staircase remain from a substantial house of c. 1700 which has been curtailed on the north and completely remodelled in the earlier 19th century.

In 1764 the curate lived in the 'Hall House'[10] and

[65] Petworth Ho. Arch., preliminary list at the West Sussex Co. Rec. Off., Chichester.
[66] E.R.R.O., DDEL/3/1-4.
[67] Rot. Hund. (Rec. Com.), i. 122.
[68] Petworth Ho. Arch., no. 3072.
[69] Ibid.; see p. 151.
[70] See p. 156.
[71] Petworth Ho. Arch., Yorks. MCR/9.
[72] Ibid./287.
[73] E.R.R.O., DDEL/3/1-4.
[74] R.D.B., 93/74/71 (1907).
[75] O.S. Map 6" (1854 edn.).
[76] 3rd Rep. Poor Law Com. 169.
[77] Census.
[78] Percy Charty. 351-2.
[79] See pp. 156-7, 163-4. [80] Reg. Giffard, p. 52.
[81] e.g. Reg. Romeyn, ii, p. 225; Reg. Corbridge, ii, p. 170; Cal. Inq. p.m. v, p. 320; x, p. 22; Cal. Inq. p.m. Hen. VII, i, p. 202; Cal. Pat. 1557-8, 188; Inst. Bks.
[82] Petworth Ho. Arch., no. 1417.
[83] B.I.H.R., Inst. AB. 3, f. 244; H.U.L., N.A.H. Lawrance, 'Clergy List', Harthill, 1 (i), p. 58.
[84] Inst. Bks.; B.I.H.R., Inst. AB. 8, p. 28.

[85] Petworth Ch. Act, 4 & 5 Wm. and Mary, c. 13 (Priv. Act).
[86] Inst. Bks. [87] Petworth Ho. Arch., no. 662.
[88] Crockford (1971-2).
[89] Tax. Eccl. (Rec. Com.), 303.
[90] Valor Eccl. (Rec. Com.), v. 140. [91] C 94/3 f. 57.
[92] Rep. Com. Eccl. Revenues, 924.
[93] B.I.H.R., Bp. V. 1884/Ret.; Bp. V. 1915/Ret.
[94] Valor Eccl. v. 140.
[95] B.I.H.R., CP. G. 278, 360, 2298; H. 3916, 4513.
[96] C 94/3 f. 57. [97] B.I.H.R., TER. I. Catton 1716.
[98] R.D.B., AH/177/5.
[99] B.I.H.R., TA. 215S, 297S, 521S, 624S, 624AS.
[1] Valor Eccl. v. 140.
[2] B.I.H.R., TER. I. Catton 1663, 1693, 1728.
[3] R.D.B., 221/37/33; 232/459/380.
[4] L. & P. Hen. VIII, xiv (2), p. 131.
[5] Petworth Ho. Arch., no. 3072.
[6] B.I.H.R., TER. I. Catton 1663 etc.
[7] Herring's Visit. i. 148.
[8] Lawton, Rer. Eccl. Dioc. Ebor. 333.
[9] Rep. Com. Eccl. Revenues, 924.
[10] B.I.H.R., Bp. V. 1764/Ret. 118.

at inclosure in 1766 the rector was awarded the Hall House by exchange, as well as a house that was presumably the old Rectory. The Hall House stood in the angle of the village street and Church Lane, in Hall Garth,[11] and was formerly the court house of the manor.[12] It was described as the Rectory in 1851.[13] It was sold in 1957[14] and replaced by a new Rectory near the church at Stamford Bridge. The central part of the east front of the old house retains internally some heavy timbers and a roof structure which may date from the 16th or early 17th century. The house was extended to the north later in the 17th century and both parts were refronted in brick in the 18th century. In the later 19th century the house was enlarged on the south, where the new work may replace part of the early range, and on the west.

An obit in the church was endowed with land in Full Sutton, which was granted by the Crown to Francis Barker and Thomas Blackway in 1566.[15]

There was a chapel, with a hermit, at Stamford Bridge in 1348.[16] In 1444 a chapel there was described as on the bridge,[17] and in 1466 a chapel of St. Edmund was mentioned.[18] It was probably suppressed as a chantry chapel in the 16th century. Materials from the building had been sold by 1556[19] and it was in decay in 1575.[20] A chapel of St. Leonard was, however, shown on a map of 1616 beside the Catton road, just south of the village street.[21] It was presumably that building which the inhabitants of Stamford Bridge claimed in 1598 to be served by a curate who took the tithes of the township for his stipend and provided all services but burial. The claim was disputed by the rector. It was decided by the chancellor of York that the rector himself or a curate should say a weekly service at Stamford Bridge and should baptize and marry there, and that the 'better and more able sort' of the inhabitants should hear service in the parish church eight times a year; the rector was to take the tithes of Stamford Bridge.[22] The matter was still in dispute in the 1630s.[23] The chapel presumably stood in the 'chapel garth' which belonged to the rector in 1716 and later,[24] and remains of the chapel are said to have been visible there in 1861.[25] Lands in Catton, formerly belonging to a chapel, which were granted to Francis Barker and Thomas Browne in 1571,[26] may have supported the Stamford Bridge chapel.

The living was often held in plurality by a non-resident rector. In 1308 Walter de Bedwind also held Aughton and three other churches, a prebend at Howden, the deanery of Tamworth (Staffs.), and the treasurership of York Minster.[27] The rector was granted a dispensation to hold more than one living in 1428.[28] In 1574 he resigned and became a fugitive papist.[29] In 1743 he was also vicar of Askham Richard, where he lived, and curate of Bilbrough (both Yorks. W.R.),[30] and in 1764 he held Scrayingham and Stockton on the Forest (Yorks. N.R.), and was master of the grammar school at York, where he lived.[31] In 1835 the rector was also vicar of Wressle and held St. Buryan (Cornw.).[32]

A parish chaplain, with an income of £4 13s. 4d., was recorded at Catton in 1525–6,[33] and there was an assistant curate in 1743, 1764, 1835, 1892, and 1900.[34]

Two services were held at Catton each Sunday in 1743 and Holy Communion was celebrated five times a year, with about 140 communicants the previous Easter.[35] Communion was received by 60–80 people in 1764; about 15 people received monthly in 1865 and fortnightly in 1868. A Friday and a Sunday service were held at Stamford Bridge in 1865 in a 'service room'[36] and in 1868 in the newly-built chapel. There were three Sunday services each week at Catton in 1884 and two in 1894. Communion was celebrated there each week by 1915.[37] There was one service each week in 1973 at both Catton and Stamford Bridge.

The church of ALL SAINTS, Catton, of ashlar and rubble, consists of chancel with north vestry, aisled nave with north transept, south porch, and south-west tower. By the early 13th century the church had, in addition to the nave and chancel, at least a north aisle and transept with a combined length of four bays. A south aisle, with a tower in its western bay, was added later in the 13th century. The only remaining evidences of change in the earlier 14th century are the west window of the north aisle and the north window of the transept, but the chancel may have been heightened and refenestrated at about that time. The tower was strengthened and its upper part completely rebuilt in the 15th century, the south aisle was extended a few feet to the east and refenestrated, and the north aisle was rebuilt. Later but in a similar style the walls of the transept were raised, a new window was put into the east wall, and the roof pitch was lowered.

The church walls and roof were described as ruinous in 1676.[38] The nave was restored by Henry Gardiner, rector 1859–64, and the chancel by his sisters in 1866, under the direction of G. E. Street. The new chancel east window is by William Morris.[39] Extensive repairs were apparently done under a faculty of 1908.[40] The north aisle contains a brass to Thomas Teyll (d. 1591) and a Royal Arms dated 1723.

There are three bells: (i) 1681, Samuel Smith the

---

[11] R.D.B., AH/177/5.
[12] See p. 155.
[13] O.S. Map 6" (1854 edn.).
[14] R.D.B., 1076/42/35.
[15] Cal. Pat. 1563–6, pp. 474–5.
[16] Ibid. 1345–8, 447.
[17] B.I.H.R., Prob. Reg. 2 f. 96.
[18] Ibid. Prob. Reg. 4 f. 36.
[19] E.R.R.O., DDCC/139/65.
[20] B.I.H.R., V. 1575/CB. 1.
[21] Petworth Ho. Arch., no. 3072.
[22] B.I.H.R., Chanc. AB. 13 ff. 204–205d.
[23] Ibid. CP. H. 800, 1875, 1928.
[24] Ibid. TER. I. Catton 1716 etc.
[25] Y.A.J. x. 84.
[26] Cal. Pat. 1569–72, p. 236.
[27] Reg. Greenfield, i, pp. 10–12, 32, 98; iii, p. 179; Cal. Papal Regs. ii. 41, 62.

[28] Cal. Papal Regs. viii. 338–9.
[29] Aveling, Post Reformation Catholicism, 11.
[30] Herring's Visit. i. 149.
[31] B.I.H.R., Bp. V. 1764/Ret. 118.
[32] Rep. Com. Eccl. Revenues, 924.
[33] Y.A.J. xxiv. 72.
[34] B.I.H.R., Bp. V. 1764/Ret. 118; Bp. V. 1900/Ret. 73; Herring's Visit. i. 148; Rep. Com. Eccl. Revenues, 924; Bulmer, Dir. E. Yorks. (1892), 573.
[35] Herring's Visit. i. 149.
[36] Perhaps St. John's Room: see p. 150.
[37] B.I.H.R., Bp. V. 1764/Ret. 118; V. 1865/Ret. 106; V. 1868/Ret. 102; Bp. V. 1884/Ret.; Bp. V. 1894/Ret.; Bp. V. 1915/Ret.
[38] Ibid. ER. V/CB. 4.
[39] Tablet in church; Y.A.J. x. 85; Pevsner, Yorks. E.R. 308.
[40] B.I.H.R., Fac. Bk. viii, p. 349.

elder of York; (ii) 1742; (iii) 1719, both by E. Seller of York.[41] The plate includes two silver cups, a silver salver, and base metal chalice and paten. One cup was made in London in 1617,[42] the other by John Thompson of York in 1636; one of them may have been that given, with a cover, by William Headlam in 1679.[43] The salver was made by Mark Gill of York in 1681 and given by Margaret Headlam the following year.[44]

The churchyard was enlarged in 1863[45] and 1927.[46]

Thomas Chapman in 1750 gave £1 to the church, the interest to be given to the three best bell-ringers ringing on Christmas Day. The charity was administered with several others in 1824 and 1s. was paid to the ringers.[47] No more is known of it.

A new chapel-of-ease was consecrated at Stamford Bridge in 1868.[48] The chapel of ST. JOHN, of yellow sandstone with limestone dressings, was designed by G. Fowler Jones in the Early English style and erected partly at the expense of C. A. Darley of Burtonfield Hall.[49] It consists of chancel with north vestry and nave with bellcot and north porch. There are two bells. The plate includes a silver paten, made in London in 1864.[50] The churchyard was enlarged in 1936.[51]

The registers of baptisms, marriages, and burials for the whole parish begin in 1592 and are complete.[52]

NONCONFORMITY. A few recusants and non-communicants were reported at Catton and Stamford Bridge in the late 16th and early 17th centuries, and up to a dozen in the late 17th and early 18th centuries.[53] There were three Roman Catholic families in 1764.[54]

Wesley preached at Stamford Bridge in 1753.[55] About 25 Methodists were reported in the parish in 1764, but a former meeting-house at Stamford Bridge was then said to be disused.[56] The Methodists had 4 members at Catton in 1789, rising to about 30 in the early 1800s, and 8 at Stamford Bridge in 1789, rising to about 20 in the 1790s.[57] Houses were registered for worship at 'Catton' in 1764, 1779, 1787, and 1799,[58] at High Catton in 1796 and 1812,[59] and at Stamford Bridge in 1781 and 1820.[60]

A Methodist chapel is said to have been built at Stamford Bridge in 1796 and later enlarged,[61] and a chapel there was certainly registered in 1818.[62] The chapel was rebuilt in 1828[63] and was still used in 1973; it is a large two-storeyed brick building with round-headed windows. A Wesleyan Methodist chapel was built at High Catton in 1810[64] and replaced by a new one in 1900;[65] it was still used in 1973. The Wesleyans met in a house at Low Catton in 1851.[66]

The Primitive Methodists met in houses at High Catton and Stamford Bridge in 1851.[67] They built a chapel at High Catton in 1856.[68] It is said to have closed in 1933[69] but was still standing in 1973. A Primitive Methodist chapel at Stamford Bridge was registered in 1868.[70] It had closed by 1935[71] and was used as a store-house in 1973.

EDUCATION. There was an unendowed school at Catton in 1743 with more than 30 children,[72] and in 1764 it was reported that a schoolmaster was occasionally hired and retained.[73] One of the schools existing in the parish in 1819[74] was probably in Catton township, and there was a school at High Catton in 1835.[75] Thereafter the school was at Low Catton. It was built in 1841 by Col. George Wyndham[76] and had about 35 children in 1865.[77] It may have been temporarily closed, for in 1871 it was said that a school was then being provided at Low Catton, while High Catton children went to Stamford Bridge.[78] Low Catton National school first received an annual government grant in 1874–5.[79] From 1906 onwards 20–30 children attended the school, and when it was closed in 1923[80] they were transferred to Stamford Bridge.[81] The school was thenceforth used as a meeting-room. It was temporarily reopened to cater for evacuees in 1939,[82] and in 1955 it was converted to a village hall.[83]

A school at Stamford Bridge was founded by Christopher Wharton, who by will dated 1787 bequeathed £600 to support a master to teach 18 children. The school was built in 1795 with the accumulated interest.[84] Two of the schools existing in the parish in 1819 may have been at Stamford Bridge,[85] and in 1835 there were three schools: Wharton's had 56 children, including the 18 taught

[41] Boulter, 'Ch. Bells', 26.
[42] Pevsner, *Yorks. E.R.* 308.
[43] B.I.H.R., PR. CATN. 1.
[44] *Yorks. Ch. Plate*, i. 233–4, 319.
[45] Ibid. CD. 340.
[46] York. Dioc. Regy., Consecration deed.
[47] *11th Rep. Com. Char.* 725; see below p. 158.
[48] B.I.H.R., CD. 384.
[49] *Yorks. Gaz.* 1 Feb. 1868.
[50] *Yorks. Ch. Plate*, i. 319.
[51] York Dioc. Regy., Consecration deed.
[52] B.I.H.R.
[53] Aveling, *Post Reformation Catholicism*, 59–60.
[54] B.I.H.R., Bp. V. 1764/Ret. 118.
[55] *Wesley's Jnl.* ed. N. Curnock, iv. 66.
[56] B.I.H.R., Bp. V. 1764/Ret. 118.
[57] E.R.R.O., MRP/1/7.
[58] G.R.O. Worship Returns, Vol. v, nos. 203, 546, 690, 1463.
[59] Ibid. nos. 1190, 2696.
[60] Ibid. no. 3352; B.I.H.R., Fac. Bk. ii, p. 262.
[61] J. Lyth, *Glimpses of Early Methodism in York & Dist.* 296.
[62] G.R.O. Worship Returns, Vol. v, no. 3214.
[63] H.O. 129/23/516; date on building.
[64] H.O. 129/23/516.
[65] G.R.O. Worship Reg. no. 37559. Foundation stones are dated 1899.
[66] H.O. 129/23/516.
[67] Ibid.
[68] Date on building.
[69] E.R.R.O., DDMM/19/1 p. 15. It was deregistered in 1937: G.R.O. Worship Reg. no. 7798.
[70] G.R.O. Worship Reg. no. 18450. It is said to have been built in 1866: Bulmer, *Dir. E. Yorks.* (1892), 573.
[71] G.R.O. Worship Reg. no. 18450.
[72] *Herring's Visit.* i. 148.
[73] B.I.H.R., Bp. V. 1764/Ret. 118.
[74] *Educ. of Poor Digest*, 1078.
[75] *Educ. Enquiry Abstract*, 1082.
[76] Sheahan and Whellan, *Hist. York & E.R.* ii. 558; date on building.
[77] B.I.H.R., V. 1865/Ret. 106.
[78] *Returns relating to Elem. Educ.* 794.
[79] *Rep. of Educ. Cttee. of Council, 1874–5* [C.1265-I], p. 434, H.C. (1875), xxiv.
[80] *Bd. of Educ. List 21* (H.M.S.O.).
[81] E.R. Educ. Cttee. *Mins.* 1923–4, 35.
[82] Ibid. 1939–40, 187.
[83] Stone on building.
[84] Ed. 7/135 no. 40a; stone on building; *11th Rep. Com. Char.* 726.
[85] *Educ. of Poor Digest*, 1078.

free, and the others had 24 and 18 respectively.[86] The endowment was represented by £630 stock in 1840.[87] The school was united to the National Society and the average attendance in 1871 was 48; the endowment income was then £19 and the school was said to have been 'built' that year,[88] presumably a reference to the extension that still stands in front of the older building. An annual government grant was first received in 1875–6.[89]

A new school was opened in 1911[90] on the Low Catton road near St. John's church. Until the 1920s the average attendance was usually 60–70, in the 1930s 70–80.[91] In 1951 senior pupils were sent to Fulford, and in 1955 they were transferred to Pocklington.[92] The school was enlarged in 1967[93] and the attendance in September 1973 was 162.[94] Under a Scheme of 1923 the income of Wharton's charity is widely applied on behalf of local children, including payments for other than elementary education.[95]

CHARITIES FOR THE POOR. Thomas Wood, by will dated 1568, devised a rent-charge of £10 from an estate at Kilnwick Percy for the benefit of the Cattons, Stamford Bridge, and many other townships. In 1824 3s. 4d. was distributed in High Catton, 3s. 4d. in Low Catton, and 1s. 6d. in Stamford Bridge East.[96] Henry Frederick, Baron Hotham, owner of the Kilnwick Percy estate, redeemed the rent-charge in 1961 and £7 stock was subsequently assigned to each of the Cattons and £3 to Stamford Bridge.[97] The combined income for the three townships in 1972–3 was 40p; it was not used that year.[98]

It was said in 1824 that a total of £10 had been given by unknown donors.[99] The donors were probably George Smeton (£1 in 1617), Richard Cook (5s. in 1622), William Ellard (10s. in 1622), Elizabeth Pearson (£1 in 1630), John Loftsome (10s. in 1641), Wilfrid Lazenby (£1 in 1642), Thomas Cowling (10s. in 1644), Francis Constable (£3 in 1668), Tristram Lecke (£1 in 1673), Christopher Horsley (£1 in 1670), and Richard Davy (£1 in 1685).[1]

At unknown date Hammond, William, George, and Margaret Dealtry gave £13 to the poor of the parish, including £8 to High Catton and £2 10s. to Low Catton. Land was bought, and 1½ a. was allotted to the charity at inclosure in 1766. The income was £1 15s. in 1824.[2]

Richard Gell, by will dated 1712, gave 3s. a year out of Nun ings to the poor of High Catton. The rent-charge was transferred to other land at inclosure in 1766 and was distributed with the Dealtrys' charity in 1824.[3]

William Headlam, before 1753, gave 1s. a week out of his estate in Kexby to be distributed in bread to the poor of the parish. In 1824 fourteen penny loaves were distributed weekly.[4]

In 1824 four other charities were administered together, along with the unknown donors' charity (see above) and Chapman's charity for bell-ringers.[5] They were those of Henry Dealtry, who gave £5 for High Catton in 1753, John Horsley (£1 for the parish at unknown date), Henry Lazenby (£1 each for High and Low Catton at unknown date), and Richard Lofthouse (£3 for the parish at unknown date). The total income in 1824 was £1 2s., which was duly distributed to the ringers and the poor.[6]

Nothing more is known about any of these various charities.

KEXBY, SCOREBY, AND STAMFORD BRIDGE WEST

Kexby lies about 5 miles east of York and with the townships of Scoreby and Stamford Bridge West it occupies some 4 miles of the west bank of the river Derwent. The village of Kexby stands at a point where firm ground approaches close to the river and where a ferry and bridge have for long afforded a crossing. The now depopulated village of Scoreby occupied a similar riverside situation just over a mile to the north, and 1½ mile further north Stamford Bridge West now forms a small adjunct of the large village in Stamford Bridge East township across the river. Kexby and Scoreby were both Scandinavian settlements. In 1850 the area of Kexby was 1,892 a. and of Scoreby and Stamford Bridge West 1,945 a.,[7] of which all but about 300 a. lay in Scoreby.

The whole of Kexby township and much of Scoreby lie at between 25 ft. and 50 ft. above sea-level, with even lower ground beside the Derwent. In the north, however, Scoreby extends on to the lower slopes of the York moraine and in places reaches nearly 100 ft. From this high ground the main road to York, on the line of a Roman road, runs down towards the Derwent crossing at Stamford Bridge. The road forms part of the parish boundary and one stretch of it is the main street of Gate Helmsley (Yorks. N.R.), a 'one-sided' village which faces the fields of Scoreby Grange across the road. In the Middle Ages the open-field land of Kexby and Scoreby lay wholly on the lower ground, but both townships were inclosed at an early date and grassland and woodland have since been dominant there. Kexby common, occupying the south-west corner of the township and projecting into Dunnington, was not inclosed until the 18th century. Riverside ings occupied the limited areas of alluvium within the bends of the Derwent.

The road from Dunnington to Wilberfoss, now forming part of the York–Hull trunk road, crosses Kexby township, and from it a minor road leads southwards to Elvington. The main road formerly

[86] *Educ. Enquiry Abstract*, 1082.
[87] White, *Dir. E. & N.R. Yorks.* (1840), 236.
[88] Ed. 7/135 no. 40a; *Returns relating to Elem. Educ.* 794.
[89] *Rep. of Educ. Cttee. of Council, 1875–6* [C.1513–I], p. 671, H.C. (1876), xxiii.
[90] Ed. 7/135 no. 40a.
[91] *List 21.*
[92] E.R. Educ. Cttee. *Mins.* 1951–2, 91; 1955–6, 152.
[93] Ibid. 1967–8, 40, 86.
[94] Ex inf. Chief Educ. Officer, County Hall, Beverley, 1973.
[95] Ed. 49/8537.
[96] *11th Rep. Com. Char.* 725–6, 735.
[97] Ex inf. Char. Com., Liverpool, 1974.
[98] Char. Com. files.
[99] *11th Rep. Com. Char.* 725, referring to char. board in church, which gives the sum as £11.
[1] B.I.H.R., PR. CATN. 1.
[2] *11th Rep. Com. Char.* 724.
[3] Ibid. 725.
[4] Ibid.
[5] See p. 157.
[6] *11th Rep. Com. Char.* 725.
[7] O.S. Map 6" Yorks. (1854 edn.). Kexby is covered by sheet 175, Scoreby and Stamford Bridge West mainly by sheet 175 and partly by sheet 158.

used a ferry across the Derwent, mentioned as early as 1315, at which tolls were taken by the lord of Catton manor.[8] A bequest was made to repair the road on either side of the ferry in 1396.[9] A ferry was last mentioned in 1650, when it crossed near the bridge and belonged to the lord of Kexby.[10] A stone bridge was apparently built in the late 1420s by Nicholas Blackburn, a York merchant.[11] About 1540 it was said to have three arches.[12] Bequests for the repair of Kexby Lane in the 16th century[13] were doubtless intended for the main road to the bridge. Much work was done to the bridge by the county in 1648–50,[14] and indeed an inscription[15] on it states that it was 'built' in 1650. Part of the older structure may have survived, however, including a representation of the arms of the Ughtreds.[16] The road was turnpiked in 1764 and the trust was continued until 1881.[17] Much work was done on the bridge in the 18th century; expenditure was especially heavy in 1780 and 1788,[18] and an inscription records repairs in 1778. The road has been widened and straightened in the 20th century and a new bridge was built in the 1960s,[19] bypassing the old one.[20] The old bridge, of stone, has three semicircular arches divided by piers with cutwaters. The eastern arch is normally dry.

The railway line from Market Weighton to York approaches the Derwent viaduct[21] in Stamford Bridge West township, and the Derwent Valley Light Railway crosses the south-west of Kexby. The latter line, opened in 1912, was closed for passenger traffic in 1926[22] and the Kexby section was closed for goods in 1972.[23]

Kexby village is strung out along the main road and consists mainly of 19th- and 20th-century houses. Near the bridge Manor Farm, formerly Coach and Horses Farm and earlier still an inn,[24] consists of an early-18th-century house with a taller later-18th-century block forming a new frontage; its outbuildings include a large barn and dovecot. Near-by Bridge Farm has extensive 19th-century cattle sheds. There are several estate houses, presumably built by the Wenlocks about the same time as the school, and eight council houses. There were two licensed houses in Kexby in the mid 18th century, later only one, and the Coach and Horses inn was recorded from the 1820s[25] until 1879.[26]

Scoreby village apparently stood by the river near Manor House Farm, where there were still indeterminate earthworks in 1974. Foundations and pottery were said to be frequently turned up in a riverside field in the 19th century.[27] Though now only a small appendage to Stamford Bridge village, Stamford Bridge West may formerly have been relatively larger; thus about 20 houses were recorded there in 1616 compared with 15 on the east side of the river.[28] Manor House is the only noteworthy surviving building.[29]

The half-dozen outlying farms in Kexby township include Old Hall,[30] and among a similar number in Scoreby is Londesborough Lodge, known as Keeper's Lodge in 1850 when there was a small park near by.[31]

Kexby may have been hard hit by the Black Death for it was relieved of about 60 per cent of its tax quota in 1354.[32] There were 40 poll-tax payers in 1377.[33] Twenty-three households were included in the hearth-tax return of 1672, 4 of them exempt; of those chargeable 15 had one hearth each, 3 had 3 or 4, and one had twelve.[34] The population of Kexby in 1801 was 129; it reached a maximum of 194 in 1871 and stood at 125 in 1901.[35] By 1931 there were only 93 inhabitants, and the combined population of Kexby and Scoreby fell from 229 in 1951 to 172 in 1971.[36]

There were 14 taxpayers in Scoreby and 15 in Stamford Bridge West in 1301,[37] and 118 people paid the poll tax in the two villages in 1377.[38] Sixteen households were included in the combined hearth-tax return in 1672, 4 of them exempt; of those chargeable 5 had one hearth each, 6 had 2–4, and one had six.[39] There were 123 inhabitants in 1801, a maximum of 196 in 1861, and 155 in 1901.[40] The population was 130 in 1931, just before the built-up area of Stamford Bridge West was transferred to Stamford Bridge civil parish.[41]

MANOR AND OTHER ESTATES. In 1086 Kexby, perhaps comprising 6 carucates, lay within the soke of Catton manor.[42] Thomas Burdon held a carucate there of Robert de Percy and he of Henry de Percy in 1284–5.[43] Brian Burdon was lord in 1316,[44] but after his death *KEXBY* manor passed in 1332–3 to his daughter Margaret, wife of Thomas Ughtred. In 1365 Ughtred was succeeded by his son, another Thomas (d. 1401), whose heir was his grandson Thomas.[45] By 1433 Kexby was in the possession of Robert Ughtred;[46] he or another

[8] C 134/41 no. 1; C 135/116 no. 1; Cal. Pat. 1405–8, 26, 68.
[9] Y.A.J. xii. 282.
[10] E.R.R.O., DDEL/32/31.
[11] Cal. Close, 1422–9, 410–11, 473; Y.A.J. iii. 241; Test. Ebor. ii, pp. 20, 50.
[12] Leland, Itin. ed. Toulmin Smith, i. 44.
[13] Test. Ebor. vi, pp. 208, 308; N. Country Wills, i (Sur. Soc. cxvi), 293.
[14] G. C. F. Forster, E.R. Justices of the Peace in the 17th Cent. (E. Yorks. Loc. Hist. Ser. xxx), 63.
[15] Made in 1778, perhaps copying an older one.
[16] See below. For the arms see V.C.H. Yorks. N.R. ii. 15.
[17] MacMahon, Roads and Turnpike Trusts, 70.
[18] E.R.R.O., QAB/2/1.
[19] e.g. E.R.C.C. Mins. 1960–1, 130; 1970–1, 179.
[20] See plate facing p. 160.   [21] See p. 150.
[22] V.C.H. City of York, 479.
[23] Local information.
[24] O.S. Map 6" (1854 edn.); SE 75 SW. (1958 and 1971 edns.); see plate facing p. 64.
[25] E.R.R.O., QDT/2/13, 15.
[26] Directories.

[27] Bulmer, Dir. E. Yorks. (1892), 574. For the house see below p. 161.
[28] Petworth Ho. Arch., no. 3072.
[29] See p. 161. The Three Cups inn is in Gate Helmsley.
[30] See p. 160.
[31] O.S. Map 6" (1854 edn.).
[32] E 179/202/53.
[33] E 179/202/58 m. 14.
[34] E 179/205/504.
[35] V.C.H. Yorks. iii. 497.
[36] Census.
[37] Yorks. Lay Subsidy, 30 Edw. I (Y.A.S. Rec. Ser. xxi), 105.
[38] E 179/202/58 m. 8.
[39] E 179/205/504.
[40] V.C.H. Yorks. iii. 497.
[41] Census.
[42] V.C.H. Yorks. ii. 219.
[43] Feud. Aids, vi. 33.
[44] Ibid. 173; Cal. Inq. p.m. v, p. 319.
[45] Yorks. Fines, 1327–47, p. 58; Yorks. Inq. Hen IV–V, p. 22.
[46] Cal. Pat. 1429–36, 306.

Robert died in 1471 and was succeeded by his son, also called Robert.[47] By 1498 the manor was held by Henry Ughtred (d. 1510).[48] In 1524 Sir Robert Ughtred sold Kexby to John Allen, but Thomas Wolsey intervened and bought it himself.[49] After Wolsey's attainder in 1530 the king granted the manor for life to Sir Anthony Ughtred and his wife Elizabeth in 1531[50] and then granted it in reversion to Sir Robert Ughtred in 1552.[51] The following year it was settled upon Sir Robert's daughter Dorothy on her marriage with John Constable.[52]

The Constables conveyed property in Kexby to the Headlam family in 1625, 1629, 1639, and 1646, and the manor to Jane Headlam in 1650.[53] Kexby was sold after the death of Charles Headlam to dame Sarah Dawes, widow of Beilby Thompson, in 1753[54] and it subsequently descended like Escrick in the Thompson and Lawley families.[55] After the death of Beilby Lawley, 3rd Baron Wenlock, in 1912, the estate was split up and sold. Kexby Bridge, Gypsey Wood, Far, and Gray Leys farms, comprising about 550 a. in Kexby, were sold in separate lots in 1914–15.[56] About 300 a. from Bridge and Mill House farms were sold to Sir Robert Walker in 1914,[57] and by J. P. E. Walker to the Ecclesiastical Commissioners in 1936.[58] The largest part of the Wenlock estate, however, was sold in 1914 to C. F. Ryder; it comprised 947 a. in Ivy House, Old Hall, Stray, and White Carr farms.[59] Francis Ryder succeeded to it in 1942[60] and still held it in 1973.

A manor-house was mentioned in 1342, when licence to crenellate was granted to Thomas Ughtred.[61] This was presumably the house later known as Old Hall, standing near the Derwent a mile south of the village. A second house was probably built in the late 16th century by the Teyll family. In 1581 Anthony and Thomas Teyll bought property in Kexby which the Constables had conveyed to Thomas and William Tanckard in 1564.[62] 'Mr. Teyll's house' stood near the river immediately north of the village c. 1616.[63] Anthony Teyll had in fact sold New Hall to the Constables in 1604; it passed to the Headlams in 1625,[64] and both houses then descended with the manor. John Marshall occupied a 12-hearth house in 1672.[65] Charles Headlam's house in the early 18th century, perhaps New Hall, was a two-storeyed building with attics. Its main front, facing west, was eight bays long and had three gabled projections, at least one of which contained a window bay rising through both storeys. In front of the house were a walled garden and stables.[66] New Hall still stood in 1772[67] but had been demolished by 1850.[68] Old Hall, where traces of a moat survive, has been replaced by a modern farmhouse.

In 1066 Cille, Alwine, and Asa each had a manor at Scoreby, and Forne and Fargrim held 6 carucates there. The estate was held in 1086 by Osbern de Percy of William de Percy, despite a claim that it had belonged after the Conquest to William Malet.[69]

Under the Percys Scoreby was held in 1166 by Stephen the Chamberlain,[70] and the heirs of the Chamberlains still had a mesne lordship in 1284–5, when 6 carucates were held from them by Robert de Percy, and from Robert by Anthony Bek, bishop of Durham.[71] Under Bek *SCOREBY* manor was held by Isabel de Vescy for life, but in 1310 Bek gave up his interest to Peter (d. 1315), son of Robert de Percy. The manor consequently passed from Isabel to Peter's daughter Eustacia, wife of Walter of Heslerton.[72] In 1336 Walter and Eustacia conveyed it to Robert of Scorborough, and he held it at his death in 1339.[73] Walter was also said to have granted the manor in 1347–8 to Sir John of Hotham and others, but despite these transactions the manor was still found to belong to the Heslertons at Walter's death in 1349.[74] In 1368–9 the heirs of another Walter of Heslerton (d. 1367) held Scoreby under the Percys,[75] and in 1394 livery of the manor was granted to Ralph Neville, earl of Westmorland (d. 1425), cousin and heir of Heslerton's widow Euphemia.[76]

The manor was subsequently held by Ralph's grandson Richard Neville (d. 1460), earl of Salisbury, and Richard's son Richard Neville (d. 1471), earl of Warwick, 'the kingmaker'. Upon the forfeiture and partition of Warwick's estates by Act of Parliament in 1474 between the dukes of Clarence and Gloucester, Scoreby was assigned to the latter and was confirmed to him in 1475.[77] On ascending the throne Richard III kept it in hand and in the 1490s it was accounted for along with Sheriff Hutton (Yorks. N.R.).[78] It is said to have been given by Henry VIII to his natural son Henry Fitzroy, probably along with Sheriff Hutton, in 1525, and it reverted to the Crown on Fitzroy's death in 1536.[79] It was let to members of the Blake family for much of the 16th century.[80]

In 1610 the Crown granted the manor for lives to Sir Henry Jenkins, and in 1624, described as a member of Sheriff Hutton manor, Scoreby was said to contain 715 a. as well as much woodland.[81] Sir Henry's son William (d. 1659) devised land there to

---

[47] C 140/521 no. 47.
[48] *Yorks. Deeds*, ii, p. 122.
[49] *L. & P. Hen. VIII*, iv (2), pp. 164–6.
[50] Ibid. v, p. 36.
[51] *Cal. Pat. 1550–3*, 295.
[52] C 3/236/5; E.R.R.O., DDEV/53/4.
[53] E.R.R.O., DDEL/32/1, 7, 19, 25, 31.
[54] Ibid. DDFA/8/116; Headlam Estate Act, 26 Geo. II, c. 23 (Priv. Act).
[55] See p. 20.
[56] R.D.B., 166/110/86; /139/113; /205/171; /373/309.
[57] Ibid. 164/370/325.
[58] Ibid. 561/501/390.
[59] Ibid. 166/456/387.
[60] Ibid. 678/158/121.
[61] *Cal. Pat. 1340–3*, 388.
[62] *Yorks. Fines*, i. 295; ii. 163.
[63] Petworth Ho. Arch., no. 3428.
[64] E.R.R.O., DDFA/8/19; DDEL/32/1.
[65] E 179/205/504.
[66] B.L. Lansd. MS. 914 no. 34.
[67] T. Jefferys, *Map of Yorks.* (1772).
[68] O.S. Map 6" (1854 edn.).
[69] *V.C.H. Yorks.* ii. 262.
[70] *E.Y.C.* xi, p. 213.
[71] *Feud. Aids*, vi. 33.
[72] *E.Y.C.* xi, p. 112; *Yorks. Lay Subsidy, 30 Edw. I*, 105; *Yorks. Fines, 1300–14*, p. 80; *Cal. Inq. p.m.* vi, pp. 82–3; vii, p. 421.
[73] *Yorks. Fines, 1327–47*, p. 98; *Cal. Inq. p.m.* viii, p. 180; *Cal. Fine R. 1337–47*, 158, 171.
[74] *Cal. Pat. 1350–4*, 337; *Percy Charty.* 228–9; *Cal. Inq. p.m.* ix, pp. 431–2.
[75] *Cal. Inq. p.m.* xii, pp. 181–2, 224.
[76] *Cal. Close, 1392–6*, 192; *D.N.B.*
[77] *Cal. Close, 1422–9*, 238; *1454–61*, 407; *Cal. Pat. 1467–77*, 483, 486–7; *D.N.B.*; see above p. 14.
[78] D.L. 29/650/10510.
[79] *Y.A.J.* x. 86; *V.C.H. Yorks. N.R.* ii. 178.
[80] *Y.A.J.* x. 87, 89, 91.
[81] B.L. Harl. MS. 6288 ff. 79–80.

Elvington Bridge

Kexby Bridge

THORGANBY: the former railway station

FANGFOSS: the former railway station

THORNTON: Walbut lock on the Pocklington canal

his brother,[82] and Tobias Jenkins was dealing in the manor in 1697 and 1707.[83] Tobias's daughter Mary married Sir Henry Goodrick and the manor was evidently settled on them. In 1715 Goodrick sold it to Mark Kirkby,[84] and in 1723 Jenkins conveyed his life interest in part of the manor to Kirkby's sons Mark and Christopher.[85] After the death of the younger Mark Kirkby in 1748 his estates were divided in 1750 and Scoreby went to his niece Sarah Horsfield.[86]

In 1803 the devisees of Sarah's son Mann Horsfield sold the manor to E. L. Hodgson, together with 1,247 a. in the township.[87] Hodgson sold much of the land to Ottiwell Wood in 1808 and the manor and remaining land in 1817.[88] Wood died in 1847 and Scoreby was sold in 1851 by John Wood and others to Albert Denison, Lord Londesborough; the estate then included Dunnington, Hagg, Lime Field, Manor, North, and South farms.[89] In 1905 W. F. H. Denison, earl of Londesborough, sold the estate, comprising 1,281 a., to C. F. Walker,[90] who already held Scoreby Grange and part of Stamford Bridge West manor. The whole estate, comprising 1,920 a., was sold by J. P. E. Walker in 1936 to the Ecclesiastical Commissioners.[91]

A manor-house was mentioned at Scoreby in 1368.[92] Tobias Jenkins had a four-hearth house in 1672.[93] The present Manor House Farm bears the date 1723 and the initials of Christopher and Mark Kirkby.

It was perhaps in the early 17th century, when Scoreby was granted to the Jenkins family, that a separate estate was created later known as Scoreby Grange. In the 18th century it belonged, along with Gate Helmsley (Yorks. N.R.), to the Wilmers and then the Worsleys.[94] In 1843, when it comprised 366 a., it was sold by Sir William Worsley to James Walker,[95] who later acquired the manorial estate.

The area later to be known as Stamford Bridge West township was perhaps included with Scoreby in Domesday Book. In 1246 it was held by Herbert de Neville and his wife Margery of Peter de Percy,[96] and it had been described as their manor of *STAMFORD BRIDGE* in 1243.[97] By 1284–5 it was held, like Scoreby, by Robert de Percy of the Chamberlains, and they of the Percys.[98] It subsequently descended like Scoreby manor, passing to the Crown in the 15th century and becoming a member of Sheriff Hutton. In 1534 it was let to Sir George Lawson[99] and in 1627 it was granted for life to George Kirk and others.[1] Probably in 1628 it was alienated by Charles I to the Ditchfield grantees, along with Sheriff Hutton, as security for the City of London's loan to the Crown.[2] As in the case of Elvington[3] it may have passed through the hands of Ralph Radcliffe and Sir Arthur Ingram. The Ingrams long retained Sheriff Hutton,[4] but Stamford Bridge manor had been acquired by the Wright family by 1721.[5]

The manor, manor-house, and about 270 a. were conveyed by the Wrights to Thomas Wilson and another in 1793.[6] The estate was subsequently split up, 109 a. being sold by George Wilson to Thomas Preston in 1864, for example.[7] Some of it became part of the Walkers' Scoreby estate.[8] The manor and 13 a. were sold by the Wilsons' trustees to Robert Danby in 1873 and by his trustees to E. A. F. W. Herbert in 1905.[9] The Herberts sold Manor House to A. N. Marsh in 1967.[10] The surviving house may have been built in the 18th century and refronted in the 19th.

The guild of St. Christopher and St. George, York, had property in Stamford Bridge West. After the Dissolution it was granted in 1549 to York corporation,[11] and in the early 17th century it was called 'St. Thomas land', perhaps because the corporation assigned it towards the upkeep of St. Thomas's hospital, York.[12] It amounted to *c.* 30 a.[13] and in 1719 was sold by the corporation to John Wright,[14] so becoming part of the manorial estate.

ECONOMIC HISTORY. Kexby was not described separately in the Domesday Survey and there are few early references to its economy. There was probably extensive woodland in the township in the Middle Ages. Thomas Ughtred was licensed to impark his woods at Kexby and elsewhere in 1334,[15] for example, and 116 oaks were bought at Kexby for York Minster in 1441–2.[16] The reclamation of woodland apparently led to the creation of open arable fields in the north of the township, where much ridge-and-furrow survives on either side of the main road to York, some of it in areas which have reverted to woodland in modern times.[17] Further south in the township assarting may have produced only inclosed land, including the meadow land known as Grey Leas, towards Elvington;[18] it is possible that this land took its name from the Grey family, one of whom conveyed property in Kexby to the Ughtreds in 1366, for example.[19]

Grey Leas had probably been subdivided into

[82] *Abstracts of Yorks. Wills, 1665–6* (Y.A.S. Rec. Ser. ix), 154.
[83] C.P. 25(2)/895/9 Wm. III Hil. no. 59; C.P. 25(2)/984/6 Anne Trin. no. 49.
[84] R.D.B., D/351/587.
[85] Ibid. H/625/1266.
[86] E.R.R.O., DDSY/108/3, 5.
[87] R.D.B., CF/530/841.
[88] Ibid. CN/385/603; DC/346/473.
[89] Ibid. GR/340/407; GS/361/456.
[90] Ibid. 75/457/435 (1905).
[91] Ibid. 561/501/390.
[92] C 135/198 no. 12.
[93] E 179/205/504.
[94] E.R.R.O., Land Tax; B.I.H.R., TER. I. Catton 1716 etc.; see *V.C.H. Yorks. N.R.* ii. 140.
[95] R.D.B., GB/263/309.
[96] *Yorks. Fines, 1232–46*, pp. 160–1; *E.Y.C.* xi, p. 109.
[97] *Cal. Pat. 1232–47*, 405.
[98] *Feud. Aids*, vi. 33.
[99] *L. & P. Hen. VIII*, vii, p. 174.

[1] E.R.R.O., DDKG/142(c); *V.C.H. Yorks. N.R.* ii. 178.
[2] R.D.B., H/227/475.
[3] See p. 14.
[4] *V.C.H. Yorks. N.R.* ii. 178.
[5] R.D.B., H/227/475.
[6] Ibid. BR/357/590.
[7] Ibid. IL/294/388.
[8] Ibid. 75/457/435 (1905).
[9] Ibid. LC/28/286; 70/157/148 (1904); 74/85/80 (1905).
[10] Ibid. 1514/549/482.
[11] *Cal. Pat. 1549–51*, 31.
[12] *V.C.H. City of York*, 422.
[13] L.R. 2/230 ff. 189–215; B.L. Harl. MS. 6288 ff. 66–9; E.R.R.O., DDKG/142(c).
[14] R.D.B., F/411/889.
[15] *Cal. Pat. 1334–8*, 36.
[16] *Fabric Rolls of York Minster* (Sur. Soc. xxxv), 56.
[17] Forestry Com. *Forest Record*, no. 62 (H.M.S.O.), including air photograph.
[18] *Yorks. Fines*, i. 39, 55.
[19] *Yorks. Fines, 1347–77*, p. 119.

several closes by the 17th century,[20] and a close called White Carr was mentioned in 1602.[21] Other named closes included Ox and Middle closes 'above the wood' in 1618.[22] The open fields had also, it seems, been inclosed by the early 17th century and had passed into single ownership. Wood was sold from Mill field, which was almost certainly a former open field, in 1616 and 1627, a settlement of 1625 having reserved timber there to the owner at twelve oak trees to the acre.[23] The moor or common of Kexby occupied the south-west corner of the township, adjoining Dunnington, and an outgang or 'stray' led to it alongside the township boundary.[24] The common was said to comprise about 200 a. in 1752.[25] An 86-acre close taken from it was mentioned in 1786[26] and it may have been inclosed about the same time as Dunnington common. In 1752 there were also 186 a. of woods, occupying much the same ground as in the 20th century; they lay between the road to Elvington on the east, Grey Leas on the south, and 'widow Robinson's farm' (the former White Carr) on the west.[27]

At Scoreby in 1086 there was said to be land for 3 ploughs, but Osbern de Percy then had 2 ploughs and 4 villeins and 2 bordars had 2 more. There was meadow measuring 3 furlongs by one and woodland ½ league long and ¼ broad. The estate had been worth £1 10s. in 1066 but was valued at £2 in 1086.[28] The continued existence of woodland in 1368 is suggested by a pasture called the Hagg, but there were also reclaimed plots of land called Holker and 'Newland of Forland', as well as open-field land. Tenants-at-will held 24 houses and probably 48 bovates of land, and the demesne was also in the hands of tenants.[29] Scoreby and Stamford Bridge West may also have shared an area of common pasture, for in 1259 Peter de Percy demised common for 10 cattle and 100 sheep in the pasture of the two villages.[30] Other evidence for the existence of open-field land is provided by the ridge-and-furrow that still survives in Scoreby, some of it in the modern plantations there.[31]

It is not known when and in what circumstances Scoreby village was depopulated.[32] The open fields may have been converted to pasture by the early 16th century, when two men were involved in a lawsuit after putting 50 cattle into a pasture called Scoreby.[33] The manor remained predominantly pastoral in the 17th century. In 1624 pasture closes, including Great Hagg, Holly Hagg, North fields, and Far field, and meadows called the Ing, North ings, and South ings, together covered 715 a., and there were woods containing c. 800 trees.[34] By 1639 much timber was said to have been felled. The manor was then estimated to comprise 1,400 a., including 80 a. of meadow and 300 a. of former waste ground, since inclosed and improved; the rest was described as very good pasture.[35] The woodland was not completely cleared and there were still 197 a. in 1798.[36]

At Stamford Bridge West little is known of early agricultural arrangements. The rents of freeholders and cottagers there were recorded in 1368, and there was a common oven.[37] In 1555 various closes were named and there were 10 a. of arable called the infields and 3 a. of meadow called Hawe ings.[38] There may have been some open-field and common meadow land surviving in the early 17th century. In 1612, when there were at least 10 houses in the village and a dozen closes totalling 132 a., there was land and meadow in Brigg field and Brigg ing.[39] Among the closes in 1624, however, was the 37-acre Brigg field, and others included Little field (13 a.) and Summer close (20 a.). Several tenants then had beast-gates, variously said to be in Brigg pasture, in Cow and Middle pastures, and in meadow called the ings. Haw ings were also mentioned.[40] In both 1612 and 1624 a common pasture was said to belong to the manor and was estimated at the latter date at 80 a. It may have been situated in the north of Scoreby township. A common outgang apparently leading towards Scoreby was mentioned in 1719, together with cow-gates in the common; the mayor of York's small estate also then included parcels of land in Brigg field and Main ings,[41] suggesting that inclosure was not yet complete.

A considerable acreage continued to be devoted to pasture and woodland in both Kexby and Scoreby in the 19th and 20th centuries. Kexby included 1,097 a. of arable, 500 a. of meadow and pasture, and 154 a. of woodland in 1843,[42] and 1,006 a. of arable, 543 a. of grass, and 261 a. of woodland in 1905.[43] Scoreby with Stamford Bridge West had 923 a. of arable, 503 a. of grassland, and 186 a. of woodland in 1841,[44] and 1,263 a. of arable, 507 a. of grass, and 213 a. of woodland in 1905.[45] The land use in Kexby was still notably mixed in the 20th century, with much pasture near the Derwent and around the village and extensive woods west of the Elvington road. In Scoreby grassland was most prominent near the river and in the north of the township; Hagg and Scoreby woods survived,[46] and since 1952 they have been managed by the Forestry Commission.[47]

There have usually been 9–12 farmers in Kexby in the 19th and 20th centuries.[48] The manorial estate included 9 farms of 100 a. and more in 1808,[49] and in the 1850s Kexby had 2 of over 250 a. each and 8–10 of 100 a. and more.[50] There were 2 farms of over 150 a. in the 1920s and 1930s. There have usually been 8 or 9 farmers in Scoreby and Stamford Bridge

[20] E.R.R.O., DDEL/32/31.
[21] C 142/25 no. 126.
[22] E.R.R.O., DDFA/8/21, 24–5.
[23] Ibid. DDFA/8/20; DDEL/32/1, 5.
[24] O.S. Map 6" (1854 edn.).
[25] E.R.R.O., DDFA/8/10.
[26] Ibid. DDFA/8/43.
[27] Ibid. DDFA/8/10.
[28] *V.C.H. Yorks.* ii. 262.
[29] C 135/198 no. 12.
[30] *Cat. Anct. D.* iii, D 236.
[31] Forestry Com. *Forest Record*, no. 62.
[32] See p. 159.
[33] C 1/402 no. 60.
[34] B.L. Harl. MS. 6288 ff. 79–80.
[35] E.R.R.O., DDKG/142(c).

[36] R.D.B., BZ/125/183.
[37] C 135/198 no. 12.
[38] *Cal. Pat.* 1555–7, 102.
[39] L.R. 2/230 ff. 189–215.
[40] B.L. Harl. MS. 6288 ff. 66–9.
[41] R.D.B., F/411/889.
[42] B.I.H.R., TA. 521S.
[43] Acreage Returns, 1905.
[44] B.I.H.R., TA. 297S.
[45] Acreage Returns, 1905.
[46] [1st] Land Util. Surv. Map, sheet 27; 2nd Land Util. Surv. Map, sheet 709 (SE 65–75).
[47] Ex inf. Forestry Com., York, 1972.
[48] Directories.
[49] E.R.R.O., DDFA/41/3.
[50] Ibid. DDFA/41/6; H.O. 107/2356.

West.[51] Six had over 120 a. in 1832,[52] one over 350 a. and 7 over 100 a. in 1851,[53] and 4 over 150 a. in the 1920s and 1930s.[54]

Markets and fairs brought trade to Stamford Bridge West over a long period, and perhaps briefly also to Kexby. A Wednesday market and a fair on Easter Monday and the following six days were granted to Thomas Ughtred at Kexby in 1347,[55] but they were not recorded again. Fairs at Stamford Bridge were mentioned c. 1200,[56] and a Tuesday market and a fair on the eve, day, and morrow of Holy Trinity were granted to Herbert de Neville in 1243.[57] In 1368 the Heslertons were holding fairs on 22 July and 20 November, as well as on Trinity Sunday.[58] A fair was held there in 1770 on 22 November for animals, brass, pewter, hardware, and cloth.[59] A cattle fair was held on 1 December in 1840,[60] a cattle, horse, and pleasure fair in 1872, and an almost wholly pleasure fair in 1892.[61] A fair on 1 December was mentioned as belonging to the manor as late as 1905.[62] The fair was held in a field on the south side of the York road not far from the Derwent.[63]

Fishing in the Derwent at Kexby was mentioned in the 16th century and later.[64] There was a wharf in 1840, when the proprietor of the Coach and Horses inn was also a maltster and timber, coal, and lime merchant.[65] The wharf lay just south of Kexby bridge and there was also an old landing near Kexby Old Hall in 1850.[66] Other non-agricultural employment has been provided in the township by a brickworks beside the Elvington road, first mentioned in 1901[67] and closed in 1972.[68] There have been refreshment rooms on the York road since the 1930s.[69]

At Stamford Bridge West there was a wharf beside the Derwent in the 19th century and near by a brewery and malting;[70] a brewer was mentioned from 1823 until 1889.[71] Derwent Plastics Ltd. was established in 1934, when the former brewery was converted to a workshop.[72] The factory site was enlarged in the 1950s and 1960s[73] and new buildings erected.

There was presumably a windmill at Kexby in the Middle Ages, giving its name to Mill field. It probably stood on a mound still existing in Millfield wood.[74] There was also a windmill at either Scoreby or Stamford Bridge West in 1339.[75]

LOCAL GOVERNMENT. At Kexby amends of the assize of bread and of ale were granted to Thomas Ughtred in 1347.[76] Court profits were recorded for Scoreby and Stamford Bridge West in 1368,[77] but a court leet at Stamford Bridge was said in 1624 to be seldom kept.[78]

There were parish poorhouses at a place called Noddy Cock in Stamford Bridge West.[79] Kexby, Scoreby, and Stamford Bridge West all joined York poor-law union in 1837.[80] They became part of Escrick rural district in 1894, Derwent rural district in 1935,[81] and the Selby district of North Yorkshire in 1974.

CHURCH. A chantry chapel at Kexby was mentioned in 1398[82] and a chaplain, with an income of £4, in 1525–6.[83] The chapel, which is said to have been dedicated to St. Mary,[84] may have been suppressed in the 16th century. It perhaps stood in Chapel close, mentioned in 1604.[85] A district chapelry was formed out of Catton parish in 1853.[86] It was at first a perpetual curacy but by 1872 was styled a vicarage.[87] The benefice was united with that of Wilberfoss in 1959.[88]

The patronage belonged to Lord Wenlock in 1853 and thereafter descended with the manor until the death of Beilby Lawley in 1912; it then passed like Escrick manor to Irene Lawley and so to the Forbes Adam family.[89] In 1937 it passed to Y. R. Vesey, 5th Viscount de Vesci, whose father Eustace had married Constance, sister of Beilby Lawley.[90] After 1959 the patrons of the united benefice were J. E. Vesey, 6th Viscount de Vesci, and J. E. R. Wyndham, 1st Baron Egremont.[91]

The living was worth £140 in 1884 and £130 net in 1915.[92] From 1889 to 1921 there was mention of 39 a. of glebe, but only 5 a. remained in 1974.[93] A parsonage house, built beside the church in 1853,[94] was still in use in 1973. It was perhaps by F. C. Penrose.

Two services each Sunday were held in 1865 and later; communion was celebrated monthly in 1865, with an average of 17 recipients, fortnightly by 1877, and weekly by 1915.[95] In 1973 a weekly service was held on Fridays and communion on Sundays.

The church of ST. PAUL, of stone, was designed

---

[51] Directories.
[52] C. Howard, *Gen. View of Agric. of E.R. Yorks.* 2.
[53] H.O. 107/2356.
[54] Directories.
[55] *Cal. Pat.* 1345–8, 527.
[56] *E.Y.C.* xi, p. 77.
[57] *Cal. Pat.* 1232–47, 405.
[58] C 135/198 no. 12.
[59] *Yorks. Fairs and Mkts.* (Thoresby Soc. xxxix), 176.
[60] White, *Dir. E. & N.R. Yorks.* (1840), 236.
[61] *Kelly's Dir. N. & E.R. Yorks.* (1872), 549; Bulmer, *Dir. E. Yorks.* (1892), 574.
[62] R.D.B., BR/357/590; LC/218/286; 74/85/80 (1905).
[63] O.S. Map 6" (1854 edn.).
[64] C 142/77 no. 18; E.R.R.O., DDFA/8/116; *Yorks. Fines*, i. 295; ii. 163.
[65] White, *Dir. E. & N.R. Yorks.* (1840), 236.
[66] O.S. Map 6" (1854 edn.).
[67] *Kelly's Dir. N. & E.R. Yorks.* (1901), 512.
[68] Local information.
[69] Directories.
[70] White, *Dir. E. & N.R. Yorks.* (1840), 236–7; O.S. Map 1/2,500, Yorks. CLVIII. 15 (1893 edn.).
[71] H.O. 107/2356; directories.
[72] *Dalesman*, Nov. 1965, 626.
[73] R.D.B., 889/470/393; 960/105/94; 1563/114/106.
[74] Shown as 'mill hill' on O.S. Map 6" (1854 and later edns.).
[75] E 152/28.
[76] *Cal. Pat.* 1345–8, 527.
[77] C 135/198 no. 12.
[78] B.L. Harl. MS. 6288 ff. 66–9.
[79] O.S. Map 6" (1854 edn.).
[80] *3rd Rep. Poor Law Com.* 169.
[81] Census.
[82] *Test Ebor.* i, p. 244.
[83] *Y.A.J.* xxiv. 72.
[84] Ibid. x. 84.
[85] E.R.R.O., DDFA/8/19.
[86] *Lond. Gaz.* 11 Feb. 1853, p. 365.
[87] Sheahan and Whellan, *Hist. York & E.R.* ii. 626; *Kelly's Dir. N. & E.R. Yorks.* (1872), 510.
[88] York Dioc. Regy., Order in Council 748.
[89] York Dioc. Handbk.; see above pp. 20, 160.
[90] York Dioc. Handbk.; Burke, *Peerage* (1967), 740–1.
[91] R.D.B., 1745/56/52.
[92] B.I.H.R., Bp. V. 1884/Ret.; Bp. V. 1915/Ret.
[93] Directories; ex inf. the vicar, 1974.
[94] Sheahan and Whellan, *Hist. York & E.R.* ii. 626.
[95] B.I.H.R., V. 1865/Ret. 285; V. 1877/Ret.; Bp. V. 1915/Ret.

in an early Gothic style by F. C. Penrose[96] and was consecrated in 1852.[97] It consists of chancel, nave, north-west bell-turret with spire, and west door with canopy. There is one bell.

NONCONFORMITY. Two Roman Catholics were reported at Kexby in 1865.[98] The Methodists had a dozen members there in the 1790s.[99] A Primitive Methodist chapel was mentioned in 1840[1] and 1851,[2] but a cottage was used in 1865 and 1877. The vicar reported in 1865 that most of the villagers were Primitives until the church was built in 1852 but that they had since attended the church.[3]

EDUCATION. A school at Kexby was begun in 1831 and had 37 children in 1835; it was supported by P. B. Lawley, who also partly clothed the children, and there was a lending library attached to the school.[4] The schoolroom at first stood close beside the York road,[5] but about 1858 it was rebuilt,[6] standing back from the road opposite the church. An annual government grant was first received in 1860–1[7] and 49 children attended in 1871.[8] The school was closed in 1905 and the children transferred to Dunnington and Wilberfoss.[9] The large schoolroom and master's house, built in the Tudor style of bright red brick with stone dressings, was used as a private house in 1973.

The children of Scoreby and Stamford Bridge West have attended schools in Stamford Bridge East, Dunnington, and Gate Helmsley (Yorks. N.R.).[10]

CHARITIES. T gift of members of the Dealtry family to the poor of the parish included £1 for Kexby.[11]

William Headlam is said to have given a rent-charge to Kexby township in respect of which Beilby Thompson paid £5 4s. a year in 1824. It was then distributed to the unrelieved poor in sums of from 5s. to £1 10s.[12] It was regularly received thereafter, but in 1973 it was redeemed for £100 which was then invested in stock.[13]

Kexby and Stamford Bridge West benefited from the charity of John Hodgson for parishes in York poor-law union.[14]

FANGFOSS

THE PARISH of Fangfoss lies some 10 miles east of York on gently shelving land between the wolds escarpment and the lower parts of the Vale of York.[1] It is drained by Fangfoss beck, perhaps the foss of the place-name, and by Salt beck; the two unite in the parish as Spittal beck. Fangfoss was apparently an Anglian settlement but Spittal, a hamlet to the south of the village where the Hospitallers had an estate, was not mentioned until 1342.[2] The compact parish covers 1,409 a.[3] In 1935 most of neighbouring Bolton civil parish was added to Fangfoss civil parish.[4]

From below 50 ft. above sea-level in the western part of the parish the ground rises to over 75 ft. in the north-east. Fangfoss village is centrally situated on a ridge of higher land but close to Fangfoss beck. At inclosure in 1723 a common lane leading to the beck was retained for the convenience of villagers fetching water.[5] Spittal stands on lower ground near a bridge over the beck. Most of the parish is covered by outwash sand, gravel, and clay, but the higher ground is formed of Keuper marl and sandstone.[6] The open fields lay around the village on the better-drained land, while ground near the streams was used as meadow and pasture. The low sandy area in the west of the parish formed an extensive common. The open fields, meadows, and common were inclosed in 1723, creating a pattern of long curving closes taken from the open fields, especially noticeable near the Full Sutton road, and contrasting rectangular closes made from the former common.[7] An area in the north-west of the parish was used during the Second World War as part of Full Sutton airfield,[8] but most of it had been reclaimed for agricultural use by 1974. The southern and eastern boundaries are largely formed by the becks, and in 1369 the obstructed Spittal beck was ordered to be repaired by Fangfoss and Bolton.[9]

A minor road from Full Sutton runs along the higher land on which Fangfoss stands and continues towards Pocklington; it is joined in the village by a road from Wilberfoss. The Pocklington road crosses Spittal beck by a bridge mentioned in 1371.[10] The present brick and stone bridge has a single arch. Other roadways ordered to be maintained in 1723 were the way leading to Ox pasture, which was called Bramer Lane by 1844, and the way to Belthorpe,[11] but both are now only field lanes. The railway from York to Market Weighton, opened in 1847,[12] passed through the west of the parish, with a station beside the

[96] Pevsner, *Yorks. E.R.* 291.
[97] B.I.H.R., CD. 232.
[98] B.I.H.R., V. 1865/Ret. 285.
[99] E.R.R.O., MRP/1/7.
[1] White, *Dir. E. & N.R. Yorks.* (1840), 236.
[2] H.O. 129/23/515.
[3] B.I.H.R., V. 1865/Ret. 285; V. 1877/Ret.
[4] *Educ. Enquiry Abstract*, 1082.
[5] O.S. Map 6" (1854 edn.).
[6] *Kelly's Dir. N. & E.R. Yorks.* (1889), 414.
[7] *Rep. of Educ. Cttee. of Council, 1860–1* [2828], p. 776, H.C. (1861), xlix.
[8] *Returns relating to Elem. Educ.* 792.
[9] E.R. Educ. Cttee. Mins. 1905–6, 217.
[10] e.g. directories.
[11] See p. 158.
[12] 11th Rep. Com. Char. 726.
[13] Char. Com. files.
[14] See p. 12.

[1] This article was written in 1974.
[2] *P.N.E.R. Yorks.* (E.P.N.S.) 3, 185.
[3] O.S. Map 6", Yorks. (1854 edn.). The parish appears on sheets 175–6.
[4] *Census.*
[5] E.R.R.O., IA. Fangfoss (typescript copy).
[6] Geol. Surv. Map 1", solid and drift, sheet 63 (1967 edn.).
[7] O.S. Map 6" (1854 edn.).
[8] See pp. 170–1.
[9] *Public Works in Med. Law*, ii (Selden Soc. xl), 336–7.
[10] The contemporary 'Damalicebrig', which has been identified with Spittal bridge, was probably near Foggathorpe: *Pub. Works in Med. Law*, ii. 336–9; *P.N.E.R. Yorks.* 185.
[11] E.R.R.O., IA. Fangfoss; B.I.H.R., TA. 167S.
[12] K. A. MacMahon, *Beginnings of E. Yorks. Rlys.* (E. Yorks. Loc. Hist. Ser. iii), 14.

Wilberfoss road. The line was closed in 1965[13] and the track has been lifted. The station and stationmaster's house, in a mid-19th-century domestic style, still stand.[14]

The older part of Fangfoss village lies just east of the road from Full Sutton to Pocklington and is reached by a short side lane. A small triangular green, with the church and Fangfoss Hall[15] to the east and the old school to the west, forms the centre of the village. It may be the remnant of a larger green: encroachment on the lord's waste and the enlargement of gardens were recorded in the late 18th century,[16] and several of the houses around the green now have large front gardens. The 18th- and 19th-century houses near by include the mid-19th-century Manor House Farm.[17] Other houses, of the 19th and 20th centuries, lie along the Belthorpe lane and the roads which meet at the village; they include 20 council houses. In the 18th century there were one or two licensed houses in Fangfoss.[18] The Carpenter's Arms, mentioned from 1823,[19] still exists.

The hamlet of Spittal consists of about ten houses, including four council houses, on the Pocklington road ½ mile south of Fangfoss. There are two outlying farms in the parish, dating from after the 18th-century inclosure. A third, Field House, was demolished when the airfield was built. Former airfield buildings still stand near the Full Sutton road.

There were 56 poll-tax payers in Fangfoss in 1377.[20] The parish was apparently much impoverished in the later Middle Ages, receiving a tax relief of 45 per cent in 1446.[21] All 25 households listed in the hearth-tax return in 1672 were chargeable; 21 had a single hearth, 2 had 2, and one each had 3 and 4 hearths.[22] There were 19 families in the parish in 1743 and 15 in 1764.[23] From 131 in 1801 the population of Fangfoss rose to 197 in 1871, fell to 142 in 1901,[24] and stood at 132 in 1931.[25]

MANORS AND OTHER ESTATES. In 1086 the king had all 8 carucates at Fangfoss as soke of his manor of Pocklington.[26] Later the overlordship was divided. Part passed to William de Forz, earl of Aumale, who had acquired Pocklington manor by c. 1260,[27] and land in Fangfoss was later referred to as part of the honor of Aumale.[28] The Forz estates were subsequently resumed by the Crown,[29] which granted Pocklington to Meaux abbey in 1294. Henry de Percy acquired the property by exchange with Meaux in 1303,[30] and Eleanor de Percy was named as one of the lords of Fangfoss in 1316.[31] The Percy overlordship at Fangfoss persisted, with a break in the 15th century,[32] until Henry Percy, earl of Northumberland (d. 1537), sold Pocklington to the Crown, along with his other northern estates, in 1537.[33] In the mid 16th century the overlordship passed by a royal grant of Pocklington and its appurtenances to Thomas Bishop, the reversion and rent being later granted to Thomas Percy, earl of Northumberland (d. 1572).[34]

Early demesne lords were members of the Grimthorpe family. Between c. 1120 and 1129 Henry I confirmed land in Fangfoss to William son of Ulf of Grimthorpe,[35] and in 1189 William's descendant Ralph son of Ralph held 4 carucates and 5 bovates there.[36] Ralph son of William was named as one of the lords of Fangfoss in 1316.[37] As a member of Grimthorpe manor, and of its superior manor of Pocklington, the Fangfoss property remained with the family, which acquired the title baron Greystoke in 1321, until the death of Ralph, Lord Greystoke, in 1487.[38] Ralph was succeeded by his granddaughter Elizabeth, who married Thomas, Lord Dacre of Gilsland, c. 1488.[39] William, Lord Dacre, held 30 bovates in Fangfoss in 1563.[40] Like Butterwick, the property descended to the Howard family, later earls of Carlisle.[41] The estate, occasionally called *FANGFOSS* manor in the 18th century, comprised nearly 600 a. belonging to Grimthorpe manor in 1794.[42] It was divided and sold in 1796–8,[43] part passing to the Overends, who already had other land in the parish.[44]

The overlordship of other land in Fangfoss passed to the Chauncy family, which had been granted land there by the late 12th century.[45] By 1203 tenants of Walter de Chauncy held 20 bovates,[46] and the Fangfoss estate was later described as a member of the Chauncy manor of Skirpenbeck.[47] The Chauncy overlordship was last mentioned in 1398.[48] In 1203 William son of Ralph held 18 bovates in Fangfoss of the Chauncy fee as mesne lord and a further 2 bovates in demesne,[49] and in 1280 the Grimthorpe family held 20 bovates there of Thomas de Chauncy.[50]

In 1203 William son of Thomas held 18 bovates and other land in Fangfoss as demesne lord under

---

[13] *Yorks. Eve. Press*, 20 Oct. 1965.
[14] See plate facing p. 161.
[15] See p. 166.
[16] E.R.R.O., DDCV/71/1a–b, 6.
[17] See p. 167.
[18] E.R.R.O., QDT/2/15.
[19] Directories.
[20] E 179/202/59 m. 65.
[21] E 179/202/120.
[22] E 179/205/504.
[23] B.I.H.R., Bp. V. 1764/Ret. 178; *Herring's Visit.* i. 220.
[24] *V.C.H. Yorks.* iii. 493.
[25] Census.
[26] *V.C.H. Yorks.* ii. 197.
[27] C 132/24 no. 6.
[28] *Cal. Inq. p.m.* vi, p. 26.
[29] *Complete Peerage*, i. 356.
[30] *Percy Charty.* (Sur. Soc. cxvii), 43–4, 151.
[31] *Feud. Aids*, vi. 168.
[32] e.g. *Cal. Inq. p.m.* vi, pp. 25–6, 304; xiv, pp. 77–8; *Yorks. Inq.* v. 143; see above p. 151.
[33] S.C. 6/Hen. VIII/4283–6; J. M. W. Bean, *Estates of Percy Family, 1416–1537*, 154.

[34] *Cal. Pat.* 1557–8, 179–80; 1560–3, 394; *Yorks. Fines*, i. 271; ii. 174.
[35] *E.Y.C.* i, pp. 348–9.
[36] *Cal. Pat.* 1391–6, 190.
[37] *Feud. Aids*, vi. 168.
[38] C 139/76 no. 34; *Cal. Inq. p.m.* vi, p. 304; xiv, pp. 77–8; *Yorks. Inq.* v. 143; *Complete Peerage*, s.v. Greystoke and FitzWilliam.
[39] *Complete Peerage*, s.v. Dacre of Gilsland; *Miscellaneas* iv (Y.A.S. Rec. Ser. xciv), 105.
[40] Castle Howard MS., Box 24, Survey of Estates, 1563.
[41] *V.C.H. Yorks. E.R.* ii. 193; *Complete Peerage*, s.v. Dacre of Gilsland, and Carlisle.
[42] R.D.B., BU/210/325; E.R.R.O., DDHB/57/199; C.P. 25(2)/1083 no. 31; C.P. 25(2)/1086/13 Geo. I Hil. [no. 7 from end].
[43] R.D.B., BW/571/818; BX/87/151–2; /88/153; BZ/87/119.
[44] See p. 166.
[45] *E.Y.C.* ii, p. 175.
[46] *Yorks. Fines, John* (Sur. Soc. xciv), p. 79.
[47] *Yorks. Fines, 1272–1300*, p. 47; *Feud. Aids*, vi. 38.
[48] *Cat. Anct. D.* iii, D 454.
[49] *Yorks. Fines, John*, p. 79.
[50] *Yorks. Fines, 1272–1300*, p. 47.

William son of Ralph.[51] Thomas son of William of Belthorpe subinfeudated all his Fangfoss property, apparently comprising only about 5 bovates, to John of Selby in 1252.[52] Hugh son of Nicholas of Selby was dealing in property in Fangfoss between 1308 and 1338,[53] but the property was not subsequently mentioned. It may have passed to the Percy family as demesne lords by the early 15th century.

Henry Percy, created earl of Northumberland, forfeited an estate at Fangfoss, in addition to his overlordship there, as a result of his rebellion in 1403.[54] The property was granted to Robert Waterton for life in 1403 and in fee tail in 1409,[55] and, as *FANGFOSS* manor, was conveyed to Sir Henry Broomfleet in 1446.[56] In 1469 the manor was conveyed by Richard Choke, a justice of Common Pleas, and others, probably as Broomfleet feoffees, to three men, perhaps also feoffees.[57] It was apparently the same estate, again called Fangfoss manor, which Robert Stillington, bishop of Bath and Wells and a former Chancellor of England, successfully defended at law in 1479[58] and granted to his collegiate foundation of St. Andrew, Acaster Selby (Yorks. W.R.) in 1483.[59] The Percy family had, however, apparently regained its Fangfoss estate by 1489, when Henry, earl of Northumberland, died seized of the manor; he was said, no doubt mistakenly, to hold it of the Hospitallers.[60] The property passed with Pocklington to the Crown in 1537.[61]

In 1546 the Crown granted former Percy lands in Fangfoss to Thomas Bishop, but they had been surrendered by 1552 when Arthur Darcy was granted the estate.[62] In 1563 Darcy's son Henry held 17 bovates there.[63] The Darcy family were not mentioned again and the estate may have passed to the Overend family by the early 18th century. In the 1720s George Overend had 14 bovates in Fangfoss, the largest estate after the earl of Carlisle's,[64] and in 1788 Catherine Overend had a house and nearly 300 a. there.[65] In 1796 a further 120 a. were bought from the earl of Carlisle.[66]

In 1834 Catherine Overend's son Cholmley sold his estate of about 500 a. in Fangfoss to George Champney.[67] The latter conveyed nearly 300 a. to Edward Radford and Robert Menzies in 1847,[68] and Radford sold them to Frederick Walker and Childers Radford in 1862.[69] In 1871 Radford and the Revd. James Palmes, Champney's son-in-law, sold Fangfoss Hall and 373 a. to Thomas Eadon, and a further 305 a. to Robert Bromley.[70] Both parts of the estate passed in 1879 to Charles Bromley, who reconveyed them to Thomas Eadon in 1886.[71] In 1912, after Eadon's death, about 520 a. of the estate were sold in separate lots.[72]

Thomas Eadon's widow Sarah acquired Fangfoss Hall and 30 a. in 1912, and they were sold by her executors to Joseph Todd in 1919.[73] In 1937 Todd's executors sold the property to Ethel Hotham.[74] The house was bought by Florence Todd in 1943[75] and by William Walton in 1952.[76] In 1957 it was bought by Josephine Truelove and subsequently sold as two residences.[77]

Fangfoss Hall, a square three-storeyed house of dark brown brick, is said to have been built in 1766.[78] The interior was partly refitted about 1840 and again after its division in 1957. The house may stand on or near the site of an earlier house, mentioned, with Hallgarth close, in 1563 and again in 1620.[79] A long fish pond near by may have been part of an earlier moat, but by the 19th century it had apparently become an ornamental pond in the small park which lay to the east of the house.[80] The 18th-century carriage approach is to the west front, and there are 18th- and 19th-century farm buildings and stables on the north-west.

In the late 11th or early 12th century Robert son of Ulf of Grimthorpe gave land in Fangfoss to the Hospitallers; in 1212 the estate comprised 12 bovates and was held of William son of Ralph, a member of the donor's family.[81] A hospital had apparently been built there by 1267 and may still have existed in the 1350s.[82] The Hospitallers held the estate, called *FANGFOSS SPITTAL* manor in 1507,[83] until the Dissolution, when it comprised 6 bovates and meadow land.[84] The order briefly regained its property in 1558.[85] Some meadow land was sold in the 1540s to William Ramsden[86] and was quitclaimed to Robert Appleton in 1572.[87] The rest of the estate was let by the Crown, generally for short terms, in the later 16th century.[88] King's Garth, the alternative name for Spittal Bridge close in the 19th century, may refer to this period of Crown occupation.[89] No more is known of the estate.

By 1275–6 Nunburnholme priory had been granted 2 bovates in Fangfoss by ancestors of Lord

---

[51] *Yorks. Fines, John*, p. 79.
[52] *Yorks. Fines, 1246–72*, p. 80. Thomas was, no doubt mistakenly, returned as tenant of 18 bovates held of Pocklington c. 1260: C 132/24 no. 6.
[53] *Yorks. Fines, 1327–47*, p. 120.
[54] *D.N.B.*
[55] *Cal. Pat. 1401–5*, 254.
[56] C.P. 25(1)/280/159 nos. 37–8.
[57] *Cal. Close, 1468–76*, pp. 116, 128.
[58] K.B. 27/872 rot. 42.
[59] *Cal. Close, 1476–85*, p. 342; *V.C.H. Yorks.* i. 452–3; iii. 360–1.
[60] *Cal. Inq. p.m. Hen. VII*, i, pp. 202–3.
[61] See p. 165.
[62] E 318/Box 6/222; *Cal. Pat. 1550–3*, 284.
[63] Castle Howard MS., Box 24, Survey of Estates, 1563; *N. Country Wills*, ii (Sur. Soc. cxxi), 30.
[64] E.R.R.O., DPX/50.
[65] R.D.B., BP/332/550.
[66] Ibid. DN/53/55; FQ/114/135; see p. 165.
[67] Ibid. FQ/114/135; E.R.R.O., DDCV/57/8.
[68] R.D.B., DM/88/106; FL/28/34; GM/326/421.
[69] Ibid. JL/14/14.
[70] Ibid. KX/380/504; /384/506; Ed. 7/135 no. 50.
[71] R.D.B., MU/207/312; 11/107/107 (1886).

[72] Ibid. 53/308/301 (1903); 146/61/56; /62/57; /79/74; /85/79; /218/195; 147/19/15; 149/101/94; /552/489.
[73] Ibid. 149/552/489; 198/501/429.
[74] Ibid. 587/232/176.
[75] Ibid. 665/395/342.
[76] Ibid. 928/449/396.
[77] Ibid. 1076/20/19; 1140/313/279; /418/368.
[78] Bulmer, *Dir. E. Yorks.* (1892), 612. For illus. see *E. Yorks. Georgian Soc. Trans.* iv (2), fig. 13; *Yorks. Life*, Oct.–Dec. 1951, 266–8.
[79] C 142/415 no. 34; Castle Howard MS., Survey of Estates, 1563.
[80] B.I.H.R., TA. 167S.
[81] *E.Y.C.* i, pp. 348–9; *Yorks. Fines, John*, p. 170; *Cur. Reg. R.* vi. 361.
[82] *V.C.H. Yorks.* iii. 308; *Yorks. Deeds*, vi, p. 168.
[83] C.P. 40/982 rot. 705.
[84] *Rot. Hund.* (Rec. Com.), i. 104; *Cal. Inq. p.m.* vi, p. 30; *Miscellanea*, iv. 104.
[85] *Cal. Pat. 1557–8*, 318–19.
[86] E 318/Box 18/919 mm. 7–8, 10.
[87] E.R.R.O., DDKP/6/1.
[88] e.g. E 309/Box 7/24 Eliz. I/11 no. 5; /Box 8/27 Eliz. I/9; E 310/31/183 no. 85; /32/194 no. 68.
[89] R.D.B., FQ/114/135.

Greystoke, but no further reference to the estate has been found.[90]

St. John's College, Cambridge, had about 3 a. at Fangfoss in 1563 and in the 18th and 19th centuries.[91]

From 1252 the rectorial estate in Fangfoss belonged to the dean of York.[92] The corn and hay tithes were leased for 21 years in 1616,[93] but in 1650 and thereafter the tithes and other rectorial properties were leased for lives. The tithes were worth £82 a year in 1650.[94] The Beaumont family, lessees of the tithes in the 17th century, were succeeded in the 18th century by the earls of Carlisle.[95] At inclosure in 1723 the dean received rent-charges of £64 for the great tithes of most of the township. The corn and hay tithes of certain old inclosures remained uncommuted, as did the corresponding wool and lamb tithes, which were assigned to the earl of Carlisle in return for a 14s. rent-charge.[96] In 1844 the latter were finally commuted for 12s. 6d. and the remaining corn and hay tithes for £21.[97]

The rectorial glebe consisted of 4 bovates in 1563, while 8 a. in two ancient closes and 9 cattle-gates in the pasture were also mentioned c. 1720.[98] At inclosure in 1723 the dean's lessee was allotted 80 a. for glebe.[99] In 1798 the earl of Carlisle sold his leasehold interest in about 85 a. of glebe to John Fawcett.[1] The rectory was vested in the Ecclesiastical Commissioners in 1844,[2] and in 1856 they sold 85 a. to Thomas Fawcett, the lessee.[3] In the later 19th century the Fawcetts were reputed lords of the manor of Fangfoss in respect of this estate.[4] The property, known as Manor farm by 1919,[5] was sold by Rose Fawcett to Wilfred Layland in 1947.[6] It was sold again in 1949 to Peter Thorpe, in 1960 to Joseph Fenner, and in 1962 to Brian Barrett.[7]

The rectorial house, mentioned from 1638, was the largest in the village, with four hearths, in 1672.[8] It presumably stood on the site of the later Manor House Farm, where there was certainly a house by 1798.[9] The present house is a yellow-brick building of the late 19th century.

ECONOMIC HISTORY. In 1203 the township contained 23 bovates and *culture* called 'Goltorpflatts', as well as meadow in the marsh.[10] The Greystoke demesne consisted of 30 a. of meadow in 1323[11] and 10 a. of meadow in 1375.[12] Bondsmen and leaseholders held most of the Grimthorpe estate in 1219, paying £5 12s. rent for 3½ carucates, while freeholders paid nearly 9s. for 6 bovates.[13] At least 7 bovates were held in socage of the Grimthorpe family in 1317.[14] In 1323 the Greystoke free tenants at Fangfoss owed £4 11s. in rent, three bondsmen paid £4 for 3 messuages and 6 bovates, and various tenants-at-will paid £10 3s. for 7 messuages and 14 bovates. Four tofts were let to cottagers for 8s. and the common bakehouse, held by a tenant-at-will, yielded 2s. a year.[15] Tenants-at-will paid £10 rent for 9 messuages and 25 bovates in 1375; 6 cottages were also let and £1 5s. rent received for unspecified properties.[16]

The open fields contained 64 bovates in 1563, of which 159 a. lay in North field, 116 a. in West field, 36 a. in East field, and 31 a. in South field.[17] North field probably incorporated the 13th-century 'Goltorp' or Gowthorpe flats, and an area towards Gowthorpe is still called the Flats. There were 185 a. of common meadow land. Bramer, beside Spittal beck to the south of the village, contained 98 a., the carr, lying east of the settlement,[18] 53 a., the Breke 30 a., and Lady meadow or ing, in the north of the parish, 5 a.[19] Bramer and the carr were divided into several furlongs, two of those in the carr called 'stinting furlongs'. A wand or measure 7 ft. 5 in. long was used to apportion the meadows among the villagers. Stinted rough pasture was provided by the 120-acre common moor in the west of the parish, adjoining the commons of Catton, Full Sutton, and Gowthorpe. A 50-acre Ox pasture, lying between the moor and Spittal beck, was stinted by the manorial court of Grimthorpe.

In 1537 there were some 20 holdings on Lord Dacre's manor. Eight freeholds included 3 bovates of land, and a further 30 bovates were held by 8 tenants-at-will with 2–5 bovates each. The tenants-at-will also included 2 cottagers and other men holding only meadow. The manor was worth nearly £26 a year. In 1563 Lord Dacre had 30 of the 64 bovates in the parish. Open fields and meadows were shared by 30 freeholders and tenants, 12 of whom had no open-field land. Henry Darcy had 121 a., and there were 10 holdings of 20–50 a., 7 of 5–19 a., and 12 of less than 5 a.

In 1629 Dacre's successor, William, Lord Howard, had about 10 tenants at Fangfoss. Five held 8 houses and 30 bovates, the largest holding being of 9 bovates. Another held a house and unspecified amounts of meadow and open-field land, and there were three cottagers. A bakehouse (an 'outside backhouse') was let, and the carr 'lately inclosed by George Farkson' was worth £4. The rents amounted to nearly £89 in all.[20] On the eve of inclosure nine men owned 64 bovates in the open fields; with the exception of the earl of Carlisle's 30 bovates and George Overend's 14, the holdings were all of 6 bovates or less. There were then 154 cow-gates in

---

[90] *Rot. Hund.* i. 104.
[91] Castle Howard MS., Survey of Estates, 1563; E.R.R.O., IA. Fangfoss; B.I.H.R., TA. 167S.
[92] See p. 144.
[93] Minster Libr., D. & C. Archives, S 1 (2) f, ff. 5, 15.
[94] C 94/3 f. 57; *T.E.R.A.S.* ii. 48.
[95] Ibid.; Minster Libr., D. & C. Arch., S 1 (2) f, ff. 5, 15; S 1 (1) e, f. 38d.; B.I.H.R., CC. DY. Fangfoss; TER. I. Fangfoss 1690; E.R.R.O., IA. Fangfoss.
[96] E.R.R.O., IA. Fangfoss.
[97] B.I.H.R., TA. 167S.
[98] E.R.R.O., DPX/50; Castle Howard MS., Survey of Estates, 1563.
[99] E.R.R.O., IA. Fangfoss.
[1] R.D.B., BZ/87/119.
[2] *Lond. Gaz.* 19 July 1844, p. 2499.
[3] R.D.B., HL/265/276.
[4] Directories.
[5] R.D.B., 205/192/168.
[6] Ibid. 773/156/134.
[7] Ibid. 834/43/31; 1172/478/429; 1266/53/49.
[8] E 179/205/504; Minster Libr., D. & C. Arch., S 1 (2) f, f. 5.
[9] R.D.B., BZ/87/119.
[10] *Yorks. Fines, John*, p. 79.
[11] C 134/82 no. 7.
[12] C 135/240 no. 11.
[13] *Bk. of Fees*, i. 246.
[14] *Cal. Inq. p.m.* vi, p. 30.
[15] C 134/82 no. 7.
[16] C 135/240 no. 11.
[17] The following paragraphs are based on Dacre surveys: Castle Howard MSS., Surveys of Estates, 1537, 1563.
[18] B.I.H.R., TA. 167S.
[19] Ibid.; E.R.R.O., DDHV/11/1; /24/2.
[20] E.R.R.O., DDPY/10/1.

the pasture, two being allowed for each bovate and one for each house or cottage. In the common householders enjoyed rights double those of cottagers.[21]

The open fields and other common lands were inclosed in 1723 after agreement between the landowners,[22] and the award was ratified by an Act of 1726.[23] Of the 1,159 a. allotted 273 a. lay in High field, 150 a. in Middlegate field, 141 a. in East field, 118 a. in Between-the-towns field, 95 a. in Bramer, 222 a. in the moor, and 160 a. in the common pasture. High field was the former North field, Middlegate field the former West field, and Between-the-towns field, situated between Fangfoss and Bolton, the former South field. The township also contained about 170 a. of old inclosure in 1723, including several pieces of meadow.[24] Other meadow land was included in the open fields, and Between-the-towns field contained land called common carr, carr acres, and St. James's ing. As in other parishes, part of the common moor may have been separated from the rest as a place to confine animals, for the Hold was among the allotments in 1723. By the award Charles, earl of Carlisle, received 560 a. for his freehold estate, as well as 80 a. as lessee of the rectorial glebe. George Overend was awarded 223 a., while five other members of his family received allotments ranging from 4 a. to 48 a. and amounting in all to 128 a. There were only 5 other allotments, 2 of 70–90 a. and 3 of 3 a. each.

When Lord Carlisle's estate was offered for sale in 1795 it amounted to nearly 600 a. and included three farms of 97 a. to 198 a.[25] There were generally 8–12 farmers at Fangfoss and Spittal in the 19th and early 20th centuries, of whom 3 in 1851 and 2 in the 1920s and 1930s had over 150 a.[26] In 1801 342 a. were under crops at Fangfoss.[27] There were 864 a. of arable, 450 a. of meadow and pasture, and 18 a. of woodland in 1844,[28] and 709 a. of arable, 526 a. of permanent grass, and 21 a. of woodland in 1905.[29] There were roughly equal amounts of arable and grassland in the parish in the 1930s and 1960s, the arable most prominent away from the settlements, notably on the former common.[30]

A brick-maker was mentioned in 1840,[31] and in 1844 and 1851 a brickyard lay in the angle between the Full Sutton and Wilberfoss roads. A hanger on the former airfield was sold by the Ministry of Defence in 1967 and acquired in 1968 by a caravan company which still occupied it, as well as some new buildings, in 1974.[32]

In 1212 the Hospitallers' estate included a mill, and in 1252 the Belthorpe family held 'Swalewe' mill.[33]

LOCAL GOVERNMENT. Amends of the assize of ale were claimed for his tenants at Fangfoss by Nicholas of Selby in 1293.[34] A tenant of the Hospitallers owed suit of court at Fangfoss twice a year in 1507.[35] Part of Fangfoss belonged to Grimthorpe manor,[36] whose court records survive from the 18th and 19th centuries. Those relating to Fangfoss include jury verdicts for 1748–1835, call rolls for 1758–1835, and court papers of the 18th and early 19th centuries.[37]

In 1748 the officers sworn at Grimthorpe included a constable and two bylawmen for Fangfoss, and a pinder was mentioned from 1762. The bylawmen were last mentioned in 1798, but the constable and pinder continued until 1835. In 1779 the inhabitants of Fangfoss complained that a man had been re-appointed constable at Grimthorpe 'contrary to the parish meeting', and it seems that the nomination of officers and inspection of their accounts took place at Fangfoss, perhaps at vestry meetings. The constable was also serving as surveyor of highways in 1779.[38]

Overseers' accounts for the period 1769–1837 reveal that parish poorhouses were being built or repaired in the 1790s.[39] In 1869 the site of two cottages sold by the overseers was used for a schoolmaster's house.[40] Fangfoss joined Pocklington poor-law union in 1836[41] and Pocklington rural district in 1894.[42] It became part of the North Wolds district of Humberside in 1974.

CHURCH. The early history of Fangfoss church is the same as that of Barmby Moor. There was a 'parson', presumably a chaplain, at Fangfoss in 1235.[43] The curacy of Fangfoss was usually held by the vicar of Barmby from the later 16th century, and in 1973 the two places still constituted a united vicarage.[44]

In 1525–6 a chaplain serving Fangfoss received £4 a year.[45] From 1684 a stipend of £5 a year was paid by the dean, and by the mid 18th century the dean had also released his right to mortuaries.[46] The curacy was worth £8 10s. in 1707.[47] It was augmented by £200 from Queen Anne's Bounty in 1747, 1779, 1791, 1798, and 1819.[48] The average net income was £46 in 1829–31.[49] In 1860 Fangfoss was endowed with tithe rent-charges of nearly £8, formerly belonging to the rectory, and with £4 from the Common Fund.[50]

Small tithes in Fangfoss contributed to the income of the joint living. At the ordination of 1252 the tithes of gardens, flax, and hemp, as well as a share of the altarage, were assigned to the vicarage.[51]

[21] E.R.R.O., DPX/50.
[22] Ibid. IA. Fangfoss.
[23] 12 Geo. I, c. 5 (Priv. Act).
[24] E.R.R.O., DPX/50; B.I.H.R., TA. 167S.
[25] E.R.R.O., DDHB/57/199.
[26] H.O. 107/2351; directories.
[27] 1801 Crop Returns.
[28] B.I.H.R., TA. 167S.
[29] Acreage Returns, 1905.
[30] [1st] Land Util. Surv. Map, sheet 27; 2nd Land Util. Surv. Map, sheet 709 (SE 65–75).
[31] White, Dir. E. & N.R. Yorks. 237.
[32] R.D.B., 1493/185/163; 1557/532/388.
[33] Yorks. Fines, John, p. 170; Yorks. Fines, 1246–72, p. 80.
[34] Plac. de Quo Warr. (Rec. Com.), 225.
[35] C.P. 40/982 rot. 705.
[36] See p. 165.
[37] E.R.R.O., DDCV/71/1a–b, 2, 4–6.
[38] Ibid. DDGR/8/1.
[39] Overseers' acct. bk., penes the vicar, 1974.
[40] R.D.B., KE/417/585; see p. 170.
[41] 3rd Rep. Poor Law Com. 169.
[42] Census.
[43] Reg. Gray, 247.
[44] See p. 144.
[45] Y.A.J. xxiv. 72.
[46] B.I.H.R., TER. I. Fangfoss 1684 etc.
[47] Lawton, Rer. Eccl. Dioc. Ebor. 338.
[48] Hodgson, Q.A.B. 439.
[49] Rep. Com. Eccl. Revenues, 932.
[50] Lond. Gaz. 30 Oct. 1860, p. 3913.
[51] Reg. Gray, 213.

The small tithes of Fangfoss were worth £5 in 1650[52] and about £4 in 1690.[53] At inclosure in 1723 the curate was awarded rent-charges of £5 for the small tithes, excluding that of rape which was commuted in 1844 for £2 a year. Small tithes from certain old inclosures were assigned to the earl of Carlisle in 1723 in return for a 5s. contribution to the £5 payable to the curate, and these were finally commuted for £2 in 1844, when they were held by Thomas Fawcett.[54]

The only glebe at Fangfoss in 1690 was a pasture gate and rights in the common,[55] for which 3 a. were awarded at inclosure in 1723.[56] Bounty money was used to buy 8 a. at Pocklington in 1791, 6 a. at Allerthorpe in 1792, and 4 a. at Tickhill (Yorks. W.R.) in 1802. By 1853 5 a. at Pocklington had been sold, and the Tickhill land was sold before 1857.[57] A house and 3 a. were bought at Barmby in 1854, and a house and 4 a. at Bolton (in Bishop Wilton) were added by 1877.[58] Six acres at Spittal and Bolton were sold in 1917, the house and 3 a. at Barmby in 1920, 3 a. at Pocklington in 1924, and 6 a. at Allerthorpe in 1967.[59] A 'vicarage house' at Fangfoss was mentioned in 1684 and 1690, but had gone by 1716.[60] A garth adjoining the churchyard was described as the vicar's in 1888.[61]

In 1566 the Crown granted lands in Fangfoss, which had formerly supported an obit in the church, to Francis Barker and Thomas Blackway.[62]

Since the 16th century Fangfoss has apparently lacked a resident minister,[63] except briefly in the late 19th century when an assistant curate lived at Bolton and served Fangfoss church.[64] Moreover, in the 18th and early 19th centuries the vicar of Barmby also held Allerthorpe and Thornton, and resided in one of the latter parishes.[65] In 1835 the incumbent also held Pocklington and Yapham.[66]

Fangfoss has consequently been poorly served at times. In the 1590s services were neglected by the vicar of Barmby.[67] In 1743 there was a service at Fangfoss once a fortnight; Holy Communion was celebrated at Christmas and Easter, and there were about 40 communicants.[68] By 1851 there was a weekly service.[69] At the monthly communion services in 1865 there were about 10 communicants.[70] In 1974 two services a month were held at Fangfoss. A cottage was built in 1875 to provide income for the religious education of children.[71] In the mid 20th century the income was applied to Sunday schools at Fangfoss and Barmby Moor.[72]

The medieval church or chapel of ST. MARTIN consisted of chancel with apsidal end and nave with south porch and west tower. The chancel was 'quite fallen down' in 1591 and 'altogether ruinous' in 1602.[73] The building was extensively repaired in the 18th century[74] and repewed in the 1820s.[75] By the 1830s the apse had gone, the tower had recently been partly rebuilt in brick, and the south porch had been stripped of much of its ornamentation.[76] The church was rebuilt in 1848-50 by R. D. Chantrell in a Norman style, use being made of stonework from the former Norman church, notably in the south doorway and the corbel table.[77] The church, called St. Mary's in 1851 and later St. John's,[78] comprises chancel with north vestry and nave with south door and west bell-turret. The fittings include an octagonal stone font and a communion table, apparently acquired at about the date of restoration.[79]

The Church Estate charity for church repairs, of unknown origin, consisted of a cottage and 2 a. in 1711.[80] At inclosure in 1723 the charity was awarded 4 a.,[81] which produced an income of £2 in 1743, £4 in 1777,[82] and £8 in 1824. By 1764 a rent-charge of 10s. from land formerly belonging to Timothy Overend had been added to the charity.[83] Two cottages were built in 1873, and in 1875 the annual income of the charity stood at £24.[84] The rent-charges were being withheld in the early 20th century. Two cottages belonging to the charity were sold in 1959 and 1964,[85] but the site of a third and 4 a. of land were retained in 1974, when income was still received.[86]

The church had two bells in 1552 and there are still two: (i) 1628; (ii) undated.[87] A silver chalice has belonged to the church since 1552. The plate also includes a pewter flagon and paten, a plated cup given by the wife of Robert Taylor, vicar 1840-85,[88] and a plated flagon.[89] The registers of baptisms begin in 1663 and are complete except for 1712-15 and 1810-13. Those of marriages begin in 1656, but lack entries for 1694-1715 and 1736-55. The burial registers begin in 1671 but lack entries for 1712-15.[90]

The churchyard was extended in 1920.[91]

---

[52] C 94/3 f. 57.
[53] B.I.H.R., TER. I. Fangfoss 1690.
[54] Ibid. TA. 167S; E.R.R.O., IA. Fangfoss; see p. 167.
[55] B.I.H.R., TER. I. Fangfoss 1690.
[56] E.R.R.O., IA. Fangfoss.
[57] B.I.H.R., TER. I. Fangfoss 1853, 1857.
[58] Ibid. 1877; R.D.B., HF/9/14.
[59] R.D.B., 181/110/95; 223/250/205; 287/292/235; 1515/151/141.
[60] B.I.H.R., TER. I. Fangfoss 1684, 1690; Barmby Moor 1716.
[61] Ibid. CC. EC. 11/57.
[62] Cal. Pat. 1563-6, p. 475.
[63] C 94/3 f. 57; Y.A.J. xviii. 317; see above p. 168.
[64] B.I.H.R., Bp. V. 1894/Ret.; Bulmer, Dir. E. Yorks. (1892), 611-12; see above p. 145.
[65] See p. 188.
[66] Rep. Com. Eccl. Revenues, 932.
[67] Y.A.J. xviii. 221, 228, 232, 317.
[68] Herring's Visit. i. 220.
[69] H.O. 129/23/516.
[70] B.I.H.R., V. 1865/Ret. 37.
[71] Ibid. Ch. Ret. s.v. Barmby Moor and Fangfoss.
[72] Ex inf. the vicar, 1974.
[73] Y.A.J. xviii. 221, 338.
[74] Yorks. Gaz. 10 Aug. 1850.
[75] B.I.H.R., DY. Fac.
[76] T. Allen, Hist. Co. York, iii. 412.
[77] B.I.H.R., Ch. Ret.; H.O. 129/23/516; Y.A.J. xxii. 253-5; Yorks. Gaz. 14 Oct. 1848, 10 Aug. 1850.
[78] H.O. 129/23/516; directories.
[79] B.I.H.R., TER. I. Fangfoss 1825, 1853.
[80] 11th Rep. Com. Char. 730.
[81] E.R.R.O., IA. Fangfoss.
[82] B.I.H.R., TER. I. Fangfoss 1777; Herring's Visit. i. 220.
[83] B.I.H.R., Bp. V. 1764/Ret. 178; 11th Rep. Com. Char. 731.
[84] B.I.H.R., Ch. Ret. s.v. Fangfoss and Barmby Moor.
[85] Char. Com. files; R.D.B., 1145/493/445; 1357/488/441.
[86] Fangfoss par. rec. penes the vicar; ex inf. the vicar, 1974.
[87] Inventories of Ch. Goods, 82; Boulter, 'Ch. Bells', 26.
[88] B.I.H.R., V. 1865/Ret. 37; W. D. Wood Rees, Hist. of Barmby Moor (Pocklington, priv. print. 1911), 49.
[89] Inventories of Ch. Goods, 82; Yorks. Ch. Plate, i. 248.
[90] Penes the vicar, 1974. Several earlier entries are illegible.
[91] York. Dioc. Regy., Consecration deed.

NONCONFORMITY. A house at Fangfoss was registered for dissenting worship in 1777,[92] and the Methodists had 17 members there in 1787 and between 8 and 23 in 1788–1816.[93] A small Wesleyan chapel and school-house were built opposite the church in 1836–7,[94] and replaced by a larger chapel on a new site in 1865.[95] The latter closed in 1974. In the mid 19th century 10–12 Primitive Methodists were meeting in a cottage,[96] but in 1865 they built a chapel on the Pocklington road.[97] Later called Canaan chapel,[98] it had closed by 1947.[99] It was used as a workshop in 1974.

EDUCATION. In 1819 the parishioners of Fangfoss paid a schoolmaster who taught about 25 children.[1] A day school belonging to the Primitive Methodists and maintained by parents had 20 pupils in 1835.[2] A school for Fangfoss and neighbouring townships, which also served as a Wesleyan chapel, was built by George Champney in 1836–7; in 1861 it had an income of £40 from voluntary contributions and the school pence of 45 pupils.[3] It had been united with the National Society and was receiving an annual government grant by 1863.[4] The school had ceased to be a Methodist meeting-place by 1865.[5] A new school was built on the same site in 1867 and a master's house added in 1869;[6] there were 41 pupils in 1871.[7] Attendance fell from 50 in 1907 to 37 in 1912, and stood at 36 in 1938.[8] In 1952 the senior pupils were transferred to Pocklington. A new school was built in 1971–2 beside the Pocklington road.[9] There were 32 pupils on the roll in January 1974.[10]

CHARITIES FOR THE POOR. Thomas Wood, by will dated 1568, devised a rent-charge of £10 a year from an estate at Kilnwick Percy for the benefit of Fangfoss and many other townships. In 1824 5s. were distributed in Fangfoss.[11] The income was spent on coal in the 1880s and cash payments were made in the early 20th century.[12] Henry Frederick, Baron Hotham (d. 1967), owner of the Kilnwick Percy estate, redeemed the rent-charge in 1961 and £10 stock was subsequently assigned to Fangfoss.[13] In 1973 the 26p income was given to one person.[14]

The Poor's Money comprised gifts at unknown dates of £4 10s. from Robert and Mary Dealtry, £2 from Priscilla Beaumont, £2 10s. from Mary Overend, and 10s. each from Edward Catton and an unknown donor.[15] The Dealtry and Beaumont gifts may date from the 17th century.[16] The £10 capital was entrusted to the overseers, who used it to make weekly cash payments. By 1824, however, £5 had been lost[17] and no more is heard of the charity.

Rent-charges of 3s. 4d. and 10s., given at unknown dates by William and Margaret Cade and Timothy Overend respectively, were received by the overseers during the 18th century, but in 1811–15 another Timothy Overend assumed the administration after the improper use of the charges. The charities benefited poor householders and widows, but no payments were made after 1815 and in 1824 it was proposed to divert the income to other uses.[18] Payments were resumed in 1860 after a long interval, and in 1884 the income from Cades' gift and Hill Garth, presumably the property bearing Overend's rent-charge, was used to buy coal. The charities were apparently later called the Church Charity and in 1907 four payments of 3s. 4d. were made,[19] but they were lost afterwards.[20]

A rent-charge of 2s. from property in Spittal was mentioned in 1786, but it had not been received for many years in 1824.[21]

FULL SUTTON

THE VILLAGE of Full Sutton, which was an Anglian settlement, lies about 9 miles east-north-east of York, at the end of the Escrick moraine.[1] It had acquired the descriptive prefix, meaning 'foul' or 'dirty', by the 13th century.[2] Much of the parish lies at about 50 ft. above sea-level and is covered by outwash sand, gravel, and clay. The land rises to over 75 ft. east of the village, however, and reaches 100 ft. at the parish boundary. The higher ground consists of boulder clay, glacial sand and gravel, and Keuper marl, and it is on a sand and gravel outcrop that the village is situated.[3] The small Winter beck flows westwards across Full Sutton towards the river Derwent. The parish, which is wedge-shaped, covers 881 a.[4]

The former open-field land lay all round the village, and Full Sutton common occupied the southernmost part of the parish. Open fields and common were inclosed in 1766. The wartime Full Sutton airfield, which was in use in 1944–6,[5] lay

---

[92] G.R.O. Worship Returns, Vol. v, no. 465; B.I.H.R., Fac. Bk. ii, p. 161.
[93] E.R.R.O., MRP/1/7.
[94] H.O. 129/23/516; O.S. Map 6" (1854 edn.).
[95] Date on building.
[96] H.O. 129/23/516; B.I.H.R., V. 1865/Ret. 37.
[97] G.R.O. Worship Reg. no. 17268.
[98] E.R.R.O., MRP/5/3; ex inf. Mrs. E. Wilkinson, Wilberfoss, 1974.
[99] G.R.O. Worship Reg. no. 17268.
[1] *Educ. of Poor Digest*, 1080.
[2] *Educ. Enquiry Abstract*, 1084.
[3] H.O. 129/23/516; Ed. 7/135 no. 50.
[4] *Rep. of Educ. Cttee. of Council, 1862–3* [3171], p. 513, H.C. (1863), xlvii.
[5] See above.
[6] Dates on buildings.
[7] *Returns relating to Elem. Educ.* 794.
[8] *Bd. of Educ. List 21* (H.M.S.O.).
[9] E.R. Educ. Cttee. *Mins.* 1951–2, 225; 1971–2, 59, 217–18.
[10] Ex inf. Chief Educ. Officer, County Hall, Beverley, 1974.
[11] *11th Rep. Com. Char.* 730.
[12] Churchwardens' accts. 1883–1929, *penes* the vicar, 1974.
[13] Ex inf. Char. Com., Liverpool, 1974.
[14] Ex inf. Mr. J. Thompson, Fangfoss, 1974.
[15] *11th Rep. Com. Char.* 730.
[16] C 94/3 f. 57; C 142/415 no. 34.
[17] *11th Rep. Com. Char.* 730.
[18] Ibid. 729–30.
[19] Churchwardens' accts. 1883–1929.
[20] Char. Com. files.
[21] *11th Rep. Com. Char.* 730.
[1] This article was written in 1974.
[2] *P.N.E.R. Yorks.* (E.P.N.S.), 185.
[3] Geol. Surv. Map 1", solid and drift, sheet 63 (1967 edn.).
[4] O.S. Map 6", Yorks. (1854 edn.). Most of the parish is on sheet 158, the rest on sheet 175.
[5] Ex inf. Ministry of Defence, 1973.

south of the village, partly in Bishop Wilton and Fangfoss parishes.[6]

From Full Sutton village minor roads lead southwards towards Fangfoss, westwards towards Catton, and northwards to join the former Roman road which leads to Stamford Bridge. The entire northern boundary of the parish follows the Stamford Bridge road. The road was turnpiked in 1765 and the trust was continued until 1872.[7] The railway line from Market Weighton to York crosses the former common.[8]

The village lies mainly around an oblong 1¼-acre green,[9] from which a footpath leads to the parish church, standing behind the outbuildings of Glebe Farm. A small pond which lay beside the road west of the green[10] has been filled in. Most of the village houses date from the 19th century. They include a farm-house built by the Revd. Richard Lucas in 1837,[11] and Full Sutton Villa or Hall, a grey-brick house built by Thomas Pearson c. 1860.[12] A village hall was opened in the outbuildings of Glebe Farm in 1949 and enlarged in 1962.[13] Fishponds north-east of the church[14] may have been associated with the manor-house. A Full Sutton innkeeper was mentioned in 1741[15] and there were one or two licensed houses in the later 18th century.[16] A beerhouse was recorded in 1840.[17]

Of the three outlying farm-houses in the parish Street Farm, on the Stamford Bridge road, was formerly known as Spence's Farm,[18] and Common House was demolished when the airfield was built.

There were 45 poll-tax payers at Full Sutton in 1377.[19] Twenty-three households were included in the hearth-tax return of 1672, 11 of them exempt. Of those that were chargeable 8 had only one hearth each, 2 had 2, and 2 had four.[20] There were 18 families in 1743 and 14 in 1764.[21] The population rose from 100 in 1801 to 174 in 1861, before falling to 119 in 1901.[22] It remained fairly constant in the earlier 20th century but fell to 92 in 1971.[23]

MANOR AND OTHER ESTATE. Full Sutton was not mentioned in 1086, when it lay within the manor and soke of Catton.[24] The lordship subsequently descended with Catton in the Percy, Seymour, and Wyndham families,[25] but little land in Full Sutton was attached to Catton manor. An allotment of 12 a. to the earl of Egremont at inclosure in 1766[26] comprised the whole of his estate there; it was sold by Lord Leconfield in 1921.[27]

Full Sutton may have been held under the Percys by Peter son of Grente in the later 12th century,[28] and all 6 carucates there were held by William Dawtry or Dealtry in 1284–5, 4½ of them in demesne.[29] William was dead by 1312.[30] John Dawtry held the estate in 1315,[31] and he and Eleanor Percy were said to be lords of the place in 1316.[32] The estate apparently descended in the Dawtry family, and in 1577 William Dawtry held the reputed manor of FULL SUTTON.[33] About 1602 it comprised 16 of the 36 bovates in the township.[34]

In 1675–6 John Dealtry conveyed the manor to Thomas Langley and Samuel Walker[35] and by 1705 it had probably passed to Francis Elwick, who then had the advowson.[36] Elwick's granddaughter Frances married John Eyre, and in 1726 she sold the manor to William Simpson.[37] The estate comprised 483 a. in 1766.[38] It was presumably another William Simpson who by will dated 1766 devised the manor to trustees to hold successively for his brothers John and Lindley Simpson. After Lindley's death it passed before 1785, under the terms of the will, to John Bridgman, son of William Simpson's niece Elizabeth and her husband Sir Henry Bridgman, Bt. John Bridgman took the name Simpson on succeeding to the estates,[39] and in 1788 he sold the manor and 349 a. to John Ramsey (d. 1801).[40] The lands remained in the hands of Ramsey's trustees until the mid 19th century.[41] In 1868 204 a. were conveyed to Robert Freer, and in 1877 they were sold by Thomas Freer to Joseph Fearnsides.[42] Susannah Fearnsides's executors sold them to Charles Mennell in 1898, and Mennell acquired more land in Full Sutton in 1903 and 1919.[43] The Mennells sold Manor House farm, comprising 187 a., to R. Q. Triffitt in 1923, and the Triffitts still had most of it in 1973.[44] The present farm-house is a 19th-century building.

Land in Full Sutton belonged to the chantry of St. Mary the Virgin in Lund church and after the suppression was granted to William Mylton in 1563.[45]

ECONOMIC HISTORY. Agricultural arrangements at Full Sutton in the Middle Ages are not documented. All the land was held by freeholders of Catton manor in the late 16th and early 17th

[6] See p. 164.
[7] K. A. MacMahon, Roads and Turnpike Trusts in E. Yorks. (E. Yorks. Loc. Hist. Ser. xviii), 23, 70.
[8] See p. 150.
[9] O.S. Map 1/2,500, Yorks. CLVIII. 16 (1910 edn.).
[10] O.S. Map 6" (1854 edn.).
[11] Inscription on house.
[12] R.D.B., HB/139/187; KS/290/383.
[13] Ibid. 831/165/140; 1269/140/127; 1270/122/108.
[14] O.S. Map 6" (1854 edn.).
[15] E.R.R.O., QSF. Mids. 1741, B.8–9.
[16] Ibid. QDT/2/15.
[17] White, Dir. E. & N.R. Yorks. (1840), 238.
[18] O.S. Map 6" (1854 edn.).
[19] E 179/202/59 m. 67.
[20] E 179/205/504.
[21] B.I.H.R., Bp. V. 1764/Ret. 202; Herring's Visit. i. 212.
[22] V.C.H. Yorks. iii. 493.
[23] Census.
[24] V.C.H. Yorks. ii. 219.
[25] See p. 151.
[26] R.D.B., AH/177/5.
[27] Ibid. 244/35/26.
[28] E.Y.C. xi, p. 255.
[29] Feud. Aids, vi. 47.
[30] Abbrev. Rot. Orig. (Rec. Com.), i. 191.
[31] Cal. Inq. p.m. v, p. 319.
[32] Feud. Aids, vi. 168, where 'Sautre' should no doubt read 'Dautre'.
[33] Petworth House Archives, no. 1417 f. 50d.
[34] Ibid. no. 1416.
[35] C.P. 25(2)/757/27–8 Chas. II Hil. no. [2 from end].
[36] See p. 172.
[37] R.D.B., K/303/622–3.
[38] Ibid. AH/177/5.
[39] 25 Geo. III, c. 30 (Priv. Act).
[40] R.D.B., BM/341/470; CD/184/277.
[41] Ibid. HI/81/108; E.R.R.O., Land Tax 1832; Sheahan and Whellan, Hist. York & E.R. ii. 559.
[42] R.D.B., KF/225/306; MK/280/439.
[43] Ibid. 6/329/30; /525/491 (1898); 57/437/416 (1903); 202/329/283.
[44] Ibid. 262/415/368; 1828/352/268.
[45] Cal. Pat. 1560–3, 619.

centuries, five men having 36 bovates c. 1602, for example.[46] By the 17th century there were three open fields, known as Hunland field, Wrengthorne, Wrainthorne, or White Cross field, and Hatkill or Sindill field.[47] There was also a stinted pasture called Ox close, mentioned as early as 1630,[48] in which the rector had a gate in 1716. The common, in the south-west of the parish and adjoining High Catton common, provided turf and whins, besides pasture.[49] Parcels of meadow called Kirkwinterbecks, mentioned in 1653,[50] were apparently held in severalty, and other closes were recorded in the 17th century, including West Flat and Furrland closes in 1630.[51] Forelands is the modern name for land adjoining Stamford Bridge township. By 1766 there were 324 a. of ancient inclosures in the parish.

The open fields and common were inclosed in 1766[52] under an Act of 1760.[53] A total of 529 a. was allotted, including 112 a. from Hunland field, 91 a. from Hatkill field, 70 a. from White Cross field, 69 a. jointly from Hunland and White Cross fields, and 187 a. from the common. The earl of Egremont, as lord of the manor, received 12 a., the rector 99 a., William Simpson 249 a., and four others 78 a., 61 a., 28 a., and 3 a. respectively. In addition exchanges were arranged involving 40 a. of ancient inclosures.

In 1795 there were 451 a. of arable and 24 a. of waste in the parish,[54] and in 1905 638 a. of arable and 228 a. of grass.[55] There was still a notable amount of pasture around the village in the 1930s and later.[56] In the 19th and 20th centuries there have usually been about six farmers in Full Sutton.[57] In 1851 one man had 300 a. and another 150 a.[58] Little non-agricultural employment has been recorded. A Full Sutton man worked as a weaver in 1580,[59] and in the 1930s there appeared a sand and gravel merchant and a motor engineer.[60]

LOCAL GOVERNMENT. Surviving court records for the manor and soke of Catton, within which Full Sutton lay, show that a constable was appointed for this township in the 1470s, the 1660s, and the 19th century.[61]

No parochial records before 1835 are known. Full Sutton joined Pocklington poor-law union in 1836[62] and Pocklington rural district in 1894.[63] It became part of the North Wolds district of Humberside in 1974.

CHURCH. Full Sutton church was first mentioned in the early 13th century when, as a chapel of Catton, it was granted independence in return for certain payments,[64] which were later resolved into an annual pension of £1 13s. 4d.[65] It was subsequently regarded as a rectory. The living was united with Skirpenbeck in 1919.[66]

The advowson belonged to Ralph Dawtry in 1234[67] and thereafter descended like the manor in the Dawtry family.[68] It was for some reason held by Thomas Fairfax and another in 1658.[69] The advowson passed with the manor to Langley and Walker in 1675–6. It was held by Francis Elwick in 1705, by Joseph Eyre in 1713–14, and later by the Simpsons.[70] It was separated from the manor between 1823 and 1829, when it was acquired by Charles Duncombe, created Baron Feversham in 1826.[71] In 1880 W. E. Duncombe, created earl of Feversham in 1868, exchanged the advowsons of Full Sutton and Holtby (Yorks. N.R.) with the Crown for Kirkbymoorside (Yorks. N.R.).[72] The Lord Chancellor still exercised the patronage on behalf of the Crown in 1972.[73]

The church was worth £6 13s. 4d. in 1291[74] and £10 12s. 8d. net in 1535.[75] Payment of the pension to Catton was disputed by the rector of Full Sutton in 1555.[76] The living was worth £40 in 1650[77] and the average net income in 1829–31 was £150.[78] The Catton pension was still being paid in 1865.[79] The living was worth £198 net in 1884 and £129 net in 1915.[80] Glebe land in 1716 comprised a close and an unspecified amount of open-field land.[81] At inclosure in 1766 the rector was awarded 105 a. in lieu of glebe and tithes, and he already had an 8-acre close.[82] All the land was sold in 1925.[83] The parsonage house was out of repair in 1704.[84] In 1777 it was a brick house containing four ground-floor rooms and four bedrooms; it was replaced by a larger house between 1825 and 1849.[85]

In the Middle Ages the living was held by several members of the Dealtry family.[86] At least two 18th-century incumbents were non-resident, living at their other cures of Hatfield (Yorks. W.R.) in 1743 and Thorne (Yorks. W.R.) in 1764.[87] After 1919 the rector lived at Skirpenbeck, and since 1941 he has also been rector of Scrayingham with Leppington and Howsham.[88]

A service was held each Sunday in 1743 and Holy Communion was celebrated four times a year with about 20 communicants.[89] There were monthly

[46] E 164/37 f. 259; Petworth Ho. Arch., nos. 1416, 1417 f. 50d.
[47] Petworth Ho. Arch., no. 1448; E.R.R.O., DC 40/1/19/6, 11; B.I.H.R., TER. I. Full Sutton 1716.
[48] E.R.R.O., DC 40/1/19/4; /1/31/36.
[49] B.I.H.R., TER. I. Full Sutton 1716.
[50] E.R.R.O., DDX/97/2.
[51] Ibid. DC 40/1/31/36.
[52] R.D.B., AH/177/5.
[53] 33 Geo. II, c. 43 (Priv. Act).
[54] E.R.R.O., DPX/(84).
[55] Acreage Returns, 1905.
[56] [1st] Land Util. Surv. Map, sheet 27; 2nd Land Util. Surv. Map, sheet 709 (SE 65–75).
[57] Directories.
[58] H.O. 107/2351.
[59] Y.A.J. xxxvi. 440.
[60] Directories.
[61] See pp. 154–5.
[62] 3rd Rep. Poor Law Com. 169.
[63] Census.
[64] Percy Charty. (Sur. Soc. cxvii), 351–2.
[65] See below.
[66] York Dioc. Regy., Order in Council 519.
[67] Reg. Gray, p. 65.
[68] See p. 171.
[69] Lamb. Pal. Libr., COMM./III/7.
[70] Inst. Bks.
[71] Ibid.; Baines, Hist. Yorks. (1823), ii. 393.
[72] Lond. Gaz. 9 Mar. 1880, p. 1958. For the Duncombes see Burke, Peerage (1967), 940–2.
[73] Crockford (1971–2).
[74] Tax. Eccl. (Rec. Com.), 303.
[75] Valor Eccl. (Rec. Com.), v. 141.
[76] B.I.H.R., CP. G. 580.
[77] C 94/3 f. 57.
[78] Rep. Com. Eccl. Revenues, 936.
[79] B.I.H.R., TER. I. Full Sutton 1777–1865.
[80] Ibid. Bp. V. 1884/Ret.; Bp. V. 1915/Ret.
[81] Ibid. TER. I. Full Sutton 1716.
[82] R.D.B., AH/177/5.
[83] Ibid. 304/97/73.
[84] B.I.H.R., ER. V/CB. 10.
[85] Ibid. TER. I. Full Sutton 1777, 1825, 1849.
[86] Minster Libr., Torre MS., 'Cleveland & E.R.', p. 1189.
[87] B.I.H.R., Bp. V. 1764/Ret. 202; Herring's Visit. i. 212; ii. 51.
[88] Notes in church, 1974.
[89] Herring's Visit. i. 212.

communions by 1868 and weekly ones by 1884, when there were about 6 communicants. By 1877 two services were held each Sunday and one on Fridays.[90] Only one service was held in January 1974 but communion was celebrated on the other Sundays.

The church of ST. MARY, of ashlar, consists of chancel with north vestry, and nave with west bellcot and south porch. The church was in decay in 1615,[91] and in 1723–4 the porch was repaired and a buttress rebuilt.[92] The whole church was rebuilt and enlarged in 1844–5, partly with old masonry.[93] The chancel is in a 14th-century style and the nave has some small reset windows of the 15th century.

There were two bells in 1770,[94] and in 1877 it was reported that two new ones had been provided.[95] The plate includes a silver chalice and a paten, presented in 1878 by Mrs. Darcy Wyvill and J. S. Salman, vicar, respectively, and a plated cup, a plate, and a flagon.[96] The registers of baptisms, marriages, and burials begin in 1713 and are complete.[97]

The churchyard was enlarged in 1909.[98]

NONCONFORMITY. The Methodists had 11–27 members at Full Sutton in 1814–16.[99] Houses were licensed for worship in 1761, 1813, 1823, and 1827,[1] and a Wesleyan chapel in 1829.[2] Most people were said in 1865 to attend both church and chapel.[3] The chapel closed in 1974.[4]

EDUCATION. A schoolmaster at Full Sutton was licensed in 1596.[5] In 1819 children attended school in a near-by parish, but a school was started at Full Sutton in 1823 and ten children attended in 1835.[6] A school supported by parents was mentioned in 1865,[7] but subsequently children were said to go to schools in Fangfoss and Skirpenbeck.[8]

CHARITIES FOR THE POOR. Thomas Wood, by will dated 1568, devised a rent-charge of £10 from an estate at Kilnwick Percy for the benefit of Full Sutton and many other townships. In 1824 2s. 6d. was distributed in Full Sutton, along with the interest of the Town Stock.[9] Henry Frederick, Baron Hotham, owner of the Kilnwick Percy estate, redeemed the rent-charge in 1961 and £5 stock was subsequently assigned to Full Sutton.[10] The income was given to one person in 1966, but in 1972 the 17p received was not distributed.[11]

The Town Stock comprised gifts of £1 by Richard Green, £1 by Elizabeth Pearson, and £1 6s. 8d. by George Dealtry, all in 1659, £1 by Dorothy Green in 1674, and £2 by William Ringrose in 1728. By 1736 a further £1 3s. 4d. had been added by the parish.[12]

John Cobb, by will of 1783, directed that bread should be distributed out of the profits of a close in the parish. His next of kin apparently gave £40 as an endowment. Two-shillings' worth of bread was subsequently given out four times a year. Elizabeth Cobb, by will dated 1809, bequeathed £72 net to the poor of Full Sutton.[13] The two bequests were used to buy £106 stock and the joint income in 1974 was over £1; in recent years the income has been allowed to accumulate and occasional grants in money or goods have been made to the sick and poor.[14]

David Beal, by will proved in 1853, bequeathed £60, the interest to be distributed in bread every third Sunday. In 1972 the income was over £1 from £61 stock; it was not distributed that year.[15] The dole shelf is now in the church vestry.

SUTTON UPON DERWENT

THE PARISH of Sutton upon Derwent lies about 7 miles south-east of York, on the east bank of the river.[1] The village stands on the slopes of the Escrick moraine, which is broken here by the Derwent, and the situation of Sutton and Elvington on opposite banks of the river suggests that this was a natural crossing point from early times. The place-name, which indicates an Anglian settlement, had received its distinctive suffix by the 13th century. In the east of the parish 'Woodhouses' had come into existence by the later 12th century,[2] and a grange of Kirkham priory was established there. Another part of the parish was apparently known by the name Cathwaite. References to it as an appurtenance of Sutton manor occur in the 14th century;[3] an inhabitant of it was mentioned in 1447[4] and Cathwaite House in 1554;[5] and land formerly belonging to one Cathwaite was in the hands of the Crown in the 16th century.[6] The Beck, on the southern parish boundary, was said in 1323 to flow through Cathwaite,[7] and ground near the stream was called Cathards in 1850. The irregularly-shaped parish

[90] B.I.H.R., V. 1868/Ret. 181; V. 1877/Ret.; Bp. V. 1884/Ret.
[91] Ibid. V. 1615/CB.
[92] Ibid. ER. V/Ret. 1 f. 132d.; ER. V/Ret. 3 f. 24.
[93] Ibid. V. 1865/Ret. 197; Sheahan and Whellan, Hist. York & E.R. ii. 560.
[94] B.I.H.R., TER. I. Full Sutton 1770.
[95] Ibid. V. 1877/Ret.
[96] Yorks. Ch. Plate, i. 253.
[97] B.I.H.R.
[98] York Dioc. Regy., Consecration deed.
[99] E.R.R.O., MRP/1/7.
[1] G.R.O. Worship Returns, Vol. v, nos. 146, 2728, 3829, 4061.
[2] Ibid. no. 4188.
[3] B.I.H.R., V. 1865/Ret. 197.
[4] Local information.
[5] B.I.H.R., Schools index.
[6] Educ. of Poor Digest, 1094; Educ. Enquiry Abstract, 1096.
[7] B.I.H.R., V. 1865/Ret. 197.
[8] Returns relating to Elem. Educ. 794; directories.
[9] 11th Rep. Com. Char. 735, 745.
[10] Ex inf. Char. Com., Liverpool, 1974.
[11] Char. Com. files.
[12] B.I.H.R., PR. Full Sutton 1.
[13] Char. Com. files; 11th Rep. Com. Char. 744–5.
[14] Char. Com. files; ex inf. the rector, 1974.
[15] Char. Com. files.
[1] This article was written in 1974.
[2] P.N.E.R. Yorks. (E.P.N.S.), 189.
[3] C 135/198 no. 12; Cal. Inq. p.m. vi, p. 83; ix, p. 431.
[4] Cal. Pat. 1446–52, 56.
[5] Select 16th Cent. Causes in Tithe (Y.A.S. Rec. Ser. cxiv), 60.
[6] See p. 176.
[7] Hist. MSS. Com. 24, Rutland, iv, p. 85.

covers 3,681 a., of which Woodhouse accounts for 1,229 a.[8]

The river Derwent forms the entire western boundary of the parish, and on the south the boundary partly follows the Beck and a dike marking an abandoned course of the Derwent. Along the eastern boundary Sails beck flows towards the Beck, and Blackfoss beck separates the townships of Sutton and Woodhouse. Most of the parish lies at more than 25 ft. above sea-level, but lower ground borders the river and streams. The ridge of the moraine exceeds 50 ft. in the north of Sutton township. The moraine is capped with glacial sand and gravel, and most of the lower ground consists of outwash silt, clay, and sand, with alluvium alongside the streams.[9] The open fields of Sutton lay mainly on the slopes of the moraine, with meadows occupying the low riverside ground, and by the 18th century commons were restricted to the southern parts of the township, where they included South wood. Final inclosure took place in 1777. Much of the township was occupied by ancient inclosures, however, including an area around North wood. Woodhouse grange, too, was inclosed at an early period. These names suggest that woodland was extensive in the parish before medieval colonization, and the large Sutton wood still survives in the north of the township.

The road from York is carried over the Derwent by a bridge mentioned as early as 1396.[10] The bridge may have replaced a ferry recorded in 1368,[11] but another ferry (*passagium*) between 'the head' (*capud*) of Sutton and Wheldrake, mentioned in 1218,[12] was presumably situated south of the village. Near the Derwent bridge the road was said in the 18th century to be frequently damaged by flooding,[13] and it now occupies a raised causeway across the meadows. In Sutton the road divides, one branch forming the main village street and continuing towards Melbourne, crossing the Beck at Hagg bridge.[14] The other branch leads through Woodhouse and on towards Barmby Moor. It crosses Blackfoss beck by Sandhill bridge, presumably the 'Wandebrugg' mentioned in 1252 and the Woodhouse or Foss bridge recorded in 1370.[15] The road was improved at that point in the 1950s and the bridge rebuilt.[16] Another road leads northwards along the moraine to Newton upon Derwent, and in Woodhouse a minor road formerly leading into Thornton[17] survives only as a field road.

The river Derwent was improved for navigation in the early 18th century, but the cut and lock near Sutton mill are on the Elvington bank.[18] A Sutton dealer used the river in 1807,[19] and there was a landing-place in Sutton, near the bridge, in 1850.[20] A cut was made across the neck of a sharp meander near the village in the 20th century.[21] In the south of the township Bank island marks an earlier change in the river's course; the 10-acre Banks close was already in 1690 'environed and compassed' by the river.[22]

Most of the houses in Sutton village are loosely strung out for about a mile along the road leading from the bridge towards Melbourne; a few others stand on the Woodhouse road. The church lies at the northern end of the village, on the edge of the Derwent flood plain, together with the manor-house and mill-house, and there was a chalybeate spring called Spa well near by. From the village street a track known as Rake Lane formerly led to the riverside meadows.[23] The most noteworthy of the 18th- and 19th-century cottages and farm-houses are Derwent and Glebe Farms; both have internal chimney plans and may be of the late 17th century in origin. Cherry Farm has a wheelhouse. There are 20 council houses, about 10 houses built by the Crown, mostly in the 1950s, and some 30 private houses contributing to the recent expansion of the village. A village hall was built in 1929–31.[24]

There was at least one alehouse in Sutton in the early 18th century[25] and two or three licensed houses later in the century.[26] By 1823 the Cross Keys and the Ram's Head were in existence. The latter was replaced by the Clarges Arms by 1840 and renamed the St. Vincent Arms by 1879.[27] The Cross Keys closed *c.* 1970 and a newly-built house on the site was opened in 1974 as Turpin's Tavern.[28]

The four or five isolated farm-houses in Sutton township include Sutton Farm, south of the village, which was sometimes called Sutton Hall,[29] and St. Loys, standing near the river north of the village.[30] About 500 yd. south of St. Loys, in Sutton wood, is the so-called Giant's Hill, which may be the site of a small moated homestead.[31] Of the three scattered farm-houses in Woodhouse township, Woodhouse Grange may stand near the site of the former monastic grange. It is not known whether 'Woodhouses' comprised a distinct hamlet in the 12th century before the grange was established. Two of the Woodhouse farm-houses, together with St. Loys, already existed before inclosure in 1777.[32]

There were 94 poll-tax payers at Sutton in 1377.[33] In 1672 57 households were included in the hearth-tax return, 7 of them exempt. Of those that were chargeable 43 had only one hearth each, 4 had 2 or 3, and 3 had six.[34] There were 40 families in the parish in 1743[35] and 38 in 1764.[36] The population in 1801 was 274, rising to 417 in 1831; it fell to 299 in 1891

---

[8] O.S. Map 6" (1854 edn.). Most of the parish is on sheet 192, the rest on sheet 175.
[9] Geol. Surv. Map 1", solid and drift, sheet 71 (1973 edn.).
[10] See p. 12.
[11] C 135/198 no. 12.
[12] C.P. 25(1)/262/13 no. 34.
[13] E.R.R.O., QSF. Mids. 1736, B.12; Christ. 1743, B.5; Mids. 1784, B.2; Christ. 1790, E.10.
[14] See p. 181.
[15] *Yorks. Fines, 1246–72*, p. 82; *Public Works in Med. Law*, ii (Selden Soc. xl), 337.
[16] R.D.B., 896/60/46; E.R.C.C. *Mins.* 1950–1, 509.
[17] T. Jefferys, *Map of Yorks.* (1772); see p. 181.
[18] See pp. 13, 149–50.
[19] B. F. Duckham, *Inland Waterways of E. Yorks. 1700–1900* (E. Yorks. Loc. Hist. Ser. xxix), 52.
[20] O.S. Map 6" (1854 edn.).
[21] Ibid. (1911 and later edns.).
[22] E.R.R.O., DDFA/16/1.
[23] O.S. Map 6" (1854 edn.).
[24] Stone on building.
[25] E.R.R.O., QSF. Christ. 1717, C.14; Christ. 1725–6, C.8; Mids. 1729, G.1.
[26] Ibid. QDT/2/15.
[27] Directories.
[28] Local information.
[29] e.g. R.D.B., 823/58/52.
[30] See p. 176.
[31] Ex inf. Royal Com. on Historical Monuments, York, 1974.
[32] Jefferys, *Map Yorks.*
[33] E 179/202/59 m. 58.
[34] E 179/205/504.
[35] *Herring's Visit.* iii. 111.
[36] B.I.H.R., Bp. V. 1764/Ret. 62.

and stood at 313 in 1901.[37] Numbers fluctuated in the 20th century, falling as low as 270 in 1931 but reaching 353 in 1971.[38]

MANOR AND OTHER ESTATES. In 1086 there were two estates of 6 carucates at Sutton upon Derwent. The first consisted in 1066 of 5 carucates held by Bernulf and Norman and one held by Segrida. Picot de Percy held the whole estate under William de Percy in 1086.[39] The overlordship descended in the main branch of the Percy family.[40] The second estate was held in 1066 by Orm, Colgrim, Ulf, and Game, and in 1086 Niel Fossard held it of the count of Mortain.[41] In the 12th century the estate was apparently held from William Fossard by William Aguilon.[42] The overlordship later passed to the Mauley family and was still mentioned in 1384. Anketin Malore had a mesne lordship in 3 carucates of it in 1284–5.[43]

Picot de Percy and succeeding demesne lords of the manor of SUTTON UPON DERWENT were members of a minor branch of the Percys whose chief estates lay in Bolton Percy (Yorks. W.R.), Carnaby, and Sutton.[44] The manor comprised both the Percy and the Mauley estates.[45] After the death of Peter de Percy in 1315 the manor was held successively by his father Robert and Robert's wife Beatrice.[46] By 1336, however, Peter's surviving heir Eustacia had come of age and held it with her husband Walter of Heslerton.[47] After Walter's death in 1349 and during the minority of his son, another Walter, the manor was in the possession of Thomas Ughtred, Martin of Skerne, and Walter de Cotes until Eustacia, an idiot, died.[48] The younger Walter died in 1367,[49] and in 1394 livery of the manor was granted to Ralph Neville, earl of Westmorland (d. 1425), cousin and heir of Walter's widow Euphemia.[50]

Like Scoreby[51] the manor was held by the Nevilles and after the partition of the earl of Warwick's estates in 1474 by the duke of Gloucester.[52] On ascending the throne Richard III kept it in hand and in the 1490s it was accounted for along with Sheriff Hutton (Yorks. N.R.).[53] In 1489 and later the Eglesfields were among those holding the bailiwick of the manor.[54]

In 1553 the Crown granted Sutton upon Derwent to John, duke of Northumberland, who was licensed to alienate it to John Eglesfield the same year.[55] In 1563 Eglesfield (d. 1566) bequeathed it to Sir Henry Gates, John Vaughan, John Herbert, and William Lakyn to the uses of his will. He was succeeded by his sisters Mary, wife of Andrew Milner, and Margaret Wallis, widow.[56] The Wallis and Milner shares were acquired in 1567 and 1570 respectively by John Vaughan.[57] The Vaughans held the manor until 1649, when it was conveyed to Sir Thomas Fairfax.[58]

Fairfax sold the manor in 1661 to George Monck, duke of Albemarle.[59] George's son Christopher, duke of Albemarle (d. 1688), left his estates in trust to several kinsmen and Sutton upon Derwent passed to one of them, Sir John Granville, created earl of Bath (d. 1701). Granville's grandson W. H. Granville, the 3rd earl, died in 1711 without issue and his estates passed to his aunts Catherine Peyton, Grace Carteret, and Jane Leveson-Gower. In 1731 Grace and Jane's son John Leveson-Gower, created Earl Gower, conveyed the manor to Sir Thomas Clarges (d. 1759).[60] Clarges's grandson Sir Thomas (d. 1783) was awarded 752 a. at inclosure in 1777,[61] and another Sir Thomas (d. 1834) had 1,955 a. in Sutton in 1823.[62] From the Clarges family the manor passed in 1857 to C. R. J. Jervis, subsequently Viscount St. Vincent (d. 1879).[63] The estate comprised 2,432 a. in 1929.[64] About 500 a. were sold by R. G. J. Jervis (b. 1905), 7th Viscount St. Vincent, in 1947,[65] and 1,744 a. more in 1948 to the Crown,[66] which already owned Woodhouse Grange.[67]

Robert de Percy had licence to crenellate his house at 'Sutton' in 1293[68] and the manor-house was probably mentioned, as 'le maners' in the park, in 1309.[69] It was certainly recorded in 1368.[70] The park had been mentioned as early as 1280[71] and ground south of the manor-house is still called the Park. It may have been in the manor-house, moreover, that the chapel was located where Aubrey, widow of Robert de Percy, was licensed to have a chaplain in 1232.[72] In 1314 Aubrey, daughter of Robert de Percy, was granted an oratory in the manor-house.[73] In the 19th century the manor-house, close to the church, was often called Manor Farm, and the lords of the manor usually lived at Sutton Hall, or Sutton Farm, an isolated house south of the village.[74] The hall was sold by Lord St. Vincent to Ena Meadowcroft in 1947.[75] Manor Farm dates from the 18th century.

[37] V.C.H. Yorks. iii. 493.
[38] Census.
[39] V.C.H. Yorks. ii. 262.
[40] e.g. Cal. Inq. p.m. i, p. 205; x, pp. 181–2; Feud. Aids, vi. 145.
[41] V.C.H. Yorks. ii. 226.
[42] Cal. Chart. R. 1327–41, 365.
[43] Cal. Close, 1381–5, 491–2; Feud. Aids, vi. 44.
[44] E.Y.C. xi, p. 10; see V.C.H. Yorks. E.R. ii. 126.
[45] e.g. Feud. Aids, vi. 44, 145; Cal. Inq. p.m. i, p. 205; ii, p. 171; vi, p. 237; xv, p. 321.
[46] Cal. Inq. p.m. vi, pp. 83, 237.
[47] Yorks. Fines, 1327–47, p. 95.
[48] Cal. Inq. p.m. ix, p. 431; xii, p. 125.
[49] Ibid. x, pp. 181–2.
[50] Cal. Close, 1392–6, 192; D.N.B.
[51] See p. 160.
[52] Cal. Pat. 1467–77, 581.
[53] D.L. 29/650/10510.
[54] Ibid.; Cal. Fine R. 1485–1509, pp. 95–6, 168; Cal. Pat. 1452–61, 582; L. & P. Hen. VIII, i (1), p. 95; i (2), p. 1464; v, p. 177; xiv (1), p. 262; N. Country Wills, i (Sur. Soc. cxvi), 281.
[55] Cal. Pat. 1553, 180, 274.
[56] C 142/144 no. 136; C 142/177 no. 58; Cal. Pat. 1560–3, 581.
[57] Yorks. Fines, i. 343, 381.
[58] C.P. 25(2)/612/1649 East. pt. 2, no. [6].
[59] C.P. 43/312 rot. 8.
[60] E.R.R.O., DDX/31/178, 182–3, 188; Burke, Peerage (1967), 2422; Burke, Dorm. & Ext. Peerages (1883), 243; Burke, Ext. & Dorm. Baronetcies (1844), 117.
[61] R.D.B., BB/4/4; Burke, Ext. & Dorm. Baronetcies, 117.
[62] E.R.R.O., DDX/31/204; Burke, Ext. & Dorm. Baronetcies, 117.
[63] R.D.B., HQ/135/164; Burke, Peerage (1967), 2211.
[64] R.D.B., 594/407/324.
[65] e.g. ibid. 760/369/304; 761/369/303.
[66] Ex inf. Crown Estate Comrs., Bracknell, 1974.
[67] See below.
[68] Cal. Pat. 1292–1301, 6, 14.
[69] E.R.R.O., DDWB/16/1.
[70] C 135/198 no. 12.
[71] Reg. Wickwane, p. 86.
[72] Reg. Gray, p. 55.
[73] Reg. Greenfield, iii, p. 238.
[74] Directories.
[75] R.D.B., 823/58/52.

That part of Sutton upon Derwent known as Woodhouse was given by Picot de Percy (d. by 1135) and others to Kirkham priory.[76] Shortly before the Dissolution the priory let the property to Thomas Manners, earl of Rutland.[77] After passing to the Crown Woodhouse Grange was granted in 1558 to the Savoy hospital, London,[78] and in the 16th and 17th centuries it was often leased by the Constable family.[79] The hospital was dissolved in 1702[80] and its property reverted to the Crown. The Coore family were lessees in the late 18th and early 19th centuries.[81] Woodhouse Grange, which comprised 1,168 a. in 1785,[82] still belonged to the Crown in 1974.

Land in Sutton worth £6 13s. 4d. which belonged to one Cathwaite was forfeited to the Crown before 1526 and granted to a succession of life tenants. In 1553 the reversion was granted to John, duke of Northumberland,[83] and the estate was thus united with the manor.

Small estates in Sutton were held by Thicket priory,[84] the Knights Hospitallers, Wilberfoss priory, and Warter priory. The Hospitallers' land was briefly regranted to them by the Crown in 1558.[85] Wilberfoss priory was licensed in 1483 to acquire land in Sutton worth £6 13s. 4d., and the former estate of Robert Hoton was granted by the Crown.[86] The former priory estate amounted to 9 bovates in 1539,[87] and in 1605 the property was in dispute between Sir Henry Vaughan, lord of the manor, and Sir Henry Lindley and John Starkey.[88]

The former Warter priory land was granted by the Crown to Thomas Manners, earl of Rutland, in 1541.[89] It had been disposed of by 1591, when it belonged to Francis Vaughan and comprised a house called St. Loys, a close in which the house stood, and a wood.[90] The name St. Loys was first recorded in 1577[91] and presumably derives from St. Eloy, or Aloysius. After 1591 the estate apparently descended with the manor and in 1964, comprising 159 a., it was sold by the Crown to T. E. Almond.[92] The house stands near a prominent moated site. The main range is at least of 17th-century origin and was timber-framed. Early in the 18th century the walls were rebuilt in brick, and later in the same century a wing was added on the west.

ECONOMIC HISTORY. In 1086 the Percy estate at Sutton upon Derwent had land for 3½ ploughs, but Picot de Percy then had one plough and 11 villeins had three. There were also 3 fisheries. The value of the estate had decreased from £1 16s. in 1066 to £1. The Mortain estate also had land for 3 ploughs, but Niel Fossard then had one plough and 6 villeins and 4 bordars had three. The estate was worth £1 in both 1066 and 1086.[93]

The manor of Sutton included 323 a. of arable and 62 a. of meadow in demesne in 1368. Free rents were of little value, but tenants-at-will paid nearly £13 and cottagers over £2, and there were seven grassmen in Cathwaite. The total value of the manor, £35, also included a small wood called the park, a pasture in Cathwaite called 'Sonetwylwes', and a fishery.[94] The park had been mentioned as early as 1280, when the rector confirmed a grant to Robert de Percy of two spinneys there called Parson bushes, as well as ground called 'Farneford'.[95] In 1309 the park was again mentioned and 'Farneforth' was described as a laund, or woodland clearing. The reclamation of new land is also indicated by 46½ a. in the Riddings in South field, and other land lay in North and East fields.[96] Hall Riddings survives as the modern name of closes south-east of the village.[97] The medieval fishery was doubtless in the river Derwent, and the Percies also claimed common fishing rights in Alemar, in Wheldrake, before 1218, when they were surrendered to Fountains abbey.[98]

In the Middle Ages most of the surviving woodland lay in the territory of Kirkham priory's grange at Woodhouse. In 1252 the prior and Peter de Percy agreed that each of them should take timber from different areas of woodland, but that they both should hunt and enjoy pannage in all the woods. Mention was made of the prior's croft, park, and field at Woodhouse.[99] A confirmation in 1336 of earlier grants to the priory referred to the toft which the canons had dug and built in their wood.[1] The woods at Woodhouse were mentioned again in 1559,[2] and timber was being felled there in the 1660s by Josias Prickett of Allerthorpe, a sub lessee of the Constables.[3]

In Sutton itself little is known of the open fields in the 16th and 17th centuries, but more of the riverside meadows and the common pastures. The meadows included several used in common. Others were inclosed and in the early 18th century there were a dozen of them, including the Mask or Marsh, the Swallow, the Dimple, and Wildgoose hill.[4] The last-named no doubt indicates the winter use made by wildfowl of the flooded ings, as in Wheldrake.[5] The Marsh was first referred to in 1554, when a single tenant was stocking it. Earlier, however, it had been leased by the inhabitants at large and fed with up to 200–300 animals from April to July and 90 from August to November. The latter number included 20 belonging to the occupier of the manor and 4 to the rector, together with 2 for each husbandman and one for each grassman; there were

---

[76] *Cal. Chart. R. 1327–41*, 365; *Whitby Charty.* ii (Sur. Soc. lxxii), 707.
[77] E.R.R.O., DDEV/1/10.
[78] *Cal. Pat. 1557–8*, 361.
[79] E.R.R.O., DDEV/1/7, 9, 16, 21, 29, 34, 39; /50/16; *Royalist Composition Papers*, iii (Y.A.S. Rec. Ser. xx), 14.
[80] *V.C.H. London*, i. 547.
[81] E.R.R.O., DDJ/34/86; Land Tax 1783 etc.
[82] M.P.E. 529.
[83] *L. & P. Hen. VIII*, iv (1), p. 955; iv (2), p. 1386; x, p. 156; xvi, p. 53; *Cal. Pat. 1550–3*, 51, 180.
[84] *Valor Eccl.* (Rec. Com.), v. 94.
[85] *Miscellanea*, iv (Y.A.S. Rec. Ser. xciv), 103; *Cal. Pat. 1557–8*, 319.
[86] *Cal. Pat. 1476–85*, 375.
[87] S.C. 6/Hen. VIII/4522.
[88] E 134/3 Jas. I Mich./27.
[89] *L. & P. Hen. VIII*, xvi, p. 325.
[90] E 178/1321.
[91] Petworth House Archives, no. 1417.
[92] R.D.B., 1366/480/446; /482/447.
[93] *V.C.H. Yorks.* ii. 226, 262.
[94] C 135/198 no. 12.
[95] *Reg. Wickwane*, p. 86.
[96] E.R.R.O., DDWB/16/1.
[97] O.S. Map 6" (1854 and later edns.).
[98] *Yorks. Fines, 1218–31*, pp. 7–8.
[99] *Yorks. Fines, 1246–72*, p. 82.
[1] *Cal. Chart. R. 1327–41*, 365.
[2] E.R.R.O., DDEV/1/7.
[3] Ibid. DDEV/1/40; see above.
[4] B.I.H.R., PR. Sutton on Derwent 2.
[5] See p. 121.

STAMFORD BRIDGE: the former water-mill

SUTTON UPON DERWENT: the disused water-mill
Elvington lock is on the right

SUTTON UPON DERWENT: fragment of an 11th-century cross-shaft

STILLINGFLEET CHURCH: the south doorway

said to be 20 or more tenants in each of those categories. The Marsh was sometimes flooded in winter.[6] The common meadows in the late 17th century included Town, Stock, and Grass carrs, Kirk ing, and Town Norlands or Northlands.[7] Of the common pastures South wood was mentioned in 1554,[8] and in the late 17th century the rector had cow-gates there and ox-gates in Wynam Bottom. In Woodhouse two men occupied their own moors or commons, but the rector was entitled to take turves there.[9]

Some inclosure evidently took place in the mid 16th century, for in 1605 it was recalled that John Eglesfield had taken seven closes out of the open fields and three from the common.[10] By the later 18th century the remaining open-field land lay in High, Prickett Gate, Stone Breach or Breck, and Moor Land fields.[11] The open fields and common meadows and pastures were inclosed in 1777[12] under an Act of 1776.[13] A total of 780 a. were allotted and there were stated to be 1,618 a. of ancient inclosures in the township, c. 200 a. of which were the subject of exchanges under the award. Allotments of 54 a. were made from Prickett Gate field, 61 a. from Stone Breck field, 56 a. from High field, and 57 a. from Moor Land field. Allotments from the meadows comprised 34 a. in Low grounds, 5 a. in the carr, and 6 a. in Northlands, and those from the common pastures amounted to 177 a. in the moor, 208 a. in South wood, and 122 a. in Wynam Bottom. Sir Thomas Clarges as lord of the manor received 752 a. of new and 14 a. of ancient inclosures, the rector got 185 a. of ancient inclosures, and Robert Wilberfoss got 30 a. all told. At Woodhouse there were two farms, of 505 a. and 663 a., in 1785; each included much land described as 'common', but there was little woodland.[14]

In the 19th and 20th centuries there have usually been a dozen farms in Sutton township and 2 in Woodhouse. In 1851 2 of those in Sutton were of over 300 a. and 6 over 150 a., while of the 3 in Woodhouse that year one exceeded 500 a. and one 200 a.[15] In the 1930s 8 farms in Sutton and one or two in Woodhouse were of 150 a. or more.[16] There were 1,084 a. under crops at Sutton in 1801, including 387 a. of oats, 202 a. of turnips or rape, and 186 a. of wheat.[17] In 1905 there were 2,274 a. of arable, 1,123 a. of grass, and 113 a. of woodland.[18] At Woodhouse in 1844 arable amounted to 460 a., grass to 232 a., heath to 122 a., and wood to 168 a., and roads and wastes covered 87 a.[19] An area of rough pasture there was known as the Warren in 1850.[20] In the 1930s and later arable land mainly occupied the higher ground and there was still extensive grassland alongside the Derwent and the becks.[21] Since 1953 98 a. of woodland, mostly in Sutton wood, have been managed by the Forestry Commission.[22]

In 1332 Walter of Heslerton was alleged to have obstructed the passage of boats by raising two weirs in the Derwent at Sutton,[23] and a fishery belonging to the manor continued to be recorded in the 17th century and later.[24] Salmon-poaching at Sutton was alleged in 1729[25] and a fisherman was among the inhabitants in 1851.[26] There were salmon 'hecks', or gratings, beside the water-mill in the 19th century.[27] Other men in non-agricultural employment included a lime and coal merchant (who was also the miller) and a timber merchant in the early 19th century,[28] and there was a brickworks at Woodhouse in the 1840s and 1850s.[29] From at least 1872 to 1905 the publican at the Clarges, later the St. Vincent, Arms was also a brewer, there was an agricultural implement maker in the late 19th and earlier 20th centuries, and a motor garage and refreshment rooms appeared in the village in the 1920s and 1930s.[30]

A water-mill on Blackfoss beck was mentioned in 1252 and 1336,[31] and there was a windmill at Sutton in 1368.[32] The later water-mill was on the Derwent. An 'old mill race' was shown crossing the meadow called the Dimple in 1850,[33] but there is no evidence of a mill there and it is likely that Sutton mill has for long stood on its present site, south of the bridge.[34] In 1597 and later the manor was said to have 'three water-mills'.[35] This may have referred to the number of pairs of stones in the mill, but it may be significant that both before and after the mill was rebuilt in 1826–7 following a fire the grinding floor was divided into 'the flour mill end', 'the corn mill', and 'the country mill end'.[36] Then and later the mill had seven pairs of stones, two water-wheels, and in adjoining buildings a granary, a drying kiln, and a shelling mill. It was used until 1960 and subsequently became derelict.[37]

LOCAL GOVERNMENT. No manorial records and no parochial records before 1835 are known. Sutton joined Pocklington poor-law union in 1836[38] and Pocklington rural district in 1894.[39] It became part of the North Wolds district of Humberside in 1974.

[6] Select 16th Cent. Causes in Tithe, 60–66.
[7] B.I.H.R., TER. I. Sutton on Derwent 1663, 1685; E.R.R.O., DDX/185/14.
[8] Select 16th Cent. Causes in Tithe, 63.
[9] B.I.H.R., TER. I. Sutton on Derwent 1663, 1685.
[10] E 134/3 Jas. I Mich./27.
[11] B.I.H.R., TER. I. Sutton on Derwent 1764.
[12] R.D.B., BB/4/4.
[13] 16 Geo. III, c. 57 (Priv. Act).
[14] M.P.E. 529.
[15] H.O. 107/2351.
[16] Directories.
[17] 1801 Crop Returns.
[18] Acreage Returns, 1905.
[19] B.I.H.R., TA. 109AS.
[20] O.S. Map 6" (1854 edn.).
[21] [1st] Land Util. Surv. Map, sheet 27; 2nd Land Util. Surv. Map, sheet 699 (SE 64–74).
[22] Ex inf. Forestry Com., York, 1972.
[23] Cal. Inq. Misc. ii, pp. 320–1.

[24] e.g. C.P. 43/228 rot. 77; C.P. 43/904 rot. 23.
[25] E.R.R.O., QSF. Christ. 1729, C.1.
[26] H.O. 107/2351.
[27] E.R.R.O., DDX/31/204, 226.
[28] e.g. Baines, Hist. Yorks. (1823), ii. 393–4.
[29] H.O. 107/2351; O.S. Map 6" (1854 edn.); White, Dir. E. & N.R. Yorks. (1840), 247.
[30] Directories.
[31] Yorks. Fines, 1246–72, p. 82; Cal. Chart. R. 1327–41, 365.
[32] C 135/198 no. 12.
[33] O.S. Map 6" (1854 edn.).
[34] See plate facing p. 176.
[35] C 142/248 no. 4; C.P. 43/228 rot. 77; C.P. 43/904 rot. 23.
[36] E.R.R.O., DDX/31/226–7.
[37] K. J. Allison, E.R. Water-mills (E. Yorks. Loc. Hist. Ser. xxvi), 50 and plate 2.
[38] 3rd Rep. Poor Law Com. 169.
[39] Census.

CHURCH. Sutton church was first mentioned between 1161 and c. 1170, when it was given by Robert de Percy to Whitby abbey.[40] No vicarage was ordained, however, and the living remained a rectory. The advowson was in dispute between the abbey and Aubrey, widow of Robert de Percy, in 1233,[41] but Whitby presented in 1299 and 1305.[42] The abbey alienated the advowson to John Mowbray in 1367.[43] At the death in 1419 of William Mowbray's widow Margaret, who had afterwards married William Cheyne, it passed to William Ingilby, son of the Mowbrays' daughter Eleanor.[44] It was perhaps the same William Ingilby who died in 1438 and was succeeded by his son John (d. 1456), whose heir was his son William. In 1473 the advowson was held by the king during William's minority. It was presumably the same William who died in 1501, and the advowson was subsequently held by John Ingilby (d. 1502).[45] In 1565 Sir William Ingilby conveyed it to John Eglesfield.[46] It passed the next year to Eglesfield's sisters, and their shares were acquired in 1567 and 1570[47] by John Vaughan. The advowson subsequently descended with the manor, though presentations were made by Miles Dodson, by grant from Sir Henry Vaughan, in 1625 and by Christopher Store in 1698.[48] Viscount St. Vincent still held it in 1972.[49]

The church was worth £10 13s. 4d. in 1291,[50] £13 6s. 8d. in 1367,[51] and £14 14s. 6d. net in 1535.[52] It was valued at £100 in 1650[53] and the average annual income in 1829–31 was £509 net.[54] The net income was £468 in 1884 and £366 in 1915.[55] Tithes accounted for the greater part of the income and produced £14 10s. in 1535.[56] For those in Sutton township, together with the glebe, the rector received an allotment of 185 a. and rent-charges of £58 4s. 5½d. at inclosure in 1777.[57] A modus of 1s. 6d. was still paid, however, for the tithes of Bank island in the 19th century.[58] The tithes of Woodhouse were commuted for £160 in 1844.[59]

Robert de Percy granted a toft, a croft, and 3 a. in the parish to the rector in 1280.[60] Glebe land and five cottages produced an income of under £2 in 1535.[61] In the late 17th and 18th centuries the glebe comprised 4 bovates, or 16 a., of open-field land, about 10 a. of meadow, 20 gates in the commons, and 6 cottages.[62] Glebe Farm, with 194 a., was sold to Lord St. Vincent in 1919.[63] The parsonage house was out of repair in the later 15th century.[64] The house mentioned from 1663 was rebuilt in 1726, and it contained three main ground-floor rooms, service rooms, and seven bedrooms in 1764.[65] The house was rebuilt in 1854–5 to designs by John Bownas and William Atkinson of York;[66] it is a substantial symmetrically-planned building of brick and slate.

Robert of Appleton, rector, was appointed in 1294 to manage the secular affairs of Wilberfoss priory.[67] John Favour, rector 1625–50, was a Puritan,[68] and Josiah Holdsworth was ejected from the rectory in 1662.[69] The rector was resident in the 18th and 19th centuries, but he was also curate of Wilberfoss in 1743 and John Sarraude held Elvington rectory in 1764 and Coleby (Lincs.), too, at his death in 1800. The rector employed an assistant curate in 1865.[70] Since 1972 the rector of Elvington has been curate-in-charge of Sutton.[71]

Two services were held at Sutton each Sunday in 1743, and Holy Communion was celebrated 4 times a year, with 52 communicants the previous Easter.[72] There was only one service a week in 1764, but again 2 by 1865, when about 12 people attended communion 6 times a year. Communion was celebrated monthly in 1868 and weekly in 1915.[73] In 1974 a service was held most Sundays.

The church of *ST. MICHAEL* is built of rubble and ashlar and consists of chancel with north vestry and organ chamber, aisled and clerestoried nave with south porch, and west tower. The western end of the chancel may be of the early 12th century and a wide arch in its north side must then have led to a transept or side chapel. The fabric of the nave that existed at that time has been largely removed by the addition of aisles. The three westernmost bays of both arcades date from the later 12th century, thus suggesting the length of the early nave, but the south is stylistically the earlier. The chancel, which is the same width as the nave, may have been rebuilt or extended in the 13th century. In the earlier 14th century the tower was built, the nave extended one bay to the west, the aisle walls rebuilt, and the porch added. The tower was largely rebuilt in the 15th century, and the nave was reroofed and provided with a clerestory and the chancel was refenestrated in the early 16th century.

The church was said to have been out of repair in 1676[74] and the east window could be of that date. The nave roof was probably renewed in the 18th century. Some repairs were carried out in 1841, when the chancel arch and the porch were rebuilt and the chancel roof may have been renewed; the north aisle was rebuilt in 1846.[75] A major restoration

---

[40] *E.Y.C.* xi, p. 117.
[41] *Reg. Gray*, p. 63.
[42] *Reg. Romeyn*, ii, p. 323; *Reg. Corbridge*, ii, p. 171.
[43] *Cal. Inq. Misc.* iii, p. 253.
[44] *Yorks. Inq. Hen. IV–V*, p. 155.
[45] e.g. C 139/90 no. 9; C 139/163 no. 11; *Cal. Pat. 1467–77*, 417; *Cal. Inq. p.m. Hen. VII*, ii, pp. 347, 353–4.
[46] *Yorks. Fines*, i. 306.
[47] Ibid. 325, 343, 374, 381; see above p. 175.
[48] Inst. Bks.; H.U.L., N.A.H. Lawrance, 'Clergy List', Harthill, 2 (ii), p. 240; B.I.H.R., Prec. Bk. 22.
[49] *Crockford* (1971–2).
[50] *Tax. Eccl.* (Rec. Com.), 303.
[51] *Cal. Inq. Misc.* iii, p. 253.
[52] *Valor Eccl.* v. 140.
[53] C 94/3 f. 57.
[54] *Rep. Com. Eccl. Revenues*, 970.
[55] B.I.H.R., Bp. V. 1884/Ret.; Bp. V. 1915/Ret.
[56] *Valor Eccl.* v. 140.
[57] R.D.B., BB/4/4.
[58] B.I.H.R., TER. I. Sutton on Derwent 1849 etc.
[59] Ibid. TA. 109AS.
[60] *Yorks. Fines, 1272–1300*, p. 33.
[61] *Valor Eccl.* v. 140.
[62] B.I.H.R., TER. I. Sutton on Derwent 1663 etc.
[63] R.D.B., 202/385/332.
[64] C 1/40 no. 228.
[65] B.I.H.R., TER. I. Sutton on Derwent 1663, 1743, 1764.
[66] Ibid. MGA. 1854/3.
[67] *Reg. Romeyn*, i, pp. xiii, 234.
[68] *Walker Revised*, ed. A. G. Matthews, 393; R. A. Marchant, *Puritans and Ch. Courts in Dioc. York 1560–1642*, 247, 323.
[69] *Calamy Revised*, ed. A. G. Matthews, 272.
[70] B.I.H.R., Bp. V. 1764/Ret. 62; V. 1865/Ret. 323; *Herring's Visit.* iii. 213; tablet in church.
[71] *Crockford*.
[72] *Herring's Visit.* iii. 112.
[73] B.I.H.R., Bp. V. 1764/Ret. 62; V. 1865/Ret. 323; V 1868/Ret. 479; Bp. V. 1915/Ret.
[74] Ibid. ER. V/CB. 4.
[75] Ibid. Ch. Ret. 1875; *Kelly's Dir. N. & E.R. Yorks.* (1872), 551; church guide.

took place in 1926–8, when the vestry was added, some walls rebuilt, the nave roof restored, and many new fittings put in.[76]

There is a fragment of an 11th-century cross shaft, with on one side a representation of the Virgin and Child, and a mutilated carved panel of St. George and the dragon, perhaps of the 14th century.[77] Monuments include a brass to Peter Cooke, rector (d. 1625), a tablet to James Blackbeard, rector (d. 1698), and one by Skelton of York (to George Beal, d. 1857).

There were three bells in 1764[78] and still three in 1974: (i) 1593; (ii) 1637; (iii) 1842, Thomas Mears of London.[79] The plate includes a 13th-century chalice and paten, discovered under the nave in 1927,[80] a silver cup and cover made in York in 1609 by Peter Pearson, two pewter plates dated 1723, and plated flagon and paten.[81] The registers of baptisms, marriages, and burials begin in 1593 and are complete.[82]

The churchyard was enlarged in 1922.[83]

NONCONFORMITY. Two recusants from Sutton were mentioned in 1669[84] and there was a Roman Catholic family in the village in 1764.[85]

A single Protestant dissenter at Sutton was reported in 1676.[86] The Methodists had 13–29 members there in 1789–1816,[87] and houses and barns were licensed for worship in 1784, 1815, 1820, 1830 (three), 1831, and 1846.[88] There was said to be a Methodist chapel in the village in 1823[89] and a Wesleyan chapel, said to have been built in 1838, was in use in 1851.[90] In 1865, however, there were c. 12 Wesleyans but no place of worship,[91] and a 'meeting-house' was used in 1872.[92] An iron Wesleyan chapel was built in 1882;[93] it was deregistered in 1937[94] and subsequently removed. A chapel was registered by the Primitive Methodists in 1861 but deregistered in 1876;[95] it was presumably the 'meeting-house' used by the Primitives in 1872.[96]

EDUCATION. A grammar school master at Sutton was mentioned in 1677 and a petty school master in 1698.[97] Schoolhouse garth was recorded in 1749.[98] There was a school with 33 pupils in 1819,[99] and a school begun in 1824 had 60 pupils in 1833, when it was partly supported by Sir Thomas Clarges and the rector, Clarges also providing a house.[1] A new building was erected in 1844, and in 1859 the average attendance was 44.[2] The school was united with the National Society.[3] An annual government grant was first received by 1850.[4] The school was enlarged c. 1906.[5] Attendance stood at 40–50 in 1906–14. It fell after the First World War but again reached c. 50 in 1926 and 1931, falling to 38 later in the 1930s.[6] Senior pupils were transferred to Pocklington in 1955.[7] The number on the roll in January 1974 was 30.[8]

CHARITIES FOR THE POOR. Thomas Wood, by will dated 1568, devised a rent-charge of £10 from an estate at Kilnwick Percy for the benefit of Sutton and many other townships. In 1824 5s. a year was distributed in Sutton.[9] Henry Frederick, Baron Hotham (d. 1967), owner of the Kilnwick Percy estate, redeemed the rent-charge in 1961 and £10 stock was subsequently assigned to Sutton.[10]

Thomas Wilberfoss (d. 1722) bequeathed £2 a year for the poor out of either Browney Hill close or 2 a. of meadow in West carr.[11] The income was distributed in bread in the late 19th century.

William Massey (d. c. 1849) bequeathed £10 for the poor and in 1854 his executors paid over the money to the rector and churchwardens.[12]

In 1972–3 the combined income of the three charities was £1 from £13 stock; money was given to two persons.[13]

THORNTON

The village of Thornton lies about 10 miles south-east of York, and with its townships of Melbourne and Storwood the parish occupies a large tract of low-lying ground around the Beck, the chief watercourse draining this part of the Vale of York.[1] Thornton, which was occasionally distinguished by the suffix 'in Spalding Moor', and Melbourne, the 'Middle Stream', were apparently Anglian settlements, but Storwood was Scandinavian. In the Middle Ages the hamlet was called Storthwaite, the 'brushwood inclosure', but the alternative name Storwood began to be used in the early 17th century. At Thornton the name Millhouse appeared in the 14th century,[2] and there was later an outlying

---

[76] B.I.H.R., Fac. Bk. x, pp. 611, 676, 699; *Y.A.J.* xxix. 237–41.
[77] *Y.A.J.* xxix. 238, 240, 326; see above plate facing p. 177.
[78] B.I.H.R., TER. I. Sutton on Derwent 1764.
[79] Boulter, 'Ch. Bells', 27.
[80] *Y.A.J.* xxix. 237.
[81] *Yorks. Ch. Plate*, i. 322–3.
[82] B.I.H.R.
[83] York Dioc. Regy., Consecration deed.
[84] *Depositions from York Castle* (Sur. Soc. xl), 171.
[85] B.I.H.R., Bp. V. 1764/Ret. 62.
[86] Bodl. MS. Tanner 150 ff. 27 sqq.
[87] E.R.R.O., MRP/1/7.
[88] G.R.O. Worship Returns, Vol. v, nos. 652, 2884, 3379, 4196–7, 4220, 4236, 4632.
[89] Baines, *Hist. Yorks.* ii. 393.
[90] H.O. 129/23/516.
[91] B.I.H.R., V. 1865/Ret. 323.
[92] *Kelly's Dir. N. & E. Yorks.* 551.
[93] Bulmer, *Dir. E. Yorks.* (1892), 718.
[94] G.R.O. Worship Reg. no. 26071.
[95] Ibid. no. 13745; E.R.R.O., MRP/4/76(d).
[96] *Kelly's Dir. N. & E.R. Yorks.* 551.
[97] B.I.H.R., Schools index.
[98] Ibid. TER. I. Sutton on Derwent 1749.
[99] *Educ. of Poor Digest*, 1094.
[1] *Educ. Enquiry Abstract*, 1096.
[2] Ed. 7/135 no. 177.
[3] *Returns relating to Elem. Educ.* 794.
[4] *Mins. of Educ. Cttee. of Council, 1849–50* [1215], p. cclxii, H.C. (1850), xliii.
[5] Y.A.S., MD. 217; E.R. Educ. Cttee. *Mins.* 1904–5, 283.
[6] Bd. of Educ. List 21 (H.M.S.O.).
[7] E.R. Educ. Cttee. *Mins.* 1955–6, 152.
[8] Ex inf. Chief Educ. Officer, County Hall, Beverley, 1974.
[9] *11th Rep. Com. Char.* 735, 744.
[10] Ex inf. Char. Com., Liverpool, 1974.
[11] *11th Rep. Com. Char.* 744; B.I.H.R., Bp. V. 1764/Ret. 62.
[12] Char. Com. files.
[13] Ibid.
[1] This article was written in 1974.
[2] *P.N.E.R. Yorks.* (E.P.N.S.), 184, 236.

A HISTORY OF YORKSHIRE: EAST RIDING

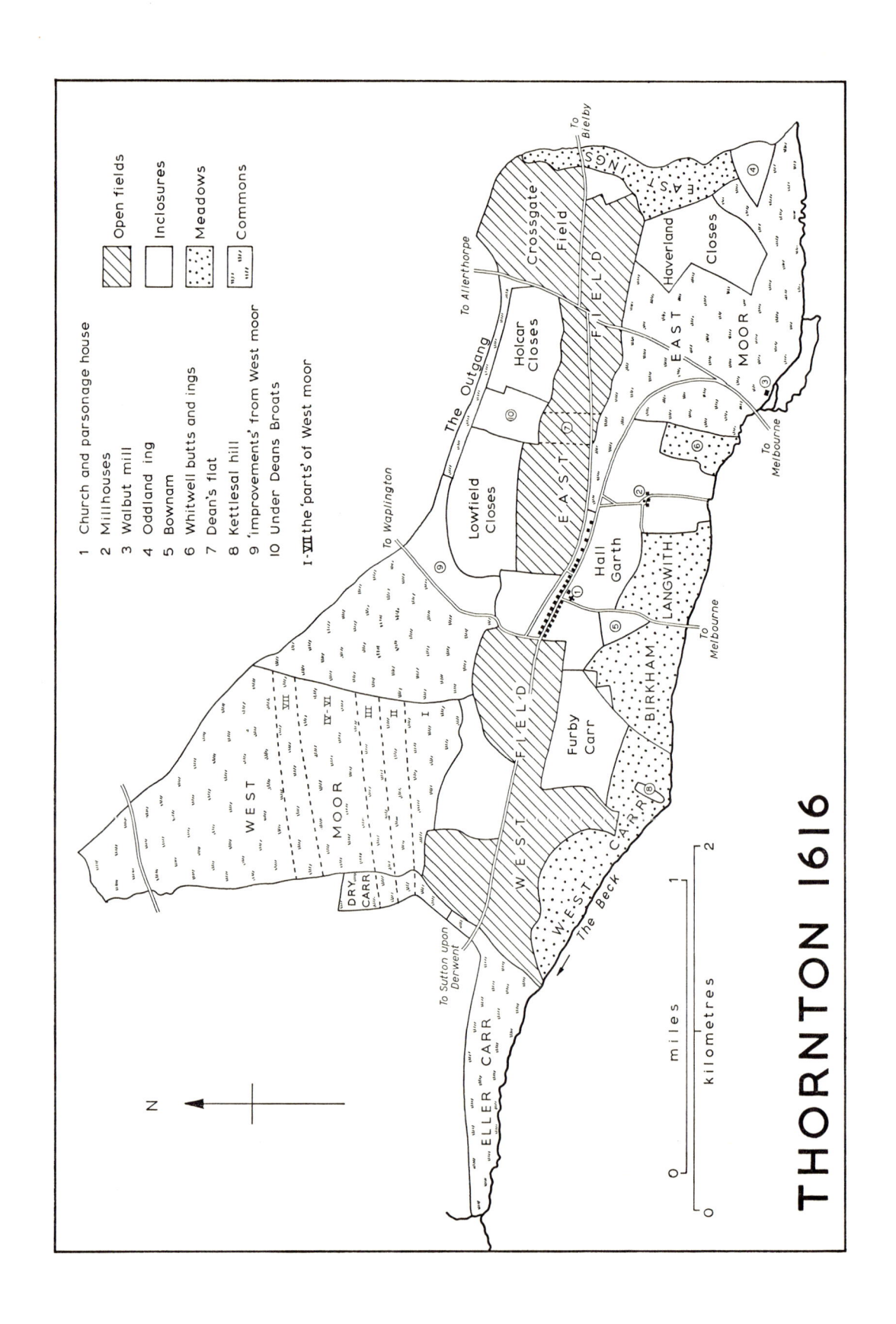

THORNTON 1616

Key:
- Open fields
- Inclosures
- Meadows
- Commons

1. Church and parsonage house
2. Millhouses
3. Walbut mill
4. Oddland ing
5. Bownam
6. Whitwell butts and ings
7. Dean's flat
8. Kettlesal hill
9. 'Improvements' from West moor
10. Under Deans Broats

I–VII the 'parts' of West moor

group of buildings known as Millhouses. The vill of 'Chetelstorp', probably in Storwood, was mentioned in 1086[3] but it was not recorded again and its site is unknown. The parish, irregular in shape, covers 6,684 a., of which Melbourne accounts for 3,148 a. and Storwood 1,222 a.[4] Several stretches of the parish boundary follow watercourses, among them the Beck, which also forms the boundary between Thornton and Melbourne townships. In Storwood the parish boundary with East Cottingwith follows Hacking and Newlands drains. For civil purposes Storwood was united with East Cottingwith in 1935.[5]

Throughout the parish the ground nowhere reaches 50 ft. above sea-level and large areas are below 25 ft. The settlements all stand on higher ground, Storwood close to the Beck but Melbourne ¼ mile and Thornton ½ mile from it. Much of the parish is covered with outwash sand, silt, and clay, but there is much alluvium on the lowest ground, alongside the Beck.[6] Thornton was described in 1797 as in general 'an entire sand and in most parts very light'.[7] The open fields of Thornton and Melbourne lay in the better drained sandy areas, with meadows and carrs on the wetter ground, and there were extensive common wastes in all the townships, including the huge Ross moor in Melbourne and Storwood on the heavier silts and clays. The open fields, commons, and meadows in Thornton were inclosed at various times from the 17th to the 19th century, and those of Melbourne and Storwood in 1782. Between 1940 and 1947 an area in the south-east of Melbourne was used as an airfield by the Royal Air Force.[8]

The drainage of the parish and the management of the Beck have long been a problem. In the 1320s flooding was caused by the neglect of drains further south in the Vale of York, as well as by interference with the stream at Walbut water-mill in Thornton, which also hindered road traffic across the Beck.[9] Frequent flooding of the road to Pocklington was referred to in 1415.[10] Flooding was again caused at Walbut mill in the 17th century, when the court of sewers ordered the construction of a new overflow channel.[11] Attempts to improve drainage in Thornton are suggested by the existence of Haverland dike, in the east of the township, in 1577.[12] Conditions were still bad in the 18th century, however, and it was said of the meadow land in Thornton in 1797 that 'for want of a better outfall, a great deal of it is very much injured'.[13] At the inclosure of the ill-drained waste in Melbourne in 1782 provision was made for five new drains on Ross and East moors.[14] Two land-drainers lived at Melbourne in 1851.[15] The lords of Thornton and Melbourne manors were in dispute over drainage in the 1850s,[16] and still in the 1880s the full rent of Park farm, Melbourne, was said to be unattainable 'until ... the undrained or imperfectly drained portion of the land was made dry'.[17]

Sir Henry Vavasour of Melbourne was a leading promoter of the Pocklington canal, which was constructed in 1816–18 alongside the entire length of the Beck in Thornton, Melbourne, and Storwood. There were three locks in the parish, and a short 'cut' branched from the canal towards Melbourne village. The canal, which carried mainly coal, fertilizers, corn, timber, and flour, was neglected after its purchase by the York & North Midland Railway in 1848. Little traffic passed beyond Melbourne by the 1890s and navigation was abandoned in the 1930s.[18]

Minor roads lead from Thornton village towards Sutton upon Derwent, Barmby Moor, Allerthorpe, Melbourne, and Bielby. The Sutton road, now called Field Lane, existed in 1616 but was only a farm road in 1974. The Barmby road apparently has a later origin. In 1616 the road running northwards from the west end of the village led instead to Waplington; by the mid 18th century its line had been moved westwards, and by 1851 it had been moved further west and its destination changed, probably at the inclosure of West moor. From the other end of the village two roads led eastwards in 1616, one continuing the line of the back lane towards Bielby, the other leading from the village street to join the Melbourne–Allerthorpe road, which crosses Thornton township. Part of the Bielby road was later stopped up, almost certainly at the inclosure of the open fields in the mid 18th century, and the second road was realigned at the inclosure of East moor at about the same time.[19] A high-backed brick bridge carries the road over the canal near Walbut mill. A more direct road to Melbourne runs southwards from the church at Thornton; it was called 'Melbourne church way' in 1577.[20] The north-west corner of Thornton township is crossed by the road from Sutton upon Derwent to Barmby, known in Thornton as the Street.

Two roads run east–west across Melbourne and Storwood townships, one through Melbourne village and the other further south; they are linked by half-a-dozen cross roads. West of the village the first of the chief roads was called 'Melbourne new road' in 1779,[21] possibly because of realignment during the inclosure then in progress. The road continues westwards to Hagg bridge, over the Beck, and so into Sutton upon Derwent. This was perhaps the bridge at Thornton which was being built of stone in the late 1420s by Nicholas Blackburn, a York merchant.[22] It was called Hagg bridge by 1735.[23] By 1806 the county was responsible for the bridge, which consisted of one brick arch in 1884. The adjoining brick bridge was built to carry the

---

[3] V.C.H. Yorks. ii. 269.
[4] O.S. Map 6", Yorks. (1854–5 edn.). Most of the parish appears on sheets 192–3 and a small part of Melbourne township on sheets 207–8. [5] Census.
[6] Geol. Surv. Map 1", solid and drift, sheet 71 (1973 edn.).
[7] Petworth House Archives, no. 3075.
[8] Ex inf. Ministry of Defence, London, 1973.
[9] Hist. MSS. Com. 24, Rutland, iv, p. 85; Cal. Pat. 1321–4, 373.
[10] Minster Libr., Torre MS., 'Peculiars', p. 718.
[11] June A. Sheppard, Draining of Marshlands of S. Holderness and Vale of York (E. Yorks. Loc. Hist. Ser. xx), 17. [12] Petworth Ho. Arch., no. 1417 f. 40.
[13] Ibid. no. 3075.
[14] R.D.B., BB/311/40. [15] H.O. 107/2351.
[16] Petworth Ho. Arch., no. 1095.
[17] E.R.R.O., DDCS/4/5.
[18] C. Hadfield, Canals of Yorks. and N.E. Eng. 328–33, 445; B. F. Duckham, Inland Waterways of E. Yorks. 1700–1900 (E. Yorks. Loc. Hist. Ser. xxix), 58–69. See above plate facing p. 161.
[19] Petworth Ho. Arch., nos. 3426, 3460; O.S. Map 6" (1854–5 edn.).
[20] Petworth Ho. Arch., no. 1417 f. 39d.
[21] E.R.R.O., QSF. East. 1779, A.
[22] Cal. Close, 1422–9, 410–11, 473; Y.A.J. iii. 241.
[23] E.R.R.O., QSF. Christ. 1735, B.5.

road over the canal in the 19th century. Eastwards the road leads into Thornton, crossing the Beck by the single brick arch of Walbut bridge, which as 'Melbourne bridge' was already being maintained by the county in the 1880s.[24]

As a through route from East Cottingwith to Seaton Ross the more southerly of the two chief roads already existed before the inclosure of the commons in 1782, but several straight sections of it were apparently newly laid out then. Some of the cross roads were also made at inclosure, either wholly or partly on new lines, and old roads across Ross moor from Ellerton and Foggathorpe were replaced. Storwood hamlet stands on the most westerly of the cross roads.[25]

Other minor roads in Melbourne include that running north to Thornton, which crosses the canal by Church bridge, another high brick structure with curving parapet walls. Several farm roads lead down to the canal and formerly crossed it by swing bridges, now fixed.

The 19th- and 20th-century houses of Thornton stand on both sides of a single village street, with the church towards the east end. Gardens in front of the houses represent the narrowing of the wide street that existed in 1616. There was also a back lane behind the northern row of houses in 1616 which was apparently stopped up at the inclosure of the open fields in the mid 18th century. There are eight council houses and a village hall. At Millhouses, just to the south-east of the village, there were ten houses in 1577 and thirteen in 1767, but by 1851 only one.[26] In the 18th century there were one or two licensed houses in Thornton.[27] The Plough existed in 1797,[28] and in 1851 and the 1870s the Grey Horse.[29] The half-dozen outlying farms in the township all date from after the 18th-century inclosures.

The straggling village of Melbourne, less than a mile south of Thornton, lies mostly along one street, though some recent houses stand to the south near the mission church and a few buildings are situated on the remnant of a former outgang into West field. Most of the houses date from the 19th and 20th centuries. They include an early-19th-century house with a central pediment, a symmetrical pair of lodges flanking a projected entrance to Melbourne Hall,[30] and Deanery Farm. A reading room, built in the late 19th century,[31] is now a private house; the present village hall stands on land acquired for the purpose in 1953.[32] Many houses and bungalows, including a dozen council houses, have been built in and around the village in recent years.

There were usually one or two, and occasionally three, licensed houses at Melbourne in the 18th century.[33] The Cross Keys inn was mentioned from 1823 onwards and still exists. The Blacksmith's Arms, mentioned from 1840, was called the Horse Shoes in 1850; it became the Melbourne Arms in the early 20th century but closed c. 1968.[34] A third inn, the Ross Moor, existed in 1840 and was perhaps renamed the Charles James Fox, which stood on the moor in 1850.[35]

The hamlet of Storwood, nearly 3 miles west of Melbourne, consisted of a dozen houses in the mid 18th century but only about six by 1850.[36] Apart from Storwood Manor[37] there were four houses in 1974. There was a licensed house at Storwood in the 18th century and an inn at Hagg bridge in 1850 and the 1870s. In 1890 the latter was called the Temperance Hotel.[38]

Most of the two dozen outlying farm-houses in Melbourne and Storwood date from after the inclosure of 1782, but Ball Hall, Park House, and East Wood (now Rossmoor Grange), all in Storwood, were then already in existence.[39] Melbourne Hall stands in parkland south of the village.[40] Rossmoor Lodge, built for Gen. James Wharton in 1816, is a large yellow-brick house with three projecting bays on the main front, which faces the former park.[41] Melbourne Grange has an early-19th-century central range extended by cross-wings with low-pitched gables of the later 19th century. Melbourne Lodges, an identical pair of red-brick houses, flank the road to Seaton Ross on the township boundary. The name Bibbill Farm derives from Bibbehale, 'Bibba's nook of land', which was referred to in the 13th century.[42] Other isolated buildings include those of a former prisoner-of-war labour camp in Storwood, opened in 1940.[43] Some of the former airfield buildings were used for agricultural purposes in 1974, while commercial development to the east of Melbourne village originally made use of others.

There were 83 poll-tax payers in Thornton township in 1377.[44] Forty-nine households were included in the hearth-tax return in 1672, of which 10 were not chargeable, 38 had a single hearth each, and one had 3 hearths.[45] There were 78 families in the parish in 1743 and 104 in 1764.[46] The population of Thornton alone was 217 in 1801; it remained at c. 200 until the mid century, but by 1901 it had fallen to 137.[47] It increased to 178 in 1951 but was only 145 in 1971.[48]

There were 143 poll-tax payers in Melbourne and Storwood in 1377,[49] and 68 households were included in the hearth-tax return in 1672, 16 of them exempt. Of those chargeable 52 had a single hearth, 4 had 2 each, and one had seven.[50] The

---

[24] E.R.R.O., QAB/1/24; /2/3; ex inf. Highways Dept., County Hall, Beverley, 1974.
[25] E.R.R.O., QSF. East. 1779, A; R.D.B., BB/311/40; T. Jefferys, *Map of Yorks.* (1772); O.S. Map 6" (1854–5 edn.).
[26] E.R.R.O., TA. Thornton; Petworth Ho. Arch., nos. 1417, 3460; O.S. Map 6" (1854–5 edn.).
[27] E.R.R.O., QSF. East. 1729, A.1; QDT/2/15.
[28] Petworth Ho. Arch., no. 3075.
[29] Directories; O.S. Map 6" (1854–5 edn.).
[30] Local information.
[31] *Kelly's Dir. N. & E.R. Yorks.* (1909), 599.
[32] Char. Com. files.
[33] E.R.R.O., QSF. Mids. 1716, C.16; QDT/2/12.
[34] Local information.
[35] Directories; O.S. Map 1/2,500, Yorks. CXCII. 11 (1910 edn.); O.S. Map 6" (1854–5 edn.).
[36] R.D.B., BB/311/40; O.S. Map 6" (1854–5 edn.).
[37] See p. 184.
[38] E.R.R.O., QDT/2/12; O.S. Map 6" (1854–5 edn.); 1/2,500, Yorks. CXCII. 11 (1892 edn.); directories.
[39] Jefferys, *Map Yorks.* (1772).
[40] See p. 184.
[41] R.D.B., 216/338/282; date and initials J.W. on rain-water head.
[42] *P.N.E.R. Yorks.* (E.P.N.S.), 236.
[43] E.R.R.O., DDMM/19/1.
[44] E 179/202/59 m. 79.
[45] E 179/205/504.
[46] B.I.H.R., Bp. V. 1764/Ret. 82; *Herring's Visit.* iii. 174.
[47] *V.C.H. Yorks.* iii. 491.
[48] *Census.*
[49] E 179/202/59 m. 42.
[50] E 179/205/504.

population of Melbourne rose from 308 in 1801 to 437 in 1821 and 568 in 1861, but had fallen to 356 by 1901. It remained about the same until 1931 but then rose to 499 in 1951; in 1971 it stood at 444. Storwood's population was 86 in 1801, rising to 119 in 1831 and falling to 76 in 1901. In 1931 it was 63.[51]

MANORS AND OTHER ESTATES. The 6-carucate estate in Thornton which Eddiva held in 1066 had passed to Ralph de Mortimer by 1086,[52] and its overlordship remained with the Mortimers until 1425.[53]

William de Vescy held 3 knight's fees in Spalding moor of Ralph de Mortimer in 1243[54] and his son John was dealing with THORNTON manor in 1275.[55] The property continued to descend in the Vescy family.[56] In 1289–90 and 1316 the 4-carucate estate was held by Clemence, wife of John de Vescy (d. 1295),[57] but before her death in 1343 it had apparently passed to Gilbert de Aton, descendant and heir of William de Vescy (d. 1183). In the early 14th century Gilbert conveyed property in Thornton and elsewhere to John de Mowbray,[58] who was returned as tenant in 1346.[59] By 1428, however, the Mowbrays had been succeeded by John, duke of Bedford,[60] and in 1489 the manor was held to the use of Henry Percy, 4th earl of Northumberland.[61] The property, which was regarded as a member of Wressle in 1577,[62] thereafter descended like Catton in the Percy, Seymour, and Wyndham families.[63] The Wyndham estate at Thornton, which consisted of 2,279 a. in 1897,[64] was broken up and sold in 1920–1.[65] The 403-acre Thornton Grange farm and the 141-acre Hall Garth farm were bought by Henry Stubbins in 1921,[66] and the Stubbins family have since acquired a further 200 a. which were formerly part of the Wyndham estate.[67]

In 1066 Eddiva had 6 carucates in Melbourne and another carucate in 'Chetelstorp'. These lands were held by Ralph de Mortimer in 1086.[68] Apart from an interruption in Edward III's reign, the overlordship remained with the Mortimers until 1425, when the family's earldom of March passed to Richard, duke of York.[69] The earldom was united with the Crown on the accession of Edward, earl of March, in 1461.[70] The overlordship was last mentioned in 1622.[71] The Vescy family were mesne lords in the late 13th century.[72]

Robert de Ros held land in Melbourne and Storwood in the early 13th century by a Vescy grant,[73] and his son William had a knight's fee there and elsewhere in 1243.[74] At his death c. 1285 William's son Robert held STORWOOD manor,[75] and the estate, comprising 6 carucates in Melbourne and Storwood in 1289–90, continued to descend in the main line of the Ros family.[76] Margery, widow of William, Lord Ros (d. 1343), held the manor as dower until her death in 1363.[77] Thomas, Lord Ros (d. 1384), held the estate jointly with his wife Beatrice, who died seised of it in 1415.[78] After Thomas, Lord Ros's attainder in 1461 the manor was granted for life to Ralph, Lord Greystoke, in 1468.[79] It may have been briefly regained that year, when it was settled on Thomas's son Richard.[80] Edmund de Ros was restored on Henry VII's accession. Edmund's sister Eleanor married Sir Robert Manners and at Edmund's death in 1508 the manor passed to her son Sir George Manners.[81]

The Manners family, earls of Rutland, held it[82] until the death of Elizabeth Manners in 1591, when her heir was her son William Cecil, Lord Ros.[83] Cecil died in 1618 and his uncle and heir Sir Richard Cecil[84] sold the manor to Sir Peter Chapman in 1620.[85] Chapman died seised of the manor of Storwood and Melbourne in 1622, leaving as coheirs John Bradley, William Blanshard, and Elizabeth Robinson, his nephews and niece. Blanshard and Elizabeth Robinson confirmed their purparties to Bradley,[86] whose son Peter later married an Elizabeth Robinson.[87] Sir Charles Bolle and John Bowles were involved in Bradley-Robinson settlements of the mid 17th century,[88] and it was by the terms of another John Bolle's will, dated 1727, that the manor passed to his niece Margaret Spencer and her husband William in 1735.[89] John Stephenson acquired an interest in the property in 1738 although it was not until 1761 that William Spencer released his remaining rights.[90] Sarah Stephenson devised the manor in 1775 to her cousin Elizabeth Danser, who had succeeded by the following year, and she sold it to John Walker in 1786.[91] The estate

[51] V.C.H. Yorks. iii. 491; Census.
[52] V.C.H. Yorks. ii. 269, 319.
[53] C 139/19 no. 32; Cal. Close, 1377–81, 87; Cal. Inq. p.m. iv, p. 162; x, p. 539; Feud. Aids, vi. 145, 167, 217, 268–9; Kirkby's Inquest (Sur. Soc. xlix), 254.
[54] E.Y.C. iii, p. 487.
[55] Yorks. Fines, 1272–1300, p. 5.
[56] For pedigree see Complete Peerage, s.v. Vescy.
[57] Kirkby's Inquest, 254, 309; Feud. Aids, vi. 167.
[58] Yorks. Fines, 1327–47, p. 93; Complete Peerage, s.v. Vescy.
[59] Feud. Aids, vi. 217; Parl. Rep. Yorks. i (Y.A.S. Rec. Ser. xci), 73.
[60] Feud. Aids, vi. 268–9.
[61] C 142/5 no. 14; S.C. 6/Hen. VIII/4283–91.
[62] Petworth Ho. Arch. no. 1417 f. 38d.
[63] See p. 151.
[64] R.D.B., 3/170/163 (1898).
[65] Ibid. 225/78/63; 231/94/76; /335/279; 232/137/118; /410/343; 233/31/26; /259/207; /460/377; 234/229/194; /232/195; /236/197.
[66] Ibid. 234/229/194.
[67] Ibid. 596/278/223; 1278/268/247.
[68] V.C.H. Yorks. ii. 269, 319.
[69] C 139/19 no. 32; C 139/50 no. 48; Kirkby's Inquest, 253; Feud. Aids, vi. 145, 217; Cal. Inq. p.m. iv, p. 162; viii, p. 335; x, p. 539.
[70] Complete Peerage, s.v. March.
[71] C 142/391 no. 79.
[72] Plac. de Quo Warr. (Rec. Com.), 189; Cal. Inq. p.m. ii, p. 345.
[73] Yorks. Fines, 1218–31, pp. 17, 107; Plac. de Quo Warr. 189.
[74] Bk. of Fees, ii. 1099.
[75] Yorks. Inq. ii, p. 35.
[76] Kirkby's Inquest, 253. For Ros pedigree see Complete Peerage, s.v. Ros.
[77] C 135/71 no. 19; Cal. Pat. 1343–5, 24; Cal. Inq. p.m. xi, p. 400.
[78] C 136/33 no. 7; C 138/245 no. 44.
[79] C 140/490 no. 50; Cal. Pat. 1461–7, 458; 1467–77, 115.
[80] Cal. Close, 1468–76, p. 48; Cal. Pat. 1485–94, 24.
[81] Complete Peerage, xi. 253; Burke, Dorm. & Ext. Peerages (1883), 460.
[82] N. Country Wills, i (Sur. Soc. cxvi), 185; ii (Sur. Soc. cxxi), 118; Yorks. Fines, ii. 68.
[83] C 142/257 no. 43.
[84] Wards 7/100 no. 96; C 142/429 no. 136.
[85] Yorks. Fines, 1614–25, 163.
[86] C 142/391 no. 79; Yorks. Fines, 1614–25, 197.
[87] Minster Libr., D. & C. Archives, T 2 (1).
[88] Ibid.; H.U.L., DRA/5, 12.
[89] R.D.B., M/461/758; O/204/496.
[90] Ibid. P/202/527; Q/131/308; /207/511; /366/936; R/23/54; AB/281/500; AD/4/9.
[91] Ibid. AU/533/1883; AW/359/627; BM/68/120.

was briefly divided by sales to Barnard Clarkson and Thomas Whitaker in 1790,[92] but was reunited when Henry Vavasour bought the parts in 1793 and 1797.[93] His grandson Sir H. M. Vavasour sold the manor in 1850 to James Christie,[94] and in 1890 the manor, Melbourne Hall, and over 1,900 a. were sold to Walter Cliff.[95] Charles Bedwell bought the estate from Cliff's executors in 1920.[96] The Bromborough Estate Co. bought the manor and about 1,400 a. in 1926,[97] but disposed of most of the estate in separate lots in the 1950s and 1960s.[98]

The Ros manor-house at Storwood was mentioned in 1285[99] and was described as ruinous in 1343;[1] the site, at the south end of the hamlet, is still surrounded by a prominent moat.[2] It may have contained a chapel, for in 1414 Beatrice de Ros left £20 for a chaplain to celebrate mass in Storwood chapel.[3] In 1639 John Bradley was living at Storwood, though apparently not in the manor-house.[4] The present Manor House is a mainly 19th-century building. By the late 18th century, however, the manor-house had been moved to Melbourne. Melbourne Hall was built soon after the inclosure of 1782; by 1790 the manorial estate included the 'lately erected' house and its gardens, as well as an adjacent piece of East moor planted with trees and presumably emparked.[5] The house was let intermittently during the 19th and early 20th centuries.[6] Together with its 71-acre park it was bought from Charles Bedwell by William Egerton in 1923,[7] and in 1940 the property passed to John Seed and his wife, the widow of Francis Egerton.[8] Melbourne Hall is a large red-brick house of two storeys, with three canted bay windows placed at the centre and ends of the south front. Its west front incorporates the original stable block, and the present stables to the north of the house date from the early 19th century.

The Ros family held Breighton manor as well as Storwood and Melbourne, and land in Melbourne became attached to Breighton. Thus in 1361 Sir James de Ros of Gedney (Lincs.) died seised of Breighton and rents from 6½ bovates in Melbourne held of Thomas, Lord Ros. Sir James's son Sir Robert succeeded to the properties[9] and died in 1381, leaving his brother Nicholas as his heir.[10] Breighton, apparently still with the land in Melbourne, passed like a manor in Hunmanby to the Paulets and Strangeways in the 16th century.[11] In 1544, however, the manor was granted by the Crown to Matthew, earl of Lennox, and his wife,[12] and in the early 17th century 167 a. of former Lennox land in Melbourne were let by the Crown.[13] The estate had passed to the archbishop of York by 1664.[14] The archbishop was awarded 140 a. at inclosure in 1782,[15] when his whole Melbourne estate comprised 314 a.[16] In the 1850s the archbishop and the Ecclesiastical Commissioners sold about 322 a. in Melbourne, some of it described as formerly belonging to Breighton manor; the largest sale, of about 137 a., was to James Christie.[17]

The chapter of York had an estate in Melbourne in the 18th century: they were awarded 23 a. at inclosure for their open-field land, and about 50 a. of old inclosed ground belonging to them were involved in exchanges.[18] Their lands probably included an unspecified amount bought in 1717 as a choir endowment.[19] In 1900 the chapter had 162 a. at Melbourne.[20] The estate was transferred to the Ecclesiastical Commissioners in 1938, and the Church Commissioners sold it as Deanery farm to J. H. Gibson in 1950.[21]

By the mid 19th century St. Peter's School, York, had an estate at Melbourne which was intermingled and administered with that of the chapter.[22] The school's 70-acre estate was sold in 1904 to Walter Cliff.[23]

Warter priory had a hermitage at Storwood in the 12th century.[24] In the 14th and 15th centuries the Ros profits at Storwood and Melbourne included £20 rent from the priory, part of it perhaps for property there.[25] Fountains abbey held a bovate in Thornton in 1428.[26]

From 1252 Thornton rectory belonged to the dean of York.[27] The tithes of Thornton and Melbourne were worth £30 and £32 a year respectively in 1650.[28] In 1802 the Thornton tithes were valued at £103,[29] and rent-charges of about £281 were awarded to the dean at their commutation in 1845.[30] The Melbourne tithes were commuted at inclosure in 1782 for 233 a. and rent-charges of about £4.[31] The tithes of corn, hay, wool, and lambs at Storwood were let for short terms from 1538 and for lives from the late 16th to the early 18th century, during which time they were held by the Constable family.[32] They were valued at £14 in 1650[33] and at their commutation in 1782 rent-charges of nearly £38 and 52 a. were awarded to the dean.[34]

---

[92] R.D.B., BG/271/32; BP/240/388.
[93] Ibid. BR/361/591; BY/226/354; C.P. 25(2)/1466 no. 395.
[94] R.D.B., GR/189/231; /200/235; GT/54/74.
[95] Ibid. 38/78/77 (1890).
[96] Ibid. 216/338/282.
[97] Ibid. 327/558/441; 504/114/87.
[98] Ibid. 861/515/432; 870/297/244; 992/336/296; 1054/80/67; 1057/514/460; 1242/199/179; 1326/296/273; 1328/76/74; 1351/420/377.
[99] *Yorks. Inq.* ii, p. 35.
[1] C 135/71 no. 40.
[2] H. E. Jean Le Patourel, *Moated Sites of Yorks.* 19, 116.
[3] *Test. Ebor.* i, p. 376.
[4] H.U.L., DRA/565.
[5] R.D.B., BB/311/40; BP/240/388.
[6] Directories.
[7] R.D.B., 273/67/50.
[8] Ibid. 1504/473/392; Burke, *Land. Gent.* (1952), 2281.
[9] *Cal. Inq. p.m.* xi, p. 165–6.
[10] Ibid. xv, p. 233.
[11] C 66/2964 mm. 23–7; C 139/106 no. 24; C 142/43 no. 56; *Yorks. Fines*, i. 89; *V.C.H. Yorks. E.R.* ii. 232–3.
[12] *L. & P. Hen. VIII*, xix (1), p. 627.
[13] E 310/33/198 no. 1.
[14] B.I.H.R., Bp. Dio. 2, p. 18.
[15] R.D.B., BB/311/40.
[16] B.I.H.R., CC. Ab. 10 Thornton, 63366.
[17] R.D.B., HM/322/387; HO/403/486; HU/401/517; /403/518; HW/298/362.
[18] Ibid. BB/311/40.
[19] Minster Libr., D. & C. Arch., T 2 (3) b.
[20] St. Peter's Sch., York, TD. 33.
[21] R.D.B., 848/502/435; Minster Libr., D. & C. Arch., Order in Council, 1938.
[22] Minster Libr., D. & C. Arch., P 2 (5) (letter of 1869).
[23] R.D.B., 70/387/367 (1904).
[24] *E.Y.C.* x, pp. 117–18, 122–4.
[25] C 139/50 no. 48; *Cal. Close*, 1381–5, 488–9.
[26] *Feud. Aids*, vi. 268–9.
[27] See p. 187.
[28] C 94/3 f. 56.
[29] Minster Libr., D. & C. Arch., T 2 (3) a.
[30] E.R.R.O., TA. Thornton.
[31] R.D.B., BB/311/40.
[32] Minster Libr., D. & C. Arch., S 3 (5) a, f. 8; Torre MS., 'York Minster', p. 547; E.R.R.O., DDEV/50/121, 126.
[33] C 94/3 f. 53.
[34] R.D.B., BB 311 40.

The rectorial glebe consisted c. 1613 of 38 a. in Hall garth, 14 a. in East field, and 7 a. in the ings, all in Thornton. It included land granted to the dean, probably at an early date,[35] in lieu of certain tithes: he was thus entitled to take the forecrop from Kettlesall hill in the west ings 'in consideration of the tithe hay of all the lord's common meadow grounds . . . and land ends' in Thornton, and he was similarly restricted to the first crop in East field and East ings.[36] The glebe at Thornton still consisted of 60 a. in the early 19th century.[37]

In 1844 the rectorial estate was vested in the Ecclesiastical Commissioners,[38] who sold all 233 a. in Melbourne to James Christie in 1854[39] and the land in Thornton to George Wyndham in 1857.[40] A house stood in Hall garth c. 1613[41] and an early-19th-century description of the dean's farm at Thornton mentions Rectory House in the garth; the house was not referred to in 1857.[42]

ECONOMIC HISTORY. There was land for three ploughs at Thornton in 1086 but the estate, which had been worth 14s. before the Conquest, was then waste.[43] Subsequent reclamation is undocumented, but by 1225 land in the field to the north of the chapel was mentioned, together with probable meadow land at 'Keteleshal'.[44]

The manor was worth about £29 in the 1530s and 1540s, the tenants' rents amounting to nearly £26 and the farm of the water-mill to £3.[45] The value of the manor was much the same c. 1570.[46]

By the late 16th and early 17th centuries[47] there were two open fields in Thornton, called East and West fields by 1577 and containing 282 a. and 248 a. respectively c. 1613. East field included one consolidated but uninclosed holding, the 14 a. of rectorial glebe known as Dean's or Dean's Broat flat. Part of East field, containing 92 a. c. 1613, was called Crossgate field. The open fields had almost certainly been diminished by this period. In 1616 East field thus had many small closes, called Holcar and Lowfield closes and Under Deans Broats, containing in all about 140 a., on its northern flank. The 8-acre Bownam, described as 'all one furlong' in 1577, may similarly represent an inclosed portion of neighbouring West field. Fifteen acres were inclosed in Scorbutts and Borow flat on the northern edge of West field c. 1613, while in 1616 one man held his 16-acre share of the field in severalty.

Alongside the Beck in the south and east of the township there were 250–300 a. of common meadows. In 1616, for example, East ings contained 50 a., West carr (or West ings) 100 a., Birkham and Langwith ings 110 a., and Whitwell butts and ings 19 a. The 13-acre Oddland or Outland ing, adjoining East ings, was shared with Lord Ros, who took the first hay crop and left the aftermath to the lord and tenants of Thornton. The 50-acre Furby carr was apparently the only sizeable meadow held in severalty at this period.

The common wastes at Thornton consisted of East and West moors, Dry carr (or Dry Acre) common, and Eller carr, which was intercommoned with the tenants of Woodhouse. The moors, described as 'very good and large' in 1577, provided 'sufficient common' for each tenant's beasts, as well as turves for which all the inhabitants paid 10s. a year. East moor had, nevertheless, been diminished by inclosure. In 1616 56 a. in Moor closes and other closes on the moor's western flank were held by the inhabitants of Millhouses, who may have been responsible for assarting them. Haverland closes to the east of the moor then contained about 70 a., and two small closes near Walbut mill had also been taken out of East moor by c. 1613. Nevertheless, just over 200 a. of the moor remained; it was apparently subject to temporary division for practically all of it was let to 'oxgangmen and grassmen' c. 1613 in plots of 3–8 a.; only 15 a. 'at the town end' was then in common use. Parts of West moor were also improved and divided. Thus by 1616 33 a. had been fully inclosed as 'improvements'. About 1613 a further 528 a. in West moor, Dry carr, and Eller carr were let to tenants in temporary divisions of 30–36 a., and in 1616 there were various 'parts' in the moor, some of 36 a. There were still 180 a. in common use.

All 40 tenants at Thornton in 1570 were leaseholders, including three cottagers; 10 of them had 2 bovates each, 18 had one, and there were also unspecified amounts of land in some of the holdings. In 1577 tenants-at-will held 46 houses and cottages in the township. The only freeholders c. 1613 were the rector and the vicar. Tenants then held 47 houses and 1,884 a. of land; 17 holdings comprised 60–79 a. each, 19 contained 20–59 a., and 16 were of under 20 a. The 17 largest holdings were held by two-oxgangmen c. 1613; with one exception each of them had a basic holding composed of 15½ a. in West field, 3 a. in Crossgate field, 3 a. in East ings and 6 a. in West ings, and 30–36 a. in Eller carr, Dry carr, and West moor. The one-oxgangmen each had 10 a. in East field, 5 a. in Birkham and Langwith, and 8 a. in East moor. The cottagers held no open-field land but rented small plots in the ings and East moor. There were about 250 a. unlet c. 1613.

The remaining open fields were inclosed c. 1760 without an Act. Crossgate was by then known as Crosswood field,[48] while parts of West field were called Town End, West Hill, and Brick Kiln fields. Inclosure was imminent in 1758, when it was specified that tenants' leases were to be void in the event of it,[49] and had been effected by 1767.[50] The common meadows were inclosed between 1767 and 1845.[51]

Much of the waste was probably inclosed at the same time as the open fields. East moor, which still contained some 50 beast-gates in 1758[52] and included 135 a. in 1767,[53] nevertheless lay in distinct parcels in the latter year and was certainly in closes

[35] See below.
[36] Petworth Ho. Arch., nos. 1417 ff. 38d.–39d.; 3073 ff. 181d.–204.
[37] Minster Libr., D. & C. Arch., T 2 (3) a; W 3 f. 63.
[38] Lond. Gaz. 19 July 1844, p. 2499.
[39] R.D.B., HE/150/182.
[40] Ibid. HQ/307/380.
[41] Petworth Ho. Arch., no. 3073 (maps).
[42] Minster Libr., D. & C. Arch., P 2 (5).
[43] V.C.H. Yorks. ii. 269.
[44] Reg. Gray, p. 3.
[45] S.C. 6/Hen. VIII/4283–91.
[46] E 164/37 ff. 273–7.
[47] The following four paragraphs are based on surveys of 1570 (E 164/37 ff. 273–7) and 1577 (Petworth Ho. Arch., no. 1417), a survey and maps of c. 1613 (ibid. no. 3073 ff. 181d.–204), and a map of 1616 (ibid. no. 3426).
[48] Petworth Ho. Arch., no. 3442.
[49] Ibid. nos. 1579, 3460.
[50] Ibid. no. 3460.
[51] Ibid.; E.R.R.O., TA. Thornton.
[52] Petworth Ho. Arch., no. 1579.
[53] Ibid. no. 3460.

by 1845.[54] In 1755 West moor contained 235 a., occupying the ground lying west of the old Waplington road and part of the temporary divisions of the early 17th century. The rest of the divisions lay in several Moor closes by 1767, and Eller carr had been fully inclosed by that date. An outgang along the township's northern boundary remained in common use in 1767.[55] The common was further reduced in the late 18th and early 19th centuries, some of the former waste being used for rabbit-farming. In 1797 one farm included 111 a. in use as a warren and another consisted of 144 a. which had 'lately been a warren'. In 1845 a 28-acre close called Rabbit Warren lay next to the common, which by then had shrunk to 77 a.[56]

On the eve of inclosure in 1758 there were 35 holdings at Thornton, 18 of 50–120 a., 8 of 20–49 a., and 9 of less than 20 a.[57] By 1797 there were 42 holdings, 14 of over 50 a., 10 of 20–49 a., and 18 of less than 20 a.[58]

In 1086 there was land for three ploughs at Melbourne. The estate had been worth 20s. before the Conquest but was then waste, like the land at 'Chetelstorp'. Pasturable woodland at Melbourne was 2 leagues long and 2 furlongs broad.[59]

By the 13th century much land in the townships of Melbourne and Storwood had been reclaimed, although extensive wastes remained. In 1285 the value of the manor, about £28, was equally divided between Storwood and Melbourne. As well as the manor-house and park, valued at £3 10s. a year, there were 80 a. of arable land in demesne at Storwood, and a turbary worth £6 13s. 4d. Twelve cottagers, who had fishing rights, paid over £1 in rents. At Melbourne three free tenants owed rents of about £2, bondsmen held 27 bovates for £9, and 20 cottagers paid about £1. There were also 12 a. of meadow, presumably in demesne, and a mill.[60] The turbary lay in the waste already known as Landrikmose in the 13th century.[61] The Ros right of free warren in Landrikmose occasioned at least one dispute with men from adjoining townships.[62] The cottagers' fishing rights were not in the Beck but in a pool in neighbouring Wheldrake parish; thus in 1218–19 the abbot of Fountains granted members of the Ros family the right to fish Alemar when they were in Yorkshire, but restricted the men of Storwood to fishing there according to custom and at certain times.[63] The park at Storwood was repeatedly alleged to have been broken by trespassers in the late 13th and 14th centuries.[64]

In 1343 the manor was worth about £30. The demesne comprised 80 a. of poor land, 14 a. of meadow, 12 a of poor-quality meadow called Oddland ing, and a close at Melbourne. The park was valued for herbage and there was a small wood. The herbage and turves of the moor were worth £5, unless there was flooding, and a fishery 'in the marsh' produced 6d. in summer. The rents of villeins and tenants-at-will at Melbourne amounted to £14, those of cottars to nearly £3, and those of freeholders to £1 6s. 8d. At Storwood the tenants-at-will owed about £1 15s. Court profits were only 3s. 4d. because of the tenants' poverty.[65]

The manor was valued at about £38 a year in 1421. In addition to the turbary and the park, which were worth £15 a year, there were 80 a. of arable and 80 a. of meadow in demesne; the rents of free tenants amounted to £1 10s. and those of 20 tenants-at-will to £10.[66] The manor was worth £55 a year in the mid 16th century.[67] In 1622 the manor of Storwood and Melbourne comprised 410 a. of arable, 236 a. of meadow land, 920 a. of pasture, and 400 a. of waste.[68] Little is known of the open fields at Storwood but ridge-and-furrow exists around the hamlet. There were common ings and carrs in the township alongside the Beck and a considerable area of waste in Landrikmose, which was usually called West moor or Ross moor, after the seigneurial family, in the 17th and 18th centuries.[69] The park, which probably lay to the east of the manor-house on ground now called the Parks, was described as a close in 1727,[70] and in 1776 the manorial estate in Storwood consisted of 55 a. in nine closes, besides 9 a. in the carrs.[71] Apart from the lord of the manor there were 22 proprietors in the township in 1782 holding 643 a. of old-inclosed land.[72]

In Melbourne township four open fields, Angram, Church, Garth End, and West fields, survived into the 18th century, though their size may have been reduced before final inclosure in 1782. Thirteen closes called Angrams, containing 25 a. in 1776, may thus have been taken from the adjacent Angram field.[73] Ings and carrs bordered the Beck, and the township had extensive waste in Ross and East moors. The turbary was still exploited by the lord in the 17th century, when every husbandman in Melbourne and Storwood was bound to render him a load of turves or 1s.[74] By 1782 there were several hundred acres of old inclosures in the south of Melbourne, including an area called New moor.[75] Old closes called Coney garths, mentioned in 1790, suggest that a rabbit warren was formerly sited in the south of the township.[76]

The remaining open fields and other common lands were inclosed in 1782[77] under an Act of 1777.[78] A total of 2,344 a. were allotted, at least 1,182 a. lying in Ross moor, about 500 a. in East moor, 60 a. in Angram field, 88 a. in Garth End field, at least 99 a. in the ings, and over 53 a. in the carrs. Awards of plots of mixed origin make it impossible to determine the areas more fully. John and Elizabeth Danser received 1,045 a. for their land and manorial rights in the waste, the dean of York 283 a. and the vicar 62 a. for their tithes, and the archbishop of York 143 a. There were also 6 allot-

---

[54] E.R.R.O., TA. Thornton.
[55] Petworth Ho. Arch., nos. 3442, 3460.
[56] Ibid. no. 3075; E.R.R.O., TA. Thornton.
[57] Petworth Ho. Arch., no. 1579.
[58] Ibid. no. 3075.
[59] V.C.H. Yorks. ii. 269.
[60] Yorks. Inq. ii, p. 35.
[61] Yorks. Fines, 1218–31, pp. 107, 127.
[62] Monastic Notes, i (Y.A.S. Rec. Ser. xvii), 54.
[63] Yorks. Fines, 1218–31, p. 17; see above p. 125.
[64] Cal. Pat. 1292–1301, 381; 1317–21, 280, 283; 1330–4, 298, 440–1; 1361–4, 450.
[65] C 135/71 no. 40.
[66] Yorks. Inq. iv, p. 176.
[67] N. Country Wills, i. 185.
[68] C 142/391 no. 79.
[69] H.U.L., DRA/558; R.D.B., A/361/518.
[70] E.R.R.O., QSF. East. 1727, B.10.
[71] R.D.B., AW/359/627.
[72] Ibid. BB/311/40.
[73] Ibid. AW/359/627.
[74] H.U.L., DRA/558.
[75] R.D.B., BB/311/40.
[76] Ibid. BP/240/388.
[77] Ibid.
[78] 17 Geo. III, c. 142 (Priv. Act).

ments of 40–80 a., 9 of 20–39 a., and 28 of less than 20 a. As provided for in the Act, the costs of inclosure were covered in the case of the dean, vicar, and archbishop by the deduction and sale of a proportion of their allotments. About 100 a. of old inclosed ground were involved in exchanges effected at inclosure.

In the 19th and early 20th centuries there were generally 13–18 farmers in Thornton, of whom about 5 had 150 a. or more in the 1850s, 1920s, and 1930s. At Melbourne there were usually 20–30 farmers, including 4 with over 150 a. in the 1850s and one in the early 20th century. There were 6–10 farmers at Storwood, only one with over 150 a.[79]

In 1801 1,299 a. in Thornton and Melbourne were under crops, mainly oats (546 a.) and wheat (370 a.).[80] There was, however, much woodland in Melbourne and Storwood following the 1782 inclosure; by 1790 part of East moor had been planted with trees, and in the late 19th century the timber on the Melbourne Hall estate was valued at nearly £10,000.[81] At Thornton in 1845 there were 1,457 a. of arable, 463 a. of meadow and pasture, 167 a. of woodland, and 77 a. of common.[82] The position was much the same in 1905, with 1,426 a. of arable, 739 a. of grassland, and 30 a. of woodland. Arable was less prominent in Melbourne in 1905, with 1,459 a. compared with 1,271 a. of grassland and 204 a. of woodland. At Storwood there were about 509 a. each of arable and grassland, and 52 a. of woodland.[83] In the 1930s and later the parish had roughly equal amounts of arable and grassland, with the former predominant in the east and grassland in the west alongside the Beck and on the former Ross moor. In the 1960s Thornton also included an area of rough pasture, comprising Seavy carr and Bownams. Most of Thornton's woodland, and notably that on the common, had disappeared by the 1930s.[84] In the 1960s the Forestry Commission acquired 49 a. of woodland in Melbourne and 25 a. in Storwood.[85]

There was little non-agricultural employment in the parish before the 19th century. A shearman was mentioned at Melbourne in 1559,[86] and two weavers in the early 18th century.[87] Brick Kiln field in Thornton was mentioned in 1758,[88] and there was a brickyard on East moor in Melbourne in 1790.[89] By 1851 Melbourne had two brick-makers and Storwood one,[90] but the occupation was not mentioned after 1892 for Melbourne and 1879 for Storwood.[91] Brick-making and marling account for the numerous pits in Melbourne.[92] The coal merchant, waterman, lock-keeper, and sailor mentioned at Melbourne in 1851 were presumably all dependent upon the canal.[93] In 1974 a firm of agricultural merchants had premises on the site of airfield buildings to the east of Melbourne village.

Walbut mill, which was mentioned in 1323[94] and frequently thereafter, stood on the Beck south-east of Thornton village. A miller was last mentioned in 1901 but the building still stood in 1974.[95] The site of another mill, probably wind-powered, lay at the east end of Hall Garth in 1577;[96] the mill presumably existed by the 14th century, when Millhouse was first mentioned.[97] A mill at Melbourne was mentioned in 1285[98] and a ruined windmill in the early 16th century.[99] It perhaps stood at the east end of the village, where the name Mill Hill still survives.

LOCAL GOVERNMENT. Surviving court rolls for Wressle from the period 1505–1663 contain information about its member Thornton,[1] and call rolls and other records of Thornton manor survive from the period 1833–57.[2] In the 16th and 17th centuries there were usually 2 constables, 2 keepers of the assize of ale and of bread, 4–5 bylawmen, and a pinder at Thornton.[3] In the mid 19th century the officers included one or 2 constables, 2 bylawmen, and one or 2 pinders. Court rolls exist for Melbourne and Storwood for a dozen years between 1521 and 1581.[4] There were 4 bylawmen for Melbourne in the 16th century, and 2 bylawmen, 2 constables, and 2 aletasters for Storwood.

Churchwardens' accounts survive from 1822 onwards.[5] There were poorhouses at Melbourne in the 19th century.[6] Thornton, Melbourne, and Storwood joined Pocklington poor-law union in 1836[7] and Pocklington rural district in 1894.[8] They became part of the North Wolds district of Humberside in 1974.

CHURCH. Although not named, Thornton, like Allerthorpe, was one of the chapels given by the king between 1100 and 1108, along with their mother-church of Pocklington, to the archbishop of York and York minster. They were apparently assigned by the archbishop to the dean, and between c. 1119 and 1129 the king confirmed the assignment.[9] The parish was subsequently within the dean's peculiar jurisdiction. In 1225 the archbishop confirmed a gift of land and the altarage of the chapel which the dean had made to one of his clerks 'in the name of a vicarage',[10] but it was not until 1252 that a vicarage was fully ordained jointly at Thornton and Allerthorpe, with provision that a minister be found for each church.[11] Subsequently Thornton was a

---

[79] H.O. 107/2351; R.D.B., 3/170/163 (1897); directories.
[80] 1801 Crop Returns.
[81] R.D.B., BP/240/388; E.R.R.O., DDCS/4/5.
[82] E.R.R.O., TA. Thornton.
[83] Acreage Returns, 1905.
[84] [1st] Land Util. Surv. Map, sheet 27; 2nd Land Util. Surv. Map, sheet 699 (SE 64–74); O.S. Map 6" (1854–5 edn.).
[85] R.D.B., 1170/464/419; 1175/67/71; 1278/312/290.
[86] Cal. Pat. 1558–60, 236.
[87] E.R.R.O., QSF. Mids. 1723, C.22.
[88] Petworth Ho. Arch., no. 1579.
[89] R.D.B., BP/240/388.
[90] H.O. 107/2351.
[91] Directories.
[92] H. E. Strickland, Gen. View of Agric. of E.R. Yorks. 23.
[93] H.O. 107/2351.
[94] Hist. MSS. Com. 24, Rutland, iv, p. 85.
[95] K. J. Allison, E.R. Water-mills (E. Yorks. Loc. Hist. Ser. xxvi), 50.
[96] Petworth Ho. Arch., no. 1417 f. 38d.
[97] See p. 179.
[98] Yorks. Inq. ii, p. 35.
[99] Belvoir Castle MS., Roos 976.
[1] Petworth Ho. Arch., preliminary list at the West Sussex Co. Rec. Off., Chichester.
[2] E.R.R.O., DDEL/17/1–5.
[3] Petworth Ho. Arch., Yorks. MCR/90, 243.
[4] Belvoir Castle MSS., Court rolls.
[5] B.I.H.R., PR. THORN. 17.
[6] H.O. 107/2351; O.S. Map 6" (1854–5 edn.).
[7] 3rd Rep. Poor Law Com. 170.
[8] Census.
[9] E.Y.C. i, pp. 333–6.
[10] Reg. Gray, p. 3.
[11] Ibid. p. 212.

vicarage and Allerthorpe a curacy. There were separate ministers in 1525–6, but from the 17th century the vicarage and curacy were usually held by one man.[12] Baptisms and marriages apparently took place at both Thornton and Allerthorpe after 1252, but the right of burial was reserved to Pocklington until 1360.[13] Thornton and Allerthorpe still constituted a united vicarage in 1974.

The advowson presumably belonged to the dean of York in the Middle Ages and later, despite a Crown grant of it, along with Thornton manor, to Thomas Percy in 1557.[14] In 1650 the advowson, said to have formerly belonged to the dean, was held by the Commonwealth.[15] The Crown presented in 1660[16] but the dean in 1662 and later.[17] With the vesting of the rectory in the Ecclesiastical Commissioners in 1844, the patronage passed automatically to the archbishop of York.[18] In 1871 it passed to the Crown by exchange,[19] and the patronage was exercised by the Lord Chancellor in 1973.[20]

The vicar's income in 1525–6 was £3 5s.[21] The vicarage was worth £7 5s. 8d. net in 1535[22] and £6 10s. in 1650.[23] The average net income of the joint living in 1829–31 was £210.[24] In 1863 rent-charges of about £86, formerly belonging to the dean of York, were transferred to the vicarage by the Ecclesiastical Commissioners, and the living was simultaneously endowed with £100 a year for a curate.[25] The net value of the living was c. £300 in 1884 and £239 in 1915.[26]

In 1252 the vicarage was endowed with the small tithes.[27] Those in Melbourne were valued at £3 a year in 1650,[28] and in 1684 an annual composition of £20 was paid for the small tithes and fees in Thornton, Melbourne, and Storwood.[29] At inclosure in 1782 the vicar was awarded 62 a. and rent-charges of 15s. in Melbourne and £8 18s. in Storwood in lieu of tithes.[30] The Thornton tithes were commuted for £92 in 1845.[31] The 66-acre Glebe farm in Melbourne was sold to Walter Cliff by the Ecclesiastical Commissioners in 1901.[32]

The parsonage house stood next to Thornton church in 1616[33] and was in need of repair in the 1620s.[34] In 1726 it consisted of three rooms 'on one floor' and a back kitchen.[35] The house, of brick and 'post and pan' with a thatched roof, had probably been enlarged by 1770, when it also had a parlour, three chambers, and a garret.[36] By 1809, however, the vicar had moved to Allerthorpe,[37] and by the mid 19th century the Thornton house had been demolished.[38]

There may have been a chantry in the church for in the 1530s and 1540s £1 6s. 8d. a year was paid out of Thornton manor to the chaplain of the chantry 'next to Thornton'.[39] In 1554 the Crown granted a bovate in Allerthorpe, which had formerly supported an obit in Thornton church, to John and Joan Constable.[40]

In addition to the vicar there were two parochial chaplains at Thornton and Melbourne in 1525–6, each receiving £4 a year.[41] During the 18th century and the first quarter of the 19th the incumbent also held the vicarage of Barmby Moor with Fangfoss.[42] An assistant curate appointed after 1863[43] later served a new church built at Melbourne in 1882,[44] and there continued to be a curate until 1926.[45]

There was a weekly service at Thornton in 1743; Holy Communion was celebrated four times a year and about 58 people communicated at Easter.[46] By 1871 two services were held each Sunday, of which one a week in summer and one a fortnight in winter were in Melbourne school; there were, however, only three communion services a year, with an average of 12 communicants.[47] Communion was celebrated monthly from 1877 but 'very few' communicated. By 1894 there was only one service a week at Thornton, but a second service was held in Melbourne mission church. In 1915 two weekly services were held at Thornton and two at Melbourne. Communion was celebrated at least monthly at Thornton and on occasion at Melbourne, and at Easter 1914 there were 14 and 38 communicants respectively.[48] In 1973 no services, apart from Holy Communion, were held in Thornton church, but there were two services a month at Melbourne church, one held with the Methodists, and a further two united services in the Methodist chapel at Melbourne.

The church of ST. MICHAEL is largely built of rubble and consists of a chancel and a nave which formerly had a north porch. No part of the fabric can be certainly dated to a period earlier than the 14th century, but the nave may now incorporate a former north aisle and the small size of both nave and chancel suggests that their plan is earlier. The 14th-century features include windows in the nave and chancel, and both doorways. The side windows in the chancel are of unusual design and may date from the 15th century.

In 1568 the windows and fabric of the chancel were in decay but they had apparently been repaired by 1590.[49] There was a restoration in 1890–2 under

---

[12] See p. 138.
[13] *Cal. Papal Pets.* i. 355.
[14] *Cal. Pat.* 1557–8, 186.
[15] C 94/3 f. 56.
[16] Inst. Bks.
[17] B.I.H.R., Inst. AB. 6, p. 380; *Rep. Com. Eccl. Revenues*, 972.
[18] Eccl. Comrs. Act, 3 & 4 Vic. c. 113, s. 41; *Lond. Gaz.* 19 July 1844, p. 2499.
[19] *Lond. Gaz.* 17 Jan. 1871, p. 158.
[20] *Crockford.*
[21] *Y.A.J.* xxiv. 64.
[22] *Valor Eccl.* (Rec. Com.), v. 141.
[23] C 94/3 f. 56.
[24] *Rep. Com. Eccl. Revenues*, 972.
[25] B.I.H.R., TER. I. Thornton 1865; *Lond. Gaz.* 1 May 1863, p. 2315.
[26] B.I.H.R., Bp. V. 1884/Ret.; Bp. V. 1915/Ret.
[27] *Reg. Gray*, pp. 212–13.
[28] C 94/3 f. 56.
[29] B.I.H.R., TER. I. Thornton 1684.
[30] R.D.B., BB/311/40.
[31] E.R.R.O., TA. Thornton.
[32] R.D.B., 39/168/162 (1901).
[33] Petworth Ho. Arch., no. 3426.
[34] B.I.H.R., CP. H. 1783.
[35] Ibid. TER. I. Thornton 1726.
[36] Ibid. 1770.
[37] See p. 138.
[38] O.S. Map 6" (1854–5 edn.).
[39] S.C. 6/Hen. VIII/4283–6.
[40] *Cal. Pat.* 1553–4, 146.
[41] *Y.A.J.* xxiv. 72.
[42] See p. 145.
[43] B.I.H.R., V. 1871/Ret. 499; see above.
[44] Ibid. PR. THORN. 17 (1888); Bulmer, *Dir. E. Yorks.* (1892), 721–2.
[45] *Crockford.*
[46] *Herring's Visit.* iii. 174.
[47] B.I.H.R., V. 1871/Ret. 499.
[48] Ibid. V. 1877/Ret.; Bp. V. 1884/Ret.; Bp. V. 1894/Ret.; Bp. V. 1915/Ret.
[49] *Y.A.J.* xviii. 210, 217.

the direction of Ewan Christian when the west end and the chancel arch appear to have been rebuilt and the roofs renewed.[50]

The church had four bells in 1552 but by 1770 only two.[51] There are still two: (i) 1767; (ii) undated.[52] In 1552 the church had a silver chalice.[53] The present plate includes a silver communion cup, inscribed in 1715 but of an earlier date, and a pewter flagon and paten. A silver service presented by J. C. Hanson, vicar, in 1892 was used at Melbourne mission church.[54]

The registers of baptisms and burials begin in 1615 and are complete; the marriage registers are complete from 1652.[55] The churchyard was extended in 1926.[56]

The iron mission church at Melbourne, dedicated to St. Monica, was made by the Windsor Iron Works, Liverpool, and erected in 1882.[57] The cruciform church, with its north-east vestry and north-west tower and spire above a porch, has a corrugated iron exterior and a pine-boarded interior. The font was given by Thomlinson Walker.[58]

NONCONFORMITY. There were 4–11 Roman Catholics at Thornton in 1615–27 and in the 1640s and 1660s, but only 2 in the mid 18th century.[59] Melbourne and Storwood had 11 recusants in 1664.[60]

The Methodists had 22 members at Thornton in 1789, the number rising to 64 in 1798 and standing at 37 in 1816. At Melbourne there were about 20 members in 1805–16, and 6–25 at Storwood in 1799–1816.[61] Houses and other buildings at Thornton were licensed for dissenting worship in 1764, 1784, 1791, 1803, 1812, 1819, 1820, 1821, 1827, and 1841.[62] Private buildings were also registered at Melbourne in 1791, 1819 (two), and 1820,[63] and at Storwood in 1820.[64] A Wesleyan schoolroom existed at Thornton by 1800 and was being used for worship in 1851;[65] a chapel was built in 1909[66] and was still in use in 1974. Wesleyan and Primitive Methodist chapels were built at Melbourne in 1811 and 1821 respectively,[67] and a Wesleyan chapel at Storwood in 1837.[68] The Storwood chapel was rebuilt on a new site and registered in 1895; it had closed by 1954 and has since been demolished.[69] The former Primitive Methodist chapel at Melbourne had ceased to be used for worship by 1949,[70] but was still standing in 1974. The former Wesleyan chapel was in use in 1974; it has pointed windows with wooden tracery.

EDUCATION. In 1743 the parish clerk taught the principles of Christian religion in a private school at Thornton,[71] and a schoolmaster was supported by parents in 1764.[72] About 1800 the Poor's Money and a sum raised by assessment were used to build a school-house.[73] Fifteen children attended a school supported by subscription in 1819,[74] and 23 pupils were paid for by their parents in 1835.[75] Although the school received £5 a year from Col. George Wyndham in 1856,[76] it was described as an unendowed church school in 1865, when about 35 were in attendance.[77] The average attendance at the school, which was united with the National Society, was 12 in 1871 and about 25 in 1877.[78] The school received an annual government grant from 1875.[79] Between 1906 and 1932 attendance was usually 20–25, but it fell to 14 in 1938.[80] A new school was built on the same site in 1927.[81] The senior pupils were transferred to Pocklington in 1955, and in 1965 the remaining pupils were sent to Melbourne primary school and Thornton school was closed.[82] The school, standing behind the former master's house, was used as a dwelling house in 1974.

At Melbourne the Poor's Money and a sum raised by subscription and assessment were used to build a school in 1810.[83] By 1835 the township had three schools, attended by 57 pupils at their parents' cost;[84] a schoolmaster lived in the village in 1851, and a dame school was mentioned in 1865.[85] There were two schools, catering for 24 children, in 1871, one of them a National school.[86] A school board was formed in 1875, and a new school built in 1878 initially had 65 pupils.[87] The school received an annual government grant from 1880.[88]

In 1906–27 attendance fluctuated between 42 and 54, but had fallen to 31 by 1938.[89] In 1953 the

---

[50] B.I.H.R., PR. THORN. 17; Bulmer, *Dir. E. Yorks.* (1892), 721–2.
[51] B.I.H.R., TER. I. Thornton 1770; *Inventories of Ch. Goods*, 75.
[52] Boulter, 'Ch. Bells', 27.
[53] *Inventories of Ch. Goods*, 75.
[54] *Yorks. Ch. Plate*, i. 325.
[55] B.I.H.R.
[56] York Dioc. Regy., Consecration deed.
[57] B.I.H.R., PR. THORN. 17 (1882–3, 1888); *Kelly's Dir. N. & E.R. Yorks.* (1897), 543–4. There is an inscribed drawing of the church in the vestry: ex inf. Mr. J. Hutchinson, 1974.
[58] Inscription.
[59] Aveling, *Post Reformation Catholicism*, 60.
[60] *Depositions from York Castle* (Sur. Soc. xl), 121.
[61] E.R.R.O., MRP/1/7.
[62] G.R.O. Worship Returns, Vol. v, nos. 220, 645, 824, 1760, 2574, 3278, 3573, 4078; B.I.H.R., DMH. Reg. 1, p. 141; Reg. 2, p. 96. It is possible that some of these registrations refer to other Yorkshire Thorntons.
[63] G.R.O. Worship Returns, Vol. v, nos. 810, 3326, 3335, 3360.
[64] B.I.H.R., DMH. Reg. 1, pp. 148–9.
[65] H.O. 129/23/516.
[66] Date on building.
[67] H.O. 129/23/516.
[68] Ibid.; Sheahan and Whellan, *Hist. York & E.R.* ii. 569–70.
[69] G.R.O. Worship Reg. no. 34663.
[70] Ibid. no. 11807.
[71] *Herring's Visit.* iii. 174.
[72] B.I.H.R., Bp. V. 1764/Ret. 82.
[73] *11th Rep. Com. Char.* 745.
[74] *Educ. of Poor Digest*, 1095.
[75] *Educ. Enquiry Abstract*, 1097.
[76] Sheahan and Whellan, *Hist. York & E.R.* ii. 569–70.
[77] B.I.H.R., V. 1865/Ret. 540.
[78] Ibid. V. 1877/Ret.; *Returns relating to Elem. Educ.* 794.
[79] *Rep. of Educ. Cttee. of Council, 1875–6* [C. 1513-I], p. 671, H.C. (1876), xxiii. The school was sometimes wrongly described as British: e.g. *Rep. of Educ. Cttee. of Council, 1890–1* [C. 6438-I], p. 706, H.C. (1890–1), xxvii; *Lists of Schs. under Admin. of Bd. 1903–4* [Cd. 2011], p. 268, H.C. (1904), lxxv.
[80] *Bd. of Educ. List 21* (H.M.S.O.).
[81] E.R. Educ. Cttee. Mins. 1927–8, 39.
[82] Ibid. 1955–6, 152; 1964–5, 121, 172.
[83] *11th Rep. Com. Char.*, 745; *Kelly's Dir. N. & E.R. Yorks.* (1872), 553.
[84] *Educ. Enquiry Abstract*, 1097.
[85] B.I.H.R., V. 1865/Ret. 540; H.O. 107/2351.
[86] *Returns relating to Elem. Educ.* 794.
[87] Ed. 7/135 no. 116; *Kelly's Dir. N. & E.R. Yorks.* (1889), 464–5.
[88] *Rep. of Educ. Cttee. of Council, 1879–80* [C. 2562-I], p. 733, H.C. (1880), xxii.
[89] *List 21*.

senior pupils were transferred to Market Weighton and the school was reorganized as a junior and infants' school.[90] A new school was opened close by in 1961 and enlarged in 1969; the old building was demolished.[91] There were 124 on the roll in January 1974.[92]

In the early 20th century children from Storwood attended the school at East Cottingwith.[93]

CHARITIES FOR THE POOR Thomas Wood, by will dated 1568, devised a rent-charge of £10 a year from an estate at Kilnwick Percy for the benefit of Thornton, Melbourne, and many other townships. In 1824 Thornton and Melbourne each received 5s.[94] Henry Frederick, Baron Hotham, owner of the Kilnwick Percy estate, redeemed the rent-charge in 1961 and £10 stock each was subsequently assigned to Thornton and Melbourne.[95] The Thornton income of 5s. was not distributed in 1968.[96]

The Poor's Estate at Thornton, comprising various small benefactions, had a stock of about £33 in 1743[97] and £28 in 1786. The interest was distributed to the poor until c. 1800, when the capital was used to build a school-house and a smithy. The income was thereafter derived from the rents of the buildings, which amounted to £2 a year in 1824, when the Poor's Estate was administered with Wood's charity.[98] No more is known of the charity.

The Poor's Estate at Melbourne comprised various gifts and had a stock of about £60 in 1743,[99] £47 in 1764,[1] and £40 in 1786. It was used c. 1810 to build a school and an adjacent house; the latter was let for the poor's benefit and produced £2 a year in 1824,[2] and after its disuse as a school the former also produced rents for the poor.[3]

Oddland ing in Thornton was said c. 1805 to be charged with annual payments of 5s. each to the Melbourne and Storwood poor.[4] It was presumably the same land from which 5s. was paid to the poor of Melbourne in 1824, when it was applied with the Poor's Estate and Wood's charity.[5] The charity may have derived from the share in Oddland ing enjoyed by the lords of Storwood and Melbourne in the 17th century.[6]

Wood's charity for Melbourne, the Melbourne Poor's Estate or Old School House charity, and the unknown donor's charity (Oddland ing) were combined as the United Charities under a Scheme of 1912. The total endowment was represented by £142 stock in 1970, and by a Scheme of that year the income was to be used for gifts in money and goods.[7] The income of £3.50 was not distributed in 1973.[8]

WILBERFOSS

THE PARISH of Wilberfoss, including Newton upon Derwent township, lies about 7 miles east of York, on the east bank of the river Derwent and astride the Escrick moraine.[1] Newton village lies on the slopes of the moraine but Wilberfoss stands just to the east of the ridge beside the substantial Foss beck, which flows southwards to become Blackfoss beck in Sutton upon Derwent. The name Wilberfoss was not recorded until c. 1150 but it seems likely that it was an Anglian settlement, possibly established near an improved natural stream. Newton was first mentioned at the same time and its suffix was added in the 13th century.[2] The irregularly-shaped parish covers 3,185 a., of which Wilberfoss township accounts for 1,472 a. and Newton 1,713 a.[3] Newton and Wilberfoss civil parishes were combined in 1935.[4]

The moraine, composed of glacial sand and gravel and boulder clay, exceeds 50 ft. above sea-level across the whole width of the parish, separating lower ground towards the Derwent on the west from other more extensive low grounds on the east. The latter are drained principally by Foss and Sails becks and Black dike. In the extreme east of the parish the ground again rises above 50 ft. Long stretches of the parish boundary are formed by the Derwent and the becks. Part of the open-field land of both villages lay on the moraine but much of it occupied the outwash sand, silt, and clay of the low ground in the middle of the parish. In the west of Newton and in the east of both townships there were extensive common pastures, and limited areas of common meadow land lay on the alluvium beside the river and streams.[5] The open fields and other common lands were inclosed in 1766.

The principal road in the parish, leading from Kexby bridge over the Derwent, through Wilberfoss village, and on towards Barmby Moor, now forms part of the York–Hull trunk road. It crosses Foss beck by Stone bridge, so named by 1850,[6] which was probably the Wilberfoss bridge mentioned in 1463[7] and in the early 18th century.[8] The present bridge consists of three brick arches. It perhaps dates from the 18th century but has been widened on both sides. The road was turnpiked in 1764 and side gates were set up at the end of roads leading from Fangfoss and Newton; the trust was discontinued in 1881.[9] Two of the milestones remain. A

---

[90] E.R. Educ. Cttee. *Mins.* 1952–3, 227.
[91] Ibid. 1968–9, 172; local information.
[92] Ex inf. Chief Educ. Officer, County Hall, Beverley, 1974.   [93] Directories.
[94] 11th Rep. Com. Char. 745–6.
[95] Ex inf. Char. Com., Liverpool, 1974.
[96] Char. Com. files.
[97] Herring's Visit. iii. 174.
[98] 11th Rep. Com. Char. 745.
[99] Herring's Visit. iii. 174.
[1] B.I.H.R., Bp. V. 1764/Ret. 82.
[2] 11th Rep. Com. Char. 745.
[3] Char. Com. files.
[4] Petworth Ho. Arch., no. 3932.
[5] 11th Rep. Com. Char. 746.   [6] See p. 185.

[7] Char. Com. files.
[8] Ex inf. Mr. T. G. Wilson, Barmby Moor, 1974.
[1] This article was written in 1974.
[2] *P.N.E.R. Yorks.* (E.P.N.S.), 188; *V.C.H. Yorks.* iii. 125.
[3] O.S. Map 6″, Yorks. (1854 edn.). Most of the parish is covered by sheet 175, with a little on sheets 176 and 192.
[4] *Census.*
[5] Geol. Surv. Map 1″, solid and drift, sheets 63 (1967 edn.) and 71 (1973 edn.).
[6] O.S. Map 6″ (1854 edn.).
[7] B.I.H.R., Prob. Reg. 4 f. 49.
[8] E.R.R.O., QSF. Mids. 1707, D.15; Mids. 1739, B.19.
[9] K. A. MacMahon, *Roads and Turnpike Trusts in E. Yorks.* (E. Yorks. Loc. Hist. Ser. xviii), 70.

bypass for Wilberfoss was built in the 1960s and the road widened and straightened on both sides of the village.[10] A straight road across the former East moor, leading to Bolton, was made at inclosure, together with an unsurfaced road to Yapham. Another minor road, running along the eastern parish boundary, crosses Foss beck by New bridge, so called by *c.* 1602; the present bridge dates from 1935.[11] The Newton road runs along the crest of the moraine and on towards Sutton upon Derwent, and from Newton village a minor road runs eastwards to join the York–Hull road and Mask Lane leads down to the Derwent. The Roman road from Brough to Stamford Bridge crossed the parish but its line was not followed by later roads.

The York–Hull road formed the main street of Wilberfoss until the village was bypassed. Near Foss beck it crossed an open area, now partly inclosed, which was presumably the Town Green mentioned in the early 19th century.[12] From the main street Beckside and Middle Street both lead towards the church, the latter crossing the beck by Church bridge, a single-arched stone footbridge of uncertain date. Back Lane forms a small loop on the south side of the main street and from it Church or Butts Lane led to a footpath formerly running towards Newton.

The earliest houses in the village stand in Middle Street and are at least 18th-century in date. Among later buildings the largest is the Villa, probably built for the cattle dealer H. Q. Gillah *c.* 1885–90;[13] it is a white-brick building with large cattle sheds in the same material. The village has greatly expanded since the Second World War and there are several private housing estates, as well as about 60 council houses. An alehouse was licensed at Wilberfoss in 1729 and there were 2–4 such houses in the later 18th century.[14] In 1823 the inns were the Horse Shoes, the True Briton, and the Waggon and Horses.[15] The first, usually called the Blacksmith's Arms, stood on the main road at the east end of the village[16] and was demolished for the building of the bypass. The second, renamed the Oddfellows' Arms by 1840,[17] still stood in the village centre in 1974. The Waggon and Horses near by had closed by 1872.[18]

The single village street of Newton lies just to the west of the road along the moraine, here called Back o' Newton, and is joined to it at each end. The most noteworthy houses are two known as Hall Farm.[19] The Poplars is dated 1868, and there are six council houses. Newton had 1–3 licensed houses in the later 18th century and 2, the Half Moon and the Sportsman, in 1840.[20] The former still exists in the village street, but the latter was last mentioned in 1851; it stood on the turnpike road near the Barmby Moor boundary.[21]

There are about ten outlying farm-houses in Wilberfoss township and six in Newton, the latter including Holly Farm with a prominent dovecot; all date from after the inclosure of 1766. Gale House and Peacock Farm in Wilberfoss probably derive their names from two local families, the Gales being impropriators in the 16th and 17th centuries.[22] In Wilberfoss a mid-19th-century house of brown brick with white-brick dressings stands on the former East moor, where more than a dozen houses and bungalows occupy small allotments made at inclosure in 1766.

There were 105 poll-tax payers in Wilberfoss in 1377 and 63 in Newton.[23] Forty-four households were listed in the hearth-tax return for Wilberfoss in 1672, 13 of them exempt; of those that were chargeable 25 had only one hearth each, 4 had 2, and 2 had 3 or four. At Newton 4 out of 36 households were exempt; of the rest 30 had one hearth each, one had 2, and one had four.[24] There were 104 families in the whole parish in 1743 and 65 in 1764.[25] The population of Wilberfoss township in 1801 was 282; it rose to a maximum of 414 in 1881 and fell to 346 in 1901. Newton had 188 inhabitants in 1801, rising to 246 in 1861 and falling to 216 in 1901. There was little change by 1931, when the two villages had 341 and 193 inhabitants respectively, but thereafter the population of the combined civil parish rose to 648 in 1951 and 860 in 1971.[26]

MANOR AND OTHER ESTATES. Wilberfoss and Newton were not mentioned in 1086, when they lay within the manor and soke of Catton.[27] The lordship subsequently descended with Catton in the Percy, Seymour, and Wyndham families.[28] Under the Percys a mesne lordship in 5 carucates in Wilberfoss was held by the Kyme family. In 1260 it belonged to William of Kyme and in 1315 to Philip of Kyme;[29] Philip was described as a lord of Wilberfoss in 1316, along with Eleanor Percy, who was then sole lord at Newton.[30]

Under the Kymes the demesne tenants included the Burdon family, lords of Kexby. Robert Burdon had 6 bovates in 1260 and Thomas Burdon possibly 20 bovates in 1284–5;[31] Thomas was granted free warren at Wilberfoss in 1290.[32] The subsequent descent of this estate is obscure but in the 15th century it belonged, like Scoreby, to the Nevilles, and after the partition of the earl of Warwick's estate in 1474 to the duke of Gloucester.[33] It was later accounted for along with Sheriff Hutton (Yorks. N.R.).[34] It was presumably this land which was said *c.* 1602 to have formerly belonged to the duchy of York: 71 a. of it had been bought by the Percys and 11 bovates belonged to freeholders.[35]

[10] R.D.B., e.g. 1310/514/463; E.R.C.C. *Mins.* 1962–3 22; 1966–7, 126.
[11] Petworth House Archives, no. 1416; date on bridge.
[12] E.R.R.O., DDEL/3/1.
[13] R.D.B., 5/310/300 (1885); O.S. Map 1/2,500, Yorks. CLXXV. 11 (1891 edn.); Bulmer, *Dir. E. Yorks.* (1892), 731.
[14] E.R.R.O., QSF. East. 1729, A.1; QDT/2/15.
[15] Baines, *Hist. Yorks.* (1823), ii. 400.
[16] Directories; O.S. Map 6" (1958 edn.).
[17] White, *Dir. E. & N.R. Yorks.* (1840), 249.
[18] Directories; O.S. Map 6" (1854 edn.). [19] See p. 193.
[20] E.R.R.O., QDT/2/15; White, *Dir. E. & N.R. Yorks.* (1840), 249.
[21] H.O. 107/2351; W.D. Wood Rees, *Hist. of Barmby Moor* (Pocklington, priv. print. 1911), 29.

[22] See p. 194. For the Peacocks see e.g. R.D.B., AH/177/5.
[23] E 179/202/59 mm. 84, 138.
[24] E 179/205/504.
[25] *V.C.H. Yorks.* iii. 493.
[26] *Census.*
[27] *V.C.H. Yorks.* ii. 219 n.
[28] See p. 151.
[29] *Cal. Inq. p.m.* i, p. 131; v, p. 319.
[30] *Feud. Aids,* vi. 168.
[31] *Cal. Inq. p.m.* i, p. 131; *Feud. Aids,* vi. 47.
[32] *Cal. Chart. R.* 1257–1300, 341.
[33] e.g. *Cal. Close,* 1422–9, 238; 1476–85, p. 189; *Cal. Pat.* 1467–77, 483; see above p. 160.
[34] D.L. 29/650/10510.
[35] Petworth Ho. Arch., no. 1416.

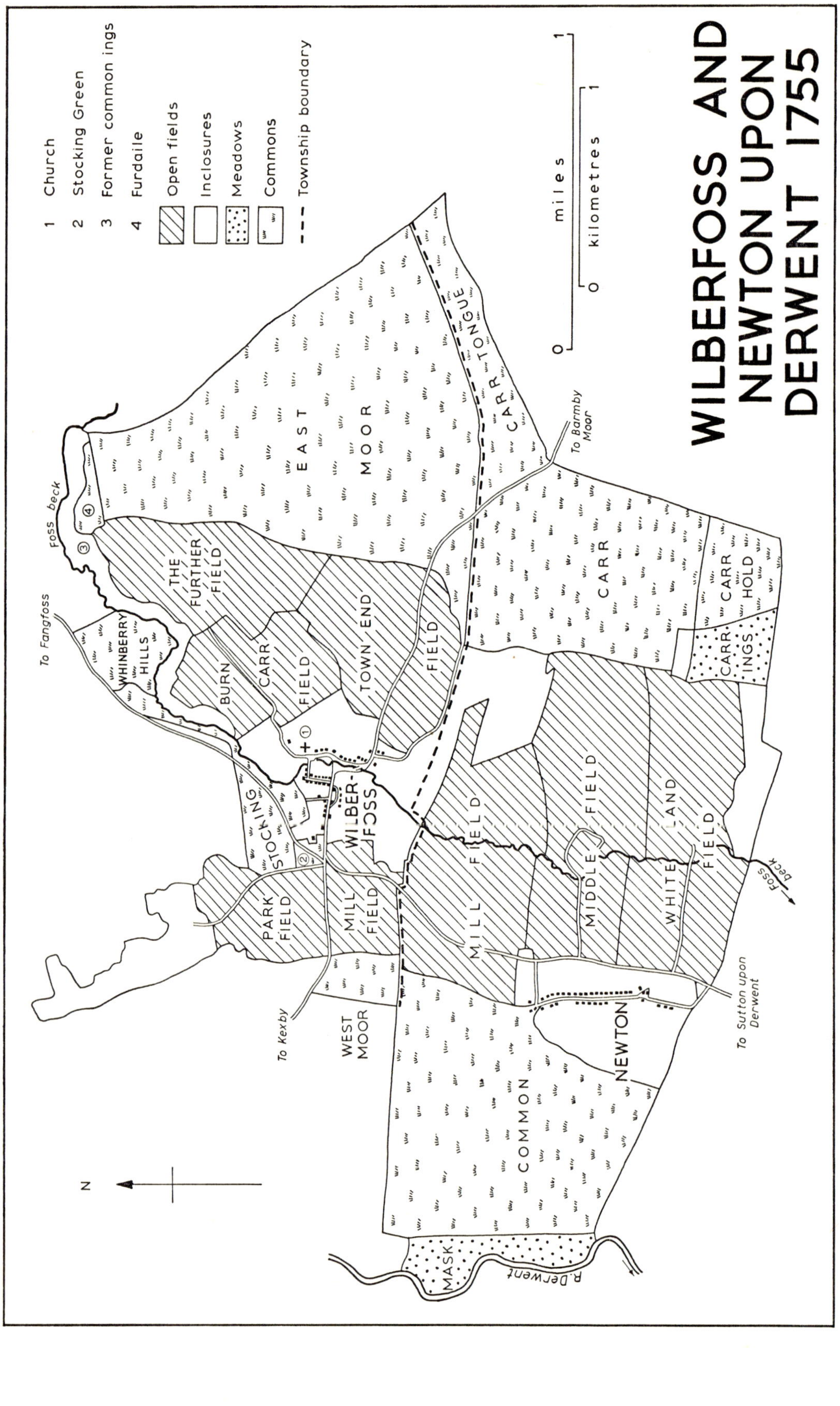
WILBERFOSS AND NEWTON UPON DERWENT 1755
1 Church
2 Stocking Green
3 Former common ings
4 Furdaile
Open fields
Inclosures
Meadows
Commons
Township boundary
miles
0
1
kilometres
0
1
N
EAST MOOR
CARR TONGUE
To Barmby Moor
CARR
CARR HOLD
CARR INGS
THE FURTHER FIELD
Foss beck
To Fangfoss
WHINBERRY HILLS
BURN CARR FIELD
TOWN END FIELD
STOCKING
WILBER-FOSS
PARK FIELD
MILL FIELD
MILL FIELD
MIDDLE FIELD
WHITE LAND FIELD
Foss beck
To Kexby
WEST MOOR
NEWTON
To Sutton upon Derwent
COMMON
MASK
R. Derwent

In 1766 the lands of the earl of Egremont, as lord of Catton, comprised 176 a. in Wilberfoss and 350 a. in Newton.[36] They descended with Catton until 1920–1, when 161 a. in Wilberfoss[37] and 370 a. in Newton were sold in separate lots by C. H. Wyndham, Lord Leconfield.[38]

Of the numerous estates held of the Percys and the Kymes only one was reputed to be a manor. In 1314 John de Rotherfeld held 5 carucates in Newton of Henry de Percy,[39] and this was perhaps the manor of NEWTON which Adam of Rotherham granted to William Clarel in 1319.[40] In 1473 Newton manor was conveyed by Nicholas Drapour to Richard FitzWilliam.[41] It was later held by Thomas FitzWilliam (d. 1513) and then by his son Sir William FitzWilliam (d. 1515).[42] Sir William was succeeded by his daughters Alice (d. 1533), wife of James Foljambe, and Margaret (d. 1557), wife of Geoffrey Foljambe.[43] Francis Foljambe had the manor in 1577 and Sir Thomas Foljambe c. 1602, when it comprised 10 bovates and some closes.[44] Sir Thomas sold it to John Molyneux in 1610, and he to Robert Tirwhit in 1614.[45] Robert Morley was said to have the manor in 1646.[46]

At least part of the estate may have passed to the Burdon family, who already had other land in the township.[47] In 1722 Richard Burdon sold a capital messuage, 7 bovates, and other land to John Nottingham,[48] and he or another of the same name had 223 a. in 1766.[49] Another John Nottingham sold a house and 132 a. to Richard Price in 1819,[50] and on Price's death in 1857 the estate passed to his grandson J. R. Haig.[51] In 1918 D. P. Haig sold the property, then called Newton Hall farm, to William Leach,[52] and the Leaches have since retained it. Hall Farm is a large plain 19th-century farm-house.

Another part of the estate, comprising a house and 61 a., was sold in 1879 by Joseph Terry and others to W. J. Bentley.[53] It passed to Bentley's nephew J. B. Scholes (d. 1944), whose executors sold it in 1948 to W. M. McNeil. In 1969 McNeil sold it to C. J. S. Wood.[54] The house, also known as Hall Farm, is an early-18th-century building with a single range of five bays.

One of the largest estates held under the Percys in Wilberfoss was that of the Wilberfoss or Wilberforce family. An early member of the family was Ilger of Wilberfoss, who is said to have married Margaret, daughter of William of Kyme.[55] William of Wilberfoss held 9 bovates of the Kymes in 1260.[56] The estate was never described as a manor. William Wilberfoss (d. 1557) was succeeded by his son Roger, who in 1577 had a capital messuage and 28 bovates.[57] In the 17th century the family also acquired the former Wilberfoss priory estate, including the rectory.[58] After the death of William Wilberfoss in 1709 the estate was divided among his four sons,[59] and other members of the family also held land in the township. In 1757 another William Wilberfoss sold the 'mansion house', 5 bovates, and 43 a. of closes to Thomas Butterfield,[60] who had 137 a. in the township in 1766.[61] Butterfield devised the estate in 1777 to his nephew William Wilkinson, who died in 1839 holding 255 a., including Hall farm.[62] His devisees sold Hall farm in 1857 to John Dalton and others, and they in 1871 to George Brown: it then comprised 143 a.[63] Brown died in 1902 and devised the estate to his son William Brown and grandson M. G. Wharram,[64] and in 1931 the latter sold it to J. D. Burton.[65] The Burtons still held it in 1974.

Hall or Church Farm, standing on the site of the former priory, was demolished c. 1950. It was a two-storeyed L-shaped house, probably of the earlier 17th century, built of brick on a stone plinth. There was a two-storeyed entrance porch on the main front.[66] The farm buildings included in 1974 a small square structure of early brickwork with a stone plinth which may have been contemporary with the house.

Several religious houses, including Wilberfoss priory itself, had estates in the parish. Land there was confirmed to Warter priory in 1178,[67] and the priory had 4 bovates in Wilberfoss in 1280.[68] After the Dissolution the estate was granted by the Crown to Thomas Manners, earl of Rutland, in 1541.[69] By 1591 it had been sold to Wilfrid Dinnis,[70] and c. 1602 it consisted of a house and 4 bovates in Newton township.[71] The Austin friary at Tickhill (Yorks. W.R.) had land at Newton worth over £5 in 1535.[72] It was held by Francis Gower c. 1602, when it included 11 houses.[73] William Gower was dealing in property in Newton in 1636.[74] A plot of land formerly belonging to Kirkham priory was granted to Joan and John Constable in 1554.[75] In 1539 the Knights Hospitallers had a house in Wilberfoss and rents there and in Newton.[76] The property was briefly restored to them in 1558[77] and their former cottage was mentioned c. 1602.[78] St. Nicholas's

---

[36] R.D.B., AH/177/5.
[37] Ibid. 226/65/55; 229/277/248; 233/456/375; 244/35/26.
[38] Ibid. 224/561/475; 226/65/56; 232/131/115; /412/344.
[39] Cal. Inq. p.m. v, p. 319.
[40] C.P. 25(1)/270/92 no. 36.
[41] C.P. 25(1)/294/76 no. 95.
[42] C 142/45 no. 47; L. & P. Hen. VIII, iv (2), p. 1105.
[43] C 142/111 no. 51; C 142/55 no. 42.
[44] Petworth Ho. Arch., nos. 1416–17, 1423.
[45] Yorks. Fines, 1603–14, 131; 1614–25, 8.
[46] Royalist Composition Papers, iii (Y.A.S. Rec. Ser. xx), 1.
[47] C 142/466 no. 12; Yorks. Fines, 1603–14, 126; 1614–25, 239.
[48] R.D.B., H/267/567.
[49] Ibid. AH/177/5.
[50] Ibid. DF/129/179.
[51] Ibid. HP/318/432; LO/244/342.
[52] Ibid. 189/193/178.
[53] Ibid. MT/336/499.
[54] Ibid. 785/523/421; 1622/163/147.
[55] Visit. Yorks. 1584–5 and 1612, ed. J. Foster, 158–9 gives pedigree.
[56] Cal. Inq. p.m. i, p. 131.
[57] Petworth Ho. Arch., no. 1417 f. 50; C 142/120 no. 86.
[58] See p. 194.
[59] R.D.B., A/178/245.
[60] Ibid. Z/265/613.
[61] Ibid. AH/177/5.
[62] Ibid. AZ/49/70; FM/74/79.
[63] Ibid. HQ/124/149–50; KT/286/399.
[64] Ibid. 51/18/17 (1903); 120/305/275.
[65] Ibid. 424/429/354.
[66] Yorks. Archit. and York Arch. Soc., Ann. Rep. 1949–50, 12–14.
[67] E.Y.C. x, p. 122.
[68] Yorks. Fines, 1272–1300, p. 37.
[69] L. & P. Hen. VIII, xvi, p. 325.
[70] E 178/1321.
[71] Petworth Ho. Arch., nos. 1416, 1423.
[72] V.C.H. Yorks. iii. 281.
[73] Petworth Ho. Arch., nos. 1416, 1423.
[74] C.P. 43/213 rot. 91; C.P. 25(2)/522/12 Chas. I East. pt. 1, no. [6].
[75] Cal. Pat. 1553–4, 146.
[76] Miscellanea, iv (Y.A.S. Rec. Ser. xciv), 104.
[77] Cal. Pat. 1557–8, 319.
[78] Petworth Ho. Arch., no. 1416.

hospital, York, had a cottage and close at Wilberfoss[79] which were granted to John Somer and Thomas Kerry in 1564.[80] St. Peter's hospital, York, was given land in Wilberfoss in the 12th century,[81] and St. Williams's college, York, had property there in 1546.[82]

Jordan son of Gilbert's gift of Wilberfoss church to Wilberfoss priory, perhaps c. 1150,[83] was followed by small gifts of land by Alan of Catton and others.[84] At the Dissolution the priory consisted of a church adjoining the parish church, cloisters, a chapter house, and many rooms and smaller buildings, as well as orchard, gardens, and farm buildings.[85] The priory site and land in Wilberfoss and Newton, together with the rectory, were granted by the Crown in 1553 to George Gale.[86] The Gales held the property[87] until 1636, when they sold the 'manor' of Wilberfoss to Roger Wilberfoss and John Agar.[88] Wilberfoss acquired the Agar share in 1656.[89] With the exception of the rectorial tithes the estate presumably descended with the Wilberfoss family's other lands in the parish.[90] Some of the former priory land in Newton had been separated from the rest by 1611, when Wilfrid Dinnis granted 2 bovates of it to George Lister; it was sold to Francis Burdon in 1623 and Thomas Horsley in 1629.[91]

There were disputes over the payment of tithes in the early 17th century.[92] The tithes of Wilberfoss were worth £30 and those of Newton £27 in 1650.[93] The Wilberfoss family sold the former to Marmaduke and John Simpson in 1736.[94] Those of Newton were subsequently divided: by 1747 half belonged to the Jeffersons and were sold by Richard Jefferson to the earl of Egremont in 1759,[95] and in 1766 a quarter belonged to John Horsley and the rest to William Hardcastle and George Simpkin. At the inclosure of 1766 combined allotments for tithes and freehold estates were made to the several impropriators.[96]

ECONOMIC HISTORY. Medieval agricultural arrangements are obscure. The extension of the cultivated lands in Wilberfoss township is probably indicated by Jordan son of Gilbert's gift to the priory in the 12th century of 6 bovates of old land and one 'of increase'. Several copses were also given to the priory.[97] A dozen sub-tenants held land of the Kymes in 1260,[98] and in the 16th century and later there were many freeholders in the township. In 1577 there were 10 freeholders and a tenant-at-will, and 38 people paid 'boons' in respect of services formerly rendered to the lord of Catton manor, of which Wilberfoss was a member.[99] About 1602 30 houses and 41 bovates belonged to freeholders, and 4 houses and 71 a. were held of Catton manor by unfree tenants;[1] and in 1616 there were 49 houses in Wilberfoss but only 4 unfree tenants.[2]

The arable land of the township lay in seven open fields by 1616, namely Burn Carr, Far, New Bridge, Mill, Park or Stone Pit, Stocking, and Town End fields. Park field had been referred to as West field in the 16th century.[3] Burn Carr ings in 1616 were presumably common meadows near Foss beck. The common pastures were then known as Low or South-east moor, containing 494 a., Stocking, of 36 a., and Furdaile, of 11 a.[4] The moor was used solely by Wilberfoss, but the inhabitants also intercommoned on East and West moors in Catton. Limited rights on West moor were enjoyed under an agreement made with Richard de Percy in the 13th century, but Wilberfoss apparently lost them in the 16th century after persistent encroachment.[5]

By the early 18th century a little inclosure had taken place. The 15-acre New close in Far field was mentioned in 1709, and Seave and Beck closes in 1716;[6] Seave close may have been in the medieval 'Seveker',[7] and it seems that it was the beckside meadows and carrs that were being inclosed. By the 1750s there was also a substantial area of closes around the village and part of Park field had been inclosed.[8] In 1766 the total extent of ancient inclosed land was about 270 a.[9] Stocking common was said in 1755 to be 'useful for a hold for calves and horses'.[10]

The remaining open fields and commons were inclosed in 1766[11] under an Act of 1760.[12] A total of 1,149 a. was allotted, comprising 97 a. in Birker, 107 a. in Far, 52 a. in Mill, 75 a. in Stone Pit, and 153 a. in Town End fields, and 551 a. in East moor, 38 a. in Stocking, 3 a. in Stocking green, 25 a. in West moor, and 48 a. in Whinberry Hills. The largest allotment, partly in lieu of tithes, went to John Simpson, and the earl of Egremont received 86 a. One other allotment exceeded 100 a., and there were 4 of 70–99 a., 4 of 30–69 a., 12 of 10–29 a., and 12 of under 10 a.

At Newton there were 15 free tenants in 1577 and 28 people paid 'boons' to the lord of Catton.[13] Newer reclaimed land is indicated by the mention of 'forby lands' in 1611,[14] and by 1662 the township's open fields were known as Middle, Mill, and Whiteland.[15] Newton apparently had the sole use of Newton carr, but Low Catton men intercommoned in Newton moor or common and in the open fields, just as Newton men did in West moor in Catton.[16] Beast-gates in the carr were mentioned in the 18th

---

[79] Petworth Ho. Arch., no. 1416; E.R.R.O., DDKP/15/2; *Valor Eccl.* (Rec. Com.), v. 21.
[80] *Cal. Pat.* 1563–6, pp. 11–12.
[81] *E.Y.C.* ii, pp. 252–3.
[82] *V.C.H. Yorks.* iii. 386.
[83] See p. 195.
[84] *V.C.H. Yorks.* iii. 125; *L. & P. Hen. VIII*, i (1), pp. 77–8; *Yorks. Fines, 1232–46*, pp. 37–8.
[85] *Y.A.J.* ix. 204–6.
[86] *Cal. Pat.* 1553, 89.
[87] C 142/109 no. 52; C 142/134 no. 224; C 142/212 no. 14; Petworth Ho. Arch., no. 1416.
[88] C.P. 25(2)/522/12 Chas. I East. pt. 1, no. [45].
[89] C.P. 25(2)/614/1656 Trin. no. 39.
[90] See p. 193.
[91] E.R.R.O., DDX/185/2–4.
[92] B.I.H.R., CP. H. 6, 2158, 2188, 2232–3.
[93] C 94/3 f. 57.   [94] R.D.B., Q/117/267.
[95] Ibid. T/63/126; AB/55/135.

[96] Ibid. AH/177/5.
[97] *Cal. Pat.* 1485–94, 466.
[98] *Cal. Inq. p.m.* i, p. 131.
[99] Petworth Ho. Arch., no. 1417 ff. 50–2, 55d.
[1] Ibid no. 1416.   [2] Ibid no. 3072.
[3] Ibid no. 1416.
[4] Ibid no. 3072.
[5] Ibid no. 1416; see p. 153.
[6] R.D.B., A/180/246; F/20/42.
[7] *Cal. Pat.* 1485–94, 467.
[8] See map on p. 192.
[9] R.D.B., AH/177/5.
[10] Petworth Ho. Arch., no. 3443.
[11] R.D.B., AH/177/5.
[12] 33 Geo. II, c. 43 (Priv. Act).
[13] Petworth Ho. Arch., no. 1417 ff. 51–2.
[14] E.R.R.O., DDX/185/2; see p. 124.
[15] B.I.H.R., TER. I. Wilberfoss 1662.
[16] Petworth Ho. Arch., nos. 1416, 1423.

century.[17] Onions, from seed bought in York, and parsnips were grown in a garden in the village in the 1590s.[18]

The open fields and commons were inclosed with those of Wilberfoss in 1766,[19] when allotments totalling 1,447 a. were made. They comprised 203 a. in Middle, 215 a. in Mill, and 202 a. in White Land fields, 31 a. in Carr ings and 45 a. in Mask, and 345 a. in the common, 51 a. in Carr Hold, and 355 a. in the carr and Carr Tongue. The largest allotments consisted of 299 a. to the earl of Egremont, 223 a. to Mann Horsfield, and 208 a. to John Nottingham. There was one other allotment of over 100 a., 3 of 70–99 a., 6 of 30–69 a., 5 of 10–29 a., and 6 of under 10 a.

In the 19th and 20th centuries there have usually been 15–25 farmers at Wilberfoss and 10–20 at Newton. In 1851 5 in each township had over 100 a., but in the 1920s and 1930s only one or 2 at Newton had 150 a. or more.[20] The arable area in 1795 amounted to 597 a. in Wilberfoss and 795 a. in Newton,[21] and in 1905 there were 1,095 a. of arable, 384 a. of grassland, and 9 a. of wood in Wilberfoss, and 979 a. of arable, 425 a. of grassland, and 5 a. of wood in Newton.[22] Arable was still predominant in the 1930s and later, with pasture mainly near the Derwent and the becks and around the two villages.[23] There have been half-a-dozen smallholders in the 20th century, mainly on the former commons in the east of the parish.[24]

There is little evidence of non-agricultural employment in the parish, but at Wilberfoss a brickmaker was mentioned in 1775,[25] a tanner in 1791,[26] and a brewer in 1823,[27] and at Newton there was an agricultural implement maker in the late 19th century.[28] The location of former brickworks is indicated by Brickyard Farm, in Carr Lane at Newton,[29] and old clay pits south of the Hull road in Wilberfoss.[30] There are large disused gravel pits on the moraine in both townships. An agricultural engineer has operated from a site on the Hull road at Wilberfoss since 1949[31] and there are now extensive warehouses.

A water-mill at Wilberfoss belonging to the priory was mentioned in the 1230s,[32] and a windmill was included in the grant of former priory property to George Gale in 1553.[33] A windmill was mentioned again in 1669[34] and from 1823 onwards, a miller being last recorded in 1933.[35] The latest mill stood on the moraine north-west of the village but was demolished c. 1970. The name Mill field in both Wilberfoss and Newton suggests that there was at least one earlier windmill site in the parish. In 1755 an oatmeal mill stood near the beck at Wilberfoss, close to Stone bridge.[36]

LOCAL GOVERNMENT. Surviving court records for the manor and soke of Catton, within which Wilberfoss lay, show that in the 1470s two constables and two aletasters were elected for Wilberfoss township and two constables and one aletaster for Newton. Two constables were chosen for each township in the 1660s, and a constable, four bylawmen, and a pinder were appointed for Wilberfoss in the 19th century.[37]

No parochial records before 1835 are known. Several poorhouses stood on Stocking green at Wilberfoss in 1755[38] and 1850,[39] and six families lived there in 1851.[40] Wilberfoss and Newton joined Pocklington poor-law union in 1836[41] and Pocklington rural district in 1894.[42] They became part of the North Wolds district of Humberside in 1974.

CHURCH. It was perhaps c. 1150 that Jordan son of Gilbert gave Wilberfoss church and its chapel at Newton upon Derwent, together with 7 bovates of land, to Wilberfoss priory.[43] The gift was confirmed in 1233[44] and the church was appropriated to the priory, though no vicarage was ordained.[45] After the Dissolution Wilberfoss remained a perpetual curacy until the 19th century; it was styled a vicarage by 1872.[46] The benefice was united with Kexby in 1959.[47]

The church was presumably served by a chaplain, found by the priory, until the Dissolution. Thereafter the appointment of curates and presentation of vicars descended with Catton manor.[48] After 1959 the patrons of the united benefice were J. E. Vesey, 6th Viscount de Vesci, and J. E. R. Wyndham, created Baron Egremont.[49]

The parochial chaplain received £4 6s. 8d. in 1525–6.[50] The curate's stipend, paid out of the rectory, was £10 in 1650[51] and £12 in the 18th century.[52] The curacy was augmented with £200 from Queen Anne's Bounty in 1764, 1786, and 1810 and with a parliamentary grant of £1,200 in 1819.[53] The average net income was £67 in 1829–31.[54] An endowment of £17 a year was made from the Common Fund in 1871 in respect of a gift of £510 to the

[17] E.R.R.O., DDPY/37/13; DDX/185/10; R.D.B., H/267/567.
[18] B.I.H.R., CP. H. 6.
[19] R.D.B., AH/177/5.
[20] H.O. 107/2351; directories.
[21] E.R.R.O., DPX/84.
[22] Acreage Returns, 1905.
[23] [1st] Land Util. Surv. Map, sheet 27; 2nd Land Util. Surv. Map, sheet 709 (SE 65–75).
[24] Directories.
[25] E.R.R.O., QSF. East. 1775, C.21.
[26] Ibid. QSF. Mids. 1791, C.10.
[27] Baines, *Hist. Yorks.* (1823), ii. 400.
[28] *Kelly's Dir. N. & E.R. Yorks.* (1872), 560; (1893), 506.
[29] H.O. 107/2351.
[30] O.S. Map 1/2,500, Yorks. CLXXV. 12 (1910 edn.).
[31] R.D.B., 813/51/38.
[32] *Percy Charty.* (Sur. Soc. cxvii), 87. See also *Cal. Pat. 1485–94*, 467; *Monastic Notes*, i (Y.A.S. Rec. Ser. xvii), 226.
[33] See p. 194.
[34] C.P. 43/345 rot. 53.
[35] Directories.
[36] Petworth Ho. Arch., no. 3443.
[37] See pp. 154–5.
[38] Petworth Ho. Arch., no. 3443.
[39] O.S. Map 6" (1854 edn.).
[40] H.O. 107/2351.
[41] *3rd Rep. Poor Law Com.* 169.
[42] *Census.*
[43] *V.C.H. Yorks.* iii. 125.
[44] *Reg. Gray*, p. 57.
[45] *Reg. Greenfield*, v, p. 231; *V.C.H. Yorks.* iii. 86 n.
[46] *Kelly's Dir. N. & E.R. Yorks.* (1872), 560.
[47] York Dioc. Regy., Order in Council 748.
[48] e.g. *Rep. Com. Eccl. Revenues*, 978; directories.
[49] R.D.B., 1745/56/52.
[50] *Y.A.J.* xxiv. 72.
[51] C 94/3 f. 57.
[52] B.I.H.R., TER. I. Wilberfoss 1716 etc.
[53] Hodgson, *Q.A.B.* 457.
[54] *Rep. Com. Eccl. Revenues*, 978.

Ecclesiastical Commissioners.[55] The net income of the vicarage was £99 in 1884 and £86 in 1915.[56]

Open-field land apparently belonged to the curacy in the late 17th century,[57] but in the 18th there was no glebe[58] until bounty money was used by 1786 to buy 6 a. in Dunsforth (Yorks. W.R.). Another 9 a. were bought at Bempton by 1809, 2 a. at Huntington (Yorks. N.R.) by 1817, and 5 a. at Wilberfoss by 1849.[59] The Wilberfoss land was sold in 1971 but that at Dunsforth and Bempton still belonged to the living in 1974.[60] In the 18th century the only other source of income was fees. A cottage belonged to the curacy in the late 17th century[61] but there was subsequently no parsonage house until one was bought, with half of the parliamentary grant, by 1825.[62] The Vicarage, a late-18th-century house standing in the west of the village on the York road, was sold in 1936.[63]

A guild of St. Mary at Wilberfoss was mentioned in 1402.[64] The dependent chapel at Newton, given with the church to Wilberfoss priory,[65] was mentioned again in 1447,[66] and in 1539 the chaplain's stipend was said to be paid by the lessee of the former priory property in the parish.[67] The chapel was perhaps suppressed along with the chantries. Chapel garth was granted by the Crown to George Gale in 1553 and the lands formerly belonging to the chapel to Francis Barker and Thomas Browne in 1571.[68] It was stated in 1582 that about sixteen years earlier a villager had taken a chalice and vestment from the chapel and kept them.[69]

The curate of Wilberfoss was also vicar of Bugthorpe in 1705,[70] and in 1743 he was rector of Sutton upon Derwent, where he lived.[71] In 1764 he lived at Wilberfoss, in a rented house.[72] From the early 20th century the vicar also held and lived at Kexby,[73] and since 1959 the incumbent of the united benefice has continued to live at Kexby.[74]

A service was held in the church weekly in summer and fortnightly in winter in 1743; communion was then celebrated four times a year and there were 98 communicants the previous Easter.[75] By 1764 there were two services a week, and the number of communicants at Easter had dropped to 68.[76] There was again only one Sunday service by 1851[77] but two once more by 1871, and in 1884 there was also a service on Wednesdays. Communion was celebrated six times a year, with 20–30 recipients, in 1865, monthly in 1871, and weekly in 1894.[78] In 1974 there were two services each Sunday.

The church of *ST. JOHN THE BAPTIST*, of rubble and ashlar, consists of chancel with north vestry, nave with south aisle and porch, and west tower. It is probable that in the late medieval period the priory church occupied the position of the present chancel and that the claustral ranges abutted upon the existing nave. The north wall of the nave is now windowless and although plastered on both faces may be dated by the stumps of two 12th-century buttresses. The nave has a south arcade of the 13th century but the aisle and porch date from the 15th century; the aisle was described as new built in 1447–8.[79] The tower was also a 15th-century addition and there was a bequest towards its building in 1461.[80] Although it incorporates some old materials the present chancel appears to date from the 19th century. On its north side the vestry, like the organ recess projecting from the nave, is a 19th- and 20th-century adaptation of the stumps of old walls running towards the priory.

From 1766 income for the repair of the church was received from a one-acre close and a 6s. rent-charge in Wilberfoss and a one-acre close and a 9-acre allotment, made at inclosure that year, in Newton.[81] Rents from the property were received by the churchwardens in 1824.[82] The joint Church and Poor's Lands charity at Newton was divided under a Scheme of 1925, when the church charity had 10 a. in Newton, £18 stock, and £84 cash. In 1962 the income of £25 was used for repairs and in 1973 £30 was so used.[83]

The bells were rehung in 1629[84] and payments were made for recasting in 1753 and 1791.[85] There are three surviving bells: (i) 1759; (ii) 1790, Dalton of York; (iii) 1667.[86] The plate includes a silver cup dated 1805 and a pewter flagon and paten.[87] The registers of baptisms, marriages, and burials begin in 1618, with a gap in 1666–77.[88]

The churchyard was enlarged in 1858[89] and 1926.[90]

NONCONFORMITY. In 1571 Roger Wilberfoss and Edward Harling were reported to have kept undefaced the timber of the rood loft and the stones of the cross from the church.[91] In the 1590s and early 17th century there were more than a dozen recusants in the parish, including members of the Gale family. There were still a few recusants in the mid 17th century,[92] and two in 1676.[93]

A house was registered for protestant nonconformist worship in 1764,[94] and there were eight

---

[55] *Lond. Gaz.* 18 Aug. 1871, p. 3648.
[56] B.I.H.R., Bp. V. 1884/Ret.; Bp. V. 1915/Ret.
[57] Ibid. TER. I. Wilberfoss 1662–90.
[58] Ibid. 1716 etc.
[59] Ibid. 1786, 1809, 1849.
[60] R.D.B., 1745/56/52; ex inf. the vicar, 1974.
[61] B.I.H.R., TER. I. Wilberfoss 1662–90.
[62] Ibid. 1825.
[63] R.D.B., 545/48/38.
[64] *Test. Ebor.* i, p. 302.
[65] See p. 195.
[66] E 315/401 f. 401.
[67] *Test. Ebor.* ii, p. 125.
[68] *Cal. Pat.* 1553, 89; 1569–72, p. 237.
[69] B.I.H.R., V. 1582/CB.
[70] Lamb. Pal. Libr., MS. 964 f. 1222.
[71] *Herring's Visit.* iii. 213.
[72] B.I.H.R., Bp. V. 1764/Ret. 134.
[73] Directories.
[74] Crockford.
[75] *Herring's Visit.* iii. 213.
[76] B.I.H.R., Bp. V. 1764/Ret. 134.
[77] H.O. 129/23/516.
[78] B.I.H.R., V. 1865/Ret. 594; V. 1871/Ret. 555; Bp. V. 1884/Ret.; Bp. V. 1894/Ret.
[79] Ibid. Prob. Reg. 2, f. 165.
[80] *Test. Ebor.* ii, p. 239.
[81] B.I.H.R., Bp. V. 1764/Ret. 134; PR. WILB. 14; R.D.B., AH/177/5.
[82] *11th Rep. Com. Char.* 748.
[83] Char. Com. files; ex inf. Messrs. Grays, Solicitors, York, 1974. See p. 197.
[84] B.I.H.R., CP. H. 1865.
[85] Ibid. PR. WILB. 14.
[86] Boulter, 'Ch. Bells', 27.
[87] *Yorks. Ch. Plate*, i. 334.
[88] B.I.H.R.
[89] Ibid. PR. WILB. 16.
[90] York Dioc. Regy., Consecration deed.
[91] J. S. Purvis, *Tudor Par. Doc. of Dioc. York*, 150.
[92] Aveling, *Post Reformation Catholicism*, 59.
[93] Bodl. MS. Tanner 150 ff. 27 sqq.
[94] G.R.O. Worship Returns, Vol. v, no. 214.

Methodist families in the parish that year.[95] The Methodists had 7–33 members in Wilberfoss and 4–22 in Newton in 1790–1816.[96] Houses in Wilberfoss were licensed for worship in 1812 and 1819,[97] and in Newton in 1820 and 1821.[98] The first chapel in the parish was registered by the Wesleyan Methodists at Newton in 1818[99] and replaced by a new one on the same site in 1901,[1] still used in 1974. A Wesleyan chapel in Wilberfoss was built facing the beck in 1841[2] and also remained in use in 1974. A Primitive Methodist chapel in Wilberfoss was built in Back Lane in 1824[3] and rebuilt on the same site in 1872.[4] It was deregistered in 1937[5] but was still standing in 1974.

EDUCATION. There was a schoolmaster at Wilberfoss in 1748–9,[6] and in 1764 a schoolmaster was hired by the inhabitants of Newton.[7] By 1835 there were two day schools with about 40 children and a boarding school for 14 boys at Wilberfoss, and a day school for 12 pupils at Newton; all were supported by the parents.[8] The boarding school was presumably that kept by the incumbent in 1840.[9] A school stood beside Wilberfoss green in 1851.[10] In 1868 60–75 children attended three schools in the parish,[11] but in 1871 there was only a school at Newton, with 24 in attendance, while Wilberfoss children went to Kexby.[12] A school at Wilberfoss was built in 1873, together with a schoolmaster's house, and opened the next year, receiving its first annual government grant in 1875; the average attendance in 1874 was 78.[13] It was united with the National Society.[14]

The attendance usually varied between 70 and 100 in 1906–37.[15] In 1955 senior pupils were transferred to Pocklington.[16] A new school on the Fangfoss road was opened in 1973, but the old building also continued to be used. There were 103 on the roll in January 1974.[17]

By a Scheme of 1884 half the income of the poor's share of the Church and Poor's Lands charity at Newton was paid to help children attending Wilberfoss school. The educational part of the income was then £10 a year, but little or none was used for the benefit of Newton children in the early 20th century. The educational part was separated from the general charity in 1905. Under a Scheme of 1925 the income was widely applied on behalf of local children, including payments towards other than elementary education. The income was then still £10 a year and there was £72 cash in hand.[18] In 1969 a grant of £15 was made to the Sunday school and in 1971 £94 was used for repairs to charity property; no grants were made in 1971–3.[19]

CHARITIES FOR THE POOR. Thomas Wood, by will dated 1568, devised a rent-charge of £10 from an estate at Kilnwick Percy for the benefit of Wilberfoss, Newton, and many other townships. In 1824 3s. 4d. each was distributed in Wilberfoss and Newton.[20] Henry Frederick, Baron Hotham, owner of the Kilnwick Percy estate, redeemed the rent-charge in 1961 and £13 stock was assigned to Wilberfoss and Newton.[21] The income of 6s. 8d. was not distributed in 1967.[22]

William Clark before 1764 devised 10s. a year from land at Newton to be distributed in the parish in cash at Christmas, Easter, and Whitsun and in bread on one Sunday each year. It was distributed largely as intended in 1824.[23]

John Horsley, by will dated 1719, bequeathed £40 after his wife's death to the poor of Newton township. She died by 1728. The churchwardens and overseers held 9 a. in Newton in respect of the charity in 1766. In 1824 the income was distributed in lots of between 5s. and £3.[24]

Clark's and Horsley's charities, along with another for Newton's share of repairs to Wilberfoss church, were later jointly administered as the Church and Poor's Lands charity; by a Scheme of 1884 half of the income of the poor's part was applied to education. The educational share was separated from the general charity in 1905. The latter was divided by a Scheme of 1925 into distinct church and poor's charities; the poor's charity then had a cottage and 9 a. in Newton and £59 cash. The poor's charity income was £42 in 1962, and payments made included gifts of £2 to each of 7 persons.[25] In 1973 gifts totalling £28 were made to 17 persons.[26]

John Bell (d. 1938) instructed his trustees to administer a fund to supply a nurse for Wilberfoss parish. By a deed of 1941 a nursing association was promoted and a nurse was provided from then until 1971. By a Scheme of 1972 the nursing association was converted to the John Bell Relief in Sickness and Infirmity Fund. Its endowment then comprised £2,075 stock and £119 cash, and the income was to be used for the general benefit of Wilberfoss and adjoining parishes.[27] In 1974 the income of £70 a year was used to employ a 'home help'.[28]

---

[95] B.I.H.R., Bp. V. 1764/Ret. 134.
[96] E.R.R.O., MRP/1/7.
[97] G.R.O. Worship Returns, Vol. v, nos. 2554, 3324.
[98] B.I.H.R., DMH. Reg. 1, pp. 155, 279.
[99] Ibid. p. 55.   [1] G.R.O. Worship Reg. no. 38317.
[2] Date on building.
[3] White, *Dir. E. & N.R. Yorks.* (1840), 248.
[4] Date on building.
[5] G.R.O. Worship Reg. no. 11811.
[6] K. F. Mills, *Hist. of Priory and Ch., Wilberfoss*, 17.
[7] B.I.H.R., Bp. V. 1764/Ret. 134.
[8] *Educ. Enquiry Abstract*, 1099.
[9] White, *Dir. E. & N.R. Yorks.* (1840), 249.
[10] O.S. Map 6" (1854 edn.).
[11] B.I.H.R., V. 1868/Ret. 551.
[12] *Returns relating to Elem. Educ.* 794.
[13] Ed. 7/135 no. 201; *Rep. of Educ. Cttee. of Council, 1875–6* [C. 1513–I], p. 672, H.C. (1876), xxiii.
[14] B.I.H.R., V. 1877/Ret. 166.
[15] *Bd. of Educ. List 21* (H.M.S.O.).
[16] E.R. Educ. Cttee. *Mins.* 1955–6, 152.
[17] Ex inf. Chief Educ. Officer, County Hall, Beverley, 1974.
[18] Ed. 49/8580–1; Char. Com. files.
[19] Ex inf. Messrs. Grays, 1974.
[20] *11th Rep. Com. Char.* 735, 746, 748.
[21] Ex inf. Char. Com., Liverpool, 1974.
[22] Char. Com. files.
[23] B.I.H.R., Bp. V. 1764/Ret. 134; *11th Rep. Com. Char.* 746.
[24] R.D.B., AH/177/5; *11th Rep. Com. Char.* 747–8.
[25] Char. Com. files; Ed. 49/8580–1; see p. 196 and above.
[26] Char. Com. files; ex inf. Messrs. Grays, 1974.
[27] Char. Com. files.
[28] Ex inf. Mrs. A. E. Ward, Wilberfoss, 1974.

INDEX

NOTE. An italic page-number denotes an illustration on that page or facing it.

Among the abbreviations used in the index the following may need elucidation: adv., advowson; Alex., Alexander; Alf., Alfred; And., Andrew; Ant., Anthony; abp., archbishop; Art., Arthur; Benj., Benjamin; bp., bishop; b., born; bro., brother; Cath., Cathedral or Catherine; chant., chantry(–ies); chap., chapel; char., charities; Chas., Charles; Chris., Christopher; ch., church(es); coll., college; ct., court(s) (manorial &c.); Cuth., Cuthbert; dau., daughter(s); Dav., David; d., died; dom. arch., domestic architecture; Edm., Edmund; Edw., Edward; Eliz., Elizabeth; Eust., Eustace; fam., family; f., father; fl., flourished; Fred., Frederick; Geof., Geoffrey; Geo., George; Gilb., Gilbert; grds., grandson; Hen., Henry; Herb., Herbert; hosp., hospital; ho., house; Humph., Humphrey; husb., husband; inc., inclosure; ind., industry; Jas., James; Jos., Joseph; jr., junior; Leon., Leonard; Ld., Lord; man., manor (ial, –s); Marg., Margaret; mkt., market; Marm., Marmaduke; m., married; Mat., Matthew; Mic., Michael; Nat., Nathaniel; Nic., Nicholas; par., parish; Pet., Peter; Phil., Philip; pop., population; prot. nonconf., protestant noncomformity; rly. stn., railway station (s); Reg., Reginald; Ric., Richard; riv., river; Rob., Robert; Rog., Roger; Rom. Cath., Roman Catholicism; Sam., Samuel; sch., school(s); sr., senior; Sim., Simon; s., son(s); Steph., Stephen; Thos., Thomas; Tim., Timothy; Vct., Viscount; Wal., Walter; wid., widow; w., wife; Wilf., Wilfred; Wm., William.

Acaster Malbis (Yorks. W.R.), 74–5, 78, 80–1
  vicar of, see Squire, Gabriel
Acaster Selby (Yorks. W.R.), 101–2, 107, 110–12
  St. Andrew's coll., 166
Acklam:
  Eliz., m. Sir Wm. Milbanke, 106
  Hen. of, 110
  John (d. 1551), 77, 106
  John (d. 1611), 111
  John (d. 1643), 106
  Mary, see Moreby
  Ric. (fl. 1490), 77, 79
  Wm. (fl. c. 1370), 106
  Wm. (d. 1567), 106
  Sir Wm. (fl. 1619), 25, 106
  fam., 77, 106, 108, 110–11
Adam, Ric. s. of, see Richard
Adam, Wm., 110
Adams:
  Chris., 95–6
  Frances, m. Jocelyn Price, 95
  John, 95
  fam., 96
Adamson, Oliver, 65
affeerors, 10, 26, 109, 138, 144
Agar, John, 194
agricultural implement making, 9, 177, 195
agricultural societies, shows, 19, 83
Aguilon, Wm., 175
Aike (in Lockington), 131
Air Ministry, 123, 138
Aire and Calder Navigation, 109
airfields, 12–13, 15, 47, 56, 83, 91, 121, 133, 138, 140–1, 164–5, 168, 170–1, 181–2, 187
Akam, Phil., 107
Alan, count of Brittany (d. 1089), 20–1, 31, 34, 69, 104–6, 123
Alan, count of Brittany (? he who d. 1093), 104
Alan, count of Brittany, earl of Richmond (d. 1146), 123
Alan son of Roald, constable of Richmond, 21
Alba, cardinal bp. of, see Ossat
Albemarle, duke of, see Monck, Chris. and Geo.
Aldborough:
  Eliz., m. 1 Brian Stapleton, 2 Ric. Redeman, 105
  Sibyl, m. Wm. of Ryther, 105
  Wm. (d. c. 1388), 105
  Wm. (d. by 1392), 105
Alden (fl. 1066), 6
aletasters, 26, 33, 80, 138, 155, 187, 195
Alford, Vct., see Home-Cust
Allanson (Allison):
  Chris., 22, 123
  John, 45–6
Allen:
  John, 160
  Rob., 42
Allerthorpe:
  John of, 115

Thos. of, 115
Allerthorpe, *112*, 131, **133–40**, 146, 169, 176, 188
  char., 139–40
  ch., 133, 138–9, 188
  common fields, 133, 136–9
  common pastures, 133, 135, 137–8
  ct., 137–8
  curates of, 138
  dom. arch., 133–4
  the Gables, 134
  Hall, 133–4
  inc., 133, 137–9
  ind., 138
  inn, 133
  lock, 133
  man., 134–8, 141
  man.-ho., 135
  par. officers, 138
  perpetual curacy, 138, 188; *and see* Thornton, vicarage
  pop., 134
  prot. nonconf., 138–9
  rectory, 134, 136
  roads, 133
  Rom. Cath., 139
  sch., 139
  tithes, 136, 138
  vicarage ho. (of Thornton), 138
  windmills, 138
  woodland, 133, 137
  and see Waplington
Allison, *see* Allanson
allotments and smallholdings, 25, 41, 53, 66, 85–6, 147, 154, 191, 195
Almond, T. E., 176
alms-houses, *see* Elvington; Escrick; Heslington; Riccall; Skipwith
Altham, Sir Jas., 114, 116
Alulf (fl. 1086), 13–14
Alwine (fl. 1066), 160
Amcotes:
  Alex., 61
  Ric. of, 61
  fam., 61
Amherst:
  Eliz., *see* Cary
  Sir Jeffery, 39
Ampleforth, prebend of, *see* York, Cath. ch. of St. Peter
ancient demesne, 41–2
Andrews, G. T., 81
Andrie, Wm., 101
Anglo-Saxon Chronicle, 149
Anlaby, Susanna, m. 1 Chas. Bowes, 2 Chas. Fenwick, 55
Anlaby (in Kirk Ella), 130, 132
Annas, Hen., 8
Annesley:
  Art., Vct. Valentia (d. 1686), 114, 120 *n*
  Art., Vct. Valentia (d. 1816), 94, 114
  Francis (d. 1750), 93, 119
  Francis (fl. 1801), 93
  Revd. Francis (fl. 1801), 93–4
  Hugh, 34
  fam., 114, 116

Appleby, Eliz., 7
Appleton:
  Rob. of (fl. 1294), rector of Sutton upon Derwent, 178
  Rob. (fl. 1572), 166
  Rob. (d. 1658), 146
Appleton, Nun, priory (Yorks. W.R.), 152
archer, Sim. the, *see* Simon
architects, *see* Andrews; Atkinson, J. B., W., and Wm.; Blore; Bownas; Carr, John; Chantrell; Christian; Etty; Fawcett, Jos.; Fowler; Hardwick, P. C.; Jones, G. F.; Matthew; Pearson, J. L.; Penrose; Pritchett; Salvin, Ant.; Sharpe; Street; Weightman & Hatfield; White, Wm.
Armstrong's Patents Co. Ltd., 75
Arram (in Leconfield), 131
Arras (in Market Weighton), 131
Asa (fl. 1066), 160
Ash:
  Eliz., 136
  Revd. Leon., 136
Ashworth, Thos., 49
Aske:
  Conan, 20
  John (fl. 1542), 21, 78, 115, 117
  John (fl. 1596), 21, 115
  Ric., 25
  Rob., 91
  fam., 21, 123
Askham Richard (Yorks. W.R.), 156
assarting, 1; *and see under places*
assizes of bread and ale, 15, 33, 59, 80, 98, 138, 163, 168, 187
Atkinson:
  J. B., 73, 145 *n*
  Rob., 116
  W., 73
  Wm., 178
Aton:
  Anastasia, m. Edw. St. John, 48
  Cath., m. Ralph Eure, 48
  Eliz., m. 1 Wm. Place, 2 Sir John Conyers, 48
  Gilb. de (d. by 1302), 48
  Gilb. de (d. 1324), 48, 183
  Wm. de, s. of Gilb. of Barlby, 48
  Wm. de (fl. 1284), 48
  Wm. (d. 1389), 48
  fam., 49, 63–4
Aubigny:
  Cecily de, *see* Bigod
  Gunnore de, 77
  Isabel de, m. Rob. de Ros (d. *c.* 1285), 77
  Ralph de, 77
  Wm. de (fl. 12th cent.), 77
  Wm. de (d. by 1242), 77
  fam., 77
Auckland St. Andrew (co. Dur.), collegiate ch., dean of, *see* Mauley, Steph. de
Aughton, 93, 114, 118, 131, 156
  and see Cottingwith, East; Laytham

INDEX

Aumale:
  earl of, *see* Forz
  honor of, 165
Austin, Wm., 114, 116
Avice daughter of Jernegan son of Hugh, m. Rob. Marmion, 106 *n*
Avranches:
  Cath. d', m. Wm. Skipwith, 63, 93
  Ric. d' (fl. 1200), 63, 93
  Ric. d' (fl. 14th cent.), 96, 99
  fam., 63, 93, 96
Ayscough, Hen., rector of Dunnington and Elvington, 10, 16

Babthorpe:
  Isabel, m. Sir John Hastings, 53
  (formerly Hunsley), Ralph of (fl. c. 1190), 53
  Ralph of (fl. 1284), 53
  Sir Ralph (d. 1490), 53
  Sir Ralph (d. 1618), 48, 78
  Rob. of, 52
  Thos., 43, 45, 65
    his f. and bro., 45
  Wm. (d. 1501), 53
  Wm. (d. 1555), 48, 54, 58, 78
  Sir Wm. (d. 1581), 40, 54, 63
  Wm. (fl. 1619), 95
  Sir Wm. (d. 1635), 48, 53, 65
  fam., 48–9, 53, 63, 65–6
Babthorpe (in Hemingbrough), 3, 50, 52–3, 55
  chap., man., 53
  dom. arch., 53
  man., 39, 49, 53, 58, 65
  man.-ho., 53
  moated site, 53
  rectory, 55
  roads, 52
  tithes, 55
Bachelor:
  Eliz., 57
  Mary, 57
Bacon, J. H., 54
Badlesmere, Margery de, m. Wm., Ld. Ros, 183
Bailey, Eleanor, 36
Baillie, Jane, 123
Bain:
  Edwin S., and his w., 95
  Frances, m. E. W. Sandys, 95
Baines:
  H. J., 22, 82
  H. M., 77
  H. V., 77
  Hen., and his w. Emily, 82
  Hewley (d. 1760), 77, 81
  Hewley (d. 1800), 79–80, 82
  J. H., 78
  John, 77
  Marg., *see* Hewley
  W. M., 77
  fam., 22, 77
Bainton, 130, 132; *and see* Neswick
Bainton Beacon division (of Harthill wapentake), 132
Baker, Clement, 70
Baldric, Hugh s. of, *see* Hugh
Baldwin, fam., 116
Ball, John, 136
Ballard, Thos., 94
Banks:
  John, 53–4, 62
  Wm., 39, 53–4
  fam., 53
Bardolf:
  John, 21
  Ralph, 94
  Rog., 94
  Wm., 21
  fam., 21
Bardwell:
  Fred., 142
  T. N. F., 142
Barker:

Frances, *see* Mason
Francis, 16, 81, 110, 119, 145, 156, 169, 196
  John, 14
  Thos. (fl. 1717), 54
  Thos. (fl. 1853), 7
Barlby, Gilb. of, 48
Barlby (in Hemingbrough), 3, 37, 42, 46, **47–52**, 57, 61, 64
  adv., 50
  assarting, 49
  Barlby, New (Barlby Bank, Bank Ho., Selby Water Ho.), 47–52
  brick-making, 50
  bridges, 47–8
  char., 50–2, 63
  ch., 47, 50–2
  common fields, 47, 49
  common meadows, 47, 49
  common pastures, 47, 49
  curates of, 50, 110; *and see* Braim; Froggott; Lecke, Thos.; Potter, Rob. and Wm.; Teasdale; Williamson, Wm.
  dom. arch., 47–8
  drainage, 47, 49
  ferries, 47
  fishing, 50
  the Grove, 47
  Hall, 48
  inc., 47, 49
  ind., 2, 37, 47–8, 50
  inns, 48
  man., 48–9, 63
  man.-ho., 48; *and see* Barlby, Hall
  mills, 48, 50
  moated site, 48
  perpetual curacy, 50
  poor relief, 50
  pop., 48
  prot. nonconf., 51
  rectory, 49, 58, 65
  roads, 47–8
  sch., 46, 51–2, 60, 62, 66, 89, 101, 112, 120
  tithes, 49, 58, 65
  vicar of, 47, 50
  vicarage, 50
  vicarage ho., 50
  wharves, 50
  woodland, 49
Barmby Moor (Barnby Moor; *also* in, on, *or* upon the Moor), 131, 135, **140–7**
  adv., 144
  chant., 145
  char., 145–7
  ch., 140, 142, 144–7, 169
  common fields, 140, 143
  common pastures, 140, 143–4
  ct., 144
  dom. arch., 141
  fair, 143
  Ho., 141
  inc., 140–4, 146
  ind., 140–1, 144
  inns, *129*, 141
  man., 140–4, 146
  man.-ho. (Barmby Man.), *129*, 141–2
  mkt., 143
  moated site, 140, 142
  par. officers, 144, 146
  poor relief, 144
  pop., 141
  prot. nonconf., 146
  rectory, 142, 144
  recusancy, 146
  roads, 133, 140
  sch., 146–7
  tithes, 142–4
  vicarage (Barmby Moor with Fangfoss), 138, 144, 168, 188
  vicarage ho., 144–5
  vicars of, 143–5, 168–9; *and see* Taylor, Rob.

windmill, 144
woodland, 143
Barmby on the Marsh (in Howden), 37, 39, 46, 52
Barnby (Barmby Moor), prebend of, *see* York, Cath. ch. of St. Peter
Barnby Moor, *see* Barmby Moor
Barrett, Brian, 167
Barstow:
  Sir Geo., 61
  Mic., 61
  Thos., 61
  fam., 61
Barton:
  Edw., 8
  Frances, *see* Redman
  John of (fl. 1353), 81
  John (d. 1506), 8
  John (d. 1553), 8
  Noel, 31
  Thos. (fl. c. 1500), 8
  Thos. (d. 1565), 8
Basinges, Geof. de, 105
Bassett, fam., 61
Bateson:
  G. W., later G. W. Bateson de Yarburgh, then G. W. de Yarburgh-Bateson, Baron Deramore, 70
  Mary, *see* Yarburgh
Bath, earl of, *see* Granville, John and W. H.
Bath and Wells, bp. of, *see* Droxford; Stillington, Rob.
Batley, Edw., 116
Baxter, Wm., 42
beacons, 132
Beal:
  Dav., 173
  Geo., 179
Beamond (Beamont), *see* Beaumont
Beauchamp, Goisfrid de, 77
Beaufort, Joan de, m. 2 Ralph de Neville, earl of Westmorland (d. 1425), 14
Beaumont (Beamond, Beamont):
  Chris., 153
  Eliz. de, m. 1 Wm. Deincourt, 2 Sir Ric. Hastings, 103
  Priscilla, 170
  Waleran de, earl of Warwick, 122
  fam., 141, 167
Beckwith:
  Leon. (fl. 16th cent.), 8, 104, 106
  Leon. (fl. 1654), 84
  Newark, 84
  Rog., 104, 106
  fam., 84, 108
Bedford, duke of, *see* Lancaster
Bedwell, Chas., 184
Bedwind, Wal. de, rector of Catton, prebend of Howden, dean of Tamworth, and treasurer of York, 156
Bek, Ant., bp. of Durham, 100, 160
Belasyse, Thos., Vct. Fauconberg, 78
Belkerthorpe, Wm. de, 106
Bell:
  Anne (fl. 1617), m. Wm. Haddlesey, 77
  Anne (fl. 1715), *see* Denton
  J. T., 22
  Jane (fl. 1617), m. —— Greenbury, 77
  Jane (fl. 16th cent.), *see* North
  John (fl. 18th cent.), 22
  John (d. 1938), 197
  Mary, *see* Denton
  Ric. (d. 1617), 77–8
  Ric. (d. 1639), 79
  Rob., 22
  Wm., 139
  fam., 77
bell-founders, *see* Blews; Dalton, Geo.; Lester & Pack; Mears, C. & G. and Thos.; Mears &

199

bell-founders (*cont.*)
    Stainbank; Seller; Smith, Sam., jr. and sr.; Wald; Warner
Belsham, Anna, 22
Belthorpe, fam., 168
Belthorpe (in Bishop Wilton), 131, 166
Belton, Hen., 32
Belvoir, Cecily de, *see* Bigod
Bempton, 196
Benedictine order, 115
Benson:
    Harriet, m. Geo. Fox (later Fox-Lane), 7
    Rob., Ld. Bingley, 7
    T. S., 96
Bentley, W. J., 193
Bentley (in Rowley), 131
Berkshire, *see* Windsor
Bernulf (fl. 1066), 175
Berwyse, Ric., 142
Beswick (in Kilwick), 131
Beverhoudt, Harriet Von, 14
Beverley:
    John, 57
    Thos., 57
Beverley, 129–30
Bewe:
    John, 57
    Josias, 57
    Mary, m. Wm. Bracebridge, 57
Bewlay, Rob., 151
bicycle manufacturers, 9
Bielby (in Hayton), 131
Bigod:
    Adelize, *see* Todeni
    Cecily (de Belvoir), m. Wm. de Aubigny, 77
    Rog., 77
    fam., 111
Bilbrough (Yorks. W.R.), 156
Bingley, Ld., *see* Benson, Rob.; Fox
Birmingham, 35
Bishop:
    Thos. (fl. 16th cent.), 135, 165–6
    Thos. (fl. 17th cent.), 135
    fam., 135
Black Death, 34, 58, 122, 134, 152, 159
Blackbeard, Jas., rector of Sutton upon Derwent, 179
Blackburn, Nic., 159, 181
Blackway, Thos., 16, 81, 110, 119, 156, 169
Blackwood, 57–8, 62, 91, 97–8
Blackwood Hall Farms Ltd., 96
Blake:
    Chas., rector of Wheldrake, 126–8
    fam., 160
Blakey:
    A. H., 62–3, 95
    T. O., 63–4, 95
Bland, Hen., 32
Blanshard:
    Jas., 64
    John, 48
    Jos., 48
    Susanna, m. Jos. Stringer, 48
    Wm., 183
bleaching, 72, 154
Blews, Wm., & Sons (bell-founders), 35
Blois:
    Sir Chas., 95–6
    Clara, *see* Price
Blore, Edw., 115
Blunt, Maurice, 57
Blythe, Ric., 120
Boland, Humph., 122
Bolle:
    Sir Chas., 183
    John, 183
Bolton:
    Cecily of, *see* Darel
    Hugh of, 115
Bolton (in Bishop Wilton), 131, 164, 168–9
Bolton Percy (Yorks. W.R.), 126, 175
Bootham (Yorks. N.R.), *see* York, St. Mary's hosp.
Bossall, *see* Buttercrambe
boundary stones and pits, 33, 79, 85–6, 91
Bousfield, E. C., 70, 123
Bowdler:
    Edw., 35
    fam., 35
Bowes:
    Chas., sr. (d. 1648), 54–5
    Chas., jr. (fl. 1665), 54
    Frances, w. of Martin, m. 2 Mat. Hutton, 54
    Ric., 48, 53–4
    Susanna, *see* Anlaby
    fam., 48, 53–4
Bowles, John, 183
Bownas, John, 178
Bowthorpe (in Hemingbrough), 3, 63–4
    bridge, 62
    Hall, 63
    man., 63–4
    man.-ho., *see* Bowthorpe, Hall
    pop., 63
    rectory, 64
    tithes, 64
    wharf, 63
    and see Menthorpe
Boyce, John, 6
Boynton:
    Boynton, 53–4
    Eliz., m. Ric. Langley, 53–4
    Judith, m. John Twisleton, 53
Bracebridge:
    Mary, *see* Bewe
    Wm., 57
Bracken (in Kilnwick), 131
Brackenholme (in Hemingbrough), 3, 37, 39–43, 47, 52–5, 128
    bridges, 52–3; *and see* Loftsome
    common fields, 55
    common pastures, 55
    ferry, 52
    man., 53–4
    man.-ho., 54
    pop., 53
    rectory, 55
    roads, 52–3
    tithes, 55
    wharf, 53
    woodland, 52, 55, 62
Bradford, Thos., 94, 114, 120
Bradley:
    John, 183–4
    Pet., 183
    fam., 183
Bradshaw:
    Dorothy, *see* Ellerker
    Ellerker, 104
    Sir Jas., 104
Braim, Thos., curate of Barlby, 50–1
Braithwaite, Grace, *see* Robinson
Bramley:
    Ric., 54, 61
    fam., 54, 61, 96
Brantingham, 131; *and see* Ellerker
Brayton (Yorks. W.R.), 43, 56
Brearley:
    Hen., 54
    Thos., 54
Breighton (in Bubwith), 63, 130, 184
Breton, Eudes s. of the, *see* Eudes
Brettanby, Geof. de, 21
Breuse:
    Ric. de, 114, 118
    Wm. de, 114
brewing and brewers, 9, 75, 163, 177, 195
brick-making and brick-makers, *see* Barlby; Catton, High and Low; Cliffe; Cottingwith, West; Deighton; Duffield, North; Elvington; Escrick; Fangfoss; Fulford, Gate; Hemingbrough; Kelfield; Kexby; Melbourne; Moreby; Naburn; Newton upon Derwent; Riccall; Stamford Bridge East; Stillingfleet; Storwood; Thorganby; Thornton; Waplington; Wheldrake; Wilberfoss; Woodhouse
bridge:
    Sim. at the, *see* Simon
    Thos. at the, *see* Thomas
bridges, *see* Barlby; Bowthorpe; Brackenholme; Catton, High and Low; Duffield, North; Dunnington; Elvington; Escrick; Heslington; Kelfield; Kexby; Loftsome; Melbourne; Moreby; Naburn; Riccall; Stamford Bridge East; Stillingfleet; Sutton upon Derwent; Thorganby; Thornton; Wheldrake; Wilberfoss; Woodhall; Woodhouse
Bridgman (Bridgeman):
    Eliz., *see* Simpson
    Frances, m. Wm., Ld. Howard, 28, 82, 89, 101, 112, 128
    Sir Hen., 171
    (later Simpson), John, 171
Bridgwater, earls of, *see* Egerton, John and John W.
Bridlington, 74, 100; *and see* Sewerby
Briggs:
    Jonathan, sr. (d. 1840), 54–5
    Jonathan, jr. (fl. 1840), 54
    Riley, 48, 65–6
Brind (in Wressle), 131
British Association for the Advancement of Science, 126
British Oil & Cake Mills Ltd., 49–50
British Sugar Corporation Ltd., 50
Brittany, John of, earl of Richmond, 105–6
Brittany, counts of, *see* Alan; Stephen
Bromborough Estate Co., 184
Bromley:
    Chas., 166
    Rob., 166
Broomfleet:
    Sir Hen., 166
    Marg., w. of Thos., *see* St. John
    Marg., m. John, Ld. Clifford, 48
    Thos., 48
Broomfleet (in South Cave), 131
Brough (*Petuaria*) (in Elloughton), 131, 140, 149
Brown (Browne):
    Geo., 193
    Ric., 54
    Rob., 104
    Thos., 145, 156, 196
    Wm., 193
Brownlow, Baron, *see* Cust
Bubwith, Wal. of, 95
Bubwith, 130; *and see* Breighton; Foggathorpe; Gribthorpe; Gunby; Harlthorpe; Spaldington; Willitoft
Buckle:
    Jos., 94
    fam., 94
Buckrose wapentake, 149
Bugthorpe, 196
Builers, Hilary de, *see* Trussebut
Bulmer, Bertram of, 7
Bulmer wapentake (Yorks. N.R.), 3
Burdett:
    Eliz., m. 1 Geo. Ridley, 2 T. F. Pritchard, 65
    John, 48, 65
    Ric., 65
    T. F., *see* Pritchard
Burdon (Burton):
    Brian, 151, 159
    Francis, 194
    Marg., m. Thos. Ughtred, 159

INDEX

Ric., 193
Rob., 191
Thos., 151, 159, 191
fam., 191, 193
and see Burton
Burland, Hannah, 142
Burn-Murdoch:
  J. F., 48
  Revd. J. M., 48–9
  Marian, *see* Carr
Burnby, 131
Burnell, Geo., 104
Burrell:
  Ric., 31
  John, 31
Bursea (in Holme upon Spalding Moor), 131
Burton:
  A. C., 136
  A. F., 57–8, 136
  Eliz. (d. 1811), *see* Keighley
  Eliz. (fl. 1878), 60
  J. D., 193
  John, 54
  Mary, *see* Henson, Mary, jr.
  Thos., 57, 60
  Wm., 57
  fam., 57–8, 193
  and see Burdon
Burton, Bishop, 130
Burton, Cherry, 131; *and see* Gardham; Newton; Raventhorpe
Burton Fields, *see* Hundburton
Burun, Erneis de, 31, 106–7, 115, 117
Bury-Barry, Judith, 14
Busfield, Wm., 145
Bush:
  Reg., 152
  fam., 152
Butler, Jas., 126
Buttercrambe (in Bossall) (Yorks. N.R.), 103
Butterfield, Thos., 193
Butterwick (in Foxholes), 165
Byard, Hen., rector of Wheldrake, 126
Byland abbey (Yorks. N.R.), 152
bylawmen, 10, 26, 33, 72–4, 80, 85–6, 98, 109, 117, 125, 138, 144, 155, 168, 187, 195

Cade:
  Marg., 170
  Wm., 170
calfherd, Warin the, *see* Warin
Calverley-Rudston, T. W., 134
Cambridge University:
  chancellor of, *see* Rickinghall
  St. John's Coll., 167
canals, 130; *and see* Pocklington
Carbury, earl of, *see* Vaughan, Ric.
Carleton, Jas., 87
Carlisle, earls of, 165, 167; *and see* Howard, Chas. (d. 1738) and Fred.
Carmelite order, 115
Carnaby, 175
Carr:
  Geo., 39
  J. F., 54–5
  John, 14, 20
  Marian, m. Revd. J. M. Burn-Murdoch, 48
  Mary (d. 1871), *see* Robinson
  Mary (dau. of Mary, d. 1871), m. T. G. Parker, 48
carrots, 143
Carteret, Grace, *see* Granville
Carus Wilson, Frances, m. Jocelyn Willye, 95
Cary:
  Cath., m. Sir John Russell, 39
  Eliz., m. Sir Jeffery Amherst, 39, 55
  Col. (later Gen.) Geo., 39
  Isabella, *see* Ingram
Casson, Sem, 81

Cathwaite, ——, 173, 176
Cathwaite (in Sutton upon Derwent), 173, 176
Catton:
  Alan of, 194
  Edw., 170
Catton, 3, 131, **147–64**, 148; *and see* Catton, High and Low; Hundburton; Kexby; Scoreby; Stamford Bridge East; Stamford Bridge West
Catton, High and Low, **147–58**, 194
  adv., 155
  assarting, 152
  brick-making, 154
  bridges, 149; *and see* Kexby
  char., 157–8
  ch., 147, 150, 153, 155–7, 158 *n*, 163, 172
  common fields, 149, 152–3, 155
  common meadows, 149, 152
  common pastures, 149, 152–3, 167, 172, 194
  ct., 151, 153–6, 172, 195
  fishing, 154
  ford, 150
  inc., 149–50, 152–6, 158
  ind., 154
  inns, 150
  man., 149, 151–2, 154–6, 158–9, 171–2, 183, 191, 193–5
  man.-ho., 150–1
  moated site, 151
  park, 149–50, 152–3
  poor relief, 150, 155
  pop., 150–1
  prot. nonconf., 157
  rectors of, 153, 155–6; *and see* Bedwind; Gardiner
  rectory, 155
  rectory ho., 155–6
  recusancy, 157
  roads, 149
  Rom. Cath., 156–7
  sch., 157
  tithes, 153, 155
  water-mills, 152, 154
  wharf, 154
  woodland, 152–4
Caulem, ——, 52
Cave, Rob., and his w. Cath., 104
Cave hundred, 2, 130–1
Cave, North, 109, 131; *and see* Cliffe, South; Drewton; Everthorpe; Kettlethorpe
Cave, South, 131; *and see* Broomfleet; Faxfleet; Weedley
Cawood, fam., 123
Caythorpe (Cawthorpe) (in Rudston), 86
Cayton (Yorks. N.R.), *see* Osgodby
Cecil:
  Eliz., *see* Manners
  Sir Ric., 183
  Wm., Ld. Ros, 57, 183, 185
Chaice, Jas., 57
Chamberlain:
  Hen. (fl. 1251), 94
  John (fl. 1196), 94
  John (fl. 1250), 142
  Rob. (? two of this name, fl. 13th cent.), 94, 142
  Steph. the, 160
  fam., 94, 135, 160–1
Champney:
  Geo., 166, 170
  Marg., *see* Freeman
  Thos., 63
Chancery, 8, 28, 71
Chantrell, R. D., 145, 169
chantries, 171; *and see* Barmby Moor; Duffield, North; Hemingbrough; Kelfield; Kexby; Naburn; Riccall; Skipwith; Stamford Bridge East; Stillingfleet; Thornton; Wheldrake; York, Cath. ch. of

St. Peter and St. John's ch., Ouse Bridge
chapels, manorial, *see* Babthorpe; Cliffe; Hagthorpe; Kelfield; Moreby; Naburn; Osgodby; Riccall; Storwood; Sutton upon Derwent
Chaplin:
  John, 64
  Rob. (fl. 1752), 64
  Rob. (fl. 1921), 64
  Wm., 63
  fam., 64
Chapman:
  Sir Pet., 183
  Thos., 157
Charles I, King, 161
Charlton, L. S., 65
Chatterton, Thos., 136
Chauncy:
  Thos. de, 165
  Wal. de, 165
  fam., 165
'Cheldale' (in Great Driffield), 130
Cheshire, *see* Darnhall
Chester:
  earl of, *see* Hugh
  honor of, 151
'Chetelstorp' (in Escrick), 3, 17, 20
'Chetelstorp' (? in Storwood), 131, 181, 183, 186
chevage, 59
Cheyne, Wm., 178
Chichester (Suss.), bp. of, *see* Rickinghall
chicory-growing and -drying, 9, 33, 72, 134, 154
Choke, Ric., justice of Common Pleas, 166
Cholmley (Cholmeley):
  Amelia, 36
  Cath., m. Geo. Overend, 166
Christian, Ewan, 45, 189
Christie, Jas., 184–5
Church Commissioners, 184
Cille (fl. 1066), 160
Clare, Bogo of, rector of Hemingbrough, treasurer and prebendary of York, dean of Stafford, 43
Clarel, Wm., 193
Clarence, duke of, *see* Plantagenet, Geo.
Clarges:
  Sir Thos. (d. 1759), 175
  Sir Thos. (d. 1783), 175, 177
  Sir Thos. (d. 1834), 175, 179
  fam., 175
Clark (Clarke):
  A. J., rector of Elvington, 13
  C. E., 54
  Revd. J. E., 13 *n*, 16
  Rob., 14
  Susannah, *see* Redman
  Wm., 197
  fam., 16, 136
Clarkson, Barnard, 104–5, 184
Cleaving (in Londesborough), 131
clerk, Durand the, *see* Durand
Cliff (Cliffe):
  Hen. of, 43
  Wal., 136, 184, 188
Cliffe, Long Cliffe, Cliffe with Lund (in Hemingbrough), 3, 37, 42, 46, 52, **55–60**, 61, 91, 110
  assarting, 56, 58
  brick-making, 59
  chap., man., 57
  char., 60
  common fields, 56, 59
  common meadows, 56, 58–9
  common pastures, 56, 58–9
  ct., 58–9
  fishing, 59
  inc., 57–60
  ind., 33, 59
  inns, 56

Cliffe (cont.)
  man., 56–9
  man.-ho., see Cliffe, Turnham Hall
  mills, 59
  mission room, 45
  moated site, 58
  poor relief, 59
  pop., 56
  prot. nonconf., 59–60
  rly. stn., 56, 59
  rectory, 49, 58
  roads, 56, 59–60
  sch., 60
  tithes, 49, 58, 65
  Turnham Hall, 45, 57
  wharves, 59
  woodland, 58–9
Cliffe, North (in Sancton), 129, 131
Cliffe, South (in North Cave), 129, 131
Clifford:
  Hen., earl of Cumberland, 48
  John de, Ld. Clifford (d. 1461), 48
  John (fl. 1866), 35
  Marg., see Broomfleet
  fam., 48
Clifton (Yorks. N.R.), 20–2, 31, 104–5, 123
Clingand, Thos., 127
Coates:
  Thos., 151
  fam., 151
Cobb:
  Eliz., 173
  John, 173
Cock, Mary, 105
Cockburn, Rob., 136
Cockermouth, Baron, see Seymour, Algernon; Wyndham, Sir Chas.
Cockshutt (later Twisleton), Thos., 53
Coker, Ebenezer, 111
Coldingham:
  Margery of, m. Wal. de Paxton, 54
  Ric. of, 54
  Thos. of, 54
Coleby (Lincs.), vicar of, see Sarraude
Coleville, Wm., 122–3
Colewenne (Curwenne), Joan de, see Lascelles
Colgrim (fl. 1066), 175
Collum, Hugh de, 55
Colston:
  Joshua, 54
  fam., 54
common fields, 1, 129; and see under places
common meadows, see under places
common ovens, 162, 167
common pastures, 1; and see under places
Common Pleas, justice of, see Choke
Conan, Hen. s. of, see Henry son of Conan (fl. 1200–10; d. c. 1285; fl. 1311; fl. 1346)
Conan son of Henry (fl. earlier 13th cent.), 104
Conan son of Henry (fl. later 13th cent.), 104–5
Consett:
  Chris., 89
  Wm., 84
Constable:
  Anne, see Hussey
  Avice le, see Lascelles
  Dakins, 116
  Dorothy, see Ughtred
  Francis, 158
  Joan, 40, 188, 193
  John, 40, 160, 188, 193
  Sir Rob., 95
  Wm. (fl. 1614), 95
  fam., 160, 176, 184
Conyers:
  Eliz., see Aton
  Sir John, 48

Cook (Cooke):
  John, and his w. Marg., 28
  Marm., prebendary of Riccall, 87–8
  Pet., rector of Sutton upon Derwent, 179
  Ric., 158
Cookson, Wm., 134
Cooper (Couper):
  Thos. (fl. 15th cent.), 142
  Thos. (fl. 18th cent.), vicar of Riccall, 87
  Wm., 142
coopering, 50
Coore, fam., 176
Copley:
  Sir Godfrey, 63
  fam., 63
Copsi, Rob. s. of, see Robert
Corney, Rob., 89
Cornwall, earldom of, 77
Cornwall, see St. Buryan
Cotes, Wal. de, 175
cottage-reeve, 33
Cottingham, 131–2; and see Newton; 'Pileford'
Cottingwith, East (in Aughton), 34, 50, 113–14, 116 n, 131, 181, 190
Cottingwith, West (in Thorganby), 3, 31, 112–20
  assarting, 115, 117
  brick-making, 118
  char., 120
  common fields, 117
  common meadows, 117
  common pastures, 117
  dom. arch., 113
  ferry, 113
  fishing, 118
  inc., 113, 116–17
  inns, 113
  man., 106, 114–15, 117
  man.-ho., 115; and see Cottingwith, West, Old Hall and Thicket Priory
  Old Hall, 113–14
  par. officers, 118
  park, 113
  pop., 113
  prot. nonconf., 119
  rly. stn., 113
  rectory, 116–17
  roads, 113
  sch., 119–20
  Thicket Priory (man.-ho.), 113, 115, 119
  Thicket priory (religious ho.), 4, 22–3, 58, 65, 115–18, 123, 136, 176
  tithes, 116–17
  windmill, 118
  woodland, 117
Cotton, Geo., 107
Council in the North, 70
Counsell, Hugh, 105, 119
Couper, see Cooper
Cowling:
  Thos., 158
  Wm., 112
'Crachetorp' (? Tranby, in Hessle), 130
Crakehall, Pet. of, 107
Cranswick (in Hutton Cranswick), 130
Crathorne:
  Jas., 104
  Ralph (d. by 1490), 104
  Ralph (d. by 1517), 104
  Ralph (fl. late 16th cent.), 104
  Thos. (d. 1509), 104
  Thos. (d. 1568), 104
  fam., 104
Crawford, H. D., 142
Crepping:
  Denise, m. Rob. Stodowe, 135, 142
  John de, 142

Remigius, and his w. Cath., 142
Rob. de (d. c. 1280), 135, 142
Rob. (fl. 1310), 142
Rob. (? another, fl. 14th cent.), 142
fam., 135
Cripling, Rob., 10
Crockey Hill, see Deighton
Crompton, Sam., 136
Cromwell:
  Marg., see Deincourt
  Ralph, Ld., 103
crops (less common), see carrots; chicory; flax; hemp; mustard; onions; parsnips; potatoes; rape; sainfoin; turnips
Crosdill, John, 104
crosses, 5, 11, 19, 29, 83, 88, 131, 179, 196
Crossum ('Gressone') (in Thorganby), 112–13, 115
Crowle:
  Wm., 57
  fam., 58
Crowther, Isaac, 61
Cumberland, earl of, see Clifford, Hen.
Currance, John, 77
Cust, Peregrine, Baron Brownlow, 10
customs and services, see chevage; leyrwite; merchet; multure; pannage; relief; serjeanty, tenures by; works, tenants'

Dacre:
  Eliz., Lady Dacre, see Greystoke
  Thos., Ld. Dacre, 165
  Wm., Ld. Dacre and Ld. Greystoke, 165, 167
Dalby:
  Thos., 50, 52
  fam., 22
Dalton:
  Geo., 196
  John, 193
  Thos., see Norcliffe
Dalton, North, 77, 131
Dalton, South, 131
Dammory:
  Nic., 21
  Rog., 20
  fam., 21
Danby, Rob., 161
Daniel, John s. of, see John
Daniel, John, 14
Danser:
  Eliz., w. of John, 183, 186
  John, 186
Darcy:
  Art., 166
  Sir Geo., 78, 107
  Hen., 166–7
  fam., 166
Darel:
  Beatrice, m. Geof. of Fitling, 122
  Cecily, m. Hugh of Bolton, 122
  Duncan, 21
  Geof. (d. by 1185), 122
  Geof. (grds. of last), see Fitling
  Thos., 122
  Wm. (fl. before 1246), 123
  Wm., and his w. (fl. 1360s), 123
  fam., 122–4, 126
Darley:
  C. A., 151, 154, 157
  H. B., 151
  Hen., 151
  Wm., 151
Darnhall abbey (Ches.), 123
Daubeney, Wm., 103
Davison, Geo., 128
Davy:
  Ric. (fl. 1685), 158
  Ric. (fl. 1477), vicar of Riccall, 87
Dawes, Sarah, see Roundell

INDEX

Dawnay:
  John (fl. 1402), 21
  Sir John (fl. 1572), 95
  John (fl. 17th cent.), 21
  Mary, m. John Legard, 21
  Thos., 95
  fam., 21
Dawson:
  G. P., 51, 65–6
  Geo. (d. 1812), 65
  Geo. (d. 1832), 66
Dawtry, see Dealtry
de Vesci, Vct., see Vesey, J. E. and Y. R.
de Yarburgh, G. W. Bateson, see Bateson
de Yarburgh-Bateson:
  G. W., see Bateson
  Lucy, see Fife
  Ric., Ld. Deramore, 74
  Rob', Ld. Deramore, 70–1, 74
Dealtry (Dawtry):
  Ant., 61
  Geo., 158, 173
  Hammond, 158
  Hen., 158
  John (fl. 1315), 171
  John (fl. 1675), 171
  Marg., 158
  Mary, 170
  Ralph, 172
  Rob., 170
  Wm. (fl. 1284), 171
  Wm. (fl. 1577), 171
  Wm. (fl. before 1766), 158
  fam., 164, 171–2
Deighton (in Escrick), 3, 17, 19–28, *24*, 29, 70, 78
  assarting, 23
  brick-making, 25
  chap., 26
  char., 28
  common fields, 17, 23, 25
  common pastures, 17, 23, 25
  ct., 26
  Crockey Hill, 19, 28
  dom. arch., 19
  Hall, see man.-ho.
  inc., 23, 25
  inn, 19
  man., 21–3, 25–6, 78
  man.-ho., 22, 26
  mills, 25–6
  mission room, 26–7
  moated site, 22
  park, 23, 25
  pop., 19–20
  prot. nonconf., 26–8
  roads, 19
  sch., 28
  tithes, 26
  woodland, 23, 25–6
Deincourt:
  Alice, m. Wm., Ld. Lovell, 103–4
  Eliz., see Beaumont
  Joan, see Grey
  John, 103
  Marg., m. Ralph, Ld. Cromwell, 103
  Wm., 103
Deira, 141
Denison:
  Albert, Baron Londesborough, 161
  Rob., 135–6
  W. F. H., earl of Londesborough, 161
  fam., 141
Denmark, 27
Dent & Co., tar distillers, 50
Denton:
  Anne, m. Rob. Bell, 22
  Eliz., see Robinson
  John, 48
  Mary, m. John Bell, 22
  Wm., 48
depopulated villages, 37; and see Babthorpe; Bowthorpe; Brackenholme; 'Chetelstorp' (in Escrick and ? in Storwood); Crossum; Hagthorpe; Hundburton; 'Janulfestorp'; Menthorpe; Moreby; Scoreby; Thornton, Millhouses; Thorp; Waplington; Waterhouses; Woodhall
Deramore, barons, 66, 70; and see Bateson; de Yarburgh-Bateson, Ric. and Rob.
Derwent, riv., 1, 12, 89, 91, 124, 129, 147, 149, 173
  as boundary, 1, 3, 12, 37, 52, 60, 89, 91, 113, 121, 129, 149, 158, 174, 190
  bridges over, see Brackenholme; Duffield, North; Elvington; Kexby; Stamford Bridge East; Thorganby; Wheldrake; Woodhall
  changes in course, 12, 52, 113, 121, 124, 174
  ferries across, see Brackenholme; Duffield, North; Hemingbrough; Kexby; Menthorpe; Sutton upon Derwent
  fords in, see Catton; Stamford Bridge East
  trade, 13, 50, 53, 60, 63–4, 98, 125, 149–50, 154, 174, 177; and see under places, s.v. wharves
  and see under places, s.v. fishing; mills
Derwent Plastics Ltd., 163
Derwent rural district, 10, 15, 26, 34, 42, 50, 55, 59, 62, 64, 66, 72, 80, 87, 91, 99, 109, 118, 126, 163
Despenser:
  Hugh, 57
  fam., 57
Dewsbury, Wm., 134
Dickering wapentake, 1, 129
Dickinson:
  J. I. C., 57
  Thos., 82
Dinnis, Wilf., 193–4
Dinsdale, G. E., 63
Ditchfield grantees, the, 14, 161
Dobby:
  John, 14
  Thos., 14
Dodson, Miles, 178
Dodsworth:
  Revd. Fred., 7
  John, 14
  Ralph, 14
Dolman (Doweman):
  Marm., 135
  Sir Rob. (d. 1628), 135
  Rob. (fl. 18th cent.), 136
  Thos. (d. 1589), 95, 135
  Thos. (d. 1639), 135
  fam., 135, 139
domestic architecture, 1, 129; and see timber-framed buildings, and under places
Dorset, see Wimborne
Douglas, Marg., m. Mat. Stewart, earl of Lennox, 184
dovecots, 22, 31, 47, 53, 56, 62, 65, 83, 103, 114, 121, 123–4, 159, 191
Doweman, see Dolman
Downing, Edm., 134
drainage, 129; and see under places
Drapour, Nic., 193
Drax (Yorks. W.R.), 56, 58
  priory, 37, 43, 55, 58, 62, 65, 135–8
  and see Rusholme
Dresser, Jos., 14
Drewton (in North Cave), 131
Driffield, Great, 130
  prebend, see York, Cath. ch. of St. Peter
  and see 'Cheldale'; Driffield, Little; Elmswell; Kelleythorpe
Driffield, Little (in Great Driffield), 130
Driffield hundred, 130
Droxford, John of, rector of Hemingbrough, bp. of Bath and Wells, chancellor of the Exchequer, 43
Drypool, see Southcoates
Ducy:
  Rob., 115
  Sir Wm., 115
Dudley, John, duke of Northumberland, 175–6
Duffield, North (in Skipwith), 3, 37, 58, 63, 89, 91–101, *92*
  assarting, 91, 97–8
  Blackwood Hall, 96
  brick-making, 98
  bridges, 91
  chant., 99
  chap., 99
  char., 101
  common fields, 91, 97–8
  common meadows, 98
  common pastures, 60, 62, 91, 97–8
  dom. arch., 93
  drainage, 97
  fair, 89, 93, 98
  ferry, 89, 91
  fishing, 98
  Hall, 95, 97, 99
  inc., 93, 95–6, 98–9
  inns, 93
  man., 94–5, 97–8
  man.-ho., 95; and see Duffield, North, Hall
  man.-ho. site, 95
  mkt., 89, 93, 98
  mills, 98
  motte, 93
  park, 97–8
  poor relief, 98–9
  pop., 93
  prot. nonconf., 100
  rly. stn., 91
  rectory, 96, 98
  recusancy, 100
  roads, 89, 91
  sch., 101
  tithes, 96, 98–9
  wharf, 98
  woodland, 62, 97–8
Duffield, South (in Hemingbrough), 3, 37, 43, 52–3, 56, 58, **60–3**, 91, 97
  assarting, 62
  char., 46, 52, 63, 66
  common fields, 60, 62
  common meadows, 60, 62
  common pastures, 60, 62, 64
  Hall, 61
  Holmes Ho., 61, *129*
  inc., 61–2
  inn, 61
  man., 61
  Man. Ho., 62
  moated sites, 61
  par. officers, 42
  poor relief, 62
  pop., 61
  prot. nonconf., 62
  rly. stn., 60
  rectory, 62
  roads, 60, 62
  sch., 62–3
  tithes, 62
  wharf, 60
  windmill, 62
  woodland, 62
Duggleby, 142
Duncombe:
  Art., 135, 139, 141–2, 146
  B. A. C., 135, 141
  C. W., 135, 141
  Chas., Baron Feversham, 172
  Charlotte, m. J. A. Sykes, 139

Duncombe (cont.)
    Delia, see Field
    G. A., 135
    W. E., earl of Feversham, 172
    fam., 141, 172
Dunn:
    Jonathan, 61
    Mary, 142
Dunnington:
    John (d. 1810), 114, 116
    (later Dunnington-Jefferson), John (d. 1840), 101, 114–17, 120
    Jos. (d. 1835), 115
    (later Dunnington-Jefferson), Revd. Jos., curate of Thorganby (d. 1880), 115, 119–20
    Thos. (fl. 1733), 120
    Thos. (fl. 1841), 95
    fam., 95, 114
Dunnington, 1, 3, **5–12**, 65
    adv., 10
    assarting, 5, 8
    bridge, 5
    char., 11–12
    ch., 10–12, 16
    common fields, 5, 8, 10
    common meadows, 5, 8
    common pastures, 5, 8, 10, 158, 162
    ct., 9
    dom. arch., 5–6
    drainage, 5
    fairs, 9
    Ho., 5
    inc., 5–11
    ind., 9, *33*
    inns, 6
    lunatic asylum, 5
    man., 6–9, 70
    man.-ho., 7
    mills, 9
    par. officers, 10, 12
    poor relief, 10
    pop., 6
    prebend of, see York, Cath. ch. of St. Peter
    prot. nonconf., 11–12
    rly. stn., 5
    rectors of, 8, 10–11; and see Ayscough; Lindley, Chris.
    rectory, 10
    rectory ho., 5, 10
    roads, 5
    sch., 11–12, 164
    tithes, 10
    woodland, 8–9
    and see Grimston; 'Janulfestorp'
Dunnington-Jefferson:
    John (d. 1840), see Dunnington
    Sir John (b. 1884), 95, 113–15
    Jos. J. (d. 1928), 123
    Revd. Jos. (d. 1880), see Dunnington
    fam., 95, 114, 117–18
Dunsforth (Yorks. W.R.), 196
Durand the clerk, 107
Dure, Eliz., 111
Durham:
    bp. of, 3–4, 39, 42, 48, 52–5, 57–9, 61–3, 65, 83–6, 93–4, 99; and see Bek
    prior of, 37, 42, 55, 99; and see Wessington
    priory, 39–43, 54, 99
Durleigh (Som.), 17
dying (cloth), 154

Eadon:
    John, 107
    Thos. (fl. 1741), 21
    Thos. (fl. 19th cent.), and his w. Sarah, 166
Earle:
    Jos., 39
    Wm., 39
earthworks, see moated sites; mottes; prehistoric remains; village earthworks; windmill mounds
Eastburn (in Kirkburn), 130
Easthorpe (in Londesborough), 131
Eastwood, J. B., 113–14
Ecclesiastical Commissioners, 7, 10, 70, 73, 84, 87, 123, 136, 141–2, 144, 160–1, 167, 184–5, 188, 196
Eddiva (fl. 1066), 183
Edward IV, King (formerly Edw. Plantagenet, earl of March), 183
Edwin (fl. 1066), 6
Egerton:
    Francis, 184
    Hen., 136
    John, earl of Bridgwater (d. 1649), 10
    John W., earl of Bridgwater (d. 1823), 10
    Wm., 184
    fam., 10
Eglesfield:
    John, 175, 177–8
    Marg., m. —— Wallis, 175, 178
    Mary, m. And. Milner, 175, 178
    fam., 14, 175
Egremont:
    Baron, see Wyndham, J. E. R.
    earls of, 155; and see Seymour, Algernon; Wyndham, Sir Chas. and Geo. (d. 1837)
Elam, Emanuel, 77
Elcock, Thos., vicar of Riccall, 87
Ella, Kirk, 130, 132; and see Anlaby; Ella, West; Willerby
Ella, West (in Kirk Ella), 132
Ellard, Wm., 158
Ellerker:
    Dorothy, m. Sir Jas. Bradshaw, 104
    (formerly Mainwaring), Eaton, 104, 107–8
    Edw., 104
    Jas., 104
    John, 104
    R. M., 104
    Ralph (fl. 1579), 104
    Sir Ralph (d. c. 1640), 104
    Randolph, 104
    fam., 104 n
Ellerker (in Brantingham), 131
Ellerton, 131
    priory, 115–18
Ellin:
    Geo., 57
    Mary, see Willbor
Ellis, Hen. s. of, see Henry
Elloughton, 131; and see Brough; Wauldby
Elmhirst, Mrs. E. L. L., 142
Elmswell (in Great Driffield), 130
Elvington, 1, 3, **12–17**, 121, 173
    adv., 15–16
    alms-ho., 15
    assarting, 14–16
    brick-making, 15
    bridges, 12–13, *160*
    Brinkworth Hall, 13
    char., 16–17
    ch., 15–17, *17*
    common fields, 12, 14–15
    common meadows, 12, 15–16
    common pastures, 12–13, 15
    ct., 15
    dom. arch., 13
    fishing, 15
    the Grange, 13
    Hall, 13–14
    inc., 12–13, 15–16
    ind., 15
    inn, 13
    lock, 13, 174, *176*
    man., 13–16, 161
    man.-ho., 14; and see Elvington, Hall
    park, 13
    poor relief, 15
    pop., 13
    prot. nonconf., 13, 16–17
    rly. stn., 13
    rectors of, 15–16, 178; and see Ayscough; Clarke, A. J.; Sarraude
    rectory, 10, 16
    rectory ho., 16
    recusancy, 16
    roads, 12–13
    sch., 13, 17
    tithes, 16
    wharf, 13
    woodland, 14–15
Elwick:
    Frances, m. John Eyre, 171
    Francis, 171–2
Ely, dean of, 126
engineering firms, 50, 144, 168, 195
Erneis, Thos. s. of, see Thomas
Ernuin (fl. 1086), 55
Ernuin the priest, 7
Escrick, 1, 3, 5, **17–28**, *18*, 75, 99, 107
    adv., 26
    alms-ho., 28
    assarting, 17, 22
    brick-making, 25
    bridge, 17
    char., 28, 82, 89, 101, 112, 128
    ch., 17, 17, 19, 23, 26–8
    common fields, 17, 19, 22–3, 26–7
    common meadows, 17, 22–3
    common pastures, 17, 22–3, 124
    dom. arch., 19
    drainage, 17
    Hall, *16*, 17, 19–21, *21*, 23, 26–8
    inc., 22–3
    inn, 19
    man., 14, 20–3, 26, 85, 94, 104, 107, 122, 160, 163
    man.-ho., 20; and see Escrick, Hall
    mills, 25
    moraine, 1, 12, 17, 25, 101–2, 113, 120–1, 125, 129, 147, 149, 170, 173–4, 190–1, 195
    par. officers, 26
    park, 17, 19–20, 22–3, 25
    poor relief, 26
    pop., 19–20
    prot. nonconf., 27–8
    Queen Margaret's Sch. for Girls, 20
    rly. stn., 19
    rectors of, 23, 26–8; and see Squire, Thos.
    rectory, 26–7
    rectory ho., 17, 19, 23, 26
    roads, 17, 19
    Rom. Cath., 27
    rural district, 10, 15, 26, 34, 72, 80, 109, 118, 126, 163
    sch., 28
    tithes, 26
    the Villa, 19
    woodland, 17, 19, 22–3, 25
    and see 'Chetelstorp'; Deighton
Escrick and District Co-operative Soc., 19
Estofte, Chris., 95, 136
Esveillechien, Wm., 61
Etherington, Ambrose, 14
Etton, 126, 131; and see 'Steintorp'; 'Torp'
Etty, Wm., 149
Eudes the marshal, son of the Breton, 21
Eure:
    Cath., see Aton
    Ralph (d. 1422), 48
    Ralph, Ld. Eure (d. 1617), 10, 48
Everingham, 131
Everthorpe (in North Cave), 131
Evesham, Hugh of, rector of Hemingbrough and prebendary of York, 43
Ewbank, Geo., 136
Exchequer, chancellor of the, see Droxford

INDEX

Eye (Suff.), 77
Eynns:
  Ric., and his w., 69
  Sir Thos. (fl. mid 16th cent.), 69
  Thos. (d. 1578), 69–70
Eyre:
  Frances, see Elwick
  John, 171
  Jos., 172
Eyville:
  Emery d', 57–8, 95
  John d', 95
  fam., 95

Fairburn, Melville, 22
Fairfax:
  Chas., Vct., 78
  Cuth., 78
  Sir Thos. (d. 1640), 78
  Sir Thos. (d. 1671), 172, 175
  Wm., 103, 106
fairs, see Barmby Moor; Duffield, North; Dunnington; Hemingbrough; Kexby; Osgodby; Riccall; Stamford Bridge West
Falkingham:
  R.H., 58
  fam., 58
Fangfoss, 131, **164–70**, 171
  brick-making, 168
  ch., 144–5, 165, 168–70
  char., 169–70
  common fields, 164, 167–8
  common meadows, 164, 167–8
  common pastures, 164, 167–9
  ct., 168
  curate of, 169; and see Taylor, Rob.
  Hall, 165–6
  inc., 164–5, 167–9
  ind., 168
  inn, 165
  man., 165–7
  man.-ho., see Fangfoss, Hall
  mill, 168
  par. officers, 168, 170
  park, 166
  perpetual curacy, 138, 144, 168; and see Barmby Moor, vicarage
  poor relief, 168, 170
  pop., 165
  prot. nonconf., 170
  rly. stn., 161, 164–5
  rectory, 167
  roads, 164
  sch., 165, 168, 170, 173
  tithes, 167–9
  'vicarage ho.', 169
  woodland, 168
Fargrim (fl. 1066), 160
Farkson, Geo., 167
Farnham, John, 99
Fauconberg, Vct., see Belasyse
Favour, John, rector of Sutton upon Derwent, 178
Fawcett:
  John, 167
  Jos., 99
  Rose, 167
  Thos., 167, 169
  fam., 167
Fawkes:
  Marm., 57, 95
  fam., 61
Faxfleet (in South Cave), 131, 136
Fearnsides:
  Jos., 171
  Susannah, 171
Fenner, Jos., 167
Fenton, John, 54
Fenwick:
  Chas., 55
  Rob., 30
  Susanna, see Anlaby
Fermor, Ric., 78
Ferriby, North, 130, 132; and see Swanland
ferries, see Barlby; Brackenholme; Cottingwith, West; Duffield, North; Hemingbrough; Kelfield; Kexby; Menthorpe; Naburn; Newhay; Stillingfleet; Sutton upon Derwent; Wheldrake
fishing, see Barlby; Catton, High and Low; Cliffe; Cottingwith, West; Duffield, North; Elvington; Fulford, Gate; Hemingbrough; Kelfield; Kexby; Menthorpe; Moreby; Naburn; Newhay; Riccall; Stillingfleet; Storwood; Sutton upon Derwent; Thorganby; Wheldrake
Feversham:
  Baron, see Duncombe, Chas.
  earl of, see Duncombe, W. E.
Fido, Ant., curate of Hemingbrough, 43
Field:
  Delia, m. Art. Duncombe, 135, 145
  J. W., 135
  Joshua, 135
  fam., 141
Fife, Lucy, m. Rob. de Yarburgh-Bateson, 74
Fisher, fam., 27, 145
Fishergate:
  John son of Hen. of, 135
  fam., 135
Fiskgate, Rob. of, 106
Fitling:
  Beatrice of, see Darel
  Geof. of, 115
  (later Darel), Geof. of, s. of last, 122–3
FitzAlan, Eleanor, m. Hen. de Percy (d. 1314), 151, 165, 171, 191
FitzHenry:
  Hen., 104
  John (fl. 1440), 104
  John (d. by 1496), 104
  ——, ? m. John Stillington, 104
FitzRanulph:
  Ralph (? fl. 13th cent.), 20
  (or Lascelles), Ralph (fl. 14th cent.), 20
  Tiffany, see Lascelles
Fitzroy, Hen., 160
FitzWilliam:
  Alice, m. Jas. Foljambe, 193
  Marg., m. Geof. Foljambe, 193
  Ric., 193
  Thos., 193
  Sir Wm., 193
FitzWilliam, earls, see Wentworth
Flasby (Yorks. W.R.), 106 n
flax-growing, -dressing, and -spinning, 50, 59, 72, 86, 91, 108, 138, 144, 168
Fletcher, Rob., 89
Fletcher's Sauce Co. Ltd., 50
Fligg, fam., 96 n
Flint Co. Ltd., landowners, 63–4, 95
flint-grinding, 80
Flohil, P. B., 48
flooding, 15, 17, 25, 47, 58, 71, 83, 85, 89, 91, 101–2, 113, 118, 121, 124, 133, 174, 176–7, 181, 186
Florence (Italy), 84
Foggathorpe (in Bubwith), 131, 164 n
Foliot:
  Jordan (d. by 1311), and his w. Marg., 103, 109
  Jordan (? another, fl. 14th cent.), 103
Foljambe:
  Alice, see FitzWilliam
  Francis, 193
  Geof., 193
  Jas., 193
  Marg., see FitzWilliam
  Sir Thos., 193
Forbes Adam:
  C. G., 20
  Irene, see Lawley
  fam., 20, 85, 94, 104, 107, 122, 163
Forestry Commission, 9, 80, 108, 125, 133, 137, 154, 162, 177, 187
Forne (fl. 1066), 160
Forz:
  Wm. de, earl of Aumale, 165
  fam., 165
Fossard:
  Joan, m. Rob. of Turnham, 57, 65, 114
  Niel, 57, 61, 64, 94, 114, 175–6
  Wm., 57, 175
  fam., 57, 65, 94
Foster:
  John, 27
  Rob., 89
Fothergill, Marm., vicar of Skipwith, 100
Fountains abbey (Yorks. W.R.), 121–5, 176, 184, 186
Fowler, C. H., 11, 50–1, 111
Fox:
  (later Fox-Lane), Geo., Ld. Bingley (d. 1773), 7
  (later Fox-Lane), Harriet, see Benson
Fox-Lane:
  Geo., see Fox
  Harriet, see Benson
  Jas., see Lane-Fox
France, 13; and see Marmoutier
franchises, see assizes of bread and ale; common ovens; free warren; gallows; infangthief; pillory; tumbril
free warren, 114, 186, 191
Freeman:
  Anne, m. Wm. Wilberfoss, 63
  Marg., m. Thos. Champney, 63
  Martin, 39
  Rob., 63
  fam., 63
Freer:
  Rob., 171
  Thos., 171
Friends, Society of (Quakers), 11, 35, 45, 100, 111, 119, 134, 146
Froggott, Thos., vicar of Riccall and curate of Barlby, 50
Fulchri (fl. 1066), 106
Fulford, **29–36**, 70, 78; and see Fulford, Gate and Water
Fulford, Gate (Over Fulford), 1, 3, 17, 25, **29–36**, 70
  adv., 34
  assarting, 32
  battle, 29, 82
  brick-making, 33
  char., 34–6
  ch., 29–30, 34–6
  common fields, 29, 32, 34
  common meadows, 32
  common pastures, 29, 32–3, 71
  ct., 32–3
  curates of, 32, 34–6; and see Sutton
  Delwood Croft, 29
  dom. arch., 29–30
  fishing, 32–3
  ford, 29
  Fulford, New, 29, 36
  Green Dykes, 29, 67, 71
  Hall, 29–30
  Ho., 29
  inc., 30–4
  inns, 30
  man., 31–5, 106
  mission room, 35
  New Walk, from York, 30
  Old Ho., 29
  par. officers, 33, 35
  Park, 29
  perpetual curacy, 34
  poor relief, 33–4

Fulford, Gate (cont.)
  pop., 30
  'prison ho.', 33
  prot. nonconf., 35–6
  recusancy, 35
  Retreat lunatic asylum, 30
  roads, 29
  Rom. Cath., 35
  Royal Masonic Benevolent Institution, 30
  sch., 36, 74, 158
  Sir J. J. Hunt Memorial Cottage Homes, 30
  Siward's Howe, 33, 69 n
  tithes, 32–3
  vicarage, 34
  vicarage ho., 34
  Well Ho. and Lady Well Ho., 30
  wharves, 33
  White Ho., 29
  windmills, 33
  woodland, 33
  York barracks, 30, 35
  York cemeteries, 30, 35
  York–Fulford tramway, 30
  York sch., 30
  York sewerage works, 30
Fulford, New, see Fulford, Gate
Fulford, Water (Nether Fulford), 3, 29–34
  common fields, 33
  common meadows, 33
  dom. arch., 30
  golf course, 30
  Hall, see Fulford, man.-ho.
  inc., 33
  man., 31–2, 34–5
  man.-ho., 30–1
  pop., 30–1
  roads, 29
  tithes, 31–2
  York City Asylum (Naburn Hosp.), 30, 75
  York hosp., 30
Fulford golf club, see Fulford, Water; Heslington
Fulfords Ambo (i.e. Gate and Water Fulford), 29
fulling mills, 154

Gale (Gayle):
  Francis (fl. 1564), 26
  Francis (fl. 1606), 22, 123
  Geo. (? two of this name), 21, 194–6
  Hen., 26
  Rob., 21
  fam., 191, 194, 196
gallows, 80
Gamel (Gam) (fl. 1066), s. of Osbert, 93
Gamel (Game) (fl. 1066), king's thegn, 105, 175
Gardham (in Cherry Burton), 131
Gardiner, Hen., rector of Catton, and his sisters, 156
Gargrave, Thos., 110
Garrard, fam., 27
Garwood, Dorothy, 14
Gascoigne:
  Nic., 105
  Wm. (d. 1422), 105
  Wm. (fl. 1449), 105
Gates, Sir Hen., 175
Gayle, see Gale
Gedney (Lincs.), 184
Gee, Sir Orlando, 155
Geere, Thos., 141
Gell, Ric., 158
Geoffrey (fl. 1086), 6, 8
Geoffrey son of Pain, 31, 106, 115
Gibson:
  J. H., 184
  John (fl. 1582), 10
  Sir John (fl. 1632), 14
  Wm., 116

Gilbert, Jordan s. of, see Jordan
Gilbert, Thos., vicar of Stillingfleet, 110
Gill:
  Mark, 157
  Ursula, 111
Gillah, H. Q., 191
Givendale, Great, 131; and see Grimthorpe
Givendale, Little (in Millington), 131
glass-painters, see Gyles; Morris, Wm.
Gleichen, Count, 27
Gloucester, duke of, see Richard III
glover, 41
Godson, Jas., 31
Goodman:
  John, sr. (fl. 1615), 32
  John, jr. (fl. 1615), 32
  John (fl. 1668), 32
  John (? another, fl. 1689, 1708), 32
Goodmanham, 131
Goodrick:
  Sir Hen., 7, 161
  Mary, see Jenkins
Gower:
  Francis, 193
  Wm., 193
Gower, Earl, see Leveson-Gower
Gowthorpe (in Bishop Wilton), 131, 167
Graham:
  Jas., 39
  John, 54
  Maria, 54
  Sophia, see Tweedy
Grainger, Harland, 62
Granville:
  Cath., m. Craven Peyton, 175
  Grace, m. Sir Geo. Carteret, 175
  Jane, m. Sir Wm. Leveson-Gower, 175
  Sir John, earl of Bath, 175
  W. H., earl of Bath, 175
Grassington (in Linton, Yorks. W.R.), 73
Gray, see Grey
Greame:
  Alicia, m. G. J. Lloyd, 73–4
  (later Yarburgh), Yarburgh, 70, 74
Greathead, Rob., 105
greave, 138
Greaves, Victor, 54
Green:
  Dorothy, 173
  Ric., 173
Greenbury, Jane, see Bell
Greenwick (in Bishop Wilton), 131
Grendon:
  Iseult, see Metham
  John, 63
Grente, Pet. s. of, see Peter
'Gressone', see Crossum
Grey (Gray):
  Avice de, see Marmion
  Joan, m. John Deincourt, 103
  John de, Ld. Grey, 103, 106 n
  Rob., Ld. Grey (d. 1388), 103
  Rob. de (fl. 1240s), 103, 106–7
  Rob. de (d. by 1295), 103, 106
  Wal. de, abp. of York, 103, 106–7
  fam., 103, 161
Greystoke:
  Eliz., m. Thos., Ld. Dacre of Gilsland, 165
  Ralph, Ld., 165, 183
  fam., 167
Greystoke, barons, see Grimthorpe
Gribthorpe (in Bubwith), 131
Griffin, Caroline, m. P. B. Lawley, 27
Grim (fl. 1066), 106, 115
Grimsby, Wm. of, 21
Grimsthorpe (later Woodhall) (in Hemingbrough), 52, 54; and see Woodhall
Grimston (in Dunnington), 3, 5–11, 29

chap., 10
common fields, 8
common pastures, 8–9
Court, 8
dom. arch., 6
Hall, 7
Hill, 7
inc., 5, 9
inns, 6
man., 7–8, 10
man.-ho., see Grimston, Court, Hall, and Hill
mission room, 11
poor relief, 10
pop., 6
roads, 5, 9
Smithy, 6
tithes, 10
woodland, 9
Grimthorpe:
  Rob. s. of Ulf of, 166
  fam. (later barons Greystoke), 165–7
Grimthorpe (in Great Givendale), 131, 165, 167–8
Grosvenor, Eliz., m. B. R. Lawley, 28
Gruggen, Revd. Fred., 142, 145
guilds (religious), see Thorganby; Wilberfoss; York, St. Christopher
Guisborough priory (Yorks. N.R.), 95
Gulliver, Nat., 88
Gunby, fam., 58
Gunby (in Bubwith), 130
Gurney, Ric., 27
Gyles, Hen., 87, 111

Haddlesey:
  Anne, see Bell
  Jane, 62
  Wm., 61
  fam., 55
Haffenden, fam., 136
Hagthorpe:
  Isabel, see Osgodby
  Joan, m. 1 Rob. Proctor, 2 Thos. Newark, 54
  Rob. of, 54
  Thos., 54, 65
  fam., 54, 65
Hagthorpe (in Hemingbrough), 3, 52–5
  chap., man., 54
  Hall, 54
  man., 48, 54–5
  man.-ho., see Hagthorpe, Hall
  moated site, 53–4
  roads, 52–3
Hague (Haig):
  Barnard, 105
  D. P., 193
  J. R., 193
  Sam., 104
Hall:
  Geo., 136, 138
  Ralph, 26
  Mr., 7
Halnaby (Yorks. N.R.), 106 n
Halsham, 43
Haltemprice priory, 132
Hambald, John, and his w. Joan, 142
Hameldon, Jordan de, see Osgodby
Hamerton, John of, 77
Hanson, J. C., vicar of Thornton, 189
Harcourt:
  E. V. V., abp. of York, 126
  W. V., rector of Wheldrake, 126
Hardcastle, Wm., 194
Hardrada, see Harold
Hardwick:
  P. C., 70
  Thos., and his w. Cath., 54
  fam., 85
Hare:
  N. E., 54
  fam., 54

INDEX

Harling, Edw., 196
Harlthorpe (in Bubwith), 131
Harold, King, 147
Harold, Earl (fl. 1066), 151
Harold Hardrada, 29, 82, 147
Harrington, Thos., 127
Harrison:
  C. H. C., 82
  Cuth., 57, 111
  Lennox, w. of Cuth., 111
  Lennox, m. Geo. Smith, 57
  Ralph, 87
  W. M., 151–2
Harswell, 131
Hart, John, 139
Harthill wapentake, 3, 129–32, *131*; *and see* Holme, Hunsley, and Wilton Beacon divisions
Hartley, Thos., 39
Harvy, Geo., 106
Hassell, Thos., 141
Hastings:
  Edw., 103
  Eliz., *see* Beaumont
  Isabel, *see* Babthorpe
  Sir John, 53
  Sir Ric., 103
Hastings (Suss.), 147
Hatfield, *see* Weightman
Hatfield (Yorks. W.R.), 172
Hatton, Chris., 69
Hawold (in Huggate), 131
Haxby, Geo., 128
Hay, fam., 115
Hayton, 131, 133; *and see* Bielby
Headlam:
  Chas., 160
  Jane, 160
  Marg., 157
  Wm., 157–8, 164
  fam., 160
Heard, Thos., 141
Heathcote:
  Bache, 53
  C. T., 49, 53, 58, 65
Hebden, John, 82
Helium, Hen. of, 142
Helmsley, Gate (Yorks. N.R.), 3, 158, 159 *n*, 161, 164
Hemingbrough, 3, **37–66**, *38*, 87
  adv., 42
  assarting, 40–1
  brick-making, 41
  chant., 40–3, 45
  chap., 43
  char., 41–3, 46–7
  ch., *frontispiece*, 37, 40, 42–3, *44*, 46–7, 50
  coll., 40, 42–3, 45
  common fields, 37, 40–1
  common meadows, 41
  ct., 42
  curates of, 43; *and see* Fido
  dom. arch., 39
  fair, 40–1
  ferries, 37, 40
  fishing, 40–1
  Hall, 39
  inc., 41
  inns, 39
  man., 37, 39–42, 49, 55, 58, 62, 64–5
  mkt., 40–1
  par. officers, 41–2, 46
  poor relief, 42
  pop., 39
  prot. nonconf., 45–6
  provost's ho. site, 40
  rly. stn., 56
  rectors of, 42–3; *and see* Clare; Droxford; Evesham; Mauley, Steph. de; Middleton, Ric. of; Ossat; Rickinghall; Robert de marisco; Walworth
  rectory, 40, 42–3, 62, 64
  rectory ho., 42

  recusancy, 45
  roads, 37
  Rom. Cath., 45
  sch., 43, 46, 62–3
  tithes, 40, 62, 64
  vicarage, 42
  vicarage ho., 39, 43
  vicars of, 42–3, 45–6, 50; *and see* Ion; Mallinson; Potter, Wm.; Revell; Teasdale
  wharf, 41
  windmill, 39–41
  woodland, 37, 40–1, 62
  and see Babthorpe; Barlby; Bowthorpe; Brackenholme; Cliffe; Duffield, South; Hagthorpe; Menthorpe; Newhay; Osgodby; Woodhall
hemp, 137–8, 168
Henry I, King, 165
Henry III, King, 98
Henry VIII, King, 160
Henry, Conan s. of, *see* Conan
Henry son of Conan (or Hen. of Kelfield, fl. 1200–10), 104, 107–8
Henry son of Conan (or Hen. of Kelfield, d. c. 1285), 104–6
Henry son of Conan (fl. 1311), 104, 108
Henry son of Conan (fl. 1346), 104
Henry son of Ellis, 103
Henry son of Thomas, 105
Henry son of Walter, 105
Henry son of William, 106
Henson:
  Mary, sr. (fl. 1717), 54
  Mary, jr. (fl. 1743), m. John Burton, 54
Herbert:
  E.A.F.W., 161
  Eliz., w. of Ric., m. 2 Geo. Toulson, 94
  Gilb., 94, 96
  John (fl. 1563), 175
  John (fl. 1628), 96
  John (fl. 1707), 96
  Phil., 96
  Ric., 94
  Rob., 94
  Roland (Rowland) (? two of this name, fl. 16th cent.), 95, 123
  Rowland (? two of this name, fl. 17th cent.), 94, 96
  fam., 94, 161
Hermer (fl. c.1100), and his fam., 104
hermits and hermitages, 95, 97, 140, 156, 184
Herring, John, 77
Hescheheld, Sim. de, 7
Hesketh:
  Anne, m. Jas. Yarburgh, 69
  Julia, w. of Sir Thos., 74
  Mary, m. Fairfax Norcliffe, 69
  Sir Thos. (d. 1605), 69, 74
  Thos. (? another, fl. 17th cent.), 69
  fam., 74
Heslerton:
  Euphemia of, *see* Neville
  Eustacia of, *see* Percy
  Norman of, 103
  Wal. of (d. 1349), 31, 160, 175, 177
  Wal. of (d. 1367), 160, 175
  fam., 160, 163
Heslington:
  Nic. (fl. 1615), 104
  Nic. (fl. 1710), 104
Heslington, 1, 3, 17, 29, **66–74**, *68*, 120
  adv., 73
  alms-ho., 74
  assarting, 71
  bridge, 71
  char., 74
  ch., 34, *65*, 67, 69, 71–3, 126
  common fields, 67, 71–2

  common pastures, 67, 71–2
  ct., 72
  curates of, 73
  dom. arch., 67, 69
  golf course, 30, 67, 72
  Hall, *65*, 66–7, 69–70, *113*
  inc., 67, 70–2
  ind., 72
  inns, 67, 69
  Little Hall, 67
  man., 7–8, 31–2, 67, 69–72
  man.-ho., *see* Heslington, Hall and Man. Ho.
  Man. Ho., 70
  mills, 67, 71–2
  Moor Hall, 67
  par. officers, 72
  park, 67
  perpetual curacy, 73
  pop., 69
  prot. nonconf., 73–4
  rectory, 71
  roads, 67, 70
  sch., 74
  tithes, 71
  vicarage, 73
  vicarage ho., 73
  woodland, 72
  York University, 1, *65*, 66, 69–70, 72
Hessle, 130–1
  hundred, 130; *and see* 'Totfled'
Hetherton, John, 151
Heversham (Westmld.), 126
Hewley:
  Sir John, 77–8, 82
  Marg., m. John Baines, 77
  Sarah, w. of Sir John, 77
Higham, Wm., 58
Hildyard, Wm., 61
Hobson, Ric., 39
Hodgson:
  E. L., 161
  John, 12, 17, 28, 36, 74, 82, 112, 120, 128, 164
Holand, Thos., earl of Kent, 103
Holderness, 73
Holdsworth, Josiah, rector of Sutton upon Derwent, 178
Holman:
  Ernest, 64
  G. & Sons, landowners, 61
  Palmer, 64
Holme, Rob., 12
Holme Beacon division (of Harthill wapentake), 132
Holme on the Wolds, 131
Holme upon Spalding Moor, 129, 131–2
  poor-law union, workho., 33, 99
  and see Bursea; Wholsea
Holtby (Yorks. N.R.), 12, 172
Home-Cust, John, Vct. Alford, 10
Hook, John of, 135
Hooton Roberts (Yorks. W.R.), 27
Hopper, A. G., 65
Hornby, fam., 5
Hornshaw's, agricultural implement makers, 9
horse-mills, 86, 98, 118, 125
Horsfield:
  Mann, 161, 195
  Sarah, 161
Horsley:
  Chris., 158
  John (fl. 1719), 197
  John (fl. 1766), 194
  John (? another), 158
  Thos., 194
Hotham:
  Ethel, 166
  Hen. Durand, Baron Hotham, 141
  Hen. Fred., Baron Hotham, 139, 141, 146, 158, 170, 173, 179, 190, 197
  Sir John of, 160
  Wm., 7

Hotham, 131
Hoton, Rob., 176
Houghton (in Sancton), 131
house-reeve, 33
Howard:
- Cath., see Knyvett
- Chas., Ld. Howard (d. 1715), 122
- Chas., earl of Carlisle (d. 1738), 166–9
- Sir Edw., later Baron Howard, 20, 122–3
- Fred., earl of Carlisle, 166–8
- Theophilus, 122
- Thos., earl of Suffolk, 20, 122
- Wm., Ld. Howard, 167
- fam., 165

Howdell, fam., 41
Howden, 43, 131
- ch., 99
- coll., 96
  - prebends, 96, 99; and see Bedwind
- ct., 42
- hundred, 2
- man., 3, 48, 53–4, 57, 59, 61, 63, 65, 84, 86, 94
- poor-law union, 42, 55, 64
- rural district, 42, 55, 64
- and see Barmby on the Marsh; Knedlington

Howdenshire liberty, see Howden hundred
Howdenshire wapentake, 3, 131
Howsham, 172
Hubie:
- Mary, 51–2
- Rob., 51
- fam., 51

Hudson:
- Geo. (fl. 1662), 89
- Geo. (? fl. 18th cent.), 145
- Jane, see Toulson
- Rob., 94

Huggate, 10, 131; and see Hawold
Hugh (fl. c. 1140), 106 n
Hugh, Jernegan s. of, see Jernegan
Hugh, earl of Chester, 151
Hugh son of Baldric, 69, 93, 96, 103, 105–8, 123
Hugh son of Nicholas, see Selby
Hull, Kingston upon, 50, 129–32
Hull, riv., 129
Hull & Selby Rly., 82
Hull valley, 129
Humber, riv., 129
Humberside (county), see North Wolds district
Hundburton (Burton Fields) (in Catton), 131, 147, 149, 151–4
- Burtonfield Hall, 151–2, 157
- common fields, 153
- common pastures, 153
- inc., 153
- man., 147, 149, 151, 153
- man.-ho., see Hundburton, Burtonfield Hall
- park, 152
- pop., 151
- tithes, 155

hundreds and wapentakes, 1–4, 129–32; and see Buckrose; Bulmer; Cave; Dickering; Driffield; Harthill; Hessle; Howden; Howdenshire; Ouse and Derwent; Pocklington; Sneculfcros; Turbar; Warter; Weighton, Market; Welton
Hunfrid (fl. 1086), 106–7
Hunmanby, 54, 184
Hunsley, Ralph of, see Babthorpe
Hunsley (in Rowley), 131–2
Hunsley Beacon division (of Harthill wapentake), 132
Hunt:
- Sir J. J., 7–8
  - Memorial Cottage Homes, see Fulford, Gate Reg., 7–8

Huntington (Yorks. N.R.), 34, 73, 196
Hussey:
- Anne (fl. 1496), see Salvin
- Anne (fl. c. 1600), m. Sir Rob. Constable, 95
- John (fl. 1486), 94
- John (fl. 1570), 95
- Thos., 123
- Sir Wm. (d. 1530), 94–5
- Wm. (d. 1570), 95, 98, 100
- fam., 95

Hustler, Geo., vicar of Stillingfleet, 111
Hutton:
- Frances, see Scrope
- Mat., dean of York, 54
- Susan, 77
- Sir Tim., 54

Hutton (in Hutton Cranswick), 130
Hutton, Sheriff (Yorks. N.R.), 12, 14, 152, 160–1, 175, 191
Hutton Cranswick, see Cranswick; Hutton; Rotsea; Sunderlandwick
Hutton Rudby (Yorks. N.R.), 74
Huxtable, John, 136

Idle:
- Anne, m. —— Suger, 134
- Frances, 134, 141
- John, 134, 141

inclosure, 1, 129; and see under places
Independents, 51
industry, 3, 130; and see agricultural implement making; bicycle manufacturers; bleaching; brewing; brick-making; coopering; dying; engineering; flax-spinning; flint-grinding; fulling; glover; mills; oil-milling; rope-making; sand and gravel extraction; sauce-making; saw-mills; steam mills; sugar-refining; tanning; tar-distilling; trade; weaving; see also under places, s.v. ind.
infangthief, 80
Ingham, Joshua, 104
Ingilby (Ingleby):
- Eleanor, see Mowbray
- John (d. 1456), 178
- John (d. 1502), 178
- Wm. (d. 1438), 178
- Wm. (d. 1501), 178
- Sir Wm. (fl. 1565), 178
- Wm. (fl. 1614), 95

Ingram:
- Sir Art. (d. 1642), 39
- Sir Art. (d. 1655), 14, 161
- Art. (d. 1742), 39
- Isabella, m. Geo. Cary, 39
- fam., 39–40, 161

inspectors of carcasses, 26
Ion:
- Jane, m. C. G. Tate, 39
- John, vicar of Hemingbrough and Halsham, 39, 43

Jack, Rob., 141
Jackson, J. M., 54
Jacques:
- A. H., 58
- Mary, m. Sim. Sterne, 14
- Sir Rog. (fl. 1646), 14
- Rog. (fl. later 17th cent.), 14
- T. P., 58
- Wm., 60

'Janulfestorp' (in Dunnington), 3, 5
Jefferson:
- Emanuel, 115, 120
- Ric., 194
- Rob., 114–15, 120
- fam., 114–15, 123, 194

Jenkins:
- Sir Hen., 7, 160
- Mary, m. Sir Hen. Goodrick, 7, 161
- Tobias (? two of this name), 6–8, 161
- Wm., and his bro., 160–1
- fam., 161

Jernegan son of Hugh, 106 n
Jervis:
- C. R. J., Vct. St. Vincent, 175
- R. C., Vct. St. Vincent, 178
- R. G. J., Vct. St. Vincent, 175, 178

Jewitt, Ric., 54
Jobson, Francis, 84
John son of Daniel, 106
John, Thos. s. of, see Thomas
Johnson:
- G. H., 58
- Hen., 135
- J. W., 65
- John (fl. 1584), 107
- John (fl. 1744), 146–7
- Judith, see Myers
- Mat., 110
- Dr. (? Hen.), 146
- fam., 141–2

Johnson-Marshall, see Matthew
Jones:
- G. F., 157
- Hen., 136

Jordan son of Gilbert, 194–5
Joseph Rowntree Social Services Trust Ltd., 70
Jurassic hills, 129

Keighley:
- Eliz., m. Wm. Burton, 57
- Jas., 57

Kelfield, Hen. of, see Henry son of Conan
Kelfield (in Stillingfleet), 3, 101–5, 107–12
- assarting, 108
- brick-making, 109
- bridge, 102
- chant., 105
- chap., 111
- chap., man., 101, 105, 111
- char., 112
- common fields, 101, 108
- common meadows, 101, 108
- common pastures, 101, 108
- ct., 109
- drainage, 102
- ferry, 102–3
- fishing, 109
- Hall, 105, 111
- inc., 102–4, 108
- inns, 103
- man., 101, 104–5, 108–9
- man.-ho., 105; and see Kelfield, Hall
- moated sites, 105
- park, 108
- poor relief, 109
- pop., 103
- prot. nonconf., 111–12
- rectory, 107
- roads, 102
- Rom. Cath., 111
- sch., 89, 110, 112
- tithes, 107, 110
- wharf, 109
- windmill, 109
- woodland, 108

Kelleythorpe (in Great Driffield), 130
Kelsey:
- A. J., 46
- Maud, 88
- Rob., 88

Kendall, Thos., 114
Kent, earls of, see Holand; Woodstock, Edm. of and John of
Kerry, Thos., 32, 194
Kettering, Wm., 65

INDEX

Kettlethorpe (in North Cave), 131
Kexby (in Catton), 3, 147, 152, **158–64**
  adv., 163
  assarting, 161
  brick-making, 163
  bridges, 149, 154, 158–9, *160*, 190
  chant., 155, 163
  chap., 155, 163
  char., 164
  ch., 155, 163–4
  common fields, 158, 161–2
  common pastures, 158, 162
  dom. arch., 159
  fairs, 163
  ferry, 158–9
  fishing, 163
  inc., 158, 162
  ind., 163
  inn, 159, 163; *and see* Man. Farm
  man., 151, 159–60, 162–3, 191
  Man. Farm (formerly an inn), *64*, 159
  man.-ho., 160; *and see* Kexby, New Hall and Old Hall
  mkt., 163
  moated site, 160
  New Hall, 160
  Old Hall, 160
  park, 161
  perpetual curacy, 163
  pop., 159
  prot. nonconf., 164
  roads, 158–9, 163
  Rom. Cath., 164
  sch., 159, 164, 197
  tithes, 155
  vicar of, 164
  vicarage, 163, 195–6
  vicarage ho., 163
  wharves, 163
  windmill, 163
  woodland, 158, 161–3
Key:
  Anne, 35
  Cath., 36
  John, 31, 34, 36
  Mary, 34, 36
  R. E., 31
  Sam., 72
  W. H., 20, 71
  fam., 31, 34, 70
Kildale (Yorks. N.R.), 105
Kilnwick, 131; *and see* Beswick; Bracken
Kilnwick Percy, 131, 136, 139, 146, 158, 170, 173, 179, 190, 197
Kiplingcotes (in Middleton on the Wolds), 131
Kirby:
  John, 151
  W. L., Ltd., millers, 50
Kirby in Cleveland (Yorks. N.R.), 126
Kirk:
  Geo., 161
  Mat., 96
Kirkburn, 130; *and see* Eastburn; Southburn; Tibthorpe
Kirkby:
  Chris., 7, 161
  Mark (fl. 1715), 7, 161
  Mark (d. 1748), 7, 161
Kirkbymoorside (Yorks. N.R.), 172
Kirkham priory, 122–3, 173, 176, 193
Kirlew:
  Edw. (? two of this name), 54–5
  Jos., 61
  Thos., 54
  fam., 54
Knaresborough (Yorks. W.R.), 16
Knedlington (in Howden), 60
Knight:
  John, 61
  fam., 61
Knights Hospitallers, 95, 135–6, 152, 164, 166, 168, 176, 193
Knights Templars, 65, 78, 134, 136, 152
Knyvett:
  Anne, *see* Pickering
  Cath., m. Thos. Howard, 20
  Sir Hen. (fl. 16th cent.) (? two of this name), 20–1
  Sir Hen. (fl. 17th cent.), 20
  Thos., Baron Knyvett, 20, 122
  fam., 20, 22–3
Kyme:
  Marg., ?m. Ilger of Wilberfoss, 193
  Phil., of, 191
  Wm. of, 191, 193
  fam., 191–4

Lacy:
  Eliz., *see* Lodge
  ———, husb. of Eliz., 48
Lakyn, Wm., 175
Lambarte, Jas., 107
Lamplugh:
  Thos., abp. of York, 126
  his s., rector of Wheldrake, 126
Lancashire, *see* Windsor Iron Works
Lancaster, John of, duke of Bedford, 151, 183
Lane-Fox:
  Geo. (d. 1896), 7
  (or Fox-Lane), Jas., 7
  fam., 7–8
Langlands, John, 111
Langley:
  Eliz., *see* Boynton
  Ric. (fl. earlier 18th cent.), 53–4
  Ric. (fl. 1784), 54
  Thos., 171–2
Langton (Lincs.), 110
Langwith (in Wheldrake), 3, 13, 67, 70, 73, 120–6
  assarting, 121
  common pastures, 121, 125
  inc., 122, 125
  moated site, 122
  pop., 122
  Thorp, 121, 123
  tithes, 126
  woodland, 123–5
Lascelles:
  Avice, m. Rob. le Constable, 20–1
  Isabel, 20
  Joan de, m. Thos. de Colewenne, 20
  Marg., m. Jas. Pickering, 20
  Maud, m. Sir Rob. de Tilliol, 20
  Picot de (fl. c. 1150), 20
  Picot de (d. c. 1252), 22
  Ralph de, *see* FitzRanulph
  Rog. de (d. c. 1218), 20
  Rog. de (d. c. 1300), 20, 22
  Rog. (fl. 15th cent.), 20
  Thos., 27
  Tiffany, m. Ralph FitzRanulph, 20
  Wm. de, 21
  fam., 20
Latham:
  Chris., 89
  Edm., 58
Latimer, Eliz. de, m. John de Neville, 103
Latimer, Ld., *see* Neville, John
Laton, fam., 61
Laurence, Hen., 105
Laver, Geo., 152
Law Life Assurance Soc., 96
Lawley:
  B. R., Baron Wenlock, 14, 27, 84–5, 87–8, 163
  Beilby, Baron Wenlock, 20, 26, 28, 84–5, 91, 94, 97, 107, 123, 160, 163
  Caroline, *see* Griffin
  Constance, m. Eust. Vesey, 163
  Eliz., *see* Grosvenor
  Irene, m. C. G. Forbes Adam, 14, 20, 26, 85, 163
  Jane, *see* Thompson
  (later Thompson), P. B., Baron Wenlock, 14, 19–20, 28, 85, 97, 105, 125, 164
  Rob., Baron Wenlock (d. 1834), 25
  Sir Rob. (fl. late 18th cent.), 20
  fam., 27–8, 84–5, 94, 159–60
Lawson:
  Sir Geo. (fl. 1534), 161
  Geo. (fl. 1604), 106
  Geo. (fl. 1638, s. of last), 106
  Grace, 111
  Marm. (? fl. early 18th cent.), 106 *n*
  Marm. (d. 1762), 106
  Susanna, *see* Preston
  fam., 106
Lax, F. B., 65
Layland, Wilf., 167
Laytham (in Aughton), 131
Layton, Wm., 146–7
Lazenby:
  Hen., 158
  Wilf., 158
Leach:
  Wm., 193
  fam., 193
Lecke:
  Thos., curate of Barlby, 50
  Tristram, 158
Leconfield, Baron, *see* Wyndham, Chas. H., Geo. (d. 1869), and J. E. R.
Leconfield, 131; *and see* Arram; Newsham
Legard:
  John, 21
  Mary, *see* Dawnay
  Sir Thos., 21
  fam., 21
Lennox, earl of, *see* Stewart
Leppington, Edw., 100
Leppington, 172
Lester & Pack, bell-founders, 88
Leveson-Gower:
  Jane, *see* Granville
  John, Earl Gower, 175
Levett:
  Faith, 77
  fam., 77
Lewkenor, Sir Ric., 69
leyrwite, 8
libraries, parochial, and reading rooms, 6, 12, 46, 102, 120, 127, 150, 164, 182
Lichfield (Staffs.), cath., treasurer of, *see* Sandale
Liddell, Geo., vicar of Naburn, 81
lights, endowed, in ch., 16, 26, 34, 110, 119
Lincoln, dean of, *see* Robert de marisco
Lincolnshire, *see* Coleby; Langton
Lindley:
  Chris., rector of Dunnington, 10
  Sir Hen., 176
Lingcroft, *see* Naburn
Linton, *see* Grassington
Lister:
  Geo., 194
  Jas., 95, 98
Liverpool, *see* Windsor Iron Works
Lloyd:
  Alicia, *see* Greame
  Edw., 75
  (later Yarburgh), G. J., 70, 72–4, 123
  Rosabella, w. of Edw., 81–2
Lockington, 131; *and see* Aike
lock-ups, 5, 33
Lodge:
  Eleanor, m. ——— Spofforth, 48
  Eliz., m. ——— Lacy, 48
  John, 52
  Ralph (d. 1661), 46, 51
  Ralph (d. 1717), 48
  fam., 48
Loftas, Edw., 82

Lofthouse, Ric., 158
Loftsome, John, 158
Loftsome (in Wressle), 52–3
    bridge, *32*, 53
    and see 'Siwarbi'
Londesborough:
    Baron, see Denison, Albert
    earl of, see Denison, W. F. H.
Londesborough, 131; and see Cleaving; Easthorpe; Towthorpe
London, 100
    bell-founders of, 27, 81, 88, 145, 179
    City of, 14, 161
    inhabitant of, 126
    plate made in, 11, 27, 81, 88, 100, 111, 157
    St. Paul's cath., canon of, see Smith, Sydney
    Savoy chap., 27
    Savoy hosp., 176
    and see Westminster
Long, Rob. the, see Robert
Lord Chancellor, 99, 118, 172, 188; and see Middleton, Ric. of; Stillington, Rob.
Louvain, Jocelin of, 6
Lovell:
    Alice, see Deincourt
    Ld. Francis, 103
    Ld. Wm., 103
Lowry, Thos., curate of Naburn, 81
Lowth, Revd. Wm., 7
Lowther, Sir Wm., 61, 63
Lucas, Revd. Ric., 171
Lund (in Harthill wapentake), 131, 171
Lund (in Hemingbrough), 43, 45–6, 56, 58–9, *64*; and see Cliffe
Luthe:
    Gilb. de, 103, 109
    Nic. de, 109
Lutterell:
    Geof., 114
    fam., 114
Lyndlawe, Wm. de, 21

McNeil, W. M., 193
Mainwaring, Eaton, see Ellerker
Malbis (de Malbis):
    Ric. (d. 1210), 77, 122–4
    Ric. (fl. 1293), 80
    fam., 57, 77, 122
Malet:
    Rob., 13, 77
    Wm., 6, 13, 57, 61, 64, 94, 122, 160
Mallinson, John, vicar of Hemingbrough, 43
Malore, Anketin, 175
malting, 9, *33*, 59, 154, 163
Malton (Yorks. N.R.), 150
Maluvel, Rob. de, 135
Manners:
    Anne, 45
    Eleanor, see Ros
    Eliz., m. Wm. Cecil, 183
    Sir Geo., 31, 183
    Hen., earl of Rutland, 31, 123
    John, 134
    Sir Rob., 31, 183
    Thos., Ld. Ros, earl of Rutland, 31, 78, 123, 176, 193
    fam., 183
Mara:
    Mabel, m. Geof. de Nevill, 21
    Ralph de, 21
March:
    earl of, see Edward IV
    earldom, 183
marisco, Rob. de, see Robert
Mark, Ant., 57
market-gardening, nurseries, 25, 30, 33, 41, 50, 59, 72, 79, 86, 108
markets, see Barmby Moor; Duffield, North; Hemingbrough; Kexby; Osgodby; Riccall; Stamford Bridge West
marl pits, marling, 9, 187
Marmion (Marmyoun):
    Avice (fl. 1280), see Avice
    Avice (fl. late 14th cent.), m. John de Grey, Ld. Grey of Rotherfield, 106 *n*
    John, 106 *n*
    Rob., 106 *n*
    Wm., 21
    fam., 106
Marmoutier (Bas-Rhin, France), abbey, 49
Marmyoun, see Marmion
Marsh:
    A. N., 161
    John, 78
    Wm., 78
marshal, Eudes the, see Eudes
Marshall:
    Anne, 96
    Art., 31
    John, 160
    Mic., 96
    Rob., 96
    Sam., 31
    Thos., 31
Martin, T. B., 141
Mason:
    Frances, m. Thos. Barker, 54
    Wm., 54
Massey, Wm., 14, 179
Masterman:
    Benj., 88
    Hen. (d. 1732), 84 *n*, 88
    Hen. (?another), 85
    Thos., 14
    fam., 84
Mather, Alex., 13
Matthew, Rob., Johnson-Marshall and Partners, architects, 69
Mauley:
    Eleanor de, 57
    Isabel de, see Turnham
    Pet. de (d. by 1241), 57, 65, 114
    Pet. de (fl. 1284), 114
    Steph. de, rector of Hemingbrough, prebendary of York, dean of Wimborne and Auckland, 43
    fam., 57–8, 94, 114–15, 175
Maunby:
    Ellen, m. Edw. of Saltmarsh, 114
    Ralph of, 114, 118
    Thos. of, 118
Maunsel:
    Edm., 79
    Ric., 78–9
    Wm., 61
    fam., 77, 79
Meadowcroft, Ena, 175
Mears:
    C. & G., bell-founders, 81
    Thos., bell-founder, 179
Mears & Stainbank, bell-founders, 145
Meaux abbey, 14, 165
Meeke:
    Francis, 32
    Geo., 32
Melbourne (in Thornton), 131, 179, 181–90
    brick-making, 187
    bridges, 182
    char., 189–90
    common fields, 181–2, 186
    common meadows, 181, 186
    common pastures, 181–2, 186
    ct., see Storwood, ct.
    dom. arch., 182
    Hall, 182, 184, 187
    inc., 181–2, 184, 186–8
    inns, 182
    lock, 181
    man., 181; and see Storwood, man.
    man.-ho., see Melbourne, Hall
    mission ch., 182, 188–9
    parks, 182, 184
    poor relief, 187
    pop., 182–3
    prot. nonconf., 188–9
    rectory, 184–5
    recusancy, 189
    roads, 181–2
    Rossmoor Lodge, 182
    sch., 188–90
    tithes, 184, 186, 188
    windmill, 186–7
    woodland, 186–7
Melton (in Welton), 131
Meltonby (in Pocklington), 131
Mennell:
    Chas., 171
    Wm., 69
    fam., 171
Menthorpe, Rob. of, 55
Menthorpe, Menthorpe with Bowthorpe (in Hemingbrough and Skipwith), 3, 37, **63–4**, 89, 93, 95–6, 100
    char., 47
    common pastures, 63–4
    ferry, 63
    fishing, 64
    inc., 63–4
    inn, 63
    man., 95
    par. officers, 42
    pop., 63
    prot. nonconf., 64
    rly. stn., 63
    rectory, 64, 96
    roads, 63–4
    Rom. Cath., 100
    tithes, 64, 96, 99
    wharf, 63
Menzies:
    Charlotte, 54
    Rob. (d. 1839), 53–5
    Rob. W. (d. 1887), 166
    fam., 54
merchet, 8, 40, 143
Merleswain (fl. 1066), 49, 114
Merston, Thos. of, 106
Metham:
    Iseult, w. of Ric. de, m. 2 John Grendon, 63
    Ric. de, 63
    Thos., and his w., 35
    fam., 63
Methley, Hugh of, 7
Methodists, see under places, s.v. prot. nonconf.
Methodists, Independent, 73
Meynell, Rob. de, 114, 118
Meysey-Thompson, Doris, m. 1 Francis Egerton, 2 John Seed, 184
Middleham (Yorks. N.R.), 126
Middleton:
    John (fl. 1673), 95
    John (fl. 18th cent.), 56, 58
    Pet. (fl. 1624), 95
    Pet. (fl. 1808), 95
    Ric. of, rector of Hemingbrough, king's chancellor, 43
    Wm. (fl. 1634), 95
    Wm. (fl. late 18th cent.), 95
    Wm. (? another, fl. 1808), 95
Middleton on the Wolds, 131; and see Kiplingcotes
Milbank (Milbanke):
    Eliz., see Acklam
    Sir Ralph, 20, 106
    Sir Wm., 106
    fam., 106
Millington, 131, 142; and see Givendale, Little
mills, 3, 43; and see fulling mills horse-mills; saw-mills; steam mills; see also under places, s.vv mills; water-mills; windmills

INDEX

Milner:
  And., 175
  Mary, see Eglesfield
  Tempest, 141
Ministry of Agriculture, Fisheries and Food, 79–80, 135
Ministry of Defence, 168
Minton, Herb., 145
Misson (Notts.), 144
Mitchell, Thos., 104–5
moated sites, see Babthorpe; Barlby; Barmby Moor; Catton, High and Low; Cliffe; Deighton; Duffield, South; Hagtorpe; Kelfield; Kexby; Langwith; Naburn; Riccall; Skipwith; Storwood; Sutton upon Derwent
Molyneux, John, 193
Monck:
  Chris., duke of Albemarle, 175
  Geo., duke of Albemarle, 175
Monkton, Nun, priory (Yorks. W.R.), 78
Monteagle, Ld., see Stanley, Wm.
Moon, Ric., 85
moor-reeves, moormen, 33, 144
Moore, Lorenzo, 105
Moorse, M. S., 65
Morcar (fl. 1066), 20, 31–2, 123
Moreby:
  Hen. of, 15, 106
  Mary, m. Wm. Acklam, 106
  Nic. of, 105 n, 110
  Rob. of, 111
  Wm. of, 106
  fam., 111
Moreby (in Stillingfleet), 3, 58, 77, 101–11
  assarting, 108
  brick-making, 109
  bridge, 75, 102
  chap., man., 106
  common fields, 108
  common meadows, 108
  fishing, 109
  Hall, 16, 101–2, 106, 108–9
  inc., 108
  man., 104–6
  man.-ho., 106; and see Moreby, Hall
  park, 101–2, 106, 108
  pop., 103
  rectory, 107
  road, 102
  Rom. Cath., 111
  tithes, 107, 110
  wharf, 109
  woodland, 108
Morers:
  Ric. de, 13
  Wm. de (fl. 12th cent.), 13–14
  Wm. de (fl. 1356, 1394, ? two of this name) 14–15
  fam., 13
Moreville:
  Agnes de, 106
  Ric. de, 134
Morley:
  John, 58
  Rob., 193
  fam., 58
Morrell, Edw., 62
Morrice, Francis, 32, 40, 96
Morris:
  Ric., 128
  Wm., 156
Morritt:
  Anne, see Sawrey
  Bacon, 61, 63
  J. S., 61, 63
Mortain, count of, see William
Mortimer:
  Chas., 32, 151
  Ralph de (fl. 1086), 183
  Ralph de (fl. 1243), 183
  Tim., 31, 151

  fam., 183
Mosley, Revd. Thos., 36
mottes, 130 n; and see Duffield, North; Thorganby
Moulin, Pet. du, rector of Wheldrake, 126
Mowbray:
  Eleanor, m. —— Ingilby, 178
  John de (d. c. 1327), 135
  John de (fl. mid 14th cent., ? two or three of this name), 135, 178, 183
  Marg., w. of Wm., 178
  Niel de, 135
  Wm., 178
  fam., 69, 135–6, 183
Moyser:
  Jas., 107
  fam., 107
Multon:
  Maud de, see Vaux
  Thos. de (d. by 1285), 114
  Thos. de (d. 1295), 114
  Thos. de (fl. c. 1300), 114
multure, 8
Murdac:
  Ric., 93
  Rob., 93
Musgrave, Cuth., 43
mustard, 72, 108
Myers:
  Jeremiah, 134
  Judith, w. of ——, m. 2 Hen. Johnson, 135
  Rob., 134
  Thos. (fl. 1625), 134
  Thos. (fl. 1650s), 134
  Thos. (fl. c. 1700), 134
  fam., see Smyth, Ann
Mylton, Wm., 171
Myton (in Hessle), 130–1
Mytton, Thos., 96

Naburn, 1, 3, 25, 32, **74–82**, 76, 102
  adv., 80, 109
  assarting, 74, 78–9
  Bell Hall, 20, 75, 77–80, 80
  brick-making, 80
  bridges, 75, 80, 102
  chant., 80–1, 110
  chap., man., 81
  char., 81–2
  ch., 78–82
  common fields, 74, 79, 81
  common meadows, 79
  common pastures, 74, 79
  ct., 80
  curate of (? incumbent), see Lowry
  dom. arch., 75
  ferries, 75, 80
  fishing, 80
  Hall, 75, 77, 81–2
  Hosp., see Fulford, Water, s.v. York City Asylum
  inc., 78–81
  inn, 75
  Lingcroft (Lincroft), 75, 78–80
  locks, 75, 80
  man., 77, 79–80
  man.-ho., 77; and see Naburn, Hall
  mills, 75, 80
  moated site, 78
  par. officers, 80
  poor relief, 80
  pop., 75, 77
  prot. nonconf., 82
  rly. stn., 75
  rectory, 78–80
  recusancy, 81
  roads, 75
  Rom. Cath., 81
  sch., 82
  tithes, 78–81
  vicar of, 79–81; and see Liddell
  vicarage, 80, 109

  vicarage ho., 81
  wharf, 80
  woodland, 74, 77–80
  York sewerage works, 75
National Soc. (and National sch.), 28, 36, 51, 74, 82, 88, 112, 120, 127, 139, 146, 157–8, 170, 179, 189, 197
nature reserves, 1, 91, 121, 133
Nelson:
  Jos., vicar of Skipwith, 100–1
  Thos., 52
Ness, John of, 107
Neswick (in Bainton), 130
Neville (Nevill):
  Chas., earl of Westmorland, 103
  Edm., 151
  Eliz. de, see Latimer
  Euphemia, m. Wal. of Heslerton (d. 1367), 160, 175
  Francis, 69
  Geof. de, 21
  Herb. de, 161, 163
  Hugh de, 21
  Joan de, see Beaufort
  John de (d. 1388), 103
  John, Ld. Latimer (d. 1543), 78
  John, benefactor at Escrick, 28
  Mabel de, see Mara
  Margery, w. of Herb., 161
  Ralph de (fl. 1284), 7
  Ralph, earl of Westmorland (d. 1425), 14, 160, 175
  Ralph, earl of Westmorland (d. 1499), 104
  Ric. de (fl. 1346), 7
  Ric., earl of Salisbury (d. 1460), 14, 151, 160
  Ric., earl of Warwick (d. 1471), 14, 160, 175, 191
  fam., 8, 151, 175, 191
New Village, 131
Newark:
  Joan, see Hagtorpe
  John, 54
  Thos., 54
  fam., 54
Newbald, 131
Newbald, North, 86
Newcastle upon Tyne (Northumb.), 111
Newhay (in Hemingbrough), 3, 43, 50, 55–6, 58–9
  ferry, 56
  fishing, 59
  grange, 1, 37, 55, 58
  man., 58
  rectory, 58
  tithes, 58
Newlove, John, vicar of Riccall, 87
Newsham, Geo., 88
Newsham (? in Leconfield), 131
Newsholme (in Wressle), 130
Newsome:
  Annie, 96
  Eleanor, 96
  Eliz., 89
  Mary, 89
  fam., 96
Newstead, Mr., 112
Newton:
  Edw. H., 7
  John of, 21
Newton (in Cherry Burton), 131
Newton (in Cottingham), 131–2
Newton upon Derwent (in Wilberfoss), 73, 131, 152–3, 190–7, 192
  assarting, 194
  brick-making, 195
  chap., 195–6
  char., 196–7
  common fields, 190, 194–5
  common meadows, 190, 195
  common pastures, 190, 194–5
  dom. arch., 193
  inc., 191, 194–6
  inns, 191

Newton upon Derwent (*cont.*)
  man., 191, 193
  pop., 191
  prot. nonconf., 197
  rectory, 193-4
  roads, 191
  sch., 197
  tithes, 194
  woodland, 195
Niel (fl. 1086), 7-8
Norais, Wm. de, 66
Norcliffe:
  Fairfax, 69
  Mary, *see* Hesketh
  (later Dalton), Thos., 69
Norfolk:
  Martin of, 78
  Nic. of, 79
  Thos. of, 78
  fam., 78
Norman (fl. 1066), 6, 64, 122, 175
North:
  Jane, m. Ric. Bell, 77
  John, 77
North Eastern Railway Co., 150
North Wolds district (of Humberside), 138, 144, 155, 168, 172, 177, 187, 195
Northumberland:
  countess of, *see* Talbot
  duke of, *see* Dudley
  earls of, *see* Percy: Hen. (d. 1408, d. 1455, d. 1489, d. 1537), Joceline, and Thos.
Nottingham:
  John (fl. 18th cent., ? two of this name), 193, 195
  John (fl. 1819), 193
Nottingham University, 57
Nunburnholme, 131
  priory, 116, 123, 166-7
  and *see* Thorpe le Street
Nurse:
  G. W., 48
  Isaac, 48

Oates:
  Rob., 31, 33-4, 72
  fam., 70
obits, 26, 87, 119, 156, 169, 188
Oglethorpe, Wm., 104
officers, manorial, *see* affeerors; aletasters; bylawmen; cottage-reeve; greave; house-reeve; inspectors of carcases; moor-reeves; pinders; *prepositus de manegreves*; reeve
O'Gram, Jas., 134-5
oil-milling and seed-crushing, 48, 50, 59
Olympia Agricultural Co. Ltd., 57
Olympia Oil and Cake Co. Ltd., 48-50, 57
onions, 195
Orm (fl. 1066), 175
Orr, Annie, 57
Osbaldeston:
  Anne, *see* Wentworth
  Wm., 54
  fam., 54
Osbaldeston-Mitford, fam., 54
Osbaldwick (Yorks. N.R.), 11
Osgodby:
  Adam of, 65
  Cecily, m. Hugh Turnyll, 65
  Denise of, m. Sampson de la Pomeray, 65
  Emme, m. John Rabace, 65
  Isabel, m. Thos. Hagthorpe, 65
  (or de Hameldon), Jordan of, 65
  Rob. of (fl. 1284), 65
  Rob. of (fl. 1302), 65-6
Osgodby (in Hemingbrough), 3, 37, 48, 50, 51, 53, **64-6**, 110
  assarting, 66

  chap., man., 65
  char., 47, 63, 66
  common fields, 64, 66
  common meadows, 64, 66
  common pastures, 47, 60, 64, 66
  ct., 66
  fair, 66
  Hall, 40, 51, 64-5
  inc., 66
  inns, 64
  man., 48, 64-6
  man.-ho., 65; and *see* Osgodby, Hall
  mkt., 66
  par. officers, 42
  park, 64-6
  poor relief, 66
  pop., 64
  prot. nonconf., 66
  rectory, 49, 58, 65-6
  roads, 64
  Rom. Cath., 66
  tithes, 49, 58, 65-6
  windmill, 66
  woodland, 66
Osgodby (in Cayton) (Yorks. N.R.), 65 *n*
Ossat, Joscelin d', rector of Hemingbrough, cardinal bp. of Alba, 43
Ouchterloney, Sir Jas., 27
Ouse, riv., 1, 29, 52, 82-3, 91, 102-3
  as boundary, 1, 3, 29, 37, 47, 56, 74, 83, 101
  bridges over, *see* Barlby; Kelfield; Naburn
  changes in course, 1, 37-8, 43, 47, 55-6, 58-9, 83
  ferries across, *see* Barlby; Hemingbrough; Kelfield; Naburn; Newhay; Stillingfleet
  ford in, *see* Fulford, Gate
  trade, 33, 41, 50, 59, 75, 80, 82-3, 86, 109
  and *see under places*, s.vv. fishing; mills
Ouse and Derwent forest, 1, 71, 123-4
Ouse and Derwent wapentake, 1, 2, 3-4, 129, 131, 147
Ousethorpe (in Pocklington), 131
Overend:
  Cath., *see* Cholmley
  Cholmley, 166
  Geo., 166-8
  Mary, 170
  Tim. (fl. early 18th cent.), 12, 169-70
  Tim. (fl. early 19th cent.), 170
  fam., 165-6, 168
Owram:
  John, 57
  Steph., 57

Pagett, Ric., 26
Pain, Geof. s. of, *see* Geoffrey
Paler, John, 27
Palmer:
  Moffatt, 58
  Nic., 106
  Wm., rector of Wheldrake, 126
Palmes (de Palmes):
  Brian, 77, 79
  Sir Geo. (fl. late 16th-early 17th cent.), 78
  Geo. (d. 1774), 77-80
  Geo. (d. 1851), 78, 81-2
  Cmdr. Geo. B. (d. 1974), 77
  Sir Guy, 65, 78
  Revd. Jas., 166
  John (fl. 16th cent.), 78
  John (d. 1784), 81
  Maud, *see* Watervill
  Nic., 77
  Wm. (fl. 13th cent.), 77, 79
  Wm. (fl. 14th cent.), 77, 79
  Wm. (fl. 17th cent.), 65

  fam., 75, 77-81
  pannage, 8, 22, 49, 176
  Parish, Geo., rector of Wheldrake, 128
Parker:
  Gilb., 85
  J. W. R., 48
  (later Toulson), John, 91, 94
  Mary, *see* Carr
  T. G., 48
Parkin, Mary, 54
parks, *see* Catton, High and Low; Cottingwith, West; Deighton; Duffield, North; Elvington; Escrick; Fangfoss; Heslington; Hundburton; Kelfield; Kexby; Melbourne; Moreby; Osgodby; Riccall; Scoreby; Storwood; Sutton upon Derwent; Waplington; Wheldrake; Woodhouse
Parnel, m. Conan s. of Hen., and her fam., 105
parsnips, 195
Pateshull:
  Isabel de, *see* Stonegrave
  Sim. de, 105
Paulet, fam., 184
Paxton:
  Margery de, *see* Coldingham
  Wal. de, 54
Payler:
  Anne, *see* Watkinson
  Edw., 151
  Mary, 151
  Sir W. P., 151
  Watkinson, 151
Paynel:
  Ralph, 49, 58, 113, 115-17
  Wm., 58
  fam., 58
Peacock, fam., 191
Pearson:
  Eliz., 158, 173
  J. L., 45, 88, 100
  Pet., 179
  Thos., 171
Peirse:
  Dorothy, 104
  Mary, m. Revd. Edw. Stillingfleet, 104, 112
Penrose, F. C., 26-7, 163-4
Percy:
  Aubrey, w. of Rob. de (d. 1226-9), 175, 178
  Aubrey, dau. of Rob. de (d. 1321), 175
  Beatrice, w. of Rob. de (d. 1321), 175
  Eleanor de, *see* FitzAlan
  Eliz., m. Chas. Seymour, duke of Somerset, 151, 155
  Eustacia de, m. Wal. of Heslerton (d. 1349), 160, 175
  Hen. de (d. 1314), 159, 165, 193
  Hen. de (d. 1352), 94
  Sir Hen. (d. 1403), 135
  Hen., earl of Northumberland (d. 1408), 135, 149, 151, 166
  Hen., earl of Northumberland (d. 1455), 135, 151
  Hen., earl of Northumberland (d. 1489), 166, 183
  Hen., earl of Northumberland (d. 1537), 135, 151, 165
  Joceline, earl of Northumberland, 151
  John, 105
  Mary, *see* Talbot
  Maud de, m. Wm., earl of Warwick, 122, 152
  Osbern de, 160, 162
  Pet. de (d. 1266-7), 161-2, 176
  Pet. de (d. 1315), 160, 175
  Picot de, 175-6
  Ric. de, 6, 8, 10, 152-3, 194
  Rob. de (d. by 1175), 178
  Rob. de (d. 1226-9), 175, 178

INDEX

Rob. de (d. 1321), 116, 159–61, 175–6, 178
Thos., earl of Northumberland, 151, 165, 188
Wm. de (d. 1096), 6–8, 13, 122, 151, 160, 175
Wm. de (d. by 1175), 122
Wm. de (? d. 1245), 152
fam., 6, 8, 10, 13, 55, 94, 105, 122, 136–7, 151–3, 155, 160–1, 165–6, 171, 175–6, 183, 191, 193
'Persene' (? in Scorborough), 131
Peruzzi, the, 84
Peter son of Grente, 171
Petit, M. A., 54
Petre:
  Laura, 49
  Rob., Ld. Petre, 49
Petuaria, *see* Brough
Peyton, Cath., *see* Granville
Philips (Phillips):
  Francis, 32, 40, 96
  H. A., 12
  Wm., 58
Pickering:
  Anne, m. Sir Hen. Knyvett, 20
  Chris., 20
  Jas., 20
  Marg., *see* Lascelles
  Rob. of, dean of York, 109
  Wm. of, dean of York, 109
Pickup, Wm., 47, 60
Picot (fl. 12th cent.), 115
Pierrepont, Sir Wm., 155
'Pileford' (in Cottingham), 131
Pilgrimage of Grace, 91
pillory, 98
Pindar, Eliz., 34
pinders, 33, 72, 80, 86, 109, 138, 144, 155, 168, 187, 195; *and see* pinfolds
pinfolds, 47, 83, 93
Pistor, Rob., 105, 119
Place (Playce):
  Eliz., *see* Aton
  W., 114
  Wm. de (fl. 1329), 114
  Wm. (fl. late 14th cent.), 48
plague, 151; *and see* Black Death
Plantagenet:
  Edw., *see* Edward IV
  Geo., duke of Clarence, 14, 160
  Ric., *see* Richard III
  Ric., duke of York, 183
Playce, *see* Place
Plumer (Plummer):
  John, 111
  Sir Thos., 63
Plumpton, Wm., and his w. Isabel, 53
Pocklington, 130–1, 133–8, 140–1, 143–4, 169
  canal, 133, *161*, 181–2, 187
  ch., 133, 139, 144–5, 169, 187–8
  Grammar Sch., 141–2, 145, 158
  hundred, 2, 130–1
  man., 61, 134–5, 142, 165–6
  poor-law union, 138, 144, 155, 168, 172, 177, 187, 195
  rural dist., 138, 144, 155, 168, 172, 177, 187, 195
  secondary sch., 139, 146, 170, 179, 189, 197
  and see Meltonby; Ousethorpe; Yapham
Poer:
  John le, 135, 142
  Wal. le, 142
  Wm. le, 142
  fam., 135
Pomeray:
  Denise de la, *see* Osgodby
  Sampson de la, 65
Pontefract, R. M., 14
Porritt, ——, 52
Portington:
  John, 63
  Rog., 63
potatoes, 72, 108
Potter:
  Rob., vicar of Stillingfleet and curate of Barlby, 50
  Wm., jr., vicar of Hemingbrough and Brayton, and curate of Barlby, 43, 50
Potts, Geo., 22
poultry-farming, 86, 141, 154
Powle, Thos., 122
Pratt:
  Jas., 85
  fam., 86
pre-Conquest remains, 100, *177*, 179
prehistoric remains, *see* Fulford, Gate; Green Dykes and Siward's Howe; Skipwith, Danes' Hills
prepositus de manegreves, 33
Presbyterians, 45
Prest, Revd. E., 7
Preston:
  A. T., 106
  Beatrice, 58, 104–6
  Hen. (d. 1837), 58, 104–6, 109
  Hen. (fl. 1847), 14
  John, 61
  Susanna, m. Marm. Lawson, 106 *n*
  Revd. Thos. (d. 1827), 14, 58, 104
  Thos. (fl. 1864), 161
  Wm., 106
  fam., 58, 104–6
Price:
  Clara, m. Sir Chas. Blois, 95
  Frances, *see* Adams
  Jocelyn, 95
  Lucy, m. Capt. Willye, 95–6
  Ric., 193
Prickett:
  Barbara, w. of Marm., 57
  Josias, 176
  Marm., 57
  Rob., 57
  fam., 134, 136
priest, Ernuin the, *see* Ernuin
Prince, Ralph, 32, 78
Pritchard:
  Eliz., *see* Burdett
  (later Burdett), T. F., 65
Pritchett, J. P., 35
Proctor:
  Geof., 54
  J. W., 65
  Joan, *see* Hagthorpe
  Rob., 54
protestant nonconformity, *see* Friends; Independents; Methodists; Methodists, Independent; Presbyterians; Wesleyan Association
Punchardun:
  Hugh de, 7
  Mat. de, 7
Puritans, 10, 16, 27, 87, 110, 178

Quakers, *see* Friends
Queen Margaret's School for Girls, *see* Escrick
Quincy:
  Rog. de, 105
  Saer de, earl of Winchester, 105
  fam., 105

Rabace:
  Emme, *see* Osgodby
  John, 65
rabbit warrens, 8–9, 25, 137, 143, 177, 186
Radcliffe, Ralph, 14, 161
Radford:
  Childers, 166
  Edw., 166
railways, 50, 130
  Derwent Valley Light, 5, 13, 56, 60, 91, 113, 121, 159
  Hull–Selby, 37, 47–8, 53, 56, 59, 64
  Market Weighton to Selby, 47–8, 56, 59–60, 63–4, 91
  Market Weighton to York, 140, 150, 159, 164–5, 171
  Selby–York, 19, 47, 75, 83
  stations, *see* Cliffe; Cottingwith, West; Duffield, North and South; Dunnington; Elvington; Escrick; Fangfoss; Hemingbrough; Menthorpe; Naburn; Riccall; Stamford Bridge East; Thorganby; Wheldrake
  and see Hull & Selby Rly.; York & North Midland Rly.
Raimes, John, 127–8
Ralph, Wm. s. of, *see* William
Ralph son of Ralph, 6
Ralph son of William, 165
Ramsden, Wm., 166
Ramsey, John, 14, 171
Ranchil (fl. 1066), 103
Rank, Jos., Ltd., 50
Rante, Rog., 134
rape, 107–8, 125, 143, 169, 177
Raper, John, 96
Raventhorpe (in Cherry Burton), 131
Reader, G. W., 81
reading rooms, *see* libraries
recreation ground, 83
recusancy, *see* Barmby Moor; Catton, High and Low; Duffield North; Elvington; Fulford Gate; Hemingbrough; Melbourne; Naburn; Riccall; Stamford Bridge East; Storwood; Sutton upon Derwent; Thorganby; Waplington; Wheldrake; Wilberfoss
Redman (Redeman, Redmayne):
  Eliz., *see* Aldborough
  Frances, m. Noel Barton, 31
  John, 31–2, 34–6
  Ric., 105
  Susannah, m. Rob. Clarke, 31
  Thos., 31
  fam., 29, 31, 34, 77
reeve, 78
Reeves:
  Chas. (fl. 18th cent.), 54
  Chas. (fl. 1835), 54
  John, 54
relief, 8, 143
Revell, Thos., vicar of Hemingbrough, 43
Rhodes, Thos., 6
Riccall, 3, 56, **82–9**, 91, 100
  adv., 87
  alms-ho., 89
  assarting, 85
  brick-making, 86
  bridges, 83, 86
  chant., 87
  chap., man., 84
  char., 88–9
  ch., *81*, 84 *n*, 87–8, 110
  common fields, 83, 85–6
  common meadows, 85–6
  common pastures, 47, 64, 83, 85–6, 88
  ct., 86
  dom. arch., 83
  drainage, 47, 83
  fair, 83
  fishing, 86
  inc., 83, 85–6
  ind., 86
  inns, 83
  man., 83–6
  man.-ho., *80*, 83–4, 87; *and see* Riccall, Wheel Hall
  mkt., 83
  mills, 86
  moated sites, 84

Riccall (*cont.*)
  par. officers, 87–8
  park, 85
  poor relief, 87, 89
  pop., 84
  prot. nonconf., 88
  rly. stn., 83
  rectory, 85
  recusancy, 88
  roads, 83
  Rom. Cath., 88
  rural district, 50, 59, 62, 66, 87, 91, 99, 109
  sch., 88–9, 112
  tithes, 85, 87
  vicarage, 87
  vicarage ho., 80, 83–4, 87–8
  vicars of, 87–9; *and see* Cooper, Thos. (fl. 18th cent.); Davy, Ric. (fl. 1477); Elcock; Froggott; Newlove
  wharves, 82–3, 86
  Wheel Hall, 84–5, 103
  woodland, 85–6
Riccall Co-operative Society, 83
Richard III, King (formerly Ric. Plantagenet, duke of Gloucester), 14, 87, 160, 175, 191
Richard son of Adam, 107
Richardson:
  Alf., 142
  Anne, 36
  Dinah, 12
  Edw., 26
  Gilb., 142
  Hubert, 142
  Jane, *see* Wormley
  Sydney, 142
  Toft, 84, 88
  W. E., 84
  Wm. (fl. 1751), 29
  Wm. (fl. 1845), 29
Richmond, earls of, 104–5; *and see* Alan, count of Brittany (d. 1146); Brittany, John of
Richmond (Yorks. N.R.):
  constable of, *see* Alan son of Roald
  honor, 20–1
Rickinghall, John, rector of Hemingbrough, chancellor of Cambridge university, bp. of Chichester, 43
Ridley:
  Chris., 116
  Eliz., *see* Burdett
  Geo., 65
Rillington poor-law union, workho., 10
Ringrose, Wm., 173
Riplingham (in Rowley), 130
Ripon (Yorks. W.R.):
  bp. of, 57, 84
  collegiate ch., prebendary of, 35
Risby (in Rowley), 131
rivers, 130; *and see* Derwent; Ouse
roads:
  Hull–Selby trunk, 37, 47, 53, 56, 64
  Hull–York trunk, 5, 67, 69, 133, 140, 144, 149, 158, 190–1
  Roman, 5, 29, 67, 133, 140, 147, 149, 158, 171, 191
  Selby–York trunk, 17, 19, 29, 47, 50, 83
  turnpike trusts, 5, 47, 56, 60, 64, 67, 91, 133, 140, 149, 154, 159, 171, 190–1
Roald, Alan s. of, *see* Alan
Roald, Alan, 7
Robert de marisco, rector of Hemingbrough, later dean of Lincoln, 43
Robert son of Copsi, 69
Robert the long, 105–6
Robins, John, 27
Robinson:
  A. A., 62
  Anne, *see* Sandys
  Art. (? two or more of this name), 21, 27, 115
  Eliz. (fl. 1622), 183
  Eliz. (fl. early 17th cent., ? another) 183
  Eliz. (fl. 1713), m. —— Denton, 21–2
  F. B., 84
  Grace, m. —— Braithwaite, 21
  Hen. (fl. 1622), 115
  Hen. W. (fl. 1752), *see* Waite
  Humph. (d. 1626), 115
  Humph. (fl. 1680s, 1718), 115
  John (d. 1601), 21, 115
  John, s. of last, 115
  John (fl. 1832), 60
  Mary, (d. 1839), 48, 51–2, 61
  Mary (d. 1871), m. J. F. Carr, 46, 48, 52, 54, 63
  Nic. (d. 1754), 115
  Revd. Nic. W. (fl. 1801), 115
  Ric. (b. by 1626), 115
  Ric., s. of last, 115
  Ric. (fl. *c.* 1800), 95
  Sarah, m. Hen. Waite, 115
  Thos. (? fl. early 18th cent.), *see* Strangeways
  Thos. (fl. 1758), 62
  Wm., 48
  ——, m. Edwin S. Bain, 95
  ——, wid., 162
  fam., 21, 27, 48, 61, 95, 115, 123, 183
Roger, Thos. s. of, *see* Thomas
Roger son of Roger, 115
Roman Catholic Church, Sacred Coll., 43
Roman Catholicism, *see* Allerthorpe; Catton, High and Low; Escrick; Fulford, Gate; Hemingbrough; Kelfield; Kexby; Menthorpe; Moreby; Naburn; Osgodby; Riccall; Stillingfleet; Sutton upon Derwent; Thorganby; Thornton; Wheldrake; *and see* recusancy
Romano-British remains, 37
rope-making, 9
Ros:
  Beatrice, *see* Stafford
  Edm. de, Ld. Ros, 31, 183
  Eleanor de, m. Sir Rob. Manners, 31, 183
  Everard de, 115
  Isabel de, *see* Aubigny
  Sir Jas. de, 184
  John de, 57
  Margery, *see* Badlesmere
  Nic. de, 184
  Ric., 183
  Rob. de (d. *c.* 1285), 31, 77, 115, 183
  Rob. de (fl. early 13th cent.), 183
  Sir Rob. de (d. 1381), 184
  Rose de, *see* Trussebut
  Thos., Ld. Ros (d. 1384), 183–4
  Thos., Ld. Ros (d. 1464), 31, 183
  Wm., Ld. Ros (d. 1343), 183
  Wm. de (?1264), 31, 103, 106, 115, 183
  fam., 31, 33–4, 57, 77, 106, 115, 183–4, 186
Ros, Ld., *see* Cecil, Wm.; Manners, Thos.; Ros, Edm., Thos., and Wm.
Rotherfeld, John de, 193
Rotherham, Adam of, 193
Rotherham (Yorks. W.R.), 110 *n*
Rotsea (in Hutton Cranswick), 130
Roucliff, Guy, 27
Roundell, Sarah, m. 1 Sir Darcy Dawes, 2 Beilby Thompson (d. 1750), 75, 122, 160
Rowley, 131; *and see* Bentley; Hunsley; Riplingham; Risby; Weighton, Little
Roxby:
  Hen., 96
  T. M., 96
Royal Air Force, 13, 83, 140, 146, 181; *and see* airfields
Royal Masonic Benevolent Institution, *see* Fulford, Gate
Rudston, *see* Caythorpe
Rufforth (Yorks. W.R.), 11
Rusholme (in Drax), 43
Russell:
  Cath., *see* Cary
  Sir John, 39, 55
Rutland, earls of, *see* Manners, Hen. and Thos.
Ryder:
  C. F., 160
  Francis, 160
  John, 31
Ryther:
  Sibyl of, *see* Aldborough
  Wm. of, 105

Sails, Wilf., 58
sainfoin, 143
St. Andrew, Rog. of, 105
St. Buryan (Cornw.), 156
St. John:
  Anastasia, *see* Aton
  Edw., 48
  Marg., m. Thos. Broomfleet, 48
St. Leger flat race, 69
St. Vincent, Vct., *see* Jervis, C. R. J., R. C., and R. G. J.
Salisbury, earl of, *see* Neville, Ric. (d. 1460)
Sallicibus, *see* Thomas
Salman, J. S., rector of Full Sutton, 173
Salmon, Chris., 40
Saltmarsh:
  Edw. of (fl. 1336), 114
  Edw. (d. 1482), 114, 119
  Edw. (d. 1548), 114, 116, 119
  Edw. (fl. 1621), 116
  Ellen of, *see* Maunby
  John, 114
  Phil., 114
  Rob., 114
  Thos. (fl. 16th cent.), 114
  Thos. (fl. 1598, 17th cent.), 114, 120
  fam., 114, 119
  and see 'Saltuiche'
'Saltuiche' (prob. Saltmarsh), Alice and Edw., 119
Salvin (Salvain):
  Anne, m. Sir Wm. Hussey, 94
  Ant., 106
  Gerard (d. 1320), 95, 98
  Gerard (fl. mid 14th cent.), 98
  Gerard (fl. 1580), 57
  Sir John (fl. 15th cent.), 94
  John (fl. 1576), 58
  Rob., 94
  Sibyl, w. of Rob., 94
  fam., 57–8, 94–5
Sancton, 131; *and see* Cliffe, North; Houghton
sand and gravel extraction, 33, 72, 97, 137, 144, 154, 172, 195
Sandale, John of, rector of Stillingfleet, treasurer of Lichfield cath., 110
Sandford:
  Edm., 21
  Wm., 21
Sandys:
  Anne, m. Ric. Robinson, 95
  E. W., 95
  Frances, *see* Bain
  W. B. R., 95
Sarraude, John, rector of Elvington and Sutton upon Derwent, and vicar of Coleby (Lincs.), 178
sauce-making, 50
Savile, Thos., and his w. Cath., 54
saw-mills, 86, 137

INDEX

Sawley abbey (Yorks. W.R.), 152
Sawrey:
    Anne, m. Bacon Morritt, 61
    Ric., 61
Scarborough (Yorks. N.R.), 20
Scawen:
    Jas., 127
    Thos., 122, 127
    Sir Wm., 122
Scholes, J. B., 193
Scholfield:
    E. P., 95
    Edw., 95
    John, 95
    R. S., 95, 101
    Rob., 95
    Wm., 95, 98
Scorborough, Rob. of, 160
Scorborough, 131; *and see* 'Persene'
Scoreby (in Catton), 3, 147, 152, 158–64
    assarting, 162
    common fields, 158, 162
    common pastures, 162
    ct., 163
    inc., 158, 162
    man., 7, 151, 160–2, 175, 191
    man.-ho., 161
    park, 159
    pop., 159
    tithes, 155
    windmill, 163
    woodland, 158, 160, 162
Scrayingham, 156, 172
Scrope, Frances (? dau. of Ric. Scrope), m. 1 Martin Bowes, 2 Mat. Hutton, 54
Sculcoates, 131–2
sculptors, *see* Fisher; Gleichen; Skelton; Thorwaldsen; Tognoli
Seaton:
    Ric., 57
    fam., 57
Seaton Ross, 131
Seed, John, 184
seed-crushing, *see* oil-milling
Segrida (fl. 1066), 175
Selby:
    Hugh son of Nic. of, 166
    John of, 166
    Nic. of, 168; *and see* Hugh s. of Nic. of
Selby (Yorks. W.R.), 2, 37, 47, 50–1
    abbey, 47, 49, 58, 65, 95, 97, 104, 106–7
    district (N. Yorks.), 10, 15, 26, 34, 42, 50, 55, 59, 62, 64, 66, 72, 80, 87, 99, 109, 118, 126, 163
    poor-law union, 50, 59, 62, 66, 87, 99, 109
    suburb of, *see* Barlby, New
    toll-bridge, 47–8, 50
Selby Warehousing & Transport Co. Ltd., 48–9
Seller, E., 45, 111, 119, 157
serjeanty, tenures by, 135–6, 142
services, *see* customs
Settrington, 10
Sewerby (in Bridlington), 74
Seymour:
    Algernon, duke of Somerset, earl of Egremont, and Baron Cockermouth, 151
    Chas., duke of Somerset, 151, 155
    Eliz., *see* Percy
    fam., 171, 183, 191
Sharpe, Edm., 65
Sharrow, W., 46
Sheffield (Yorks. W.R.), 11, 13, 39, 99
Sherbourne:
    John, 151
    Ronald, 151
Shilleto, Eliz., 96
Shipton (in Market Weighton), 131
shops, 19, 40–1, 83, 86, 125, 154
Simon at the bridge, 115

Simon the archer, 134
Simpkin, Geo., 194
Simpson:
    Eliz., m. Sir Hen. Bridgman, 171
    John (fl. mid 18th cent.), 171, 194
    John (fl. 1780s), *see* Bridgman
    Lindley, 171
    Marm., 194
    R. H., 65
    T. H., 65
    Wm. (fl. 1726), 171
    Wm. (fl. 1766), 171–2
    fam., 65, 172
'Siwarbi' (? Loftsome, in Wressle), 130
Skelton, ———, 179
Skerne, Martin of, 175
Skerne, 130
Skidby, 131
Skinner:
    Anne, 57
    Eliz., 57
    Jane, 57
    Mary, m. Jeremiah Smith, 57
Skipwith:
    Cath., *see* Avranches
    John, 95
    Mary, w. of Willoughby, 93
    Osbert of, 93
    Sir Thos., 93
    Wm. (fl. before 1400), 63, 93
    Wm. (fl. 1454), 94
    Sir Wm. (fl. 1536), 96
    Willoughby, 93
    (earlier Thorpe), fam., 63, 93–6
Skipwith, 3, 28, **89–101**, *90*, 119
    adv., 99
    alms-ho., 98
    assarting, 91, 96–7
    chant., 99
    char., 100–1
    ch., *81*, 91, 98–100
    common fields, 91, 94, 96–7
    common meadows, 96
    common pastures, 1, 60, 62, 83, 89, 91, 96–7, 100
    ct., 98
    Danes' Hills, 91
    Hall, *see* man.-ho.
    inc., 94, 96–7
    inns, 93
    man., 49, 91, 93–8
    man.-ho., 94
    moated site, 94
    par. officers, 98, 100
    poor relief, 98–9
    pop., 93
    prebend of, *see* Howden, coll.
    prot. nonconf., 100
    rector of, 99
    rectory, 95–6
    roads, 91
    sch., 62, 100–1, 120
    Skipwith, Little, 91
    tithes, 96, 99
    vicarage, 99, 118
    vicarage ho., 99
    vicars of, 96, 98–100; *and see* Fothergill; Nelson, Jos.; Woodburne, Rob.
    windmill, 97
    woodland, 62, 89, 91, 96–7
    and see Duffield, North; Menthorpe
Skirpenbeck, 153, 165, 172–3
Sledge, Francis, 104
Sledmere, 123
Slettan (fl. 1066), 6
Slingsby, Hen., 106
smallholdings, *see* allotments
Smedley-H.P. Foods, Ltd., 50
Smeton, Geo., 158
Smith:
    Annie, 54
    Geo., 57
    Humph., 32
    J. S., 6, 8

    Sir Jeremiah (d. 1675), 40, 65
    Jeremiah (d. 1714), 57, 65
    John, 36
    Lennox, *see* Harrison
    Mary, *see* Skinner
    Sam. (d. 1709), 11, 51, 81, 100, 156–7
    Sam. (d. 1731), 11, 127
    Sydney, canon of St. Paul's cath., 69
    T. R., 39
    Sir Thos. (fl. 1615), 32
    Thos. (d. 1810), 39, 62
    Thos. (d. 1841), 40, 49, 55, 58
    Wm., 36
Smyth, Ann (Myers heir), 134
Smythe, Sir Edw., 27
Sneculfcros hundred, 2, 130–1
societies, friendly, 102, 121, 147
Somer, John, 32, 194
Somerset:
    duchess of, *see* Percy, Eliz.
    duke of, *see* Seymour, Algernon and Chas.
Somerset, *see* Bath; Wells
Sonulf (fl. 1066), 7
Southburn (in Kirkburn), 130
Southcoates (in Drypool), 34
Southwell (Notts.), minster, canon of, 110
Spalding moor, 140, 179, 183
Spaldington, Osbert of, 31
Spaldington (in Bubwith), 130
Spence:
    Rob., 17
    Susannah, 14
Spencer:
    Marg., w. of Wm., 183
    Wm., 183
Spittal (in Fangfoss), 164–70
    bridge, 164
    char., 170
    hosp., 166
    man., 166
Spofforth:
    Eleanor, *see* Lodge
    Rob., sr., 96, 98
    Rob., jr., 95, 98
    S. A., 70, 123
    Sam., 96
    ———, husb. of Eleanor, 48
spring, medicinal, 174
Squire:
    Gabriel, vicar of Acaster Malbis, 81
    Thos., rector of Escrick, 27
Stable, Geo., 116
Stablers, Messrs., of York, 72
Stafford, Beatrice de, m. 2 Thos. Ros, Ld. Ros (d. 1384), 183–4
Stafford, collegiate ch., dean of, *see* Clare
Staffordshire, *see* Stoke-upon-Trent; Tamworth
Stainbank, *see* Mears
Stamford Bridge East (in Catton), 131, 147–58, *148*, 159
    battle, 29, 147, 149–50
    brick-making, 150, 154
    bridges, 147, 149–50, 156
    chant., 155–6
    chap., 140, 150, 155–7
    char., 157–8
    common fields, 152–3
    common meadows, 149, 152
    common pastures, 153
    Derwent Hill, 150
    dom. arch., 150
    ford, 147–50
    inc., 153–4
    ind., 154
    inns, 150
    man., 149, 151
    mission room, 156
    poor relief, 154–5
    pop., 150–1
    prot. nonconf., 157

Stamford Bridge East (*cont.*)
  rly. stn., 150
  recusancy, 157
  roads, 147, 149–50
  sch., 157–8, 164
  tithes, 156
  viaduct, *33*, 150, 159
  water-mills, 149–50, 152–5, *176*
  woodland, 154
Stamford Bridge West (in Catton), 147, *148*, 152, 158–9, 161–4
  char., 164
  common fields, 162
  common meadows, 162
  common pastures, 162
  ct., 163
  fairs, 163
  inc., 162
  ind., 163
  lock, 149–50
  man., 161–3
  man.-ho., 161
  mkt., 163
  poor relief, 163
  pop., 151, 159
  roads, 149
  wharf, 163
  windmill, 163
  woodland, 162
Stanegrave, *see* Stonegrave
Stanley:
  Chas., 133, 136
  Wm., Ld. Monteagle, 155
Stapleton:
  Brian (fl. *c.* 1400), 105
  Brian (fl. 1589), 57
  Eliz., *see* Aldborough
  Nic. de, 61
Starkey, John, 176
Staughton, Adrian, 69
steam mills, 26, 50, 59, 86, 118, 137
Steele, Thos., 42, 46
'Steintorp' (? in Etton), 131
Stephen, count of Brittany, 20, 31, 34, 123–4
Stephenson:
  John, 183
  Sarah, 183
Sterne:
  Mary, *see* Jacques
  Laurence, writer, 14
  Ric. (d. 1744), 15
  Ric. (d. 1791), 14
  Sim., 14
  fam., 14
Stewart:
  Marg., *see* Douglas
  Mat., earl of Lennox, 184
Stillingfleet:
  Revd. Edw., 104
  Mary, *see* Peirse
Stillingfleet, 3, 81, **101–12**, *112*
  adv., 109
  assarting, 107
  brick-making, 109
  bridge, 102
  chant., 81, 110–11
  char., 102, 109–10, 112
  ch., 101–2, 109–12, *177*
  common fields, 101, 107
  common meadows, 107
  common pastures, 101, 107–8
  ct., 109
  dom. arch., 102, 104
  drainage, 102
  ferry, 102
  fishing, 109
  Ho., 104
  inc., 102–4, 107, 110
  inns, 102
  man., 103–9
  man.-ho., 104
  poor relief, 109
  pop., 103
  prot. nonconf., 111
  rectors of, 109–10; *and see* Sandale
  rectory, 107–8
  roads, 102
  Rom. Cath., 111
  sch., 112
  tithes, 107, 110
  vicarage, 80, 109–10
  vicarage ho., 110
  vicars of, 103, 108–12; *and see* Gilbert, Thos.; Hustler; Potter, Rob.
  wharf, 109
  windmill, 109
  woodland, 107–8
  and see Kelfield; Moreby
Stillington:
  John (d. 1534), 104
  John (fl. 17th cent.), 104
  Jos., 104, 108–9
  Mary, 104
  Rob., bp. of Bath and Wells, Ld. Chancellor, 166
  Thos., 104–5
  Wm., 104
  ———, *see* FitzHenry
  fam., 105, 108, 111
Stockton on the Forest (Yorks. N.R.), 81, 156
Stodowe:
  Denise, *see* Crepping
  Rob. (d. by 1389), 142
  Rob. (fl. 1414), 135, 142
  fam., 135
Stoke-upon-Trent (Staffs.), 145
Stonegrave (Stanegrave):
  Isabel of, m. Sim. de Pateshull, 105
  John of, 59, 105
  Sim. of, 114
  fam., 58, 115
Store, Chris., 178
Storey, Ann, 89
Storwood (Storthwaite) (in Thornton), 131, 179, 181–90
  brick-makers, 187
  bridges, 181–2
  chap., man., 184
  common fields, 181, 186
  common meadows, 181, 186
  common pastures, 181–2, 186
  ct. (Storwood and Melbourne), 186–7
  fishing, 186
  inc., 182, 186–8
  inn, 182
  lock, 181
  man. (Storwood and Melbourne), 183–4, 186, 190
  man.-ho., 184, 186
  moated site, 184
  park, 186
  pop., 182–3
  prot. nonconf., 189
  rectory, 184–5
  recusancy, 189
  roads, 181–2
  tithes, 184, 188
  woodland, 187
  and see 'Chetelstorp'
Stott, Eliz., 112
Strangeways:
  Jas., 48, 53–4
  Thos. (d. 1702), 48, 53–4
  (later Robinson), Thos., s. of last, 48, 53–4
  fam., 184
Straw, Cath., 147
Street, G. E., 156
Strickland, Sir Geo., 142
Stringer:
  J. B., 48
  Jos., 48
  Ric., 89
  Susanna, *see* Blanshard
  fam., 48
Stubbins:
  Hen. E., 135, 183
  fam., 135, 183
Stutville:
  Eust. de, 105
  Joan de, m. Hugh Wake, 93, 103
  Nichole, w. of Eust., m. 2 Wm. de Percy, 105
  Nic. de, 103
  Rob. de (fl. *c.* 1100), 93, 103, 106
  Rob. de (d. by 1275), 103
  Rob. de (fl. 1275), 109
  Wm. de, 103
  fam., 93, 95, 105–6
Suffolk, earl of, *see* Howard, Thos.
sugar-refining, 50
Suger:
  Anne, *see* Idle
  Eliz., 134–5
  Jane, m. ——— Wilmer, 135, 141, 143
  Martha, 134
  Revd. Zachary, 134
  fam., 141
Sunderlandwick (in Hutton Cranswick), 130
Sutton, Rob., curate of Fulford, 34
Sutton, Full, 131, 152, 156, 164, **170–3**
  adv., 171–2
  char., 173
  ch., 155, 171–3
  common fields, 170, 172
  common pastures, 153, 167, 170, 172
  dom. arch., 171
  Hall, 171
  inc., 171–2
  inn, 171
  man., 171–2
  man.-ho., 171
  pop., 171
  prot. nonconf., 173
  rectors of, 155, 172–3; *and see* Salman
  rectory, 172
  rectory ho., 172
  roads, 171
  sch., 173
  tithes, 172
Sutton upon Derwent, 12, 131, **173–9**
  adv., 178
  assarting, 176
  bridges, 174; *and see* Elvington; Storwood
  chap., man., 175
  char., 179
  ch., 16, 174, *177*, 178–9
  common fields, 174, 176–8
  common meadows, 176–7
  common pastures, 174, 176–8
  dom. arch., 174, 176
  ferries, 174
  fishing, 176–7
  Hall, 174–5
  inc., 175, 177–8
  inns, 174, 177
  man., 173, 175–8
  man.-ho., 174–5; *and see* Sutton upon Derwent, Hall
  mills, 15, 174, *176*, 177
  moated sites, 174, 176
  par. officers, 179
  park, 175–6
  pop., 174–5
  prot. nonconf., 179
  rectors of, 176–9, 196; *and see* Appleton, Rob. of (fl. 1294); Blackbeard; Cooke, Pet.; Favour; Holdsworth; Sarraude
  rectory, 178
  rectory ho., 178
  recusancy, 179
  roads, 174
  Rom. Cath., 179
  St. Loys, 174, 176
  sch., 179
  tithes, 178
  wharf, 174

INDEX

woodland, 174, 176–7
Swale, John, 72
Swane (fl. 11th cent.), 95
Swanland (in North Ferriby), 131–2
Swann:
    Geo., 142
    John (fl. 1748), 20
    John (fl. 1853), 142
    fam., 20, 142
Sygrave, Wm., 123
Sykes:
    Charlotte, see Duncombe
    Chris., 123
    Sir Tatton, 142

Talbot:
    Edw., 106
    Mary, m. Hen. Percy, earl of Northumberland (d. 1537), 151, 155
Tamworth (Staffs.), coll. ch., dean of, 156
Tanckard:
    Thos., 160
    Wm., 7–9, 160
tanning, 9, 41, 195
tar-distilling, 50
Tate:
    C. G., 39
    Jane, see Ion
Taylor:
    Francis, 32
    Hugh, 58
    John (d. 1705), 31, 35
    John, grds. of last, 31–4
    Ric., 114
    Rob., vicar of Barmby Moor with Fangfoss, 145
    Thos., 31
    Wm., 31
    ——, w. of Rob., 169
    fam., 31, 70
Teasdale, Marm., vicar of Hemingbrough and curate of Barlby, 50
Tempest, Francis, 45
Temple Hirst (Yorks. W.R.), 65
Terrick, Sam., rector of Wheldrake, 128
Terry, Jos., 193
Teyll:
    Ant., 160
    Thos., 156, 160
    fam., 160
Thicket Priory, see Cottingwith, West
Thomas, Hen. s. of, see Henry
Thomas, Wm. s. of, see William
Thomas 'at the bridge', 102
Thomas in the willows (in *Sallicibus*), 116
Thomas son of Erneis, 21
Thomas son of John, 106
Thomas son of Roger, 115
Thomas son of William, 166
Thompson:
    Beilby (d. 1750), 20–1, 75, 160
    Beilby (d. 1799), 17, 19–21, 23, 26–8, 85, 125, 128
    Eliz., w. of Beilby (d. 1799), 27
    Hen. (d. 1700), 17, 20, 22
    J. H., 61
    Jane, m. Sir Rob. Lawley, 20, 27
    Jas., 61
    John, 157
    Nic., 96
    P. B., see Lawley
    Ric., 20, 94, 104
    Sarah, see Roundell
    fam., 20–1, 23, 26–8, 75, 84, 94, 100, 104, 107, 122, 160
Thorganby, 3, 95, **112–20**, 121
    adv., 114, 118
    assarting, 116
    Association for the Prosecution of Felons, 113
    brick-making, 118

bridges, 113, 118
char., 118, 120
ch., 113, 118–19, *128*
common fields, 113, 116–17
common meadows, 113, 116–17
common pastures, 113, 116–17
curates of, 118–20; and see Dunnington, Revd. Jos.
dom. arch., 113
drainage, 113
fishing, 118
guild, 119
Hall, *64*, 113–14
Hedley Ho., 113
inc., 113, 116–17
inn, 113
man., 113–19
man.-ho., 114; and see Thorganby, Hall
mills, 118
motte, 113
par. officers, 113, 118, 120
perpetual curacy, 118
poor relief, 118
pop., 113
prot. nonconf., 119–20
rly. stn., 113, *161*
rectory, 116, 118–19
recusancy, 119
roads, 113, 118
Rom. Cath., 119
sch., 101, 120
tithes, 116
vicar of, 119
vicarage, 99, 118–19
vicarage ho., 119
woodland, 116–18
and see Cottingwith, West; Crossum
Thorne (Yorks. W.R.), 172
Thornton (Thornton in Spalding Moor), 131, **179–90**, *180*
    adv., 188
    assarting, 185
    brick-making, 187
    bridges, 181–2
    chant., 188
    char., 189–90
    ch., 133, 138–9, 145, 182, 185, 187–9
    common fields, 181–2, 185
    common meadows, 181, 185
    common pastures, 181, 185–7
    ct., 187
    drainage, 181
    inc., 181–2, 185–6
    inns, 182
    lock, *161*, 181
    man., 181, 183, 185, 188
    Millhouses, 179, 181–2, 185
    mills, 153, 181, 185, 187
    par. officers, 187, 189
    pop., 182
    prot. nonconf., 189
    rector of, 185
    rectory, 184–5
    roads, 181
    Rom. Cath., 189
    sch., 189–90
    tithes, 184–5, 188
    vicarage (Thornton with Allerthorpe), 138, 145, 169, 187–8
    vicarage ho., 188; and see Allerthorpe
    vicars of, 138, 185–8; and see Hanson
    woodland, 187
    and see Melbourne, Storwood
Thornton (? which one of this name) (Yorks.), 189 n
Thorp (in Wheldrake), see Langwith
Thorpe (Thorp):
    Adam of, 126
    Pet., 167
    Ralph of, 103
    fam., see Skipwith

Thorpe, see 'Torp'
Thorpe (? in Harswell), 131
Thorpe le Street (in Nunburnholme), 131
Thorwaldsen, Bertil, 27
Thurkelby, Rog. of, 94, 98
Thurkill, Thos., 32
Tibthorpe (in Kirkburn), 130
Tickhill (Yorks. W.R.), 169
    friary, 193
Tilliol, Maud, see Lascelles
Tilmire, 5, 9, 17, 25, 29, 32–3, 71–2
timber-framed buildings, 1, 31, 75, 81, 83, 102, 121, 126, 156, 176
Tindall:
    Francis, 61
    Nellie, 61
Tireman:
    Anne, see Willbor
    Jemima, 57
    Thos., 57
    fam., 57
Tirwhit, Rob., 193
Tison, Gilb., 55, 58, 95
Tochi (fl. 1066), 64
Todd:
    Florence, 166
    Jos., 166
Todeni:
    Adelize de, m. Rog. Bigod, 77
    Berenger de, 77
    Rob. de, 77–8
Tognoli, Giovanni, 27
Tooke, Edw., 135
Topcliffe (Yorks. N.R.), 87
Topham:
    Art., 61
    Eliz., w. of Art., 61
    Mat., 61
    fam., 61
Torall, Ulf s. of, see Ulf
Torchil (fl. 1066), 77
'Torp' (in Driffield hundred), 130
'Torp' (? in Etton), 131
Tosti (fl. 1066), 39–40
Tostig, Earl, 29, 82, 147
'Totfled' (in Hessle hundred), 130
Toulson:
    Eliz., see Herbert
    Geo. (fl. 1706), 94
    Geo. (d. 1766), 94, 96
    J. A. P., 94, 96
    J. P., see Parker, John
    Jane, m. 1 Banastre Walton, 2 Rob. Hudson, 49, 94
Towthorpe (in Londesborough), 131
trade:
    agricultural marketing and supply, 50, 138, 187
    carrots, 143
    coal, 13, 80, 86, 149–50, 163, 177, 181, 187
    corn, 9, 86, 149, 181
    fertilizers, 181
    flour, 150, 181
    fuel storage, 144
    gravel, 72
    lime, 149, 163, 177
    mercer, merchant, 41
    potatoes, 86, 143
    timber, 50, 86, 163, 177, 181
    wool, 50
    and see fairs; markets; shops; warehousing
Tranby (in Hessle), 132; and see 'Crachetorp'
Triffitt:
    R. Q., 171
    fam., 171
Truelove, Josephine, 166
Trussebut:
    Hilary, m. —— de Builers, 31–2, 106, 115
    Rob., 103, 115
    Rose, m. Everard de Ros, 115
    Wm., 31, 106–7, 115

Trussebut (*cont.*)
  fam., 103
Tryon, Cecily, 142
Tuler, Steph. le, 105
tumbril, 98
Turbar hundred, 130
turbaries, turf, 15, 32, 59, 66, 71, 79, 96–9, 137–8, 143, 172, 177, 185–6
Turey, *see* Turie
Turgot (fl. 1066), 77
Turie (Turey), Rob., 88, (? as the Revd. Mr.) 112
Turner:
  John, 104
  Sharon, 96
Turnham:
  Isabel of, m. Pet. de Mauley (d. by 1241), 57, 65, 114
  Joan of, *see* Fossard
  Rob. of (fl. c. 1200), 57, 65, 114
  Rob. of (fl. c. 1220), 57
  fam., 57
turnips, 72, 125, 137, 177
Turnyll:
  Cecily, *see* Osgodby
  Hugh, 65
  Ralph, 65
Tweedy:
  John, 39–40, 49, 55, 58, 62
  Sophia, m. Jas. Graham, 39
Twinam, Jas., 12
Twisleton:
  John (fl. 1612), 58
  John (d. 1757), 53
  Josias C., 53
  Judith, *see* Boynton
  Thos., *see* Cockshutt
  fam., 53

Ughtred:
  Sir Ant., 160
  Dorothy, m. John Constable, 160
  Eliz., w. of Sir Ant., 160
  Hen., 160
  Marg., *see* Burdon
  Rob. (d. 1471), 159–60
  Rob., s. of Rob. (d. 1471), 160
  Sir Rob. (fl. 1524), 160
  Sir Rob. (fl. 1552), 160
  Thos. (fl. early 14th cent.), 159–61, 163, 175
  Thos. (d. 1401), 159
  Thos., grds. of Thos. (d. 1401), 159
  fam., 159, 161
Ulchil (fl. 1066), 8, 13
Ulf (fl. before 1066), 141
Ulf (fl. 1066), 175
Ulf, Wm. s. of, *see* William
Underwood, Jos., 46

Valentia, Vct., *see* Annesley, Art.
Vaughan:
  Francis, 176
  Sir Hen., 176, 178
  John, 175, 178
  Ric., earl of Carbury, 114
  fam., 175
Vaux:
  Hubert de, 114
  Maud, m. Thos. de Multon, 114–15
Vavasour:
  Hen. (fl. 1449), 105
  Hen. (d. 1813), 184
  Sir Hen. (d. 1838), 181
  Sir Hen. M. (fl. 1850), 184
  John (d. 1524), 105
  John (fl. 1577), 105
  Leon., 107
  Wm. (d. 1500), 105
  Wm. (d. by 1566), 105
  fam., 105
Venur, Ric. le, 62
Verdenel, fam., 70
Vescy:

Clemence de, w. of John, 183
Eust. de, 55
Isabel de, 160
John de (d. 1289), 183
John de (d. 1295), 55, 114–15, 183
Wm. de (d. 1183), 114, 183
Wm. de (d. 1253), 183
fam., 55, 115, 183
Vesey:
  Constance, *see* Lawley
  Eust., 163
  J. E., Vct. de Vesci, 163, 195
  Y. R., Vct. de Vesci, 163
vestries, 26, 33, 118, 168
Vickers, John, 50–1
village and parish halls, institutes, 13, 17, 19, 35, 46, 51, 56, 73, 75, 84, 89, 93, 101–2, 112–13, 138, 141, 150, 157, 171, 174, 182
village earthworks, 6, 159
village feasts, 41, 75, 141
village greens, 13, 83, 93, 101–2, 107–8, *112*, 133, 140–1, 165, 171, 191, 197

Wadham, K., 14
Waite:
  Geo., 36
  (later Robinson), Hen., 115
  Sarah, *see* Robinson
Wake:
  Baldwin, 103
  Hugh, 93, 103
  Joan, *see* Stutville
  Marg., m. Edm. of Woodstock, 93, 103
  Thos., 103
  fam., 93, 103
Wakefield (Yorks. W.R.), 126
Wald, Thos. de, 16
Walker:
  Ambrose, 82
  C. F., 161
  Eliz., 81
  Fred., 166
  Geo., 136
  J. P. E., 160–1
  Jas., 63–4, 161
  John, 183
  Sir Rob., 63, 160
  Sam., 171–2
  Silvester, 127–8
  Thomlinson, 189
  ⸺, 52
  fam., 63, 161
Walkington, 34, 131
Wallis, Marg., *see* Eglesfield
Walmesley:
  Thos., 63
  fam., 63
Walter, Hen. s. of, *see* Henry
Walton:
  Banastre, 49, 94
  Jane, *see* Toulson
  Wm., 166
Walworth, Thos. of, rector of Hemingbrough, prebendary of York, master of St. Nicholas's hosp. York, 43
Wandesford, Rowland, 87
Wanstall, Marg., 142
wapentakes, *see* hundreds
Waplington:
  Rog. of, *see* Waplington, Wm.
  Thos. of, 137
  Wm. s. of Rog. of, 134
Waplington (in Allerthorpe), 131, 133–9
  brick-making, 137
  char., 139
  common fields, 133, 137
  common pastures, 133, 137
  Hall, 136–7
  inc., 133, 137
  man., 134–7, 139

man.-ho., *see* Waplington, Hall
park, 136
pop., 134
rectory, 136
recusancy, 135, 139
tithes, 136, 138
woodland, 137
War Department, 48
Ward:
  Hen., 62
  John, 27
  Jos., 100
  Sim., 20
  Wm., 57
Ware:
  H. J., 39
  Wm., 39
warehousing firm, 144
Warin the calfherd, 106
Warner, John, & Sons, 27
Warter, 131
  hundred, 2, 130–1
  priory, 32, 78, 123–4, 126, 176, 184, 193
Warwick:
  ctss. of, *see* Percy, Maud de
  earls of, *see* Beaumont, Waleran de; Neville, Ric. (d. 1471)
Warwickshire, *see* Birmingham
Wastehose:
  Alan, 61
  Emme, 62
Waterhouses (in Wheldrake), 120, 122
Waterton, Rob., 166
Watervill:
  Maud de, m. Wm. Palmes (fl. 13th cent.), 77
  Reynold de, 77
  Ric. de, 77
  Rog. de, 77
  fam., 77
Waterworth, Ric., 63
Watkinson:
  Anne, m. Edw. Payler, 151
  T. S., 7
  Thos. (fl. 1572), 95
  Thos. (fl. 1650), 96
  Wm., jr. (d. 1614), and his w., 151
  Wm., sr. (fl. 1611), and his s., 151
  fam., 95–6, 100
Watson:
  John (fl. 1784), 54
  John (fl. 1811), 54–5
Watton, 131
Waud:
  John, 50
  Mary, 60
  Sam., 136
Wauldby (in Elloughton), 130–1
weaving, weavers, 9, 15, 41, 62, 72, 86, 97–8, 109, 118, 124–5, 144, 172, 187
Weddall:
  Chas., 96
  Edw., 63
  Rob., 52
  fam., 96
Weedley (in South Cave), 136
Weightman & Hatfield, architects, 39
Weighton, Little (in Rowley), 131
Weighton, Market, 130–2, 190
  hundred, 130
  and see Arras; Shipton
Wellisburne, John, 106
Wells (Som.):
  cath. ch., canon of, 126
  and see Bath
Welton, 131
  hundred, 130–1
  and see Melton
Wendy, Thos., 69
Wenlock, Baron, *see* Lawley, B. R., Beilby, P. B., and Rob.
Wentworth:
  Anne, m. Wm. Osbaldeston, 54

INDEX

Geo. (fl. 1620), 53
Sir Geo. (d. 1660), 53
fam., earls FitzWilliam, 150
Wesley, John, 157
Wesleyan Association, 73
Wessington, John of, prior of Durham, 45
West, John, 40–1, 43
Westminster Abbey, dean of, 126
Westmorland, earl of, *see* Neville, Chas., Ralph (d. 1425), and Ralph (d. 1499)
Westmorland, *see* Heversham
Westoby, Wm., 139, 146
Wharram, M. G., 193
Wharton:
  Chris., 157–8
  Gen. Jas., 182
wheelhouses, 19, 53, 56, 61, *64*, 75, 93, 102–3, 113–14, 121, 174
Wheldrake, Pet. of, 21
Wheldrake, 1, 3, 14, 23, 67, 78, **120–8**
  adv., 126
  assarting, 121, 124
  brick-making, 125
  bridges, *32*, 121–2, 125
  castle, 122–3
  chant., 126
  char., 127–8
  ch., 73, 123, 125–7, *128*
  common fields, 121, 124–5
  common meadows, 121–2, 124–5, 176
  common pastures, 23, 121, 124–5
  ct., 125
  dom. arch., 121, 127, *129*
  ferry, 174
  fishing, 122–3, 125, 176, 186
  inc., 121–2, 125–6
  inns, 121
  man., 14, 122–3, 124–5, 127
  man.-ho., 121 *n*, 123
  mills, 125
  par. officers, 125
  park, 123
  poor relief, 125–6
  pop., 122
  prot. nonconf., 127
  rly. stn., 121
  rectors of, 125–7; *and see* Blake; Byard; Harcourt, W. V.; Lamplugh; Moulin; Palmer, Wm.; Parish; Terrick
  rectory, 126
  rectory ho., 126
  recusancy, 127
  roads, 121, 125
  Rom. Cath., 127
  sch., 127–8
  tithes, 125–6
  wharf, 125
  woodland, 121–5
  and see Langwith; Waterhouses
Wheldrick:
  Wm., 62
  fam., 62
Whitaker:
  Harriet, 14
  Thos., 184
  and see Whittaker
Whitby abbey (Yorks. N.R.), 178
White:
  John, 114
  Wm., 16
Whitehorse, Wal., 77
Whittaker, E. A., 65; *and see* Whitaker
Whittall, Benj., 60
Whitworth:
  H. P., 135, 141
  Hen., 135, 141
Wholsea (in Holme upon Spalding Moor), 131
Wickham:
  Hen. (fl. 1707), 7–8
  Revd. Hen. (fl. 1772), 7–8

fam., 70
Widdowes (Widhouse), Wm., 46
Wightman:
  Sir Owen W., 110
  fam., 70
Wilberfoss (Wilberforce):
  Anne, *see* Freeman
  Ilger of, 193
  Marg., *see* Kyme
  Rob., 63, 177
  Rog. (fl. 1570s), 193, 196
  Rog. (fl. 1636), 194
  Thos. (d. 1722), 179
  Thos. (fl. 1804), 63
  Wm. of (fl. 1260), 193
  Wm. (d. 1557), 193
  Wm. (d. 1709), and his s., 193
  Wm. (fl. 1757), 63, 193
  fam., 193–4
Wilberfoss, 131, 152–3, **190–7**, *192*
  adv., 163, 195
  assarting, 194
  brick-making, 195
  bridges, 190–1
  char., 196–7
  ch., 194–7
  common fields, 190, 194–6
  common meadows, 190, 194
  common pastures, 153, 190, 194
  curates of, 178, 195–7
  dom. arch., 191, 193
  drainage, 190
  guild, 196
  Hall (or Ch.) Farm, 193
  inc., 191, 194
  ind., 195
  inns, 191
  mills, 195
  par. officers, 196–7
  perpetual curacy, 195–6
  poor relief, 195
  pop., 191
  priory, 22, 123, 136, 152, 176, 178, 193–6
  prot. nonconf., 196–7
  rectory, 191, 193–5
  recusancy, 196
  roads, 190–1
  sch., 164, 197
  tithes, 194
  the Villa, 191
  vicarage, 163, 195–6
  vicarage ho., 196
  vicars of, 195–6
  woodland, 194–5
  and see Newton upon Derwent
Wilkes, Susannah, 88
Wilkinson:
  Francis, 112
  Wm., 193
Willans, Martin, 95
Willerby (in Kirk Ella), 130, 132
Willbor:
  Anne, m. Thos. Tireman, 57
  Mary, m. Geo. Ellin, 57
  Ric., 57
William I, King, 39, 121
William, count of Mortain, 7–8, 57, 61, 64, 96–7, 114, 117, 175–6
William, Hen. s. of, *see* Henry
William, Ralph s. of, *see* Ralph
William, Thos. s. of, *see* Thomas
William son of Ralph, 165–6
William son of Thomas, 165
William son of Ulf, 165
Williamson:
  Thos., 57
  Wm., curate of Barlby, 50
  fam., 57
Willitoft (in Bubwith), 130
Willye:
  Frances, *see* Carus Wilson
  Jocelyn, 95
  Lucy, *see* Price
  Capt., 95
Wilmer:

Jane, *see* Suger
fam., 161
Wilson:
  Sir Chas. H., 65, 95
  Dorothy, 100–1
  Eliz., 88–9
  Geo., 161
  Nat., 96
  Ric., 96
  T. W., 36, 39
  Thos., 12, 39–40, 49, 55, 58, 62, 161
  fam., 161
Wilson & Tweedy, bankers, 39
Wilton, Bishop, 129, 131–2, 171; *and see* Belthorpe; Bolton; Gowthorpe; Greenwick; Youlthorpe
Wilton Beacon division (of Harthill wapentake), 3, *130–1*, 132, 147
Wimborne (Dors.), dean of, *see* Mauley, Steph. de
Winchester, earl of, *see* Quincy, Saer de
Winder, L. A., 84
windmill mounds, 25, 97, 118, 163
Windsor (Berks.), St. George's chap., canon of, 110
Windsor Iron Works (Liverpool), 189
Wistow, John of, 106
Wistow (Yorks. W.R.), 83
Witham (Wytham):
  Wm. (fl. 1540), 115
  Wm. (fl. 1639), 7
Witherington, John, 43
Wolfreton (in Kirk Ella), 130, 132
Wolsey, Thos., 160
Wood:
  C. J. S., 193
  Jas., 104
  John, 161
  Ottiwell, 161
  Thos., 139–40, 146, 158, 170, 173, 179, 190, 197
Woodard Society, 20, 26
Woodburne:
  Faith, w. of Rob., 95
  Jas., 95
  Rob., vicar of Skipwith, 95
Woodhall (formerly Grimsthorpe) (in Hemingbrough), 3, 37, 39, 42–3, 47, 52–5
  bridge, 53
  common fields, 55
  inc., 55
  man., 54–5
  man.-ho., 54; *and see* Woodhall, Wood Hall
  pop., 53
  rectory, 55
  roads, 52–3
  tithes, 55
  Wood Hall, 53–5
Woodhouse (Woodhouses) (in Sutton upon Derwent), 173–8, 185
  assarting, 176
  brick-making, 177
  bridge, 174
  inc., 174
  park, 176
  roads, 174
  tithes, 178
  woodland, 176–7
woodland (haggs, springs), 1; *and see under* places
Woodstock:
  Edm. of, earl of Kent, 93, 103
  John of, earl of Kent, 103
  Marg. of, *see* Wake
workhouses, *see* Holme upon Spalding Moor; Rillington
works, tenants', 8, 23, 33, 40, 42, 71, 85, 116–17, 136, 142–3, 152–3, 194
Wormald:
  Smith, 14
  Wm., 31

Wormley:
  Chris., 84, 88
  Edw. (fl. 1654), 84
  Edw. (d. 1787), 84
  Edw. (? same as last), 86
  Hen., 84
  Jane, w. of Chris., m. 2 Toft Richardson, 84, 88
  Rob., 88
  fam., 84
Worsley:
  Sir Wm., 161
  fam., 161
Wray:
  Revd. C. D., 104–5
  Eleanor, 112
Wressle, 37, 58, 130, 156, 183, 187; *and see* Brind; Loftsome; Newsholme
Wright:
  Fred. (fl. *c.* 1880), 150
  Fred. (fl. 1938), 39
  John, 161
  fam., 20, 161
Wyndham:
  Sir Chas., earl of Egremont and Baron Cockermouth, 151, 194
  Chas. H., Ld. Leconfield, 151, 171, 193
  Geo., earl of Egremont (d. 1837), 151, 153–4, 171–2, 193–5
  Col. Geo., Baron Leconfield (d. 1869), 151, 157, 185, 189
  J. E. R., Baron Egremont and Baron Leconfield, 155, 163, 195
  fam., 171, 183, 191
Wytham, *see* Witham
Wyvill, Mrs. Darcy, 173

Yapham (in Pocklington), 131
Yarburgh:
  Anne, *see* Hesketh
  Chas., 70, 72
  G. J., *see* Lloyd
  Hen., 69, 74
  Jas., 69
  Mary, m. G. W. Bateson, 70
  N. E., 32, 69–70
  Yarburgh, *see* Greame
  fam., 67, 69–70, 72–3, 123
York, of, *see* Plantagenet, Ric.
York, 9, 17, 23, 73, 113, 125–6, 195
  abp. of, 70, 126, 187
  as owner of estates, 31, 70, 79, 84, 181–2, 184, 186–7
  as patron, 42, 73, 80, 87, 126, 144, 188
  and see Cre… de; Harcourt, E. V. …plugh
  Archbishop Holgate's Grammar Sch., 69
  architects of, 14, 20, 73, 81, 149, 178
  barracks, *see* Fulford, Gate
  bell-founders of, 11, 45, 51, 81, 111, 119, 127, 157, 196

  boundaries, 29–30, 36, 67
  castle, 4, 135, 142
  Castle Mills, 74
  Cath. ch. of St. Peter (York minster), 7, 43, 141, 144, 161, 187
    canons of, 84–5, 126
    chancellor of, 156
    chant., 7
    choir endowment, 184
    dean and chapter, 6–8, 70–1, 107, 109, 116, 123, 125, 184
    dean of, 136, 142–4, 167–8, 184–8; *and see* Hutton, Mat.; Pickering, Rob. of and Wm. of
    liberty of, 3, 30, 69, 84
    prebends: Ampleforth, 7–8, 10, 31–4, 67, 70–3; Barnby (Barmby Moor), 141–4; Driffield, 70–1; Dunnington, 6–9; Riccall, 83–7; *and see* Clare; Cooke, Marm.; Evesham; Mauley, Steph. de; Walworth
    precentor, 71
    treasurer, *see* Bedwind; Clare
    vicar-choral, sub-chanter, 73
  cemeteries, *see* Fulford, Gate
  City Asylum, *see* Fulford, Water
  communications with, 5, 30, 67, 75, 147, 149; *and see* railways; roads; rivers
  Corpus Christi guild, 78
  County Hosp., 75, 121
  ct. held at, 4, 42
  dormitory villages for, 1, 5, 13, 19, 74, 83, 121, 147, 149
  Dorothy Wilson's hosp., 100
  duchy of, 152, 191
  Fishergate Board Sch., 36
  fishpond of the Foss, 43
  Friends' Quarterly Meeting, 100
  glass-painters of, 87, 111
  grammar sch., 156
  Holy Trinity priory, 49, 122
  inhabitants of, 1, 6, 11–12, 16, 32–6, 39, 61, 72–3, 81, 101, 122–3, 146, 159, 181
  mayor and corporation, 29–30, 33, 40–1, 74, 86, 161–2
  moraine, 1, 5, 29, 33, 66–7, 69, 72, 147, 158
  New Walk, *see* Fulford, Gate
  plate made in, 45, 100, 111, 127, 139, 145, 157, 179
  poor-law union, 10, 12, 15, 17, 26, 28, 34, 36, 72, 74, 80, 82, 109, 112, 118, 120, 125–6, 128, 163–4
  property in, 28, 32, 81, 128, 136
  Retreat lunatic asylum, *see* Fulford, Gate
  St. Andrew's priory, 32, 78
  St. Christopher and St. George, guild of, 40, 161
  St. Crux's ch., 73
  St. Denys's ch., 80–1
  St. George's ch., 78, 80–1
  St. John's ch., Ouse Bridge, 107
  St. John's Coll., 69
  St. Lawrence's ch., 29, 67, 69, 71–3

  St. Leonard's hosp., *see* York, St. Peter's hosp.
  St. Margaret's ch., Walmgate, 81
  St. Martin's ch., Micklegate, 32, 34
  St. Mary's abbey, 3, 20–3, 26, 31–4, 78, 106–8, 115–16
  St. Mary's hosp., 107, 109
  St. Michael's ch., Spurriergate, 35
  St. Nicholas's hosp., 7–8, 32, 193–4; *and see* Walworth
  St. Olave's ch., 34
  St. Peter's (later St. Leonard's) hosp., 3, 32, 69, 71, 78, 106, 123, 152, 194
  St. Peter's Sch., 107, 184
  St. Thomas's hosp., 161
  St. William's chap., Ouse Bridge, 27
  St. William's Coll., 194
  sch., *see* Fulford, Gate
  sculptors of, 27, 145, 179
  sewerage works, *see* Fulford, Gate; Naburn
  suburbs, 1, 29–30, 66, 69, 72–3, 83
  tramway, *see* Fulford, Gate
  University, *see* Heslington
  Vale of, 1, 37, 129–30, 147, 164, 179, 181
  Well Ho., *see* Fulford, Gate
York & North Midland Rly., 181
York Co-operative Society, 19
York Diocesan Board of Finance, 139–40
York Waterworks Co., 69
Yorkshire, sheriff of, 4, 42, 71, 132
Yorkshire, East Riding:
  county council, 41, 46, 53, 66, 86, 91, 101, 150
  ct. of sewers for west parts, 5, 181
  quarter sessions, 147
  'the county', 12, 83, 102, 149, 159, 181–2
Yorkshire, North, *see* Selby district
Yorkshire, North Riding, 1, 3; *and see* Bootham; Bulmer; Buttercrambe; Clifton; Guisborough; Halnaby; Helmsley, Gate; Holtby; Huntington; Hutton, Sheriff; Hutton Rudby; Kildale; Kirby in Cleveland; Kirkbymoorside; Malton; Middleham; Osbaldwick; Osgodby; Richmond; Scarborough; Stockton; Topcliffe; Whitby
Yorkshire, West Riding, 1, 3, 80; *and see* Acaster Malbis; Acaster Selby; Askham Richard; Bilbrough; Bolton Percy; Brayton; Drax; Dunsforth; Flasby; Grassington; Hatfield; Knaresborough; Monkton, Nun; Ripon; Rotherham; Rufforth; Selby; Sheffield; Temple Hirst; Thorne; Tickhill; Wakefield; Wistow
Yorkshire Ouse and Hull Riv. Authority, 86
Yorkshire Ouse Sailing Club, 75
Yorkshire Sugar Co. Ltd., 50
Yorkshire Wolds, 1, 129–30, 164
Youlthorpe (in Bishop Wilton), 131

SO 5-6-76

DECK COLLECTIONS

REFERENCE
DO NOT CIRCULATE